PROFESSING
THE NEW
RHETORICS

PROFESSING THE NEW RHETORICS

A SOURCEBOOK

EDITED BY

THERESA ENOS
UNIVERSITY OF ARIZONA

STUART C. BROWN
NEW MEXICO STATE UNIVERSITY

A BLAIR PRESS BOOK

PRENTICE HALL, ENGLEWOOD CLIFFS, NJ 07632

Library of Congress Cataloging-in-Publication Data

Professing the new rhetorics : a sourcebook / edited by Theresa Enos,
   Stuart C. Brown.
      p.   cm.
   "A Blair Press book."
   Includes bibliographical references and index.
   ISBN 0-13-014317-0
      1. English language—Rhetoric—Study and teaching—History—20th century.   I. Enos,
   Theresa.   II. Brown, Stuart C. (Stuart Cameron), 1955-   .
   PE1404.P66   1994
   808'.042—dc20

                                                          93-20931
                                                             CIP

Cover design: Kirchoff-Wohlerg, Inc.
Production coordinator: Robert Anderson

Acknowledgments appear on pages 487-88, which constitute a continuation of the
copyright page.

Blair Press
The Statler Building
20 Park Plaza, Suite 1113
Boston, MA 02116-4399

© 1994 by Prentice Hall, Inc.
A Paramount Communications Company
Englewood Cliffs, NJ 07632

Printed in the United States of America
10 9 8 7 6 5 4 3 2 1

ISBN   0-13-014317-0

Prentice-Hall International (UK) Limited, *London*
Prentice-Hall of Australia Pty. Limited, *Sydney*
Prentice-Hall Canada Inc., *Toronto*
Prentice-Hall Hispanoamericana, S.A., *Mexico*
Prentice-Hall of India Private Limited, *New Delhi*
Prentice-Hall of Japan, Inc., *Tokyo*
Simon & Schuster Asia Pte. Ltd., *Singapore*
Editora Prentice-Hall do Brasil, Ltda., *Rio de Janeiro*

PREFACE

Rhetoric is a history of new rhetorics, a continuing history. We propose this collection as a demonstration of the continuity and diversity of approaches to rhetoric in the twentieth century. By providing representative texts from a variety of perspectives and disciplines, *Professing the New Rhetorics* is an attempt to fill a gap in contemporary rhetorical theory and practice, to find a philosophical and chronological frame in which to understand what rhetoric is and how it is of value to students and teachers of language and culture.

As we hope the readings in this collection suggest, rhetoric as a discipline necessarily involves recognizing the importance of theory, practice, and history as integral processes. We further envision these readings as providing a conceptual means of moving away from the closed nature of "technical" or "practical" rhetoric that has been—and still is—the dominant approach to writing instruction in American colleges. Rhetoric is more than an application encountered in the first-year writing courses, just as it is more than an accusation made by political commentators.

Professing the New Rhetorics has three purposes. First, it illustrates the diversity of sources and thought that both enrich and complicate understanding of rhetoric in the twentieth century. Second, it provides a sense of rhetoric encapsulated in an era, one connected to rhetorics past, but distinctly its own. Third, it offers selected, essential readings that will initiate students and others to the vast and dazzling realm called *rhetoric*.

A great many people have provided invaluable suggestions, advice, and encouragement over the development of this project, but we wish specifically to recognize Ann Berthoff, Robert Connors, Edward Corbett, Richard Enos, Richard Fulkerson, Winifred Bryan Horner, Andrea Lunsford, Carolyn Miller, the late Donald Stewart, John Trimbur, Thomas Willard, and Ross Winterowd as well as a number of anonymous reviewers, who generously gave their time and insights during the several revisions of the selections. We are grateful to the graduate students in Rhetoric, Composition, and the Teaching of English at the University of Arizona, who, during the spring 1990 seminar on twentieth-century rhetoric, waded into the 1200-page collection of readings that was our earliest manuscript. And of course we would not have been able to do this book at all had we not had the assistance and confidence of Nancy Perry at Blair Press—should everyone be blessed with such an editor.

We dedicate this book to rhetoricians the world over, and to the spirit of rhetorics past, present, and future.

T. E.
S. C. B.

CONTENTS

The New Rhetorics: Commentary and Application

Introduction

Histories make men wise; poets, witty; the
mathematics, subtile; natural philosophy, deep; moral,
grave; logic and rhetoric, able to contend.

—FRANCIS BACON

Peristasis

This collection is an historical sketch of the evolution of rhetoric in the twentieth century. All but abandoned by the end of the nineteenth century, the study of rhetoric flowers as we end the twentieth. Graduate programs, scholarly journals, books, conferences, and scholars now actively engage in its study. Rhetoric is being transformed once again, from a pejorative to an honorific term. Although it is still used by many to indicate bombast and empty gesture, *rhetoric* is being revived as an all-encompassing term, one that concerns inquiry and the making of knowledge, and the communication of that inquiry.

Our title, *Professing the New Rhetorics: A Sourcebook,* indicates our intentions to represent this transformation of rhetoric. We chose *Professing* to imply suggestiveness and articulation; the word also hints at the tentativeness and flux found in attempts to circumscribe rhetoric narrowly. Individuals have grappled with the nature of rhetoric and how to use it since its inception. But our focus is on *New,* the rhetorics that have recently distinguished themselves in some way, or ways, from the methodology and substantive art known as *rhetoric;* at the same time we recognize that what we know as new rhetorics can be but modifications or extensions of the 2,500-year history of rhetoric. We have taken but a narrow slice from the tradition's rich and vibrant life.

Rhetorics in a plural form is perhaps a cleverness, but we want to emphasize the multiplicity of rhetorical study and its inclusiveness—its nature to encompass rather than circumscribe. As we note in the introduction to the collection *Defining the New Rhetorics,* "Just as an ecology is best represented by its diversity, the various voices in this volume represent the richness and value of rhetoric and the plurality of perceptions that both sustain and hinder rhetoric as a discipline." As such, the concept of a sourcebook, in its fullest sense, becomes integral. We foresee this collection used as a starting point, its purpose to tantalize and to provoke more than to prescribe or to limit. Many of the scholars represented here by one brief selection are worth extensive study in their own right; and they all point to other figures and inquiries that bear investigating.

Selecting one scholar or work over another to represent the New Rhetorics is a dangerous precept, one we have struggled with continually. Our selections risk being defined too narrowly, their meanings pinned down and their uses prescribed; we risk exclusion of valuable and necessary contributions. But we urge readers to think of this collection in terms of initiation, of an open-ended description, and of an introduction, not an attempt to present a canon. Rather than let any single individual represent what the New Rhetorics is, we must allow New Rhetorics, in the fullest and most complicated sense, to represent themselves.

As in all histories, what is left out is often as important as what is included. We began this project with the idea of assembling as many of the important contributors to the contemporary revival and understanding of rhetoric as we could discover. That we view rhetoric as a plurality made the selection of contributors all the more expansive. Thus the selections that follow might be construed by some as attempts toward canonizing. Others might question our exclusion of certain figures. Reviewers will justly note that we have not included selections by theory builders such as Bachelard, Max Black, Chomsky, Cixous, Derrida, Eco, Feyerabend, Gadamer, Gates, Geertz, Stuart Hall, Jacobson, Kristeva, Kuhn, Latour, Lyotard, Ricoeur, Rorty, Sapir, Todorov, Hayden White, and Whorf—figures of such contemporary importance that they are most often known by their last names alone. We have also left out many of the valuable works by those who have worked in speech communication such as Lloyd Bitzer, Ernest Bormann, Wayne Brockriede, Hoyt Hudson, Richard Johannesen, Henry Johnstone, Maurice Natanson, Marie Hochmuth Nichols, Karl Wallace, Eugene White, and Herbert Wichelns. And we have not included important figures such as Ann Berthoff, Gertrude Buck, Edward Corbett, Frank D'Angelo, Peter Elbow, Linda Flower and John Hayes, Daniel Fogarty, Walker Gibson, Richard Lanham, Janice Lauer, Josephine Miles, James Moffett, James Murphy, William Riley Parker, D. Gordon Rohman and Albert O. Wlecke, Louise Rosenblatt, Robert Scholes, Fred Newton Scott, Martin Steinmann, Donald Stewart, Ross Winterowd, Richard Young. . . .

And even this listing is incomplete; study of contributions to the New Rhetorics is best regarded as ending on an ellipsis. These and many other scholars have made rhetoric vital in the twentieth century. All have contributed to what we know as rhetoric. Their contributions will continue influencing what rhetoric becomes as they are joined by the host of younger scholars now adding to our understandings of rhetoric and its newest forms. One has only to look at the two bibliographies of suggested further reading we have included and in the books and journals of the profession to extend and to update this list.

Divisio

Our intention behind the structuring of the selections both complicates and simplifies approaches to rhetoric. We begin with "Overviews and Theory" and follow this section with "Commentary and Application." The first section offers both an historical introduction to the revival of rhetoric in the twentieth century and a view of some of the dominant strands that influence contemporary thought on rhetoric. We attempt to provide a sense of the breadth and depth of inquiry that has occurred in the study of rhetoric up to current perspectives and to provide an overview of the nature and necessity of that inquiry. Many of these figures and the selections that represent them have been instrumental in reviving and directing rhetorical study along its many paths. De Saussure, Richards, Burke, Bahktin, Weaver, Grassi, Toulmin, McKeon, Perelman, Foucault, Polanyi, Habermas, Barthes, and Booth each provide a point of departure that has generated new ideas about what rhetoric is and what it is becoming. Historically, these modern influences have helped create the rhetoric we know and study at this point.

The second section, "Commentary and Application," represents current approaches to the New Rhetorics. In this section we see the inclusiveness and breadth of the discipline of rhetoric. The section illustrates current attention to the role language has in making and recording knowledge as well as directs attention to the study of rhetoric itself—its value and its reemergence as a discipline. Here we find attention to rhetorical studies within speech and communication departments being paid by Bryant, Scott, Ehninger, and Fisher. We also find the resurgence of rhetoric in English studies after decades of isolation in speech and communication studies. Ohmann in the 1960s and Halloran in the 1970s signal the revival of rhetoric as a legitimate enterprise for English departments. Eagleton, Hirsch, and Freire recognize and contribute to this emergence in unique ways. The selections by Lunsford and Ede, Corder, Bizzell, and Berlin demonstrate our sense of rhetoric as having achieved legitimacy as a discipline in its own right once again.

As an opportunity to further extend readings in both sections, each selection has a brief headnote that situates the author within the framework of the New Rhetorics and provides further glimpses into the nature of rhetoric. Additionally, at the end of each section we provide an extensive, although by no means complete, bibliography of further readings to aid readers in their own explorations of the richness and diversity of twentieth-century rhetoric.

Some readers will find the following selections idiosyncratic. Perhaps they are. In *Rosencrantz and Guildenstern Are Dead*, the playwright Tom Stoppard has a character argue

> I can do you blood and love without the rhetoric, and I can do you blood and
> rhetoric without the love and I can do you all three concurrent or consecutive
> but I can't do you love and rhetoric without the blood.

In the five-year development of this collection, we have often felt bloodied
by the decisions for exclusion that we have had to make. We discovered a
startling lack of consensus among colleagues and reviewers as to what are
the key texts to introduce, explain, and substantiate rhetorical study in the
twentieth century; nor could we find agreement on what rhetoric is and its
purview.

Apologia and an Invitation

Following Renato Barilli, who, in his book *Rhetoric,* argues that the spirit
of rhetoric is one of conciliation and integration, we began this project with
the conception of a much larger text—but realized that any text would likely
encounter criticisms of exclusion no matter its size. The division of this
book into two sections conveys neither the diversity of the New Rhetorics
nor their contributions to the other disciplines. Discussions over definitions
of rhetoric, other taxonomies, different lists of sources, and individual conceptions are all essential to maintaining the vitality and usefulness of the
New Rhetorics. James Kinneavy's "Contemporary Rhetoric" (a bibliographic
study of contemporary rhetoric) is representative of this diversity with its
seventeen categories. A truly definitive collection would encompass the
texts he cites and many others. Such definitiveness is unlikely and even
undesirable. Rhetoric, fully conceived, is too inclusive and too individualized a concept to allow any one text to determine its scope.

Pragmatic concerns such as space constraints, permissions fees, and the
desire to provide a usable text, whether for reference or for a course, put us
in the position of leaving out authors and of limiting to one piece each
author we do include. Determining who to include and who to exclude,
however, has led to an important feature of this collection, an undercurrent
that should be made explicit. The selections presented here rely on not only
the interaction of the reader with the authors we include, but also the
involvement of the reader in providing extensions, additions, and elaborations. The reader must take it upon herself or himself to personalize and
refine these selections to her or his own sense of what we call New
Rhetorics. We urge disagreement with our choices and extend the invitation
to engage the selections here dialectically—use this text as an opportunity
to create an alternative one.

We must finally apologize for the seeming exclusion of minority and
women authors. In our defense, we did try to include these voices. We
attempted to fit voices as diverse as Suzanne Langer, Louise Rosenblatt,

Henry Louis Gates, Toni Morrison, Pamela Annas, Sonja Foss, and other "powerful users and crafters of rhetoric" as one reviewer phrased it. They are not here, however. As Patricia Bizzell recounts in "Opportunities for Feminist Research in the History of Rhetoric," a recent article about her own anthology efforts for *The Rhetorical Tradition,* the history of rhetoric demonstrates the exclusion of women and others who have not had access to an elite education: "we were dismayed to find so little of this critical work—and indeed, little nontraditional material as well." Our collection represents this paucity.

We suggest, however, that this lack be seen as reminder that, until recently, the rhetorical canon has been dominated by white, male contributors. But rather than view this as an exclusion or reification, we might more constructively use this knowledge as a call for future inquiry. To ignore our history and its shortcomings is to deny it. Rather than try to alter its history, we will perhaps best serve the profession of rhetoric by recognizing what has been missing, and by ensuring that future generations will find that rhetorical study awoke in the late twentieth century to find new voices, new contributions, and even more new rhetorics.

THE
NEW
RHETORICS

Overview and Theory

FERDINAND DE SAUSSURE
1857–1913

Born into a distinguished Swiss family, Ferdinand de Saussure entered the University of Leipzig in 1876 to study linguistics and later studied in Berlin. On earning his doctorate from Leipzig, he taught in Paris from 1881–1891, his fame becoming so great that Paris replaced Leipzig as center of linguistic studies. In 1891 he accepted a professorship at Geneva. During his lifetime, Saussure published little, but three lectures he delivered on general linguistics were published as the Cours de linguistique generale *(1916). Saussure viewed the underlying structure of language as an abstract social system, a departure from the psychological emphasis of other theorists. The* Cours *foreshadowed structuralism in linguistics; in the lectures Saussure refers to language in general as* langage, *to the underlying structure as* langue, *and to spoken language as* parole. *The following reading was translated by Wade Baskin.*

Nature of the Linguistic Sign

1. Sign, Signified, Signifier

Some people regard language, when reduced to its elements, as a naming-process only—a list of words, each corresponding to the thing that it names. For example:

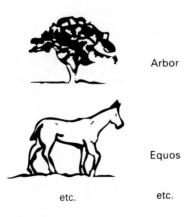

Arbor

Equos

etc.   etc.

This conception is open to criticism at several points. It assumes that ready-made ideas exist before words; it does not tell us whether a name is vocal or psychological in nature (*arbor,* for instance, can be considered from either viewpoint); finally, it lets us assume that the linking of a name and a thing is a very simple operation—an assumption that is anything but true. But this rather naive approach can bring us near the truth by showing us that the linguistic unit is a double entity, one formed by the associating of two terms.

We have seen in considering the speaking-circuit that both terms involved in the linguistic sign are psychological and are united in the brain by an associative bond. This point must be emphasized.

The linguistic sign unites, not a thing and a name, but a concept and a sound-image. The latter is not the material sound, a purely physical thing, but the psychological imprint of the sound, the impression that it makes on our senses. The sound-image is sensory, and if I happen to call it "material," it is only in that sense, and by way of opposing it to the other term of the association, the concept, which is generally more abstract.

The psychological character of our sound-images becomes apparent when we observe our own speech. Without moving our lips or tongue, we can talk to ourselves or recite mentally a selection of verse. Because we regard the words of our language as sound-images, we must avoid speaking of the "phonemes" that make up the words. This term, which suggests vocal activity, is applicable to the spoken word only, to the realization of the inner image in discourse. We can avoid that misunderstanding by speaking of the *sounds* and *syllables* of a word provided we remember that the names refer to the sound-image.

The linguistic sign is then a two-sided psychological entity that can be represented by the drawing:

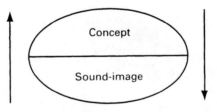

The two elements are intimately united, and each recalls the other. Whether we try to find the meaning of the Latin word *arbor* or the word that Latin uses to designate the concept "tree," it is clear that only the associations sanctioned by that language appear to us to conform to reality, and we disregard whatever others might be imagined.

Our definition of the linguistic sign poses an important question of terminology. I call the combination of a concept and a sound-image a *sign,* but in current usage the term generally designates only a sound-image, a word, for example (*arbor,* etc.). One tends to forget that *arbor* is called a sign only because it carries the concept "tree," with the result that the idea of the sensory part implies the idea of the whole.

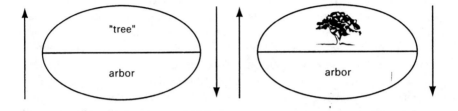

Ambiguity would disappear if the three notions involved here were designated by three names, each suggesting and opposing the others. I propose to retain the word *sign (signe)* to designate the whole and to replace *concept* and *sound-image* respectively by *signified (signifié)* and *signifier (significant);* the last two terms have the advantage of indicating the opposition that separates them from each other and from the whole of which they are parts. As regards *sign,* if I am satisfied with it, this is simply because I do not know of any word to replace it, the ordinary language suggesting no other.

The linguistic sign, as defined, has two primordial characteristics. In enunciating them I am also positing the basic principles of any study of this type.

2. Principle I: The Arbitrary Nature of the Sign

The bond between the signifier and the signified is arbitrary. Since I mean by sign the whole that results from the associating of the signifier with the signified, I can simply say: *the linguistic sign is arbitrary.*

The idea of "sister" is not linked by any inner relationship to the succession of sounds *s-ö-r* which serves as its signifier in French; that it could be represented equally by just any other sequence is proved by differences among languages and by the very existence of different languages: the signified "ox" has as its signifier *b-ö-f* on one side of the border and *o-k-s (Ochs)* on the other.

No one disputes the principle of the arbitrary nature of the sign, but it is often easier to discover a truth than to assign to it its proper place. Principle I dominates all the linguistics of language; its consequences are numberless. It is true that not all of them are equally obvious at first glance; only after many detours does one discover them, and with them the primordial importance of the principle.

One remark in passing: when semiology becomes organized as a science, the question will arise whether or not it properly includes modes of expression based on completely natural signs, such as pantomime. Supposing that the new science welcomes them, its main concern will still be the whole group of systems grounded on the arbitrariness of the sign. In fact, every means of expression used in society is based, in principle, on collective behaviour or—what amounts to the same thing—on convention. Polite formulas, for instance, though often imbued with a certain natural expressiveness (as in the case of a Chinese who greets his emperor by bowing down to the ground nine times), are none the less fixed by rule; it is this rule and not the intrinsic value of the gestures that obliges one to use them. Signs that are wholly arbitrary realize better than the others the ideal of the semiological process; that is why language, the most complex and universal of all systems of expression, is also the most characteristic; in this sense linguistics can become the master-pattern for all branches of semiology although language is only one particular semiological system.

The word *symbol* has been used to designate the linguistic sign, or, more specifically, what is here called the signifier. Principle I in particular weighs against the use of this term. One characteristic of the symbol is that it is never wholly arbitrary; it is not empty, for there is the rudiment of a natural bond between the signifier and the signified. The symbol of justice, a pair of scales, could not be replaced by just any other symbol, such as a chariot.

The word *arbitrary* also calls for comment. The term should not imply that the choice of the signifier is left entirely to the speaker; I mean that it is unmotivated, i.e., arbitrary in that it actually has no natural connection with the signified. . . .

3. Principle II: The Linear Nature of the Signifier

The signifier, being auditory, is unfolded solely in time from which it gets the following characteristics: (a) it represents a span, and (b) the span is measurable in a single dimension; it is a line.

While Principle II is obvious, apparently linguists have always neglected to state it, doubtless because they found it too simple; nevertheless, it is fundamental, and its consequences are incalculable. Its importance equals that of Principle I; the whole mechanism of language depends upon it. In contrast to visual signifiers (nautical signals, etc.) which can offer simultaneous groupings in several dimensions, auditory signifiers have at their command only the dimension of time. Their elements are presented in succession; they form a chain. This feature becomes readily apparent when they are represented in writing and the spatial line of graphic marks is substituted for succession in time.

Sometimes the linear nature of the signifier is not obvious. When I accent a syllable, for instance, it seems that I am concentrating more than one significant element on the same point. But this is an illusion; the syllable and its accent constitute only one phonational act. There is no duality within the act but only different oppositions to what precedes and what follows.

Immutability and Mutability of the Sign

1. Immutability

The signifier, though to all appearances freely chosen with respect to the idea that it represents, is fixed, not free, with respect to the linguistic community that uses it. The masses have no voice in the matter, and the signifier chosen by language could be replaced by no other. This fact, which seems to embody a contradiction, might be called colloquially "the stacked deck." We say to language: "Choose!" but we add: "It must be this sign and no other." No individual, even if he willed it, could modify in any way at all the choice that has been made; and what is more, the community itself cannot control so much as a single word; it is bound to the existing language.

No longer can language be identified with a contract pure and simple, and it is precisely from this viewpoint that the linguistic sign is a particularly interesting object of study; for language furnishes the best proof that a law accepted by a community is a thing that is tolerated and not a rule to which all freely consent.

Let us first see why we cannot control the linguistic sign and then draw together the important consequences that issue from the phenomenon.

No matter what period we choose or how far back we go, language always appears as a heritage of the preceding period. We might conceive of an act by which, at a given moment, names were assigned to things and a contract was formed between concepts and sound-images; but such an act has never been recorded. The notion that things might have happened like that was prompted by our acute awareness of the arbitrary nature of the sign.

No society, in fact, knows or has ever known language other than as a product inherited from preceding generations, and one to be accepted as such. That is why the question of the origin of speech is not so important as it is generally assumed to be. The question is not even worth asking; the only real object of linguistics is the normal, regular life of an existing idiom. A particular language-state is always the product of historical forces, and these forces explain why the sign is unchangeable, i.e., why it resists any arbitrary substitution.

Nothing is explained by saying that language is something inherited and leaving it at that. Cannot existing and inherited laws be modified from one moment to the next?

To meet that objection, we must put language into its social setting and frame the question just as we would for any other social institution. How are other social institutions transmitted? This more general question includes the question of immutability. We must first determine the greater or lesser amounts of freedom that the other institutions enjoy; in each instance it will be seen that a different proportion exists between fixed tradition and the free action of society. The next step is to discover why, in a given category, the forces of the first type carry more weight or less weight than those of the second. Finally, coming back to language, we must ask why the historical factor of transmission dominates it entirely and prohibits any sudden widespread change.

There are many possible answers to the question. For example, one might point to the fact that succeeding generations are not superimposed on one another like the drawers of a piece of furniture, but fuse and interpenetrate, each generation embracing individuals of all ages—with the result that modifications of language are not tied to the succession of generations. One might also recall the sum of the efforts required for learning the mother language and conclude that a general change would be impossible. Again, it might be added that reflection does not enter into the active use of an idiom—speakers are largely unconscious of the laws of language; and if they are unaware of them, how can they modify them? Even if they were aware of these laws, we may be sure that their awareness would seldom lead to criticism, for people are generally satisfied with the language they have received.

The foregoing considerations are important but not topical. The following are more basic and direct, and all the others depend on them.

(i) *The arbitrary nature of the sign*   Above, we had to accept the theoretical possibility of change; further reflection suggests that the arbitrary nature of the sign is really what protects language from any attempt to modify it. Even if people were more conscious of language than they are, they would still not know how to discuss it. The reason is simply that any subject in order to be discussed must have a reasonable basis. It is possible, for instance, to discuss whether the monogamous form of marriage is more reasonable than the polygamous form and to advance arguments to support either side. One could also argue about a system of symbols, for the symbol has a rational relationship with the thing signified; but language is a system of arbitrary signs and lacks the necessary basis, the solid ground for discussion. There is no reason for preferring *soeur* to *sister, Ochs* to *boeuf,* etc.

(ii) *The multiplicity of signs necessary to form any language*   Another important deterrent to linguistic change is the great number of signs that must go into the making of any language. A system of writing comprising twenty to forty letters can in case of need be replaced by another system. The same would be true of language if it contained a limited number of elements; but linguistic signs are numberless.

(iii) *The over-complexity of the system*   A language constitutes a system. In this one respect language is not completely arbitrary but is ruled to some extent by logic; it is here also, however, that the inability of the masses to transform it becomes apparent. The system is a complex mechanism that can be grasped only through reflection; the very ones who use it daily are ignorant of it. We can conceive of a change only through the intervention of specialists, grammarians, logicians, etc.; but experience shows us that all such meddlings have failed.

(iv) *Collective inertia towards innovation*   Language—and this consideration surpasses all the others—is at every moment everybody's concern; spread throughout society and manipulated by it, language is something used daily by all. Here we are unable to set up any comparison between it and other institutions. The prescriptions of codes, religious rites, nautical signals, etc., involve only a certain number of individuals simultaneously and then only during a limited period of time; in language, on the contrary, everyone participates at all times, and that is why it is constantly being influenced by all. This capital fact suffices to show the impossibility of revolution. Of all social institutions, language is least amenable to initiative. It blends with the life of society, and the latter, inert by nature, is a prime conservative force.

But to say that language is a product of social forces does not suffice to show clearly that it is unfree; remembering that it is always the heritage of the preceding period, we must add that these social forces are linked with time. Language is checked not only by the weight of the collectivity but also by time. These two are inseparable. At every moment solidarity with the past checks freedom of choice. We say *man* and *dog*. This does not prevent the existence in the total phenomenon of a bond between the two antithetical forces—arbitrary convention, by virtue of which choice is free, and time, which causes choice to be fixed. Because the sign is arbitrary, it follows no law other than that of tradition, and because it is based on tradition, it is arbitrary.

2. Mutability

Time, which insures the continuity of language, wields another influence apparently contradictory to the first: the more or less rapid change of linguistic signs. In a certain sense, therefore, we can speak of both the immutability and the mutability of the sign.

In the last analysis, the two facts are interdependent: the sign is exposed to alteration because it perpetuates itself. What predominates in all change is the persistence of the old substance; disregard for the past is only relative. That is why the principle of change is based on the principle of continuity.

Change in time takes many forms, on any one of which an important chapter in linguistics might be written. Without entering into detail, let us see what things need to be delineated.

First, let there be no mistake about the meaning that we attach to the word "change." One might think that it deals especially with phonetic changes undergone by the signifier, or perhaps changes in meaning which affect the signified concept. That view would be inadequate. Regardless of what the forces of change are, whether in isolation or in combination, they always result in *a shift in the relationship between the signified and the signifier.*

Here are some examples. Latin *necāre* "kill" became *noyer* "drown" in French. Both the sound-image and the concept changed; but it is useless to separate the two parts of the phenomenon; it is sufficient to state with respect to the whole that the bond between the idea and the sign was loosened, and that there was a shift in their relationship. If, instead of comparing Classical Latin *necāre* with French *noyer,* we contrast the former term with *necare* of Vulgar Latin of the fourth or fifth century meaning "drown," the case is a little different; but here again, although there is no appreciable change in the signifier, there is a shift in the relationship between the idea and the sign.

Old German *dritteil* "one-third" became *Drittel* in Modern German. Here, although the concept remained the same, the relationship was changed in two ways: the signifier was changed not only in its material aspect but also in its grammatical form; the idea of *Teil* "part" is no longer implied; *Drittel* is a simple word. In one way or another there is always a shift in the relationship.

In Anglo-Saxon the pre-literary form *fot* "foot" remained while its plural *⋆fōti* became *fēt* (Modern English *feet*). Regardless of the other changes that are implied, one thing is certain: there was a shift in their relationship; other correspondences between the phonetic substance and the idea emerged.

Language is radically powerless to defend itself against the forces which from one moment to the next are shifting the relationship between the signified and the signifier. This is one of the consequences of the arbitrary nature of the sign.

Unlike language, other human institutions—customs, laws, etc.—are all based in varying degrees on the natural relations of things; all have of necessity adapted the means employed to the ends pursued. Even fashion in dress is not entirely arbitrary; we can deviate only slightly from the conditions dictated by the human body. Language is limited by nothing in the choice of means, for apparently nothing would prevent the associating of any idea whatsoever with just any sequence of sounds.

To emphasize the fact that language is a genuine institution, Whitney quite justly insisted upon the arbitrary nature of signs; and, by so doing, he placed linguistics on its true axis. But he did not follow through and see that the arbitrariness of language radically separates it from all other institutions. This is apparent from the way in which language evolves. Nothing could be more complex. As it is a product of both the social force and time, no one can change anything in it, and, on the other hand, the arbitrariness of its signs theoretically entails the freedom of establishing just any relationship between phonetic substance and ideas. The result is that each of the two elements united in the sign maintains its own life to a degree unknown elsewhere, and that language changes, or rather evolves, under the influence of all the forces which can affect either sounds or meanings. The evolution is inevitable; there is no example of a single language that resists it. After a certain period of time, some obvious shifts can always be recorded.

Mutability is so inescapable that it even holds true for artificial languages: Whoever creates a language controls it only so long as it is not in circulation; from the moment when it fulfils its mission and becomes the property of everyone, control is lost. Take Esperanto as an example; if it succeeds, will it escape the inexorable law? Once launched, it is quite likely that Esperanto will enter upon a fully semiological life; it will be transmitted according to laws which have nothing in common with those of its logical creation, and there will be no turning back. A man proposing a fixed language that posterity would have to accept for what it was would be like a hen hatching a duck's egg: the language created by him would be borne along, willy-nilly, by the current that engulfs all languages.

Signs are governed by a principle of general semiology: continuity in time is coupled to change in time; this is confirmed by orthographic systems, the speech of deaf-mutes, etc.

But what supports the necessity for change? I might be reproached for not having been as explicit on this point as on the principle of immutability. This is because I failed to distinguish between the different forces of change. We must consider their great variety in order to understand the extent to which they are necessary.

The causes of continuity are a priori within the scope of the observer, but the causes of change in time are not. It is better not to attempt giving an exact account at this point, but to restrict discussion to the shifting of relationships in general. Time changes all things; there is no reason why language should escape this universal law.

Let us review the main points of our discussion. . . .

1. Avoiding sterile word definitions, within the total phenomenon repre-sented by speech we first singled out two parts: "langue" and "parole." Langue is speech less speaking. It is the whole set of linguistic habits which allow an individual to understand and to be understood.
2. But this definition still leaves language outside its social context; it makes language something artificial, since it includes only the individual part of reality; for the realization of language, a community of speakers *(masse parlante)* is necessary. Contrary to all appearances, language never exists apart from the social fact, for it is a semiological phenomenon. Its social nature is one of its inner characteristics. Its complete definition confronts us with two inseparable entities.

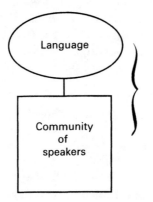

But under the conditions described language is not living—it has only potential life; we have considered only the social, not the historical, fact.
3. The linguistic sign is arbitrary; language, as defined, would therefore seem to be a system which, because it depends solely on a rational princi-ple, is free and can be organized at will. Its social nature, considered inde-pendently, does not definitely rule out this viewpoint. Doubtless it is not on a purely logical basis that group psychology operates; one must con-sider everything that deflects reason in actual contacts between individu-als. But the thing which keeps language from being a simple convention that can be modified at the whim of interested parties is not its social nature; it is rather the action of time combined with the social force. If time is left out, the linguistic facts are incomplete and no conclusion is possible.

If we considered language in time, without the community of speak-ers—imagine an isolated individual living for several centuries—we should probably notice no change; time would not influence language. Conversely, if we considered the community of the social forces that influence language. To represent the actual facts, we must then add to our first drawing a sign to indicate the passage of time:

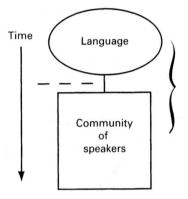

Language is no longer free, for time will allow the social forces at work on it to carry out their effects. This brings us back to the principle of continuity, which cancels freedom. But continuity necessarily implies change, varying degrees of shifts in the relationship between the signified and the signifier.

Static and Evolutionary Linguistics

Inner Duality of All Sciences Concerned with Values

Very few linguists suspect that the intervention of the factor of time creates difficulties peculiar to linguistics and opens to their science two completely divergent paths.

Most other sciences are unaffected by this radical duality; time produces no special effects in them. Astronomy has found that the stars undergo considerable changes but has not been obliged on this account to split itself into two disciplines. Geology is concerned with successions at almost every instant, but its study of strata does not thereby become a radically distinct discipline. Law has its descriptive science and its historical science; no one opposes one to the other. The political history of states is unfolded solely in time, but an historian depicting a particular period does not work apart from history. Conversely, the science of political institutions is essentially descriptive, but if the need arises it can easily deal with an historical question without disturbing its unity.

On the other hand, that duality is already forcing itself upon the economic sciences. Here, in contrast to the other sciences, political economy and economic history constitute two clearly separated disciplines within a single science; the works that have recently appeared on these subjects point up the distinction. Proceeding as they have, economists are—without being well aware of it—obeying an inner necessity. A similar necessity obliges us to divide linguistics into two parts, each with its own principle. Here as in political economy we are confronted with the notion of *value;* both sciences are concerned with *a system for equating things of different orders*—labour and wages in one and a signified and a signifier in the other.

Certainly all sciences would profit by indicating more precisely the co-ordinates along which their subject-matter is aligned. Everywhere distinctions should be made, according to the following illustration, between (1) *the axis of simultaneities (AB),* which stands for the relations of coexisting things and from which the intervention of time is excluded; and (2) *the axis of successions (CD),* on which only one thing can be considered at a time but upon which are located all things on the first axis together with their changes.

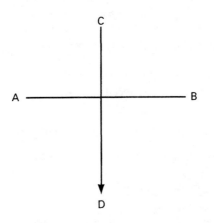

For a science concerned with values the distinction is a practical necessity and sometimes an absolute one. In these fields scholars cannot organize their research rigorously without considering both co-ordinates and making a distinction between the system of values *per se* and the same values as they relate to time.

This distinction has to be heeded by the linguist above all others, for language is a system of pure values which are determined by nothing except the momentary arrangement of its terms. A value—so long as it is somehow rooted in things and in their natural relations, as happens with economics (the value of a plot of ground, for instance, is related to its productivity)—can to some extent be traced in time if we remember that it depends at each moment upon a system of coexisting values. Its link with things gives it, perforce, a natural basis, and the judgments that we base on such values are therefore never completely arbitrary; their variability is limited. But we have just seen that natural data have no place in linguistics.

Again, the more complex and rigorously organized a system of values is, the more it is necessary, because of its very complexity, to study it according to both co-ordinates. No other system embodies this feature to the same extent as language. Nowhere else do we find such precise values at stake and such a great number and diversity of terms, all so rigidly interdependent. The multiplicity of signs, which we have already used to explain the continuity of language, makes it absolutely impossible to study simultaneously relations in time and relations within the system.

The reasons for distinguishing two sciences of language are clear. How should the sciences be designated? Available terms do not all bring out the distinction with equal sharpness. "Linguistic history" and "Historical linguistics" are too vague. Since political history includes the description of different periods as well as the narration of events, the student might think that he is studying a language according to the axis of time when he describes its successive states, but this would require a separate study of the phenomena that make language pass from one state to another. *Evolution and evolutionary linguistics* are more precise, and I shall use these expressions often; in contrast, we can speak of the science of *language-states (états de langue)* or *static linguistics.*

But to indicate more clearly the opposition and crossing of two orders of phenomena that relate to the same object, I prefer to speak of *synchronic* and *diachronic* linguistics. Everything that relates to the static side of our science is synchronic; everything that has to do with evolution is diachronic. Similarly, *synchrony* and *diachrony* designate respectively a language-state and an evolutionary phase. . . .

I. A. RICHARDS
1893-1979

Focusing on "how words work" and "the study of misunderstanding and its reme-dies," the Englishman Ivor Armstrong Richards proposed a new role for rhetoric in the twentieth century in Philosophy of Rhetoric *(1936). Richards was educated in moral sciences at Magdalen College, Cambridge, where he taught in the first litera-ture studies program. While in Cambridge, Richardson collaborated with C. K. Ogden on* The Meaning of Meaning *(1923), a study that begins his investigations into meaning as an aspect of interpretation. Teaching at Cambridge and encoun-tering student interpretations of poems led to his writing* Practical Criticism *(1929) and* Principles of Literary Criticism *(1925), texts that became foundations for the New Criticism, which was developing in North America at the time. After visits to China (where he worked to establish Basic English, a simplified form of teaching English as a second language that he developed with Ogden), Richards settled at Harvard University to teach in its College of Education. Convinced that theory without application is useless, Richards argued for revising concepts of lan-guage teaching in* How to Read a Page *(1942) and* Speculative Instruments *(1955). Richards's most notable contributions to current understandings of rhetoric include revival of the rhetorical triangle (drawing on the work of C. S. Peirce), context as a crucial component of meaning-making, an enhanced model of com-munication, and the establishment of metaphor as the basis of language. Arguing that language is the key to understanding, Richards proposes rhetoric as a foun-dational discipline, one that encompasses the disciplines of linguistics, psychology, philosophy, anthropology, education, and literary studies.*

How to Read a Page

A slip of the log I am sitting on by my campfire under Mount Sir Donald has given me as an alternative title, "How to *reap* a page," which perhaps better suggests the aim. We assume we know how to read: spell it r e a *p*, and we begin to wonder how we do it.

Twenty years ago a very inexperienced writer commenced authorship with the remark, "A book is a machine to think with" *(Principles of Literary Criticism)*. Here he is trying to devise another sort of verbal machine: some-thing which may be a help in using books as machines to *think* with. He seems to have been uneasy about the word "think" then, for he added in a later edition, "but it need not usurp the functions either of the bellows or the locomotive." Some books endeavor to transport their readers or to drag them passively hither and thither; others aim to stuff them, with facts or other supposedly fattening matter; others are microscopes, as it were, which can take the most familiar things and lay scraps and details of them before us, so transmuted by the new conditions under which we see them that we lose all power of recognizing or putting them together again; others behave rather as pulverizers or consolidators. My readers here will have to choose for themselves what sort of machine they will compare this book to. I do not believe that either a washing machine or a combination harvester is the right comparison.

How a page was read has often been a matter of life and death. Misread orders on the battlefield have sent thousands to unnecessary destruction. Their readings of a page of Scripture have led as many to the stake. Written words are very dangerous things:

Who hath given man speech
Or who hath set therein
A thorn for peril and a snare for sin

wrote Swinburne *(Atlanta in Calydon)*. He was thinking of quarrels, but we are perhaps in most danger when we agree too readily, or think we agree when in fact we do not. One thing here, at least, I am clear about and I hope I can make myself clear on. Neither this book nor any other can say how a page *should* be *read*—if by that we mean that it can give a recipe for discovering what the page *really says*. All it could do—and that would be much— would be to help us to understand some of the difficulties in the way of such discoveries. "How the page should be read" is a typically ambiguous phrase. Everyone can see that it may mean: (a) the right reading, the authentic interpretation; or (b) the right general procedure, or way of tackling the page. I need hardly say that this book keeps its eye on the second of these, and will be content if it can display some of the things which make it easy for us to twist pages to mean what we please—whether in order to damn or to praise them.

It is concerned with pages of all sorts—from plain exposition or instruction, the battle order for example, to poetry or philosophy, or the pages of Scripture referred to above. With the *first* there should be no doubt that there is one right reading which can be discovered or the writer is horribly at fault. But with the pages which on a long view have mattered most to the world, the utterances of the great poets and sages, we may reasonably doubt whether there is one right and only right reading. These greatest sayings of man have an inexhaustible fertility. Different minds have found such different things in them that we would be very rash if we assumed that some one way of reading them which commends itself to us is the right one. And yet . . . to assume so, to suppose that some one reading is the only right one, is our natural and our traditional approach. We feel very strongly that unless there is a right reading, and unless our business is to find it, we are wasting our time with such writings. This would certainly be so if they were like the specifications of an airplane, say, or like a map. A map on which hills and valleys could reasonably change places according to the consulting eye would be condemned as worthless by all. But with the highest poetry and philosophy and moral teaching, something like this happens and rightly. And the great pages lose nothing of their perpetual value because it happens. Indeed, their value is perpetual because through them, as through nothing else, we gain such opportunities of surveying the possibilities of ourselves and our worlds. There are limitations here clearly. Not every vague saying becomes precious. You will not succeed in making up a sentence which, because it might mean anything, will be permanently interesting. The immortal pages are no such puzzles, though they are the great exercisers of the spirit. But if we read them as though they could say one thing only, or condemn them because they can say many different things, we will be cutting ourselves off from the best which has been known and thought in the world—to use Matthew Arnold's phrase.

A list of the vices of reading should put first, as worst and most disabling, the expectation that everything should be easily understood. Things worth thought and reflection cannot be taken in at a glance. The writer should, of course, have done his utmost to make things easy for us. He could have had nothing (could he?) more important than *that* to do. But where there is still some difficulty remaining, let us beware of blaming it on the author rather than on our own imperfect command of the language. To blame the writer will teach us nothing. To wonder if we are reading right may.

Next to this vice should come that shallow indifference which says, "Well, if the page can mean almost anything, what does it matter how I take it? One reading is as good as another." It isn't. All the value comes from the depth and honesty, the sincerity and stress of the reflection through which we choose which meanings among its possibilities we will take seriously into our considerations. These things have many meanings because they touch us at points at which each one of us is himself many-minded. Understanding them is very much more than picking a possible reasonable interpretation, clarifying that, and sticking to it. Understanding them is seeing how the varied possible meanings hang together, which of them depend upon what else, how and why the meanings which matter most to us form a part of our world—seeing thereby more clearly what our world is and what we are who are building it to live in.

A chief modern difficulty in such understanding comes from the recent development of the historical sense. Compared with our great-grandfathers, we know incredibly much about the past. Scholarship has made the authors, their times and social conditions, etc., etc., known to us as to no other generation ever. This, at first sight, should make good reading easier. In many ways it does. We can turn to a dictionary such as Dr. Johnson never dreamed of and see how a troublesome word has been used century after century in varying ways. Concordances show us all the other uses the author made of the word. On wider points we can consult histories and biographies. Vast collections of disparate interpretations and comments are available. Around almost every important author an enormous critical apparatus has come into being. Its prime aim is just to help us to read better. But somehow all this wealth of scholarly aid does not lift up our hearts as it should. It spreads attention out too thinly and daunts us with the thought that we would have to know everything before we could know anything. Doubtless this is true, philosophically, but to readers in search of a method it is unhelpful.

Modern historical scholarship especially terrorizes us with the suggestion that somewhere in the jungle of evidence there is something we happen not to know which would make the point clear, which would show us just what the author did in fact mean. That suspicion of a missing clue is paralyzing—unless we remember firmly that from the very nature of the case essential clues are always missing. However much evidence we amass, we still have to jump to our conclusions. Reading is not detection as the perfect detective practices it. We are never concerned with facts pointing conclusively to a central fact—what happened in an author's mind at a given moment. No facts could ever establish that. If psychoanalysis has done nothing else for the world it has at least helped us to realize that minds—including authors' minds—are private. All we can ever prove by factual evidence is *an act*—that the author wrote such and such words. But what he meant by them is another matter. Our conclusions there must rest, as best they may, upon another sort of consideration. Fundamentally they rest upon analogies—certain very broad similarities in structure between minds: "The all-in-each of every mind," as Coleridge called it.

To go deeper, the reader, as opposed to the biographer, is not concerned with what as historical fact was going on in the author's mind when he penned the sentence, but with what the words—given the rest of the language—may mean. We do not read Shakespeare, or Plato, or Lao Tzu, or Homer, or the Bible, to discover what their authors—about whom otherwise we know so little—were thinking. We read them for the sake of the things their words—if we understand them—can do for us. But understanding them, of course, is not making them mean something we know and approve of already, nor is it detecting their ignorance and limitations. It is using them to stretch our minds as they have stretched the minds of so many different readers through the centuries. The interest they have so long had for man is the proof of their importance for us.

Emerson estimated that a man might have, if he were fortunate, some hundreds of reasonable moments in a long life. He was thinking probably of moments of inspiration from sources less traceable than the book in one's hand. The great pages are the most constant and dependable sources of "reasonable moments," if we mean by them moments when we know more completely what we are, and why we are so, and thus "see into the life of things" more deeply than in our everyday routine of existence. Such reasonable moments are the highest aim of reading. In them we do more than communicate with our authors—in the humble sense of communicate. We partake with them of wisdom. This aim is not attained unless we also gain such skills in reading as serves us in all our communications with our fellow human beings. The arts of reading are a pyramid whose pinnacle rests on the stages below. No one can understand poetry well whose mind cannot take in the prose of discussion and necessary business.

We all enjoy the illusion that we read better than we do; not least, no doubt, those who set out to write about *How to read*. But most of us—or those at least, who are likely to open a book with this title—are satisfied that other people read badly, that they can miss any point and will put their own wild interpretations on even the most obvious remark. In recent years books, papers, and articles which labor this point and accuse the general reader of incompetence with language have been coming out in plenty. Some of them hint despondingly that things are getting worse and threaten us even with universal intellectual collapse unless something is done about it. Authorities tell vast conferences of English teachers every few weeks that they are failing to teach reading. Texts simplified and written down to tenth-grade level are adopted in university courses because the undergraduates cannot, it is alleged, read anything harder. Publicists lament, in popular volumes, the plain man's helpless acceptance of verbal nonsense. Specialists complain that their contributions are wasted because the other specialists do nothing but misread them. And prophets foretell the downfall of democracy through a decline in the citizen's ability to follow any discussion worth a hearing.

Behind all this there is enough solid evidence to make anyone who studies it very uncomfortable. If most people's reading is really as inefficient as it seems when carefully enough examined, the main staff of education is hardly worth leaning on. What is the advantage of toiling on through thousands of pages, if a chief outcome is an accumulation of misunderstandings? Surely it should be possible to go directly to the root of the trouble, to study verbal misunderstanding, its nature and causes, deeply enough to find and apply a cure?

Accordingly, a considerable literature is coming into being which discusses the theory of language: classification, abstraction, naming, metaphor, and the rest. Unfortunately, it cannot be said to offer us much hope of immediate remedies. And this is not surprising. The questions which our theory of language has to discuss are hardest of all to write clearly about. They are the meeting points of tremendous pressures coming from rival philosophic systems used consciously or unconsciously by those who discuss them. We should expect not only great divergences of view but persistent drastic misinterpretations among their students. Everyone who writes on such matters sighs to think how often he seems to be misread. The layman who looks into this literature extensively enough will be shocked to discover how much seemingly fundamental disagreement it contains. If he does not go into it far enough to see this, he should be warned not to suppose there is anything at present there corresponding to the agreed doctrines the sciences can offer him. There is no agreed theory of language—as elementary mechanics, for example, is an agreed theory. Later on in this book we will see why there cannot be. Moreover, to get any adequate view of what the rival professors are maintaining, the inquiring layman would have to become an adept at a peculiarly difficult sort of reading in which one is specially apt to suppose he has understood when in fact he has not. It is not likely, therefore, that perusal of those confusing pages will make many people better readers. There is evidence, on the contrary, that misunderstandings acquired from them have made intelligent people more foolish and imperceptive as readers than they would otherwise have been.

The belief that knowledge of linguistic theory will make a man a better reader comes itself from such a misunderstanding. Theory and practice are not so simply connected. It is true that bad theory does lead to bad reading. But good theory will not necessarily produce good reading. Between the principles in the theory and the actual words to be read comes the task of seeing which principles apply to which cases, the problem of recognizing what the actual situation is. Theory can give us no *direct* help in this, more's the pity! We have to rely on whatever sagacity we have developed. Nothing, alas, is easier than to fit our distinctions to the wrong instances. And in most reading there are strong motives at work which tempt us to do this.

We are all of us learning to read all the time. All our thinking is a part of the process as affecting the way we will on some occasion take some sentence. Whenever we use words in forming some judgment or decision, we are, in what may be a painfully sharp sense, "learning to read." The lover scanning his mistress's scribble or her scowling brows is learning to read. So is the theologian comparing the ideas of *eros* and *agape*.

There is an ambiguity here which is brought out by asking, learning to read what?—the written word? or by means of that word the face, or the heart, of Nature?

The answer, of course, is, "Both." We cannot separate them. We always read for some purpose—unless some sad, bad, mad schoolteacher has got hold of us. There is no such thing as merely reading words; always through the words we are trafficking or trying to traffic with things—things gone by, present, to come or eternal. So a person who sets up to teach reading should recognize that he may be more ambitious than he seems. He may pretend he is only concerned to help people not to mistake one word for another, or one construction for another. *That,* so far, doesn't look like an attempt to finger the steering wheel of the universe. But "Which word is it?" turns into "Which use?"; and the question "Which construction?" into "What implications?" Before long the would-be authority on interpretation has become indistinguishable from an authority on "What's what?"—a question which belongs to a more divine science than he may wittingly aspire to.

Nonetheless, by being more aware of this he will be better able to pursue his main task—the cultivation of general verbal sagacity.

Whence comes, then, the development of this sagacity so much needed if we are to see what is happening? The answer is "Experience," of course; experience of a certain sort. But "experience" is one of the words we are all always most likely to misunderstand, because we all use it in so many ways. As a rule, we are not more than dimly aware of the great differences between its possible meanings. In most sentences it can say very different, sometimes even contradictory, things to different readers. And these different meanings will, as a rule, all make fairly good sense. There is an interesting and not too obvious reason for this. With most uses of "experience," the other words round about in the neighboring sentences are ready to shift their meanings to conform with its meanings. Most explanations of "experience" will be found to contain words like "mind," "observation," "attention," "knowledge," "feeling," "consciousness," which systematically vary in meaning in corresponding ways. So to say what we may mean or what anyone else may mean by "experience" or by any of these words is no easy undertaking—though it is what these pages attempt.

It is no one's fault that these words behave so. It is a sign of their importance. All ꟼunderstandingꟼ of anything of general importance turns on our mastery of the ranges of ideas which such words cover. I put ꟼunderstandingꟼ here in these specialized quotation marks (*q* for *query*) to note the fact that it is another of them and to suggest that in reading it we have to make out, if we can, which of its possible meanings it probably has. To assume that we know this too soon with any such word is the most frequent cause of bad reading.

This *systematic* ambiguity of all our most important words is a first cardinal point to note. But "ambiguity" is a sinister-looking word and it is better to say "resourcefulness." They are *the most important words* for two reasons:

1. They cover the ideas we can least avoid using, those which are concerned in all that we do as thinking begins.

2. They are words we are forced to use in explaining other words because it is in terms of the ideas they cover that the meanings of other words must be given.

A short list of a hundred such words will help to make these reasons for their importance clearer.

Amount, Argument, Art, Be, Beautiful, Belief, Cause, Certain, Chance, Change, Clear, Common, Comparison, Condition, Connection, Copy, Decision, Degree, Desire, Development, Different, Do, Education, End, Event, Example, Existence, Experience, Fact, Fear, Feeling, Fiction, Force, Form, Free, General, Get, Give, Good, Government, Happy, Have, History, Idea, Important, Interest, Knowledge, Law, Let, Level, Living, Love, Make, Material, Measure, Mind, Motion, Name, Nation, Natural, Necessary, Normal, Number, Observation, Opposite, Order, Organization, Part, Place, Pleasure, Possible, Power, Probable, Property, Purpose, Quality, Question, Reason, Relation, Representative, Respect, Responsible, Right, Same, Say, Science, See, Seem, Sense, Sign, Simple, Society, Sort, Special, Substance, Thing, Thought, True, Use, Way, Wise, Word, Work.

I have, in fact, left 103 words in this list—to incite the reader to the task of cutting out those he sees no point in and adding any he pleases, and to discourage the notion that there is anything sacrosanct about a hundred, or any other number. The very usefulness which gives them their importance explains their ambiguity. They are the servants of too many interests to keep to single, clearly defined jobs. Technical words in the sciences are like adzes, planes, gimlets, or razors. A word like "experience," or "feeling," or "true" is like a pocketknife. In good hands it will do most things—not very well. In general we will find that the more important a word is, and the more central and necessary its meanings are in our pictures of ourselves and the world, the more ambiguous and possibly deceiving the word will be. Naturally these words are also those which have been most used in philosophy. But it is not the philosophers who have made them ambiguous; it is the position of their ideas, as the very hinges of all thought.

To say, then, that a reader's sagacity comes from *experience* in reading is not to say much unless we can do something to clear up what is meant here by "experience." In a rough way everyone will agree. A good doctor gets his ability to diagnose from experience. A good judge gets his discernment from experience. But what is this experience which gives some men so much and others so little? It is not having many things happen to one merely. Some who have read little read well; others who have read much read badly. What happened and how it happened matter more than the quantity or variety of happenings. If we are to get any light on the reading process, on why it goes wrong and on how it might be improved, we must look as closely as we can into our own minds as we read and form as live a conception as we may of the sort of experience with words in sentences which makes better readers. . . .

The main source of any view, sound or silly, which we have of how we read must be our own observations of our own doings while we are reading. We should supplement this by observations of others' behavior and their reports, but inevitably in interpreting such other evidence we start from and return to that picture of a mind at work which only introspection can supply.

We do not realize what an opportunity our reading affords us for these self-observations. There, in the most convenient form, is an admirable experimental setup. We need no colleague to set us tasks; the author takes that duty over. All that we have to do is to cultivate the trick of changing our easily observed reactions from a communion or dispute with him into notes on our own deliberations. There must, however, be some difficulty in the page we face to stir us to noteworthy maneuvers. Otherwise this page prefaced by "I saw that . . ." would serve as a record of our doings. Any page which stretches our power of comprehending can teach us much about how we grope, and comparison of a number of pages—if we did not let our interest in the search too soon overcome our interest in the searching—could show us useful differences between guessing and grasping. On the other hand, there must be something on the page we really care about understanding. Otherwise we will go through the motions of reading only and the result will be uninstructive.

It is an advantage if the passages we use for these experiments form a series presenting in different settings and with different verbal expression somewhat similar problems to thought. The operations with which we work at them—generalization, abstraction, deduction, induction, division, exemplification, assumption, definition—have flavors of their own, which we learn to recognize as we become clearer as to what we are doing in them. As topics to *discuss* they are all but stupefying. Logicians long ago proved that to us. Only adepts long inured to them can keep awake. Only a minimum of such discussion will appear in these pages. We propose to practice these operations rather than to discuss them. And through practice we can become better aware of what they do than through even the clearest discussion.

In reading we are performing these operations all the time. Each has its own characteristic mishaps, and these stumblings have their own distinctive feelings. We can sometimes know that we are going wrong without being able yet to see what has happened. It is such observations that we will be on the lookout for.

I will add after each passage a commentary designed to help a reader:

1. to notice what he does with them in a first perusal.
2. to compare this with what happens in later, more questioning attention.
3. to compare both with various suggested possibilities.
4. to notice upon what points any decision about the meaning of the passage turns for him.

Inevitably I will have my own views about the interpretations of the passages. To hide them would be artificial and the attempt would probably fail. My aim will not be to get the reader to agree with me in my readings. I have no very robust confidence that they are right. So I will not be expounding them as I would if persuasion were the aim. Just what our passages say is, for our purpose here, less important than *how* they say it and how they may say different things to different readers. It is the reading process rather than the products we are to study.

On the other hand, it would be idle to invite so much attention to passages which could not say rather important things, or in which the ambiguities were not of a sort which recur everywhere in writing. My extracts will therefore be, most of them, from great writers, and will treat questions of the first order of importance. And these questions will be those we will inevitably have in mind in considering our experience while reading. Thus we may with them sometimes be catching more than one bird with the same throw of the net. Most of the passages will be difficult, some very. It is the difficulties of reading we are studying. In each case please read through once carefully. Then sit back and try to collect and survey what you have gathered before reading my remarks and returning to study the passage.

My first passage, which is among the hardest, gives us Aristotle's account of "learning by experience." It comes from the last pages of the *Posterior Analytics.*

It will be followed by a version in Basic English. I shall be making much use of the techniques of Basic English throughout. Being pinched within the limits of 850 words forces one to look at the original one in translating with an intentness hard to keep up otherwise. By cutting out the easy synonym it makes one go into the possibilities of the forbidden words more deeply. Here "perception" (which Aristotle is describing for us) will be the only non-Basic word used.

Aristotle has asked how we get to know the basic, primary or immediate, premises from which demonstration leading to scientific knowledge sets out. Demonstration has to start from things undemonstrated. How have we come to know such things? Are we born with the knowledge and does the infant just fail to notice he has it? That would be too strange. On the other hand, it can't just pop into our minds complete without there being anything from which it is developed.

Therefore we must possess a capacity of some sort, but not such as to rank higher in accuracy than these developed states. And this at least is an obvious characteristic of all animals, for they possess a congenital discriminative capacity which is called sense-perception. But though sense-perception is innate in
5 all animals, in some the sense-impression comes to persist, in others it does not. So animals in which this persistence does not come to be have either no knowledge at all outside the act of perceiving, or no knowledge of objects of which no impression persists; animals in which it does come into being have perception and can continue to retain the sense-impression in the soul: and
10 when such persistence is frequently repeated a further distinction at once arises between those which out of the persistence of such sense-impressions develop a power of systematizing them and those which do not. So out of sense-perception comes to be what we call memory, and out of frequently repeated memories of the same thing develops experience; for a number of
15 memories constitute a single experience. From experience again—i.e., from the universal now stabilized in its entirety within the soul, the one beside the many which is a single identity within them all—originate the skill of the craftsman and the knowledge of the man of science, skill in the sphere of coming to be and science in the sphere of being.

The first time we read through this we are likely at places to feel a little like those animals in whom no impression persists. What is said seems too cloudy or too folded over upon itself to be taken in. One such place will be perhaps at lines 6-7, where the *either . . . or* comes. This feels like a crumple in the discourse. It is as though Aristotle were saying the thing twice, or we were seeing double. And we may notice the same effect at other places, as in the following sentence: "animals in which it [What's *it?* The persistence of course] does come into being have perception and can continue to retain the sense-impression in the soul." Here if "the persistence does come into being" it seems unnecessary to add that the animals "can continue to retain the sense-impression in the soul." That is said already. This redundancy of expression is very characteristic of Aristotle and may have something to do with his lecturing technique. These are lecture notes, and the repetitions can be so inflected by the voice that they amount to emphasis, or a sort of soothing confirmation to the listener that he *has* got the point. In reading with the eye we miss these pointers as to when it is a new nail being driven or just another tap on one already home. It will be found in general that reading a passage aloud with this sort of thing in mind is an enormous help in giving perspective to an argument, making its structure more evident, and focusing one's attention on the right places.

Developing the structure of the argument in this way goes, of course, along with questioning the meaning of its words and phrases and with tentative decisions as to what is said. As a means of getting that ready for discussion, let me offer here a simplified translation. (Of the English passage as it stands, I have no pretensions to be able to comment on the fidelity of the

Oxford version to the Greek.) This version may both bring out the structure, as I see it, and give you something to compare with what you have found.

> So we have to be able to get this knowledge in some way but not in a way which makes it righter than the knowledge which comes out of it. And this is clearly true of all animals, for they have from birth a power to see different things as different, which is named "sense-perception." But though all animals
> 5 have sense-perception by birth, some of them keep what it takes in, and some of them don't. Those which don't ever become able to keep these things have no knowledge at all when the act of sensing isn't going on. Those that are able to keep the effects of sensing and keep them again and again are of two sorts. There are those which become able through keeping them to put them into
> 10 some order and those which don't. So out of sense-perception comes to be what is named "memory." And out of frequent memories of the same thing comes experience; for a number of memories make up one experience. From experience again—that is, from the general form now fixed as a complete thing in the mind, the one thing which is the same in any number of exam-
> 15 ples—come the art of the workman and the knowledge of the man of science, art as having to do with changing things and science as having to do with what is ever the same.

Now let us compare this rendering with the original and note some of the problems which came up in making it:

1. line *2, higher in accuracy: righter,* as one answer to a question is nearer to the right answer than another. *Accuracy, precision, exactness* are difficult words to be clear about. They share some of the troubles of *true* and some of those of *definite.* A definite answer need not be true, nor a true one definite. If we try hard enough to see what *true* and *definite* may mean we will not be surprised that true and definite interpretations are so hard to arrive at.

2. line *3, congenital discriminative capacity: power to see different things as different. See* is (by metaphor) short for "perceive through any of the senses." That would not mislead. But *see* might suggest that all animals do more than respond differently to some sorts of different things, that they *see* (i.e., understand as a philosopher might) what the differences are. Aristotle is thinking of no such intellectual feat. This discriminative capacity is just the ability to be affected differently when their surroundings are different in certain ways, that is, to vary with their surroundings in certain ways. Lifeless bodies have this ability too—in very limited ways, however. A billiard ball is affected differently by different pushes, but it is little influenced by smells if at all.

3. line *5, innate: by birth.* I hesitated between *by, from,* and *at birth* here. *By* might suggest that the process of birth gave them the power, but that is not a likely interpretation. *From* and *at* suggest that they have it the moment they are born. But an innate power may come into operation only

later. Kittens have to open their eyes before they see different things as different. The notion of innate powers, like that of inheritance, collapses if we look at it too closely, as Aristotle knew. "Innate" and "congenital" say no more than that an animal has the power under the right conditions. What we are born with has to have certain conditions if it is to come out. So the contrast between heredity and environment is a false one if we make them independent. Under different conditions we would be found to have inherited different powers.

4. line 7–8, *and when such persistence is frequently repeated: those that are able to keep the effects of sensing and keep them again and again.* The problem here is whether the impressions which have to be kept if the power of systematizing them is to develop are of the same sort or not. I was tempted to write "able to keep the different effects of sensing." That would make a more satisfactory theory. But Aristotle might only have in view the return again and again of the same impression $a_1 a_2 a_3 \ldots a_n$ leading to A, the universal or form which they share. On the other theory the thing would be more complex. By "the persistence is frequently repeated" he would mean that $a_1 a_2 a_3 \ldots$

and $b_1 b_2 b_3 \ldots$

and $c_1 c_2 c_3 \ldots$ came

back. Not only that but there would be such repetitions as

$a_1 b_1 a_2 b_2 a_3 b_3 \ldots$

$a_1 c_1 a_2 c_2 a_3 c_3 \ldots$

$a_1 b_1 c_1 a_2 b_2 c_2 a_3 b_3 c_3 \ldots$

The same sense impressions come back *in varying frames of other impressions,* and it would be through *that,* not through mere unvarying repetition, that "the power of systematizing them" would be developed. It is hard to see why any number of repetitions of the same impression, however well they are retained, should become anything other than an embarrassing crowd of them. But "the universal . . . the one beside the many which is a single identity within them all" is certainly not a swarm of impressions. The impressions are the many; the one is their form, that which makes them the same. The evidence *here* that Aristotle held the more complex theory is the next phase I now discuss.

5. line 9, *systematizing them: putting them into some order.* I might have written (still in Basic), "sorting and ordering them and separating their different connections with one another," for that is what has to be done if this kind of knowledge is to arise. The systematizing which constitutes experience and supplies our basic premises is very much more than merely noting "thingumbob again!" A typical basic premise, guaranteed by experience, is: *tapping with one's fingernail on a table makes a sharp little sound.* This is woven in with such other premises as *tapping so on a can, on a stove . . . makes a different sound,* and *tapping so with the soft tip of the*

finger makes hardly any sound. The fabric these belong to is so vast that I could easily fill this book with nothing but such commonplaces of experience all connected with one another through universals. The universal which my wording makes prominent here is *tapping.* These are all instances of tapping. A much more embracing universal is *make,* which is indeed one of the topmost powers in the hierarchy (makes a sound, makes sense, etc.). *Tapping* is a fairly specific universal. It divides up into light-impacts-between-surfaces-of-solids, say, all of which are more general universals. *Make* is a very general universal and is perhaps indivisible. We meet a baffling simplicity if we try to say what making is. *Systematizing* here is the coming into the soul of universals and the growth of their connections with one another there. It is these connections which stabilize them. "The soul is the place of forms," says Aristotle elsewhere. Here he says, "within the soul." Maybe we confuse ourselves with this spatial metaphor *in* the soul. We would if we took it seriously. But the metaphor is too convenient to be abandoned. It might be more accurate to say that the soul just is the universals which knit together all it knows, as we might say that its knowledge (compare the metaphor in *cognition*) was that knitting together. But these are hardly lucid ways of talking. (Or overlucid? We have with them the same difficulty that we have in seeing empty space.)

6. line *14, soul: mind.* Basic does not include the word "soul," but adds it for its version of the Bible. "Soul" identifies for us Aristotle's word here (ψυκή), but we should not lightly identify Aristotle's conception of the soul with a Christian one or with any other. He is writing psychology here, and modern psychology in spite of its name has for such uses replaced "soul" by "mind." My change would therefore not mislead unless the reader were thinking of other Greek words which would have to be translated by "mind."

7. line *11, memory.* Psychology distinguishes memory from retention, the persistence Aristotle is talking of here, and limits "memory" to remembering and what is remembered. When we remember some event we look back to it. But the effects of the event may persist without our remembering it. We do not have to remember former acts of tapping tables in order to know what sound will be made. It is retention—the persistence of past events—which forms experience here. It is not memory in the sense in which you will use your memory when you write your memoirs.

8. line *12,* a number of memories *constitute a single experience: making up one experience.* "Experience" here plainly means something very different from the most frequent current use—"That raid was a terrific experience"—or the sense in which teachers, for example, talk so much about "worth-while experiences." In Aristotle's sense we do not get experience by just going through events but by learning something *general* or universal therein. "I regard as genuine knowledge only that which returns again as power," said Coleridge. The power is the ability to recognize, to know again

that universal (or *with* that universal, if we make it the power of knowing rather than what is known).

Constitute is a troublesome word. Does it mean "set up" or "actually are"? A number of words have this same trick: *compose, consist* ("By Him all things consist"—*Colossians* 1:17), *form,* and *make* are examples. They are very convenient when we do not know which we mean, or when it does not matter, but they are a nuisance at places like this. The only thing to do is to explore both possibilities as far as we can. We get two theories:

A. That Aristotle is stating as a matter of fact that a number of persisting impressions develop into or cause to come into being *something else,* a universal.
B. That he is pointing out that, after all, an experience (as a universal) really is what is common to a number of persisting impressions. As soon as the impressions are taken together by the mind as being *of the same thing,* the universal is at work. They couldn't be of the *same* thing, without it.

Why a *single* experience? To raise the contrast driven home in the next sentence between the plural impressions and the one universal. We keep this use in sentences like "My experience is that such men don't go far." On the other hand, most pedagogic talk about "worth-while experiences" is about multifarious impressions.

9. line *13, in its entirety: as a complete thing.* Universals seem hard to think of, or even self-contradictory, chiefly because we try to imagine them, to see them in the mind's eye as if they existed in space. So when we say a universal is *in* many things and *in* many minds, if we do not take these *in*'s literally, at least we give them a ghost's body. We think of universals as having parts: the phrase "in its entirety" is there to defend us from this habit.

10. line *16, the sphere of being: what is ever the same.* Science is knowledge of the unchanging. This may seem odd since the scientific worker is studying changes all the time. But what he is trying to know is the law of some change; and laws are unchanging. *Art,* since for Aristotle here it is concerned with making things, or with practical activity as in medical treatment, is a knowledge of how to make changes. Both originate in experience. The scientist would have no changes to study and the artist-workman no *things* to change, if the universals had not been stabilized in their soul as experience. They would merely be indescribable chaoses.

We may now pause to consider what, so far, in the process of reading as we have been observing it here in our minds, offers any suggestion toward a technique for improving reading. A number of points seem worth noting. I believe most readers will confirm them.

1. When eye reading alone does not give us a clear sense of the grammar and of the logical structure, we tend to switch speaking and hearing on. We

can do this in two ways which are, as it were, degrees of realization or actualization of the sentences.

A. We read it in imagination—producing *images* of the speech movements and of the sound of the words.
B. We really utter the words faintly or out loud.

Vocal reading can aid in giving structure to the argument. It is an experimental manipulation, a testing procedure on trial-and-error lines. While noting that reading a thing out loud may be a great help, we should not forget that it can be a great hindrance. As the name "trial and error" (rather than "trial and triumph") suggests, there are likely to be more errors than successes. The eye is a more neutral agent than the voice. Or, to put it more fairly, the voice, if there has been failure, can easily add a very persuasive garb or garble of rhythm and intonation to support the misinterpretation. This commonly happens when the cause of the misinterpretation has been prejudice—the interference of some sentiment. Nothing is easier than to make words ring out or fall flat as we please, to our own ears—especially if we don't know we are doing it. So the chances of our detecting the twist we are giving in our reading are much reduced. When other people read things to us, we often think, "So long as you read it *that way* you can't possibly understand what it says!" We should more often be saying the same thing to ourselves. In particular, a certain querulous questioning tone—"What *can* it mean?"—is an enemy of comprehension. Read it as though it made sense and perhaps it will.

2. In addition to reading the words on the page to ourselves in various ways and with various tones, we can add to them—anything from ejaculations, delighted or derisive, to an analytic commentary. Some people do no little talking to themselves while reading. For them, it is very much a part of the reading process. With argumentative matter the reader should talk back as much as possible unless he is merely fighting, talking for a victory there will be no one but himself to award. Though debate is silly, reasoning is still dialogue, as Plato said.

This touches a large theme—the different modes of reading suited to different types of writing. It is absurd to read everything—poetry, prose, pulp—alike, especially to read it all as *fast* as possible. Whom are they fleeing from, these running readers? I fear the only answer is, "Themselves." Anything that is worth *studying* should be read *as slowly* as it will let you, and read again and again till you have it by heart. Only so will the persistencies be repeated frequently enough for a power of systematizing them to develop. Most of us read too fast rather than too slowly. This opinion goes bang in the teeth, I know, of the massed professional teachers of the reading art, those who are telling one another so often that they are failing to teach it. They will brandish their figures to show that the fastest readers get most.

One may still ask: How do you know they would not have got something of another order if they had not sped so fast? Have their speeding teachers themselves got quite enough out of their reading to be able to judge? And these are things which no "comprehension test" yet devised can measure. But all this belongs to our conclusions, when we have studied the process of reading in much greater detail.

3. From internal dialogue to rephrasing is a small step. Most people find that having two versions of a passage before them opens up the task of exploration immensely. This is true even when one version is clearly very inferior; its presence still throws the implications of the other into relief. So a black-and-white reproduction of a picture can make us see what the color in the original is doing. A better parallel, perhaps, is with photographic surveying. Two versions are like two views from slightly different angles. If we can fit them together, each tells us much about the things seen in the other.

These effects are striking enough to promise (if we can study them successfully) some real improvement in reading. And tradition in teaching backs up this hope. Translation work has been the main technique of literary education in the past. Now no one who knows how translation—whether from Latin into English or back again or with French or German either way—is ordinarily done and has ordinarily been done in the past will see in that dreary and largely mechanical routine any saving virtue. It is only in the best translation work, which comes after the mechanics of the strange tongue have been mastered, and only in the hands of teachers who are themselves exacting readers, that the incessant comparisons required between different ways of saying more or less the same thing become any royal road to good reading. *Thorough* mastery of a foreign language, no doubt, always improves our understanding of the mother tongue in some degree. Getting a smattering does not. Even the first steps in a foreign tongue *can* be made a profitable study of our own language, but current practice fails to do this; and the grim toil which follows consists mainly in replacing, one by one, words we hardly understand at all with words we have not time to consider—or vice versa. So my reference here to translation as a method of improving reading will not cheer up anyone to whom translation means primarily that. But there is an altogether different sort of translation in which both languages, as to the routine handling of their mechanics and the pocket-dictionary senses of their words, are fully grasped. The task then can become a deep exploration of meaning, a perfect exercise for developing resource and justice in interpretation.

The same merits can be possessed by English–English translation, if we put certain controls on it which bar out synonym trading and glosses which dodge or veil the difficulties. (Basic English offers us many possibilities of such controls.)

Comparison seems to be the key to all learning of this type. Learning to read is not fundamentally different from learning to be a good judge of wine, or of horses, or of men. Persistence of effects must be repeated frequently enough to become systematized. And, for progress to be rapid, effects whose similarities and differences—their sameness amid difference rather— are instructive should persist together. Some people can compare things across wide intervals of time. They go ahead faster than the rest of us. Others cannot make subtle comparisons between things which do not overlap in their effects. Everything depends, of course, on what things are being compared by whom. What I have just been saying applies chiefly to first comparisons between somewhat novel things in somewhat novel respects— the earliest stages of the systematization about which Aristotle was talking. The more any body of perceptions becomes systematized, the easier it becomes to span vast stretches of time in comparing examples within it. A real expert can identify a wine and its condition even though he has not tasted any similar wine for years. But that is only because his experience became well systematized in the bygone days when he was tasting such wines. And then, no doubt, his comparisons were not very widely spaced apart.

Now, if reading is a matter of organized comparisons between meanings, as it certainly is, it should not be difficult to arrange things so that the best opportunities for the growth of this organization or systematization are secured. What we have to do is put the materials for distinctions and connections about which we are not clear enough *together,* so that the universals can develop through comparison. And we will do this best by using different ways of saying "the same thing" in close collocation.

But four very important qualifications must be made or this program will lead us into nothing but folly:

A. We must know which are the important distinctions and connections.
B. We must be very much on our guard with the phrase "the same thing."
C. We must respect the fundamental conditions of interest.
D. We must recognize that failure to see an important distinction or connection is most often due to our not *wanting* to see it.

I will take these up in turn, and then pass on to some experiments with another passage in the light of these reflections.

a. I have mentioned already—when listing my hundred great words—the chief reasons which make some distinctions and connections more important than others. Let me restate them here in another form. The most important ideas (and an idea here is a form of distinction and connection) are the *necessary* ones in the sense that we cannot do without them. They enter inevitably into all our thinking, for thinking is just another name for the operation of these ideas. Typical among them are the ideas covered by *same, different, change, cause, thing, idea, part, whole, abstract, concrete, general, special, form, implies, matter, quality,* and *relation.* Language has an inexhaustible variety of ways of expressing these ideas, and we may easily fail to notice that they are serving still as the structure of our thought. Sometimes, too, we may handle them better through language which does not make them prominent by using these bald and somewhat formidable words. More often, though, we miss a point or confuse an argument by failing to see that under the attractively novel phrasing, and behind its special graces, we have to do with the same familiar joints and muscles and bones.

To say we cannot do without these ideas may seem to get us into a difficulty. If we have them and use them all the time already, what is the point of working up great programs for teaching ourselves about them? The point is that no one is as skillful with them as he might be, and that much of the inefficiency of thought and language comes from needless blundering with these ideas. But here again we must note that skill with them is not in the least the same thing as being able to propound even the best theories about them. A first-rate authority on the foundations of mathematics might well be a poor mathematician. And so it is throughout. Our aim will not be improved theory of language but improved conduct with it.

If we can improve our conduct of these ideas, our reward is everywhere. That is why time given to the words which can handle them least confusingly is better spent than time given to distinctions and connections which are only locally useful.

If we open a dictionary of synonyms we are faced with thousands of subtle problems. The early nineteenth-century compilers used to attempt to *state* distinctions between usages—with all but uniformly absurd results. The only thing that will show us what these different implications are is watching them at work. And only then, when we see with the help of all around it what a word is doing, can we fruitfully attempt to state this, or by experiment explore differentiations. When we do so we discover that there is a certain limited set of words which we use most in such attempted elucidations. They form a language within a language—the words needed in explaining the rest of the language. The ideas these words cover are fewer than we suppose, though there is something very artificial about pretending that we can *count* such things as ideas. All we can say is that the meanings of words are relatively compound or simple, and that careful analysis *in contexts* can as a rule break down a complex meaning into simpler ideas acting together in a certain form. It is the simpler ideas (and the words which handle them best) that are the most important for us to study if we are to improve our reading. No one will pretend, of course, that an improved understanding of these ideas will by itself teach us what different things different complexes of them will do. For that we need experience of the complexes themselves at work. But better knowledge of the simples will certainly help to form that experience of complexes at work.

b. We have now to take a look at some of the problems behind the innocent-seeming words "say the same thing." Both "say" and "same" need our best attention. Their meanings are closely intertwined.

When something is *said,* words are uttered (whether through waves in the air or patterns of rays from the surface of paper does not matter here) which have certain effects. How widely and generally, or how narrowly and specifically, are we to take these effects? Looked at closely enough, they are never the same for two readers or for the same reader twice. Looked at undiscriminately enough, they are much the same always. (What other words come with them, what the situation is, and so on, must, of course, be kept in mind throughout.) Whether for practical purposes we account them *the same* depends upon two things: upon our purpose and upon the respects in which they are the same and different.

All this we all know in a sense very well. Yet we endlessly talk and frequently think as if in forgetfulness of it. We assert that two phrases say the same or that they do not, as if that were something which turned on the phrases alone—in utter independence of who reads them and when and why and within what setting. Probably when we do this we are assuming a host of things: including a standard reader with some sort of normal purpose and a standard setting and range of situations. We would be very hard put to it, indeed, if we had to be specific about these assumptions. But we are rather suspiciously careful not to explore them. We take them for granted and people are only too ready, in fact, to grant them. We seem even to suffer from a fear that questioning these assumptions will lead to no good, will shake the foundations of communication perhaps and let anyone with any word mean anything he pleases.

This background fear is empty, though its roots are perhaps deep in man's first speculations about language when he first began to experience its magical powers. Nobody perhaps, after reflection, now believes that words have their meanings in their own right, as our bodies have their minds. We have replaced that old belief with another which looks much more plausible but is as groundless. It is the belief in a sort of compact or agreement between all good users of the language to use words only in certain limited ways. It is true enough that we do behave with words *as if* some such compact ruled their uses. But the explanation in terms of usage agreement is wrong. The stability of the language has other causes. It comes from our experience of the ways in which words are tied up with one another. A language is a fabric which holds itself together. It is a fabric which, for the most part brokenly and confusedly but sometimes with startling and heartbreaking clarity, reflects the fabric of universals which is our world.

There is no risk whatever, then, in questioning the assumptions which make us say two phrases must or can't mean the same. And to be able to question them—not as a piece of linguistic theory but in practice as they come up—is a large part of the art of reading. We ought to be incessantly ready to ask of two phrases which seem "more or less to mean the same" just wherein (and for whom) are their effects alike and wherein different. And to decide whether—for the purpose in hand, which is what the whole passage is swayed by—the differences are relevant. If they are not, we can be indifferent to them. But with a slight change in the purpose they might become very important. Any ruling on such points which does not take the purpose into account *is* an attack on language. We ought to fear pedants who cry, "But that *isn't* the meaning of the word," much more than any rash or wanton innovator.

One other quirk in our behavior with phrases said to mean the same is also perhaps connected with remnants of magical beliefs. My Basic English version of the Aristotle passage, for example, says, *more or less,* what the Oxford translation says. In comparing two versions our minds sometimes perform this antic: instead of regarding them as two sets of words which in some ways have similar outcomes, in other ways different, we may suddenly find ourselves thinking, of one, "So *that* is what he was trying to say!" We are then likely to follow it up with, "It's a pity he didn't say it!" In extreme cases (and none such will probably occur in this instance) what happens is that the reader then identifies the thought with the *words* of the version he prefers. They become for him what the other passage is (inefficiently) saying, and he makes no comparison between meanings. He is helped in this by the chief regular systematic ambiguity of *say:* We say certain words and then *they* may say more than we are saying with them. These three *say*'s say very different things—as we see if we replace them with more explicit phrases: We give voice to certain words and then they may be taken to mean more than we have in mind.

c. There are few important words which are not in varying patterns systematically ambiguous; *say* is typical. These *regular* shifts of sense as a rule give us little trouble in reading, but all untechnical words also *change* their meanings from place to place in discourse under the pressures of the purpose and the setting. And these Sense Content Changes, because they are so closely related to the purpose, are specially important to follow. We need not *notice* them and usually do not; but we must submit to them if we are not to misread. But because they are made against the resistance of the word's normal relations with other words, the likelihood of misreading is considerable. If we accept the change we will probably never be aware that it occurred. If we don't, then we will either boggle at the passage and find discontinuity or nonsense in it, or more probably we will go on happily assured of a meaning which a better reader would see was not intended. If an author's purposes lead him to change the meanings of too many words, people do not go on reading them. He becomes too hard to follow—unless he is so great a writer and so adroit in relating his changes to one another that he reshapes language for us. Shakespeare is the great example. The interest of what he is doing has made us accept an experimental handling of language which otherwise would have been unreadable. He wrote, though, for an audience which was very skillful in interpretation. Thus language protects itself.

It is possible to collect examples of important words pushed out of their normal uses by various pressures. The great dictionaries contain such collections in an early, as yet little organized, stage of development. By drawing on these collections and appending paraphrases to show how words which in one place say one thing in another say another, tables and exercises affording unlimited opportunities for comparisons can be prepared. It might well be thought that these would provide the best means of improving reading. The traditional grammar books, however, by failing to teach the lessons they intended, have taught us another, of more value perhaps. We do not learn linguistic points from tables and examples; we learn through using the language—not in exercises but in the pursuit of a meaning we are seeking for a specific not a general purpose. In other words, the desire to improve our reading, worthy though it is, won't help us unless it operates through the work of puzzling out a passage because we care what it says. The persistencies of effects—no matter how well we make them overlap—will not systematize themselves into experience (knowledge that returns as power) unless they are heated by an immediate sustaining interest.

d. But interest, the great weldor (as the weldors spell it now, a *welder* being a machine: compare *actor* and *sailor*) of universals, is also the great logic-breaker. If we want to, or if something in us wants to establish something, we grow blind to any thwarting idea, however familiar it is or however obvious it might otherwise be; we deform our distinctions and connections to meet our aim, commit every sort of injustice and make the very word "argument" a term of derision. Mercury, the interpreter and messenger of Heaven, was also the patron god of rogues.

Most mistakes in reading look willful—not only to the man in the other camp but to the impartial eye. Few of them are, but it is harder to be fairminded in reading than we know, and a passion for the truth is misinterpretation's favorite guise. . . .

Speculative Instruments

A well-designed inquiry into the resourcefulness of the words which most occasion misunderstandings would amount to a study of metaphysic. (I don't know a subject in which study of the resourcefulness of its key terms doesn't amount to the subject, properly studied, itself.) It is perfectly compatible with close attention to selected passages from great books. I would say it required that. But it would be metaphysic approached from a different angle. We would not be attempting to show our students (much less tell them) what Plato or Aristotle really meant. That is a job for a superhuman historian of human thought a million years hence perhaps. We would be trying to help them to see for themselves some of the more important things the great texts may mean. And, since misunderstandings and corruptions of their thought may have played a great part in our tradition, we would be including these also. We would, I suggest, be giving little time to refutation or to the formal logical technique of philosophical proof or contention. Training in that is best given within a technically rigidified vocabulary; and we would above all try to defend our pupils from supposing that one philosophical view must necessarily be irreconcilable with another. This last amounts to throwing aside what has traditionally been held to be the chief business of philosophers. If you think it too drastic I can only confess that my own commerce with the disputatious has left me with a sad conviction that when you are refuting a view you become too busy to see what it is.

What we would aim at is a knowledge of *how* and *why* these central intellectual terms—*being, have, cause, connection, same,* and the like—can shift their meanings and thus give rise to varied misunderstandings. To develop the spatial metaphor here, which being all but unavoidable should be made as explicit as possible, all these words wander in many directions in this figurative space of meaning. But they wander *systematically,* as do those other wanderers, the Planets. By fixing a limited number of positions, meanings, for them, we may help ourselves to plot their courses. But we should not persuade ourselves that they must be at one or other of these marked points. The laws of their motions are what we need to know: their dependence upon the positions of the other words that should be taken into account with them.

To early astronomers and travellers the wanderings of the planets may have seemed troublesome. Or, more probably, portentous. Full of significance indeed they were! When understood they became the key to all the other motions in the heavens that we have yet ascertained or conjectured. A similar human preference for "fixities" and "definites" and "absolutes" is perhaps the source of some of the opposition which these suggestions may encounter.

I have said that the wandering—the resourcefulness—of these central terms of discourse is systematic. I ought to say a word or two more on that; to be brief, the same misunderstandings endlessly recur. Few people ever commit a new and original misunderstanding. Misinterpretations run to type, to a small number of types. An adequate study of one intellectual mistake can be made to illumine countless other fields where invitations to similar mistakes are offered. It is this which makes insight into *the patterns of resource* able to knit different studies together. The same problems in interpretation arise in them all. We do not at present benefit as we should from the limited variety of our stupidities. This may be, in part, because we have not developed appropriate exercises. Are we perhaps like mathematicians who had never thought of using the working of examples as a technique of instruction?

KENNETH BURKE
b. 1897

Born in Pittsburgh, Kenneth Duva Burke attended Ohio State University and Columbia University, but he left a promising scholastic career to devote himself to writing. During a career that began in the 1920s, Burke has written in so many forms and on so many subjects that he is thought of as the finest speculative mind and the foremost rhetorician of the twentieth century. Burke has reached his present stature by his lifelong study of humankind and our language-using habits; he makes social and psychoanalytic extensions of the Aristotelian philosophy of rhetoric with his theory of verbalized motivation. Burke's entire system is wrapped up in dramatism, *a technique of analysis of language and thought as modes of action rather than as means of conveying information. The backbone of this system is the* pentad, *a set of conceptual tools for the attributing of motives: act, scene, agent, agency, and purpose (later a hexad with the addition of attitude). Dramatism affirms language as the basis of all knowledge; all human activities stem from Burke's assertion that we are symbol-using animals. The purpose of Burke's work is to show us the function and inclusiveness of rhetoric—how humans as symbol-using animals use words to bridge social estrangements. Burke's key term in his system of dramatism is* identification, *a concept on which the New Rhetorics draw for a comprehensive understanding of ethos. Burke develops his conceptual framework of rhetoric in* Attitudes toward History *(1937),* The Philosophy of Literary Form *(1941),* A Grammar of Motives *(1945),* A Rhetoric of Motives *(1950), and* Language as Symbolic Action *(1966).*

Definition of Man

I

First, a few words on definition in general. Let's admit it: I see in a definition the critic's equivalent of a lyric, or of an aria in opera. Also, we might note that, when used in an essay, as with Aristotle's definition of tragedy in his *Poetics,* a definition so sums things up that all the properties attributed to the thing defined can be as though "derived" from the definition. In actual development, the definition may be the last thing a writer hits upon. Or it may be formulated somewhere along the line. But logically it is prior to the observations that it summarizes. Thus, insofar as all the attributes of the thing defined fit the definition, the definition should be viewed as "prior" in this purely nontemporal sense of priority.

Definitions are also the critic's equivalent of the lyric (though a poet might not think so!) in that the writer usually "hits on them." They are "breakthroughs," and thus are somewhat hard to come by. We should always keep trying for them—but they don't always seem to "click."

A definition should have just enough clauses, and no more. However, each clause should be like a chapter head, under which appropriate observations might be assembled, as though derived from it.

I am offering my Definition of Man in the hope of either persuading the reader that it fills the bill, or of prompting him to decide what should be added, or subtracted, or in some way modified.

II

Man is the symbol-using animal.

Granted, it doesn't come as much of a surprise. But our definition is being offered not for any possible paradoxical value. The aim is to get as essential a set of clauses as possible, and to meditate on each of them.

I remember one day at college when, on entering my philosophy class, I found all blinds up and the windows open from the top, while a bird kept flying nervously about the ceiling. The windows were high, they extended almost to the ceiling; yet the bird kept trying to escape by batting against the ceiling rather than dipping down and flying out one of the open windows. While it kept circling thus helplessly over our heads, the instructor explained that this was an example of a "tropism." This particular bird's instinct was to escape by flying *up*, he said; hence it ignored the easy exit through the windows.

But how different things would be if the bird could speak and we could speak his language. What a simple statement would have served to solve his problem. "Fly down just a foot or so, and out one of those windows."

Later, I ran across another example that I cite because it has further implications, with regard to a later clause in our definition. I witnessed the behavior of a wren that was unquestionably a genius within the terms of its species. The parents had succeeded in getting all of a brood off the nest except one particularly stubborn or backward fellow who still remained for a couple of days after the others had flown. Despite all kinds of threats and cajolery, he still lingered, demanding and getting the rations which all concerned seem to consider his rightful lot. Then came the moment of genius. One of the parent wrens came to the nest with a morsel of food. But instead of simply giving it to the noisy youngster, the parent bird held it at a distance. The fledgling in the nest kept stretching its neck out farther and farther with its beak gaping until, of a sudden, instead of merely putting the morsel of food into the bird's mouth, the parent wren clamped its beak shut on the young one's lower mandible, and with a slight jerk caused the youngster, with his outstretched neck, to lose balance and tumble out of the nest.

Surely this was an "act" of genius. This wren had discovered how to use the principle of leverage as a way of getting a young bird off the nest. Had that exceptionally brilliant wren been able to conceptualize this discovery in such terms as come easy to symbol systems, we can imagine him giving a dissertation on "The Use of the Principle of Leverage as an Improved Method for Unnesting Birds or Debirding a Nest." And within a few years the invention would spread throughout all birddom, with an incalculable saving in bird-hours as compared with the traditional turbulent and inefficient method still in general practice.

There are three things to note about this incident:

1. The ability to describe this method in words would have readily made it possible for all other birds to take over this same "act" of genius, though they themselves might never have hit upon it.
2. The likelihood is that even this one wren never used the method again. For the ability to conceptualize implies a kind of *attention* without which this innovation could probably not advance beyond the condition of a mere accident to the condition of an invention.
3. On the happier side, there is the thought that at least, through lack of such ability, birds are spared our many susceptibilities to the ways of demagogic spellbinders. They cannot be filled with fantastic hatreds for alien populations they know about mainly by mere hearsay, or with all sorts of unsettling new expectations, most of which could not possibly turn out as promised.

The "symbol-using animal," yes, obviously. But can we bring ourselves to realize just what that formula implies, just how overwhelmingly much of what we mean by "reality" has been built up for us through nothing but our symbol systems? Take away our books, and what little do we know about history, biography, even something so "down to earth" as the relative position of seas and continents? What is our "reality" for today (beyond the paper-thin line of our own particular lives) but all this clutter of symbols about the past combined with whatever things we know mainly through maps, magazines, newspapers, and the like about the present? In school, as they go from class to class, students turn from one idiom to another. The various courses in the curriculum are in effect but so many different terminologies. And however important to us is the tiny sliver of reality each of us has experienced firsthand, the whole overall "picture" is but a construct of our symbol systems. To meditate on this fact until one sees its full implications is much like peering over the edge of things into an ultimate abyss. And doubtless that's one reason why, though man is typically the symbol-using animal, he clings to a kind of naive verbal realism that refuses to realize the full extent of the role played by symbolicity in his notions of reality.

In responding to words, with their overt and covert modes of persuasion ("progress" is a typical one that usually sets expectations to vibrating), we like to forget the kind of relation that really prevails between the verbal and the nonverbal. In being a link between us and the nonverbal, words are by the same token a screen separating us from the nonverbal—though the statement gets tangled in its own traces, since so much of the "we" that is separated from the nonverbal by the verbal would not even exist were it not for the verbal (or for our symbolicity in general, since the same applies to the symbol systems of dance, music, painting, and the like).

A road map that helps us easily find our way from one side of the continent to the other owes its great utility to its exceptional existential poverty. It tells us absurdly little about the trip that is to be experienced in a welter of detail. Indeed, its value for us is in the very fact that it is so essentially inane.

Language referring to the realm of the nonverbal is necessarily talk about things in terms of what they are not—and in this sense we start out beset by a paradox. Such language is but a set of labels, signs for helping us find our way about. Indeed, they can even be so useful that they help us to invent ingenious ways of threatening to destroy ourselves. But even accuracy of this powerful sort does not get around the fact that such terms are sheer emptiness, as compared with the substance of the things they name. Nor is such abstractness confined to the language of scientific prose. Despite the concrete richness of the imagery in Keats's poems, his letters repeatedly refer to his art as "abstract." And the same kind of considerations would apply to the symbol systems of all other arts. Even so bodily a form of expression as the dance is abstract in this sense. (Indeed, in this regard it is so abstract that, when asking students to sum up the gist of a plot, I usually got the best results from dance majors, with music students a close second. Students specializing in literature or the social sciences tended to get bogged down in details. They were less apt at "abstracting.")

When a bit of talking takes place, just what is doing the talking? Just where are the words coming from? Some of the motivation must derive from our animality, and some from our symbolicity. We hear of "brainwashing," of schemes whereby an "ideology" is imposed upon people. But should we stop at that? Should we not also see the situation the other way around? For was not the "brainwasher" also similarly motivated? Do we simply use words, or do they not also use us? An "ideology" is like a god coming down to earth, where it will inhabit a place pervaded by its presence. An "ideology" is like a spirit taking up its abode in a body: it makes that body hop around in certain ways; and that same body would have hopped around in different ways had a different ideology happened to inhabit it.

I am saying in one way what Paul said in another when he told his listeners that "Faith comes from hearing." He had a doctrine which, if his hearers were persuaded to accept it, would direct a body somewhat differently from the way it would have moved and been moved in its daily rounds under the earlier pagan dispensation. Consider the kind of German boys and girls, for instance, who became burghers in the old days, who during the period of inflation and U.S.-financed reparation payments after World War I wanted but to be Wandering Birds, and who with the rise of the Third Reich were got to functioning as Hitlerite fiends.

With regard to this first clause in our definition (man as the "symbol-using" animal) it has often been suggested that "symbol-making" would be a better term. I can go along with that emendation. But I'd want to add one further step. Then, for the whole formula we'd have: the "symbol-using, symbol-making, and symbol-misusing animal."

In referring to the misuse of symbols, I have in mind not only such demagogic tricks as I have already mentioned. I also think of "psychogenic illnesses," violent dislocations of bodily motion due to the improperly criticized action of symbolicity. A certain kind of food may be perfectly wholesome, so far as its sheer material nature is concerned. And people in some areas may particularly prize it. But our habits may be such that it seems to us loathsome; and under those conditions, the very thought of eating it may be nauseating to us. (The most drastic instance is, of course, provided by the ideal diets of cannibals.) When the body rebels at such thoughts, we have a clear instance of the ways whereby the realm of symbolicity may affect the sheerly biologic motions of animality. Instances of "hexing" are of the same sort (as when a tribesman, on entering his tent, finds there the sign that for some reason those in authority have decreed his death by magic, and he promptly begins to waste away and die under the burden of this sheer thought).

A merely funny example concerns an anecdote told by the anthropologist, Franz Boas. He had gone to a feast being given by Esquimaux. As a good anthropologist, he would establish rapport by eating what they ate. But there was a pot full of what he took to be blubber. He dutifully took some, and felt sick. He went outside the igloo to recover. There he met an Esquimau woman, who was scandalized when she heard that they were serving blubber. For they hadn't told her! She rushed in—but came out soon after in great disgust. It wasn't blubber at all, it was simply dumplings. Had the good savant only known, he could have taken dumplings in his stride. But it was a battle indeed for him to hold them down when he thought of them as blubber!

So, in defining man as the symbol-using animal, we thereby set the conditions for asking: Which motives derive from man's animality, which from his symbolicity, and which from the combination of the two? Physicality is, of course, subsumed in animality. And though the *principles* of symbolism are not reducible to sheerly physical terms (quite as the rules of football are not so reducible despite the physicality of the players' hulks and motions as such), the meanings cannot be conceived by empirical organisms except by the aid of a sheerly physical dimension.

One further point, and we shall have finished with our first clause. In his analysis of dream symbolism, Freud laid great stress upon the two processes of "condensation" and "displacement." His observations are well taken. But, since we are here using the term "symbolism" in a much wider sense, we might remind ourselves that the processes of "condensation" and "displacement" are not confined merely to the symbolism of dreams and neuroses, but are also an aspect of normal symbol systems. A fundamental resource "natural" to symbolism is *substitution*. For instance, we can paraphrase a statement; if you don't get it one way, we can try another way. We translate English into French, Fahrenheit into Centigrade, or use the Greek letter *pi* to designate the ratio of the circumference of a circle to its diameter, otherwise stated as 3.14159. . . . In this sense, substitution is a quite rational resource of symbolism. Yet it is but a more general aspect of what Freud meant by "displacement" (which is a confused kind of substitution).

Or, as Horne Tooke pointed out a century and a half ago, a typical resource of language is abbreviation. And obviously, abbreviation is also a kind of substitution, hence a kind of "displacement," while it is also necessarily a kind of "condensation." And language is an abbreviation radically. If I refer to Mr. Jones by name, I have cut countless corners, as regards the particularities of that particular person. Or if I say, "Let's make a fire," think of what all I have left out, as regards the specific doing. Or if I give a book a title, I thereby refer to, while leaving unsaid, all that is subsumed under that title. Thus, condensation also can be viewed as a species of substitution. And a quite "rational" kind of "condensation" has taken place if, instead of referring to "tables," "chairs," and "rugs," I refer to "furniture," or if we put "parents" for "mother and father," and "siblings" for "brothers or sisters."

To say as much is to realize how many muddles such as Freud is concerned with may also be implicit in the symbols of "condensation" in his particular sense of the term. For my remarks are not intended as a "refutation" of Freud's terminology. By all means, my haggling about "condensation" and "displacement" as aspects of *all* symbolizing is not meant to question his line of investigation. All I am saying is that there still are some dividing lines to be drawn between the two realms (of symbolism in his sense and symbolism in general).

In any case, Freud (like Frazer) gives us ample grounds for trying never to forget that, once emotional involvement is added to symbolism's resources of substitution (which included the invitations to both condensation and displacement) the conditions are set for the symbol-using animal, with its ailments both physically and symbolically engendered, to tinker with such varying kinds of substitution as we encounter in men's modes of penance, expiation, compensation, paying of fines in lieu of bodily punishment, and cult of the scapegoat.

Obviously, to illustrate this point, there is an embarrassment of riches everywhere we choose to look, in the history of mankind. But, almost by accident, let us pick one, from a book, *Realm of the Incas,* by Victor W. Von Hagen. I refer to the picture of a

> propitiatory cairn, called *apacheta,* found in all of the high places of Peru on the ancient road. As heavily laden travelers passed along the road, they placed a stone on the *apacheta* as a symbol of the burden, "and so left their tiredness behind."

We are further told that "The Persians, the Chinese, and the Greeks adopted more or less the same custom."

Substitution sets the condition for "transcendence," since there is a technical sense in which the name for a thing can be said to "transcend" the thing named (by making for a kind of "ascent" from the realm of motion and matter to the realm of essence and spirit). The subterfuges of euphemism can carry this process still further, culminating in the resources of idealization that Plato perfected through his dialectic of the Upward Way and Downward Way.

The designation of man as the symbol-using animal parallels the traditional formulas, "rational animal" and *Homo sapiens*—but with one notable difference. These earlier versions are honorific, whereas the idea of symbolicity implies no such temptation to self-flattery, and to this extent is more admonitory. Such definitions as "two-footed land-animal" (referred to in Aristotle's *Topics*) or "featherless biped" (referred to in Spinoza's *Ethics*) would be inadequate because they would confine the horizon to the realm of motion.

So much for our first clause.

III

The second clause is: *Inventor of the negative.* I am not wholly happy with the word, "inventor." For we could not properly say that man "invented" the negative unless we can also say that man is the "inventor" of language itself. So far as sheerly empirical development is concerned, it might be more accurate to say that language and the negative "invented" man. In any case, we are here concerned with the fact that there are no negatives in nature, and that this ingenious addition to the universe is solely a product of human symbol systems. In an age when we are told, even in song, to "accentuate the positive," and when some experts in verbalization make big money writing inspirational works that praise "the power of positive thinking," the second clause of my definition must take on the difficult and thankless task of celebrating that peculiarly human marvel, the negative.

I have discussed elsewhere what an eye-opener the chapter, "The Idea of Nothing," was to me, in Bergson's *Creative Evolution*. It jolted me into realizing that there are no negatives in nature, where everything simply is what it is and as it is. To look for negatives in nature would be as absurd as though you were to go out hunting for the square root of minus-one. The negative is a function peculiar to symbol systems, quite as the square root of minus-one is an implication of a certain mathematical symbol system.

The quickest way to demonstrate the sheer symbolicity of the negative is to look at any object, say, a table, and to remind yourself that, though it is exactly what it is, you could go on for the rest of your life saying all the things that it is not. "It is not a book, it is not a house, it is not Times Square," etc., etc.

One of the negative's prime uses, as Bergson points out, involves its role with regard to unfulfilled expectations. If I am expecting a certain situation, and a different situation occurs, I can say that the expected situation did *not* occur. But so far as the actual state of affairs is concerned, some situation positively prevails, and that's that. If you are here but someone is expecting to meet you elsewhere, he will *not* meet you elsewhere because you positively *are* here. I can ask, "Does the thermometer read 54?" And if it registers anything in the world but 54, your proper answer can be "It is not 54." Yet there's no such thing as it's simply *not* being 54; it *is* 53, or 55, or whatever.

However, I would make one change of emphasis with regard to Bergson's fertile chapter. His stress is a bit too "Scientific" for specifically "Dramatistic" purposes. Thus, in keeping with the stress upon matters of knowledge, he stresses the propositional negative, "It *is* not." Dramatistically, the stress should be upon the hortatory negative, "Thou *shalt* not." The negative begins not as a resource of definition or information, but as a command, as "Don't." Its more "Scientistic" potentialities develop later. And whereas Bergson is right in observing that we can't have an "idea of nothing" (that we must imagine a black spot, or something being annihilated, or an abyss, or some such), I submit that we *can* have an "idea of No," an "idea of don't." The Existentialists may amuse themselves and bewilder us with paradoxes about *le Néant*, by the sheer linguistic trick of treating no-thing as an abstruse kind of something. It's good showmanship. But there's no paradox about the idea of "don't," and a child can learn its meaning early.

No, I must revise that statement somewhat. In one sense, there is a paradox about "don't." For the negative is but a *principle*, an *idea*, not a name for a *thing*. And thus, whereas an injunction such as "thou shalt not kill" is understandable enough as a negative *idea*, it also has about its edges the positive *image* of killing. But the main point is: Though a child may not always obey the "thou shalt not," and though there may inevitably be, in the offing, an image positively inviting disobedience, the child "gets the idea."

In this sense, though we can't have an "idea of nothing," we can have an "idea of no." When first working on the negative, I thought of looking through the documents on the training of Helen Keller and Laura Bridgeman, whose physical privations made it so difficult to teach them language. And in both cases the records showed that the hortatory negative was taught first, and it was later applied for use as propositional negative, without explicit recognition of the change in application.

There is a superbly relevant passage in Emerson's early long essay, *Nature,* in the chapter "Discipline," a paragraph ending thus: All things "shall hint or thunder to man the laws of right and wrong, and echo the ten commandments." In our scheme, this could be presented thus: "Reverse the statement, start with the principle of negation as in the Mosaic Decalogue, and everything encountered along your way will be negatively infused."

In other words, if our character is built of our responses (positive or negative) to the thou-shalt-not's of morality, and if we necessarily approach life from the standpoint of our personalities, will not all experience reflect the genius of this negativity? Laws are essentially negative; "mine" equals "not thine"; insofar as property is not protected by the thou-shalt-not's of either moral or civil law, it is not protected at all.

The negative principle in morals is often hidden behind a realm of quasi-positives. One can appreciate this situation most readily by thinking of monastic discipline. The day may be filled with a constant succession of positive acts. Yet they are ultimately guided or regulated by proscriptive principles, involving acquiescence to vows consciously and conscientiously taken, while such vows come to fulfillment formally in such admonitions as are embodied in the Decalogue. Next, bearing in mind such clear evidence of the moralistic negativity that underlies the "quasi-positives" of the monastic rituals and routines, look at sheerly secular ambitions, with their countless ways of "justifying" oneself—and all such efforts too will be seen for what they are, not simply positives, but "quasi-positives," countless improvised ways of responding to the negativity so basic to man as moral agent.

Thus, all definitions stressing man as moral agent would tie in with this clause (if I may quote a relevant passage from a recent book of mine, *The Rhetoric of Religion*):

> *Action* involves *character,* which involves *choice*—and the *form* of choice attains its perfection in the distinction between Yes and No (shall and shall-

not, will and will-not). Though the concept of sheer *motion* is non-ethical, *action* implies the ethical, the human personality. Hence the obvious close connection between the ethical and negativity, as indicated in the Decalogue.[1]

Is more needed on this point? We might say a few words about the role of antithesis in what are often called "polar" terms, not just Yes-No, but such similarly constructed pairs as: true-false, order-disorder, cosmos-chaos, success-failure, peace-war, pleasure-pain, clean-unclean, life-death, love-hate. These are to be distinguished from sheerly positive terms. The word "table," for instance, involves no thought of counter-table, anti-table, non-table, or un-table (except perhaps in the inventions of our quite positively negative-minded poet, E. E. Cummings).

We need not now decide whether, in such paired opposites, the positive or the negative member of the pair is to be considered as essentially prior. We can settle for the indubitable fact that all *moral* terms are of this polar sort. And we can settle merely for the fact that such positives and negatives imply each other. However, in a hit-and-run sort of way, before hurrying on, I might avow that I personally would treat the negative as in principle prior, for this reason: (1) Yes and No imply each other; (2) in their role as opposites, they *limit* each other; (3) but limitation itself is the "negation of part of a divisible quantum." (I am quoting from the article on Fichte in the *Encyclopaedia Britannica,* eleventh edition.)

There is an implied sense of negativity in the ability to use words at all. For to use them properly, we must know that they are *not* the things they stand for. Next, since language is extended by metaphor which gradually becomes the kind of dead metaphor we call abstraction, we must know that metaphor is *not* literal. Further, we cannot use language maturely until we are spontaneously at home in irony. (That is, if the weather is bad, and someone says, "What a beautiful day!" we spontaneously know that he does *not* mean what the words say on their face. Children, before reaching "the age of reason," usually find this twist quite disturbing, and are likely to object that it is *not* a good day. Dramatic irony, of course, carries such a principle of negativity to its most complicated perfection.)

Our tendency to write works on such topics as "The Spirit of Christianity," or "The Soul of Islam," or "The Meaning of Judaism," or "Buddha and Eternity," or "Hinduism and Metempsychosis," leads us to overlook a strongly negativistic aspect of religions. I refer here not just to the principle of moral negativity already discussed, but also to the fact that religions are so often built *antithetically* to other persuasions. Negative motivation of this sort is

---

[1] It suggests the thought that our second clause might be rephrased: "Moralized by the negative."

attested by such steps as the formation of Christianity in opposition to paganism, the formation of Protestant offshoots in opposition to Catholicism, and the current reinvigoration of churchgoing, if not exactly of religion, in opposition to communism. So goes the dialectic!

Only one more consideration, and we are through with thoughts on this clause in our definition:

In an advertising world that is so strong on the glorification of the positive (as a way of selling either goods or bads), how make the negative enticing? At times the job has been done negatively, yet effectively, by the threat of hell. But what sanctions can we best build on now?

What a notable irony we here confront! For some of man's greatest acts of genius are in danger of transforming millions and millions of human agents into positive particles of sheer motion that go on somehow, but that are negative indeed as regards even the minimum expectations to which we might feel entitled.

And what is this new astounding irony? Precisely the fact that all these new positive powers developed by the new technology have introduced a vast new era of negativity. For they are deadly indeed, unless we make haste to develop the controls (the negatives, the thou-shalt-not's) that become necessary, if these great powers are to be kept from getting out of hand.

Somewhat ironically, even as the possibilities of ultimate man-made suicide beset us, we also face an opposite kind of positive technologic threat to the resources of our moral negativity. I refer to the current "population explosion." In earlier days, the problem was solved automatically by plagues, famines, high rate of infant mortality, and such. But now the positive resources of technology have undone much of those natural "adjustments," so that new burdens are placed upon the Muscles of Negativity as the need arises for greater deliberate limitation of offspring.

However, ironically again, we should not end our discussion of this clause until we have reminded ourselves: There is a kind of aesthetic negativity whereby any moralistic thou-shalt-not provides material for our entertainment, as we pay to follow imaginary accounts of "deviants" who, in all sorts of ingenious ways, are represented as violating these very Don'ts.

IV

Third clause: *Separated from his natural condition by instruments of his own making.* It concerns the fact that even the most primitive of tribes are led by inventions to depart somewhat from the needs of food, shelter, sex as defined by the survival standards of sheer animality. The implements of hunting and husbandry, with corresponding implements of war, make for a set of habits that become a kind of "second nature," as a special set of expectations, shaped by custom, comes to seem "natural." (I recall once when there was a breakdown of the lighting equipment in New York City. As the newspapers the next day told of the event, one got almost a sense of mystical terror from the description of the darkened streets. Yet but fifty miles away, that same evening, we had been walking on an unlit road by our house in the country, in a darkness wholly "natural." In the "second nature" of the city, something so natural as dark roadways at night was weirdly "unnatural.")

This clause is designed to take care of those who would define man as the "tool-using animal" (*homo faber, homo economicus,* and such). In adding this clause, we are immediately reminded of the close tie-up between tools and language. Imagine trying to run a modern factory, for instance, without the vast and often ungainly nomenclatures of the various technological specialties, without instructions, education, specifications, filing systems, accountancy (including mathematics and money or some similar counters). And I already referred to the likelihood that the development of tools requires a kind of attention not possible without symbolic means of conceptualization. The connection between tools and language is also observable in what we might call the "second level" aspect of both. I refer to the fact that, whereas one might think of other animals as using certain rudiments of symbolism and rudimentary tools (for instance, when an ape learns to use a stick as a means of raking in a banana that the experimenter has purposely put beyond arm's length), in both cases the "reflexive" dimension is missing. Animals do not use words about words (as with the definitions of a dictionary)—and though an ape may even learn to put two sticks together as a way of extending his reach in case the sticks are so made that one can be fitted into the other, he would not take a knife and deliberately hollow out the end of one stick to make possible the insertion of the other stick. This is what we mean by the reflexive or second-level aspect of human symbolism. And it would presumably apply also to such complex sign systems as bees apparently have, to spread information about the distance and direction of a newly discovered food supply. Apparently investigators really have "cracked" such a code in certain dancelike motions of bees—but we should hardly expect ever to find that student bees are taught the language by teacher bees, or that there are apiaries where bees formulate the grammar and syntax of such signaling. "Information" in the sense of sheer motion is not thus "reflexive," but rather is like that of an electric circuit where, if a car is on a certain stretch of track, it automatically turns off the current on the adjoining piece of track, so that any car on that other piece of track would stop through lack of power. The car could be said to behave in accordance with this "information."

However, in saying that the human powers of symbolicity are interwoven with the capacity for making tools (and particularly for making tools that make tools), we still haven't answered one objection. If the two powers involve each other, if the same reflexive trait is characteristic of both, why start with symbol-using rather than with toolmaking? I'd propose an answer of this sort:

Formally, is not the choice implicit in the very act of definition itself? If we defined man first of all as the tool-using animal (or, old style, as *homo faber* rather than as *homo sapiens*), our definition would not be taking into account the "priority" of its very own nature as a definition. Inasmuch as definition is a symbolic act, it must begin by explicitly recognizing its formal grounding in the *principle* of definition as an act. In choosing *any definition at all*, one implicitly represents man as the kind of animal that is capable of definition (that is to say, capable of symbolic action). Thus, even if one views the powers of speech and mechanical invention as mutually involving each other, in a technical or formal sense one should make the implications explicit by treating the gifts of symbolicity as the "prior" member of the pair.

Also, we should note that one especially good result follows from this choice. Those who begin with the stress upon *tools* proceed to define language itself as a species of tool. But though instrumentality is an important aspect of language, we could not properly treat it as the *essence* of language. To define language simply as a species of tool would be like defining metals merely as species of tools. Or like defining sticks and stones simply as primitive weapons. Edward Sapir's view of language as "a collective means of expression" points in a more appropriate direction. The instrumental value of language certainly accounts for much of its development, and this instrumental value of language may even have been responsible for the survival of language itself (by helping the language-using animal to survive), quite as the instrumental value of language in developing atomic power now threatens the survival of the language-using animal; but to say as much is not by any means to say that language is in its essence a tool. Language is a species of action, symbolic action—and its nature is such that it can be used as a tool.

In any case, the toolmaking propensities envisioned in our third clause result in the complex network of material operations and properties, public or private, that arise through men's ways of livelihood, with the different *classes* of society that arise through the division of labor and the varying relationships to the property structure. And that brings us to our fourth clause.

V

Fourth clause: *Goaded by the spirit of hierarchy.* But if that sounds too weighted, we could settle for, "Moved by a sense of order." Under this clause, of course, would fall the incentives of organization and status. In my

Rhetoric of Motives, I tried to trace the relation between social hierarchy and mystery, or guilt. And I carried such speculations further in my *Rhetoric of Religion.* Here we encounter secular analogues of "original sin." For, despite any cult of good manners and humility, to the extent that a social structure becomes differentiated, with privileges to some that are denied to others, there are the conditions for a kind of "built in" pride. King and peasant are "mysteries" to each other. Those "Up" are guilty of not being "Down," those "Down" are certainly guilty of not being "Up."

Here man's skill with symbols combines with his negativity and with the tendencies towards different modes of livelihood implicit in the inventions that make for division of labor, the result being definitions and differentiations and allocations of property protected by the negativities of the law. I particularly like E. M. Forster's novel, *A Passage to India,* for its ingenious ways of showing how social mystery can become interwoven with ideas of cosmic mystery. The grotesque fictions of Franz Kafka are marvelous in this regard. The use of the word "Lord," to designate sometimes the Deity and sometimes an aristocrat, in itself indicates the shift between the two kinds of "worship." In *Book of the Courtier* Castiglione brings out the relationship nicely when he writes of kneeling on one knee to the sovereign, on both knees to God. Or, in ancient Rome, the application of the term *pontifex maximus* to the Emperor specifically recognized his "bridging" relationship as both a god and the head of the social hierarchy. Milton's use of terms such as Cherubim, Seraphim, Thrones, Dominations, Powers, reflects the conceiving of supernatural relations after the analogy of a social ladder. The religious vision of the city on a hill is similarly infused—making in all a ziggurat-like structure without skyscrapers. (Recall a related image, El Greco's painting of Toledo.) And, of course, the principles of such hierarchal order are worked out with imaginative and intellectual fullness in Dante's *Divine Comedy.* The medieval pageant probably represents the perfection of this design. All the various "mysteries" were represented, each distinct from all the others, yet all parts of the same overarching order.

VI

By now we should also have taken care of such definitions as man the "political animal" or the "culture-bearing animal." And for a while, I felt that these clauses sufficiently covered the ground. However, for reasons yet to be explained, I decided that a final codicil was still needed, thus making in all:

Man is
the symbol-using (symbol-making, symbol-misusing) animal
inventor of the negative (or moralized by the negative)

separated from his natural condition by instruments of his own making
goaded by the spirit of hierarchy (or moved by the sense of order)
and rotten with perfection.

I must hurry to explain and justify this wry codicil.

The principle of perfection is central to the nature of language as motive. The mere desire to name something by its "proper" name, or to speak a language in its distinctive ways is intrinsically "perfectionist." What is more "perfectionist" in essence than the impulse, when one is in dire need of something, to so state this need that one in effect "defines" the situation? And even a poet who works out cunning ways of distorting language does so with perfectionist principles in mind, though his ideas of improvement involve recondite stylistic twists that may not disclose their true nature as judged by less perverse tests.

Thoughts on this subject induce us to attempt adapting, for sheerly logological purposes, the Aristotelian concept of the "entelechy," the notion that each being aims at the perfection natural to its kind (or, etymologically, is marked by a "possession of telos within"). The stone would be all that is needed to make it a stone; the tree would be all that is needed to make it a tree; and man would (or should!) be all that is needed to make him the perfectly "rational" being (presumably a harder entelechial job to accomplish than lower kinds of entities confront). Our point is: Whereas Aristotle seems to have thought of all beings in terms of the entelechy (in keeping with the ambiguities of his term, *kinesis*, which includes something of both "action" and "motion"), we are confining our use of the principle to the realm of symbolic action. And in keeping with this view, we would state merely: There is a principle of perfection implicit in the nature of symbol systems; and in keeping with his nature as symbol-using animal, man is moved by this principle.

At this point we must pause to answer an objection. In *Beyond the Pleasure Principle* (near the end of Chapter V) Freud explicitly calls upon us "to abandon our belief that in man there dwells an impulse towards perfection, which has brought him to his present heights of intellectual prowess and sublimation." Yet a few sentences later in that same closing paragraph, we find him saying, "The repressive instinct never ceases to strive after its complete satisfaction." But are not these two sentences mutually contradictory? For what could more clearly represent an "impulse to perfection" than a "striving" after "complete satisfaction"?

The alternative that Freud proposes to the striving after perfection is what he calls a "repetition compulsion." And near the end of Chapter III he has described it thus:

One knows people with whom every human relationship ends in the same way: benefactors whose protégés, however different they may otherwise have been, invariably after a time desert them in ill-will, so that they are apparently condemned to drain to the dregs all the bitterness of ingratitude; men with whom every friendship ends in the friend's treachery; others who indefinitely often in their lives invest some other person with authority either in their own eyes or generally, and themselves overthrow such authority after a given time, only to replace it by a new one; lovers whose tender relationships with women each and all run through the same phases and come to the same end, and so on. We are less astonished at this "endless repetition of the same" if there is involved a question of active behaviour on the part of the person concerned, and if we detect in his character an unalterable trait which must always manifest itself in the repetition of identical experiences. Far more striking are those cases where the person seems to be experiencing something passively, without exerting any influence of his own, and yet always meets with the same fate over and over again.

Freud next mentions in Tasso's *Gerusalemme Liberata* the story of the hero Tancred who, having unwittingly slain his beloved Clorinda, later in an enchanted wood hews down a tall tree with his sword, and when blood streams from the gash in the tree, he hears the voice of Clorinda whose soul was imprisoned in the tree, and who reproaches him for having again "wrought" the same "baleful deed."

Freud sees in all such instances the workings of what he calls the neurotic attempt to so shape one's later life that some earlier unresolved problem is lived over and over again. Freud also calls it a "destiny compulsion," to bring out the thought that the sufferer unconsciously strives to form his destiny in accordance with this earlier pattern.

My point is: Why should such a "destiny compulsion" or "repetition compulsion" be viewed as antithetical to the "principle of perfection"? Is not the sufferer exerting almost superhuman efforts in the attempt to give his life a certain *form*, so shaping his relations to people in later years that they will conform perfectly to an emotional or psychological pattern already established in some earlier formative situation? What more thorough illustrations could one want, of a drive to make one's life "perfect," despite the fact that such efforts at perfection might cause the unconscious striver great suffering?

To get the point, we need simply widen the concept of perfection to the point where we can also use the term *ironically*, as when we speak of a "perfect fool" or a "perfect villain." And, of course, I had precisely such possibilities in mind when in my codicil I refer to man as being "rotten" with perfection.

The ironic aspect of the principle is itself revealed most perfectly in our tendency to conceive of a "perfect" enemy. The Nazi version of the Jew, as developed in Hitler's *Mein Kampf,* is the most thoroughgoing instance of such ironic "perfection" in recent times, though strongly similar trends keep manifesting themselves in current controversies between "East" and "West."

I suppose the most "perfect" definition of man along these lines is the formula derived from *Plautus: homo homini lupus,* or one to suit the sort of imaginary herding animal that would fit Hobbes's notion of the *bellum omnium contra omnes.*

The principle of perfection in this dangerous sense derives sustenance from other primary aspects of symbolicity. Thus, the principle of drama is implicit in the idea of action, and the principle of victimage is implicit in the nature of drama. The negative helps radically to define the elements to be victimized. And inasmuch as substitution is a prime resource of symbol systems, the conditions are set for catharsis by scapegoat (including the "natural" invitation to "project" upon the enemy any troublesome traits of our own that we would negate). And the unresolved problems of "pride" that are intrinsic to privilege also bring the motive of hierarchy to bear here; for many kinds of guilt, resentment, and fear tend to cluster about the hierarchal psychosis, with its corresponding search for a sacrificial principle such as can become embodied in a political scapegoat.

Similar ominous invitations along these lines derive from the terministic fact that, as Aristotle observes in his *Rhetoric,* antithesis is an exceptionally effective rhetorical device. There is its sheerly *formal* lure, in giving dramatic saliency and at least apparent clarity to any issue. One may find himself hard put to define a policy purely in its own terms, but one can advocate it persuasively by an urgent assurance that it is decidedly *against* such-and-such other policy with which people may be disgruntled. For this reason also, the use of antithesis helps deflect embarrassing criticism (as when rulers silence domestic controversy by turning public attention to animosity against some foreign country's policies). And in this way, of course, antithesis helps reinforce unification by scapegoat.

The principle of perfection (the "entelechial" principle) figures in other notable ways as regards the genius of symbolism. A given terminology contains various *implications,* and there is a corresponding "perfectionist" tendency for men to attempt carrying out those implications. Thus, each of our scientific nomenclatures suggests its own special range of possible developments, with specialists vowed to carry out these terministic possibilities to the extent of their personal ability and technical resources. Each such specialty is like the situation of an author who has an idea for a novel, and who will never rest until he has completely embodied it in a book. Insofar as any of these terminologies happen also to contain the risks of destroying the world, that's just too bad; but the fact remains that, so far as the sheer principles of the investigation are concerned, they are no different from those of the writer who strives to complete his novel. There is a kind of "terministic compulsion" to carry out the implications of one's terminology, quite as, if an astronomer discovered by his observations and computations that a certain wandering body was likely to hit the earth and destroy us, he would nonetheless feel compelled to *argue for the correctness of his computa-*

tions, despite the ominousness of the outcome. Similarly, of course, men will so draw out the implications of their terminologies that new expectations are aroused (promises that are now largely interwoven with the state of Big Technology, and that may prove to be true or false, but that can have revolutionary effects upon persons who agree with such terministic "extrapolations").

Whereas there seems to be no principle of control intrinsic to the ideal of carrying out any such set of possibilities to its "perfect" conclusion, and whereas all sorts of people are variously goaded to track down their particular sets of terministically directed insights, there is at least the fact that the schemes get in one another's way, thus being to some extent checked by rivalry with one another. And such is especially the case where *allocation of funds* is concerned.

To round out the subject of "perfection," in both honorific and ironic senses, we might end by observing that, without regard for the ontological truth or falsity of the case, there are sheerly technical reasons, intrinsic to the nature of language, for belief in God and the Devil. Insofar as language is intrinsically hortatory (a medium by which men can obtain the cooperation of one another), God perfectly embodies the petition. Similarly, insofar as vituperation is a "natural" resource of speech, the Devil provides a perfect butt for invective. Heaven and Hell together provide the ultimate, or perfect, grounding for sanctions. God is also the perfect audience for praise and lamentation (two primary modes of symbolic action, with lamentation perhaps the "first" of all, as regards tests of biological priority). Such considerations would provide a strictly logological treatment of Martin Buber's "I-Thou Relation."

VII

So much for the clauses of our Definition, a definition which most people would probably want to characterize as "descriptive" rather than "normative," yet which is surely normative in the sense that its implications are strongly admonitory, suggesting the kind of foibles and crotchets which a "comic" theory of education[2] would feature, in asking man to center his

---

[2] In his *Parts of Animals,* Chapter X, Aristotle mentions the definition of man as the "laughing animal," but he does not consider it adequate. Though I would hasten to agree, I obviously have a big investment in it, owing to my conviction that mankind's only hope is a cult of comedy. (The cult of tragedy is too eager to help out with the holocaust. And in the last analysis, it is too pretentious to allow for the proper recognition of our animality.) Also, I'd file "risibility" under "symbolicity." Insofar as man's laughter is to be distinguished from that of the Hyena, the difference derives from ideas of *incongruity* that are in turn derived from principles of *congruity* necessarily implicit in any given symbol system.

attention on the understanding of his "natural temptations" towards kinds of turbulence that, when reinforced with the powers of the new weapons, threaten to undo us.

I'm not too sure that, in the present state of Big Technology's confusions, any educational policy, even if it were itself perfect and were adopted throughout the world, would be able to help much, when the world is so ardently beset by so much distress and malice. The dreary likelihood is that, if we do avoid the holocaust, we shall do so mainly by bits of political patch-work here and there, with alliances falling sufficiently on the bias across one another, and thus getting sufficiently in one another's road, so that there's not enough "symmetrical perfection" among the contestants to set up the "right" alignment and touch it off.

Perhaps because of my special liking for the sympathetically ironic point of view in E. M. Forster's novel, *A Passage to India*, I place a wan hope in the sheer muddle of current international relations. That is, there is the chance that the problem, in its very insolubility, also contains enough elements of self-cancellation to keep things from coming to a perfect fulfillment in a perfect Apocalyptic holocaust. Meanwhile, the most that one can do, when speculating on a definition, is to ask oneself whether it is turned somewhat in the right direction.

But what of an ending for this discussion? After so much talk about "perfection," I feel quite self-conscious. For obviously, my discussion should itself have a perfect ending.

A perfect ending should promise something. In this regard, I guess the most perfect ending is provided by a sermon in which, after a threat of total loss unless we mend our ways, we are promised the hope of total salvation if we do mend our ways. But even though, today, we stand as close as mankind ever has stood, in secular regards, to a choice precisely as radical as that, I can build up no such perfectly urgent pattern (partly because, as we generally recognize now, it is impossible for us truly to imagine that next day, no matter how earnestly some writers try to help us by inventing imaginary accounts of it, accounts which even they can't believe, despite the enterprise of their imaginings).

The best I can do is state my belief that things might be improved somewhat if enough people began thinking along the lines of this definition; my belief that, if such an approach could be perfected by many kinds of critics and educators and self-admonishers in general, things might be a little less ominous than otherwise.

However, at this point I hit upon a kind of *Ersatz* promise for an ending. As you will see, it is concerned with perfection on a grand scale. And it has in its favor the further fact that it involves the modernizing, or perfecting, of a traditional vision, one even so primal as to be expressed in a nursery jingle. I shall give the traditional jingle first, and then my proposed modernized perfecting of it. The older form ran thus:

If all the trees were one tree
What a great tree that would be

If all the axes were one axe
What a great axe that would be.

If all the men were one man
What a great man he would be.

And if all the seas were one sea
What a great sea that would be.

And if the great man
Took the great axe
And chopped down the great tree
And let it fall into the great sea

What a Splish-Splash that would be!

Modernized, perfected, the form runs thus:

If all the thermo-nuclear warheads
Were one thermo-nuclear warhead
What a great thermo-nuclear warhead that would be.

If all the intercontinental ballistic missiles
Were one intercontinental ballistic missile
What a great intercontinental ballistic missile that would be.

If all the military men
Were one military man
What a great military man he would be.

And if all the land masses
Were one land mass
What a great land mass that would be.

And if the great military man
Took the great thermo-nuclear warhead
And put it into the great intercontinental ballistic missile
And dropped it on the great land mass,

What great PROGRESS that would be!

• • •

Comments

One might ask the question: "What does it mean, to approach reality through one language rather than another?" Or one might ask: "What does it mean to be the kind of animal that uses *any* language (to view reality through *any* kind of highly developed symbol system)?" Benjamin Lee Whorf's ingenious speculations (many of them collected in his volume, *Language, Thought, and Reality*) suggest answers to the first question. The present "Definition" has been concerned rather with answers to the second.

Men can be studied as individuals, as members of groups (tribes, classes, organizations, and the like), or as generically "human." The present essay has been concerned with the most "universal" of such classifications. But elsewhere we deal with the fact that the analysis of particular idioms can be methodically narrowed even to the study of one particular writer's terminology (with its own unique set of "personal equations").

Given the range of meanings in the ancient Greeks' concept of "politics," the anthropologists' definition of man as the "culture-bearing animal" is not far from Aristotle's view of man as the "political animal." Both imply the ability to develop and transmit conventions and institutions. Just as Aristotle's definition serves most directly for his book on politics, so the anthropologists' definition serves most directly for their studies of tribal cultures. "Social animal" might most directly suit sociologists. Our point is simply that for our purposes a still more general starting point is necessary, analogous to *homo sapiens,* but minus the "built-in" honorific connotations of that formula (though perhaps it did perform a notable rhetorical function in prodding many of the perverse to cherish after the manner of Flaubert the lore of *la bêtise humaine*). For the psychologist, man is a "psychological" animal; for the psychoanalyst a mentally sick animal (a psychopathology being a natural part of even the average or "normal" Everyman's everyday life); for the chemist man should be a congeries of chemicals; and so on. But since man can't be called any of these various things except insofar as, encompassing the lot, he is the kind of animal that can haggle about the definition of himself, in this sense he is what Ernst Cassirer has called the *animal symbolicum;* yet I feel that the post-Kantian way of understanding such a formula tends to get epistemologically ("Scientistically") sidetracked from the more ontological ('Dramatistic") approach grounded in the older scholastic tradition.

The idealizing of man as a species of machine has again gained considerable popularity, owing to the great advances in automation and "sophisticated" computers. But such things are obviously inadequate as models since, not being biological organisms, machines lack the capacity for pleasure or pain (to say nothing of such subtler affective states as malice, envy, amusement, condescension, friendliness, sentimentality, embarrassment, etc., *ad nauseam*). One might so construct a computer that, if its signals got into a traffic jam, it would give forth a cry like a child in agony. And this "information" might make you impulsively, despite yourself, feel compassion for it. Yet, not being an organism, the ingenious artificial construct would all the while be as impassive as a Stoic's ideal of the perfect philosopher. For though the contraption might be so designed that it could *record* its own outcry, it could not "hear" that cry in the sense in which you, as an organism of pleasure and pain, would hear it. Until, like the robots in Capek's *R.U.R.*, men's contrivances can be made actually to ache, they cannot possibly serve as adequate models for the total human condition (that is, for a definition of "man in general").

When two machines get cruelly smashed in an accident, it's all the same to them, so far as pain goes. Hence a definition of man without reference to the animality of pain is, on its face, as inadequate as a definition would be that reduced man to the sheer kinetics of chemistry. Unquestionably, such a reduction could tell us much about the realm of motions that underlies our modes of action, and without which we could not act. But we *intuitively* recognize that such terms alone cannot deal with the qualities of experience as we necessarily suffer and enact it. (Awareness itself, by the way, is ambiguously on the dividing line between "action" and "knowledge"; or, otherwise put, intuitive knowledge is a spontaneous activity much like what we call an "act of faith," as per Santayana's ingenious concept of "animal faith.")

Insofar as the concept of "action" gets reduced to terms of "work," conditions are set for an antithetical stress upon play, as with Huizinga's formula, *homo ludens*. While obviously not general enough to cover all cases, it serves well as an instrument to warn us against an overly instrumentalist view of man's ways with symbols. Here would belong also a related view of man, as the "laughing animal." While laughter, like tears, is grounded in the motions of animality, it also depends upon principles of congruity that are due to conventions or proprieties developed through the resources of symbolicity. It embodies these norms of congruity in reverse, by their violation within limits, a kind of "planned incongruity" (as discussed in my *Permanence and Change*). Thus the incongruously perfect definition of man as a wolf (in keeping with man's traditional attitude towards that much maligned, but highly social-minded animal) comes down to us through comedy.

The reference to proprieties suggests the observation that the definition of man as a "moral being" centers in that mighty symbolic invention, the negative, involving the "thou-shalt-not's" (and corresponding "thou shalt's") of law and conscience, and the saying yes or no to such proscriptions and prescriptions. Here would belong Whitman's celebration of the "Answerer," and Nietzsche's paradoxical, negativity-saturated idea of the "Yea-sayer." I remember having heard that William Blackstone somewhere defines man as a being endowed with the capacity for all kinds of crime. Though I have not been able to verify the reference, such a definition would be the most direct fit for commentaries on the law; yet "crime" is but a reflex of human prowess in the making of laws, that is, man's "symbolicity." And Goethe has offered us an attenuated variant of the same notion when confessing an ability to *imagine* all kinds of crime.

The third essay will illustrate the basic symbolic devices under which one should class man as a being typically endowed with the powers of "transcendence." And many subsequent chapters will provide other instances of such resourcefulness (for instance, the piece on Emersonian transcendentalism) including its relation to the hierarchal motive, as embodied in the social order.

Man's "time-binding" propensities would be a subdivision of his traffic with symbols, though the fourth chapter will also consider a sense in which the past is preserved "unconsciously" in the animal tissues.

All told, we should by now have reviewed a sufficient range of cases to indicate why we feel that any possible definition of man will necessarily fall somewhere within the five clauses in our "Definition." Basically, these involve concepts of motion and action (or otherwise put, physicality, animality, and symbolicity). And above all, we would want to emphasize: Whereas many other animals seem sensitive in a rudimentary way to the motivating force of symbols, they seem to lack the "second-level" aspect of symbolicity that is characteristically human, the "reflexive" capacity to develop highly complex symbol systems about symbol systems, the pattern of which is indicated in Aristotle's definition of God as "thought of thought," or in Hegel's dialectics of "self-consciousness."

As we proceed, there will be other chances to consider these matters.

MIKHAIL BAKHTIN
1895–1975

The Russian Mikhail Bakhtin's work was not readily available to an international scholarly community until mid-twentieth century because of Soviet political events. Like Ferdinand de Saussure, who influenced him greatly, Bakhtin believed that language is a system of arbitrary signs. But his system goes beyond Saussure's sociopsychological approach; Bakhtin's theory is based on the dialogic nature of language and shows how historical and social contexts create meaning. Bakhtin, like Kenneth Burke, thought we should draw on rhetoric for analyses of all genres. Although he is best known by literary critics for Problems of Dostoevsky's Poetics *(1984),* The Formal Method in Literary Scholarship *(1928) also has been influential. Perhaps the richest resources for students of rhetoric are* The Dialogic Imagination *(1981) and "The Problem of Speech Genres" (1953) (*Speech Genres and Other Late Essays*).*

Toward a Methodology for the Human Sciences

Understanding. The dismemberment of understanding into individual acts. In actual, real concrete understanding these acts merge inseparably into a unified process, but each individual act has its ideal semantic (content-filled) independence and can be singled out from the concrete empirical act. 1. Psychophysiologically perceiving a physical sign (word, color, spatial form). 2. *Recognizing* it (as familiar or unfamiliar). 3. Understanding its *significance* in the given context (immediate and more remote). 4. Active-dialogic understanding (disagreement/agreement). Inclusion in the dialogic context. The evaluative aspect of understanding and the degree of its depth and universality.

Converting an image into a symbol gives it semantic *depth* and semantic perspective. The dialogic correlation between identity and nonidentity. The image must be understood for what it is and for what it designates. The content of a true symbol, through mediated semantic coupling, is correlated with the idea of worldwide wholeness, the fullness of the cosmic and human universe. The world has contextual meaning. "The image of the world appears miraculously in the word."[1] Each particular phenomenon is submerged in the primordial elements of the *origins of existence*. As distinct from myth, this is an awareness that one does not coincide with one's own individual meaning.

The symbol has a "warmth of fused mystery."[2] The aspect of contrasting *one's own* to *another's*. The warmth of love and the coldness of alienation. Contrast and comparison. Any interpretation of a symbol itself remains a symbol, but it is somewhat rationalized, that is, brought somewhat closer to the concept.

A definition of *contextual meaning* in all the profundity and complexity of its essence. Interpretation as the discovery of a path to seeing (contemplating) and supplementing through creative thinking. Anticipation of the further growing context, its relation to the finalized whole, and its relation to the unfinalized context. This meaning (in the unfinalized context) cannot be peaceful and cozy (one cannot curl up comfortably and die within it).

Formal definition and contextual meaning. *Filled-in* recollections and *anticipated* possibilities (understanding in remote contexts). In recollections we also take subsequent events (within the past) into account, that is, we perceive and understand what is remembered in the context of the unfinalized past. In what forms is the whole present in the consciousness (in Plato and in Husserl)?

To what extent can the *contextual meaning* (of an image or symbol) be revealed and commented upon? Only with the aid of another (isomorphous) meaning (of a symbol or image). It cannot be dissolved into concepts. The role of commentary. There can be a *relative* rationalization of the contextual meaning (ordinary scientific analysis) or a deepening with the help of other meanings (philosophical-artistic interpretation). Deepening through expansion of the remote context.

The interpretation of symbolic structures is forced into an infinity of symbolic contextual meanings and therefore it cannot be scientific in the way precise sciences are scientific.

The interpretation of contextual meanings cannot be scientific, but it is profoundly cognitive. It can directly serve practice, practice that deals with things.

". . . it will be necessary to recognize that symbology is not an unscientific, but a *differently scientific* form of knowledge that has its own internal laws and criteria for precision."[3]

A work's author is present only in the whole of the work, not in one separate aspect of this whole, and least of all in content that is severed from the whole. He is located in that inseparable aspect of the work where content and form merge inseparably, and we feel his presence most of all in form. Literary scholarship usually looks for him in *content* excised from the whole. This makes it easy to identify him with that author who is a person of a particular time, with a particular biography and a particular world view. Here the image of the author almost merges with the image of a real person.

The true author cannot become an image, for he is the creator of every image, of everything imagistic in the work. Therefore, the so-called image of the author can only be one of the images of a given work (true, a special kind of image). The artist frequently depicts himself in a picture (near the edge of it) and he also draws his self-portrait. But in a self-portrait we *do not see* the author as such (he cannot be seen); in any case, we see him no more than in any of the author's other work. He is revealed most of all in the author's best pictures. The author-creator cannot be created in that sphere in which he himself appears as the creator. This is *natura naturans* and not *natura naturata*. We see the creator only in his creation, and never outside it.

The exact sciences constitute a monologic form of knowledge: the intellect contemplates a *thing* and expounds upon it. There is only one subject here—cognizing (contemplating) and speaking (expounding). In opposition to the subject there is only a *voiceless thing*. Any object of knowledge (including man) can be perceived and cognized as a thing. But a subject as such cannot be perceived and studied as a thing, for as a subject it cannot, while remaining a subject, become voiceless, and, consequently, cognition of it can only be *dialogic*. Dilthey and the problem of understanding. Various ways of *being active* in cognitive activity. The activity of the one who acknowledges a voiceless thing and the activity of one who acknowledges another subject, that is, the *dialogic* activity of the acknowledger. The dialogic activity of the acknowledged subject, and the degrees of this activity. The thing and the personality (subject) as *limits* of cognition. Degrees of thing-ness and personality-ness. The event-potential of dialogic cognition. Meeting. Evaluation as a necessary aspect of dialogic cognition.

The human sciences—sciences of the spirit—philological sciences (as part of and at the same time common to all of them—the word).

Historicity. Immanence. Enclosure of analysis (cognition and understanding) in one given *text*. The problem of the boundaries between text and context. Each word (each sign) of the text exceeds its boundaries. Any understanding is a correlation of a given text with other texts. Commentary. The dialogic nature of this correlation.

The place of philosophy. It begins where precise science ends and a different science begins. It can be defined as the metalanguage of all sciences (and of all kinds of cognition and consciousness).

Understanding as correlation with other texts and reinterpretation, in a new context (in my own context, in a contemporary context, and in a future one). The anticipated context of the future: a sense that I am taking a new step (have progressed). Stages in the dialogic movement of *understanding:* the point of departure, the given text; movement backward, past contexts; movement forward, anticipation (and the beginning) of a future context.

Dialectics was born of dialogue so as to return again to dialogue on a higher level (a dialogue of *personalities*).

The monologism of Hegel's "Phenomenology of the Spirit."

Dilthey's monologism has not been completely surmounted.

Thought about the world and thought in the world. Thought striving to embrace the world and thought experiencing itself in the world (as part of it). An event in the world and participation in it. The world as an event (and not as existence in ready-made form).

The text lives only by coming into contact with another text (with context). Only at the point of this contact between texts does a light flash, illuminating both the posterior and anterior, joining a given text to a dialogue. We emphasize that this contact is a dialogic contact between texts (utterances) and not a mechanical contact of "oppositions," which is possible only within a single text (and not between a text and context) among abstract elements (signs within a text), and is necessary only in the first stage of understanding (understanding formal definition, but not contextual meaning). Behind this contact is a contact of personalities and not of things (at the extreme). If we transform dialogue into one continuous text, that is, erase the divisions between voices (changes of speaking subjects), which is possible at the extreme (Hegel's monological dialectic), then the deep-seated (infinite) contextual meaning disappears (we hit the bottom, reach a standstill).

Complete maximum reification would inevitably lead to the disappearance of the infinitude and bottomlessness of meaning (any meaning).

A thought that, like a fish in an aquarium, knocks against the bottom and the sides and cannot swim farther or deeper. Dogmatic thoughts.

Thought knows only conditional points; thought erodes all previously established points.

The elucidation of a text not by means of other texts (contexts) but with extratextual thinglike (reified) reality. This usually takes place in biographical, vulgar sociological and causal explanations (in the spirit of the natural sciences) and also in depersonalized historicity ("a history without names").[4] True understanding in literature and literary scholarship is always historical and personified. The position and limits of the so-called *realia. Things fraught with the word.*

The unity of monologue and the special unity of dialogue.

Pure epic and pure lyric know no provisos. Provisionary speech appears only in the novel.

The influence of extratextual reality in the shaping of the writer's artistic vision and the artistic thought (and the vision and thought of others who create culture).

Extratextual influences are especially important in the early stages of a person's development. These influences are invested in the word (or in other signs), and these words are the words of other people, above all, words from the mother. Then these "others' words" are processed dialogically into "one's own/others' words" with the help of different "others' words" (heard previously) and then in one's own words, so to speak (dropping the quotation marks), which are already creative in nature. The role of meetings, visions, "insights," "revelations," and so forth. See, incidentally: Aleksey Remizov, "Close-cropped eyes. A book of knots and twists of memory." Here, the role of drawings as signs for self-expression. "Klim Samgin" (man as a system of phrases),[5] "The Unsaid" and its special nature and role are interesting from this standpoint. The early stages of verbal cognition. The "unconscious" can become a creative factor only on the threshold of consciousness and of the word (semiverbal/semisignifying consciousness). They are fraught with the word and the potential word. The "unsaid" as a *shifting boundary*, as a "regulative idea" (in the Kantian sense) of creative consciousness.

The process of gradual obliteration of authors as bearers of others' words. Others' words become anonymous and are assimilated (in reworked form, of course); consciousness is *monologized*. Primary dialogic relations to others' words are also obliterated—they are, as it were, taken in, absorbed into assimilated others' words (passing through the stage of "one's own/others' words"). Creative consciousness, when monologized, is supplemented by anonymous authors. This process of monologization is very important. Then this monologized consciousness enters as one single whole into a new dialogue (with the new external voices of others). Monologized creative consciousness frequently joins and personifies others' words, others' voices that have become anonymous, in special symbols: "the voice of life itself," "the voice of nature," "the voice of the people," "the voice of God," and so forth. The role of the *authoritative word* in this process, which usually does not lose its bearer, does not become anonymous.

The striving to reify extraverbal anonymous contexts (to surround oneself with nonverbal life). I only am a creative speaking personality, everything else outside me is only thinglike, material conditions, which as *causes* call forth and define my word. I do not converse with them—I *react* to them mechanically, as a thing reacts to external stimuli.

Such speech phenomena as orders, demands, precepts, prohibitions, promises (oaths), threats, praises, reprimands, abuse, curses, blessings, and so forth comprise a very important part of extracontextual reality. They all are linked with a sharply expressed *intonation* capable of passing (being transferred) to any words or expressions that do not have the direct formal definition of an order, a threat, and so forth.

Tone, released from phonetic and semantic elements of the word (and other signs) is important. Those signs determine the complex *tonality* of our consciousness, which serves as an emotional-evaluative context for our understanding (complete, semantic understanding) of the text we read (or hear) and also, in more complex form, for our creative writing (origination) of a text.

The task consists in forcing the *thinglike* environment, which mechanically influences the personality, to begin to speak, that is, to reveal in it the potential word and tone, to transform it into a semantic context for the thinking, speaking, and acting (as well as creating) personality. In essence any serious and probing self-examination/confession, autobiography, pure lyric, and so forth, does this.[6] Among writers, Dostoevsky, by revealing the actions and thoughts of his main heroes, achieved the greatest profundity in this transformation of the thing into contextual meaning. A thing, as long as it remains a thing, can affect only other things; in order to affect a personality it must reveal its *semantic potential,* become a word, that is, assimilate to a potential verbal-semantic context.

When analyzing Shakespeare's tragedies, we also observe a sequential transformation of all reality that affects the heroes into the semantic context of their actions, thoughts, and experiences: either they are actually words (the words of witches, of a father's ghost, and so forth) or they are events and circumstances translated into the language of the interpretive potential word.[7]

One must emphasize that this is not a direct and pure reduction of everything to a common denominator: the thing remains a thing and the word, a word; they retain their essences and are only augmented by contextual meaning.

One must not forget that "thing" and "personality" are *limits* and not absolute substances. Meaning cannot (and does not wish to) change physical, material, and other phenomena; it cannot act as a material force. And it does not need to do this: it itself is stronger than any force, it changes the total contextual meaning of an event and reality without changing its actual (existential) composition one iota; everything remains as it was but it acquires a completely different contextual meaning (the semantic transformation of existence). Each word of a text is transformed in a new context.

The inclusion of the listener (reader, viewer) in the system (structure) of the work. The author (bearer of the word) and the person who *understands.* The author when creating his work does not intend it for a literary scholar and does not presuppose a specific scholarly *understanding;* he does not aim to create a collective of literary scholars. He does not invite literary scholars to his banquet table.

Contemporary literary scholars (the majority of them Structuralists) usually define a listener who is immanent in the work as an all-understanding, ideal listener. Precisely this kind of listener is postulated in the work. This, of course, is neither an *empirical* listener nor a psychological idea, an image of the listener in the soul of the author. It is an abstract ideological formulation. Counterposed to it is the same kind of abstract ideal author. In this understanding the ideal listener is essentially a mirror image of the author who replicates him. He cannot introduce anything of his own, anything new, into the ideally understood work or into the ideally complete plan of the author. He is in the same time and space as the author or, rather, like the author he is outside time and space (as is any abstract ideal formulation), and therefore he cannot be *an-other* or other for the author, he cannot have any *surplus* that is determined by this otherness. There can be no interaction between the author and this kind of listener, no active dramatic relations, for these are not voices but abstract concepts that are equal to themselves and to one another.[8] Only mechanistic or mathematical, empty tautological abstractions are possible here. There is not a bit of personification.

Content as *new;* form as stereotyped, congealed, old (familiar) content. Form serves as a necessary bridge to new, still unknown content. Form was a familiar and generally understood congealed old world view. In precapitalistic epochs there was a less abrupt, smoother transition between form and content: form was content that had not yet hardened up, was still unfixed, was not hackneyed. Form was linked to the results of general collective creativity, to mythological systems, for example. Form was, as it were, implicit context: the content of a work developed content that was already embedded in the form and did not create it as something new, by some individual-creative initiative. Content, consequently, preceded the work to a certain degree. The author did not invent the content of his work; he only developed that which was already embedded in tradition.

Symbols are the most stable and at the same time the most emotional elements; they pertain to form and not to content.

The strictly semantic aspect of the work, that is, the *formal meaning* of its elements (the first stage of understanding) is in principle accessible to any individual consciousness. But its evaluative-semantic aspect (including symbols) is meaningful only to individuals who are related by some common conditions of life (see the formal definition of the word "symbol")—in the final analysis, by the bonds of brotherhood on a high level. Here we have *assimilation* and, at higher stages, assimilation to higher value (at the extreme, absolute value).

The meaning of emotional-evaluative exclamations in the speech life of peoples. But the expression of emotional-evaluative relations can be explicitly verbal while their *intonation* is, so to speak, implicit. The most essential and stable intonations form the intonational background of a particular social group (nation, class, professional collective, social circle, and so forth). To a certain degree, one can speak by means of intonations alone, making the verbally expressed part of speech relative and replaceable, almost indifferent. How often we use words whose meaning is unnecessary, or repeat the same word or phrase, just in order to have a material bearer for some necessary intonation.

The extratextual intonational-evaluative context can be only partially realized in the reading (performance) of a given text, and the largest part of it, especially in its more essential and profound strata, remains outside the given text as the dialogizing background for its perception. To some degree, the problem of the *social* (extraverbal) conditioning of the work reduces to this.

The text—printed, written, or orally recorded—is not equal to the work as a whole (or to the "aesthetic object"). The work also includes its necessary extratextual context. The work, as it were, is enveloped in the music of the intonational-evaluative context in which it is understood and evaluated (of course, this context changes in the various epochs in which it is perceived, which creates a new resonance in the work).

The mutual understanding of centuries and millennia, of peoples, nations, and cultures, provides a complex unity of all humanity, all human cultures (a complex unity of human culture), and a complex unity of human literature. All this is revealed only on the level of great time. Each image must be understood and evaluated on the level of great time. Analysis usually fusses about in the narrow space of small time, that is, in the space of the present day and the recent past and the imaginable—desired or frightening—future. Emotional-evaluative forms for anticipating the future in language-speech (order, desire, warning, incantation, and so forth), the trivially human attitude toward the future (desire, hope, fear); there is no understanding of evaluative nonpredetermination, unexpectedness, as it were, "surprisingness," absolute innovation, miracle, and so forth. The special nature of the *prophetic* attitude toward the future. Abstraction from the self in ideas about the future (the future without me).

> The time of the theatrical spectacle and its laws. Perception of the spectacle in those epochs when religious-cultic and state-ceremonial forms were present and reigned supreme. Everyday etiquette in the theater.

Nature juxtaposed to man. The Sophists, Socrates ("not the trees in the forest, but the people in the cities interest me").[9]

Two limits of thought and practice (deed) or two types of relations (thing and personality). The deeper the personality, that is, the closer to the personality extreme, the less applicable generalizing methods are. Generalization and formalization erase the boundaries between genius and lack of talent.

Experiment and mathematical elaboration. One raises a question and obtains an answer—this is the personal interpretation of the process of natural scientific cognition and of its subject (the experimenter). The history of cognition in terms of its results and the history of cognizing people. . . .

The process of reification and the process of personalization. But personalization is never subjectivization. The limit here is not *I* but *I* in interrelationship with other personalities, that is, *I* and *other*, *I* and *thou*.

Is there anything in the natural sciences that corresponds to "context"? Context is always personalized (infinite dialogue in which there is neither a first nor a last word—natural sciences have an object system (subjectless).

Our *thought* and our *practice*, not technical but *moral* (that is, our responsible deeds), are accomplished between two limits: attitudes toward the *thing* and attitudes toward the *personality. Reification* and *personification.* Some of our acts (cognitive and moral) strive toward the limit of reification, but never reach it; other acts strive toward the limit of personification, and never reach it completely.

Question and *answer* are not logical relations (categories); they cannot be placed in one consciousness (unified and closed in itself); any response gives rise to a new question. Question and answer presuppose mutual outsideness. If an answer does not give rise to a new question from itself, it falls out of the dialogue and enters systemic cognition, which is essentially impersonal.

The various chronotopes of the questioner and the answerer, and various semantic worlds (*I* and *other*). From the standpoint of a third consciousness and its "neutral" world, where everything is *replaceable,* question and answer are inevitably depersonified.

The difference between *stupidity* (ambivalent) and dullness (monosemantic).

Others' assimilated words ("one's own/others'"), eternally living, and creatively renewed in new contexts; and others' inert, dead words, "word-mummies."

Humboldt's main problem: the multiplicity of languages (the premise and the background of the problem—the unity of the human race). This is in the sphere of languages and their formal structures (phonetic and grammatical). But in the sphere of *speech* (within a single or any language) there arises the problem of one's own and another's word.

1. Reification and personification. The distinction between reification and "alienation." Two limits of thinking; the application of the principle of augmentation.
2. One's own and another's word. Understanding as the transformation of the other's into "one's own/another's." The principle of outsideness. The complex interrelations of the understood and the understanding subjects,

of the created and understanding, and of the creatively rejuvenating chronotopes. The importance of reaching, digging down to the creative nucleus of the personality (in the creative nucleus the personality continues to live, that is, it is immortal).

3. Precision and depth in the human sciences. The limit of precision in the natural sciences is identity ($a = a$). In the human sciences precision is surmounting the otherness of the other without transforming him into purely one's own (any kind of substitution, modernization, nonrecognition of the other, and so forth).

The ancient stage of personification (naive mythological personification). The epoch of reification of nature and man. The contemporary stage of personification of nature (and man), but without loss of reification. . . . In this stage, personification is not mythic, and yet it is not hostile to the mythic, and frequently utilizes its language (transformation into the language of symbols).

4. Contexts of understanding. The problem of *remote contexts*. The eternal renewal of meanings in all new contexts. *Small time* (the present day, the recent past, and the foreseeable [desired] future) and great time—infinite and unfinalized dialogue in which no meaning dies. The living in nature (organic). Everything inorganic is drawn into life in the process of exchange (only in abstraction can things be juxtaposed by taking them separately from life).

My attitude toward Formalism: a different understanding of specification; ignoring content leads to "material aesthetics" (criticism of this in my article of 1924); not "making" but creativity (only an "item" is obtained from material); the lack of understanding of historicity and change (a mechanical perception of change). The positive significance of formalism (new problems and new aspects of art); what is new always assumes one-sided and extreme forms in the early, more creative stages of its development.

My attitude toward structuralism: I am against enclosure in a text. Mechanical categories: "opposition," "change of codes" (the many styles of *Eugene Onegin* in Lotman's interpretation and in my interpretation). Sequential formalization and depersonalization: all relations are logical (in the broad sense of the word). But I hear *voices* in everything and dialogic relations among them. I also perceive the principle of augmentation dialogically. High evaluations of structuralism. The problem of "precision" and "depth." Depth of penetration into the *object* (thinglike) and depth of penetration into the *subject* (personal).

Structuralism has only one subject—the subject of the research himself. Things are transformed into *concepts* (a different degree of abstraction); the subject can never become a concept (he himself speaks and responds). Contextual meaning is personalistic; it always includes a question, an address, and the anticipation of a response, it always includes two (as a dialogic minimum). This personalism is not psychological, but semantic.

There is neither a first nor a last word and there are no limits to the dialogic context (it extends into the boundless past and the boundless future). Even *past* meanings, that is, those born in the dialogue of past centuries, can never be stable (finalized, ended once and for all)—they will always change (be renewed) in the process of subsequent, future development of the dialogue. At any moment in the development of the dialogue there are immense, boundless masses of forgotten contextual meanings, but at certain moments of the dialogue's subsequent development along the way they are recalled and invigorated in renewed form (in a new context). Nothing is absolutely dead: every meaning will have its homecoming festival. The problem of *great time.*

Notes

1. Taken from Pasternak's poem "August" from his 1946-53 period (when he was at work on *Dr. Zhivago*). This line appears in the last stanza of the poem, which is part of a quotation from the poet's "former, clairvoyant voice":

   Farewell, spread of the wings out-straightened
   The free stubbornness of pure flight,
   The word that gives the world its image,
   Creation: miracles and light.

   As translated in Vladimir Markov and Merrill Sparks, *Modern Russian Poetry* (New York: Bobbs-Merrill Co., 1967) p. 607.
2. See S. S. Averintsev, "The Symbol," in *Kratkaja literaturnaja entsiklopedija* (Moscow, 1972), vol. 7, column 827.
3. Ibid., column 828.
4. Reference here is to attempts by such figures as Alois Riegl and, above all, Edward Hanslick (1825-1904) to conceive art as perfectly immanent: the history of music, for instance, was a function only of a logic internal to music and had very little to do with composers themselves. See Edward Hanslick, *The Beautiful in Music,* tr. Gustav Cohen (Indianapolis: Bobbs-Merrill Co., 1957). Bakhtin was an acute student of philosophical attempts to found new bases for aesthetics, and his earlier works are peppered with commentary on them. See "Author and Hero in Aesthetic Activity," and *The Formal Method in Literary Scholarship* (pp. 50ff. in Eng. ed.).
5. The eponymous hero of Maksim Gorky's novel *Zhizn Klima Samgina* (1927-36).
6. See the analysis of these forms in Bakhtin's early work, where he concentrates on the way authors relate to their heroes; of particular relevance is the chapter on "The Semantic Whole of the Hero" in the forthcoming translation of "Author and Hero" by Vadim Liapunov included in *The Architectonics of Responsibility* (Austin: University of Texas Press, forthcoming).
7. In the spring of 1970, Bakhtin wrote an internal review for the future publishers of a book on Shakespeare by his good friend L. E. Pinsky (*Shekspir* [Moscow, 1971]).

In the review, a copy of which is in the Bakhtin archives, he said among other things:

> The stage of the Shakespearean theater is the entire world (*Theatrum mundi*). This is what gives that special significance . . . to each image, each action, and each word in Shakespeare's tragedies, which has never again returned to European drama (after Shakespeare, everything in drama became trivial). . . . This peculiarity of Shakespeare's . . . is a direct legacy of the medieval theater and forms of public spectacles, determining the evaluative-cosmic coloring of above and below . . . the main thing is the perception (or, more precisely, the living sense unaccompanied by any clear awareness) of all action in the theater as some kind of special symbolic ritual.

8. Compare similar ideas in Bakhtin's earlier work (V. N. Voloshinov, "Discourse in Life and Discourse in Art," tr. I. R. Titunik, in *Freudianism: A Marxist Critique* [New York: Academic Press, 1976], p. 112):

> Nothing is more perilous for aesthetics than to ignore the autonomous role of the listener. A very commonly held opinion has it that the listener is to be regarded as equal to the author, excepting the latter's technical performance, and that the position of a competent listener is supposed to be a simple reproduction of the author's position. In actual fact this is not so. Indeed, the opposite may sooner be said to be true: the listener never equals the author. The listener has *his own independent place* in the event of the artistic creation; he must occupy a special, and, what is more, a *two*-sided position in it—with respect to the author and with respect to the hero—and it is this position that has determinative effect on the style of the utterance.

9. In the "Phaedrus," Socrates says, "it is true I rarely venture outside my gates, and I hope that you will excuse me when you hear the reason, which is that I am a lover of knowledge, and the men who dwell in the city are my teachers, and not the trees of the country" (*The Dialogues of Plato*, tr. B. Jowett, 3rd ed. [London: Oxford University Press, 1892], vol. 1, p. 435).

RICHARD WEAVER
1910-1963

Born in North Carolina, Richard Weaver received his BA in English (with a minor in philosophy) from the University of Kentucky and his MA in 1934 from Vanderbilt University. After teaching at Texas A&M University, he enrolled in the doctoral program at Louisiana State University. Weaver earned his PhD in 1943 and then joined the faculty at the University of Chicago, where he rose to the rank of professor in 1957. Weaver was familiar with classical rhetoric and was drawn especially to Plato's views on rhetoric. To Weaver, rhetoric, because it reflects choices, shows us a better vision of what we can become. The "good" rhetorician always holds in mind the ideal and the ethical for a particular audience in a particular situation. Weaver also maintains that rhetoric is the force that shapes a community or culture; it is a striving toward some ultimate good. Therefore, by its very nature, language is sermonic. For Weaver's views on rhetoric, see also Ideas Have Consequences *(1948) and "Phaedrus and the Nature of Rhetoric" in* The Ethics of Rhetoric *(1953).*

The Cultural Role of Rhetoric

One of the most alarming results of the disparagement of memory is the tide of prejudice which is currently running against rhetoric. Everyone is aware that the old-style orator is no more, and even those speeches which suggest traditional oratory arouse skepticism and suspicion. The discourse that is favored today is without feeling and resonance, so that it is no exaggeration to say that eloquence itself has fallen into disfavor. Moments of great crisis do indeed encourage people to listen for a while to a Churchill or a MacArthur, and this is proof of the indispensability of rhetoric when men feel that great things are at stake. But today when the danger is past, they lapse again into their dislike of the rhetorical mode, labeling all discourse which has discernible emotional appeal "propaganda."

Rhetoric is involved along with memory in this trend because rhetoric depends upon history. All questions that are susceptible to rhetorical treatment arise out of history, and it is to history that the rhetorician turns for his means of persuasion. Now simultaneous with the loss of historical consciousness there emerges a conviction that man should dispense with persuasive speech and limit himself to mere communication. Viewed in the long perspective this must be considered a phase of the perennial issue between rhetoric and dialectic. But great danger lies in the fact that the present attitude represents a victory for a false conception of the role of dialectic in cultural life. States and societies cannot be secure unless there is in their public expression a partnership of dialectic and rhetoric. Dialectic is abstract reasoning upon the basis of propositions; rhetoric is the relation of the terms of these to the existential world in which facts are regarded with sympathy and are treated with that kind of historical understanding and appreciation which lie outside the dialectical process.

The current favor which rational and soulless discourse enjoys over rhetoric is a mask for the triumph of dialectic. This triumph is directly owing to the great prestige of modern science. Dialectic must be recognized as a counterpart in expression in language of the activity of science. We can affirm this, despite certain differences between them, because they are both rational and they are both neutral. The first point we need not labor; the second is important for this discussion because it is the quality of neutrality in science which has caused many moderns to suppose that it should be the model for linguistic discourse.

We hear it regularly asserted that the investigations and conclusions of science are not made to serve *ad hoc* causes. It is usually granted that the scientist is indifferent to the potencies which he makes available. His work is finished when he can say, "Here are these potencies." He is a solver of intellectual problems, as is evidenced by his reliance upon number.

Now, in a fashion similar enough to make the resemblance consequential, the dialectician is neutral toward the bearing of his reasoning upon actuality. The dialectician says, "If you assume these propositions, you must face these implications," and so forth. His work is with logical inference, not historical discovery. If we define dialectic in its pure form, we are compelled to say that it is indifferent to truth, or at least that its truth is something contained in its own operation. Professor Mortimer Adler has pointed out that "truth when it is taken to mean an extrinsic relation of thinking to entities beyond the process of thought cannot be achieved by dialectical thinking."[1] What is said here assumes the possibility of a pure dialectician, and it may be doubted, because of the nature of things, that such a person could exist. But the question I am here pursuing is whether one can become too committed to dialectic for his own good and the good of those whom he influences. I expect to show presently through a famous instance how this can happen.

My thesis is that a too exclusive reliance upon dialectic is a mistake of the most serious consequence because *dialectic alone in the social realm is subversive.* The widespread overturning of institutions in recent history and the frustration man now feels over his inability to guide his destiny begin, at the most profound level, with the disastrous notion that dialectic, unaided by rhetoric, is sufficient for human counsels. We have heard it contended by

---

[1] Mortimer Adler, *Dialectic* (New York, 1927), 31.

many leaders of opinion that if man will only avoid emotional approaches and will utilize science in coping with his problems, he will be able to conduct his affairs with a success hitherto unknown. That is to say, if he will rely upon a dialectic which is a counterpart to that of science in arriving at his decisions, he will have the advantage of pure knowledge whereas in the past he has tried to get along with a mass of knowledge and feeling. The point of this chapter will be the contrary: to give up the role of rhetoric and to trust all to dialectic is a fast road to social subversion.

For the introduction of this argument I am going back to the trial and condemnation of Socrates. Certain features of this extraordinary incident will help to illuminate the difficult problem of the relation of dialectic to rhetoric and of both of these to practical policy.

The reflective portion of mankind has wondered for centuries how so brilliant and civilized a people as the Greeks could condemn to death this famous philosopher. It would be blasphemous for anyone to suggest that the Athenian assembly did not commit a dreadful injustice. But since the condemnation occurred, there must have been some cause; and I think the cause lies much deeper than the fact that a few men with whom Socrates associated turned out badly and deeper than the resentment of a few Athenians whose vanity he had wounded through his questioning. The people of Athens had a case against Socrates which can be understood and elucidated. Set against their own attitudes and behavior, the case may not look very good to us, and we can still say that they put to death the most virtuous man in the city. Yet they had a certain cause, possibly more felt than reasoned out, but enough to account practically for the final judgment.

Socrates has come down to us as one of the greatest ethical teachers of all times. But by the Athenians who indicted him he was charged with being a subverter and a corrupter. Before we set down these two ascriptions as wholly incompatible, let us remember that Socrates was also the greatest dialectician of his time. We who study him at this remote date are chiefly impressed with the ethical aspect of his teaching, but those who listened to him in Athens may have been more impressed by his method, which was that of dialectic. By turning his great dialectical skill upon persons and institutions, Socrates could well have produced the feeling that he was an enemy of the culture which the Greeks had created. He was, in one sense of course, the highest expression of it, but the kind of skill he brought to a peak of development needs harmonizing with other things. When a dialectic operates independently of the concrete facts of a situation, it can be destructive. These facts are not determinative logically of the course which the dialectical inquiry must take, but they are the ground from which it must operate in actual discourse. A dialectic which becomes irresponsibly independent shatters the matrix which provides the base for its operation. In this fact must have lain the real source of the hostility toward Socrates. Nietzsche· has perceived this brilliantly in a passage of *The Birth of Tragedy:* "From this point onward Socrates conceives it his duty to correct existence; and with an air of irreverence and superiority, as the precursor of an altogether different culture, art, and morality, he enters single-handed into a world, to touch whose very hem would give us the greatest happiness."[2]

We must remember that Socrates begins the *Apology* by telling his auditors that they are not going to hear a clever speaker; that is to say, they are not going to hear an orator of the kind they are accustomed to; if Socrates is a good speaker, it is not in the style of his accusers. They have said nothing that is true; he proposes to speak only the truth. Further along, he professes to be "an utter foreigner to the manner of speech here." Obviously this is not the way in which a speaker consolidates himself with an audience; it betokens alienation rather than identification. Socrates has in effect said at the beginning, "Your way is not my way."

Thereafter Socrates gives an account of the origin of his unpopularity. He had gone around to men who were reputed to be wise and had questioned them about matters of which they were supposed to have knowledge. He found it easy to prove that they were not wise but ignorant or that their knowledge was so confined that it could scarcely be termed wisdom. Among those who underwent his examination were public men, or political leaders, and poets. This story is too well known to readers of the *Dialogues* to need rehearsing in detail. Suffice it to say that Socrates gives a candid relation of how his dialectic had irritated important elements in the population. But it is to the role of dialectic in the defense itself that I wish to direct chief attention. For Socrates, when his life was at stake, could not or would not give up the instrumentality by which he had been offending.

Let us look at the literal charge which has come down to us. "Socrates is a transgressor and a busybody, investigating things beneath the earth and in the heavens, and making the worse appear the better reason and teaching these things to others." Added to this was the further charge that he did not recognize the gods which were acknowledged by the state but insisted on introducing an idea of new spiritual beings. No doubt there are several ways in which this latter charge could have been answered. But the way in which Socrates chose to meet it was exactly the way to exacerbate the feelings of those whom he had earlier offended. It is significant that at one point he feels compelled to say to the assembly: "Please bear in mind not to make a disturbance if I conduct my argument in my accustomed manner." Here is the passage which follows that request:

> SOCRATES: You say what is incredible, Melitus, and that, as appears to me, even to yourself. For this man, O Athenians! appears to me to be very insolent

---

[2] *The Birth of Tragedy,* trans. Clifton Fadiman, Volume V in *The Philosophy of Nietzsche* (Modern Library Edition; 5 vols.; New York, 1937), 253.

and intemperate, and to have preferred this indictment through downright insolence, intemperance, and wantonness. For he seems, as it were, to have composed an enigma for the purpose of making an experiment. Whether will Socrates the wise know that I am jesting, and contradict myself, or shall I deceive him and all who hear me. For, in my opinion, he clearly contradicts himself in the indictment, as if he should say, Socrates is guilty of wrong in not believing that there are gods, and in believing that there are gods. And this, surely, is the act of one who is trifling.

Consider with me now, Athenians, in what respect he appears to me to say so. And do you, Melitus, answer me, and do ye, as I besought you at the outset, remember not to make an uproar if I speak after my usual manner.

Is there any man, Melitus, who believes that there are human affairs, but does not believe that there are men? Let him answer, judges, and not make so much noise. Is there anyone who does not believe that there are horses, but that there are things pertaining to horses? or who does not believe that there are pipers, but that there are things pertaining to pipes? There is not, O best of men! For since you are not willing to answer, I say it to you and to all here present. But answer to this at least: is there anyone who believes that there are things relating to demons, but does not believe that there are demons?

MELITUS: There is not.

SOCRATES: How obliging you are in having hardly answered, though compelled by these judges! You assert, then, that I do believe and teach things relating to demons, whether they be new or old; therefore, according to your admission, I do believe in things relating to demons, and this you have sworn in the bill of indictment. If, then, I believe in things relating to demons, there is surely an absolute necessity that I should believe that there are demons. Is it not so? It is. For I suppose you assent, since you do not answer. But with respect to demons, do we not allow that they are gods, or the children of gods? Do you admit this or not?

MELITUS: Certainly.

SOCRATES: Since, then, I allow that there are demons, as you admit, if demons are a kind of gods, this is the point in which I say you speak enigmatically and divert yourself in saying that I do not allow there are gods, and again that I do allow there are, since I allow that there are demons? But if demons are the children of gods, spurious ones, either from nymphs or any others, of whom they are reported to be, what man can think that there are sons of gods, and yet that there are not gods? For it would be just as absurd if anyone would think that there are mules, the offspring of horses and asses, but should not think that there are horses and asses. However, Melitus, it cannot be otherwise than that you have preferred this indictment for the purpose of trying me, or because you were at loss what real crime to allege against me; for that you should persuade any man who has the smallest degree of sense that the same person can think there are things relating to demons and to gods, and yet that there are neither demons, nor gods, nor heroes, is utterly impossible.[5]

---

[5] Henry Cary (trans.), *The Apology*, Volume I in *The Works of Plato* (6 vols.; London, 1858).

This shows in a clear way the weapon that Socrates had wielded against so many of his contemporaries. It is, in fact, a fine example of the dialectical method: first the establishment of a class; then the drawing out of implications; and finally the exposure of the contradiction. As far as pure logic goes, it is undeniably convincing; yet after all, this is not the way in which one talks about one's belief in the gods. The very rationality of it suggests some lack of organic feeling. It has about it something of the look of a trap or a trick, and one can imagine hearers not very sympathetic to the accused saying to themselves: "There is Socrates up to his old tricks again. That is the way he got into trouble. He is showing that he will never be any different." We may imagine that the mean and sullen Melitus, his interlocutor at this point—nothing good is intended of him here—was pleased rather than otherwise that Socrates was conducting himself so true to form. It underscored the allegations that were implied in the indictment.

This is not the only kind of argument offered by Socrates in his defense, it is true. In fact this particular argument is followed by a noble one based upon analogy, in which he declared that just as he would not desert the station he was commanded to guard while he was a soldier, so he would not give up his duty of being a gadfly to the men of Athens, which role he felt had been assigned him by the gods. Yet there is in the *Apology,* as a whole, enough of the clever dialectician—of the man who is concerned merely with logical inferences—to bring to the minds of the audience the side of Socrates which had aroused enmity.

The issue comes to a focus on this: Socrates professed to be a teacher of virtue, but his method of teaching it did not commend itself to all people. Now we come to the possibility that they had some justice on their side, apart from the forms which the clash took in this particular trial. We have noted that Socrates had derided poets and politicians; and to these the rhetoricians must be added, for despite the equivocal attitude taken toward rhetoric in the *Phaedrus,* Socrates rarely lost an opportunity for a sally against speechmakers. The result of his procedure was to make the dialectician appear to stand alone as the professor of wisdom and to exclude certain forms of cognition and expression which have a part in holding a culture together. It is not surprising that to the practitioners of these arts, his dialectic looked overgrown, even menacing. In truth it does require an extreme stand to rule out poetry, politics, and rhetoric. The use of a body of poetry in expressing the values of a culture will not be questioned except by one who takes the radical view presented by Plato in Book III of the *Republic.* But Socrates says in an early part of the *Apology* that when he went to the poets, he was ashamed to find that there was hardly a man present "who could not speak better than they about the poems they themselves had composed." But speak how? Poets are often lamentably poor dialecticians if you drag them away from their poetry and force them to use explicit discourse;

however, if they are good poets, they show reasoning power enough for their poetry and contribute something to the mind of which dialectic is incapable: feeling and motion.

The art of politics, although it often repels us in its degraded forms, cannot be totally abandoned in favor of pure speculation. Politics is a practical art. As such, it is concerned with man as a spatiotemporal creature; hence some political activity must take the form of compromise and adjustment. There is a certain relativism in it as a process, which fact is entailed by the *conditio humana*. But dialectic itself can stray too far from the human condition, as Pericles no doubt could have told him. We need not question that Socrates was an incomparably better man than most of the politicians who ruled Athens. He makes the point himself, however, that had he entered public life, he would have been proceeded against much earlier. That may well have been true, yet one can hardly conclude from its likelihood that human society can do without political leadership. It may be granted too that the men of Athens needed to learn from his dialectic; still they could not have depended upon it exclusively. The trend of Socrates' remarks, here and elsewhere, is that dialectic is sufficient for all the needs of man.

The fact that Socrates had excited the rhetoricians against him is a point of special significance for our argument. We have noted that he liked to indulge in raillery against speechmakers. Now it is one thing to attack those who make verbal jugglery their stock-in-trade, but it is another to attack rhetoric as an art. This is the matter over which the *Phaedrus* arrives at its point of hesitation: Can rhetoric be saved by being divorced from those methods and techniques which are merely seductive? The answer which is given in the *Phaedrus* can be regarded as ambiguous. At the end of the dialogue the rhetorician seems to wind up, by the force of the argument, a dialectician. But no reader can be unaware that Plato has made extensive use of his great rhetorical skill to buttress his case, to help it over certain places, and to make it more persuasive. His instinct in practice told him that rhetoric must supply something that dialectic lacks. This calls for looking further at the nature of rhetoric.

Rhetoric is designed to move men's feelings in the direction of a goal. As such, it is concerned not with abstract individuals, but with men in being. Moreover, these men in being it has to consider in relation to forces in being. Rhetoric begins with the assumption that man is born into history. If he is to be moved, the arguments addressed to him must have historicity as well as logicality. To explain: when Aristotle opens his discussion of rhetoric in the celebrated treatise of that name, he asserts that it is a counterpart of dialectic. The two are distinguished by the fact that dialectic always tries to discover the real syllogism in the argument whereas rhetoric tries to discover the real means of persuasion. From this emerges a difference of procedure, in which dialectic makes use of inductions and syllogisms, whereas rhetoric makes use of examples and enthymemes. In fact, Aristotle explicitly calls the use of example "rhetorical induction," and he calls the enthymeme the "rhetorical syllogism." This bears out our idea that rhetoric must be concerned with real or historical situations, although dialectic can attain its goal in a self-existing realm of discourse. Now the example is something taken from life, and the force of the example comes from the fact that it *is* or *was.* It is the thing already possessed in experience and so it is the property of everyone through the sharing of a common past. Through examples, the rhetorician appeals to matters that everybody has in a sense participated in. These are the possible already made the actual, and the audience is expected to be moved by their historicity.

The relation of rhetoric to "things-in-being" appears even more closely in the "rhetorical syllogism." The enthymeme, as students of logic learn, is a syllogism with one of the propositions missing. The reason the missing proposition is omitted is that it is presumed to exist already in the mind of the one to whom the argument is addressed. The rhetorician simply recognizes the wide acceptance of this proposition and assumes it as part of his argument. Propositions which can be assumed in this manner are settled beliefs, standing convictions, and attitudes of the people. They are the "topics" to which he goes for his sources of persuasion.

Through employment of the enthymeme, the rhetorician enters into a solidarity with the audience by tacitly agreeing with one of its perceptions of reality. This step of course enables him to pass on to his conclusion. If the rhetorician should say, "The magistrate is an elected official and must therefore heed the will of the people," he would be assuming a major premise, which is that "all elected officials must heed the will of the people." That unsupplied, yet conceded proposition, gives him a means by which he can obtain force for his argument. Therefore, quite as in the case of the example, he is resorting to something already acknowledged as "actual."

Aristotle continues his discussion of the two methods by pointing out that some persons cannot be reached by mere instruction. By the term "instruction" he signifies something of the order of logical demonstration. "Further, in dealing with certain persons, even if we possessed the most accurate scientific knowledge, we should not find it easy to persuade them by such knowledge. For scientific discourse is concerned with instruction, but in the case of such persons instruction is impossible; our proofs and arguments must rest on generally accepted principles, as we said in the *Topics,* when speaking of converse with the multitude."[4]

This also puts dialectic in a separate, though adjunct, realm. The mere demonstration of logical connections is not enough to persuade the com-

---

[4] *Rhetoric,* trans. Lane Cooper (London, 1932), 1355a.

monalty, who instead have to be approached through certain "places" or common perceptions of reality. It is these, as we have now seen, which rhetoric assumes in its enthymemes, taking the ordinary man's understanding of things and working from that to something that needs to be made evident and compulsive. As for dialectic, if the motive for it is bad, it becomes sophistry; if it is good, it becomes a scientific demonstration, which may lie behind the rhetorical argument, but which is not equivalent to it.

In sum, dialectic is epistemological and logical; it is concerned with discriminating into categories and knowing definitions. While this has the indispensable function of promoting understanding in the realm of thought, by its very nature it does not tell man what he must do. It tells him how the terms and propositions which he uses are related. It permits him to use the name of a species as a term without ever attending to whether the species exists and therefore is a force in being. That would be sufficient if the whole destiny of man were to know. But we are reminded that the end of living is activity and not mere cognition. Dialectic, though being rational and intellectual, simply does not heed the imperatives of living, which help give direction to the thought of the man of wisdom. The individual who makes his approach to life through dialectic alone does violence to life through his abstractive process. At the same time he makes himself antisocial because his discriminations are apart from the organic feeling of the community for what goes on. By this analysis the dialectician is only half a wise man and hence something less than a philosopher king, inasmuch as he leaves out the urgent reality of the actual, with which all rulers and judges know they have to deal.

The conclusion of this is that a society cannot live without rhetoric. There are some things in which the group needs to believe which cannot be demonstrated to everyone rationally. Their acceptance is pressed upon us by a kind of moral imperative arising from the group as a whole. To put them to the test of dialectic alone is to destroy the basis of belief in them and to weaken the cohesiveness of society. Such beliefs always come to us couched in rhetorical terms, which tell us what attitudes to take. The crucial defect of dialectic alone is that it ends in what might be called social agnosticism. The dialectician knows, but he knows in a vacuum; or, he knows, but he is without knowledge of how to act. Unless he is sustained by faith at one end or the other—unless he embraced something before he began the dialectical process or unless he embraces it afterward—he remains an unassimilable social agnostic. Society does not know what to do with him because his very existence is a kind of satire or aspersion upon its necessity to act. Or, it does know what to do with him, in a very crude and unpleasant form: it will put him away. Those who have to cope with passing reality feel that neutrality is a kind of desertion. In addition to understanding, they expect a rhetoric of action, and we must concede them some claim to this.

In thus trying to isolate the pure dialectician, we have momentarily lost sight of Socrates. We recall, of course, that he did not in all of his acts evince this determination to separate himself from the life of his culture. He served the state loyally as a soldier, and he refused opportunity to escape after the state had condemned him. His reasoning, in some of its lines, supports the kind of identification with history which I am describing as that of the whole man. There is one telltale fact near the very end of his career which gives interesting if indirect confirmation that Socrates had his own doubts about the omnicompetence of dialectic. When Phaedo and his friends visited Socrates in the prison, they found him composing verses. A dream had told him to "make music and work at it." Previously he had supposed that philosophy was the highest kind of music, but now, near the time of his execution, being visited by the dream again, he obeyed literally by composing a hymn to the god whose festival had just been celebrated and by turning some stories of Aesop into verse. Perhaps this was a way of acknowledging that a part of his nature—the poetical, rhetorical part—had been too neglected as a result of his devotion to dialectic and of making a kind of atonement at the end.

Still, the indictment "too much of a dialectician" has not been quashed. The trial itself can be viewed as a supremely dramatic incident in a far longer and broader struggle between rationalism on the one hand and poetry and rhetoric (and belief) on the other. This conflict reappears in the later battle, between Hellenic philosophy with its strong rational bias and Christianity, which ended after centuries in sweeping victory for the latter. Christianity provided all that Greek dialectic left out. It spoke to the feelings, and what seems of paramount significance, it had its inception in an historical fact. The Christian always had the story of Jesus with which to start his homilies. He could argue from a fact, or at least what was accepted as one, and this at once put him on grounds to persuade. We may recall here Aristotle's observation that in conversing with the multitude you do not aim at fresh scientific instruction; you rest your arguments upon generally accepted principles and beliefs, or broadly speaking, on things received. Practically, the victory of Christianity over Hellenic rationalism bears out the soundness of this insight. The Christians have worked through the poetry of their great allegory and through appeal to many facts as having happened, for example, the lives of the saints. Dialectic has been present, because it is never absent from rational discourse, but rhetoric and poetry were there to make up the winning combination.

Hellenic rationalism waned before man's need for some kind of faith and before a pessimism about human nature which seems to develop as history lengthens. We have emphasized that dialectic leads toward an agnosticism of action. Even Socrates was constantly saying, "The one thing that I know is that I know nothing." The fiercely positive Hebrew and Christian faiths contain nothing of this. As for the darker side of man's nature, what can set this forth but a powerful rhetoric? Dialectic may prove it in a conditional way, but it is up to the elaboration and iteration of rhetoric to make it real and overwhelming. Dialectic alone leads to an unwarranted confidence, and this evidently is the reason that Nietzsche refers to Socrates as an "optimist." If there is one thing which the great preachers of Christianity have inculcated, it is the proneness of man to fall.[5] Without extensive use of the art of rhetoric, they would have been unable to accomplish this. The triumph and continuance of Christianity and Christian culture attest the power of rhetoric in holding men together and maintaining institutions. It is generally admitted that there is a strong element of Platonism in Christianity. But if Plato provided the reasoning, Paul and Augustine supplied the persuasion. What emerged from this could not be withstood even by the power of Rome.

One cannot doubt that the decay of this great support of Western culture is closely connected with the decline of rhetoric. I spoke earlier of a growing resentment against the orator. This resentment arises from a feeling, perhaps not consciously articulated in many who possess it, that the orator is a teacher and a moral teacher at that. He cannot avoid being this if he uses words which will move men in a direction which he has chosen. But here is where the chief point of theoretical contention arises. There are persons today, some of them holding high positions in education, who believe (in theory, of course) that it is improper for any person to try to persuade another person. A name which has been invented for this act of persuading is "psychological coercion," which is obviously itself a highly loaded rhetorical phrase. From some such notion have come the extraordinary doctrines of modern semantics. According to the followers of this movement, the duty of anyone using language is to express the "facts" and avoid studiously the use of emotional coloring. The very use of facts in this kind of context reveals an astonishing naiveté about the nature of language. Yet there can be no doubt that this doctrine carries a great danger in that it represents a new attempt of dialectic to discredit and displace rhetoric. The writings of this group contain such a curious mélange of positivist dogma, modern prejudice, and liberal clichés that one runs a risk even in trying to digest it for purposes of analysis. Nevertheless, there are reasons for believing that it is in essence a new threat to fractionate society by enthroning dialectic as the only legitimate language of discourse.

The advocates of the "semantic" approach try to ascertain definitely the relationship between words and the things they stand for with the object of making signification more "scientific." These semanticists believe generally

---

[5] This is also the point of the great tragedies written before Euripides, who, significantly, was the only tragedian that Socrates admired.

that traditional speech is filled with terms which stand for nonexistent things, empty ideas, and primitive beliefs which get in the way of man's adaptation to environment. For them the function of speech is communication, and communication should be about things that really are. (One cannot read their literature very long without sensing the strong political motivation that inspires their position. A considerable part of their writing is a more or less open polemic against those features of speech which they regard as reflecting or upholding our traditional form of society. At a level below this, but for the same reason, they are antimetaphysical.) Unless we can establish that the world we are talking about is the world that exists empirically, then, the semanticists feel, we had better not talk at all. They want a vocabulary that is purified of all terms that originate in the subjectivity of the user, or at least they want to identify all such terms and place them in a quarantine ward.

The attempt must be identified as a fresh eruption of pure dialectic because it is concerned primarily with defining. Just as Socrates tried to define "justice" or "love" by now widening, now narrowing the categories, so they try, in a supposedly scientific way, to make the term fit the thing. The two are not engaged in exactly the same quest, and I shall come to their difference later, but they are both relying exclusively upon accurate verbal identification of something that is by them considered objective. As Socrates searched for the pure idea, so they search for the expression of the pure thing or fact. Moreover, they regard this as having the same power of salvation as the archetypal idea.

The quest of semantics cannot succeed, because the very theory of it is fallacious. The connection between a word and what it stands for cannot be determined in the way that they seem to believe. They operate on the assumption that there is some extralinguistic way of deciding what a word should mean, some point outside language from which one can judge the appropriateness of any choice of words for expression. The effort to get around language and to apply extralinguistic yardsticks is doomed to failure even in the cases of words symbolizing physical objects. A word stands for these things, but does not stand for them in the shape of the things. Language is a closed system, into which there is only one mode of entrance, and that is through meaning. And what a word means is going to be determined by the whole context of the vocabulary, with all the intermodification that this involves. A word does not get in through its fidelity to an object, but through its capacity to render what that object means to us.

But they do not even discriminate rightly the kinds of things for which words must stand. They assume that all words must stand for phenomena or things which are observable and classifiable by science. Indeed, this is their first principle: if a thing cannot be proved to exist scientifically—if it cannot be classified *with* phenomena—we are not supposed to bring it into expression at all, except in those relaxed moments when we are telling fairy stories and the like. Obviously they are ignoring the immensely important role of the subjective in life. There are numberless ideas, images, feelings, and intuitions which cannot be described and classified in the way of scientific phenomena but which have great effect upon our decisions. A rhetoric can take these into account, modify, direct, and use them because rhetoric deals in depth and tendency. A dialectic in the form of semantics cannot do this because it is interested only in defining words on the assumption that definitions are determined by the physical order. Just as the physical scientist discovers a law or a regularity in nature, so they endeavor to locate the source of terms in physical reality, and indeed their prime concern is to decide whether a referent really "exists." On first thought this might seem to give them the kind of respect for the actual order that I have claimed for believers in history. But a distinction is necessary: history is not the simple data of the perceptive consciousness; it is the experience of man after this has been assimilated and worked upon by the spirit. The appeal to history is an appeal to events made meaningful, and the meaning of events cannot be conveyed through the simple empirical references that semantic analysis puts forward as an ideal. Hence it is that the semanticist too is a neutralist, who would say, "Here is the world expressed in language that has been freed from tendency and subjective coloration." What is to be done with this world is postponed until another meeting, as it were, or it is assigned to a different kind of activity. His great mistake is the failure to see that language is intended to be sermonic. Because of its nature and of its intimacy with our feelings, it is always preaching. This type of agnostic will not listen to the sermon because he is unwilling to credit the existence of values. Yet even after it has been decided that the referent does exist, there is nothing to do with the word except turn it over to others whose horizons are not bounded by logical positivism.

This brings us to the necessity of concluding that the upholders of mere dialectic, whether they appear in this modern form or in another, are among the most subversive enemies of society and culture. They are attacking an ultimate source of cohesion in the interest of a doctrine which can issue only in nullity. It is of no service to man to impugn his feeling about the world qua feeling. Feeling is the source of that healthful tension between man and what *is*—both objectively and subjectively. If man could be brought to believe that all feeling about the world is wrong, there would be nothing for him but collapse.

Socrates was saved from trivialization of their kind by his initial commitment to the Beautiful and the Good. He is also saved in our eyes by the marvelous rhetoric of Plato. These were not enough to save him personally in the great crisis of his life, but they give high seriousness to the quest which he represents. The modern exponents of dialectic have nothing like these to give respectability to their undertaking or persuasiveness to their cause. But both, in the long view, are the victims of supposing that definition and classification are sufficient as the ends of speech.

In a summing up we can see that dialectic, when not accompanied by a historical consciousness and responsibility, works to dissolve those opinions, based partly on feeling, which hold a society together. It tends, therefore, to be essentially revolutionary and without commitment to practical realities. It is even contumacious toward the "given," ignoring it or seeking to banish it in favor of a merely self-consistent exposition of ideas.

Rhetoric, on the other hand, tries to bring opinion into closer line with the truth which dialectic pursues. It is therefore cognizant of the facts of situations and it is at least understanding of popular attitudes.

There is a school of thinking, greatly influenced by the Socratic tradition, which holds that it is intellectually treasonable to take popular opinion into account. The side that one espouses in this issue will be determined by his attitude toward creation. When we look upon the "given" of the world, we find two things: the world itself and the opinions which mankind has about the world. Both of these must be seen as parts of the totality. The world is a primary creation, and the opinions of men are creations of the men who live in it. Next the question becomes: can we regard the world as infinitely correctible and men's opinions of it as of no account? Socrates could do this because he believed in a god or gods. The world is by him from the beginning condemned; it is a prison house, a dark cave; it is the realm of becoming which is destined to pass away. All things tend toward realizing themselves in a godlikeness, at which time the mortal and earthly will have been shuffled off. A complete reliance upon dialectic becomes possible only if one accepts something like this Socratic theodicy. But the important point is that it denies the axiological status of creation.

The modern counterpart thinks he can affirm that creation is infinitely correctible because he believes only in man and speaks only on his behalf. When we examine his position, however, we find that he believes only in the natural order. This he reveals by his insistence upon positivistic proof for everything. But from the positive order he cannot draw the right inferences about man. He can find no place for those creations like affections and opinions which are distinctly human and which are part of the settlement of any culture. For him an opinion, instead of being a stage of historical consciousness which may reflect a perfectly bona fide if narrow experience, is just an impediment in the way of the facts. His dialectic would move toward the facts and seek to destroy that which holds the facts in a cohesive picture. On his principle a cohesive or systematized outlook must involve distortion, and this explains why he automatically refers to rhetoric as "propaganda."

In brief the dialectician of our day has no adequate theory of man. Lacking such a theory, he of course cannot find a place for rhetoric, which is the most humanistic of all the diciplines. Rhetoric speaks to man in his whole being and out of his whole past and with reference to values which only a human being can intuit. The semanticists have in view only a denatured speech to suit a denatured man. Theirs is a major intellectual error, committed by supposing that they were going to help man by bringing language under the surveillance of science.

There is never any question that rhetoric ultimately will survive this scientistic attack. The pity is that the attacks should ever have been made at all since, proceeding from contempt for history and ignorance of the nature of man, they must produce confusion, skepticism, and inaction. In the restored man dialectic and rhetoric will go along hand in hand as the regime of the human faculties intended that they should do. That is why the recovery of value and of community in our time calls for a restatement of the broadly cultural role of rhetoric.

ERNESTO GRASSI
b. 1902

That rhetoric is our principal means of knowing lies at the center of Ernesto Grassi's humanistic theory building. Born in Italy, he has taught philosophy at universities in Italy and South America. Grassi is important to the New Rhetorics because he subsumes rationalism (as do Stephen Toulmin and Chaim Perelman) as the method of showing truth to the epistemic nature of rhetoric. Although he is influenced by and extends the thinking of Plato, Aristotle, Cicero, and Quintilian, it is primarily through Vico and the Italian humanists that he has formed his humanistic theory of rhetoric, focusing on its epistemic nature. Grassi's work is an example of how rhetoric as its central act theorizes practice and applies theory. His Rhetoric as Philosophy: The Humanist Tradition *(1980) and his work on Vico (for example, "The Priority of Common Sense and Imagination: Vico's Philosophical Relevance Today" in* Vico and Contemporary Thought. *Eds., George Tagliacozzo, Michael Mooney, and Donald P. Verene. Humanities Press, 1979) are of special importance to the New Rhetorics.*

Rhetoric and Philosophy

The Primacy of Rhetorical Speech

The problem of rhetoric—as the speech that acts on the emotions—can be treated from two points of view. It can be considered simply as a doctrine of a type of speech that the traditional rhetors, politicians, and preachers need, i.e., only as an art, as a technique of persuading. In this case the problems of rhetoric will be limited to questions of practical directions for persuading people and will not have a theoretical character.

From another point of view, however, the problems of rhetoric can be seen as involving a relation to philosophy, to theoretical speech. We can formulate this in the following way: If philosophy aims at being a theoretical mode of thought and speech, can it have a rhetorical character and be expressed in rhetorical forms? The answer seems obvious. Theoretical thinking, as a rational process, excludes every rhetorical element because pathetic influences—the influences of feeling—disturb the clarity of rational thought.

Locke and Kant, for example, express this view, and their statements are characteristic of the rationalistic attitude toward rhetoric. Locke writes:

I confess, in discourses where we seek rather pleasure and delight than information and improvement, such ornaments as are borrowed from them can
scarce pass for faults. But yet if we would speak of things as they are, we must
allow that all the art of rhetoric, besides order and clearness; all the artificial
and figurative application of words eloquence hath invented, are for nothing
else but to insinuate wrong ideas, move the passions, and thereby mislead the
judgment; and so are perfect cheats.[1]

Kant writes:

Rhetoric, so far as this is taken to mean the art of persuasion, i.e., the art of
deluding by means of a fair semblance [as *ars oratoria*], and not merely excellence of speech (eloquence and style), is a dialectic, which borrows from
poetry only so much as is necessary to win over men's minds to the side of the
speaker before they have weighed the matter, and to rob their verdict of its
freedom. . . . Force and elegance of speech (which together constitute
rhetoric) belong to fine art; but oratory [*ars oratoria*], being the art of playing
for one's own purpose upon the weaknesses of men (let this purpose be ever
so good in intention or even in fact) merits no *respect* whatever.[2]

It is obvious that the problem of rhetoric as conceived here places philosophy in a position preeminent to rhetoric. Rhetoric is seen only as a technical doctrine of speech. Only the clarification of rhetoric in its relation to
theoretical thought can allow us to delimit the function of rhetoric. Only
this will allow us to decide whether rhetoric has a purely technical, exterior,
and practical aim of persuading, or whether it has an essentially philosophical structure and function.

The solution to this problem can be worked out only if we establish the
following fact: We claim that we know something when we are able to
prove it. To prove means to *show* something to be something, on the basis
of something. To have something through which something is shown and
explained definitively is the foundation of our knowledge. Apodictic, demonstrative speech is the kind of speech which establishes the definition of
a phenomenon by tracing it back to ultimate principles, or *archai*. It is clear
that the first *archai* of any proof and hence of knowledge cannot be proved
themselves because they cannot be the object of apodictic, demonstrative,
logical speech; otherwise they would not be the first assertions. Their non-
derivable, primary character is evident from the fact that we neither can
speak nor comport ourselves without them, for both speech and human
activity simply presuppose them. But if the original assertions are not
demonstrable, what is the character of the speech in which we express
them? Obviously this type of speech cannot have a rational-theoretical
character.

In other words it is evident that the rational process and consequently
rational speech must move from the formulation of primary assertions. Here
we are confronted with the fundamental question of the character necessary

to the formulation of basic premises. Evidently by using this kind of expression, which belongs to the original, to the nondeductible, they cannot have an apodictic, demonstrative character and structure but are thoroughly *indicative*. It is only the indicative character of *archai* that makes demonstration possible at all.

The indicative or allusive speech provides the framework within which the proof can come into existence. Furthermore if rationality is identified with the process of clarification, we are forced to admit that the primal clarity of the principles is not rational and recognize that the corresponding language in its indicative structure has an "evangelic" character, in the original Greek sense of this word, i.e., "noticing."

Such speech is immediately a "showing"—and for this reason "figurative" or "imaginative," and thus in the original sense "theoretical" [i.e., to see]. It is metaphorical, i.e., it shows something which has a sense, and this means that to the figure, to that which is shown, the speech transfers a signification; in this way the speech which realizes this showing "leads before the eyes" a significance. This speech is and must be in its structure an imaginative language.

If the image, the metaphor, belongs to rhetorical speech (and for this reason it has a pathetic character), we also are obliged to recognize that every original, former, "archaic" speech (archaic in the sense of dominant, *arche, archomai; archontes* or the dominants) cannot have a rational but only a rhetorical character. Thus the term "rhetoric" assumes a fundamentally new significance; "rhetoric" is not, nor can it be the art, the technique of an exterior persuasion; it is rather the speech which is the basis of the rational thought.

This original speech, because of its "archaic" character, sketches the framework for every rational consideration, and for this reason we are obliged to say that rhetorical speech "comes before" every rational speech, i.e., it has a "prophetic" character and never again can be comprehended from a rational, deductive point of view. This is the tragedy of the rationalistic process.

Furthermore knowledge, or the explanation of something through its cause, constitutes a process which is as such of a temporal nature, for as something that has happened it is a historical phenomenon which has passed through different moments in time. The primary speech instead reveals itself instantaneously. It does not lie within historical time; it is the origin and criterion of the movement of the rational process of clarification.

If the essence of the speech, which expresses the original, has to be purely semantic, because it is only through this kind of speech that the demonstrative language becomes at all possible, we must distinguish between two kinds of language: the *rational language,* which is dialectical, mediating, and demonstrative, i.e., apodictic and without any pathetic character, and the *semantic language,* which is immediate, not deductive or demonstrative, illuminating, purely indicative, and which has a preeminence opposite the rational language. On the basis of its figurative, metaphorical character, this language has an original pathetic essence.

This is the reason why only from a formal point of view the original, immediate, purely semantic word belongs necessarily to the sacred, religious word, while the mediating, step-by-step, demonstrating and proof-giving (apodictic) word is covered by the rational and historical word.

Now we are in a position to understand the meaning of a sentence of Heraclitus who, at the beginning of the Western tradition, expressed what we have taken to develop here: "The lord to whom the oracle of Delphi belongs says nothing and conceals nothing; he indicates, shows."

Cassandra's Tragic Movement from Rhetoric to Rationality

The consciousness of all these problems—the admission of the structure of original language as not rational but rhetorical; the interpretation of rhetoric primarily not as an expression of an art of conviction but as an expression of the original and, in this sense, of the religious speech with its "evangelic" and "prophetic" character; and finally the admission that through rational language and thought, we never comprehend the primary and original thought and speech—all these points are expressed in the tragedy of Cassandra in the *Agamemnon* of Aeschylus.

I wish to develop what I have said previously by interpreting the Greek text that, from this point of view and in this manner, demonstrates the original framework in which the Greeks have treated, in a nonrational manner, the problem of original rhetorical speech and its original philosophical dimension.

The background of Cassandra's personal tragedy is well known. She was chosen as mistress by Apollo and promised to yield to him if he would grant her, in exchange, the gift of prophecy. Having received this gift she denied herself to the god, who thereupon punished her by depriving her of her sight and providing that no one in the future should believe in her prophecies or understand her utterances.

Who is Cassandra? Homer mentions her in the *Iliad* as the daughter of the king of Troy, but he does not elaborate on her fatal gift of prophecy. Pindar describes her as a prophet. Factually, of the texts that have come down to us, the *Agamemnon* provides the final comprehensive interpretation of the Cassandra figure; the gravity of her "external" tragedy rests on the myth of Apollo and his beloved. But is Aeschylus merely concerned with this story, or does he have in mind a tragedy that lies deeper and points to a fundamental phenomenon of human existence?

How is Cassandra's semantic language constructed? At the beginning of the Cassandra tragedy one can see already that the Chorus is trying in vain to enter into a dialogue with the seer. Here its first reaction is the reproach that Cassandra's invocation of the god Apollo as well as the way she invoked him were unseemly; it considers her exclamation senseless and improper. Cassandra does not hear the words of the Chorus; she repeats her invocation, and again the Chorus reacts in a rational manner. Once more Cassandra takes no notice of it. Until the passage referred to previously, the Chorus will at no price give up the attempt to enter into a conversation with Cassandra; in the same measure it refuses to alter its own explanatory attitude.

The contrast between Cassandra and the Chorus is obvious; each moves in a space and in a time of its own. The Chorus moves in the realm of expoundable rationality and in a time which makes the future appear simply as a *possibility*. It speaks, in the text, in the grammatical form used for reporting the past. Its language, therefore, is temporal, in the sense that it attempts to grasp and to reflect the unfolding of events and their relations.

Cassandra's space, on the other hand, is determined by the simultaneous nature of the vision in which the movements of time are fused, and turn into parts of an immovable, necessary, and no longer merely possible instant. In accordance with her "seer's" gifts Cassandra speaks a pictorial language which is distinguished from that of the Chorus by frequently falling back on participial phrases. The contrast between the world of Cassandra and that of the Chorus definitely illustrates the fact that the semantic approach cannot be attained or derived through a logical process.

Never does an explanatory word pass over Cassandra's lips, for she herself knows nothing of cause and effect. She speaks only through images and symbols. Death itself is symbolized by a net in which the animal (bull or cow, as a metaphor for Agamemnon) will be ensnared; the ruse, the snare, "dawns" upon him ("What is it? What appears there?/A fishing-net of Hades? A snare to catch the husband, an accomplice for/the murder").

In the second main passage the transition takes place from Cassandra's ecstatic, mantic condition to her human sphere; rational elements come into the foreground and thus provide the beginning of a dialogical relation between Cassandra and the Chorus. How does this transition occur? Cassandra begins with a lament about her own death, though here she still addresses the god rather than the Chorus. In this speech she no longer asks the god where she is, as she did at the beginning of her appearance on stage, but *why* he has led her hither. So for the first time she asks for an *explanation*, a reason for her being here. By entering the plane of *explanation* and abandoning the world of allusion with this question, she causes her historical reality to be outlined, and she herself moves into a historical framework of time and space.

The manner in which the poet lures Cassandra from her purely semantic and mantic plane into the rational historical world, and thus makes it possible for the Chorus to enter into a dialogue with her, is characteristic and significant. This conversational passage becomes a sign of her departure from the world of the inexplicable, the original, the purely semantic. The change is brought about through a *metaphor,* as though this were the only possible bridge between the rational and the semantic realms. The Chorus compares her complaints with those of Prokne, the nightingale. This *image* touches Cassandra in her longing for the human world to which she originally belonged, and at the same time touches her in connection with her impending lot: *For the first time,* stimulated by this *image,* Cassandra hears the words of the Chorus and reacts to them.

The question which the Chorus now asks Cassandra, and the ensuing conversation (that is, the beginning of a dialogue between the protagonist of the semantic, original world and that of the rational, proving world of the Chorus) is founded on an image, a metaphor. This metaphor has an emotional impact and appeals to a longing—a human passion—which lures the human being standing in the semantic realm into the world of explanation, of occurrence, of sequence, in other words, into the realm of time dominated by death. In the purely semantic sphere there was merely the presence of images, of indications; there was a lack of causal explanations. In accordance with this abrupt change Cassandra's language also changes; suddenly she uses the past form indispensably within a perspective involving time.

Lured by the images of the past Cassandra also talks about her relation with Apollo. The text does not justify the assumption that it was love that made Cassandra promise herself to the god, but rather that she did it with an ulterior motive. She wanted to receive the gift warranted by the god's possession of her, by the fusion with him, the divine ecstasy of the prophet which eliminates the order of the temporal sequence of cause and effect and also rational speech. The divine gift—to encompass all in an instant—is something Cassandra desired not for herself alone; she wanted to communicate it to others, to be mediator between the divine and the human. However, her real aim was to obtain the gift *through a ruse.* Ruse is rational design, and no rational process or attitude can ever lead to the origins of being, to the divine, for the divine conditions the rational process.

The tragedy of Cassandra, the curse pursuing her, is based on her rationality, odd though that may sound. Since it is impossible to grasp the divine by rational methods, a failure to recognize this fact becomes a cure. Rationality also prevents the Chorus from having any communication, any dialogue, with Cassandra while she is still on a semantic plane. Her figure is uncanny because it is her rational intention to communicate timelessness to the historical and rational world; men lack the means to understand her pronouncements and illuminations by way of reason. This access can be opened only through images, metaphor, semantic speech. The "seeing" thus gains absolute precedence over the other senses in semantic language.

The Relation of Rhetoric to the Rational Process

Let us consider the rational, logical process more closely. The fruitfulness of any deductions obviously grows out of the fruitfulness of the premises; the more productive the premises, the more productive the deductions. The validity and framework of the conclusions depend on the validity and framework of the premises.

If we question this conception of the rational process as to the kind of premises from which the syllogism or the deduction set out, we again come up against the *archai*, "the principles." Here we have to remember the original meaning of *arche* and of the verb *archomai*, "to lead, to guide, to rule." To lead or to guide was expressed in Latin as *inducere* and in Greek as *epagein*. From this we can derive that "principles" alone can be the only true and original point of departure, the real foundation of induction, of *epagoge* as the process of reducing the multiplicity to a unity; therefore the real and valid concept of induction cannot be identified with a process that has its point of departure in the multiplicity and arises to a unity through abstraction.

Aristotle, in his meditation about the essence of the logical process and its inevitable premises, gives the term *pistis* or "faith," "belief" (which is so important in rhetoric), a meaning which was forgotten completely and which no longer coincides with the meaning of *doxa*, much less with the special form of rational conviction founded on proof. In the *Posterior Analytics* Aristotle defines knowledge and conviction, that is, the *rational* belief [*pistis*] arising from conviction, as "One believes and knows something when a deduction is carried out which we call proof." It is clear that Aristotle here assigns a rational character to the concept of *pistis*, conviction, understanding, and knowledge from a special perspective; the determining factor is *deduction*. Proof consists in "giving the reason." The reason becomes evident in connection with the deduction, which necessarily starts from premises and hence depends on their validity.

Aristotle continues: "Since the conclusion obtains its true validity from the fact that the reason on which it is based is evident, it necessarily follows that with each proof, the first principles in which it has origin must not only be known completely or partially prior to the proof, they must *also be known to a higher degree* than that which is deduced from them."

So when we *know* and *believe* in connection with a proof, we must necessarily *believe* and *know* the premises on which the proof is based *on more forceful grounds*. Aristotle accentuates this fundamental condition: "If we *know and believe* an object by means of the first principle to a more forceful degree than that which is derived from it, *we know and believe* the latter on the basis of the first."

Are we conscious of the change in the meaning of knowledge and belief, as expressed in this passage? Hitherto there has been mention only of a belief, and knowledge and belief, which is more primary than the rational form and of necessity radically different in structure. We must remember, nevertheless, that the nonrational character of the principles is by no means identical with irrationality; the necessity and universal validity in the non-rational character of the *archai* impose themselves equally or to a higher degree than the universal validity and necessity effective in the deductive process and resting on the foundation of strict logic.

It seems useful to quote another Aristotelian passage: "The principles—all or some—must necessarily be lent *more belief* than what is deduced. He who arrives at a certain knowledge through proof must necessarily . . . *know and believe the principles to a higher degree than what is deduced from them.*" The task resulting from this consists in a further elucidation of the structure of this knowledge and belief, and this task belongs to the problems resulting from the relation between philosophical and rhetorical speech. Here we must point out the following: The *techne* of rhetoric, as the art of persuasion, of forming belief, structures the emotive framework which creates the tension within which words, questions that are dealt with, and actions that are discussed, acquire their passionate significance. It creates a tension through which the audience is literally "sucked into" the framework designed by the author.

The emotive word affects us through its directness. Since emotional life unrolls in the framework of directly indicative signs, a word must evoke these signs in order to relieve or to soothe the passions. As a passionate, and not exclusively rational, being, man is in need of the emotive word.

So over the centuries, under the aspect of the relationship between *content* and *form*, the thesis was again and again developed that images and rhetoric were to be appreciated primarily from outside, for *pedagogical reasons*, that is, as aids to "alleviate" the "severity" and "dryness" of rational language. To resort to images and metaphors, to the full set of implements proper to rhetoric and artistic language, in this sense, merely serves to make it "easier" to absorb rational truth.

Therefore rhetoric generally was assigned a *formal* function, whereas philosophy, as *episteme*, as rational knowledge, was to supply the true, factual content. This distinction is significant because the essence of man is determined both by logical and emotional elements, and as a result speech can reach the human being as a union of *logos* and *pathos* only if it appeals to both these aspects.

A statement of this kind carries important implications: (1) The only true educational method, the only true way of teaching, is rational deduction and demonstration, which can be taught and learned in its rules and its proceedings. Education is based on explanation. (2) Attestation loses its significance altogether; the only valid testimony is the logical process. Its structure is conditioned by the rationality of proof. Problems, so-called problems of form and style, which cannot be identified with the structure of rational demonstration, are rhetorical and not theoretical, i.e., they are external. In other words the rational content determines the form; in the realm of theoretical thought there exists no problem of form which can be divorced from the rational content. (3) Knowledge is unhistorical in its essence because logical evidence *always* is valid when it has been acknowledged on the basis of its necessity and universal validity, which it possesses by definition. The historical character of knowledge at most may be of significance as regards a reconstruction of the process leading to knowledge. (4) Every cognition is necessarily *anonymous* because the rational grounds, with their necessity and universal validity, are not bound up with individual persons.

But is this conception of pedagogy which involves a determined theory of rhetoric valid? Has it not been shown already that the original, archaic (in the sense which I gave to this term) assertions have in their structure a belief, a figurative, imaginative character, so that every original speech is in its aim illuminating and persuading? In this original speech evidently it is impossible to separate content and form and also, in pedagogical terms, to look for a "posterior" unity of them.

Plato's Union of Knowledge and Passion

Now I wish to clarify the relations between rhetoric and philosophy with reference to classical antiquity; my aim is to find out whether the need was felt, and if so, in what manner, to establish a union between knowledge and passion, a union that can be reached neither through the external emotive disguise of a rational "content," nor through pouring a rational content into an emotive "form." To this end let us consider Plato's dialogues the *Gorgias* and the *Phaedrus*. An examination of what I consider a misinterpretation of Plato regarding the dualism between rhetoric and philosophy will be helpful in classifying the problem.

According to the traditional interpretation Plato's attitude against rhetoric is a rejection of the *doxa*, or opinion, and of the impact of images, upon which the art of rhetoric relies; at the same time his attitude is considered as a defense of the theoretical, rational speech, that is, of *episteme*. The fundamental argument of Plato's critique of rhetoric usually is exemplified by the thesis, maintained, among other things, in the *Gorgias*, that only he who "knows" can speak correctly; for what would be the use of the "beautiful," of the rhetorical speech, if it merely sprang from opinions, hence from not knowing? This interpretation of Plato's attitude in his dialogue *Gorgias,* however, fails to take account of some unmistakable factual difficulties.

His rejection of rhetoric, when understood in this manner, assumes that Plato rejects every emotive element in the realm of knowledge. But in several of his dialogues Plato connects the philosophical process, for example, with *eros,* which would lead to the conclusion that he attributes a decisive role to the emotive, seen even in philosophy as the absolute science. So we will have to ask ourselves how those apparently contradictory tenets are to be explained and to what extent the essence of philosophy is not exhausted for Plato in the *episteme,* i.e., in the typical rational process it requires. Will we find here a deeper meaning of rhetoric?

Plato's *Gorgias* comes to terms with the claims of rhetorical art. Gorgias here supports the thesis that rhetoric can rightly claim "to carry out and fulfil *everything* through speech." How shall we interpret this "everything"? Gorgias's answer is: The greatest and most important of all things human, that is, health, richness, beauty; to attain all that belongs to the aim of rhetoric. But is rhetoric capable of attaining these gifts of mankind? The physician, for example, will deny that anyone can be cured merely through speech, without special knowledge. What then is the use of the art of convincing, of *peithein?* So Socrates decides to find out "what kind of persuasion is the kind accomplished by the art of rhetoric."

He comes to distinguish between true and false belief and proves that in contradiction to belief, to *doxa,* there can be no true or false *episteme* or rational knowledge because it is rooted in grounds, in reasons. As a result rational knowledge and rational speech is superior; it admits no form of opinion besides itself, no form that is not covered by founded knowledge. Since rhetoric does not convince by means of such rational knowledge, it remains always in the realm of pseudoknowledge.

This radically negative judgment of rhetoric traditionally is considered to be Plato's definitive attitude to rhetoric, and that in view of the thesis that rational knowledge, i.e., philosophy, represents the only true and valid rhetorical art. This, however, leaves the problem of the relationship between passion, instinct, and the rational process unsolved. The belief inspired in man on the basis of emotive speeches accordingly would have to yield to rational knowledge, or be canceled by it; but knowledge alone, as a rational process, can neither move the human being nor carry him away to certain actions.

Gorgias answers Socrates with the following objection: Of what use is all the physician's knowledge if the patient does not pluck up courage to do what the physician has prescribed? So one does need rhetoric. A similar objection: A community rarely opts for what the specialist advises, but rather for what a capable orator proposes. The dilemma we perceived earlier seems insurmountable; on one side, there is an ineffectual rational knowledge, on the other speech as pure "seduction." Therefore how can we resolve the problem?

The problem of the *pathos* (and with it, of rhetoric) in its relationship to theoretical, i.e., epistemic, speech forms the central theme of the *Phaedrus,* the second dialogue with which I propose to deal. Its first part, as is well known, concerns *eros*. Phaedrus (a disciple of the rhetorician Lycias) holds a speech against *eros*. The subsequent speech of Socrates is equally directed against *eros* and so against *pathos;* suddenly, however, Socrates stops short. Since he is ashamed of having spoken against *eros,* he holds a third speech, which develops into a praise of *eros*.

These three speeches on *eros* are followed by the second part of the dialogue, which has as its subject the nature and structure of rhetoric and begins with a solemn reference to the Muses, in connection with a myth, namely, of the cicadas. The cicadas, Socrates explains, originally descended from human beings who lived before the time of the Muses. When the Muses were conceived and began to sing, a few of these human beings were so enthralled by them that they forgot about food and only wanted to sing, so that they almost died unnoticed. These lovers of Muses were turned into cicadas; their task was to report to the Muses, after their death, who among humans was most devoted to which one of the Muses, and Socrates comes to speak about the Muse of philosophy. In general, as we have seen, a speech is called "philosophical" when it is based on a knowledge of reasons. Statements based on knowledge possess a rational character; they belong to the field of *epistemé,* of theoretical thought. But rational speech itself, as we know, starts out from premises that are not rational because they are based on first affirmations. The rational process *does* forbid the insertion of any element connected with the Muses. But if Plato, as for example in *Gorgias,* identifies the only art of convincing which he accepts, with rational knowledge, i.e., *epistemé,* how are we to understand the fact that here he places philosophy under the sign of the Muses? Is it only a casual reference?

We can answer this question only when we ask: What is the meaning of the condition of man *before* the birth of the Muses? Why should men have been so fascinated by the Muses and their work that they went so far as to forget about food, and what has this to do with philosophy?

We cannot develop here the different meanings and interpretations of the Muses. The problem is why Plato, in his *Phaedrus,* refers to the Muses with his myth of the cicadas, speaking of the essence and structure of philosophy and what he meant by the condition of men *before* the creation of the "Muses" and their "enraptured" condition after the appearance of these goddesses. What relation can there be between the work of Muses and philosophy?

The meaning of the word "muse" remains unknown. Attempts at an etymological derivation of the term began in classical times, namely, with Plato. In the *Cratylus* he says: "The Muses, however, and music in general, were evidently thus named by Apollo from *musing* [*moosthai*]." The word *moosthai* contains in its implication a process of *searching,* of "storm and stress." Plutarch, in addition to his derivation of the word from *homou ousai* "existing at once, simultaneously," whereby he points to their union, also mentions a second one, which he considers a result of the analogy between *mousai* and *mneiai,* those who remember.

In the activities of the Muses, the concept of order clearly plays a prevalent and unifying part. The order of *movements* appears in the dance, the order of *tones* in song, and the order of *words* in verse. Furthermore order is the starting point of *rhythm* and *harmony.* Plato says in the *Laws:* "The order of movement is named *rhythm,* the order of voice, of the connection between high and low tones, is called *harmony.*"

The reference made in the *Laws* to the "order of movement" seems particularly significant because movement represents a fundamental phenomenon in the realm of existence; whatever is perceived through the senses shows a *becoming,* that is, a movement in itself (change) or a movement in space. Through the application of a *measure,* movement proceeds within certain barriers and under certain laws; it is, as one might put it, "arranged." Thus we can understand how numbers, as expressions of measure, of proportions in arts, were originally given a religious significance, and also we can understand the sacred character of dance, song, and music. Plato complains in the *Laws* about the decadence of the arts insofar as they are no longer a manifestation of the original, objective harmony. This complaint refers to the decadence of the *mousike,* which is not only music but the union of song, verse, and dance in their original objectiveness. The Muses, on the contrary, represent the link with the objective, which makes the original order of the human world possible in the face of the arbitrary, the subjective, the relative, and the changeable. The reference to the ground in which knowledge, *episteme,* is anchored is a remembrance of the original. This explains the connection between Mnemosyne and fame; the man who is surrounded by fame steps into the presence of the eternally valid. This explains also the connection between the Muses and the "view" in which, through the roots of every original science, we put the chaos in order with the aid of our founded knowledge."

Now we can begin to understand what Plato meant when he spoke of the condition of men before the birth of the Muses, in other words, what the Muses brought men and why those who devoted themselves to them forgot everything in favor of musical activities; the chaos was overcome, order was created, a cosmos appeared. We also must consider rhetoric from this aspect. On the basis of what we have just said, Plato cannot possibly identify true rhetoric with *episteme* which, due to its rational character, excludes all musical elements.

In the second part of the *Phaedrus* Plato attempts to clarify the nature of "true" rhetoric. He starts out with the demonstration that the process, which has its roots in the *nous* [*dia-noia*] as the insight into original "ideas," is the requisite for a true speech. The *dianoia* is the process which can be realized only on the basis of—or "through" [*dia*]—the *nous*. Socrates maintains that the orator must possess *dianoia* with respect to the subject he is talking about. *Dia-noia* is the faculty which leads us to a discernment through the *nous*, i.e., on the basis of an insight into the *archai*. *Nous* forms the prerequisite of *episteme* insofar as *episteme* can only prove or explain something following an insight into the original indicative, commanding, and showing images. The corresponding speech is neither purely rational nor purely pathetic.

Also it does not arise from a posterior unity which presupposes the duality of *ratio* and *passio*, but illuminates and influences the passions through its original, imaginative characters. Thus philosophy is not a posterior synthesis of *pathos* and *logos but the original unity* of the two under the power of the original *archai*. Plato sees true rhetoric as psychology which can fulfill its truly "moving" function only if it masters original images. Thus the true philosophy is rhetoric, and the true rhetoric is philosophy, a philosophy which does not need an "external" rhetoric to convince, and a rhetoric that does not need an "external" content of verity.

To sum up we are forced to distinguish between three kinds of speech:

1. The *external, "rhetorical speech,"* in the common meaning of this expression, which only refers to images because they affect the passions. Since these images do not stem from insight, however, they remain an object of opinion. This is the case of the purely emotive, false speech: "rhetoric" in the usual negative sense.

2. The *speech which arises exclusively from a rational proceeding*. It is true that this is of a demonstrative character, but it cannot have a rhetorical effect because purely rational arguments do not attain to the passions, i.e., "theoretical" speech in the usual sense.

3. The *true rhetorical speech*. This springs from the *archai*, nondeducible, moving, and indicative, due to its original images. The original speech is that of the wise man, of the *sophos*, who is not only *epistetai*, but who with insight leads, guides, and attracts.

The Metaphorical Basis of Rhetoric and Philosophy

I have attempted here to demonstrate that the problem of rhetoric in every sense cannot be separated from a discussion of its relation to philosophy. One problem, however, seems yet unsolved, namely, that an essential moment of rhetorical speech is metaphor. Can we claim that the original, archaic assertions on which rational proofs depend have a metaphorical character? Can we maintain the thesis that the *archai* have any connection with images as the subject of a "transferred" meaning? Surprisingly enough, perhaps, we can speak about first principles only through metaphors; we speak of them as "premises," as "grounds," as "foundations," as "axioms." Even logical language must resort to metaphors, involving a transposition from the empirical realm of senses, in which "seeing" and the "pictorial" move to the foreground: to "clarify," to "gain insight," to "found," to "conclude," to "deduce." We also must not forget that the term "metaphor" is itself a metaphor; it is derived from the verb *metapherein* "to transfer," which originally described a concrete activity.

Some authors limit the function of the metaphor to the transposition of words, i.e., of a word from its "own" field to another. Yet this transposition cannot be effected without an immediate insight into the *similarity* which appears in different fields. Aristotle says: "A good transposition is the sight of similar things." Thus this kind of "literary" metaphor already is based on the "discovery" of a *similar nature;* its function is to make visible a "common" quality between fields. It presupposes a "vision" of something hitherto concealed; it "shows" to the reader or to the spectator a common quality which is not rationally deducible.

But we must go a step deeper than the "literary" plane. The metaphor lies at the root of our human world. Insofar as metaphor has its roots in the analogy between different things and makes this analogy immediately spring into "sight," it makes a fundamental contribution to the structure of our world. Empirical observation itself takes place through the "reduction" of sensory phenomena to types of meanings existing in the living being; and this "reduction" consists in the "transferring" of a meaning to sensory phenomena. It is only through this "transference" that phenomena can be recognized as similar or dissimilar, useful or useless, for our human realization. In order to make "sensory" observations we are forced to "reach back" for a transposition, for a metaphor. Man can manifest himself only through his own "transpositions," and this is the essence of his work in every field of human activity.

On the theoretical level, types, which are based on the analogical process (i.e., reduction of multiplicity to unity on the basis of the *"transference" of a meaning* to the multiplicity), a process which when carried out culminates in philosophical knowledge, only can be expressed metaphorically in their nature and in their function. The metaphor lies at the root of our knowledge in which rhetoric and philosophy attain their original unity. Therefore we cannot speak of rhetoric *and* philosophy, but every original philosophy is rhetoric and every true and not exterior rhetoric is philosophy.

The metaphorical, pictorial nature of every original insight links insight with *pathos,* content with the form of speech. Thus the following words regarding effective instruction acquire a topical meaning:

> But if we regard speech with a view to its aim, it serves *to express, to teach, and to move.* But it always expresses something by means *of an image,* it teaches by means *of a force of light.* Now it is true that all this only happens through an *inner image, an inner light, and an inner force that are internally* connected with the soul.
>
> (Bonaventura, *Itinerarium mentis in Deum,* 18)

This is why the Middle Ages metaphorically saw nature, the environment of man and animal, as a book, as a transposition of the absolute. Philosophy itself becomes possible only on the basis of metaphors, on the basis of the ingenuity which supplies the foundation of every rational, derivative process.

Notes

1. *An Essay Concerning Human Understanding*, 2 vols., ed. Alexander Campbell Fraser (Oxford: Clarendon Press, 1894), II, bk. 3, ch. 10, sec. 34.
2. *The Critique of Judgement: Part I, Critique of Aesthetic Judgement,* trans. James Creed Meredith (Oxford: Clarendon Press, 1952), sec. 53.

Born and educated in England, the educator and philosopher Stephen Toulmin, like Chaïm Perelman, is most interested in a logic of value judgments, a system of bringing ethics into the process of decision making. That rhetoric is epistemic (a way of knowing rather than a method for proclaiming truth) is the underlying philosophy of Toulmin's Uses of Argument *(1969), in which he develops his idea of effective argument as the process of moving from accepted* data, *through a* warrant, *to a* claim. *Other resources to his ideas are* Introduction to Reasoning *(1978) and* Human Understanding *(1972).*

The Layout of Arguments

An argument is like an organism. It has both a gross, anatomical structure and a finer, as-it-were physiological one. When set out explicitly in all its detail, it may occupy a number of printed pages or take perhaps a quarter of an hour to deliver; and within this time or space one can distinguish the main phases marking the progress of the argument from the initial statement of an unsettled problem to the final presentation of a conclusion. These main phases will each of them occupy some minutes or paragraphs, and represent the chief anatomical units of the argument—its "organs," so to speak. But within each paragraph, when one gets down to the level of individual sentences, a finer structure can be recognized, and this is the structure with which logicians have mainly concerned themselves. It is at this physiological level that the idea of logical form has been introduced, and here that the validity of our arguments has ultimately to be established or refuted.

The time has come to change the focus of our inquiry, and to concentrate on this finer level. Yet we cannot afford to forget what we have learned by our study of the grosser anatomy of arguments, for here as with organisms the detailed physiology proves most intelligible when expounded against a background of coarser anatomical distinctions. Physiological processes are interesting not least for the part they play in maintaining the functions of the major organs in which they take place; and micro-arguments (as one may christen them) need to be looked at from time to time with one eye on the macro-arguments in which they figure; since the precise manner in which we phrase them and set them out, to mention only the least important thing, may be affected by the role they have to play in the larger context.

In the inquiry which follows, we shall be studying the operation of arguments sentence by sentence, in order to see how their validity or invalidity is connected with the manner of laying them out, and what relevance this connection has to the traditional notion of "logical form." Certainly the same argument may be set out in quite a number of different forms, and some of these patterns of analysis will be more candid than others—some of them, that is, will show the validity or invalidity of an argument more clearly than others, and make more explicit the grounds it relies on and the bearing of these on the conclusion. How, then, should we lay an argument out, if we want to show the sources of its validity? And in what sense does the acceptability or unacceptability of arguments depend upon their "formal" merits and defects?

We have before us two rival models, one mathematical, the other jurisprudential. Is the logical form of a valid argument something quasi-geometrical, comparable to the shape of a triangle or the parallelism of two straight lines? Or alternatively, is it something procedural: is a formally valid argument one *in proper form,* as lawyers would say, rather than one laid out in a tidy and simple *geometrical* form? Or does the notion of logical form somehow combine both these aspects, so that to lay an argument out in proper form necessarily requires the adoption of a particular geometrical layout? If this last answer is the right one, it at once creates a further problem for us: to see how and why proper procedure demands the adoption of simple geometrical shape, and how that shape guarantees in its turn the validity of our procedures. Supposing valid arguments can be cast in a geometrically tidy form, how does this help to make them any the more cogent?

These are the problems to be studied in the present inquiry. If we can see our way to unravelling them, their solution will be of some importance—particularly for a proper understanding of logic. But to begin with we must go cautiously, and steer clear of the philosophical issues on which we shall hope later to throw some light, concentrating for the moment on questions of a most prosaic and straightforward kind. Keeping our eyes on the categories of applied logic—on the practical business of argumentation, that is, and the notions it requires us to employ—we must ask what features a logically candid layout of arguments will need to have. The establishment of conclusions raises a number of issues of different sorts, and a practical layout will make allowance for these differences: our first question is—what are these issues, and how can we do justice to them all in subjecting our arguments to rational assessment?

Two last remarks may be made by way of introduction, the first of them simply adding one more question to our agenda. Ever since Aristotle it has been customary, when analysing the micro-structure of arguments, to set them out in a very simple manner: they have been presented three propositions at a time, "minor premiss; major premiss; *so* conclusion." The question now arises, whether this standard form is sufficiently elaborate or candid. Simplicity is of course a merit, but may it not in this case have been bought too dearly? Can we properly classify all the elements in our arguments under the three headings, "major premiss," "minor premiss" and "conclusion," or are these categories misleadingly few in number? Is there even enough similarity between major and minor premisses for them usefully to be yoked together by the single name of "premiss"?

Light is thrown on these questions by the analogy with jurisprudence. This would naturally lead us to adopt a layout of greater complexity than has been customary, for the questions we are asking here are, once again, more general versions of questions already familiar in jurisprudence, and in that more specialized field a whole battery of distinctions has grown up. "What different sorts of propositions," a legal philosopher will ask, "are uttered in the course of a law-case, and in what different ways can such propositions bear on the soundness of a legal claim?" This has always been and still is a central question for the student of jurisprudence, and we soon find that the nature of a legal process can be properly understood only if we draw a large number of distinctions. Legal utterances have many distinct functions. Statements of claim, evidence of identification, testimony about events in dispute, interpretations of a statute or discussions of its validity, claims to exemption from the application of a law, pleas in extenuation, verdicts, sentences: all these different classes of proposition have their parts to play in the legal process, and the differences between them are in practice far from trifling. When we turn from the special case of the law to consider rational arguments in general, we are faced at once by the question whether these must not be analyzed in terms of an equally complex set of categories. If we are to set our arguments out with complete logical candor, and understand properly the nature of "the logical process," surely we shall need to employ a pattern of argument no less sophisticated than is required in the law.

The Pattern of an Argument: Data and Warrants

"What, then, is involved in establishing conclusions by the production of arguments?" Can we, by considering this question in a general form, build up from scratch a pattern of analysis which will do justice to all the distinctions which proper procedure forces upon us? That is the problem facing us.

Let it be supposed that we make an assertion, and commit ourselves thereby to the claim which any assertion necessarily involves. If this claim is challenged, we must be able to establish it—that is, make it good, and show that it was justifiable. How is this to be done? Unless the assertion was made quite wildly and irresponsibly, we shall normally have some facts to which we can point in its support: if the claim is challenged, it is up to us to appeal to these facts, and present them as the foundation upon which our claim is based. Of course we may not get the challenger even to agree about the correctness of these facts, and in that case we have to clear his objection out of the way by a preliminary argument: only when this prior issue or "lemma," as geometers would call it, has been dealt with, are we in a position to return to the original argument. But this complication we need only mention: supposing the lemma to have been disposed of, our question is how to set the original argument out most fully and explicitly. "Harry's hair is not black," we assert. What have we got to go on? we are asked. Our personal knowledge that it is in fact red: that is our datum, the ground which we produce as support for the original assertion. Petersen, we may say, will not be a Roman Catholic: why?: we base our claim on the knowledge that he is a Swede, which makes it very unlikely that he will be a Roman Catholic. Wilkinson, asserts the prosecutor in Court, has committed an offence against the Road Traffic Acts: in support of this claim, two policemen are prepared to testify that they timed him driving at 45 m.p.h. in a built-up area. In each case, an original assertion is supported by producing other facts bearing on it.

We already have, therefore, one distinction to start with: between the *claim* or conclusion whose merits we are seeking to establish (C) and the facts we appeal to as a foundation for the claim—what I shall refer to as our *data* (D). If our challenger's question is, "What have you got to go on?" producing the data or information on which the claim is based may serve to answer him; but this is only one of the ways in which our conclusion may be challenged. Even after we have produced our data, we may find ourselves being asked further questions of another kind. We may now be required not to add more factual information to that which we have already provided, but rather to indicate the bearing on our conclusion of the data already produced. Colloquially, the question may now be, not "What have you got to go on?" but "How do you get there?" To present a particular set of data as the basis for some specified conclusion commits us to a certain *step;* and the question is now one about the nature and justification of this step.

Supposing we encounter this fresh challenge, we must bring forward not further data, for about these the same query may immediately be raised again, but propositions of a rather different kind: rules, principles, inference-licences or what you will, instead of additional items of information. Our task is no longer to strengthen the ground on which our argument is constructed, but is rather to show that, taking these data as a starting point, the step to the original claim or conclusion is an appropriate and legitimate one. At this point, therefore, what are needed are general, hypothetical statements, which can act as bridges, and authorise the sort of step to which our particular argument commits us. These may normally be written very briefly (in the form "If D, then C"); but, for candour's sake, they can profitably be expanded, and made more explicit: "Data such as D entitle one to draw conclusions, or make claims, such as C," or alternatively "Given data D, one may take it that C."

Propositions of this kind I shall call *warrants* (W), to distinguish them from both conclusions and data. (These "warrants," it will be observed, correspond to the practical standards or canons of argument referred to in our earlier essays.) To pursue our previous examples: the knowledge that Harry's hair is red entitles us to set aside any suggestion that it is black, on account of the warrant, "If anything is red, it will not also be black." (The very triviality of this warrant is connected with the fact that we are concerned here as much with a counter-assertion as with an argument.) The fact that Petersen is a Swede is directly relevant to the question of his religious denomination for, as we should probably put it, "A Swede can be taken almost certainly not to be a Roman Catholic." (The step involved here is not trivial, so the warrant is not self-authenticating.) Likewise in the third case: our warrant will now be some such statement as that "A man who is proved to have driven at more than 30 m.p.h. in a built-up area can be found to have committed an offence against the Road Traffic Acts."

The question will at once be asked, how absolute is this distinction between data, on the one hand, and warrants, on the other. Will it always be clear whether a man who challenges an assertion is calling for the production of his adversary's data, or for the warrants authorising his steps? Can one, in other words, draw any sharp distinction between the force of the two questions, "What have you got to go on?" and "How do you get there?" By grammatical tests alone, the distinction may appear far from absolute, and the same English sentence may serve a double function: it may be uttered, that is, in one situation to convey a piece of information, in another to authorize a step in an argument, and even perhaps in some contexts to do both these things at once. (All these possibilities will be illustrated before too long.) For the moment, the important thing is not to be too cut-and-dried in our treatment of the subject, nor to commit ourselves in advance to a rigid terminology. At any rate we shall find it possible in *some* situations to distinguish clearly two different logical functions; and the nature of this distinction is hinted at if one contrasts the two sentences, "Whenever A, one *has found* that B" and "Whenever A, one *may take it* that B."

We now have the terms we need to compose the first skeleton of a pattern for analysing arguments. We may symbolise the relation between the data and the claim in support of which they are produced by an arrow, and indicate the authority for taking the step from one to the other by writing the warrant immediately below the arrow:

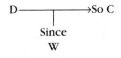

Or, to give an example:

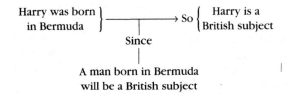

As this pattern makes clear, the explicit appeal in this argument goes directly back from the claim to the data relied on as foundation: the warrant is, in a sense, incidental and explanatory, its task being simply to register explicitly the legitimacy of the step involved and to refer it back to the larger class of steps whose legitimacy is being presupposed.

This is one of the reasons for distinguishing between data and warrants: data are appealed to explicitly, warrants implicitly. In addition, one may remark that warrants are general, certifying the soundness of *all* arguments of the appropriate type, and have accordingly to be established in quite a different way from the facts we produce as data. This distinction, between data and warrants, is similar to the distinction drawn in the law-courts between questions of fact and questions of law, and the legal distinction is indeed a special case of the more general one—we may argue, for instance, that a man whom we know to have been born in Bermuda is presumably a British subject, simply because the relevant laws give us a warrant to draw this conclusion.

One more general point in passing: unless, in any particular field of argument, we are prepared to work with warrants of *some* kind, it will become impossible in that field to subject arguments to rational assessment. The data we cite if a claim is challenged depend on the warrants we are prepared to operate with in that field, and the warrants to which we commit ourselves are implicit in the particular steps from data to claims we are prepared to take and to admit. But supposing a man rejects all warrants whatever authorising (say) steps from data about the present and past to conclusions about the future, then for him rational prediction will become impossible; and many philosophers have in fact denied the possibility of rational prediction just because they thought they could discredit equally the claims of all past-to-future warrants.

The skeleton of a pattern which we have obtained so far is only a beginning. Further questions may now arise, to which we must pay attention.

Warrants are of different kinds, and may confer different degrees of force on the conclusions they justify. Some warrants authorise us to accept a claim unequivocally, given the appropriate data—these warrants entitle us in suitable cases to qualify our conclusion with the adverb "necessarily"; others authorise us to make the step from data to conclusion either tentatively, or else subject to conditions, exceptions, or qualifications—in these cases other modal qualifiers, such as "probably" and "presumably," are in place. It may not be sufficient, therefore, simply to specify our data, warrant and claim: we may need to add some explicit reference to the degree of force which our data confer on our claim in virtue of our warrant. In a word, we may have to put in a *qualifier.* Again, it is often necessary in the law-courts, not just to appeal to a given statute or common-law doctrine, but to discuss explicitly the extent to which this particular law fits the case under consideration, whether it must inevitably be applied in this particular case, or whether special facts may make the case an exception to the rule or one in which the law can be applied only subject to certain qualifications.

If we are to take account of these features of our argument also, our pattern will become more complex. Modal qualifiers (Q) and conditions of exception or rebuttal (R) are distinct both from data and from warrants, and need to be given separate places in our layout. Just as a warrant (W) is itself neither a datum (D) nor a claim (C), since it implies in itself something about both D and C—namely, that the step from the one to the other is legitimate; so, in turn, Q and R are themselves distinct from W, since they comment implicitly on the bearing of W on this step—qualifiers (Q) indicating the strength conferred by the warrant on this step, conditions of rebuttal (R) indicating circumstances in which the general authority of the warrant would have to be set aside. To mark these further distinctions, we may write the qualifier (Q) immediately beside the conclusion which it qualifies (C), and the exceptional conditions which might be capable of defeating or rebutting the warranted conclusion (R) immediately below the qualifier.

To illustrate: our claim that Harry is a British subject may normally be defended by appeal to the information that he was born in Bermuda, for this datum lends support to our conclusion on account of the warrants implicit in the British Nationality Acts; but the argument is not by itself conclusive in the absence of assurances about his parentage and about his not having changed his nationality since birth. What our information does do is to establish that the conclusion holds good "presumably," and subject to the appropriate provisos. The argument now assumes the form:

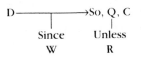

i.e.,

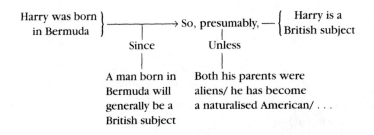

We must remark, in addition, on two further distinctions. The first is that between a statement of a warrant, and statements about its applicability— between "A man born in Bermuda will be British," and "This presumption holds good provided his parents were not both aliens, etc." The distinction is relevant not only to the law of the land, but also for an understanding of scientific laws or "laws of nature": it is important, indeed, in all cases where the application of a law may be subject to exceptions, or where a warrant can be supported by pointing to a general correlation only, and not to an absolutely invariable one. We can distinguish also two purposes which may be served by the production of additional facts: these can serve as further data, or they can be cited to confirm or rebut the applicability of a warrant. Thus, the fact that Harry was born in Bermuda and the fact that his parents were not aliens are both of them directly relevant to the question of his present nationality; but they are relevant in different ways. The one fact is a datum, which by itself establishes a presumption of British nationality; the other fact, by setting aside one possible rebuttal, tends to confirm the presumption thereby created.

One particular problem about applicability we shall have to discuss more fully later: when we set out a piece of applied mathematics, in which some system of mathematical relations is used to throw light on a question of (say) physics, the correctness of the calculations will be one thing, their appropriateness to the problem in hand may be quite another. So the question "Is this calculation mathematically impeccable?" may be a very different one from the question "Is this the relevant calculation?" Here too, the applicability of a particular warrant is one question: the result we shall get from applying the warrant is another matter, and in asking about the *correctness* of the result we may have to inquire into both these things independently.

The Pattern of an Argument: Backing Our Warrants

One last distinction, which we have already touched on in passing, must be discussed at some length. In addition to the question whether or on what conditions a warrant is applicable in a *particular* case, we may be asked why *in general* this warrant should be accepted as having authority. In defending a claim, that is, we may produce our data, our warrant, and the relevant qualifications and conditions, and yet find that we have still not satisfied our challenger; for he may be dubious not only about this particular argument but about the more general question whether the warrant (W) is acceptable at all. Presuming the general acceptability of this warrant (he may allow) our argument would no doubt be impeccable—if D-ish facts really do suffice as backing for C-ish claims, all well and good. But does not that warrant in its turn rest on something else? Challenging a particular claim may in this way lead on to challenging, more generally, the legitimacy of a whole range of arguments. "You presume that a man born in Bermuda can be taken to be a British subject," he may say, "but why do you think that?" Standing behind our warrants, as this example reminds us, there will normally be other assurances, without which the warrants themselves would possess neither authority nor currency—these other things we may refer to as the *backing* (B) of the warrants. This "backing" of our warrants is something which we shall have to scrutinise very carefully: its precise relations to our data, claims, warrants and conditions of rebuttal deserve some clarification, for confusion at this point can lead to trouble later.

We shall have to notice particularly how the sort of backing called for by our warrants varies from one field of argument to another. The *form* of argument we employ in different fields

need not vary very much as between fields. "A whale will be a mammal," "A Bermudan will be a Briton," "A Saudi Arabian will be a Muslim": here are three different warrants to which we might appeal in the course of a practical argument, each of which can justify the same sort of straightforward step from a datum to a conclusion. We might add for variety examples of even more diverse sorts, taken from moral, mathematical or psychological fields. But the moment we start asking about the *backing* which a warrant relies on in each field, great differences begin to appear: the kind of backing we must point to if we are to establish its authority will change greatly as we move from one field of argument to another. "A whale will be (i.e., *is classifiable as*) a mammal," "A Bermudan will be (*in the eyes of the law*) a Briton," "A Saudi Arabian will be (*found to be*) a Muslim"—the words in parentheses indicate what these differences are. One warrant is defended by relating it to a system of taxonomical classification, another by appealing to the statutes governing the nationality of people born in the British colonies, the third by referring to the statistics which record how religious beliefs are distributed among people of different nationalities. We can for the moment leave open the more contentious question, how we establish our warrants in the fields of morals, mathematics and psychology: for the moment all we are trying to show is the *variability* or *field-dependence* of the backing needed to establish our warrants.

We can make room for this additional element in our argument-pattern by writing it below the bare statement of the warrant for which it serves as backing (B):

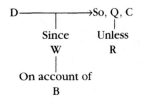

This form may not be final, but it will be complex enough for the purpose of our present discussions. To take a particular example: in support of the claim (C) that Harry is a British subject, we appeal to the datum (D) that he was born in Bermuda, and the warrant can then be stated in the form, "A man born in Bermuda may be taken to be a British subject": since, however, questions of nationality are always subject to qualifications and conditions, we shall have to insert a qualifying "presumably" (Q) in front of the conclusion, and note the possibility that our conclusion may be rebutted in case (R) it turns out that both his parents were aliens or he has since become a naturalised American. Finally, in case the warrant itself is challenged, its backing can be put in: this will record the terms and the dates of enactment of the Acts of Parliament and other legal provisions governing the nationality of persons born in the British colonies. The result will be an argument set out as follows:

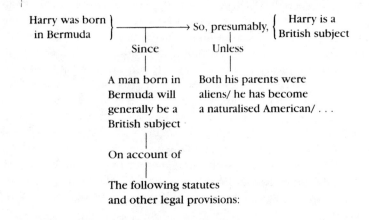

In what ways does the backing of warrants differ from the other elements in our arguments? To begin with the differences between B and W: statements of warrants, we saw, are hypothetical, bridge-like statements, but the backing for warrants can be expressed in the form of categorical statements of fact quite as well as can the data appealed to in direct support of our conclusions. So long as our statements reflect these functional differences explicitly, there is no danger of confusing the backing (B) for a warrant with the warrant itself (W): such confusions arise only when these differences are disguised by our forms of expression. In our present example, at any rate, there need be no difficulty. The fact that the relevant statutes have been validly passed into law, and contain the provisions they do, can be ascertained simply by going to the records of the parliamentary proceedings concerned and to the relevant volumes in the books of statute law: the resulting discovery, that such-and-such a statute enacted on such-and-such a date contains a provision specifying that people born in the British colonies of suitable parentage shall be entitled to British citizenship, is a straightforward statement of fact. On the other hand, the warrant which we apply *in virtue of* the statute containing this provision is logically of a very different character—"*If* a man was born in a British colony, he *may be presumed to be* British*."* Though the facts about the statute may provide all the backing required by this warrant, the explicit statement of the warrant itself is more than a repetition of these facts: it is a general *moral* of a practical character, about the ways in which we can safely argue in view of these facts.

We can also distinguish backing (B) from data (D). Though the data we appeal to in an argument and the backing lending authority to our warrants may alike be stated as straightforward matters-of-fact, the roles which these statements play in our argument are decidedly different. Data of some kind must be produced, if there is to be an argument there at all: a bare conclusion, without any data produced in its support, is no argument. But the backing of the warrants we invoke need not be made explicit—at any rate to begin with: the warrants may be conceded without challenge, and their backing left understood. Indeed, if we demanded the credentials of all warrants at sight and never let one pass unchallenged, argument could scarcely begin. Jones puts forward an argument invoking warrant W_1, and Smith challenges that warrant; Jones is obliged, as a lemma, to produce another argument in the hope of establishing the acceptability of the first warrant, but in the course of this lemma employs a second warrant W_2; Smith challenges the credentials of this second warrant in turn; and so the game goes on. Some warrants must be accepted provisionally without further challenge, if argument is to be open to us in the field in question: we should not even know what sort of data were of the slightest relevance to a conclusion, if we had not at least a provisional idea of the warrants acceptable in the situation confronting us. The existence of considerations such as would establish the acceptability of the most reliable warrants is something we are entitled to take for granted.

Finally, a word about the ways in which B differs from Q and R: these are too obvious to need expanding upon, since the grounds for regarding a warrant as generally acceptable are clearly one thing, the force which the warrant lends to a conclusion another, and the sorts of exceptional circumstance which may in particular cases rebut the presumptions the warrant creates a third. They correspond, in our example, to the three statements, (i) that the statutes about British nationality *have in fact* been validly passed into law, and say this: . . . , (ii) that Harry *may be presumed* to be a British subject, and (iii) that Harry, having recently become a naturalised American, *is no longer covered* by these statutes.

One incidental point should be made, about the interpretation to be put upon the symbols in our pattern of argument: this may throw light on a slightly puzzling example which we came across when discussing Kneale's views on probability. Consider the arrow joining D and C. It may seem natural to suggest at first that this arrow should be read as "so" in one direction and as "because" in the other. Other interpretations are however possible. As we saw earlier, the step from the information that Jones has Bright's Disease to the conclusion that he cannot be expected to live to eighty does not reverse perfectly: we find it natural enough to say, "Jones cannot be expected to live to eighty, *because* he has Bright's Disease," but the fuller statement, "Jones cannot be expected to live to eighty, *because* the probability of his living that long is low, *because* he has Bright's Disease," strikes us as cumbrous and artificial, for it puts in an extra step which is trivial and unnecessary. On the other hand, we do not mind saying, "Jones has Bright's Disease, *so* the chances of his living to eighty are slight, *so* he cannot be expected to live that long," for the last clause is (so to speak) an *inter alia* clause—it states one of the many particular morals one can draw from the middle clause, which tells us his general expectation of life.

So also in our present case: reading along the arrow from right to left or from left to right we can normally say both "C, because D" and "D, so C." But it may sometimes happen that some more general conclusion than C may be warranted, given D: where this is so, we shall often find it natural to write, not only "D, so C," but also "D, so C', so C," C' being the more general conclusion warranted in view of data D, from which in turn we infer *inter alia* that C. Where this is the case, our "so" and "because" are no longer reversible: if we now read the argument backwards the statement we get— "C, because C', because D"—is again more cumbrous than the situation really requires.

Ambiguities in the Syllogism

The time has come to compare the distinctions we have found of practical importance in the layout and criticism of arguments with those which have traditionally been made in books on the theory of logic: let us start by seeing how our present distinctions apply to the syllogism or syllogistic argument. For the purposes of our present argument we can confine our attention to one of the many forms of syllogism—that represented by the time-honoured example:

Socrates is a man;
All men are mortal;
So Socrates is mortal.

This type of syllogism has certain special features. The first premiss is "singular" and refers to a particular individual, while the second premiss alone is "universal." Aristotle himself was, of course, much concerned with syllogisms in which both the premisses were universal, since to his mind many of the arguments within scientific theory must be expected to be of this sort. But we are interested primarily in arguments by which general propositions are applied to justify particular conclusions about individuals; so this initial limitation will be convenient. Many of the conclusions we reach will, in any case, have an obvious application—*mutatis mutandis*—to syllogisms of other types. We can begin by asking the question "What corresponds in the syllogism to our distinction between data, warrant, and backing?" If we press this question, we shall find that the apparently innocent forms used in syllogistic arguments turn out to have a hidden complexity. This internal complexity is comparable with that we observed in the case of modally-qualified conclusions: here, as before, we shall be obliged to disentangle two distinct things—the force of universal premisses, when regarded as warrants, and the backing on which they depend for their authority.

In order to bring these points clearly to light, let us keep in view not only the two universal premisses on which logicians normally concentrate —"All A's are B's" and "No A's are B's"—but also two other forms of statement which we probably have just as much occasion to use in practice— "Almost all A's are B's" and "Scarcely any A's are B's." The internal complexity of such statements can be illustrated first, and most clearly, in the latter cases.

Consider, for instance, the statement, "Scarcely any Swedes are Roman Catholics." This statement can have two distinct aspects: both of them are liable to be operative at once when the statement figures in an argument, but they can nevertheless be distinguished. To begin with, it may serve as a simple statistical report: in that case, it can equally well be written in the fuller form, "The proportion of Swedes who are Roman Catholics is less than (say) 2%"—to which we may add a parenthetical reference to the source of our information, "(According to the tables in *Whittaker's Almanac*)." Alternatively, the same statement may serve as a genuine inference-warrant: in that case, it will be natural to expand it rather differently, so as to obtain the more candid statement, "A Swede can be taken almost certainly not to be a Roman Catholic."

So long as we look at the single sentence "Scarcely any Swedes are Roman Catholics" by itself, this distinction may appear trifling enough: but if we apply it to the analysis of an argument in which this appears as one premiss, we obtain results of some significance. So let us construct an argument of quasi-syllogistic form, in which this statement figures in the position of a "major premiss." This argument could be, for instance, the following:

> Petersen is a Swede;
> Scarcely any Swedes are Roman Catholics;
> So, almost certainly, Petersen is not a Roman Catholic.

The conclusion of this argument is only tentative, but in other respects the argument is exactly like a syllogism.

As we have seen, the second of these statements can be expanded in each of two ways, so that it becomes either, "The proportion of Swedes who are Roman Catholics is less than 2%," or else, "A Swede can be taken almost certainly not to be a Roman Catholic." Let us now see what happens if we substitute each of these two expanded versions in turn for the second of our three original statements. In one case we obtain the argument:

> Petersen is a Swede;
> A Swede can be taken almost certainly not to be a Roman Catholic;
> So, almost certainly, Petersen is not a Roman Catholic.

Here the successive lines correspond in our terminology to the statement of a datum (D), a warrant (W), and a conclusion (C). On the other hand, if we make the alternative substitution, we obtain:

> Petersen is a Swede;
> The proportion of Roman Catholic Swedes is less than 2%;
> So, almost certainly, Petersen is not a Roman Catholic.

In this case we again have the same datum and conclusion, but the second line now states the backing (B) for the warrant (W), which is itself left unstated.

For tidiness' sake, we may now be tempted to abbreviate these two expanded versions. If we do so, we can obtain respectively the two arguments:

> (D) Petersen is a Swede;
> (W) A Swede is almost certainly not a Roman Catholic;
> So, (C) Petersen is almost certainly not a Roman Catholic;

and,

> (D) Petersen is a Swede;
> (B) The proportion of Roman Catholic Swedes is minute;
> So, (C) Petersen is almost certainly not a Roman Catholic.

The relevance of our distinction to the traditional conception of "formal validity" should already be becoming apparent, and we shall return to the subject shortly.

Turning to the form "No A's are B's" (e.g., "No Swedes are Roman Catholics"), we can make a similar distinction. This form of statement also can be employed in two alternative ways, either as a statistical report, or as an inference-warrant. It can serve simply to report a statistician's discovery—say, that the proportion of Roman Catholic Swedes is in fact zero; or alternatively it can serve to justify the drawing of conclusions in argument, becoming equivalent to the explicit statement, "A Swede can be taken certainly not to be a Roman Catholic." Corresponding interpretations are again open to us if we look at an argument which includes our sample statement as the universal premise. Consider the argument:

> Petersen is a Swede;
> No Swedes are Roman Catholics;
> So, certainly, Petersen is not a Roman Catholic.

This can be understood in two ways: we may write it in the form:

> Petersen is a Swede;
> The proportion of Roman Catholic Swedes is zero;
> So, certainly, Petersen is not a Roman Catholic,

or alternatively in the form:

> Petersen is a Swede;
> A Swede is certainly not a Roman Catholic;
> So, certainly, Petersen is not a Roman Catholic.

Here again the first formulation amounts, in our terminology, to putting the argument in the form "D, B, so C"; while the second formulation is equivalent to putting it in the form "D, W, so C." So, whether we are concerned with a "scarcely any . . ." argument or a "no . . ." argument, the customary form of expression will tend in either case to conceal from us the distinction between an inference-warrant and its backing. The same will be true in the case of "all" and "nearly all": there, too, the distinction between saying "Every, or nearly every single A *has been found* to be a B" and saying "An A *can be taken*, certainly or almost certainly, to be a B" is concealed by the over-simple form of words "All A's are B's." A crucial difference in practical function can in this way pass unmarked and unnoticed.

Our own more complex pattern of analysis, by contrast, avoids this defect. It leaves no room for ambiguity: entirely separate places are left in the pattern for a warrant and for the backing upon which its authority depends. For instance, our "scarcely any . . ." argument will have to be set out in the following way:

D (Petersen is ⟶⟶⟶⟶⟶ So, Q (almost   C (Petersen is not a
a Swede)   certainly)   Roman Catholic)

Since
W
(A Swede can be taken to be
almost certainly not a
Roman Catholic)

Because
B
(The proportion of Roman
Catholic Swedes is less
than 2%)

Corresponding transcriptions will be needed for arguments of the other three types.

When we are theorising about the syllogism, in which a central part is played by propositions of the forms "All A's are B's" and "No A's are B's," it will accordingly be as well to bear this distinction in mind. The form of statement "All A's are B's" is as it stands deceptively simple: it may have in use both the force of a warrant and the factual content of its backing, two aspects which we can bring out by expanding it in different ways. Sometimes it may be used, standing alone, in only one of these two ways at once; but often enough, especially in arguments, we make the single statement do both jobs at once and gloss over, for brevity's sake, the transition from backing to warrant—from the factual information we are presupposing to the inference-licence which that information justifies us in employing. The practical economy of this habit may be obvious; but for philosophical purposes it leaves the effective structure of our arguments insufficiently candid.

There is a clear parallel between the complexity of "all . . ." statements and that of modal statements. As before, the *force* of the statements is invariant for all fields of argument. When we consider this aspect of the statements, the form "All A's are B's" may always be replaced by the form "An A can certainly be taken to be a B": this will be true regardless of the field, holding good equally of "All Swedes are Roman Catholics," "All those born in British colonies are entitled to British citizenship," "All whales are mammals," and "All lying is reprehensible"—in each case, the general statement will serve as a warrant authorising an argument of precisely the same form, D→C, whether the step goes from "Harry was born in Bermuda" to "Harry is a British citizen" or from "Wilkinson told a lie" to "Wilkinson acted reprehensibly." Nor should there be any mystery about the nature of the step from D to C, since the whole *force* of the general statement "All A's are B's," as so understood, is to authorise just this sort of step.

By contrast, the kind of *grounds* or *backing* supporting a warrant of this form will depend on the field of argument: here the parallel with modal statements is maintained. From this point of view, the important thing is the factual content, not the force of "all . . ." statements. Though a warrant of the form "An A can certainly be taken to be a B" must hold good in any field in virtue of *some* facts, the actual sort of facts in virtue of which any warrant will have currency and authority will vary according to the field of argument within which that warrant operates; so, when we expand the simple form "All A's are B's" in order to make explicit the nature of the backing it is used to express, the expansion we must make will also depend upon the field with which we are concerned. In one case, the statement will become "The proportion of A's found to be B's is 100%," in another, "A's are ruled by statute to count unconditionally as B's," in a third, "The class of B's includes taxonomically the entire class of A's," and in a fourth, "The practice of doing A leads to the following intolerable consequences, etc." Yet, despite the striking differences between them, all these elaborate propositions are expressed on occasion in the compact and simple form "All A's are B's."

Similar distinctions can be made in the case of the forms, "Nearly all A's are B's," "Scarcely any A's are B's," and "No A's are B's." Used to express warrants, these differ from "All A's are B's" in only one respect, that where before we wrote "certainly" we must now write "almost certainly," "almost certainly not" or "certainly not." Likewise, when we are using them to state not warrants but backing: in a statistical case we shall simply have to replace "100%" by (say) "at least 95%," "less than 5%" or "zero"; in the case of a statute replace "unconditionally" by "unless exceptional conditions hold," "only in exceptional circumstances" or "in no circumstances whatever"; and in a taxonomical case replace "the entirety of the class of A's" by "all but a small sub-class . . . ," "only a small sub-class . . ." or "no part of. . . ." Once we have filled out the skeletal forms "all . . ." and "no . . ." in this way, the field-dependence of the backing for our warrants is as clear as it could be.

The Notion of "Universal Premisses"

The full implications of the distinction between force and backing, as applied to propositions of the form "All A's are B's," will become clear only after one further distinction has been introduced—that between "analytic" and "substantial" arguments. This cannot be done immediately, so for the moment all we can do is to hint at ways in which the traditional way of setting out arguments—in the form of two premises followed by a conclusion—may be misleading.

Most obviously, this pattern of analysis is liable to create an exaggerated appearance of uniformity as between arguments in different fields, but what is probably as important is its power of disguising also the great differences between the things traditionally classed together as "premisses." Consider again examples of our standard type, in which a particular conclusion is justified by appeal to a particular datum about an individual—the singular, minor premiss—taken together with a general piece of information serving as warrant and/or backing—the universal, major premiss. So long as we interpret universal premisses as expressing not warrants but their backing, both major and minor premisses are at any rate categorical and factual: in this respect, the information that not a single Swede is recorded as being a Roman Catholic is on a par with the information that Karl Henrik Petersen is a Swede. Even so, the different roles played in practical argument by one's data and by the backing for one's warrants make it rather unfortunate to label them alike "premisses." But supposing we adopt the alternative interpretation of our major premisses, treating them instead as warrants, the differences between major and minor premisses are even more striking. A "singular premiss" expresses a piece of information *from* which we are drawing a conclusion, a "universal premiss" now expresses, not a piece of information at all, but a guarantee *in accordance with* which we can safely take the step from our datum to our conclusion. Such a guarantee, for all its backing, will be neither factual nor categorical but rather hypothetical and permissive. Once again, the two-fold distinction between "premisses" and "conclusion" appears insufficiently complex and, to do justice to the situation, one needs to adopt in its place at least the four-fold distinction between "datum," "conclusion," "warrant" and "backing."

One way in which the distinction between the various possible interpretations of the "universal premiss" may prove important to logicians can be illustrated by referring to an old logical puzzle. The question has often been debated, whether the form of statement "All A's are B's" has or has not any existential implications: whether, that is, its use commits one to the belief that some A's do exist. Statements of the form "Some A's are B's" have given rise to no such difficulty, for the use of this latter form always implies the existence of some A's, but the form "All A's are B's" seems to be more ambiguous. It has been argued, for instance, that such a statement as "All club-footed men have difficulty in walking" need not be taken as implying the existence of any club-footed men: this is a general truth, it is said, which would remain equally true even though, for once in a while, there were no living men having club feet, and it would not suddenly cease to be true that club-footedness made walking difficult just because the last club-footed man had been freed of his deformity by a skilful surgeon. Yet this leaves us uncomfortable: has our assertion then no existential force? Surely, we feel, club-footed men must at any rate *have* existed if we are to be able to make this assertion at all?

This conundrum illustrates very well the weaknesses of the term "universal premiss." Suppose that we rely on the traditional mode of analysis of arguments:

Jack is club-footed;
All club-footed men have difficulty in walking;
So, Jack has difficulty in walking.

For so long as we do, the present difficulty will be liable to recur, since this pattern of analysis leaves it unclear whether the general statement "All . . ." is to be construed as a permissive inference-warrant or as a factual report of our observations. Is it to be construed as meaning "A club-footed man will (i.e., may be expected to) have difficulty in walking," or as meaning "Every club-footed man of whom we have records had (i.e., was found to have) difficulty in walking"? We are not bound, except by long habit, to employ the form "All A's are B's," with all the ambiguities it involves. We are at liberty to scrap it in favour of forms of expression which are more explicit, even if more cumbersome; and if we make this change, the problem about existential implications will simply no longer trouble us. The statement "Every club-footed man of whom we have records . . ." implies, of course, that there have been at any rate *some* club-footed men, since otherwise we should have no records to refer to; while the warrant "A club-footed man will have difficulty in walking," equally of course, leaves the existential question open. We can truthfully say that club-footedness would be a handicap to any pedestrian, even if we knew that at this moment everyone was lying on his back and nobody was so deformed. We are therefore not compelled to answer as it stands the question whether "All A's are B's" has existential implications: certainly we can refuse a clear Yes or No. Some of the statements which logicians represent in this rather crude form do have such implications; others do not. No entirely general answer can be given to the question, for what determines whether there are or are not existential implications in any particular case is not the form of statement itself, but rather the practical use to which this form is put on that occasion.

Can we say then that the form "All A's are B's" has existential implications when used to express the backing of a warrant, but not when used to express the warrant itself? Even this way of putting the point turns out to be too neat. For the other thing which excessive reliance on the form "All A's are B's" tends to conceal from us is the different sorts of backing which our general beliefs may require, and these differences are relevant here. No doubt the statement that every club-footed man of whom we have any record found his deformity a handicap in walking, which we have here cited as backing, implies that there have been some such people; but we can back the same warrant by appeal to considerations of other kinds as well, e.g., by arguments explaining from anatomical principles in what way club-footedness may be expected to lead to disability—just how this shape of foot will prove a handicap. In these theoretical terms we could discuss the disabilities which would result from any kind of deformity we cared to imagine, including ones which nobody is known ever to have had: this sort of backing accordingly leaves the existential question open.

Again, if we consider warrants of other types, we find plenty of cases in which the backing for a warrant has, as it stands, no existential implication. This may be true, for instance, in the case of warrants backed by statutory provisions: legislation may refer to persons or situations which have yet to be—for instance, to all married women who will reach the age of 70 after 1 January 1984—or alternatively to classes of persons none of whom may ever exist, such as men found guilty on separate occasions of ten different murders. Statutes referring to people of these types can provide backing for inference-warrants entitling us to take all kinds of steps in argument, without either the warrants or their backing implying anything about the existence of such people at all. To sum up: if we pay closer attention to the differences between warrants and backing, and between different sorts of backing for one and the same warrant, and between the backing for warrants of different sorts, and if we refuse to focus our attention hypnotically on the traditional form "All A's are B's," we can not only come to see *that* sometimes "All A's are B's" does have existential implications and sometimes not, but furthermore begin to understand *why* this should be so.

Once one has become accustomed to expanding statements of the form "All A's are B's," and replacing them, as occasion requires, by explicit warrants or explicit statements of backing, one will find it a puzzle that logicians have been wedded to this form of statement for so long. The reasons for this will concern us in a later essay: for the moment, we may remark that they have done so only at the expense of impoverishing our language and disregarding a large number of clues to the proper solutions of their conundrums. For the form "All A's are B's" occurs in practical argument much less than one would suppose from logic text-books: indeed, a great deal of effort has to be expended in order to train students in ways of rephrasing in this special form the idiomatic statements to which they are already accustomed, thereby making these idiomatic utterances apparently amenable to traditional syllogistic analysis. There is no need, in complaining of this, to argue that idiom is sacrosanct, or provides by itself understanding of a kind we could not have had before. Nevertheless, in our normal ways of expressing ourselves, one will find many points of idiom which can serve as very definite clues, and are capable in this case of leading us in the right direction.

Where the logician has in the past cramped all general statements into his predetermined form, practical speech has habitually employed a dozen different forms—"Every single A is a B," "Each A is a B," "An A will be a B,"

"A's are generally B's" and "The A is a B" being only a selection. By contrasting these idioms, instead of ignoring them or insisting that they all fall into line, logicians would long ago have been led on to the distinctions we have found crucial. The contrast between "Every A" and "Not a single A," on the one hand, and "Any A" or "An A," on the other, points one immediately towards the distinction between statistical reports and the warrants for which they can be the backing. The differences between warrants in different fields are also reflected in idiom. A biologist would hardly ever utter the words "All whales are mammals"; though sentences such as "Whales are mammals" or "The whale is a mammal" might quite naturally come from his lips or his pen. Warrants are one thing, backing another; backing by enumerative observation is one thing, backing by taxonomic classification another; and our choices of idiom, though perhaps subtle, reflect these differences fairly exactly.

Even in so remote a field as philosophical ethics, some hoary problems have been generated in just this way. Practice forces us to recognize that general ethical truths can aspire at best to hold good in the absence of effective counter-claims: conflicts of duty are an inescapable feature of the moral life. Where logic demands the form "*All* lying is reprehensible" or "*All* promise-keeping is right," idiom therefore replies "Lying is reprehensible" and "promise-keeping is right." The logician's "all" imports unfortunate expectations, which in practice are bound on occasion to be disappointed. Even the most general warrants in ethical arguments are yet liable in unusual situations to suffer exceptions, and so at strongest can authorise only presumptive conclusions. If we insist on the "all," conflicts of duties land us in paradox, and much of moral theory is concerned with getting us out of this morass. Few people insist on trying to put into practice the consequences of insisting on the extra "all," for to do so one must resort to desperate measures: it can be done only by adopting an eccentric moral position, such as absolute pacifism, in which one principle and one alone is admitted to be genuinely universal, and this principle is defended through thick and thin, in the face of all the conflicts and counter-claims which would normally qualify its application. The road from nice points about logic and idiom to the most difficult problems of conduct is not, after all, such a long one.

RICHARD MCKEON
1900–1985

Practical philosopher and historian of rhetoric, Richard McKeon most often is classified as a neo-Aristotelian of the "Chicago School." During his long career at the University of Chicago, he remained interested in rhetoric's fundamental qualities and its relationship to the arts and sciences. His continuing argument was that we should not study rhetoric as unaltered forms from the past, but seek to understand rhetoric's history of transforming itself to become a philosophy of communication that reflects a culture. For rhetoric, to McKeon, goes beyond being a verbal art; it is the organizational principle by which we can create, systematize, and analyze any discipline. Thus our rhetoric is an art of discovery. McKeon calls this new rhetoric an "architectonic productive art." His essays have been published in Rhetoric: Essays in Invention and Discovery *(1987). For a personal perspective, see* Richard McKeon: A Study *by George Kimball Plochmann (U of Chicago P, 1990).*

The Uses of Rhetoric in a Technological Age: Architectonic Productive Arts

I. CONTINUITIES AND REVOLUTIONS IN THE DEVELOPMENT OF RHETORIC

Rhetoric has had a long and variegated history. It has been influential in the development of theory, practice, and art, and methods to produce and use the products of knowledge, action, and production. It has been influenced by truths of sciences, circumstances of times and communities, and analogies of arts; and it has been expounded in propositions of theory, in rules of practice, and in maxims of art. Its history has been a continuous one, because basic terms, distinctions, and schemata reappear and are put to new uses. It has been an ambiguous history, because continuing terms assume new meanings in their new applications, and the innovations are seldom guided by knowledge of how renewed terms were used in earlier traditions. Histories of rhetoric, which throw little light on the principles or purposes by which present methods and uses of rhetoric might be evaluated or changed, tend to be pedantic explorations of traditions of rhetoric as an art of persuasion and belief, of deception and proof, of image-making and communication, which follow through the consequences of pejorative or positive judgments posited as premises. Discussions of rhetoric in the past and in the present and projections of rhetoric in the future reflect estimations of its nature and operation. Apparently it has been practiced widely as an art of deception, public relations, alienation, and self-interest, and it has been one of the factors contributing to the degradation of knowledge, morality, and culture. Apparently it has also been practiced as an art of revolution and renaissance, and it has been one of the factors contributing to innovation and growth in theory, practice, and production.

Rhetoric is an instrument of continuity and of change, of tradition and of revolution. The history of rhetoric is the history of a continuing art undergoing revolutionary changes. It has played an important part at some points in the formation of culture in the West, notably during the Roman Republic and the Renaissance. In both periods it was enlarged in its operation, using an extended form of the rhetorical device of "amplification," to become a productive or poetic art, an art of making in all phases of human activity. It was systematized in its organization, using a comprehensive form of the rhetorical device of "schematization," to become an architectonic art, an art of structuring all principles and products of knowing, doing, and making. If rhetoric is to be used to contribute to the formation of the culture of the modern world, it should function productively in the resolution of new problems and architectonically in the formation of new inclusive communities. Rhetoric can be used to produce a new rhetoric constructed as a productive art and schematized as an architectonic art. At a second stage the new rhetoric can be used to reorganize the subject-matter and arts of education and life. What rhetoric should be and to what conditions it is adapted are not separate theoretic questions but the single practical question of producing schemata to guide the use of the productive arts in transforming circumstances.

The nature and methods of an architectonic productive art and the technical languages in which arts and sciences are classified, like many of the processes of inquiry and analysis and much of the technical language of distinction and systematization in the West, can be clarified by going back to beginnings made in the distinctions and analyses of Aristotle. He gave a technical meaning to the ordinary Greek expression *architecton*—"architectonic artist" or "master craftsman"—and used it in his schema of the organization of the sciences. In that organization he gave a technical meaning to the Greek expression *poiesis*—"production" or "poetry" or "making"—and used it to name one of his three sciences "poetic science" or "productive science." Later thinkers, doers, and makers have revolted against Aristotle's metaphysics and poetics more frequently than they have used them. Nevertheless they have constructed like devices for making principles and relations, and the ambiguous history of architectonic productive arts affords some guidance in understanding and changing the uses of the productive arts in an age of technology.

Aristotle distinguished between the art of the user, who knows the form, and that of the master-craftsman, who knows the matter and makes the product, although the art of a user, such as a helmsman, has architectonic functions in determining the form in which the product, the helm, is to be made. In the transition from things better known to us by sensation to things better known in nature by science the sequence runs from sensation to experience, to art, to architectonic art, to productive sciences, to theoretic sciences. The architectonic arts are themselves principles, and wisdom (or as it was later to be called, metaphysics) is the science of first causes or principles. Metaphysics functions as an authoritative or architectonic art by organizing the sciences according to principles, subject-matters, and methods into the theoretic, practical, and productive sciences—the sciences of knowing, doing, and making.

An architectonic art is an art of doing. Architectonic arts treat ends which order the ends of subordinate arts. The architectonic art is the most authoritative art. The practical science, politics, which has as its end action, not knowledge, is such an art, "for it ordains which of the sciences are to be pursued in a state, and what branches of knowledge each of the classes of citizens is to learn, and up to what point, and even the most esteemed capacities fall under it, such as strategy, domestic economy, and oratory." The moral virtues are the sources of actions in accordance with the rule of right reason. The rule of right reason is put into effect by prudence, which is a calculative intellectual virtue, engaged in ordering and interpreting the variables of action, and it is in turn under the guidance of wisdom. Prudence and wisdom make use of architectonic arts to guide subordinate arts of doing.

The second calculative intellectual virtue, art, likewise makes use of an architectonic art. Prudence is architectonic with respect to doing (and its sphere of doing includes sciences, actions, institutions, and arts). Art is architectonic with respect to making, and the architectonic art of making is rhetoric, in so far as rhetoric is an art of thought. Diction and thought are two of the six parts of tragedy which Aristotle distinguishes in the *Poetics*. Poetic diction is treated in the *Poetics*, and it is distinguished from elocution or the architectonic art of speech, which includes not only propositions, which are treated in logic, but statements in general, in aspects which do not bear directly on their truth or falsity—commands, prayers, threats, questions, answers, and other modes of simple and connected discourse. Thought is not treated in the *Poetics;* in the *Rhetoric* to which Aristotle refers in the *Poetics* for the treatment of thought, account is taken not only of cognitive processes of proof and disproof, but also of noncognitive devices of amplifying and restricting, that is, enlarging and diminishing, maximizing and minimizing.

Later ages continued to use the vocabulary of these distinctions; and the overall characteristics and problems of ages may be stated by determining the architectonic productive arts by which theoretic, practical, and productive arts are organized and related to each other in production, and by which products of the arts and sciences are set up and justified in experience. Aristotle formulated rhetoric as a "universal art," limited to no one subject-matter but applicable to all. For Aristotle rhetoric is not a "science," because each science has a particular "method" suited to its particular subject-matter and operative according to its proper principles. One of the sciences, politics, is an architectonic art, for it is a science of doing, and it is architectonic of actions, individual and communal, including actions which bear on the cultivation of sciences and arts. But the architectonic art of politics is to be distinguished from rhetoric. The vocabulary of the distinctions between architectonic and subordinate arts, and between practical and theoretical arts and sciences, continues to be used, but the distinctions are shuffled and the meanings and applications of the terms are altered: all the basic terms and relations undergo this transformation and transportation—art and method; theoretic, practical, and productive; being, thought, action, and statement.

Cicero enlarged rhetoric into a universal productive art, an *ars disserendi,* and applied it to resolve what he conceived to be the basic problem of Roman culture, the separation of wisdom and eloquence, of philosophy and rhetoric. The diremption between wisdom and eloquence had been a consequence of Socrates' great achievements in philosophy: earlier Greek philosophers and statesmen had practiced both arts, but after the development of the philosophical arts by Socrates, those who learned to analyze problems were unlearned in the arts of speech, while those who acquired eloquence were ignorant of what they talked about. Socrates had also been the first to bring philosophy down from the heavens to find its subject-matter in the homes and cities of men. Cicero therefore made use of Hellenistic readjustments of the earlier Greek philosophic distinctions and vocabulary to reformulate the practical subject-matter and methods of a philosophy rejoined to rhetoric. He based his method on questions or issues, the *constitutiones* of rhetoric operating as a productive art to construct or constitute the matter of problems or cases and of conclusions or judgments. The four constitutions are practical transformations of Aristotle's four scientific questions. Aristotle distinguished the methods of the sciences, which are applicable to particular fields, from the universal arts, which are applicable to all subject-matters. Both "methods" and "arts" are presented problematically, however, and in terms of the questions for which they provide means of inquiry. Aristotle enumerates four scientific questions—ways of discovering and establishing facts and causes in subject-matters—(1) is it? (2) what is it? (3) what properties does it have? and (4) why? These are transformed from theoretic methodological questions into practical operational questions in

Cicero's use of rhetoric as a productive architectonic science—(1) the conjectural constitution for the establishment of fact, (2) the definitive constitution for the definition of name, (3) the general or qualitative constitution for the justification of qualifications or evaluations, and (4) the translative constitution for the choice of proper or competent judges. Aristotle's questions provide principles for the methods of particular sciences which explore the structure of fact and cause within the subject-matters of those sciences. Cicero's questions construct issues for the arts of rhetoric which establish the facts and resolve the "causes" by relating facts, words, values, and judgments; they are not adapted to a pre-existent particular subject-matter but are used to constitute or produce a determined subject-matter.

Since differences of subject-matter are produced by discovering and justifying answers to questions, the arts and the sciences will not be organized according to differences in the subject-matter which they treat, but according to differences of question, action, statement, valuation, and judgment. Aristotle divided the sciences into theoretic, practical, and productive on the basis of differences of subject, method, and purpose or principle. He also divided rhetoric into three kinds on the basis of differences of audience, speaker, and subject, and he treated dialectic as a universal art and a counterpart of rhetoric. A productive architectonic art produces subject-matters and organizes them in relation to each other and to the problems to be solved. The changes in the names of the kinds of rhetoric are signs of the transformations they underwent when they became fields of action, production, or knowledge. Aristotle's "forensic" rhetoric, which is concerned with accusation and defense, with past actions, and with justice and injustice, became "judicial." His "political" rhetoric, which is concerned with exhortation and dehortation, with future actions, and with expediency and inexpediency, with utility and inutility, became "deliberative." His "epideictic" rhetoric, which is concerned with praise and blame, with present persons, their characters and actions, and with honor and dishonor, became "demonstrative." The difference between rhetoric and dialectic became the difference between eloquence and wisdom and is found in the difference between particular and universal questions.

Cicero's use of rhetoric as a productive architectonic art laid down the structure of a program of education and culture designed to reunite eloquence and wisdom in action. The great architectonic achievement of the Romans was the organization of Roman Law. But with the institution of the Roman Empire, political deliberative rhetoric ceased to play an important part in political deliberation and action, and the old dichotomy reappeared between eloquence and wisdom, between language and action, words and deeds. Justice, prudence, and wisdom were determined by the actions of the emperor, not by deliberation. Judicial and demonstrative rhetoric became verbal arts, the one an art of disputation, debate, and controversy in

Roman Jurisprudence, the other an art of verbal construction and exhibition in the Second Sophistic. In the Empire two branches of rhetoric were cultivated, judicial or legal and demonstrative or sophistic. Judicial rhetoric exercised a productive architectonic function in the formation and organization of law by the jurisconsults, both the civil law of Rome and the *jus gentium* which universalized law to all peoples. It exercised a productive architectonic function in ordering the actions of men toward universal peace and justice in the *Pax Romana*. Sophistic rhetoric exercised a productive architectonic function in the formation of a literature of consolation, instruction, pleasure, and sublimity, of adroitly differentiated styles and intricately elaborated figures, of tales and histories, prose, poetry, and the merging of the two in *satura*, of drama, satire, philosophy, and the history of philosophy and of sophistry. With the spread of Christianity the dichotomy of eloquence and wisdom continued. Honor and dishonor, merit and sin, good and evil were determined by interpretation of revealed truths and by action of the church, not by *deliberative* rhetoric. The art of disputation developed in *judicial* rhetoric was used in canon law to establish the concordance of discordant canons and was adapted to education and to theology in the development of the scholastic method. Political or deliberative rhetoric was dichotomized in its productive architectonic function between the city of God and terrestrial cities, divine laws and human laws, and *demonstrative* or artistic rhetoric became one of the verbal arts of the trivium, and in the development the arts of words and the arts of things became technical, abstract, and empty of content and subject-matter.

Renaissance philosophers and rhetoricians sought to rejoin eloquence and wisdom and developed within the new rhetoric they constructed a new universal subject-matter. They sought to make rhetoric a productive architectonic art of all arts and of all products rather than a productive technical art of language and persuasion. To make that transformation they transformed the architectonic functions of rhetoric from the practical or legal organization of actions in virtues and institutions to the productive or poetic organization of constructions in art objects and cultures. They made use of Cicero in this rebirth and innovation, as Medieval rhetoricians and philosophers had used the schemata of Ciceronian rhetoric to build a unified religion and tradition. Indeed, Renaissance rhetoricians invented the "Middle Ages" first by revolting against "middle Latinity" to return to the Latin of Cicero, and they continued the task by discovering in that middle period, which separated them from ancient Latin and Greek wisdom, further dichotomies of language and content to be removed by rejoining rhetoric and wisdom. Instead of distinguishing divine and human letters, they edited and interpreted Greek and Latin authors and applied the philology and hermeneutics of the study of literature to interpret Moses and the prophets, Paul and the evangelists, as poets. Instead of distinguishing divine and human law, they constructed history and political theory from the study of the history of ancient institutions and of the problems of the new nation states and international relations. Instead of distinguishing knowledge of universal laws of nature from empirical experience of natural occurrences, they constructed heuristic devices of discovery in which they borrowed from the common and proper places of rhetorical invention. Nizolius, in *On the True Principles and True Method [Ratio] of Philosophizing against the Pseudophilosophers* (which was later edited by Leibniz under the title *The Philosophical Anti-barbarus*), placed among the five general principles of philosophizing, (a) knowledge of the science of precepts and documents developed by the grammarians and the rhetoricians, and (b) assiduous reading of approved Greek and Latin authors and understanding of language of authors and people. Francis Bacon made use of the Topics in the formulation of his New Organon for scientific discovery. Ramus exposed the errors of the rhetoric of Aristotle, Cicero, and Quintilian (Cicero adds to the errors of Aristotle, and Quintilian to the errors of both), and reformulated the disciplines of the liberal arts using materials from ancient literature, oratory, and history. A long line of commentators on Aristotle's *Poetics* make part of their interpretation the adjustment of Aristotle's *Poetics* to the rhetorical criteria employed in Horace's *Ars Poetica*.

The Renaissance use of rhetoric as a productive architectonic art laid down the structure of a program of education and culture designed to reunite eloquence and wisdom in art. The great architectonic achievement of the Renaissance was the discovery and organization of the beautiful arts and the beautiful letters, for which the names *beaux arts* and *belles lettres* had to be invented. But with the accelerating progress of science, poetic demonstrative rhetoric ceased to play an important part in poetic insight and construction, and the old dichotomy between eloquence and wisdom reappeared, not in its practical form as a distinction between words and actions, but in its poetic form as a distinction between art and nature. This was to develop into a distinction between values and facts, and then between the humanities and the sciences. Philosophers, philologists, and historians began to imitate the methods of the sciences in the seventeenth century. They found and used methods of proof, not methods of discovery, although seventeenth century scientists worked to develop a heuristic method. By the nineteenth century, scientific method was conceived as a method of proof, and even philosophers like Mill and Whewell who disputed concerning the processes of scientific discovery, agreed that there was no "method" of discovery. The architectonic processes initiated in the Renaissance to rejoin the poles of medieval dichotomies have been conceived as phases of a process of "secularization" in which arts and sciences have been turned from the contemplation of another heavenly world to the production of this secular world for secular men. The productive processes have produced new subject-matters—literature, history, philosophy, and science, each with its proper methods or arts, and the continuation of these processes have been conceived as phases of the "fragmentation" of knowledge, community, and communication. Rhetoric ceased to operate as the productive architectonic art initiating and guiding these processes. It was replaced by the numerous arts of making and disposing which prepared for and produced a technological age, and rhetoric itself became technical: it turned from applications in other subject-matters, even *belles lettres,* except as they could be treated as instances of the proper subject-matter of rhetoric conceived as the art of speech. The fragmentation of knowledge is diagnosed and treated by juxtaposing subject-matters in "interdisciplinary" inquiry and study, and the rival productive arts of the associated fields compete for the role of architectonic art in relating and organizing the parts.

At each stage of the evolution of the arts and sciences since the Renaissance, an architectonic art was sought and used. Seventeenth century philosophers sought to apply the methods of the physical sciences or the mathematical sciences to human thought and action and to construct a "universal mechanics" or a "universal mathesis." The revolt of Kant against theoretic or speculative or dogmatic metaphysics was a revolt against that architectonic art. His Copernican revolution consisted in turning from the search for an architectonic science in the principles of being to seek it in the analysis of the forms of pure reason. "Human reason," he says, "is by nature architectonic. That is to say, it regards all our knowledge as belonging to a possible system, and therefore allows only such principles as do not at any rate make it impossible for any knowledge that we may attain to combine into a system with other knowledge." An architectonic is an art of constructing systems, and the final chapters of the "Transcendental Doctrine of Method," with which the *Critique of Pure Reason* closes, are a chapter on the "Architectonic of Pure Reason" and one on the "History of Pure Reason." The architectonic science against which Kant revolted was theoretic metaphysics or ontology; his critical epistemology was to provide an architectonic basis for treating the problems of Theology, Cosmology, and Psychology, the parts of the old metaphysics. It provided in fact a beginning to the controversies of the nineteenth century concerning theology and science (which have been conceived as phases of a warfare of science and religion), concerning the "methodologies" of the sciences (which have been conceived as phases of the developing opposition between materialism and idealism), and concerning the concepts and methods of sciences of facts and sciences of values, *Naturwissenschaft* as contrasted first to *Geisteswissenschaft* and then to *Kulturwissenschaft,* the natural sciences as contrasted to the human sciences or humanities and the social sciences (and the contrast has been conceived as an opposition and separation of two cultures based respectively on knowledge of universal, necessary laws and awareness of concrete, contingent facts). The twentieth century began with a series of revolts against metaphysics which were revolts against the methodologies of idealism and materialism rather than simple repetitions of Kant's revolt against the ontologies of empiricism and rationalism. Feuerbach placed the beginnings of modern philosophy in the "critique" of Hegel; G. E. Moore used critique of idealism and of utilitarianism as a propaedeutic to common sense.

As we enter into the final decades of this century, we boast of a vast increase of output in all arts, and we are puzzled by the absence of interdisciplinary connection and by the breakdown of interpersonal, intergroup, and intercultural communication. We need a new architectonic productive art. Rhetoric exercised such functions in the Roman republic and in the Renaissance. Rhetoric provides the devices by which to determine the characteristics and problems of our times and to form the art by which to guide actions for the solution of our problems and the improvement of our circumstances. The history of the development of culture in the West sketched in the preceding paragraphs is an application of the methods of rhetoric to the discovery of ourselves and our times. It is in opposition and refutation of many accepted or advocated interpretations, but more important than its use in adversary opposition, it opens up possible methods of directing and relating knowledge, action, and production, by instituting an architectonic productive art of improving and increasing both the production of utilities and goods (*utilia* and *honesta*) and the use and enjoyment (*uti* and *frui*) of the products. The guidelines for both tasks are found in the continuing use of basic distinctions made in the fundamental vocabulary of rhetoric, and the mark of the validity and relevance of those distinctions is found in the fact that the common vocabulary in which we discuss the problems of our times is already structured on those distinctions and that facts are as much determined by orientations as orientations are determined by facts.

The architectonic productive art in an age of "technology" is obviously technology itself given a rhetorical transformation. The architectonic productive art of the Romans was rhetoric with a practical orientation. In the Renaissance it was rhetoric with a poetic orientation. There is every reason to think that the art we seek is rhetoric with a theoretic orientation, and a rhetorical sign that this is the case is seen in the fact that, whereas the orientation of the seventeenth century, at the beginning of the modern period, found expression in "ontology," and that of the nineteenth century in "methodology," contemporary culture makes use of "technology," which combines a main stem meaning "art" with a suffix meaning "science," suggesting that it would be well to elaborate a "science of art." The subject-matter determined as the field of such problems and the methods to be instituted to treat them are foreshadowed in structure and direction, as they have been found in other innovations, by following the lead of rhetorical constitutions for questions and methods and the lead of rhetorical kinds for subject-matters and fields of activity.

II. THE NEW RHETORIC, ITS METHODS AND ITS PROBLEMS

Determination of the problems of our times, and action to resolve them, stand in need of an architectonic productive art. The problem of constituting such an art and applying it once constituted is one of rejoining eloquence and wisdom, rhetoric and philosophy. The continuing vocabulary and schemata, of words and of things, afford guidance in the constitution of such an art. The initial exploratory applications of devices borrowed from older rhetorics is facilitated by the fact that the data of experience are labeled and classified in common language using the same vocabulary and schemata. The new architectonic productive art should become a universal art, an art of producing things and arts, and not merely one of producing words and arguments; but the first step in constituting and using an enlarged objective rhetoric should be the reformulation of the structure and program of verbal rhetoric and its subject-matter. Roman rhetoricians and philosophers made rhetoric an architectonic art which related all things by means of law and the actions of men. Renaissance rhetoricians and philosophers made rhetoric an architectonic art which related all things by means of art and the constructions of men. Rhetoricians and philosophers today might make rhetoric an architectonic art which relates all things by means of science and the experiences of men. Rhetoric in all its applications is focused on the particular, not the universal—particular questions or constitutions in law, particular works or compositions in art, or particular facts or data in experience and existence. In an age of technology the diremption to be removed is the separation of theory and practice by the constitution of a technology which is theory applied, the *logos* of *techne*. We seek to produce it in concrete experience and existence by rejoining reason and sense, cognition and emotion, universal law and concrete occurrence. A first step can be taken by sketching the methods and the fields of rhetoric on the analogy of revolutions in rhetoric in earlier periods.

A. The Methods and Principles of Rhetoric

Aristotle distinguished between productive *sciences*, like Poetics (which have particular *subject-matters*, kinds of things made or produced, genres of artificial objects or objects of art) and architectonic *arts*, like Rhetoric (which direct and organize thought concerning *any subject-matter*). The sciences have become, more and more, sources of production, of new matters and new forms, in need of organizing methods and principles. We have seen how Aristotle's four scientific questions concerning objective causes were transformed into four rhetorical questions concerning verbal issues. In the latter form, they have been enlarged from time to time to become universal in their scope and productive in their operation. The traces of such past distinctions and structures are present in our search today for inclusive methods, by which to understand our situation and problems, and operative principles, by which to reorient and open up actions. The echoes take on meaning when placed in their rhetorical contexts and suggest directions of inquiry and construction which might be followed to transform the methods of rhetoric and make them applicable to new problems.

(1) Creativity and Invention

Creativity has taken a conspicuous place in modern discussions of the objectives and methods of education, action, art, and inquiry. "Creativity" usually has no meaning and provides no guiding criterion for learning or doing other than those implicit in "innovation," in the sense of setting and following a course different from those pursued by others in the past or the present. There is no method or standard of creation, discovery, or innovation. "Invention" has always been an important part of rhetoric. During the nineteenth century, under the influence of the dichotomy of language and wisdom, it was questioned whether invention is essentially the same as, or fundamentally different from, discovery. This is one of the dichotomies which the new architectonic rhetoric must eradicate. Invention can be joined to discovery in an art which is productive of things and arts or skills rather than of words and arguments or beliefs. When a productive inventive art deals with content as well as form, it is an art of active modification—rather than of passive reception—of the data of existence.

The art by which the orator discovered or created arguments in the midst of debate and controversy was based on the topics, the places or seats of argument. From the beginning, on the testimony of Quintilian, commonplaces have commonly been degraded from instruments for discovery of new ideas or arguments to repertories for repetition of old devices or adages. Existence as well as documents is approached and illuminated by places which guide discovery, and experience is limited and obscured by commonplaces of existence which are often borrowed from commonplaces of literature and speech. We need a new art of invention and discovery in which places are used as means by which to light up modes and meanings of works of art and natural occurrences and to open up aspects and connections in existence and possibility. The data and qualifications of existence are made by attention and interest; and discoveries made in a book or a work of art should provide places by which to perceive creatively what might otherwise not be experienced in the existent world we constitute. It is a long time since topics have been used as an art of invention in rhetoric. Ancient and Renaissance treatises on invention can be used to rediscover the art of invention in the use of words, which can be applied to discovering invention in reading and to using the art of invention in one's own constructions from the elements of discourse and from the data of experience. A reconstituted verbal art of invention, adapted to our circumstances and arts, might be used to shadow forth the methods and principles of an architectonic productive art generalized from invention in language to discovery in existence.

(2) Fact and Judgment

Recent revolts against metaphysics have been motivated by distrust and distaste for *a priori* methods and universal principles. We seek to apply our methods to concrete facts, to what is happening in the world here and now, and we find our principles operative in concrete occurrences and processes. Older rhetorics had methods by which to determine what is the case, and these methods of judgment or definition by which facts were characterized in answer to the question, what is it? or what did he do? were distinguished from, and related to, the methods of invention by which data were discovered in answer to the question, is it? or did he do it? Cicero makes the difference between a conjectural issue and a definitional issue a difference between the determination of what the fact is and the determination of what word should be used to describe it. The dichotomy of words and things has been subject to question in our times, and the methods of rhetoric suggest that invention of words and symbols contributes to discovery of things and that things are delimited in the definition of words.

Judgment of the issue concerning what the fact is and how it is defined and named starts from hypotheses advanced for consideration and transforms one of the hypotheses entertained into a sentence or a true proposition. A sentence or a true proposition makes or states a truth or a fact. We need a new art of judgment to relate experience to existence, an art of recovery or recognition of facts to be used with the art of discovery or apperception of data to provide instrumentalities for our contemporary respect for concrete facts of experience and for our determination to adhere to them and use them in the formation of knowledge and attitudes, in the constitution of science, experience, and expression. A beginning can be made by reexamining rhetorical methods of interpretation of the facts and artifacts of past times which are subjected to reinterpretation in the perspectives of one's own age. A reconstituted verbal art of judgment, adapted to the recovery and reinterpretation of past circumstances and arts in their present significances and relevances, might be used as a step in the development of the methods and principles of an architectonic productive art generalized from judgment of motivations and acts in narratives and histories to judgment of hypotheses and facts in experience.

(3) Sequences and Consequences in Discourse and in Fact

Facts are questioned, and are defended when questioned, by argument. The adversary oppositions of court-room trials set the basic form of Roman rhetorical argumentation. Argument as debate continued in the concordance and systematization of medieval canon-law. In the scholastic method it was supplemented by methods of dialectical dialogue and of logical refutation and proof. Renaissance rhetoric took into account arguments of dramas, tales, and histories, and in the eighteenth century rhetoric was applied systematically to the judgment and criticism of *belles lettres,* as in the *Lectures on Rhetoric and Belles Lettres* of Hugh Blair. This enlargement of the construction of sequences and consequences from pleading or persuasion to proof, question-answer, plot, action, motivation-action-reaction, cause-effect, experiment has never been brought together in schematic organization or by productive methods. They can be related to each other as answers to the third rhetorical question, the qualitative constitution: How is the fact or occurrence qualified or characterized? Approached in that perspective the arts of making connections can be related to the arts of invention and the arts of judgment. A universalized verbal art of making, and modifying, connections could be used to relate the separated fields of the arts and sciences and to trace themes as they move in variations from field to field; and a reconstituted verbal art of connections could prepare the way for moving from formulating the consequences of discourse to tracing the sequences of processes and actions and events in a generalized architectonic productive art of structures.

(4) Objectivity and Intersubjectivity in Communication and Knowledge

Metaphysicians and ontologists sought principles in the causes of things. Epistemologists and methodologists sought principles in the forms of thought and in the consensus of experts. We are suspicious of causes and concepts, and when the suspicion becomes doubt, we posit principles in postulates and theses. Yet the function of "principles" remains the same: they provide beginning points of verbal discourse and discursive thought which we can defend as beginning points of sequences of occurrences, facts, and objective relations. Theses are posited to account for positions, and positions are consequences derived from theses. We are suspicious of systems of being and of knowledge, but we organize and systematize information and raise questions and draw consequences from schematized data, facts, and relations. The arts of objective designation and intersubjective communication are practiced in new forms by machines and men in decision-making and mass-communication. A reexamination of the verbal arts of reference and systematization, of validification and justification, could be made a first step to the constitution of a generalized architectonic art of objectification and systematization in forming, and exploring the operations of, compositions of things, constitutions of communities, and constructs of communications.

B. The Fields and Problems of Rhetoric

Our concern with the "fragmentation" of knowledge and our "interdisciplinary" innovations to constitute new fields more relevant to the problems we encounter, and more viable to processes of inquiry and action, are indications that we do not find subject-matters ready made nor do we encounter problems distributed precisely in fields. We make subject-matters to fit the examination and resolution of problems, and the solution of problems brings to our attention further, consequent problems, which frequently require the setting up and examination of new fields. Rhetoric has replaced metaphysics as an architectonic art, in the past, when the organization and application of the arts and sciences was based, not on supposed natures of things or perceived forms of thought, but on recognition of the consequences of what men say and do. Cicero did not make use of Aristotle's classification of kinds of sciences according to subject-matter and method to provide subject-matter and data for the issues and decisions of rhetoric. He did make use of the Aristotelian differentiation of kinds of rhetoric and of dialectic according to speaker, audience, and subject, according to method, time, and objective, to constitute the fields and the subject-matters under discussion and adjudication. He did not adjust rhetoric to a subject-matter, but used the four kinds of issues or constitutions to develop the three kinds of oratory, that is, he used rhetorical methods to constitute relevant fields. We may well follow his example. Having examined the methods and principles of invention, judgment, disposition, and systematization, we can abandon the rigidities of accepted classifications of knowledge—institutionalized under headings like theoretical, practical, and productive; physics, logic, and ethics; science, poetry, and history; natural sciences, social sciences, and humanities—and return to rhetoric for hints concerning how to construct new interdisciplinary substantive fields by the use of the methods and principles formed for the resolution of problems for which new fields are needed. As in the case of our inquiry into methods and principles, we shall find signs of the relevance of the enterprise, and criteria by which to plan and judge steps to be taken in it, by the remnants of the terms of the art of rhetoric—"demonstrative," "judicial," "deliberative," and "dialectical"— which are found scattered in contemporary analyses and discussions of fields and problems.

(1) Demonstrative Rhetoric and the Data of Existence

"Demonstration" is a term which has wrapped up—in the meanings which we attach to it consciously as well as those which come to our attention unexpectedly, and in the applications which we make of it intentionally as well as those which extend the scope of "demonstration" unexpectedly— a rich variegated history of human thought, action, and production. Aristotle had two Greek words, *apodeiktikos* and *epideiktikos,* to apply to processes of presentation and manifestation: they are constructed from the same verb and, therefore, both mean "exhibit," "show forth," "make known," modified by prepositional prefixes which make "apodeictic" also mean "prove," that is, show forth "from" or "by," and "epideictic" also mean "display," that is, show forth "on" or "for." For Aristotle apodeictic proof was scientific proof, and epideictic oratory was display oratory. When "epideictic" became "demonstrative" oratory in the writings of Cicero, the certainties and necessities of proof were merged with the estimations and necessities of action. Aristotle distinguished three kinds of necessity, one absolute and two hypothetical, which are used in the apodeictic proofs of the three theoretical sciences. He argued that praise and honor are not reliable guides in the practical sciences, although praise and blame are the proper functions of epideictic oratory. For Cicero praise and blame are the functions of demonstrative discourse and action, in which he distinguished simple or absolute necessity from three necessities which govern actions taken to avoid or gain something: the necessity of the honorable (*honestas*), the necessity of security (*incolumitas*), and the necessity of convenience (*commoditas*). Our most recent revolt against metaphysics has been a revolt against, or an adjustment of, the apodeictic certainties of nineteenth century idealism and materialism. Yet we seem to be surprised that "demonstrations" have become exhibitions, presentations, manifestations rather than inferences, inductions, proofs.

The architectonic productive arts are not adapted to pre-existent subject-matters for the solution of recognized problems. The transformation of demonstration from proof to manifestation is not an error to be corrected by returning from agitation to evidence: it is a phenomenon of our times to be recognized as a datum to be studied and an instrumentality to be reduced to art. We have had enough experience of demonstrations to recognize not only the problems they "presented" as demonstrations but also the problems they "presented" in the insufficiencies of our conceptions of subject-matters and problems and the need for an architectonic productive art to change them.

1. Verbal demonstrative rhetoric is discourse for praise or blame. Recent demonstrations have not exhibited virtues and accomplishments for praise, but wrongs, injustices, and evils for blame. They have been effective as methods of discovery, of bringing to attention neglected data, but they have also made some use of the methods of judgment, disposition, and systematization.

2. Demonstrative rhetoric is designed to be productive of action as well as of words, that is, to arouse others to action and to accept a common opinion, to form groups that share that opinion, and to initiate participation in action based on that opinion.

3. The scope of demonstrative rhetoric is not limited to specific social, legal, and moral questions: it extends, even in application to those initial problems, to the whole field of human activity and knowledge, to all arts, sciences, and institutions.

4. Demonstration uncovers data, that is, "makes" them since data depend on the perspective in which they are "given." An assertion or demonstration by any one constitutes a datum, and affects the processes of judgment, disposition, and systematization. We need to constitute the field of demonstration in which such data can be treated without the distortions we feel justified in introducing by appeal to the assertions or demonstrations of experts.

5. The modality of demonstrative statements and actions is different from the necessities, contingencies, and possibilities of judicial, deliberative, and dialectical discourse. Epideictic oratory and modern demonstrations are about the present, and the statements they employ are assertoric. Judicial rhetoric is about the past, and judgments about the past can be necessary; deliberative rhetoric is about the future, and its proposals are contingent.

6. The field of demonstrative rhetoric is epideictic not apodeictic: it is not fenced off from, but fenced off for. In the nineteenth century when philosophers were seeking apodeictic certainties they explored the limits of concepts and of reason. The field of demonstrative rhetoric should provide the grounds for discovery and invention, going beyond the bounds of what is already known and the fields of that knowledge. The field of demonstrative rhetoric, set forth in assertions and explored by the art of invention or discovery, is a field of "topics" in the two senses which the term has acquired: subject-matters for consideration and places for invention.

(2) Judicial Rhetoric and the Facts of Experience

"Judgment" is a term which has been employed in action, art, and knowl-edge. Judgments are decisions or "sentences" in law-courts concerning past actions; they are appreciations or "criticisms" of works of art; they are con-clusions or "propositions" which are true or false. After "forensic" rhetoric became "judicial" rhetoric in the vocabulary of Cicero, the interrelations among judgments as "sentences," "evaluations," and "propositions" have been uncovered at each turn of development. The methods of accusation and defense have been enlarged to become the methods of verification and falsification, and their field has been universalized from past actions to be judged to facts and values to be determined and to general truths and laws to be established. "Cause" shares the productive ambiguity of "judgment": "causes" are discovered in things, pleaded before judges, pushed against established powers, and won in the progressive solution of problems. Judg-ments are a central theme in Kant's three Critiques, and the *Critique of Judgment* forms a connecting link between theoretical and practical reason by analyzing aesthetic judgments and purposiveness. We have revolted against the separation of facts and values, and we have turned to actions and circumstances to rejoin them. This reformulation of our problems makes it necessary to constitute and explore the field of judgment in which the facts and values of experience are related to each other and to the data of exis-tence uncovered in the newly constituted field of demonstration.

The growing interest in the new hermeneutics is further sign of the need to establish a working domain of judgments of knowledge and action. In that enlarged field the controversial opposition of verification and falsification is not resolved by victory or defeat of a protagonist but by the establishment or refutation of a hypothesis. Since the art of interpretation and judgment applies to known truths and values, the field of judgment includes all recorded literature, which is the subject of hermeneutics or semantics, but it includes the facts as well as the records of experience. It is in this field that hypotheses can become facts and the elements of invention and discovery can be joined in a statement or apperception of fact. One of the important tasks to be accomplished by the new architectonic productive art of rhetoric is to clarify the topology of the relation of the field of invention to the field of judgment. This will make it possible once more for the semantics of known facts and values to contribute to the discovery of new truths and the production of new accomplishments, and for places and elements to be used heuristically in the establishment of ideas and arguments, facts and values.

(3) Deliberative Rhetoric and the Structure of Connections

"Deliberation" and its companion terms "choice" and "decision" have already been universalized in our common language of diagnosis and action. They were terms in the practical science of ethics for Aristotle: they were limited to actions within our power; with respect to such actions we can deliberate and choose means, but not ends. The subject-matter of political rhetoric was future actions. When "political" oratory became "deliberative" oratory after Cicero, the terms of art, of ethics, politics, and rhetoric merged, and deliberation could be applied not only to ends as well as means, but to theoretic and productive as well as practical problems. We deliberate not only about the expedient and the inexpedient, but also about the good and the bad, the true and the false, the pleasurable and the distasteful. Decision-making and methods-analysis require a universal field, and our universal methods could be used more effectively if that field could be subjected to positive definition rather than only the negative limitations provided by lack of limits, infinity, or indefiniteness. When the verbal rhetoric was universalized, it included all discursive sequences—inference, narrative, plot, lyric, history, aphorism, paradox—with related forms and methods. We have become accustomed to statements of the relations among their arts—that poetry presents truths, that mathematics expresses beauties, that history sets forth universal laws—but we have not constructed the subject-matter which provides the content for the operation and interrelation of these arts. As we proceeded with its constitution we would give substantive meaning to the "structures" which appear so frequently in our discussion of problems of education and action and which need grounding if the formal precision derived from mathematics is to be translated into concrete processes of operation determined by context and subject-matter. A beginning can be made by using the fields of invention and of judgment for data and facts to be related in structured sequences and intelligible consequences. This is the field of "arts" and "methods," in which themes are continued and undergo variations which reflect changing arts and constitute changing regions of the structure of connections which constitute the field of deliberation.

(4) Dialectic and the Principles of Objectivity and Communication

Aristotle treated dialectic as a counterpart of rhetoric. The differences between them were in part consequences of the difference between the particular audiences of rhetoric and the universal audience of dialectic. Arguments can be adapted to the predilections of groups or communities of men. They can also be framed by art so that anyone who uses art or intelligence can follow them and appreciate them. The difference between dialectic and rhetoric became for Cicero a difference between universal questions of philosophy and science and particular questions concerning particular actions of particular men at particular times and places. The growth of science and communication, the increase of knowledge and the formation of world community, have begun to lay out the field of systematic organization both as a system of operation of an ongoing development and inquiry, technology. It is a field which provides grounding for the intersubjectivity of communications of persons and groups and for the objectivity of conclusions of inquiry and action. It is within this field that the possible worlds, which are discussed in plans and policy, are constructed, and theses which are posited are stabilized into principles. Theses and principles have a history which carries back in tradition to principles that were called eternal and universal but were also derived from theses which posit being in the context of an agent, his environment, and his subject. It is the field of reflexivity and responsibility, which must be explored in rational action concerning rights and justice, laws and conventions, sanctions and obligations, utilities and values, and opinions and truths. The field of the new dialectical rhetoric, of debate and dialogue, is being travelled and cultivated by chance and by art. An architectonic-productive survey of the field of these activities could make its beginning by orienting rhetoric from the oppositions of the past to the understanding and projection of the new processes and needs of the present.

Verbal rhetoric is productive of arguments and architectonic of attitudes. It provides the principle, in both the sense of beginning-point and of guideline, for the construction of an architectonic productive art of rhetoric and philosophy which can be used to create a method productive of the arts and a subject-matter substantive to the problems of an age of technology. It should be a rhetoric which relates form to matter, instrumentality to product, presentation to content, agent to audience, intention to reason. It should not make technology the operation of a machine, in which the message is a massage; it should not take its form from its medium and it should not be adapted to use to communicate established judgments (which are jostled commonplaces) or revolutionary convictions (which are repeated dogmas) on the supposition and intimation that they might be related to traditional ends or novel objectives and that they are somehow means to those ends. It should be adapted to inquiry into what is the case rather than to semantic analysis of what somebody else has said. It should be positive in the creation, not passive in the reception, of data, facts, consequences, and objective organization. It should be an art in which what any one says to be the case, judges to be good or evil, connects in relations, and establishes with some show of system and principles, is relevant as subject-matter, content, and product. In a technological age all men should have an art of creativity, of judgment, of disposition, and of organization. This should be adapted to their individual development and to their contribution to forming a common field in which the subject of inquiry is not how to devise means to achieve accepted ends arranged in hierarchies but the calculation of uses and applications that might be made of the vastly increased available means in order to devise new ends and to eliminate oppositions and segregations based on past competitions for scarce means.

Chaïm Perelman
1912–1984

Born in Poland, Chaïm Perelman was educated in Belgium, where he earned doctorates in both philosophy and law. His interest in law and justice led to his studying the traditional distinction between philosophical or formal logic and everyday reasoning and finding them arbitrary and unproductive. Focusing on the similarities between formal and informal reasoning, Perelman gave us a new rhetorical theory of argument: the use of argument in the production of knowledge, the role of audience in the determination of argumentative strategy, and the necessity of beginning from mutually agreed-upon premises. With his colleague, Lucie Olbrechts-Tyteca, Perelman combined the traditional functions of rhetoric and dialectic in The New Rhetoric: A Treatise on Argumentation *(1969).*

The New Rhetoric: A Theory of Practical Reasoning

The Loss of a Humanistic Tradition.—The last two years of secondary education in Belgium used to be called traditionally "Poetry" and "Rhetoric." I still remember that, over forty years ago, I had to study the "Elements of Rhetoric" for a final high-school examination, and I learned more or less by heart the contents of a small manual, the first part of which concerned the syllogism and the second the figures of style. Later, in the university, I took a course of logic which covered, among other things, the analysis of the syllogism. I then learned that logic is a formal discipline that studies the structure of hypothetico-deductive reasoning. Since then I have often wondered what link a professor of rhetoric could possibly discover between the syllogism and the figures of style with their exotic names that are so difficult to remember.

Lack of clarity concerning the idea of rhetoric is also apparent in the article on the subject in the *Encyclopedia Britannica*, where rhetoric is defined as "the use of language as an art based on a body of organized knowledge." But what does this mean? The technique or art of language in general, or only that of literary prose as distinct from poetry? Must rhetoric be conceived of as the art of oratory—that is, as the art of public speaking? The author of the article notes that for Aristotle rhetoric is the art of persuasion. We are further told that the orator's purpose, according to Cicero's definition, is to instruct, to move, and to please. Quintilian sums up this

145

view in his lapidary style as *ars bene dicendi*, the art of speaking well. This phrase can refer either to the efficacy, or the morality, or the beauty of a speech, this ambiguity being both an advantage and a drawback.

For those of us who have been educated in a time when rhetoric has ceased to play an essential part in education, the idea of rhetoric has been definitely associated with the "flowers of rhetoric"—the name used for the figures of style with their learned and incomprehensible names. This tradition is represented by two French authors, César Chesneau, sieur Dumarsais, and Pierre Fontanier, who provided the basic texts for teaching what was taken for rhetoric in the eighteenth and nineteenth centuries. The work of Dumarsais, which first appeared in 1730 and enjoyed an enormous success, is entitled *Concerning tropes or the different ways in which one word can be taken in a language*. Fontanier's book, reprinted in 1968 under the title *The figures of discourse*, unites in one volume two works, which appeared respectively in 1821 and 1827, under the titles *A classical manual for the study of tropes* and *Figures other than tropes*.

These works are the outcome of what might be called the stylistic tradition of rhetoric, which was started by Omer Talon, the friend of Petrus Ramus, in his two books on rhetoric published in 1572. The extraordinary influence of Ramus hindered, and to a large extent actually destroyed, the tradition of classical rhetoric that had been developed over the course of twenty centuries and with which are associated the names of such writers as Aristotle, Cicero, Quintilian, and St. Augustine.

For the ancients, rhetoric was the theory of persuasive discourse and included five parts: *inventio, dispositio, elocutio, memoria,* and *actio.* The first part dealt with the art of finding the materials of discourse, especially arguments, by using common or specific *loci*—the *topoi* studied in works which, following Aristotle's example, were called *Topics*. The second part gave advice on the purposive arrangement or order of discourse, the *method,* as the Renaissance humanists called it. The third part dealt mainly with style, the choice of terms and phrases; the fourth with the art of memorizing the speech; while the fifth concerned the art of delivering it.

Ramus also worked for the reform of logic and dialectic along the lines laid down by Rodolphus Agricola in his *De inventione dialectica* (1479) and by the humanists who followed him in seeking to break away from scholastic formalism by restoring the union of eloquence and philosophy advocated by Cicero. This reform consisted essentially in rejecting the classical opposition between science and opinion that had led Aristotle to draw a distinction between analytical and dialectical reasoning—the former dealing with necessary reasonings, the latter with probable ones. Analytical reasoning is the concern of Aristotle's *Analytics,* dialectical reasoning that of the *Topics, On Sophistical Refutations,* and the *Rhetoric.*

Against this distinction, this is what Ramus has to say in his *Dialectic:*

Aristotle, or more precisely the exponents of Aristotle's theories, thought that there are two arts of discussion and reasoning, one applying to science and called Logic, the other dealing with opinion and called Dialectic. In this—with all due respect to such great masters—they were greatly mistaken. Indeed these two names, Dialectic and Logic, generally mean the very same thing, like the words *dialegesthai* and *logizesthai* from which they are derived and descended, that is, dispute or reason. . . . Furthermore, although things known are either necessary and scientific, or contingent and a matter of opinion, just as our sight can perceive all colors, both unchanging and changeable, in the same way the art of knowing, that is Dialectic or Logic, is one and the same doctrine of reasoning well about anything whatsoever. . . .

As a result of this rejection, Ramus unites in his *Dialectic* what Aristotle had separated. He divides his work into two parts, one concerning invention, the other judgment. Further, he includes in dialectic parts that were formerly regarded as belonging to rhetoric: the theory of invention or *loci* and that of disposition, called *method*. Memory is considered as merely a reflection of these first two parts, and rhetoric—the "art of speaking well," of "eloquent and ornate language"—includes the study of tropes, of figures of style, and of oratorical delivery, all of which are considered as of lesser importance.

Thus was born the tradition of modern rhetoric, better called stylistic, as the study of techniques of unusual expression. For Fontanier, as we have seen, rhetoric is reduced to the study of figures of style, which he defines as "the more or less remarkable traits and forms, the phrases with a more or less happy turn, by which the expression of ideas, thoughts, and feelings removes the discourse more or less far away from what would have been its simple, common expression."

Rhetoric, on this conception, is essentially an art of expression and, more especially, of literary conventionalized expression; it is an art of style. So it is still regarded by Jean Paulhan in his book *Les fleurs de Tarbes ou la terreur dans les lettres* (1941, but published first as articles in 1936).

The same view of rhetoric was taken in Italy during the Renaissance, despite the success of humanism. Inspired by the Ciceronian ideal of the union of philosophy with eloquence, humanists such as Lorenzo Valla sought to unite dialectic and rhetoric. But they gave definite primacy to rhetoric, thus expressing their revolt against scholastic formalism.

This humanistic tradition continued for over a century and finally produced in the *De principiis* by Mario Nizolio (1553) its most significant work from a philosophical point of view. Less than ten years later, however, in 1562, Francesco Patrizi published in his *Rhetoric* the most violent attack upon this discipline, to which he denied any philosophical interest whatsoever. Giambattista Vico's reaction came late and produced no immediate result. Rhetoric became a wholly formal discipline—any living ideas that it contained being included in Aesthetics.

Germany is one country where classical rhetoric has continued to be carefully studied, especially by scholars such as Friedrich Blass, Wilhelm Kroll, and Friedrich Solmsen, who devoted most of their lives to this study. Yet, even so, rhetoric has been regarded only as the theory of literary prose. Heinrich Lausberg has produced a most remarkable work, which is the best tool in existence for the study of rhetorical terminology and the structure of discourse, and yet in the author's own eyes it is only a contribution to the study of literary language and tradition.

The old tradition of rhetoric has been kept longest in Great Britain—it is still very much alive among Scots jurists—thanks to the importance of psychology in the empiricism of Bacon, Locke, and Hume, and to the influence of the Scottish philosophy of common sense. This tradition, in which the theory of invention is reduced to a minimum and interest is focused on the persuasive aspect of discourse, is represented by such original works as George Campbell's *The Philosophy of Rhetoric* (1776) and Richard Whately's *Elements of Rhetoric* (1828). In this work, Whately, who was a logician, deals with argumentative composition in general and the art of establishing the truth of a proposition so as to convince others, rhetoric being reduced to "a purely managerial or supervisory science." His disciple, the future Cardinal John Henry Newman, applied Whately's ideas to the problems of faith in his *Grammar of Assent* (1870). This outlook still consists in seeing in rhetoric only a theory of expression. It was the view adopted by Ivor Armstrong Richards in his *Principles of Literary Criticism* (published in 1924) and in his *Philosophy of Rhetoric* (1936).

While in Europe rhetoric has been reduced to stylistics and literary criticism, becoming merely a part of the study of literature insofar as it was taught at all, in the United States the appearance of a speech profession brought about a unique development.

Samuel Silas Curry, in a book entitled *The Province of Expression* (1891), was the first to emphasize spoken discourse and its delivery, rather than the composition of literary prose, and to claim autonomy for speech as opposed to written composition. "Expression," as he understood it, did not mean the way in which ideas and feelings are expressed in a literary form, but instead the manner in which they are communicated by means of an art of "delivery." Concern for this element, apparently one of lesser importance, clearly reveals a renewed interest in the audience, and this interest helped to promote the creation of a new "speech profession," separate from the teaching of English and of English literature. Under the influence of William James, James Albert Winans published a volume entitled *Public Speaking* (1915) that firmly established a union between professors of speech and those of psychology. With the cooperation of specialists in ancient and medieval rhetoric, such as Charles S. Baldwin, Harry Caplan, Lane Cooper, Everett Lee Hunt, and Richard McKeon, the whole tradition of classical rhetoric has been retraced. This study has been continued and further developed in the works of Wilbur Samuel Howell, Donald C. Bryant, Karl R. Wallace, Walter J. Ong, Lloyd F. Bitzer, Douglas Ehninger, and Marie K. Hochmuth. The work of these scholars—the titles of which can be found in the Bibliography that has been regularly published by the *Quarterly Journal of Speech* since 1915—constitutes a unique achievement which is as yet too little known outside the United States.

An Ornamental or a Practical Art?

There is nothing of philosophical interest in a rhetoric that has turned into an art of expression, whether literary or verbal. Hence it is not surprising that the term is missing entirely from both André Lalande's *Vocabulaire technique et critique de la philosophie* and the recent American *Encyclopedia of Philosophy* (1967). In the Western tradition, "Rhetoric" has frequently been identified with verbalism and an empty, unnatural, stilted mode of expression. Rhetoric then becomes the symbol of the most outdated elements in the education of the old regime, the elements that were the most formal, most useless, and most opposed to the needs of an equalitarian, progressive democracy.

This view of rhetoric as declamation—ostentatious and artificial discourse—is not a new one. The same view was taken of the rhetoric of the Roman Empire. Once serious matters, both political and judiciary, had been withdrawn from its influence, rhetoric became perforce limited to school exercises, to set speeches treating either a theme of the past or an imaginary situation, but, in any case, one without any real bearing. Serious people, especially the Stoics, made fun of it. Thus Epictetus declares: "But this faculty of speaking and of ornamenting words, if there is indeed any such peculiar faculty, what else does it do, when there happens to be discourse about a thing, than to ornament the words and arrange them as hairdressers do the hair?"

Aristotle would have disagreed with this conception of rhetoric as an ornamental art bearing the same relation to prose as poetics does to verse. For Aristotle, rhetoric is a practical discipline that aims, not at producing a work of art, but at exerting through speech a persuasive action on an audience. Unfortunately, however, those responsible for the confusion between the two have been able to appeal to Aristotle's own authority because of the misleading analysis he gave of the epideictic or ceremonial form of oratory.

In his *Rhetoric* Aristotle distinguishes three genres of oratory: deliberative, forensic, and ceremonial. "Political speaking," he writes, "urges us either to do or not to do something: one of these two courses is always taken by private counsellors, as well as by men who address public assemblies. Forensic speaking either attacks or defends somebody: one or other of these two things must always be done by the parties in a case. The ceremonial oratory of display either praises or censures somebody." But whereas the audience is supposed to act as a judge and make a decision concerning either the future (deliberative genre) or the past (forensic genre), in the case of an epideictic discourse the task of the audience consists in judging, not about the matter of discourse, but about the orator's skill. In political and forensic discourse the subject of the discourse is itself under discussion, and the orator aims at persuading the audience to take part in deciding the matter, but in epideictic discourse the subject—such as, for example, the praise of soldiers who have died for their country—is not at all a matter of debate. Such set speeches were often delivered before large assemblies, as at the Olympic Games, where competition between orators provided a welcome complement to the athletic contests. On such occasions, the only decision that the audience was called upon to make concerned the talent of the orator, by awarding the crown to the victor.

One might well ask how an oratorical genre can be defined by its literary imitation. We know that Cicero, after having lost the suit, rewrote his *Pro Milone* and published it as a literary work. He hoped that by artistically improving the speech, which had failed to convince Milo's judges, he might gain the approbation of lovers of literature. Are those who read this speech long after its practical bearing has disappeared any more than spectators? In that case, all discourses automatically become literature once they cease to exert a persuasive effect, and there is no particular reason to distinguish different genres of oratory. Yet it can be maintained, on the contrary, that the epideictic genre is not only important but essential from an educational point of view, since it too has an effective and distinctive part to play—that, namely, of bringing about a consensus in the minds of the audience regarding the values that are celebrated in the speech.

The moralists rightly satirize the view of epideictic oratory as spectacle. La Bruyère writes derisively of those who "are so deeply moved and touched by Theodorus's sermon that they resolve in their hearts that it is even more beautiful than the last one he preached." And Bossuet, fearful lest the real point of a sermon be missed, exclaims: "You should now be convinced that preachers of the Gospel do not ascend into pulpits to utter empty speeches to be listened to for amusement."

Bossuet here is following St. Augustine's precepts concerning sacred discourse as set forth in the fourth book of his work *On Christian Doctrine*. The orator is not content if his listener merely accepts the truth of his words and praises his eloquence, because he wants his full assent:

> If the truths taught are such that to believe or to know them is enough, to give one's assent implies nothing more than to confess that they are true. When, however, the truth taught is one that must be carried into practice, and that is taught for the very purpose of being practiced, it is useless to be persuaded of

the truth of what is said, it is useless to be pleased with the manner in which it is said, if it be not so learnt as to be practiced. The eloquent divine, then, when he is urging a practical truth, must not only teach so as to give instruction, and please so as to keep up the attention, but he must also sway the mind so as to subdue the will.

The listener will be persuaded, Augustine also claims:

if he be drawn by your promises, and awed by your threats; if he reject what you condemn, and embrace what you commend; if he grieve when you heap up objects for grief, and rejoice when you point out an object for joy; if he pity those whom you present to him as objects of pity, and shrink from those whom you set before him as men to be feared and shunned.

The orator's aim in the epideictic genre is not just to gain a passive adherence from his audience but to provoke the action wished for or, at least, to awaken a disposition so to act. This is achieved by forming a community of minds, which Kenneth Burke, who is well aware of the importance of this genre, calls *identification*. As he writes, rhetoric "is rooted in an essential function of language itself, a function that is wholly realistic and is continually born anew; the use of language as a symbolic means of inducing cooperation in beings that by nature respond to symbols." In fact, any persuasive discourse seeks to have an effect on an audience, although the audience may consist of only one person and the discourse be an inward deliberation.

The distinction of the different genres of oratory is highly artificial, as the study of a speech shows. Mark Antony's famous speech in Shakespeare's *Julius Caesar* opens with a funeral eulogy, a typical case of epideictic discourse, and ends by provoking a riot that is clearly political. Its goal is to intensify an adherence to values, to create a disposition to act, and finally to bring people to act. Seen in such perspective, rhetoric becomes a subject of great philosophical interest.

Thinking about Values

In 1945, when I published my first study of justice, I was completely ignorant of the importance of rhetoric. This study, undertaken in the spirit of logical empiricism, succeeded in showing that *formal justice* is a principle of action, according to which beings of one and the same essential category must be treated in the same way. The application of this principle to actual situations, however, requires criteria to indicate which categories are relevant and how their members should be treated, and such decisions involve a recourse to judgments of value. But on positivistic methods I could not see how such judgments could have any foundation or justification. Indeed, as I entirely accepted the principle that one cannot draw an "ought" from an "is"—a judgment of value from a judgment of fact—I was led inevitably to the conclusion that if justice consists in the systematic implementation of certain value judgments, it does not rest on any rational foundation: "As for the value that is the foundation of the normative system, we cannot subject it to any rational criterion: it is utterly arbitrary and logically indeterminate. . . . The idea of value is, in effect, incompatible both with formal necessity and with experiential universality. There is no value which is not logically arbitrary."

I was deeply dissatisfied with this conclusion, however interesting the analysis, since the philosophical inquiry, carried on within the limits of logical empiricism, could not provide an ideal of practical reason, that is, the establishment of rules and models for reasonable action. By admitting the soundness of Hume's analysis, I found myself in a situation similar to Kant's. If Hume is right in maintaining that empiricism cannot provide a basis for either science or morals, must we not then look to other than empirical methods to justify them? Similarly, if experience and calculation, combined according to the precepts of logical empiricism, leave no place for practical reason and do not enable us to justify our decisions and choices, must we not seek other techniques of reasoning for that purpose? In other words, is there a logic of value judgments that makes it possible for us to reason about values instead of making them depend solely on irrational choices, based on interest, passion, prejudice, and myth? Recent history has shown abundantly the sad excesses to which such an attitude can lead.

Critical investigation of the philosophical literature yielded no satisfactory results. The French logician Edmond Goblot, in his work *La logique des jugements de valeur,* restricted his analysis to derived or instrumental value judgments, that is, to those judgments that use values as a means to already accepted ends, or as obstacles to their attainment. The ends themselves, however, could not be subjected to deliberation unless they were transformed into instrumental values, but such a transformation only pushes further back the problem of ultimate ends.

We thus seem to be faced with two extreme attitudes, neither of which is acceptable: subjectivism, which, as far as values are concerned, leads to skepticism for lack of an intersubjective criterion; or an absolutism founded on intuitionism. In the latter case, judgments of value are assimilated to judgments of a reality that is *sui generis.* In other words, must we choose between A. J. Ayer's view in *Language, Truth, and Logic* and G. E. Moore's view in *Principia Ethica*? Both seem to give a distorted notion of the actual process of deliberation that leads to decision making in practical fields such as politics, law, and morals.

Then too, I agreed with the criticisms made by various types of existentialism against both positivist empiricism and rationalistic idealism, but I could find no satisfaction in their justification of action by purely subjective projects or commitments.

I could see but one way to solve the dilemma to which most currents of contemporary philosophy had led. Instead of working out *a priori* possible structures for a logic of value judgments, might we not do better to follow the method adopted by the German logician Gottlob Frege, who, to cast new light on logic, decided to analyze the reasoning used by mathematicians? Could we not undertake, in the same way, an extensive inquiry into the manner in which the most diverse authors in all fields do in fact reason about values? By analyzing political discourse, the reasons given by judges, the reasoning of moralists, the daily discussions carried on in deliberating about making a choice or reaching a decision or nominating a person, we might be able to trace the actual logic of value judgments which seems continually to elude the grasp of specialists in the theory of knowledge.

For almost ten years Mme L. Olbrechts-Tyteca and I conducted such an inquiry and analysis. We obtained results that neither of us had ever expected. Without either knowing or wishing it, we had rediscovered a part of Aristotelian logic that had been long forgotten or, at any rate, ignored and despised. It was the part dealing with dialectical reasoning, as distinguished from demonstrative reasoning—called by Aristotle *analytics*—which is analyzed at length in the *Rhetoric, Topics,* and *On Sophistical Refutations.* We called this new, or revived, branch of study, devoted to the analysis of informal reasoning, *The New Rhetoric.*

Argumentation and Demonstration

The new rhetoric is a theory of argumentation. But the specific part that is played by argumentation could not be fully understood until the modern theory of demonstration—to which it is complementary—had been developed. In its contemporary form, demonstration is a calculation made in accordance with rules that have been laid down beforehand. No recourse is allowed to evidence or to any intuition other than that of the senses. The only requirement is the ability to distinguish signs and to perform operations according to rules. A demonstration is regarded as correct or incorrect according as it conforms, or fails to conform, to the rules. A conclusion is held to be demonstrated if it can be reached by means of a series of correct operations starting from premises accepted as axioms. Whether these axioms be considered as evident, necessary, true, or hypothetical, the relation between them and the demonstrated theorems remains unchanged. To pass from a correct inference to the truth or to the computable probability of the conclusion, one must admit both the truth of the premises and the coherence of the axiomatic system.

The acceptance of these assumptions compels us to abandon pure formalism and to accept certain conventions and to admit the reality of certain models or structures. According to the classical theory of demonstration, which is rejected by formalism, the validity of the deductive method was guaranteed by intuition or evidence—by the natural light of reason. But if we reject such a foundation, we are not compelled to accept formalism. It is still insufficient, since we need good reasons to accept the premises from which we start, and these reasons can be good only for a mind capable of judging them. However, once we have accepted the framework of a formal system and know that it is free from ambiguity, then the demonstrations that can be made within it are compelling and impersonal; in fact, their validity is capable of being controlled mechanically. It is this specific character of formal demonstration that distinguishes it from dialectical reasoning founded on opinion and concerned with contingent realities. Ramus failed to see this distinction and confused the two by using a faulty analogy with the sight of moving and unmoving colors. It is sometimes possible, by resorting to prior arrangements and conventions, to transform an argument into a demonstration of a more or less probabilistic character. It remains true, nonetheless, that we must distinguish carefully between the two types of reasoning if we want to understand properly how they are related.

An argumentation is always addressed by a person called the orator—whether by speech or in writing—to an audience of listeners or readers. It aims at obtaining or reinforcing the adherence of the audience to some thesis, assent to which is hoped for. The new rhetoric, like the old, seeks to persuade or convince, to obtain an adherence which may be *theoretical* to start with, although it may eventually be manifested through a disposition to act, or *practical,* as provoking either immediate action, the making of a decision, or a commitment to act.

Thus argumentation, unlike demonstration, presupposes a meeting of minds: the will on the part of the orator to persuade and not to compel or command, and a disposition on the part of the audience to listen. Such mutual goodwill must not only be general but must also apply to the particular question at issue; it must not be forgotten that all argumentation aims somehow at modifying an existing state of affairs. This is why every society possesses institutions to further discussion between competent persons and to prevent others. Not everybody can start debating about anything whatever, no matter where. To be a man people listen to is a precious quality and is still more necessary as a preliminary condition for an efficacious argumentation.

In some cases there are detailed rules drawn up for establishing this contact before a question can be debated. The main purpose of procedure in civil and criminal law is to ensure a balanced unfolding of the judicial debate. Even in matters where there are no explicit rules for discussion, there are still customs and habits that cannot be disregarded without sufficient reason.

Argumentation also presupposes a means of communicating, a common language. The use of it in a given situation, however, may admit of variation according to the position of the interlocutors. Sometimes only certain persons are entitled to ask questions or to conduct the debate.

From these specifications it is apparent that the new rhetoric cannot tolerate the more or less conventional, and even arbitrary, limitations traditionally imposed upon classical rhetoric. For Aristotle, the similarity between rhetoric and dialectic was all-important. According to him, they differ only in that dialectic provides us with techniques of discussion for a common search for truth, while rhetoric teaches how to conduct a debate in which various points of view are expressed and the decision is left up to the audience. This distinction shows why dialectic has been traditionally considered as a serious matter by philosophers, whereas rhetoric has been regarded with contempt. Truth, it was held, presided over a dialectical discussion, and the interlocutors had to reach agreement about it by themselves, whereas rhetoric taught only how to present a point of view—that is to say, a partial aspect of the question—and the decision of the issue was left up to a third person.

It should be noted, however, that for Plato dialectic alone does not attain to metaphysical truth. The latter requires an intuition for which dialectic can only pave the way by eliminating untenable hypotheses. However, truth is the keynote for dialectic, which seeks to get as close to the truth as possible through the discursive method. The rhetorician, on the other hand, is described as trying to outdo his rivals in debate, and, if his judges are gross and ignorant, the triumph of the orator who shows the greatest skill in flattery will by no means always be the victory of the best cause. Plato emphasizes this point strongly in the *Gorgias,* where he shows that the demagogue, to achieve victory, will not hesitate to use techniques unworthy of a philosopher. This criticism gains justification from Aristotle's observation, based evidently on Athenian practice, that it belongs to rhetoric "to deal with such matters as we deliberate upon without arts or systems to guide us, in the hearing of persons who cannot take in at a glance a complicated argument, or follow a long chain of reasoning."

For the new rhetoric, however, argumentation has a wider scope as nonformal reasoning that aims at obtaining or reinforcing the adherence of an audience. It is manifest in discussion as well as in debate, and it matters not whether the aim be the search for truth or the triumph of a cause, and the audience may have any degree of competence. The reason that rhetoric has been deemed unworthy of the philosopher's efforts is not because dialectic employs a technique of questions and answers while rhetoric proceeds by speeches from opposing sides. It is not this but rather the idea of the unicity of truth that has disqualified rhetoric in the Western philosophical tradition. Thus Descartes declares: "Whenever two men come to opposite decisions about the same matter one of them at least must certainly be in the wrong, and apparently there is not even one of them who knows; for if the reasoning of the second was sound and clear he would be able so to lay it before the other as finally to succeed in convincing *his* understanding also." Both Descartes and Plato hold this idea because of their rejection of opinion, which is variable, and their adoption of an ideal of science based on the model of geometry and mathematical reasoning—the very model according to which the world was supposed to have been created. *Dum Deus calculat, fit mundus* [While God calculates, the world is created] is the conviction not only of Leibniz but of all rationalists.

Things are very different within a tradition that follows a juridical, rather than a mathematical, model. Thus in the tradition of the Talmud, for example, it is accepted that opposed positions can be equally reasonable; one of them does not have to be right. Indeed, "in the Talmud two schools of biblical interpretation are in constant opposition, the school of Hillel and that of Shammai. Rabbi Abba relates that, bothered by these contradictory interpretations of the sacred text, Rabbi Samuel addresses himself to heaven in order to know who speaks the truth. A voice from above answers him that these two theses both expressed the word of the Living God."

So too, for Plato, the subject of discussion is always one for which men possess no techniques for reaching agreement immediately:

> Suppose for example that you and I, my good friend [Socrates remarks to Euthyphro], differ about a number; do differences of this sort make us enemies and set us at variance with one another? Do we not go at once to arithmetic, and put an end to them by a sum? . . . Or suppose that we differ about magnitudes, do we not quickly end the differences by measuring? . . . And we end a controversy about heavy and light by resorting to a weighing machine? . . . But what differences are there which cannot be thus decided, and which therefore make us angry and set us at enmity with one another? I dare say the answer does not occur to you at the moment, and therefore I will suggest that these enmities arise when the matters of difference are the just and unjust, good and evil, honorable and dishonorable.

When agreement can easily be reached by means of calculation, measuring, or weighing, when a result can be either demonstrated or verified, nobody would think of resorting to dialectical discussion. The latter concerns only what cannot be so decided and, especially, disagreements about values. In fact, in matters of opinion, it is often the case that neither rhetoric nor dialectic can reconcile all the positions that are taken.

Such is exactly how matters stand in philosophy. The philosopher's appeal to reason gives no guarantee whatever that everyone will agree with his point of view. Different philosophies present different points of view, and it is significant that a historian of pre-Socratic philosophy has been able to show that the different points of view can be regarded as antilogies or discourses on opposite sides, in that an antithesis is opposed in each case to a thesis. One might even wonder with Alexandre Kojève, the late expert in Hegelian philosophy, whether Hegelian dialectic did not have its origin, not in Platonic dialectic, but rather in the development of philosophical systems that can be opposed as thesis to antithesis, followed by a synthesis of the two. The process is similar to a lawsuit in which the judge identifies the elements he regards as valid in the claims of the opposed parties. For Kant as well as for Hegel, opinions are supposed to be excluded from philosophy, which aims at rationality. But to explain the divergencies that are systematically encountered in the history of philosophy, we need only call these opinions the natural illusions of reason as submitted to the tribunal of critical reason (as in Kant) or successive moments in the progress of reason toward Absolute Spirit (as in Hegel).

To reconcile philosophic claims to rationality with the plurality of philosophic systems, we must recognize that the appeal to reason must be identified not as an appeal to a single truth but instead as an appeal for the adherence of an audience, which can be thought of, after the manner of Kant's categorical imperative, as encompassing all reasonable and competent men. The characteristic aspect of philosophical controversy and of the history of philosophy can only be understood if the appeal to reason is conceived as an appeal to an ideal audience—which I call the universal audience—whether embodied in God, in all reasonable and competent men, in the man deliberating or in an elite. Instead of identifying philosophy with a science, which, on the positivist ideal, could make only analytical judgments, both indisputable and empty, we would do better to abandon the ideal of an apodictic philosophy. We would then have to admit that in the discharge of his specific task, the philosopher has at his disposal only an argumentation that he can endeavor to make as reasonable and systematic as possible without ever being able to make it absolutely compelling or a demonstrative proof. Besides, it is highly unlikely that any reasoning from which we could draw reasons for acting could be conducted under the sign of truth, for these reasons must enable us to justify our actions and decisions. Thus, indirectly, the analysis of philosophical reasoning brings us back to views that are familiar in existentialism.

Audiences display an infinite variety in both extension and competence: in extent, from the audience consisting of a single subject engaged in inward deliberation up to the universal audience; and in competence, from those who know only *loci* up to the specialists who have acquired their knowledge only through a long and painstaking preparation. By thus generalizing the idea of the audience, we can ward off Plato's attack against the rhetoricians for showing greater concern for success than for the truth. To this criticism we can reply that the techniques suited for persuading a crowd in a public place would not be convincing to a better educated and more critical audience, and that the worth of an argumentation is not measured solely by its efficacy but also by the quality of the audience at which it is aimed. Consequently, the idea of a rational argumentation cannot be defined *in abstracto*, since it depends on the historically grounded conception of the universal audience.

The part played by the audience in rhetoric is crucially important, because all argumentation, in aiming to persuade, must be adapted to the audience and, hence, based on beliefs accepted by the audience with such conviction that the rest of the discourse can be securely based upon it. Where this is not the case, one must reinforce adherence to these starting points by means of all available rhetorical techniques before attempting to join the controverted points to them. Indeed, the orator who builds his discourse on premises not accepted by the audience commits a classical fallacy in argumentation—a *petitio principii*. This is not a mistake in formal logic, since formally any proposition implies itself, but it is a mistake in argumentation, because the orator begs the question by presupposing the existence of an adherence that does not exist and to the obtaining of which his efforts should be directed.

The Basis of Agreement

The objects of agreement on which the orator can build his argument are various. On the one hand, there are facts, truths, and presumptions; on the other, values, hierarchies, and *loci* of the preferable.

Facts and truths can be characterized as objects that are already agreed to by the universal audience, and, hence, there is no need to increase the intensity of adherence to them. If we presuppose the coherence of reality and of our truths taken as a whole, there cannot be any conflict between facts or truths on which we would be called to make a decision. What happens when such a conflict seems to occur is that the incompatible element loses its status and becomes either an illusory fact or an apparent truth, unless we can eliminate the incompatibility by showing that the two apparently incompatible truths apply to different fields. We shall return to this argumentative method later when dealing with the dissociation of ideas.

Presumptions are opinions which need not be proved, although adherence to them can be either reinforced, if necessary, or suppressed by proving the opposite. Legal procedure makes abundant use of presumptions, for which it has worked out refined definitions and elaborate rules for their use.

Values are appealed to in order to influence our choices of action. They supply reasons for preferring one type of behavior to another, although not all would necessarily accept them as good reasons. Indeed, most values are particular in that they are accepted only by a particular group. The values that are called universal can be regarded in so many different ways that their universality is better considered as only an aspiration for agreement, since it disappears as soon as one tries to apply one such value to a concrete situation. For argumentation, it is useful to distinguish concrete values, such as one's country, from abstract values, such as justice and truth. It is characteristic of values that they can become the center of conflict without thereby ceasing to be values. This fact explains how real sacrifice is possible, the object renounced being by no means a mere appearance. For this reason, the effort to reinforce adherence to values is never superfluous. Such an effort is undertaken in epideictic discourse, and, in general, all education also endeavors to make certain values preferred to others.

After values, we find that accepted hierarchies play a part in argumentation. Such, for example, are the superiority of men over animals and of adults over children. We also find double hierarchies as in the case in which we rank behavior in accordance with an accepted ranking of the agents. For this reason, such a statement as "You are behaving like a beast" is pejorative, whereas an exhortation to "act like a man" calls for more laudable behavior.

Among all the *loci* studied by Aristotle in his *Topics,* we shall consider only those examined in the third book, which we shall call *loci of the preferable.* They are very general propositions, which can serve, at need, to justify values or hierarchies, but which also have as a special characteristic the ability to evaluate complementary aspects of reality. To *loci of quantity,* such as "That which is more lasting is worth more than that which is less so" or "A thing useful for a large number of persons is worth more than one useful for a smaller number," we can oppose *loci of quality,* which set value upon the unique, the irremediable, the opportune, the rare—that is, to what is exceptional instead of to what is normal. By the use of these *loci,* it is possible to describe the difference between the classical and the romantic spirit.

While it establishes a framework for all nonformal reasoning, whatever its nature, its subject, or audience, the new rhetoric does not pretend to supply a list of all the *loci* and common opinions which can serve as starting points for argumentation. It is sufficient to stress that, in all cases, the orator must know the opinion of his audience on all the questions he intends to deal with, the type of arguments and reasons which seem relevant with regard to both subject and audience, what they are likely to consider as a strong or weak argument, and what might arouse them, as well as what would leave them indifferent.

Quintilian, in his *Institutes of Oratory,* points out the advantage of a public-school education for future orators: it puts them on a par and in fellowship with their audience. This advice is sound as regards argumentation on matters requiring no special knowledge. Otherwise, however, it is indispensable for holding an audience to have had a preliminary initiation into the body of ideas to be discussed.

In discussion with a single person or a small group, the establishment of a starting point is very different from before a large group. The particular opinions and convictions needed may have already been expressed previously, and the orator has no reason to believe that his interlocutors have changed their minds. Or he can use the technique of question and answer to set the premises of his argument on firm ground. Socrates proceeded in this way, taking the interlocutor's assent as a sign of the truth of the accepted thesis. Thus Socrates says to Callicles in the *Gorgias:*

> If you agree with me in an argument about any point, that point will have been sufficiently tested by us, and will not require to be submitted to any further test. For you could not have agreed with me, either from lack of knowledge or from superfluity of modesty, nor yet from a desire to deceive me, for you are my friend, as you tell me yourself. And therefore when you and I are agreed, the result will be the attainment of perfect truth.

It is obvious that such a dialogue is out of the question when one is addressing a numerous assembly. In this case, the discourse must take as premises the presumptions that the orator has learned the audience will accept.

Creating "Presence"

What an audience accepts forms a body of opinion, convictions, and commitments that is both vast and indeterminate. From this body the orator must select certain elements on which he focuses attention by endowing them, as it were, with a "presence." This does not mean that the elements left out are entirely ignored, but they are pushed into the background. Such a choice implicitly sets a value on some aspects of reality rather than others. Recall the lovely Chinese story told by Meng-Tseu: "A king sees an ox on its way to sacrifice. He is moved to pity for it and orders that a sheep be used in its place. He confesses he did so because he could see the ox, but not the sheep."

Things present, things near to us in space and time, act directly on our sensibility. The orator's endeavors often consist, however, in bringing to mind things that are not immediately present. Bacon was well aware of this function of eloquence:

> The affection beholdeth merely the present; reason beholdeth the future and sum of time. And therefore the present filling the imagination more, reason is commonly vanquished; but after that force of eloquence and persuasion hath made things future and remote appear as present, then upon the revolt of the imagination reason prevaileth.

To make "things future and remote appear as present," that is, to create presence, calls for special efforts of presentation. For this purpose all kinds of literary techniques and a number of rhetorical figures have been developed. *Hypotyposis* or *demonstratio,* for example, is defined as a figure "which sets things out in such a way that the matter seems to unfold, and the thing to happen, before our very eyes." Obviously, such a figure is highly important as a persuasive factor. In fact, if their argumentative role is disregarded, the study of figures is a useless pastime, a search for strange names for rather farfetched and affected turns of speech. Other figures, such as *repetition, anaphora, amplification, congerie, metabole, pseudo direct discourse, enallage,* are all various means of increasing the feeling of presence in the audience.

In his description of facts, truths, and values, the orator must employ language that takes into account the classifications and valuations implicit in the audience's acceptance of them. For placing his discourse at the level of generality that he considers best adapted to his purpose and his audience, he has at hand a whole arsenal of linguistic categories—substantives, adjectives, verbs, adverbs—and a vocabulary and phrasing that enable him, under the guise of a descriptive narrative, to stress the main elements and indicate which are merely secondary.

In the selection of data and the interpretation and presentation of them, the orator is subject to the accusation of partiality. Indeed, there is no proof that his presentation has not been distorted by a tendentious vision of things. Hence, in law, the legal counsel must reply to the attorney general, while the judge forms an opinion and renders his decision only after hearing both parties. Although his judgment may appear more balanced, it cannot achieve perfect objectivity—which can only be an ideal. Even with the elimination of tendentious views and of errors, one does not thereby reach a perfectly just decision. So too in scientific or technical discourse, where the orator's freedom of choice is less because he cannot depart, without special reason, from the accepted terminology, value judgments are implicit, and their justification resides in the theories, classifications, and methodology that gave birth to the technical terminology. The idea that science consists of nothing but a body of timeless, objective truths has been increasingly challenged in recent years.

The Structure of Argument

Nonformal argument consists, not of a chain of ideas of which some are derived from others according to accepted rules of inference, but rather of a web formed from all the arguments and all the reasons that combine to achieve the desired result. The purpose of the discourse in general is to bring the audience to the conclusions offered by the orator, starting from premises that they already accept—which is the case unless the orator has been guilty of a *petitio principii.* The argumentative process consists in establishing a link by which acceptance, or adherence, is passed from one element to another, and this end can be reached either by leaving the various elements of the discourse unchanged and associated as they are or by making a dissociation of ideas.

We shall now consider the various types of association and of dissociation that the orator has at his command. To simplify classification, we have grouped the processes of association into three classes: quasi-logical arguments, arguments based upon the structure of the real, and arguments that start from particular cases that are then either generalized or transposed from one sphere of reality to another.

Quasi-Logical Arguments

These arguments are similar to the formal structures of logic and mathematics. In fact, men apparently first came to an understanding of purely formal proof by submitting quasi-logical arguments, such as many of the *loci* listed in Aristotle's *Topics,* to an analysis that yielded precision and formalization. There is a difference of paramount importance between an argument and a formal proof. Instead of using a natural language in which the same word can be used with different meanings, a logical calculus employs an artificial language so constructed that one sign can have only one meaning. In logic, the principle of identity designates a tautology, an indisputable but empty truth, whatever its formulation. But this is not the case in ordinary language. When I say "Business is business," or "Boys will be boys," or "War is war," those hearing the words give preference, not to the univocity of the statement, but to its significant character. They will never take the statements as tautologies, which would make them meaningless, but will look for different plausible interpretations of the same term that will render the whole statement both meaningful and acceptable. Similarly, when faced with a statement that is formally a contradiction—"When two persons do the same thing it is not the same thing," or "We step and we do not step into the same river,"—we look for an interpretation that eliminates the incoherence.

To understand an orator, we must make the effort required to render his discourse coherent and meaningful. This effort requires goodwill and respect for the person who speaks and for what he says. The techniques of formalization make calculation possible, and, as a result, the correctness of the reasoning is capable of mechanical control. This result is not obtained without a certain linguistic rigidity. The language of mathematics is not used for poetry any more than it is used for diplomacy.

Because of its adaptability, ordinary language can always avoid purely formal contradictions. Yet it is not free from incompatibilities, as, for instance, when two norms are recommended which cannot both apply to the same situation. Thus, telling a child not to lie and to obey his parents lays one open to ridicule if the child asks, "What must I do if my father orders me to lie?" When such an antinomy occurs, one seeks for qualifications or amendments—and recommends the primacy of one norm over the other or points out that there are exceptions to the rule. Theoretically, the most elegant way of eliminating an incompatibility is to have recourse to a dissociation of concepts—but of this, more later. Incompatibility is an important element in Socratic irony. By exposing the incompatibility of the answers given to his insidious questions, Socrates compels his interlocutor to abandon certain commonly accepted opinions.

Definitions play a very different role in argumentation from the one they have in a formal system. There they are mostly abbreviations. But in argumentation they determine the choice of one particular meaning over others—sometimes by establishing a relation between an old term and a new one. Definition is regarded as a rhetorical figure—the oratorical definition—when it aims, not at clarifying the meaning of an idea, but at stressing aspects that will produce the persuasive effect that is sought. It is a figure relating to choice: the selection of facts brought to the fore in the definition is unusual because the *definiens* is not serving the purpose of giving the meaning of a term.

Analysis that aims at dividing a concept into all its parts and interpretation that aims at elucidating a text without bringing anything new to it are also quasi-logical arguments and call to mind the principle of identity. This method can give way to figures of speech called *aggregation* and *interpretation* when they serve some purpose other than clarification and tend to reinforce the feeling of presence.

These few examples make it clear that expressions are called figures of style when they display a fixed structure that is easily recognizable and are used for a purpose different from their normal one—this new purpose being mainly one of persuasion. If the figure is so closely interwoven into the argumentation that it appears to be an expression suited to the occasion, it is regarded as an argumentative figure, and its unusual character will often escape notice.

Some reasoning processes—unlike definition or analysis, which aim at complete identification—are content with a partial reduction, that is, with an identification of the main elements. We have an example of this in the rule of justice that equals should be treated equally. If the agents and situations were identical, the application of the rule would take the form of an exact demonstration. As this is never the case, however, a decision will have to be taken about whether the differences are to be disregarded. This is why the recourse to precedent in legal matters is not a completely impersonal procedure but always requires the intervention of a judge.

Arguments of reciprocity are those that claim the same treatment for the antecedent as for the consequent of a relation—buyers-sellers, spectators-actors, etc. These arguments presuppose that the relation is symmetrical. Unseasonable use of them is apt to have comic results, such as the following story, known to have made Kant laugh:

> At Surat an Englishman is pouring out a bottle of ale which is foaming freely. He asks an Indian who is amazed at the sight what it is that he finds so strange. "What bothers me," replies the native, "isn't what is coming out of the bottle, but how you got it in there in the first place."

Other quasi-logical arguments take the transitivity of a relation for granted, even though it is only probable: "My friends' friends are my friends." Still other arguments apply to all kinds of other relations such as that between part and whole or between parts, relations of division, comparison, probability. They are clearly distinct from exact demonstration, since, in each case, complementary, nonformal hypotheses are necessary to render the argument compelling.

Appeal to the Real

Arguments based on the structure of reality can be divided into two groups according as they establish associations of succession or of coexistence.

Among relations of succession, that of causality plays an essential role. Thus we may be attempting to find the causes of an effect, the means to an end, the consequences of a fact, or to judge an action or a rule by the consequences that it has. This last process might be called the pragmatic argument, since it is typical of utilitarianism in morals and of pragmaticism in general.

Arguments establishing relations of coexistence are based on the link that unites a person to his actions. When generalized, this argument establishes the relation between the essence and the act, a relation of paramount importance in the social sciences. From this model have come the classification of periods in history (Antiquity, the Middle Ages), all literary classifications (classicism, romanticism), styles (Gothic, baroque), economic or political systems (feudalism, capitalism, fascism), and institutions (marriage, the church). Rhetoric, conceived as the theory of argumentation, provides a guidance for the understanding both of the manner in which these categories were constituted and of the reasons for doing so. It helps us grasp the advantages and the disadvantages of using them and provides an insight into the value judgments that were present, explicitly or implicitly, when they took shape. The specificity of the social sciences can be best understood by considering the methodological reasons justifying the constitution of their categories—Max Weber's *Idealtypus*.

Thanks to the relations of coexistence, we are also able to gain an understanding of the argument from authority in all its shapes as well as an appreciation of the persuasive role of *ethos* in argumentation, since the discourse can be regarded as an act on the orator's part.

Establishing the Real

Arguments attempting to establish the structure of reality are first arguments by example, illustration, and model; second, arguments by analogy.

The example leads to the formulation of a rule through generalization from a particular case or through putting a new case on the same footing as an older one. Illustration aims at achieving presence for a rule by illustrating it with a concrete case. The argument from a model justifies an action by showing that it conforms to a model. One should also mention the argument from an antimodel; for example, the drunken Helot to whom the Spartans referred as a foil to show their sons how they should not behave.

In the various religions, God and all divine or quasi-divine persons are obviously preeminent models for their believers. Christian morality can be defined as the imitation of Christ, whereas Buddhist morality consists in imitating Buddha. The models that a culture proposes to its members for imitation provide a convenient way of characterizing it.

The argument from analogy is extremely important in nonformal reasoning. Starting from a relation between two terms *A* and *B*, which we call the *theme* since it provides the proper subject matter of the discourse, we can by analogy present its structure or establish its value by relating it to the terms *C* and *D*, which constitute the *phoros* of the analogy, so that *A* is to *B* as *C* is to *D*. Analogy, which derives its name from the Greek word for proportion, is nevertheless different from mathematical proportion. In the latter the characteristic relation of equality is symmetrical, whereas the *phoros* called upon to clarify the structure or establish the value of the *theme* must, as a rule, be better known than the *theme*. When Heraclitus says that in the eyes of God man is as childish as a child is in the eyes of an adult, it is impossible to change the *phoros* for the *theme*, and vice versa, unless the audience is one that knows the relationship between God and man better than that between a child and an adult. It is also worth noting that when *man* is identified with *adult*, the analogy reduces to three terms, the middle one being repeated twice: *C* is to *B* as *B* is to *A*. This technique of argumentation is typical of Plato, Plotinus, and all those who establish hierarchies within reality.

Within the natural sciences the use of analogy is mainly heuristic, and the intent is ultimately to eliminate the analogy and replace it with a formula of a mathematical type. Things are different, however, in the social sciences and in philosophy, where the whole body of facts under study only offers reasons for or against a particular analogical vision of things. This is one of the differences to which Wilhelm Dilthey refers when he claims that the natural sciences aim at explaining whereas the human sciences seek for understanding.

The metaphor is the figure of style corresponding to the argument from analogy. It consists of a condensed analogy in which one term of the *theme* is associated with one term of the *phoros*. Thus "the morning of life" is a metaphor that summarizes the analogy: Morning is to day what youth is to life. Of course, in the case of a good many metaphors, the reconstruction of the complete analogy is neither easy nor unambiguous. When Berkeley, in his *Dialogues,* speaks of "an ocean of false learning," there are various ways to supply the missing terms of the analogy, each one of which stresses a different relation unexpressed in the metaphor.

The use of analogies and metaphors best reveals the creative and literary aspects of argumentation. For some audiences their use should be avoided as much as possible, whereas for others the lack of them may make the discourse appear too technical and too difficult to follow. Specialists tend to hold analogies in suspicion and use them only to initiate students into their discipline. Scientific popularization makes extensive use of analogy, and only from time to time will the audience be reminded of the danger of identification of *theme* and *phoros.*

The Dissociation of Ideas

Besides argumentative associations, we must also make room for the dissociation of ideas, the study of which is too often neglected by the rhetorical tradition. Dissociation is the classical solution for incompatibilities that call for an alteration of conventional ways of thinking. Philosophers, by using dissociation, often depart from common sense and form a vision of reality that is free from the contradictions of opinion. The whole of the great metaphysical tradition, from Parmenides to our own day, displays a succession of dissociations where, in each case, reality is opposed to appearance.

Normally, reality is perceived through appearances that are taken as signs referring to it. When, however, appearances are incompatible—an oar in water looks broken but feels straight to the touch—we must admit, if we are to have a coherent picture of reality, that some appearances are illusory and may lead us to error regarding the real. One is thus brought to the construction of a conception of reality that at the same time is capable of being used as a criterion for judging appearances. Whatever is conformable to it is given value, whereas whatever is opposed is denied value and is considered a mere appearance.

Any idea can be subjected to a similar dissociation. To real justice we can oppose apparent justice and with real democracy contrast apparent democracy, or formal or nominal democracy, or quasi democracy, or even "democracy" (in quotes). What is thus referred to as apparent is usually what the audience would normally call justice, democracy, etc. It only becomes apparent after the criterion of real justice or real democracy has been applied to it and reveals the error concealed under the name. The dissociation results in a depreciation of what had until then been an accepted value and in its replacement by another conception to which is accorded the original value. To effect such a depreciation, one will need a conception that can be shown to be valuable, relevant, as well as incompatible with the common use of the same notion.

We may call "philosophical pairs" all sets of notions that are formed on the model of the "appearance-reality" pair. The use of such pairs makes clear how philosophical ideas are developed and also shows how they cannot be dissociated from the process of giving or denying value that is typical of all ontologies. One thus comes to see the importance of argumentative devices in the development of thought, and especially of philosophy.

Interaction of Arguments

An argumentation is ordinarily a spoken or written discourse, of variable length, that combines a great number of arguments with the aim of winning the adherence of an audience to one or more theses. These arguments interact within the minds of the audience, reinforcing or weakening each other. They also interact with the arguments of the opponents as well as with those that arise spontaneously in the minds of the audience. This situation gives rise to a number of theoretical questions.

Are there limits, for example, to the number of arguments that can be usefully accumulated? Does the choice of arguments and the scope of the argumentation raise special problems? What is a weak or an irrelevant argument? What is the effect of a weak argument on the whole argumentation? Are there any criteria for assessing the strength or relevance of an argument? Are such matters relative to the audience, or can they be determined objectively?

We have no general answer to such questions. The answer seems to depend on the field of study and on the philosophy that controls its organization. In any case, they are questions that have seldom been raised and that never have received a satisfactory answer. Before any satisfactory answer can be given, it will be necessary to make many detailed studies in the various disciplines, taking account of the most varied audiences.

Once our arguments have been formulated, does it make any difference what order they are presented in? Should one start, or finish, with strong arguments, or do both by putting the weaker arguments in the middle—the so-called Nestorian order? This way of presenting the problem implies that the force of an argument is independent of its place in the discourse. Yet, in fact, the opposite seems to be true, for what appears as a weak argument to one audience often appears as a strong argument to another, depending on whether the presuppositions rejected by one audience are accepted by the other. Should we present our arguments then in the order that lends them the greatest force? If so, there should be a special technique devoted to the organization of a discourse.

Such a technique would have to point out that an exordium is all-important in some cases, while in others it is entirely superfluous. Sometimes the objections of one's opponent ought to be anticipated beforehand and refuted, whereas in other cases it is better to let the objections arise spontaneously lest one appear to be tearing down straw men.

In all such matters it seems unlikely that any hard-and-fast rules can be laid down, since one must take account of the particular character of the audience, of its evolution during the debate, and of the fact that habits and procedures that prove good in one sphere are no good in another. A general rhetoric cannot be fixed by precepts and rules laid down once for all. But it must be able to adapt itself to the most varied circumstances, matters, and audiences.

Reason and Rhetoric

The birth of a new period of culture is marked by an eruption of original ideas and a neglect of methodological concerns and of academic classifications and divisions. Ideas are used with various meanings that the future will distinguish and disentangle. The fundamental ideas of Greek philosophy offer a good example of this process. One of the richest and most confused of all is that expressed by the term *logos,* which means among other things: word, reason, discourse, reasoning, calculation, and all that was later to become the subject of logic and the expression of reason. Reason was opposed to desire and the passions, being regarded as the faculty that ought to govern human behavior in the name of truth and wisdom. The operation of *logos* takes effect either through long speeches or through questions and answers, thus giving rise to the distinction noted above between rhetoric and dialectic, even before logic was established as an autonomous discipline.

Aristotle's discovery of the syllogism and his development of the theory of demonstrative science raised the problem of the relation of syllogistic—the first formal logic—with dialectic and rhetoric. Can any and every form of reasoning be expressed syllogistically? Aristotle is often thought to have aimed at such a result, at least for deductive reasoning, since he was well aware that inductive reasoning and argument by example are entirely different from deduction. He knew too that the dialectical reasoning characteristic of discussion, and essentially critical in purpose, differed widely from demonstrative reasoning deducing from principles the conclusions of a science. Yet he was content to locate the difference in the kind of premises used in the two cases. In analytical, or demonstrative, reasoning, the premises, according to Aristotle, are true and ultimate, or else derived from such premises, whereas in dialectical reasoning the premises consist of generally accepted opinions. The nature of reasoning in both cases was held to be the same, consisting in drawing conclusions from propositions posited as premises.

Rhetoric, on the other hand, was supposed to use syllogisms in a peculiar way, by leaving some premises unexpressed and so transforming them into enthymemes. The orator, as Aristotle saw, could not be said to use regular syllogisms; hence, his reasoning was said to consist of abbreviated syllogisms and of arguments from example, corresponding to induction.

What are we to think of this reduction to two forms of reasoning of all the wide variety of arguments that men use in their discussions and in pleading a cause or justifying an action? Yet, since the time of Aristotle, logic has confined its study to deductive and inductive reasoning, as though any argument differing from these was due to the variety of its content and not to its form. As a result, an argument that cannot be reduced to canonical form is regarded as logically valueless. What then about reasoning from analogy? What about the *a fortiori* argument? Must we, in using such arguments, always be able to introduce a fictive unexpressed major premise, so as to make them conform to the syllogism?

It can be shown that the practical reasoning involved in choice or decision making can always be expressed in the form of theoretical reasoning by introducing additional premises. But what is gained by such a move? The reasoning by which new premises are introduced is merely concealed, and resort to these premises appears entirely arbitrary, although in reality it too is the outcome of a decision that can be justified only in an argumentative, and not in a demonstrative, manner.

At first sight, it appears that the main difference between rhetoric and dialectic, according to Aristotle, is that the latter employs impersonal techniques of reasoning, whereas rhetoric relies on the orator's *ethos* (or character) and on the manner in which he appeals to the passions of his audience (or *pathos*). For Aristotle, however, the *logos* or use of reasoning is the main thing, and he criticizes those authors before him, who laid the emphasis upon oratorical devices designed to arouse the passions. Thus he writes:

> If the rules for trials which are now laid down in some states—especially in well-governed states—were applied everywhere, such people would have nothing to say. All men, no doubt, *think* that the laws should prescribe such rules, but some, as in the court of Areopagus, give practical effect to their thoughts and forbid talk about non-essentials. This is sound law and custom. It

is not right to pervert the judge by moving him to anger or envy or pity—one might as well warp a carpenter's rule before using it.

For this reason, after a long discussion devoted to the role of passion in oratorical art, he concludes:

As a matter of fact, it [rhetoric] is a branch of dialectic and similar to it, as we said at the outset.

To sum up, it appears that Aristotle's conception, which is essentially empirical and based on the analysis of the material he had at his disposal, distinguishes dialectic from rhetoric only by the type of audience and, especially, by the nature of the questions examined in practice. His precepts are easy to understand when we keep in mind that he was thinking primarily of the debates held before assemblies of citizens gathered together either to deliberate on political or legal matters or to celebrate some public ceremony. There is no reason, however, why we should not also consider theoretical and, especially, philosophical questions expounded in unbroken discourse. In this case, the techniques Aristotle would have presumably recommended would be those he himself used in his own work, following the golden rule that he laid down in his *Nicomachean Ethics,* that the method used for the examination and exposition of each particular subject must be appropriate to the matter, whatever its manner of presentation.

After Aristotle, dialectic became identified with logic as a technique of reasoning, due to the influence of the Stoics. As a result, rhetoric came to be regarded as concerned only with the irrational parts of our being, whether will, the passions, imagination, or the faculty for aesthetic pleasure. Those who, like Seneca and Epictetus, believed that the philosopher's role was to bring man to submit to reason were opposed to rhetoric, even when they used it, in the name of philosophy. Those like Cicero, on the other hand, who thought that in order to induce man to submit to reason one had to have recourse to rhetoric, recommended the union of philosophy and eloquence. The thinkers of the Renaissance followed suit, such as Valla, and Bacon too, who expected rhetoric to act on the imagination to secure the triumph of reason.

The more rationalist thinkers, like Ramus, as we have already noted, considered rhetoric as merely an ornament and insisted on a separation of form and content, the latter alone being thought worthy of a philosopher's attention. Descartes adopted the same conception and reinforced it. He regarded the geometrical method as the only method fit for the sciences as well as for philosophy and opposed rhetoric as exerting an action upon the will contrary to reason—thus adopting the position of the Stoics but with a different methodological justification. But to make room for eloquence within this scheme, we need only deny that reason possesses a monopoly of the approved way of influencing the will. Thus, Pascal, while professing a rationalism in a Cartesian manner, does not hesitate to declare that the truths that are most significant for him—that is, the truths of faith—have to be received by the heart before they can be accepted by reason:

> We all know that opinions are admitted into the soul through two entrances, which are its chief powers, understanding and will. The more natural entrance is the understanding, for we should never agree to anything but demonstrated truths, but the more usual entrance, although against nature, is the will; for all men whatsoever are almost always led into belief not because a thing is proved but because it is pleasing. This way is low, unworthy, and foreign to our nature. Therefore everybody disavows it. Each of us professes to give his belief and even his love only where he knows it is deserved.
>
> I am not speaking here of divine truths, which I am far from bringing under the art of persuasion, for they are infinitely above nature. God alone can put them into the soul, and in whatever way He pleases. I know He has willed they should enter into the mind from the heart and not into the heart from the mind, that He might make humble that proud power of reason. . . .

To persuade about divine matters, grace is necessary; it will make us love that which religion orders us to love. Yet it is also Pascal's intention to conduce to this result by his eloquence, although he has to admit that he can lay down the precepts of this eloquence only in a very general way:

> It is apparent that, no matter what we wish to persuade of, we must consider the person concerned, whose mind and heart we must know, what principles he admits, what things he loves, and then observe in the thing in question what relations it has to these admitted principles or to these objects of delight. So that the art of persuasion consists as much in knowing how to please as in knowing how to convince, so much more do men follow caprice than reason.
>
> Now of these two, the art of convincing and the art of pleasing, I shall confine myself here to the rules of the first, and to them only in the case where the principles have been granted and are held to unwaveringly; otherwise I do not know whether there would be an art for adjusting the proofs to the inconstancy of our caprices.
>
> But the art of pleasing is incomparably more difficult, more subtle, more useful, and more wonderful, and therefore if I do not deal with it, it is because I am not able. Indeed I feel myself so unequal to its regulation that I believe it to be a thing impossible.
>
> Not that I do not believe there are as certain rules for pleasing as for demonstrating, and that whoever should be able perfectly to know and to practice them would be as certain to succeed in making himself loved by kings and by every kind of person as in demonstrating the elements of geometry to those who have imagination enough to grasp the hypotheses. But I consider, and it is perhaps my weakness that leads me to think so, that it is impossible to lay hold of the rules.

Pascal's reaction here with regard to formal rules of rhetoric already heralds romanticism with its reverence for the great orator's genius. But before romanticism held sway, associationist psychology developed in eighteenth-century England. According to the thinkers of this school, feeling, not reason, determines man's behavior, and books on rhetoric were written based on this psychology. The best known of these is Campbell's *The Philosophy of Rhetoric,* noted above. Fifty years later, Whately, following Bacon's lead, defined the subject of logic and of rhetoric as follows:

> I remarked in treating of that Science [Logic], that Reasoning may be considered as applicable to two purposes, which I ventured to designate respectively by the terms "Inferring" and "Proving," i.e., the *ascertainment* of the truth by investigation and the *establishment* of it to the satisfaction of *another;* and I there remarked that Bacon, in his *Organon,* has laid down rules for the conduct of the former of these processes, and that the latter belongs to the province of Rhetoric; and it was added, that to *infer,* is to be regarded as the proper office of the Philosopher, or the Judge;—to *prove,* of the Advocate.

This conception, while stressing the social importance of rhetoric, makes it a negligible factor for the philosopher. This tendency increases under the influence of Kant and of the German idealists, who boasted of removing all matters of opinion from philosophy, for which only apodictic truths are of any importance.

The relation between the idea that we form of reason and the role assigned to rhetoric is of sufficient importance to deserve studies of all the great thinkers who have said anything about the matter—studies similar to those of Bacon by Prof. Karl Wallace and of Ramus by Prof. Walter J. Ong. In what follows, I would like to sketch how the positivist climate of logical empiricism makes possible a new, or renovated, conception of rhetoric.

Within the perspective of neopositivism, the rational is restricted to what experience and formal logic enable us to verify and demonstrate. As a result, the vast sphere of all that is concerned with action—except for the choice of the most adequate means to reach a designated end—is turned over to the irrational. The very idea of a reasonable decision has no meaning and cannot even be defined satisfactorily with respect to the *whole* action in which it occurs. Logical empiricism has at its disposal no technique of justification except one founded on the theory of probability. But why should one prefer one action to another? Only because it is more efficacious? How can one choose between the various ends that one can aim at? If quantitative measures are the only ones that can be taken into account, the only reasonable decision would seem to be one that is in conformity with utilitarian calculations. If so, all ends would be reduced to a single one of pleasure or utility, and all conflicts of values would be dismissed as based on futile ideologies.

Now if one is not prepared to accept such a limitation to a monism of values in the world of action and would reject such a reduction on the ground that the irreducibility of many values is the basis of our freedom and of our spiritual life; if one considers how justification takes place in the most varied spheres—in politics, morals, law, the social sciences, and, above all, in philosophy—it seems obvious that our intellectual tools cannot all be reduced to formal logic, even when that is enlarged by a theory for the control of induction and the choice of the most efficacious techniques. In this situation, we are compelled to develop a theory of argumentation as an indispensable tool for practical reason.

In such a theory, as we have seen, argumentation is made relative to the adherence of minds, that is, to an audience, whether an individual deliberating or mankind as addressed by the philosopher in his appeal to reason. Whately's distinction between logic, as supplying rules of reasoning for the judge, and rhetoric, providing precepts for the counsel, falls to the ground as being without foundation. Indeed, the counsel's speech that aims at convincing the judge cannot rest on any different kind of reasoning than that which the judge uses himself. The judge, having heard both parties, will be better informed and able to compare the arguments on both sides, but his judgment will contain a justification in no way different in kind from that of the counsel's argumentation. Indeed, the ideal counsel's speech is precisely one that provides the judge with all the information that he needs to state the grounds for his decision.

If rhetoric is regarded as complementary to formal logic and argumentation as complementary to demonstrative proof, it becomes of paramount importance in philosophy, since no philosophic discourse can develop without resorting to it. This became clear when, under the influence of logical empiricism, all philosophy that could not be reduced to calculation was considered as nonsense and of no worth. Philosophy, as a consequence, lost its status in contemporary culture. This situation can be changed only by developing a philosophy and a methodology of the reasonable. For if the rational is restricted to the field of calculation, measuring, and weighing, the reasonable is left with the vast field of all that is not amenable to quantitative and formal techniques. This field, which Plato and Aristotle began to explore by means of dialectical and rhetorical devices, lies open for investigation by the new rhetoric.

Further Developments

I introduced the new rhetoric to the public for the first time over twenty years ago, in a lecture delivered in 1949 at the Institut des Hautes Etudes de Belgique. In the course of the same year, the Centre National de Recherches de Logique was founded with the collaboration of the professors of logic in the Belgian universities. In 1953 this group organized an international colloquium on the theory of proof, in which the use and method of proof was studied in the deductive sciences, in the natural sciences, in law, and in philosophy—that is, in the fields where recourse to reasoning is essential. On that occasion Prof. Gilbert Ryle presented his famous paper entitled "Proofs in Philosophy," which claims that there are no proofs in philosophy: "Philosophers do not provide proofs any more than tennis players score goals. Tennis players do not try in vain to score goals. Nor do philosophers try in vain to provide proofs; they are not inefficient or tentative provers. Goals do not belong to tennis, nor proofs to philosophy."

What, then, is philosophical reasoning? What are "philosophical arguments"? According to Ryle, "they are operations not *with* premises and conclusions, but operations *upon* operations with premises and conclusions. In proving something, we are putting propositions through inference-hoops. In some philosophical arguments, we are matching the hoops through which certain batches of propositions will go against a worded recipe declaring what hoops they should go through. Proving is a one-level business; philosophical arguing is, anyhow sometimes, an interlevel business."

If the notion of proof is restricted to the operation of drawing valid inferences, it is undeniable that philosophers and jurists only rarely prove what they assert. Their reasoning, however, does aim at justifying the points that they make, and such reasoning provides an example of the argumentation with which the new rhetoric is concerned.

The part played by argumentation in philosophy has given rise to numerous discussions and to increasing interest, as is shown by the special issue of the *Revue Internationale de Philosophie* of 1961 devoted to the subject, by the colloquium on philosophical argumentation held in Mexico City in 1963, by the collection of studies published by Maurice Natanson and Henry W. Johnstone, Jr., entitled *Philosophy, Rhetoric and Argumentation,* and by the special number of *The Monist* in 1964 on the same subject.

Professor Johnstone has for many years been particularly interested in this topic and has published a book and many papers on it. To further the study of the relation between philosophy and rhetoric, he organized with Prof. Robert T. Oliver, then head of the Speech Department at Pennsylvania State University, a colloquium in which philosophers and members of the speech profession met in equal numbers to discuss the question. The interest aroused by this initiative led to the founding in 1968 of a journal called *Philosophy and Rhetoric,* edited jointly by Professor Johnstone and Prof. Carroll C. Arnold.

That so much attention should be focused on argumentation in philosophical thought cannot be understood unless one appreciates the paramount importance of practical reason—that is, of finding "good reasons" to justify a decision. In 1954 I drew attention to the role of decision in the theory of knowledge, and Gidon Gottlieb further developed it, with particular attention to law, in his book *The Logic of Choice.*

Argumentation concerning decision, choice, and action in general is closely connected with the idea of justification, which also is an important element in the idea of justice. I have attempted to show that the traditional view is mistaken in claiming that justification is like demonstration but based on normative principles. In fact, justification never directly concerns a proposition but looks instead to an attitude, a decision, or an action. "Justifying a proposition" actually consists in justifying one's adherence to it, whether it is a statement capable of verification or an unverifiable norm. A question of justification ordinarily arises only in a situation that has given rise to criticism: no one is called upon to justify behavior that is beyond reproach. Such criticism, however, would be meaningless unless some accepted norm, end, or value had been infringed upon or violated. A decision or an action is criticized on the ground that it is immoral, illegal, unreasonable, or inefficient—that is, it fails to respect certain accepted rules or values. It always occurs within a social context; it is always "situated." Criticism and justification are two forms of argumentation that call for the giving of reasons for or against, and it is these reasons that ultimately enable us to call the action or decision reasonable or unreasonable.

In 1967 a colloquium was held on the subject of demonstration, verification, justification, organized jointly by the Institut International de Philosophie and the Centre National de Recherches de Logique. At that meeting I emphasized the central role of justification in philosophy. Among other things, it enables us to understand the part played by the principle of induction in scientific methodology. Prof. A. J. Ayer claimed that the principle of induction cannot be based on probability theory; yet it did seem possible to give good reasons for using induction as a heuristic principle. But this is only a particular case of the use of justification in philosophy. It is essential wherever practical reason is involved.

In morals, for example, reasoning is neither deductive nor inductive, but justificative. Lucien Lévy-Bruhl, in his famous book *La Morale et la science des moeurs* (1903), criticized the deductive character of much traditional moral philosophy and proposed the conception of the science of morals that made it a sociological discipline, inductive in character. Yet in morals absolute preeminence cannot be given either to principles—which would make morals a deductive discipline—or to the particular case—which would make it an inductive discipline. Instead, judgments regarding particulars are compared with principles, and preference is given to one or the other according to a decision that is reached by resorting to the techniques of justification and argumentation.

The idea of natural law is also misconceived when it is posed in ontological terms. Are there rules of natural law that can be known objectively? Or is positive law entirely arbitrary as embodying the lawmaker's sovereign will? A satisfactory positive answer cannot be given to either question. We know that it is imperative for a lawmaker not to make unreasonable laws; yet we know too that there is no one single manner, objectively given, for making just and reasonable laws. Natural law is better considered as a body of general principles or *loci*, consisting of ideas such as "the nature of things," "the rule of law," and of rules such as "No one is expected to perform impossibilities," "Both sides should be heard"—all of which are capable of being applied in different ways. It is the task of the legislator or judge to decide which of the not unreasonable solutions should become a rule of positive law. Such a view, according to Michel Villey, corresponds to the idea of natural law found in Aristotle and St. Thomas Aquinas—what he calls the classical natural law.

For government to be considered legitimate, to have authority, there must be some way of justifying it. Without some reasonable argumentation for it, political power would be based solely on force. If it is to obtain respect, and not only obedience, and gain the citizens' acceptance, it must have some justification other than force. All political philosophy, in fact, aims at criticizing and justifying claims to the legitimate exercise of power.

Argumentation establishes a link between political philosophy and law and shows that the legislator's activity is not merely an expression of unenlightened will. From lack of such a theory, Hume and Kelsen were right in making a sharp distinction between what is and what ought to be and claiming that no inference can be made from one to the other. Things take a different outlook, however, when one recognizes the importance of argumentation in supplying good reasons for establishing and interpreting norms. Kelsen's pure theory of the law then loses the main part of its logical justification. The same befalls Alf Ross's realist theory of the law, as has been shown in the remarkable essay by Prof. Stig Jørgensen.

The new rhetoric has also been used to throw new light upon the educator's task, on the analysis of political propaganda, on the process of literary creation, as well as on the reasoning of the historian. But it is in the field of law that it has made the largest impact. Recent studies and colloquia devoted to the logic of law testify to the keen interest that the subject has aroused, especially among French-speaking jurists. The faculty of law at Brussels has just inaugurated a new series of lectures, entitled "Logic and Argumentation."

Lawyers and philosophers working in collaboration have shown that the theory of argumentation can greatly illuminate the nature of legal reasoning. The judge is obliged by law to pass sentence on a case that comes before him. Thus Article 4 of the Code Napoléon declares: "The judge who, under pretext of the silence, the obscurity, or the incompleteness of the law, refuses to pass sentence is liable to prosecution for the denial of justice." He may not limit himself to declaring that there is an antinomy or lacuna in the legal system that he has to apply. He cannot, like the mathematician or formal logician, point out that the system is incoherent or incomplete. He must himself solve the antinomy or fill in the lacuna. Ordinary logic by itself would suffice to show the existence of either an antinomy or a lacuna, but it cannot get him out of the resulting dilemma: only legal logic based on argumentation can accomplish that.

To conclude this general, but far from exhaustive, survey, it is necessary to stress again the import that the new rhetoric is having for philosophy and the study of its history. Twenty years ago, for example, the *Topics* and *Rhetoric* of Aristotle were completely ignored by philosophers, whereas today they are receiving much attention. Renewed interest in this hitherto ignored side of Aristotle has thrown new light upon his entire metaphysics and attached new importance to his notion of *phronesis* or prudence. Renewed attention is being given to the classical rhetoric of Cicero, and we are now gaining a better understanding of the historical development of rhetoric and logic during the Middle Ages and the Renaissance.

It is possible too that the new rhetoric may provoke a reconsideration of the Hegelian conception of dialectic with its thesis and antithesis culminating in a synthesis, which might be compared to a reasonable judge who retains the valid part from antilogies. This new rhetorical perspective may also help us to a better understanding of the American pragmatists, especially of C. S. Peirce, who, in his approximation to Hegel's objective logic, aimed at developing a *rhetorica speculativa*.

For these inquiries to be pursued, however, the theory of argumentation must awaken the interest of philosophers and not merely that of lawyers and members of the speech profession. In a synoptic study of the subject, Professor Johnstone deplores the fact that the theory of argumentation is still little known in the United States, although it is now well known in Europe. Attention has been focused on the problems raised by the use of practical reason, and the field has been explored and mapped by theoreticians and practitioners of the law. There is much that philosophers could learn from this work if they would cease confining their methodological inquiries to what can be accomplished by formal logic and the analysis of language. A more dynamic approach to the problems of language would also reveal the extent to which language, far from being only an instrument for communication, is also a tool for action and is well adapted to such a purpose. It may even prove possible to achieve a synthesis of the different and seemingly opposed tendencies of contemporary philosophy, such as existentialism, pragmaticism, analytical philosophy, and perhaps even a new version of Hegelian and Marxist dialectic.

MICHEL FOUCAULT
1926–1984

A French historian who used philosophy to develop his theories, Michel Foucault is known for his method of examining discourse that mirrors a society within some historical time frame. He taught in the 1960s and in 1970 was awarded the highest position in the French university system, a professorship at the College de France. Drawing on rhetoric to blur boundaries among social science disciplines, Foucault argued that because society constructs its own knowledge through patterns of discourse that reflect shared values or knowledge, it thus controls received knowledge. More specifically, socially constructed knowledge extends to the author's function. Rather than always being in superior position to the text, the author's role changes historically, sometimes foregrounded, sometimes disappearing. One of Foucault's particular interests was the history of attitudes toward mental illness, which he traced in Madness and Civilization *(1961). Other books that have influenced both rhetoric and literary theory are* Discipline and Punish *(1979),* The History of Sexuality *(1976),* The Order of Things *(1973), and* The Archaeology of Knowledge *(1972).*

What Is an Author?

In proposing this slightly odd question, I am conscious of the need for an explanation. To this day, the "author" remains an open question both with respect to its general function within discourse and in my own writings; that is, this question permits me to return to certain aspects of my own work which now appear ill-advised and misleading. In this regard, I wish to propose a necessary criticism and reevaluation.

For instance, my objective in *The Order of Things* had been to analyze verbal clusters as discursive layers which fall outside the familiar categories of a book, a work, or an author. But while I considered "natural history," the "analysis of wealth," and "political economy" in general terms, I neglected a similar analysis of the author and his works; it is perhaps due to this omission that I employed the names of authors throughout this book in a naive and often crude fashion. I spoke of Buffon, Cuvier, Ricardo, and others as well, but failed to realize that I had allowed their names to function ambiguously. This has proved an embarassment to me in that my oversight has served to raise two pertinent objections.

It was argued that I had not properly described Buffon or his work and that my handling of Marx was pitifully inadequate in terms of the totality of his thought. Although these objections were obviously justified, they ignored the task I had set myself: I had no intention of describing Buffon or Marx or of reproducing their statements or implicit meanings, but, simply stated, I wanted to locate the rules that formed a certain number of concepts and theoretical relationships in their works. In addition, it was argued that I had created monstrous families by bringing together names as disparate as Buffon and Linnaeus or in placing Cuvier next to Darwin in defiance of the most readily observable family resemblances and natural ties. This objection also seems inappropriate since I had never tried to establish a genealogical table of exceptional individuals, nor was I concerned in forming an intellectual daguerreotype of the scholar or naturalist of the seventeenth and eighteenth century. In fact, I had no intention of forming any family, whether holy or perverse. On the contrary, I wanted to determine—a much more modest task—the functional conditions of specific discursive practices.

Then why did I use the names of authors in *The Order of Things?* Why not avoid their use altogether, or, short of that, why not define the manner in which they were used? These questions appear fully justified and I have tried to gauge their implications and consequences in a book that will appear shortly. These questions have determined my effort to situate comprehensive discursive units, such as "natural history" or "political economy," and to establish the methods and instruments for delimiting, analyzing, and describing these unities. Nevertheless, as a privileged moment of individualization in the history of ideas, knowledge, and literature, or in the history of philosophy and science, the question of the author demands a more direct response. Even now, when we study the history of a concept, a literary genre, or a branch of philosophy, these concerns assume a relatively weak and secondary position in relation to the solid and fundamental role of an author and his works.

For the purposes of this paper, I will set aside a sociohistorical analysis of the author as an individual and the numerous questions that deserve attention in this context: how the author was individualized in a culture such as ours; the status we have given the author, for instance, when we began our research into authenticity and attribution; the systems of valorization in which he was included; or the moment when the stories of heroes gave way to an author's biography; the conditions that fostered the formulation of the fundamental critical category of "the man and his work." For the time being, I wish to restrict myself to the singular relationship that holds between an author and a text, the manner in which a text apparently points to this figure who is outside and precedes it.

Beckett supplies a direction: "What matter who's speaking, someone said, what matter who's speaking." In an indifference such as this we must recognize one of the fundamental ethical principles of contemporary writing. It is not simply "ethical" because it characterizes our way of speaking and writing, but because it stands as an immanent rule, endlessly adopted and yet never fully applied. As a principle, it dominates writing as an ongoing practice and slights our customary attention to the finished product. For the sake of illustration, we need only consider two of its major themes. First, the writing of our day has freed itself from the necessity of "expression"; it only refers to itself, yet it is not restricted to the confines of interiority. On the contrary, we recognize it in its exterior deployment. This reversal transforms writing into an interplay of signs, regulated less by the content it signifies than by the very nature of the signifier. Moreover, it implies an action that is always testing the limits of its regularity, transgressing and reversing an order that it accepts and manipulates. Writing unfolds like a game that inevitably moves beyond its own rules and finally leaves them behind. Thus, the essential basis of this writing is not the exalted emotions related to the act of composition or the insertion of a subject into language. Rather, it is primarily concerned with creating an opening where the writing subject endlessly disappears.

The second theme is even more familiar: it is the kinship between writing and death. This relationship inverts the age-old conception of Greek narrative or epic, which was designed to guarantee the immortality of a hero. The hero accepted an early death because his life, consecrated and magnified by death, passed into immortality; and the narrative redeemed his acceptance of death. In a different sense, Arabic stories, and *The Arabian Nights* in particular, had as their motivation, their theme and pretext, this strategy for defeating death. Storytellers continued their narratives late into the night to forestall death and to delay the inevitable moment when everyone must fall silent. Scheherazade's story is a desperate inversion of murder; it is the effort, throughout all those nights, to exclude death from the circle of existence. This conception of a spoken or written narrative as a protection against death has been transformed by our culture. Writing is now linked to sacrifice and to the sacrifice of life itself; it is a voluntary obliteration of the self that does not require representation in books because it takes place in the everyday existence of the writer. Where a work had the duty of creating immortality, it now attains the right to kill, to become the murderer of its author. Flaubert, Proust, and Kafka are obvious examples of this reversal. In addition, we find the link between writing and death manifested in the total effacement of the individual characteristics of the writer; the quibbling and confrontations that a writer generates between himself and his text cancel out the signs of his particular individuality. If we wish to know the writer in our day, it will be through the singularity of his absence and in his link to death, which has transformed him into a victim of his own writing. While all of this is familiar in philosophy, as in literary criticism, I am not certain that the consequences derived from the disappearance or death of the author have been fully explored or that the importance of this event has been appreciated. To be specific, it seems to me that the themes destined to replace the privileged position accorded the author have merely served to arrest the possibility of genuine change. Of these, I will examine two that seem particularly important.

To begin with, the thesis concerning a work. It has been understood that the task of criticism is not to reestablish the ties between an author and his work or to reconstitute an author's thought and experience through his works and, further, that criticism should concern itself with the structures of a work, its architectonic forms, which are studied for their intrinsic and internal relationships. Yet, what of a context that questions the concept of a work? What, in short, is the strange unit designated by the term, work? What is necessary to its composition, if a work is not something written by a person called an "author"? Difficulties arise on all sides if we raise the question in this way. If an individual is not an author, what are we to make of those things he has written or said, left among his papers or communicated to others? Is this not properly a work? What, for instance, were Sade's papers before he was consecrated as an author? Little more, perhaps, than rolls of paper on which he endlessly unravelled his fantasies while in prison.

Assuming that we are dealing with an author, is everything he wrote and said, everything he left behind, to be included in his work? This problem is both theoretical and practical. If we wish to publish the complete works of Nietzsche, for example, where do we draw the line? Certainly, everything must be published, but can we agree on what "everything" means? We will, of course, include everything that Nietzsche himself published, along with the drafts of his works, his plans for aphorisms, his marginal notations and corrections. But what if, in a notebook filled with aphorisms, we find a reference, a reminder of an appointment, an address, or a laundry bill, should this be included in his works? Why not? These practical considerations are endless once we consider how a work can be extracted from the millions of traces left by an individual after his death. Plainly, we lack a theory to encompass the questions generated by a work and the empirical activity of those who naively undertake the publication of the complete works of an author often suffers from the absence of this framework. Yet more questions arise. Can we say that *The Arabian Nights*, and *Stromates* of Clement of Alexandria, or the *Lives* of Diogenes Laertes constitute works? Such questions only begin to suggest the range of our difficulties, and, if some have found it convenient to bypass the individuality of the writer or his status as an author to concentrate on a work, they have failed to appreciate the equally problematic nature of the word "work" and the unity it designates.

Another thesis has detained us from taking full measure of the author's disappearance. It avoids confronting the specific event that makes it possible and, in subtle ways, continues to preserve the existence of the author.

This is the notion of *écriture*. Strictly speaking, it should allow us not only to circumvent references to an author, but to situate his recent absence. The conception of *écriture*, as currently employed, is concerned with neither the act of writing nor the indications, as symptoms or signs within a text, of an author's meaning; rather, it stands for a remarkably profound attempt to elaborate the conditions of any text, both the conditions of its spatial dispersion and its temporal deployment.

It appears, however, that this concept, as currently employed, has merely transposed the empirical characteristics of an author to a transcendental anonymity. The extremely visible signs of the author's empirical activity are effaced to allow the play, in parallel or opposition, of religious and critical modes of characterization. In granting a primordial status to writing, do we not, in effect, simply reinscribe in transcendental terms the theological affirmation of its sacred origin or a critical belief in its creative nature? To say that writing, in terms of the particular history it made possible, is subjected to forgetfulness and repression, is this not to reintroduce in transcendental terms the religious principle of hidden meanings (which require interpretation) and the critical assumption of implicit significations, silent purposes, and obscure contents (which give rise to commentary)? Finally, is not the conception of writing as absence a transposition into transcendental terms of the religious belief in a fixed and continuous tradition or the aesthetic principle that proclaims the survival of the work as a kind of enigmatic supplement of the author beyond his own death?

This conception of *écriture* sustains the privileges of the author through the safeguard of the a priori; the play of representations that formed a particular image of the author is extended within a gray neutrality. The disappearance of the author—since Mallarmé, an event of our time—is held in check by the transcendental. Is it not necessary to draw a line between those who believe that we can continue to situate our present discontinuities within the historical and transcendental tradition of the nineteenth century and those who are making a great effort to liberate themselves, once and for all, from this conceptual framework?

• • •

It is obviously insufficient to repeat empty slogans: the author has disappeared; God and man died a common death. Rather, we should reexamine the empty space left by the author's disappearance; we should attentively observe, along its gaps and fault lines, its new demarcations, and the reapportionment of this void; we should await the fluid functions released by this disappearance. In this context we can briefly consider the problems that arise in the use of an author's name. What is the name of an author? How does it function? Far from offering a solution, I will attempt to indicate some of the difficulties related to these questions.

The name of an author poses all the problems related to the category of the proper name. (Here, I am referring to the work of John Searle, among others.) Obviously not a pure and simple reference, the proper name (and the author's name as well) has other than indicative functions. It is more than a gesture, a finger pointed at someone; it is, to a certain extent, the equivalent of a description. When we say "Aristotle," we are using a word that means one or a series of definite descriptions of the type: "the author of the *Analytics*," or "the founder of ontology," and so forth. Furthermore, a proper name has other functions than that of signification: when we discover that Rimbaud has not written *La Chasse spirituelle*, we cannot maintain that the meaning of the proper name or this author's name has been altered. The proper name and the name of an author oscillate between the poles of description and designation, and, granting that they are linked to what they name, they are not totally determined either by their descriptive or designative functions. Yet—and it is here that the specific difficulties attending an author's name appear—the link between a proper name and the individual being named and the link between an author's name and that which it names are not isomorphous and do not function in the same way; and these differences require clarification.

To learn, for example, that Pierre Dupont does not have blue eyes, does not live in Paris, and is not a doctor does not invalidate the fact that the name, Pierre Dupont, continues to refer to the same person; there has been no modification of the designation that links the name to the person. With the name of an author, however, the problems are far more complex. The disclosure that Shakespeare was not born in the house that tourists now visit would not modify the functioning of the author's name, but, if it were proved that he had not written the sonnets that we attribute to him, this would constitute a significant change and affect the manner in which the author's name functions. Moreover, if we establish that Shakespeare wrote Bacon's *Organon* and that the same author was responsible for both the works of Shakespeare and those of Bacon, we would have introduced a third type of alteration which completely modifies the functioning of the author's name. Consequently, the name of an author is not precisely a proper name among others.

Many other factors sustain this paradoxical singularity of the name of an author. It is altogether different to maintain that Pierre Dupont does not exist and that Homer or Hermes Trismegistes have never existed. While the first negation merely implies that there is no one by the name of Pierre Dupont, the second indicates that several individuals have been referred to by one name or that the real author possessed none of the traits traditionally associated with Homer or Hermes. Neither is it the same thing to say that Jacques Durand, not Pierre Dupont, is the real name of *X* and that Stendhal's name was Henri Beyle. We could also examine the function and meaning of such statements as "Bourbaki is this or that person," and "Victor Eremita, Climacus, Anticlimacus, Frater Taciturnus, Constantin Constantius, all of these are Kierkegaard."

These differences indicate that an author's name is not simply an element of speech (as a subject, a complement, or an element that could be replaced by a pronoun or other parts of speech). Its presence is functional in that it serves as a means of classification. A name can group together a number of texts and thus differentiate them from others. A name also establishes different forms of relationships among texts. Neither Hermes nor Hippocrates existed in the sense that we can say Balzac existed, but the fact that a number of texts were attached to a single name implies that relationships of homogeneity, filiation, reciprocal explanation, authentification, or of common utilization were established among them. Finally, the author's name characterizes a particular manner of existence of discourse. Discourse that possesses an author's name is not to be immediately consumed and forgotten; neither is it accorded the momentary attention given to ordinary, fleeting words. Rather, its status and its manner of reception are regulated by the culture in which it circulates.

We can conclude that, unlike a proper name, which moves from the interior of a discourse to the real person outside who produced it, the name of the author remains at the contours of texts—separating one from the other, defining their form, and characterizing their mode of existence. It points to the existence of certain groups of discourse and refers to the status of this discourse within a society and culture. The author's name is not a function of a man's civil status, nor is it fictional; it is situated in the breach, among the discontinuities, which gives rise to new groups of discourse and their singular mode of existence. Consequently, we can say that in our culture, the name of an author is a variable that accompanies only certain texts to the exclusion of others: a private letter may have a signatory, but it does not have an author; a contract can have an underwriter, but not an author; and, similarly, an anonymous poster attached to a wall may have a writer, but he cannot be an author. In this sense, the function of an author is to characterize the existence, circulation, and operation of certain discourses within a society.

• • •

In dealing with the "author" as a function of discourse, we must consider the characteristics of a discourse that support this use and determine its difference from other discourses. If we limit our remarks to only those books or texts with authors, we can isolate four different features.

First, they are objects of appropriation; the form of property they have become is of a particular type whose legal codification was accomplished some years ago. It is important to notice, as well, that its status as property is historically secondary to the penal code controlling its appropriation. Speeches and books were assigned real authors, other than mythical or important religious figures, only when the author became subject to punishment and to the extent that his discourse was considered transgressive. In our culture—undoubtedly in others as well—discourse was not originally a thing, a product, or a possession, but an action situated in a bipolar field of sacred and profane, lawful and unlawful, religious and blasphemous. It was a gesture charged with risks long before it became a possession caught in a circuit of property values. But it was at the moment when a system of ownership and strict copyright rules were established (toward the end of the eighteenth and beginning of the nineteenth century) that the transgressive properties always intrinsic to the act of writing became the forceful imperative of literature. It is as if the author, at the moment he was accepted into the social order of property which governs our culture, was compensating for his new status by reviving the older bipolar field of discourse in a systematic practice of transgression and by restoring the danger of writing which, on another side, had been conferred the benefits of property.

Secondly, the "author-function" is not universal or constant in all discourse. Even within our civilization, the same types of texts have not always required authors; there was a time when those texts which we now call "literary" (stories, folk tales, epics, and tragedies) were accepted, circulated, and valorized without any question about the identity of their author. Their anonymity was ignored because their real or supposed age was a sufficient guarantee of their authenticity. Texts, however, that we now call "scientific" (dealing with cosmology and the heavens, medicine or illness, the natural sciences or geography) were only considered truthful during the Middle Ages if the name of the author was indicated. Statements on the order of "Hippocrates said . . ." or "Pliny tells us that . . ." were not merely formulas for an argument based on authority; they marked a proven discourse. In the seventeenth and eighteenth centuries, a totally new conception was developed when scientific texts were accepted on their own merits and positioned within an anonymous and coherent conceptual system of established truths and methods of verification. Authentification no longer required reference to the individual who had produced them; the role of the author disappeared as an index of truthfulness and, where it remained as an inventor's name, it was merely to denote a specific theorem or proposition, a strange effect, a property, a body, a group of elements, or pathological syndrome.

At the same time, however, "literary" discourse was acceptable only if it carried an author's name; every text of poetry or fiction was obliged to state its author and the date, place, and circumstance of its writing. The meaning and value attributed to the text depended on this information. If by accident or design a text was presented anonymously, every effort was made to locate its author. Literary anonymity was of interest only as a puzzle to be solved as, in our day, literary works are totally dominated by the sovereignty of the author. (Undoubtedly, these remarks are far too categorical. Criticism has been concerned for some time now with aspects of a text not fully dependent on the notion of an individual creator; studies of genre or the analysis of recurring textual motifs and their variations from a norm other than the author. Furthermore, where in mathematics the author has become little more than a handy reference for a particular theorem or group of propositions, the reference to an author in biology and medicine, or to the date of his research has a substantially different bearing. This latter reference, more than simply indicating the source of information, attests to the "reliability" of the evidence, since it entails an appreciation of the techniques and experimental materials available at a given time and in a particular laboratory.)

The third point concerning this "author-function" is that it is not formed spontaneously through the simple attribution of a discourse to an individual. It results from a complex operation whose purpose is to construct the rational entity we call an author. Undoubtedly, this construction is assigned a "realistic" dimension as we speak of an individual's "profundity" or "creative" power, his intentions or the original inspiration manifested in writing. Nevertheless, these aspects of an individual, which we designate as an author (or which comprise an individual as an author), are projections, in terms always more or less psychological, of our way of handling texts: in the comparisons we make, the traits we extract as pertinent, the continuities we assign, or the exclusions we practice. In addition, all these operations vary according to the period and the form of discourse concerned. A "philosopher" and a "poet" are not constructed in the same manner; and the author of an eighteenth-century novel was formed differently from the modern novelist. There are, nevertheless, transhistorical constants in the rules that govern the construction of an author.

In literary criticism, for example, the traditional methods for defining an author—or, rather, for determining the configuration of the author from existing texts—derive in large part from those used in the Christian tradition to authenticate (or to reject) the particular texts in its possession. Modern criticism, in its desire to "recover" the author from a work, employs devices strongly reminiscent of Christian exegesis when it wished to prove the value of a text by ascertaining the holiness of its author. In *De Viris Illustribus,* Saint Jerome maintains that homonymy is not proof of the common authorship of several works, since many individuals could have the same name or someone could have perversely appropriated another's name. The name, as an individual mark, is not sufficient as it relates to a textual tradition. How, then, can several texts be attributed to an individual author? What norms, related to the function of the author, will disclose the involvement of several authors? According to Saint Jerome, there are four criteria: the texts that must be eliminated from the list of works attributed to a single author are those inferior to the others (thus, the author is defined as a standard level of quality); those whose ideas conflict with the doctrine expressed in the others (here the author is defined as a certain field of conceptual or theoretical coherence); those written in a different style and containing words and phrases not ordinarily found in the other works (the author is seen as a stylistic uniformity); and those referring to events or historical figures subsequent to the death of the author (the author is thus a definite historical figure in which a series of events converge). Although modern criticism does not appear to have these same suspicions concerning authentication, its strategies for defining the author present striking similarities. The author explains the presence of certain events within a text, as well as their transformations, distortions, and their various modifications (and this through an author's biography or by reference to his particular point of view, in the analysis of his social preferences and his position within a class or by delineating his fundamental objectives). The author also constitutes a principle of unity in writing where any unevenness of production is ascribed to changes caused by evolution, maturation, or outside influence. In addition, the author serves to neutralize the contradictions that are found in a series of texts. Governing this function is the belief that there must be—at a particular level of an author's thought, of his conscious or unconscious desire—a point where contradictions are resolved, where the incompatible elements can be shown to relate to one another or to cohere around a fundamental and originating contradiction. Finally, the author is a particular source of expression who, in more or less finished forms, is manifested equally well and with similar validity, in a text, in letters, fragments, drafts, and so forth. Thus, even while Saint Jerome's four principles of authenticity might seem largely inadequate to modern critics, they, nevertheless, define the critical modalities now used to display the function of the author.

However, it would be false to consider the function of the author as a pure and simple reconstruction after the fact of a text given as passive material, since a text always bears a number of signs that refer to the author. Well known to grammarians, these textual signs are personal pronouns, adverbs of time and place, and the conjugation of verbs. But it is important to note that these elements have a different bearing on texts with an author and on those without one. In the latter, these "shifters" refer to a real speaker and to an actual deictic situation, with certain exceptions such as the case of indirect speech in the first person. When discourse is linked to an author, however, the role of "shifters" is more complex and variable. It is well known that in a novel narrated in the first person, neither the first person pronoun, the present indicative tense, nor, for that matter, its signs of localization refer directly to the writer, either to the time when he wrote, or to the specific act of writing; rather, they stand for a "second self" whose similarity to the author is never fixed and undergoes considerable alteration within the course of a single book. It would be as false to seek the author in relation to the actual writer as to the fictional narrator; the "author-function" arises out of their scission—in the division and distance of the two. One might object that this phenomenon only applies to novels or poetry, to a context of "quasi-discourse," but, in fact, all discourse that supports this "author-function" is characterized by this plurality of egos. In a mathematical treatise, the ego who indicates the circumstances of composition in the preface is not identical, either in terms of his position or his function, to the "I" who concludes a demonstration within the body of the text. The former implies a unique individual who, at a given time and place, succeeded in completing a project, whereas the latter indicates an instance and plan of demonstration that anyone could perform provided the same set of axioms, preliminary operations, and an identical set of symbols were used. It is also possible to locate a third ego: one who speaks of the goals of his investigation, the obstacles encountered, its results, and the problems yet to be solved and this "I" would function in a field of existing or future mathematical discourses. We are not dealing with a system of dependencies where a first and essential use of the "I" is reduplicated, as a kind of fiction, by the other two. On the contrary, the "author-function" in such discourses operates so as to effect the simultaneous dispersion of the three egos.

Further elaboration would, of course, disclose other characteristics of the "author-function," but I have limited myself to the four that seemed the most obvious and important. They can be summarized in the following manner: the "author-function" is tied to the legal and institutional systems that circumscribe, determine, and articulate the realm of discourses; it does not operate in a uniform manner in all discourses, at all times, and in any given culture; it is not defined by the spontaneous attribution of a text to its creator, but through a series of precise and complex procedures; it does not refer, purely and simply, to an actual individual insofar as it simultaneously gives rise to a variety of egos and to a series of subjective positions that individuals of any class may come to occupy.

* * *

I am aware that until now I have kept my subject within unjustifiable limits; I should also have spoken of the "author-function" in painting, music, technical fields, and so forth. Admitting that my analysis is restricted to the domain of discourse, it seems that I have given the term "author" an excessively narrow meaning. I have discussed the author only in the limited sense of a person to whom the production of a text, a book, or a work can be legitimately attributed. However, it is obvious that even within the realm of discourse a person can be the author of much more than a book—of a theory, for instance, of a tradition or a discipline within which new books and authors can proliferate. For convenience, we could say that such authors occupy a "transdiscursive" position.

Homer, Aristotle, and the Church Fathers played this role, as did the first mathematicians and the originators of the Hippocratic tradition. This type of author is surely as old as our civilization. But I believe that the nineteenth century in Europe produced a singular type of author who should not be confused with "great" literary authors, or the authors of canonical religious texts, and the founders of sciences. Somewhat arbitrarily, we might call them "initiators of discursive practices."

The distinctive contribution of these authors is that they produced not only their own work, but the possibility and the rules of formation of other texts. In this sense, their role differs entirely from that of a novelist, for example, who is basically never more than the author of his own text. Freud is not simply the author of *The Interpretation of Dreams* or of *Wit and its Relation to the Unconscious* and Marx is not simply the author of the *Communist Manifesto* or *Capital:* they both established the endless possibility of discourse. Obviously, an easy objection can be made. The author of a novel may be responsible for more than his own text; if he acquires some "importance" in the literary world, his influence can have significant ramifications. To take a very simple example, one could say that Ann Radcliffe did not simply write *The Mysteries of Udolpho* and a few other novels, but also made possible the appearance of Gothic Romances at the beginning of the nineteenth century. To this extent, her function as an author exceeds the limits of her work. However, this objection can be answered by the fact that the possibilities disclosed by the initiators of discursive practices (using the examples of Marx and Freud, whom I believe to be the first and the most important) are significantly different from those suggested by novelists. The novels of Ann Radcliffe put into circulation a certain number of resemblances and analogies patterned on her work—various characteristic signs, figures, relationships, and structures that could be integrated into other books. In short, to say that Ann Radcliffe created the Gothic Romance means that there are certain elements common to her works and to the nineteenth-century Gothic romance: the heroine ruined by her own innocence, the secret fortress that functions as a counter-city, the outlaw-hero who swears revenge on the world that has cursed him, etc. On the other hand, Marx and Freud, as "initiators of discursive practices," not only made possible a certain number of analogies that could be adopted by future texts, but, as importantly, they also made possible a certain number of differences. They cleared a space for the introduction of elements other than their own, which, nevertheless, remain within the field of discourse they initiated. In saying that Freud founded psychoanalysis, we do not simply mean that the concept of libido or the techniques of dream analysis reappear in the writings of Karl

Abraham or Melanie Klein, but that he made possible a certain number of differences with respect to his books, concepts, and hypotheses, which all arise out of psychoanalytic discourse.

Is this not the case, however, with the founder of any new science or of any author who successfully transforms an existing science? After all, Galileo is indirectly responsible for the texts of those who mechanically applied the laws he formulated, in addition to having paved the way for the production of statements far different from his own. If Cuvier is the founder of biology and Saussure of linguistics, it is not because they were imitated or that an organic concept or a theory of the sign was uncritically integrated into new texts, but because Cuvier, to a certain extent, made possible a theory of evolution diametrically opposed to his own system and because Saussure made possible a generative grammar radically different from his own structural analysis. Superficially, then, the initiation of discursive practices appears similar to the founding of any scientific endeavor, but I believe there is a fundamental difference.

In a scientific program, the founding act is on an equal footing with its future transformations: it is merely one among the many modifications that it makes possible. This interdependence can take several forms. In the future development of a science, the founding act may appear as little more than a single instance of a more general phenomenon that has been discovered. It might be questioned, in retrospect, for being too intuitive or empirical and submitted to the rigors of new theoretical operations in order to situate it in a formal domain. Finally, it might be thought a hasty generalization whose validity should be restricted. In other words, the founding act of a science can always be rechanneled through the machinery of transformations it has instituted.

On the other hand, the initiation of a discursive practice is heterogeneous to its ulterior transformations. To extend psychoanalytic practice, as initiated by Freud, is not to presume a formal generality that was not claimed at the outset; it is to explore a number of possible applications. To limit it is to isolate in the original texts a small set of propositions or statements that are recognized as having an inaugurative value and that mark other Freudian concepts or theories as derivative. Finally, there are no "false" statements in the work of these initiators; those statements considered inessential or "prehistoric," in that they are associated with another discourse, are simply neglected in favor of the more pertinent aspects of the work. The initiation of a discursive practice, unlike the founding of a science, overshadows and is necessarily detached from its later developments and transformations. As a consequence, we define the theoretical validity of a statement with respect to the work of the initiator, whereas in the case of Galileo or Newton, it is based on the structural and intrinsic norms established in cosmology or physics. Stated schematically, the work of these initiators is not situated in relation to a science or in the space it defines; rather, it is science or discursive practice that relates to their works as the primary points of reference.

In keeping with this distinction, we can understand why it is inevitable that practitioners of such discourses must "return to the origin." Here, as well, it is necessary to distinguish a "return" from scientific "rediscoveries" or "reactivations." "Rediscoveries" are the effects of analogy or isomorphism with current forms of knowledge that allow the perception of forgotten or obscured figures. For instance, Chomsky in his book on Cartesian grammar "rediscovered" a form of knowledge that had been in use from Cordemoy to Humboldt. It could only be understood from the perspective of generative grammar because this later manifestation held the key to its construction: in effect, a retrospective codification of an historical position. "Reactivation" refers to something quite different: the insertion of discourse into totally new domains of generalization, practice, and transformations. The history of mathematics abounds in examples of this phenomenon as the work of Michel Serres on mathematical anamnesis shows.

The phrase, "return to," designates a movement with its proper specificity, which characterizes the initiation of discursive practices. If we return, it is because of a basic and constructive omission, an omission that is not the result of accident or incomprehension. In effect, the act of initiation is such, in its essence, that it is inevitably subjected to its own distortions; that which displays this act and derives from it is, at the same time, the root of its divergences and travesties. This nonaccidental omission must be regulated by precise operations that can be situated, analysed, and reduced in a return to the act of initiation. The barrier imposed by omission was not added from the outside; it arises from the discursive practice in question, which gives it its law. Both the cause of the barrier and the means for its removal, this omission—also responsible for the obstacles that prevent returning to the act of initiation—can only be resolved by a return. In addition, it is always a return to a text in itself, specifically, to a primary and unadorned text with particular attention to those things registered in the interstices of the text, its gaps and absences. We return to those empty spaces that have been masked by omission or concealed in a false and misleading plenitude. In these rediscoveries of an essential lack, we find the oscillation of two characteristic responses: "This point was made—you can't help seeing it if you know how to read"; or, inversely, "No, that point is not made in any of the printed words in the text, but it is expressed through the words, in their relationships and in the distance that separates them." It follows naturally that this return, which is a part of the discursive mechanism, constantly introduces modifications and that the return to a text is not a historical supplement that would come to fix itself upon the primary discursivity and redouble it in the form of an ornament which, after all, is not essential. Rather, it is an effective and necessary means of transforming discursive practice. A study of Galileo's works could alter our knowledge of the history, but not the science, of mechanics; whereas, a reexamination of the books of Freud or Marx can transform our understanding of psychoanalysis or Marxism.

A last feature of these returns is that they tend to reinforce the enigmatic link between an author and his works. A text has an inaugurative value precisely because it is the work of a particular author, and our returns are conditioned by this knowledge. The rediscovery of an unknown text by Newton or Cantor will not modify classical cosmology or group theory; at most, it will change our appreciation of their historical genesis. Bringing to light, however, *An Outline of Psychoanalysis,* to the extent that we recognize it as a book by Freud, can transform not only our historical knowledge, but the field of psychoanalytic theory—if only through a shift of accent or of the center of gravity. These returns, an important component of discursive practices, form a relationship between "fundamental" and mediate authors, which is not identical to that which links an ordinary text to its immediate author.

These remarks concerning the initiation of discursive practices have been extremely schematic, especially with regard to the opposition I have tried to trace between this initiation and the founding of sciences. The distinction between the two is not readily discernible; moreover, there is no proof that the two procedures are mutually exclusive. My only purpose in setting up this opposition, however, was to show that the "author-function," sufficiently complex at the level of a book or a series of texts that bear a definite signature, has other determining factors when analyzed in terms of larger entities—groups of works or entire disciplines.

• • •

Unfortunately, there is a decided absence of positive propositions in this essay, as it applies to analytic procedures or directions for future research, but I ought at least to give the reasons why I attach such importance to a continuation of this work. Developing a similar analysis could provide the basis for a typology of discourse. A typology of this sort cannot be adequately understood in relation to the grammatical features, formal structures, and objects of discourse, because there undoubtedly exist specific discursive properties or relationships that are irreducible to the rules of grammar and logic and to the laws that govern objects. These properties require investigation if we hope to distinguish the larger categories of discourse. The different forms of relationships (or nonrelationships) that an author can assume are evidently one of these discursive properties.

This form of investigation might also permit the introduction of an historical analysis of discourse. Perhaps the time has come to study not only the expressive value and formal transformations of discourse, but its mode of existence: the modifications and variations, within any culture, of modes of circulation, valorization, attribution, and appropriation. Partially at the expense of themes and concepts that an author places in his work, the "author-function" could also reveal the manner in which discourse is articulated on the basis of social relationships.

Is it not possible to reexamine, as a legitimate extension of this kind of analysis, the privileges of the subject? Clearly, in undertaking an internal and architectonic analysis of a work (whether it be a literary text, a philosophical system, or a scientific work) and in delimiting psychological and biographical references, suspicions arise concerning the absolute nature and creative role of the subject. But the subject should not be entirely abandoned. It should be reconsidered, not to restore the theme of an originating subject, but to seize its functions, its intervention in discourse, and its system of dependencies. We should suspend the typical questions: how does a free subject penetrate the density of things and endow them with meaning; how does it accomplish its design by animating the rules of discourse from within? Rather, we should ask: under what conditions and through what forms can an entity like the subject appear in the order of discourse; what position does it occupy; what functions does it exhibit; and what rules does it follow in each type of discourse? In short, the subject (and its substitutes) must be stripped of its creative role and analyzed as a complex and variable function of discourse.

The author—or what I have called the "author-function"—is undoubtedly only one of the possible specifications of the subject and, considering past historical transformations, it appears that the form, the complexity, and even the existence of this function are far from immutable. We can easily imagine a culture where discourse would circulate without any need for an author. Discourses, whatever their status, form, or value, and regardless of our manner of handling them, would unfold in a pervasive anonymity. No longer the tiresome repetitions:

"Who is the real author?"
"Have we proof of his authenticity and originality?"
"What has he revealed of his most profound self in his language?"

New questions will be heard:

"What are the modes of existence of this discourse?"
"Where does it come from; how is it circulated; who controls it?"
"What placements are determined for possible subjects?"
"Who can fulfill these diverse functions of the subject?"

Behind all these questions we would hear little more than the murmur of indifference:

"What matter who's speaking?"

MICHAEL POLANYI
1891–1976

*Born in Budapest, Michael Polanyi served as a physician in the Austro-Hungarian
army and also had a successful career as a research chemist in Berlin. He left Germany for England in 1933 for a professorship first at the University of Manchester
and then at Oxford University. Polanyi became interested in philosophy and
rhetoric as ways of understanding and countering the persuasive power of ideologies, particularly Nazism and Marxism. He believed that twentieth-century society
must turn away from objectivist epistemology and dependence on science for certain knowledge toward an epistemology of personal knowledge. What he calls
tacit knowing is socially constructed by a particular interpretive community in
which members accept and share disciplinary frameworks. The reader who wants
to know more about Polanyi would do well to read* Knowing and Being *(1969)
and* The Tacit Dimension *(1966).*

Scientific Controversy

Heuristic passion seeks no personal possession. It sets out not to conquer, but to enrich the world. Yet such a move is also an attack. It raises a
claim and makes a tremendous demand on other men; for it asks that its gift
to humanity be accepted by all. In order to be satisfied, our intellectual passions must find response. This universal intent creates a tension: we suffer
when a vision of reality to which we have committed ourselves is contemp-
tuously ignored by others. For a general unbelief imperils our own convictions by evoking an echo in us. Our vision must conquer or die.

Like the heuristic passion from which it flows, the *persuasive passion*
too finds itself facing a logical gap. To the extent to which a discoverer has
committed himself to a new vision of reality, he has separated himself from
others who still think on the old lines. His persuasive passion spurs him now
to cross this gap by converting everybody to his way of seeing things, even
as his heuristic passion has spurred him to cross the heuristic gap which
separated him from discovery.

We can see, therefore, why scientific controversies never lie altogether
within science. For when a new system of thought concerning a whole class
of alleged facts is at issue, the question will be whether it should be
accepted or rejected in principle, and those who reject it on such comprehensive grounds will inevitably regard it as altogether incompetent and
unsound. Take, for example, four contemporary issues: Freud's psycho-

analysis, Eddington's *a priori* system of physics, Rhine's "Reach of the Mind," or Lysenko's environmental genetics. Each of the four authors mentioned here has his own conceptual framework, by which he identifies his facts and within which he conducts his arguments, and each expresses his conceptions in his own distinctive terminology. Any such framework is relatively stable, for it can account for most of the evidence which it accepts as well established, and it is sufficiently coherent in itself to justify to the satisfaction of its followers the neglect for the time being of facts, or alleged facts, which it cannot interpret. It is correspondingly segregated from any knowledge or alleged knowledge rooted in different conceptions of experience. The two conflicting systems of thought are separated by a logical gap, in the same sense as a problem is separated from the discovery which solves the problem. Formal operations relying on *one* framework of interpretation cannot demonstrate a proposition to persons who rely on *another* framework. Its advocates may not even succeed in getting a hearing from these, since they must first teach them a new language, and no one can learn a new language unless he first trusts that it means something. A hostile audience may in fact deliberately refuse to entertain novel conceptions such as those of Freud, Eddington, Rhine or Lysenko, precisely because its members fear that once they have accepted this framework they will be led to conclusions which they—rightly or wrongly—abhor. Proponents of a new system can convince their audience only by first winning their intellectual sympathy for a doctrine they have not yet grasped. Those who listen sympathetically will discover for themselves what they would otherwise never have understood. Such an acceptance is a heuristic process, a self-modifying act, and to this extent a conversion. It produces disciples forming a school, the members of which are separated for the time being by a logical gap from those outside it. They think differently, speak a different language, live in a different world, and at least one of the two schools is excluded to this extent for the time being (whether rightly or wrongly) from the community of science.

We can now see, also, the great difficulty that may arise in the attempt to persuade others to accept a new idea in science. We have seen that to the extent to which it represents a new way of reasoning, we cannot convince others of it by formal argument, for so long as we argue within their framework, we can never induce them to abandon it. Demonstration must be supplemented, therefore, by forms of persuasion which can induce a conversion. The refusal to enter on the opponent's way of arguing must be justified by making it appear altogether unreasonable.

Such comprehensive rejection cannot fail to discredit the opponent. He will be made to appear as thoroughly deluded, which in the heat of the battle will easily come to imply that he was a fool, a crank or a fraud. And once we are out to establish such charges we shall readily go on to expose our opponent as a "metaphysician," a "Jesuit," a "Jew," or a "Bolshevik," as the case may be—or, speaking from the other side of the Iron Curtain—as an "objectivist," an "idealist" and a "cosmopolitan." In a clash of intellectual passions each side must inevitably attack the opponent's person.

Even in retrospect such conflicts can often be appreciated only in these terms. They do not appear as scientific arguments, but as conflicts between rival scientific visions, or else between scientific values and extraneous interests interfering illegitimately with the due process of scientific enquiry. I shall recall here four controversies to illustrate this. The first is the Copernican, to which I have already had occasion to refer. The other three occurred in the nineteenth century and their outcome, like that of the earlier one, had an effective part in developing our present sense of scientific value.

The Ptolemaic and Copernican theories opposed each other for a long time as two virtually complete systems separated by a logical gap. The facts known at any time during the 148 years from the publication of Copernicus' *De Revolutionibus* to the appearance of Newton's *Principia* could be accounted for by either theory. By 1619 the discovery of Kepler's third law may have tipped the balance in favor of Copernicanism,[1] but the non-appearance of any seasonal variation in the angle at which the fixed stars are seen continued to present a serious difficulty to this system. The mistaken argument that falling bodies would not descend vertically to earth if it were in motion was disproved by Galileo; but his explanation of the tides, which he regarded as a crucial proof of terrestrial rotation, fell into a similar error. His discovery of Jupiter's moons was perhaps suggestive, but its significance hardly justified his scornful invective against those who refused to look at these moons through his telescope.[2] The real ground of Galileo's conviction lay in his passionate appreciation of the greater scientific value of the heliocentric view: a feeling which was accentuated by his angry rebellion against Aristotle's authority over science. His opponents had on their side the common-sense view which sees the earth at rest, and, above all, a vivid consciousness of man's uniqueness as the only particle of the universe that feels responsible to God. Their craving to retain for man a location which corresponds to his importance in the universe was the emotional force opposed to the intellectual appeal of Copernicanism.

---

[1] Galileo never made use of this argument, which was the strongest available to him. He seems never to have accepted Kepler's elliptical planetary paths, presumably because his Pythagoreanism was even more rigid than Kepler's.

[2] Admittedly, the phases of Venus discovered by Galileo could not be accounted for by the Ptolemaic system, but they were compatible with Tycho Brahe's assumption that the planets circled round the Sun which itself circled round the Earth. Fortunately, no experiment of the Michelson Morley type was carried out at the time, for its negative result would have served as decisive proof that the Earth was at rest.

The victory of Copernicanism rejected and suppressed this demand as an illegitimate interference with the pursuit of science, and established the principle that scientific truth shall take no account of its religious or moral repercussions. But this principle is not incontestable. It is rejected today by the Soviet theory that all science is class science and must be guided by "partynost," party-spirit. It is contested also by the Catholic Church, as for example in the Encyclical *Humani Generis* of 1950, and similarly by biblical fundamentalists everywhere. My opposition to a universal mechanical interpretation of things, on the ground that it impairs man's moral consciousness, also implies some measure of dissent from the absolute moral neutrality of science. Yet though the issue is not altogether closed, the principle of moral and religious indifference prevails throughout modern science without facing so far any effective rival to its rule, and the outcome of the Copernican controversy continues to form an eminent support for this principle.[3]

Another tenet of modern science which emerged at an early stage from its conflict with the Aristotelian and scholastic tradition is its ideal of empiricism. Though I dissent from this ideal in its absolute form, since I hold that the elimination of personal knowledge from science would destroy science, I acknowledge the decisive achievements of empiricism in opening the way to modern science. Nor do I deny, of course, that science is constantly in danger from the incursion of empty speculations, which must be watchfully resisted and cast out; but I hold that the part played by personal knowledge in science makes it impossible to formulate any precise rule by which such speculations can be distinguished from properly conducted empirical investigations. Empiricism is valid only as a maxim, the application of which itself forms a part of the art of knowing. Some examples of the scientific controversies in which maxims of scientific empiricism have acquired their current meaning will show how controversial and misleading the claims of empiricism have proved in some important instances.

The quixotic attack of the young Hegel on the empirical method of science and his swift defeat at the hands of the scientists was one of the great formative experiences of modern science. In the year 1800 a band of six German astronomers, led by Bode, set out to search for a new planet to fill a gap between Mars and Jupiter in the numerical series of planetary distances, discovered by Titius and known as Bode's Law. The series is obtained by writing down the number 4, followed by the series $3 + 4, 2 \times 3 + 4, 2^2 \times 3 + 4, 2^3 \times 3 + 4 \ldots$ etc. This gives for the first eight places: 4, 7, 10, 16, 28, 52,

---

[3] See R. A. Fisher, *Creative Aspects of Natural Law*, Eddington Memorial Lecture, Cambridge, 1950, p. 15: 'We attempt, so far as our powers allow, to understand the world, by reasoning, by experimentation, and again by reasoning. In this process moral or emotional grounds for preferring one conclusion to another are completely out of place.'

100, 196, which can be shown to correspond pretty well to the relative distances of the seven planets known in 1800, provided you leave out the fifth number. Setting the distance of the Earth arbitrarily at 10 you have the table:

Bode's Law in 1800

	Predicted	Observed
Mercury	4	3.9
Venus	7	7.2
Earth	(10)	(10)
Mars	16	15.2
...?	28	?
Jupiter	52	52
Saturn	100	95
Uranus	196	192

The young Hegel poured scorn on an enquiry following up a numerical rule which, being meaningless, could only be accidental. Arguing that nature, shaped by immanent reason, must be governed by a rational sequence of numbers, he postulated that the relative spacing of the planets must conform to the Pythagorean series 1, 2, 3, $4(2^2)$, $9(3^2)$, $8(2^3)$, $27(3^3)$— in which, however, he substituted 16 for 8. This would limit the number of planets to 7 and allow a large gap between the fourth and fifth planet, i.e., Mars and Jupiter. The quest for an eighth planet to fill this gap was therefore chimerical.[4]

However, on January 1st, 1801, Bode's party of astronomers discovered the small planet Ceres in the region in question. Since then over 500 small planets have been found in that neighbourhood, and it may be that these are fragments of a full sized planet that once occupied this place.

Hegel was discomfited and the astronomers triumphed gleefully. This was all to the good, for it confirmed a juster sense of scientific value. But we should realize that it had little else to support it. Whether Bode's Law has any rational foundation or has been fulfilled so far by mere coincidence (as Hegel had thought) is still open to question today; opinions have changed on

---

[4] Hegel, Dissertatio philosophica de Orbitis Planetarum (1801), *Werke*, Berlin, 1834, 16, p. 28. In his lectures on the Philosophy of Nature, Hegel admitted the presence of Ceres and other asteroids in this gap. He still referred to the numbers of the *Timaeus*, but he now declared that the law of the planetary distances was still unknown, and that one day the scientists would have to turn to the philosophers to find it. Bertrand Beaumont, in discussing Hegel's position, suggests that the Platonic series could be extended beyond the original seven; but in terms of Greek mathematics this is impossible.

the subject repeatedly during the last 20 years.[5] Thus Hegel may have been right in rejecting the astronomers' grounds for the search for a new planet.

Yet I agree that the astronomers were right and Hegel was wrong. Why so? Because the astronomers' guess lay within a conceivable scientific system, and so it was a kind of guess to which astronomers as scientists are entitled. It was a competent guess, and—if Bode's Law has any truth in it—even a true guess; while Hegel's inference was altogether unscientific, *incompetent*. Fortunately Hegel guessed wrong and the astronomers, though their guess was perhaps unjustified, did hit the mark. But even if Hegel's guess had proved right and the astronomers' wrong, we would still reject Hegel's vision of reality and cleave to that of the astronomers.

The revulsion of scientists against *Naturphilosophie* was violent and lasting. By the middle of the century empiricism ruled unchallenged.[6] But unfortunately the empirical method of enquiry—with its associated conceptions of scientific value and of the nature of reality—is far from unambiguous, and conflicting interpretations of it had therefore ever again to fight each other from either side of a logical gap.

In his doctoral thesis, presented in 1875 to the University of Utrecht, J. H. van't Hoff had put forward the theory that compounds containing an asymmetric carbon atom are optically active. In 1877 there appeared a German translation of this work with a commendatory introduction by Wislicenus, a distinguished German chemist and an authority on optical activity. This publication evoked a furious attack from Kolbe, another leading German chemist, who had recently published an article called "Signs of the Times," in which he castigated the decline of rigorous scientific training among German chemists; a decline which, he said, had led to a renewed sprouting of

> the weeds of a seemingly learned and brilliant but actually trivial and empty Philosophy of Nature, which, after having been replaced some 50 years ago by the exact sciences, is now once more dug up by pseudo-scientists from the lumber room of human fallacies, and like a trollop, newly attired in elegant dress and make-up, is smuggled into respectable company, to which she does not belong.

In a second paper, he gave as a further example of this aberration an account of van't Hoff's work which "he would have ignored like many other

---

[5] An attempt to interpret Bode's Law rationally by deriving it from a theory of the planetary system was made by C. F. von Weizsäcker in 1943. But from a later paper it appears that the problem is still in flux.

[6] *Naturphilosophie* lingered on longest in botany, where eminent scientists were ranged on both sides, with Braun and Agassiz standing largely under the influence of Goethe's morphology and of the nature philosophy of Schelling, opposed from the middle of the nineteenth century onward by others, notably Schleiden and Hofmeister, who developed the science of plant morphology on an experimental basis.

efforts of its kind" but for "the incomprehensible fact" of its warm recommendation by so distinguished a chemist as Wislicenus. So Kolbe wrote:

> A certain Dr. J. H. van't Hoff, employed by the Veterinary Academy at Utrecht, appears to have no taste for exact chemical research. He found it more convenient to mount Pegasus (borrowed no doubt from the Veterinary Academy) and to proclaim in his *La Chimie dans l'espace* how on his daring flight to the chemical Parnassus the atoms appeared to him disposed in world space.

Kolbe's comment on the introduction given by Wislicenus to van't Hoff's theory reveals even further the principles of his criticism. Wislicenus had written of "this real and important step in the advancement of the theory of carbon compounds, a step which was organic and internally necessary." Kolbe asks: What is "the theory of carbon compounds"? What is meant by saying that "this step was organic and necessary"? And he goes on: "Wislicenus has here expelled himself from the ranks of exact scientists and has joined instead the nature philosophers of ominous memory who are separated only by a slender 'medium' from the spiritists."

Scientific opinion eventually repudiated Kolbe's attack on van't Hoff and Wislicenus, but his suspicion of speculative chemistry ("paper chemistry") continues to be shared by most of the leading chemical journals, which refuse up to this day contributions containing no new experimental results. In spite of the fact that chemistry is largely based on the speculations by Dalton, Kekulé and van't Hoff, which were initially unaccompanied by any experimental observations, chemists still remain suspicious of this kind of work. Since they do not sufficiently trust themselves to distinguish true theoretical discoveries from empty speculations, they feel compelled to act on a presumption which may one day cause the rejection of a theoretical paper of supreme importance in favor of comparatively trivial experimental studies. So difficult is it even for the expert in his own field to distinguish, by the criteria of empiricism, scientific merit from incompetent chatter.

Nor does this apply only to purely theoretical discoveries. The great controversy on the nature of alcoholic fermentation which, starting in 1839, went on for almost forty years, showed that the verification of an experimental observation may run into precisely the same difficulties. From 1835 to 1837 no less than four independent observers (Caignard de la Tour, Schwann, Kützing and Turpin) had reported that yeast produced during fermentation was not a chemical precipitate, but consisted of living cellular organisms which multiplied by budding, and had concluded that fermentation was a living function of yeast cells. But this went against the dominant intellectual passion of contemporary scientists. In 1828, Wöhler had synthetized urea from inorganic materials and had triumphantly disproved thereby the existence of powers hitherto ascribed exclusively to living beings. Liebig had followed suit by laying the foundations of a chemical approach to all living matter, and Berzelius recognized that platinum could speed up reactions occurring in its presence, in the same way in which fermentation was caused by yeast. All three great masters poured scorn on claims which they regarded as a fantastic resurgence of the kind of "vitalism" they had banned for ever. Wöhler and Liebig published an elaborate skit making fun of these absurd speculations.

In 1857 Pasteur entered the lists on the side of the "vitalists." His investigations on yeast and putrefaction involved him at the same time in another fierce controversy of longer standing, the question of "spontaneous generation." In this, too, he was on the side considered at the time reactionary (and still so considered, at the time of writing this, in the Soviet Union), which denied that living beings could be produced experimentally from dead matter.[7]

The reason why both these controversies dragged on indefinitely is revealed by a remark of Pasteur concerning his own arguments for regarding fermentation as a function of the living cells of yeast: "If anyone should say that my conclusions go beyond the established facts (he wrote) I would agree, in the sense that I have taken my stand unreservedly in an order of ideas which, strictly speaking, cannot be irrefutably demonstrated."[8] This order of ideas was therefore separated by a logical gap from that entertained by Liebig, Wöhler and many other great men of his time. The schism was eventually bridged by a conceptual reform induced by Buchner's discovery, in 1897, of zymase in the liquor squeezed out of yeast cells. The agent of fermentation was proved a dead catalyst of the kind imagined by Liebig and Berzelius, but it also proved a vital organ of yeast cells, as Pasteur and his precursors since Caignard de la Tour had affirmed; the new conception of intracellular enzymes combined these two aspects.[9]

The great scientific controversies which I have just recalled were conducted in passionate accents, as was inevitable between contestants who

---

[7] See the violent attacks on Pasteur by Pisarev published in 1865. Experiments acknowledged until recently in the Soviet Union as proofs of the spontaneous generation of cellular organisms were carried out by Lepeshinskaia.

[8] J. B. Conant (Pasteur's and Tyndall's Study of Spontaneous Generation, Harvard Univ. Press, 1953) suggests (p. 15) that the most convincing evidence for the impossibility of spontaneous generation is to be found "in the whole fabric of the results of the study of pure bacterial cultures in the last sixty or seventy years." The author implies that all the experiments made to decide this question, from the inception of Spallanzani's studies in 1768 up to 1880-90, could be interpreted in terms of either of the opposing systems of thought.

[9] I have illustrated before how an apposite new conception can reconcile two alternative systems of interpretation which hitherto violently opposed each other. Braid's conception of "hypnosis" acknowledged the reality of the very features of Mesmerism hitherto taken to prove its fraudulence, while rejecting the evidence for "animal magnetism" which had been advanced as its claim to scientific solidity.

shared no common framework within which a more impersonal procedure could be followed. Kolbe could not argue against van't Hoff. He quoted with ironical glee van't Hoff's description of the disposition of atoms in spirals, which to him was sufficient evidence that the new theory was a tissue of fancies. And from his own point of view he was right in refusing to enter into any detailed argument on these lines, since he denied that one could argue rationally in terms of such wild ideas. The ironical caricature by which Wöhler and Liebig replied to the papers of Caignard de la Tour, Schwann and others, who claimed that fermentation is a function of living yeast cells, sprang from the same view that an argument believed to be wholly specious cannot be seriously discussed point by point. A Western scientist challenged to answer Lysenko's biological theories would similarly refuse to discuss them on the Marxist-Leninist grounds on which they were put forward; while, on the other hand, Lysenko refuses to consider the statistical evidence for Mendelism on the grounds that "in science there is no place for chance."

We may conclude that empiricism, like the moral neutrality of science, is a principle laid down and interpreted for us by the outcome of past controversies about the scientific value of particular sets of ideas. Our appreciation of scientific value has developed historically from the outcome of such controversies, much as our sense of justice has taken shape from the outcome of judicial decisions through past centuries. Indeed, all our cultural values are the deposits of a similar historic succession of intellectual upheavals. But ultimately, all past mental strife can be interpreted today only in the light of what we ourselves decide to be the true outcome and lesson of this history. And we have to take this decision within the context of contemporary controversies which perhaps challenge these lessons afresh and raise in their turn quite novel questions of principle. The lesson of history is what we ourselves accept as such.

There are serious questions still open today concerning the nature of things. At least, I believe them to be open, though the great majority of scientists are convinced that the view they themselves hold is right and scorn any challenge to it. A notorious example is offered by extra-sensory perception. The evidence for it is ignored today by scientists in the hope that it will one day find some trivial explanation. In this they may be right, but I respect those too who think they may be wrong; and no profitable discussion is possible between the two sides at this stage.

Another example. Neurologists today accept almost without exception the assumption that all conscious mental processes can be interpreted as epiphenomena of a chain of material events occurring in the nervous system. Some writers, like Dr. Mays, myself and Professor R. O. Kapp, have tried to show that this is logically untenable, but to my knowledge only one neurologist, namely Professor J. C. Eccles, has gone so far as to amend the neurological model of the brain, by introducing an influence by which the will intervenes to determine the choice between two possible alternative decisions. This suggestion is scornfully ignored by all other neurologists, and indeed, it is difficult to argue profitably about it from their point of view.

A similar schism is present today between the ruling school of genetics, which explains evolution as a result of a haphazard sequence of mutations, and writers like Graham Cannon in England, Dalcq in Belgium, Vandel and others in France, who consider this explanation inadequate and support the assumption of a harmonious adaptive power controlling the most important innovations in the origin of higher forms of life.

Some people may listen to these illustrations with impatience, for they believe that science provides a procedure for deciding any such issues by systematic and dispassionate empirical investigations. However, if that were clearly the case, there would be no reason to be annoyed with me. My argument would have no persuasive force, and could be ignored without anger.

At any rate, let me make quite clear what I have urged here. I have said that intellectual passions have an affirmative content; in science they affirm the scientific interest and value of certain facts, as against any lack of such interest and value in others. This *selective* function—in the absence of which science could not be defined at all—is closely linked to another function of the same passions in which their cognitive content is supplemented by a conative component. This is their *heuristic* function. The heuristic impulse links our appreciation of scientific value to a vision of reality, which serves as a guide to enquiry. Heuristic passion is also the mainspring of originality—the force which impels us to abandon an accepted framework of interpretation and commit ourselves, by the crossing of a logical gap, to the use of a new framework. Finally, heuristic passion will often turn (and have to turn) into *persuasive* passion, the mainspring of all fundamental controversy.

I am not applauding the outbreak of such passions. I do not like to see a scientist trying to bring an opponent into intellectual contempt, or to silence him in order to gain attention for himself; but I acknowledge that such means of controversy may be tragically inevitable.

JÜRGEN HABERMAS
b. 1929

Influenced by the Frankfort School, Jürgen Habermas applies neo-Marxism to social theories to meet postmodern society's needs. Perhaps best known for what he calls "universal pragmatics," he uses speech act theory to show how one constructs discourse to achieve communicative competence. To Habermas, the ideal speech situation is composed of five kinds of utterances: objective, intersubjective, explanation, ethical, reflexive. The speaker/writer freely uses all five speech acts to effect sound reasoning. Thus, Habermas regards rhetoric as doing *(symbolic action) rather than* creating *"truth." Of most interest to rhetoricians are* Communication and the Evolution of Society *(1979) and* The Theory of Communicative Action, Volume I: Reason and the Rationalization of Society.

Intermediate Reflections:
Social Action, Purposive Activity,
and Communication

On the Classification of Speech Acts

If it is true that the validity of speech acts oriented to reaching understanding can be contested under precisely three universal aspects, we might conjecture that a system of validity claims also underlies the differentiation of types of speech acts. If so, the universality thesis would also have implications for attempts to classify speech acts from theoretical points of view. Up to this point I have been tacitly employing a division into regulative, expressive, and constative speech acts. I would like now to justify this division by way of a critical examination of other classificatory schemes.

As is well known, at the end of his series of lectures on "How to Do Things with Words," Austin had a go at a typology of speech acts. He ordered illocutionary acts in terms of performative verbs and distinguished five types (verdictives, exercitives, commissives, behabitives, and expositives), without denying the provisional character of this division. In fact, it is only for the class of commissives that Austin gives us a clear criterion of demarcation: With promises, threats, announcements, vows, contracts, and the like, the speaker commits himself to carry out certain actions in the future. The speaker enters into a normative bond that obliges him to act in a certain way. The remaining classes are not satisfactorily defined, even if one takes into account the descriptive character of the division. They do not meet the requirements of distinctness and disjunctiveness; we are not forced by Austin's classificatory scheme always to assign different phenomena to different categories nor to assign each phenomenon to at most one category.

The class of verdictives comprises utterances with which "judgments" or "verdicts"—in the sense of appraisals and assessments—are made. Austin does not distinguish here between judgments with descriptive content and those with normative content. Thus there is some overlap with both the expositives and the exercitives. The class of exercitives comprises, to begin with, all declaratives, that is, expressions of institutionally—for the most part, legally—authorized decisions (such as sentencing, adopting, appointing, nominating, resigning). There is overlap with both verdictives (such as naming and awarding) and behabitives (such as protesting). These behabitives in turn form a class that is quite heterogeneous in composition. In addition to verbs for standardized expressions of feeling (such as complaints and expressions of sympathy), it contains expressions for institutionally bound utterances (congratulations, curses, toasts, greetings of welcome) as well as expressions for satisfactions (apologies, thanks, all sorts of making good). Finally, the class of expositives does not discriminate between constatives, which serve to represent states of affairs, and communicatives, which (like asking, replying, addressing, citing, and the like) refer to speech itself. Also to be distinguished from these are the expressions with which we designate the execution of operations (such as deducing, identifying, calculating, classifying, and the like).

Searle has attempted to sharpen Austin's classification. He no longer orients himself to a list of performative verbs differentiated in a specific language, but to the illocutionary aim, the particular "point" or "purpose" that speakers pursue with various types of speech acts, independently of the forms in which they are realized in individual languages. He arrives at a clear and intuitively evident classification: assertive (or constative), commissive, directive, declarative, and expressive speech acts. To start with, Searle introduces assertive (constative, representative) speech acts as a well-defined class. Then he takes over from Austin the class of commissives and contrasts these with the directives. Whereas with the former the speaker commits himself to an action, with the latter he tries to get the hearer to carry out a certain action. Among the directives Searle counts order, command, request, invite, as well as ask, pray, and entreat. He does not discriminate here between normatively authorized imperatives—such as petition, reprimand, order, and the like—and simple imperatives, that is, nonauthorized expressions of will. For this reason, the delimitation of directives from declaratives is also not very sharp. It is true that for declarative utterances we need particular institutions that secure the obligatory character of, for instance, appointing, abdicating, declaring war, and giving notice; but their normative meaning is similar to that of commands and directions. The last class comprises expressive speech acts. These are defined by their illocutionary point: with them the speaker brings sincerely to expression his psychic attitudes. But Searle is uncertain in his application of this criterion; thus the exemplary cases of avowals, disclosures, and revelations are missing. Apologies and expressions of joy and sympathy are mentioned. Apparently Searle has let himself be misled by Austin's characterization of behabitives to tack onto this class institutionally bound speech acts like congratulations and greetings as well.

Searle's sharpened version of Austin's speech act typology marks the starting point of a discussion that has developed in two different directions. The first is characterized by Searle's own efforts to provide an ontological grounding for the five types of speech acts; the other is marked by the attempt to develop the classification of speech acts from the standpoint of empirical pragmatics so as to make it fruitful for the analysis of speech-act sequences in everyday communication.

It is along this latter path that we find the work of linguists and sociolinguists like Wunderlich, Campbell, and Kreckel. In empirical pragmatics social-life contexts are represented as communicative actions that intermesh in social spaces and historical times. The patterns of illocutionary forces realized in particular languages reflect the structures of this network of actions. The linguistic possibilities for performing illocutionary acts—whether in the fixed form of grammatical modes or in the more flexible form of performative verbs, sentence particles, sentence intonations, and the like—provide schemata for establishing interpersonal relations. The illocutionary forces constitute the knots in the network of communicative sociation; the illocutionary lexicon is, as it were, the sectional plane in which the language and the institutional order of a society interpenetrate. This societal infrastructure·of language is itself in flux; it varies in dependence on institutions and forms of life. But these variations *also* embody a linguistic creativity that gives new forms of expression to the innovative mastery of unforeseen situations.

Indicators that relate to the general dimensions of the speech situation are important for a pragmatic classification of speech acts. In the *temporal dimension* there is the question of whether participants are oriented more to the future, the past, or the present, or whether the speech acts are temporally neutral. In the *social dimension* there is the question of whether obligations relevant for the sequence of interaction arise for the speaker, the hearer, or for both parties. And for the *dimension of content* there arises the question of whether the thematic center of gravity lies more with the objects, the actions, or the actors themselves. M. Kreckel uses these indicators to propose a classification on which she bases her analyses of everyday communication (see Table 1).

Table 1
Classification According to Three Pragmatic Indicators

	Speaker (S)	Hearer (H)
	Cognition oriented (C)	*Cognition oriented (C)*

Present	Does the speaker indicate that he has taken up the hearer's message?
	
	Examples: agreeing
	          acknowledging
	          rejecting
		Does the speaker try to influence the hearer's view of the world?
		
		Examples: asserting
		          arguing
		          declaring

	Person oriented (P)	*Person oriented (P)*

Past	Does the speaker refer to himself and/or his past action?
	
	Examples: justifying
	          defending
	          lamenting
		Does the speaker refer to the person of the hearer and/or his past action?
		
		Examples: accusing
		          criticizing
		          teasing

	Action oriented (A)	*Action oriented (A)*

Future	Does the speaker commit himself to future action?
	
	Examples: promising
	          refusing
	          giving in
		Does the speaker try to make the hearer do something?
		
		Examples: advising
		          challenging
		          ordering

The advantage of this and similar classifications consists in the fact that they provide us with a guideline for ethnolinguistic and sociolinguistic descriptive systems and are more of a match for the complexity of natural scenes than are typologies that start from illocutionary points and purposes rather than from features of situations. But they pay for this advantage by relinquishing the intuitive evidence of classifications that link up with semantic analyses and take account of the elementary functions of language (such as the representation of states of affairs, the expression of experiences, and the establishment of interpersonal relations). The classes of speech acts that are arrived at inductively and constructed in accordance with pragmatic indicators do not consolidate into intuitive types; they lack the theoretical power to illuminate our intuitions. Searle takes the step to *a theoretically motivated typology of speech acts* by giving an ontological characterization of the illocutionary aims and the propositional attitudes that a speaker pursues or adopts when he performs assertive (or constative), directive, commissive, declarative, and expressive speech acts. In doing so he draws upon the familiar model that defines the world as the totality of states of affairs, sets up the speaker/actor outside of this world, and allows for precisely two linguistically mediated relations between actor and world: the cognitive relation of ascertaining facts and the interventionist relation of realizing a goal of action. The illocutionary aims can be characterized in terms of the direction in which sentences and facts are supposed to be brought into accord. The arrow pointing downwards says that the sentences are supposed to fit the facts; the arrow pointing upwards says that the facts are to be fit to the sentences. Thus the assertoric force of constative speech acts and the imperative force of directive speech acts appear as follows:

Constative	$\vdash$		$\downarrow$ C (p)
Directive	!		$\uparrow$ I (H brings about p)

where C stands for cognitions or the propositional attitudes of thinking, believing, supposing, and the like, and I stands for intentions or the propositional attitudes of wanting, desiring, intending, and the like. The assertoric force signifies that S raises a truth claim for p vis-a-vis H, that is, he assumes responsibility for the agreement of the assertoric sentence with the facts ($\downarrow$); the imperative force signifies that S raises a power claim vis-a-vis H for seeing to it that "H brings about p," that is, he assumes responsibility for having the facts brought into agreement with the imperative sentence ($\uparrow$). In describing illocutionary forces by means of the relations between language and the world, Searle has recourse to the conditions of satisfaction for assertoric and imperative sentences. He finds his theoretical standpoint for classifying speech acts in the dimension of validity. But he restricts himself to the perspective of the speaker and disregards the dynamics of the negotiation and intersubjective recognition of validity claims—that is, the building of consensus. The model of two linguistically mediated relations between a solitary actor and the one objective world has no place for the intersubjective relation between participants in communication who come to an understanding with one another about something in the world. In being worked out, this ontological concept proves to be too narrow.

The commissive speech acts seem at first to fit easily into the model. With a speech act of this type S assumes vis-a-vis H responsibility for bringing the facts into agreement with the intentional sentence ($\uparrow$):

Commissive C'		$\uparrow$ I (S brings about p)

In analyzing the use of intentional sentences in announcements, we saw that the illocutionary force of commissive speech acts cannot be explained through the conditions of satisfaction, that is, the conditions for fulfilling the announced intention. But it is only this that is meant by ($\uparrow$). With commissive speech acts the speaker *binds* his will in the sense of a *normative obligation;* and the conditions for *the reliability of a declaration* of intention are of quite another sort than the conditions that the speaker satisfies when he lives up to his intention as an actor. Searle would have to distinguish conditions of validity from conditions of satisfaction.

In a similar way, we distinguished normatively authorized imperatives such as directions, commands, ordinances, and the like from mere imperatives; with the former the speaker raises a normative validity claim, with the latter an externally sanctioned claim to power. For this reason, not even the full modal meaning of simple imperatives can be explained by the conditions for fulfilling the imperative sentences thereby employed. Even if that would do, Searle would have difficulty in reducing the class of directives to the class of simple imperatives, or in delimiting genuine imperatives from directions, orders, or commands, since his model does not allow for conditions of validity other than those for propositional truth and efficiency. This lack is especially noticeable when Searle tries to accommodate declarative and expressive speech acts in his system.

It is evident that the illocutionary force of a declaration of war, a resignation, the opening of a session, the reading of a bill, or the like cannot be interpreted according to the schema of two directions of fit. In producing institutional facts, a speaker does not at all refer to something in the objective world; rather he acts in accord with the legitimate orders of the social world and at the same time initiates new interpersonal relations. It is purely out of embarrassment that Searle symbolizes this meaning, which belongs to *another* world, by a double arrow coined in respect to the objective world:

declarative $\qquad\qquad\qquad\qquad$ D $\updownarrow$ (p)

where no special propositional attitudes are supposed to be required. This embarrassment turns up once again in the case of expressive speech acts, whose illocutionary force can just as little be characterized in terms of an actor's relations to the world of existing states of affairs. Searle is consistent enough to give expression to the inapplicability of his scheme through a neither/nor sign:

expressive speech acts $\qquad\qquad\qquad$ E $\emptyset$ (p)

where any propositional attitude is possible.

We can avoid the difficulties of Searle's attempts at classification, while retaining his fruitful theoretical approach, if we start from the fact that the illocutionary aims of speech acts are achieved through the intersubjective recognition of claims to power or validity, and if, further, we introduce normative rightness and subjective truthfulness as validity claims analogous to truth and interpret them too in terms of actor/world relations. This revision yields the following classification:

- With *imperatives* the speaker refers to a desired state in the objective world, and in such a way that he would like to get *H* to bring about this state. Imperatives can be criticized only from the standpoint of whether the action demanded can be carried out, that is, in connection with conditions of satisfaction. However, refusing imperatives normally means rejecting a claim to power; it is not based on criticism but itself *expresses a will.*
- With *constative speech acts* the speaker refers to something in the objective world, and in such a way that he would like to represent a state of affairs. The negation of such an utterance means that *H contests* the validity claim raised by *S* for the proposition stated.
- With *regulative speech acts* the speaker refers to something in a common social world, and in such a way that he would like to establish an interpersonal relation recognized as legitimate. The negation of such an utterance means that *H contests* the normative rightness claimed by *S* for his action (or for an underlying norm).
- With *expressive speech acts* the speaker refers to something in his subjective world, and in such a way that he would like to reveal to a public an experience to which he has privileged access. The negation of such an utterance means that *H doubts* the claim to sincerity of self-representation raised by *S.*

Communicatives constitute another class of speech acts. They can also be understood as that subclass of regulative speech acts—questioning and answering, addressing, objecting, admitting, and the like—that serve *the organization of speech,* its arrangement into themes and contributions, the distribution of conversational roles, the regulation of turn-taking in conversation, and the like. But it is more convenient to regard the communicatives as an independent class instead and to define them through their *reflexive relation to the process of communication;* for then we can also include those speech acts that refer directly to validity claims (affirming, denying, assuring, confirming, and the like).

Finally, there is the class of *operatives,* that is, of speech acts—such as inferring, identifying, calculating, classifying, counting, predicting, and the like—that signify the application of generative rules (of logic, grammar, mathematics, and the like). Operative speech acts have a performative sense but *no genuine communicative intent;* they serve at the same time to *describe* what one does in constructing symbolic expressions in conformity with generative rules.

If one takes this classification as basic, commissives and declaratives, as well as institutionally bound speech acts (betting, marrying, oath-taking) and satisfactives (which relate to excuses and apologies for violating norms, as well as to reparations), must all be subsumed under the same class of regulative speech acts. One can see from this that the basic modes have to be further differentiated. They cannot be used for the analysis of everyday communication until we succeed in developing taxonomies for *the whole spectrum of illocutionary forces* differentiated out in a given language within the boundaries of a specific basic mode. Only very few illocutionary acts—like assertions and statements, promises and directions, avowals and disclosures—are so general that they can characterize a basic mode as such. Of course, the possibilities of expression standardized in particular languages mark not only the relation to validity claims in general, but the *way* in which a speaker claims truth, rightness, or truthfulness for a symbolic expression. Pragmatic indicators—such as the degree of institutional dependence of speech acts, the orientation to past and future, the speaker/hearer orientation, the thematic focus, and so forth—can now help us to grasp systematically *the illocutionary modifications of validity claims.* Only an empirical pragmatics that is theoretically guided will be able to develop speech-act taxonomies which are informative, that is, which are neither blind nor empty.

The pure types of language-use oriented to reaching understanding are suitable as guidelines for constructing typologies of linguistically mediated interaction. In communicative action the plans of individual participants are coordinated by means of the illocutionary binding (or bonding) effects of speech acts. Thus we might conjecture that constative, regulative, and expressive speech acts also constitute corresponding types of linguistically mediated interaction. This is obviously true of regulative and expressive speech acts, which are constitutive for what we have discussed under the titles of normatively regulated and dramaturgical action. At first glance there seems to be no type of interaction that would correspond in the same way to constative speech acts. However, there are contexts of action that do not *primarily* serve the carrying out of communicatively harmonized plans of action (that is, the purposive activities of the participants) but make communication possible and stabilize it—for instance, chatting, conversing, and arguing—in general conversation that becomes an end in itself. In such cases the process of reaching understanding is detached from the instrumental role of serving as a mechanism for coordinating individual actions, and the discussion of themes becomes independent for purposes of conversation. I shall speak of "conversation" when the weight is shifted in this way from purposive activity to communication; argumentation is perhaps the most important special case of conversation. As interest in the topics discussed is here predominant, we could perhaps say that constative speech acts have constitutive significance for conversations.

Thus our classification of speech acts can serve to introduce three pure types—or better, *limit cases*—of communicative action: conversation, normatively regulated action, and dramaturgical action. If we further take into account the internal relation of strategic action to perlocutionary acts and imperatives, we get the classification of linguistically mediated interactions in Table 2.

Formal and Empirical Pragmatics

Even if the program I have outlined for a theory of speech acts were carried out, one might ask what would be gained for a useful sociological theory of action by such a formal-pragmatic approach. The question arises, why would not an empirical-pragmatic approach be better for this, an approach that did not dwell on the rational reconstruction of isolated, highly idealized speech acts but started at once with the communicative practice of everyday life? From the side of linguistics there are interesting contributions to the analysis of stories and texts, from sociology contributions to conversational analysis, from anthropology contributions to the ethnography of speech, and from psychology investigations into the pragmatic variables of linguistic interaction. By comparison, formal pragmatics—which, in its reconstructive intention (that is, in the sense of a theory of competence) is directed to the universal presuppositions of communicative action—seems to be hopelessly removed from actual language use. Under these circumstances, does it make any sense to insist on a formal-pragmatic grounding for an action theory?

I would like to respond to this question by first (a) enumerating the methodological steps through which formal pragmatics gains a connection to empirical pragmatics; then I shall (b) identify the problems that make it necessary to clarify the rational foundations of processes of reaching understanding; finally, I would like (c) to take up a strategically important argument, about which empirical pragmatics has to learn from formal pragmatics if the problem of rationality is not to end up in the wrong place—that is, in the orientations for action, as it does in Max Weber's theory of action—but in the general structures of the lifeworld to which acting subjects belong.

(a) The pure types of linguistically mediated interaction can be brought progressively closer to the complexity of natural situations without sacrificing all theoretical perspectives for analyzing the coordination of interactions. This task consists in reversing step by step the strong idealizations by which we have built up the concept of communicative action:

- In addition to the basic modes, we first admit the concretely shaped illocutionary forces that form the culture-specific net of possible interpersonal relations standardized in each individual language;

Table 2
Pure Types of Linguistically Mediated Interaction

Formal-Pragmatic Features / Types of Action	Characteristic Speech Acts	Functions of Speech	Action Orientations	Basic Attitudes	Validity Claims	World Relations
Strategic Action	Perlocutions Imperatives	Influencing one's opposite number	Oriented to success	Objectivating	(Effectiveness)	Objective world
Conversation	Constatives	Representation of states of affairs	Oriented to reaching understanding	Objectivating	Truth	Objective world
Normatively Regulated Action	Regulatives	Establishment of interpersonal relations	Oriented to reaching understanding	Norm-conformative	Rightness	Social world
Dramaturgical Action	Expressives	Self-representation	Oriented to reaching understanding	Expressive	Truthfulness	Subjective world

- In addition to the standard forms of speech acts, we admit other forms of linguistic realization of speech acts;
- In addition to explicit speech acts, we admit elliptically foreshortened, extraverbally supplemented, implicit utterances, for understanding which the hearer is thrown back upon the knowledge of nonstandardized, contingent contexts;
- In addition to direct speech acts, we admit indirect, transposed, and ambiguous expressions, the meaning of which has to be inferred from the context;
- The focus is enlarged from isolated acts of communication (and yes/no responses) to sequences of speech acts, to texts or conversations, so that conversational implications can come into view;
- In addition to the objectivating, norm-conformative and expressive basic attitudes, we admit an overlapping performative attitude, to take account of the fact that with each speech act participants in communication relate simultaneously to something in the objective, social, and subjective worlds;
- In addition to the level of acts of communication (that is, speech), we bring in the level of communicative action (that is, the coordination of the plans of individual participants);
- Finally, in addition to communicative action, we include in our analysis the resources of the background knowledge (that is, lifeworlds) from which participants feed their interpretations.

These extensions amount to dropping the methodological provisions that we began with in introducing standard speech acts. In the standard case the literal meaning of the sentences uttered coincides with what the speaker means with his speech act. However, the more that what the speaker means with his utterance is made to depend on a background knowledge that remains implicit, the more the context-specific meaning of the utterance can diverge from the literal meaning of what is said.

When one drops the idealization of a complete and literal representation of the meaning of utterances, the resolution of another problem is also made easier—namely, distinguishing and identifying in natural situations actions oriented to understanding and actions oriented to success. Here we must take into consideration that not only do illocutions appear in strategic-action contexts, but perlocutions appear in contexts of communicative action as well. Cooperative interpretive processes run through different phases. In the initial phase participants are often handicapped by the fact that their interpretations do not overlap sufficiently for the purpose of coordinating actions. In this phase participants have either to shift to the level of metacommunication or to employ means of indirectly achieving understanding.

Coming indirectly to an understanding proceeds according to the model of intentionalist semantics. Through perlocutionary effects, the speaker gives the hearer something to understand which he cannot (yet) directly communicate. In this phase, then, the perlocutionary acts have to be embedded in contexts of communicative action. These strategic *elements* within a use of language oriented to reaching understanding can be distinguished from strategic *actions* through the fact that the entire sequence of a stretch of talk stands—on the part of all participants—under the presuppositions of communicative action.

(*b*) An empirical pragmatics without a formal-pragmatic point of departure would not have the conceptual instruments needed to recognize the rational basis of linguistic communication in the confusing complexity of the everyday scenes observed. It is only in formal-pragmatic investigations that we can secure for ourselves an idea of reaching understanding that can guide empirical analysis into particular problems—such as the linguistic representation of different levels of reality, the manifestation of communication pathologies, or the development of a decentered understanding of the world.

The linguistic *demarcation of the levels of reality* of "play" and "seriousness," the linguistic construction of a fictive reality, wit and irony, transposed and paradoxical uses of language, allusions and the contradictory withdrawal of validity claims at a metacommunicative level—all these accomplishments rest on intentionally confusing modalities of being. For clarifying the mechanisms of deception that a speaker has to master to do this, formal pragmatics can do more than even the most precise empirical description of the phenomena to be explained. With training in the basic modes of language use, the growing child gains the ability to demarcate the subjectivity of his own expressions from the objectivity of an external reality, from the normativity of society, and from the intersubjectivity of the medium of language itself. In learning to deal hypothetically with the corresponding validity claims, he practices drawing the categorial distinctions between essence and appearance, being and illusion, "is" and "ought," sign and meaning. With these modalities of being he gets hold of the deceptive phenomena that first spring from the unwilling confusion between his own subjectivity, on the one hand, and the domains of the objective, the normative, and the intersubjective, on the other. He now knows how one can master the confusions, produce de-differentiations intentionally, and employ them in fiction, wit, irony, and the like.

The situation is similar with manifestations of *systematically distorted communication.* Here too formal pragmatics can contribute to the explanation of phenomena that are first identified only on the basis of an intuitive understanding matured by clinical experience. Such communication pathologies can be conceived of as the result of a confusion between actions oriented to reaching understanding and actions oriented to success. In situations of concealed strategic action, at least one of the parties behaves with an orientation to success, but leaves others to believe that all the presuppositions of communicative action are satisfied. This is the case of manipulation which we mentioned in connection with perlocutionary acts. On the other hand, the kind of unconscious repression of conflicts that the psychoanalyst explains in terms of defense mechanisms leads to disturbances of communication on both the intrapsychic and interpersonal levels. In such cases at least one of the parties is deceiving himself about the fact that he is acting with an attitude oriented to success and is only keeping up the appearance of communicative action. The place of systematically distorted communication within a framework of a theory of communicative action can be seen in Figure 1.

Figure 1

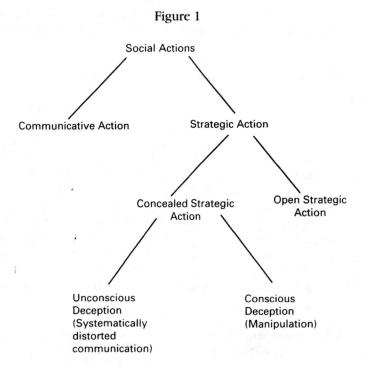

In the present context, the main advantage of a formal pragmatics is that it highlights, in the pure types of linguistically mediated interaction, precisely those aspects under which social actions embody different sorts of knowledge. The theory of communicative action can make good the weaknesses we found in Weber's action theory, inasmuch as it does not remain fixated on purposive rationality as the only aspect under which action can be criticized and improved. Drawing on the types of action introduced above, I would like now to comment briefly on the different aspects of the rationality of action.

Teleological actions can be judged under the aspect of effectiveness. The rules of action embody technically and strategically useful knowledge, which can be criticized in reference to truth claims and can be improved through a feedback relation with the growth of empirical-theoretical knowledge. This knowledge is stored in the form of technologies and strategies.

Constative speech acts, which not only embody knowledge but explicitly represent it and make conversations possible, can be criticized under the aspect of truth. In cases of more obstinate controversy concerning the truth of statements, theoretical discourse offers its services as a continuation, with different means, of action oriented to reaching understanding. When discursive examination loses its ad hoc character and empirical knowledge is systematically placed in question, when quasi-natural learning processes are guided through the sluices of argumentation, there results a cumulative effect—this knowledge is stored in the form of theories.

Normatively regulated speech acts embody moral-practical knowledge. They can be contested under the aspect of rightness. Like claims to truth, controversial claims to rightness can be made thematic and examined discursively. In cases of disturbance of the regulative use of language, practical discourse offers its services as a continuation of consensual action with other means. In moral-practical argumentation, participants can test both the rightness of a given action in relation to a given norm, and, at the next level, the rightness of such a norm itself. This knowledge is handed down in the form of legal and moral representations.

Dramaturgical actions embody a knowledge of the agent's own subjectivity. These expressions can be criticized as untruthful, that is, rejected as deceptions or self-deceptions. Self-deceptions can be dissolved in therapeutic dialogue by argumentative means. Expressive knowledge can be explicated in terms of those values that underlie need interpretations, the interpretations of desires and emotional attitudes. Value standards are dependent in turn on innovations in the domain of evaluative expressions. These are reflected in an exemplary manner in works of art. The aspects of the rationality of action are summarized in Table 3.

(c) This interconnection of action orientations, types of knowledge, and forms of argumentation is, of course, inspired by Weber's idea that in modern Europe, with the development of science, morals, and art, stores of explicit knowledge were differentiated out; these flowed into various domains of institutionalized everyday action and, as it were, put under the pressure of rationalization certain action orientations that had been determined in a traditionalist manner. The aspects of the rationality of action that

Table 3
Aspects of the Rationality of Action

Types of Action	Type of Knowledge Embodied	Form of Argumentation	Model of Transmitted Knowledge
Teleological Action: instrumental, strategic	Technically and strategically useful knowledge	Theoretical discourse	Technologies, Strategies
Constative Speech Acts (conversation)	Empirical-theoretical knowledge	Theoretical discourse	Theories
Normatively Regulated Action	Moral-practical knowledge	Practical discourse	Legal and moral representations
Dramaturgical Action	Aesthetic practical knowledge	Therapeutic and aesthetic critique	Works of art

we found in communicative action should now permit us to grasp processes of societal rationalization across their whole breadth, and no longer solely from the selective viewpoint of the rationalization of purposive-rational action.

In posing the problem in this way, the role of implicit knowledge is not given its due. We are not yet clear about the horizon of everyday action into which the explicit knowledge of cultural experts comes rushing, nor about how the communicative practice of everyday life actually changes with this influx. The concept of action oriented to reaching understanding has the additional—and quite different—advantage of throwing light on this background of implicit knowledge which enters *a tergo* into cooperative processes of interpretation. Communicative action takes place within a lifeworld that remains at the backs of participants in communication. It is present to them only in the prereflective form of taken-for-granted background assumptions and naively mastered skills.

If the investigations of the last decade in socio-, ethno-, and psycholinguistics converge in any one respect, it is on the often and variously demonstrated point that the collective background and context of speakers and hearers determines interpretations of their explicit utterances to an extraordinarily high degree. Searle has taken up this doctrine of empirical pragmatics and criticized the long dominant view that sentences get *literal meaning* only by virtue of the rules for using the expressions contained in them. So far, I have also construed the meaning of speech acts as literal meaning in this sense. Naturally this meaning could not be thought independently of contextual conditions altogether; for each type of speech act there are *general* contextual conditions that must be met if the speaker is to be able to achieve illocutionary success. But these general contextual conditions could supposedly be derived in turn from the literal meaning of the linguistic expressions employed in the standard speech acts. And as a matter of fact, if formal pragmatics is not to lose its object, knowledge of the conditions under which speech acts may be accepted as valid cannot depend *completely* on contingent background knowledge.

However, Searle has now shown—in connection with such simple assertions as "The cat is on the mat" and such imperatives as "Give me a hamburger"—that the truth conditions of the assertoric and imperative sentences employed therein cannot be completely determined independently of implicit contextual knowledge. If we begin to vary relatively deep-seated and trivial background assumptions, we notice that the (only) seemingly context-invariant conditions of validity change meaning and are thus by no means absolute. Searle does not go so far as to deny to sentences and utterances a literal meaning; but he does defend the thesis that the literal meaning of an expression must be completed by the background of an implicit knowledge that participants normally regard as trivial and obvious.

The sense of this thesis is not to reduce the meaning of a speech act to what a speaker means by it in a contingent context. Searle is not maintaining a simple relativism of the meaning of linguistic expressions; for their meaning does not change as we pass from one contingent context to the next. We discover the incompleteness of the literal meaning of expressions only through a sort of problematizing that is not directly under our control. It emerges as a result of problems that appear objectively and have an unsettling effect on our natural worldview. The fundamental background knowledge that must tacitly supplement our knowledge of the acceptability conditions of linguistically standardized expressions if hearers are to be able to understand their literal meanings, has remarkable features: It is an *implicit* knowledge that cannot be represented in a finite number of propositions; it is a *holistically structured* knowledge, the basic elements of which intrinsically define one another; and it is a knowledge that *does not stand at our disposition*, inasmuch as we cannot make it conscious and place it in doubt as we please. When philosophers nevertheless seek to do so, then that knowledge comes to light in the form of the commonsense certainties in which G. E. Moore, for instance, took an interest, and to which Wittgenstein referred in his reflections "On Certainty."

Wittgenstein calls these certainties elements of a worldview that are "anchored in all my questions and answers, so anchored that I cannot touch [them]." Beliefs that do not fit such convictions—convictions that are as beyond question as they are fundamental—appear to be absurd. "Not that I could describe the system of these convictions. Yet my convictions do form a system, a structure." Wittgenstein characterizes the dogmatism of everyday background assumptions and skills in a way similar to that in which Schutz describes the mode of taken-for-grantedness in which the lifeworld is present as a prereflexive background.

> The child learns to believe a host of things. I.e. it learns to act according to these beliefs. Bit by bit there forms a system of what is believed, and in that system some things stand unshakeably fast and some are more or less liable to shift. What stands fast does so, not because it is intrinsically obvious or convincing; it is rather held fast by what lies around it.

Literal meanings are, then, relative to a deep-seated, implicit knowledge, *about* which we normally know nothing, because it is simply unproblematic and does not pass the threshold of communicative utterances that can be valid or invalid. "If the true is what is grounded, then the ground is not true, nor yet false."

Searle encounters this layer of worldview knowledge functioning in everyday life as the background with which a hearer has to be familiar if he is to be able to understand the literal meaning of speech acts and to act communicatively. He thereby directs our gaze to a continent that remains hidden so long as the theoretician analyzes speech acts only from the perspective of the speaker who relates with his utterances to something in the objective, social, and subjective worlds. It is only with the turn back to the context-forming horizon of the lifeworld, from within which participants in communication come to an understanding with one another about something, that our field of vision changes in such a way that we can see the points of connection for social theory within the theory of communicative action: The concept of society has to be linked to a concept of the lifeworld that is complementary to the concept of communicative action. Then communicative action becomes interesting primarily as a principle of sociation: Communicative action provides the medium for the reproduction of lifeworlds. At the same time, processes of societal rationalization are given a different place. They transpire more in implicitly known structures of the lifeworld than in explicitly known action orientations (as Weber suggested). I shall take up this topic once more in the second set of "intermediate reflections."

ROLAND BARTHES
1915-1980

Roland Barthes is considered the foremost French literary critic of his generation. His work in semiotics is particularly influential. Barthes never achieved a position at the center of contemporary criticism because of his nontraditional, noncanonical approaches to literature. He laid out his theory in Elements of Semiology *(1960),* Criticism and Truth *(1967),* S/Z *(1970), and* New Critical Essays *(1980). Of special interest to rhetoricians is his inclusive view of rhetoric as encompassing nonlinguistic symbol systems as well as writing and speaking.*

The Pleasure of the Text

I am offered a text. This text bores me. It might be said to *prattle*. The prattle of the text is merely that foam of language which forms by the effect of a simple need of writing. Here we are not dealing with perversion but with demand. The writer of this text employs an unweaned language: imperative, automatic, unaffectionate, a minor disaster of static (those milky phonemes which the remarkable Jesuit, van Ginnekin, posited between writing and language): these are the motions of ungratified sucking, of an undifferentiated orality, intersecting the orality which produces the pleasures of gastrosophy and of language. You address yourself to me so that I may read you, but I am nothing to you except this address; in your eyes, I am the substitute for nothing, for no figure (hardly that of the mother); for you I am neither a body nor even an object (and I couldn't care less: I am not the one whose soul demands recognition), but merely a field, a vessel for expansion. It can be said that after all you have written this text quite apart from bliss; and this prattling text is then a frigid text, as any demand is frigid until desire, until neurosis forms in it.

Neurosis is a makeshift: not with regard to "health" but with regard to the "impossible" Bataille speaks of ("Neurosis is the fearful apprehension of an ultimate impossible," etc.); but this makeshift is the only one that allows for writing (and reading). So we arrive at this paradox: the texts, like those by Bataille—or by others—which are written against neurosis, from the center of madness, contain within themselves, *if they want to be read,* that bit of neurosis necessary to the seduction of their readers: these terrible texts are *all the same* flirtatious texts.

221

Thus every writer's motto reads: *mad I cannot be, sane I do not deign to be, neurotic I am.*

The text you write must prove to me *that it desires me.* This proof exists: it is writing. Writing is: the science of the various blisses of language, its Kama Sutra (this science has but one treatise: writing itself).

Sade: the pleasure of reading him clearly proceeds from certain breaks (or certain collisions): antipathetic codes (the noble and the trivial, for example) come into contact; pompous and ridiculous neologisms are created; pornographic messages are embodied in sentences so pure they might be used as grammatical models. As textual theory has it: the language is redistributed. Now, *such redistribution is always achieved by cutting.* Two edges are created: an obedient, conformist, plagiarizing edge (the language is to be copied in its canonical state, as it has been established by schooling, good usage, literature, culture), and *another edge,* mobile, blank (ready to assume any contours), which is never anything but the site of its effect: the place where the death of language is glimpsed. These two edges, *the compromise they bring about,* are necessary. Neither culture nor its destruction is erotic; it is the seam between them, the fault, the flaw, which becomes so. The pleasure of the text is like that untenable, impossible, purely *novelistic* instant so relished by Sade's libertine when he manages to be hanged and then to cut the rope at the very moment of his orgasm, his bliss.

Whence, perhaps, a means of evaluating the works of our modernity: their value would proceed from their duplicity. By which it must be understood that they always have two edges. The subversive edge may seem privileged because it is the edge of violence; but it is not violence which affects pleasure, nor is it destruction which interests it; what pleasure wants is the site of a loss, the seam, the cut, the deflation, the *dissolve* which seizes the subject in the midst of bliss. Culture thus recurs as an edge: in no matter what form.

. . .

The stereotype is the word repeated without any magic, any enthusiasm, as though it were natural, as though by some miracle this recurring word were adequate on each occasion for different reasons, as though to imitate could no longer be sensed as an imitation: an unconstrained word that claims consistency and is unaware of its own insistence. Nietzsche has observed that "truth" is only the solidification of old metaphors. So in this regard the stereotype is the present path of "truth," the palpable feature which shifts the invented ornament to the canonical, constraining form of the signified. (It would be good to imagine a new linguistic science that would no longer study the origin of words, or etymology, or even their diffusion, or lexicology, but the progress of their solidification, their densification throughout historical discourse; this science would doubtless be subversive, manifesting much more than the historical origin of truth: its rhetorical, *languaging* nature.)

The distrust of the stereotype (linked to the bliss of the new word or the untenable discourse) is a principle of absolute instability which respects nothing (no content, no choice). Nausea occurs whenever the liaison of two important words *follows of itself.* And when something follows of itself, I abandon it: that is bliss. A futile annoyance? In Poe's story, M. Valdemar, hypnotized and moribund, is kept alive in a cataleptic state by the repetition of the questions put to him ("Are you asleep, M. Valdemar?"); however, this survival is untenable: the false death, the atrocious death, is what has no end, the interminable. ("For God's sake!—quick!—put me to sleep—or, quick—waken me!—quick!—I say to you that I am dead!") The stereotype is this nauseating impossibility of dying.

In the intellectual field, political choice is a suspension of language—thus a bliss. Yet language resumes, in its consistent stable form (the political stereotype). Which language must then be swallowed, without nausea.

Another bliss (other edges): it consists in de-politicizing what is apparently political, and in politicizing what apparently is not.—Come now, surely one politicizes what *must* be politicized, and that's all.

Nihilism: "superior goals depreciate." This is an unstable, jeopardized moment, for other superior values tend, immediately and before the former are destroyed, to prevail; dialectics only links successive positivities; whence the suffocation at the very heart of anarchism. How *install* the deficiency of any superior value? Irony? It always proceeds from a *sure* site. Violence? Violence too is a superior value, and among the best coded. Bliss? Yes, if it is not spoken, doctrinal. The most consistent nihilism is perhaps *masked:* in some way *interior* to institutions, to conformist discourse, to apparent finalities.

• • •

Why do some people, including myself, enjoy in certain novels, biographies, and historical works the representation of the "daily life" of an epoch, of a character? Why this curiosity about petty details: schedules, habits, meals, lodging, clothing, etc.? Is it the hallucinatory relish of "reality" (the very materiality of "*that once existed*")? And is it not the fantasy itself which invokes the "detail," the tiny private scene, in which I can easily take my place? Are there, in short, "minor hysterics" (these very readers) who receive bliss from a singular theater: not one of grandeur but one of mediocrity (might there not be dreams, fantasies of mediocrity)?

Thus, impossible to imagine a more tenuous, a more insignificant notation than that of "today's weather" (or yesterday's); and yet, the other day, reading, trying to read Amiel, irritation that the well-meaning editor (another person foreclosing pleasure) had seen fit to omit from this Journal the everyday details, what the weather was like on the shores of Lake Geneva, and retain only insipid moral musing: yet it is this weather that has not aged, not Amiel's philosophy.

Art seems compromised, historically, socially. Whence the effort on the part of the artist himself to destroy it.

I see this effort taking three forms. The artist can shift to another signifier: if he is a writer, he becomes a filmmaker, a painter, or, contrariwise, if he is a painter, a filmmaker, he works up interminable critiques of the cinema, painting, deliberately reduces the art to his criticism. He can also "dismiss" writing and become a scientist, a scholar, an intellectual theorist, no longer speaking except from a moral site cleansed of any linguistic sensuality. Finally, he can purely and simply scuttle himself, stop writing, change trades, change desires.

Unfortunately, this destruction is always inadequate; either it occurs outside the art, but thereby becomes impertinent, or else it consents to remain within the practice of the art, but quickly exposes itself to recuperation (the avant-garde is that restive language which is going to be recuperated). The awkwardness of this alternative is the consequence of the fact that destruction of discourse is not a dialectic term *but a semantic term:* it docilely takes its place within the great semiological "versus" myth (*white* versus *black*); whence the destruction of art is doomed to only *paradoxical* formulae (those which proceed literally against the *doxa*): both sides of the paradigm are glued together in an ultimately complicitous fashion: there is a structural agreement between the contesting and the contested forms.

(By *subtle subversion* I mean, on the contrary, what is not directly concerned with destruction, evades the paradigm, and seeks some *other* term: a third term, which is not, however, a synthesizing term but an eccentric, extraordinary term. An example? Perhaps Bataille, who eludes the idealist term by an *unexpected* materialism in which we find vice, devotion, play, impossible eroticism, etc.; thus Bataille does not counter modesty with sexual freedom but . . . with *laughter.*)

The text of pleasure is not necessarily the text that recounts pleasures; the text of bliss is never the text that recounts the kind of bliss afforded literally by an ejaculation. The pleasure of representation is not attached to its object: pornography is not *sure*. In zoological terms, one could say that the site of textual pleasure is not the relation of mimic and model (imitative relation) but solely that of dupe and mimic (relation of desire, of production).

We must, however, distinguish between *figuration* and *representation.*

Figuration is the way in which the erotic body appears (to whatever degree and in whatever form that may be) in the profile of the text. For example: the author may appear in his text (Genet, Proust), but not in the guise of direct biography (which would exceed the body, give a meaning to life, forge a destiny). Or again: one can feel desire for a character in a novel (in fleeting impulses). Or finally: the text itself, a diagrammatic and not an imitative structure, can reveal itself in the form of a body, split into fetish objects, into erotic sites. All these movements attest to a *figure* of the text, necessary to the bliss of reading. Similarly, and even more than the text, the film will *always* be figurative (which is why films are still worth making)— even if it represents nothing.

Representation, on the other hand, is *embarrassed figuration,* encumbered with other meanings than that of desire: a space of alibis (reality, morality, likelihood, readability, truth, etc.). Here is a text of pure representation: Barbey d'Aurevilly writes on Memling's Virgin: "She stands upright, very perpendicularly posed. Pure beings are upright. By posture and by movement, we know the chaste woman; wantons droop, languish and lean, always about to fall." Note in passing that the representative undertaking has managed to engender an art (the classical novel) as well as a "science" (graphology, for example, which deduces from the attenuation of a single letter the listlessness of the writer), and that it is consequently fair, without any sophistry, to call it immediately ideological (by the historical extent of its signification). Of course, it very often happens that representation takes desire itself as an object of imitation; but then, such desire never leaves the frame, the picture; it circulates among the characters; if it has a recipient, that recipient remains interior to the fiction (consequently, we can say that any semiotics that keeps desire within the configuration of those upon whom it acts, however new it may be, is a semiotics of representation. That is what representation is: when nothing emerges, when nothing leaps out of the frame: of the picture, the book, the screen).

No sooner has a word been said, somewhere, about the pleasure of the text, than two policemen are ready to jump on you: the political policeman and the psychoanalytical policeman: futility and/or guilt, pleasure is either idle or vain, a class notion or an illusion.

An old, a very old tradition: hedonism has been repressed by nearly every philosophy; we find it defended only by marginal figures, Sade, Fourier; for Nietzsche, hedonism is a pessimism. Pleasure is continually disappointed, reduced, deflated, in favor of strong, noble values: Truth, Death, Progress, Struggle, Joy, etc. Its victorious rival is Desire: we are always being told about Desire, never about Pleasure; Desire has an epistemic dignity, Pleasure does not. It seems that (our) society refuses (and ends up by ignoring) bliss to such a point that it can produce only epistemologies of the law (and of its contestation), never of its absence, or better still: of its nullity. Odd, this philosophical permanence of Desire (insofar as it is never satisfied): doesn't the word itself denote a "class notion"? (A rather crude presumption of proof, and yet noteworthy: the "populace" does not know Desire—only pleasures.)

So-called erotic books (one must add: of recent vintage, in order to except Sade and a few others) *represent* not so much the erotic scene as the expectation of it, the preparation for it, its ascent; that is what makes them "exciting"; and when the scene occurs, naturally there is disappointment, deflation. In other words, these are books of Desire, not of Pleasure. Or, more mischievously, they represent Pleasure *as seen by psychoanalysis*. A like meaning says, in both instances, that *the whole thing is very disappointing.*

(The monument of psychoanalysis must be traversed—not bypassed— like the fine thoroughfares of a very large city, across which we can play, dream, etc.: a fiction.)

There is supposed to be a mystique of the Text. —On the contrary, the whole effort consists in materializing the pleasure of the text, in making the text *an object of pleasure like the others.* That is: either relate the text to the "pleasures" of life (a dish, a garden, an encounter, a voice, a moment, etc.) and to it join the personal catalogue of our sensualities, or force the text to breach bliss, that immense subjective loss, thereby identifying this text with the purest moments of perversion, with its clandestine sites. The important thing is to equalize the field of pleasure, to abolish the false opposition of practical life and contemplative life. The pleasure of the text is just that: claim lodged against the separation of the text; for what the text says, through the particularity of its name, is the ubiquity of pleasure, the atopia of bliss.

Notion of a book (of a text) in which is braided, woven, in the most personal way, the relation of every kind of bliss: those of "life" and those of the text, in which reading and the risks of real life are subject to the same anamnesis.

Imagine an aesthetic (if the word has not become too depreciated) based entirely (completely, radically, in every sense of the word) on the *pleasure of the consumer,* whoever he may be, to whatever class, whatever group he may belong, without respect to cultures or languages: the consequences would be huge, perhaps even harrowing (Brecht has sketched such an aesthetic of pleasure; of all his proposals, this is the one most frequently forgotten).

• • •

In antiquity, rhetoric included a section which is forgotten, censored by classical commentators: the *actio*, a group of formulae designed to allow for the corporeal exteriorization of discourse: it dealt with a theater of expression, the actor-orator "expressing" his indignation, his compassion, etc. *Writing aloud* is not expressive; it leaves expression to the pheno-text, to the regular code of communication; it belongs to the geno-text, to significance; it is carried not by dramatic inflections, subtle stresses, sympathetic accents, but by the *grain* of the voice, which is an erotic mixture of timbre and language, and can therefore also be, along with diction, the substance of an art: the art of guiding one's body (whence its importance in Far Eastern theaters). Due allowance being made for the sounds of the language, *writing aloud* is not phonological but phonetic; its aim is not the clarity of messages, the theater of emotions; what it searches for (in a perspective of bliss) are the pulsional incidents, the language lined with flesh, a text where we can hear the grain of the throat, the patina of consonants, the voluptuousness of vowels, a whole carnal stereophony: the articulation of the body, of the tongue, not that of meaning, of language. A certain art of singing can give an idea of this vocal writing; but since melody is dead, we may find it more easily today at the cinema. In fact, it suffices that the cinema capture the sound of speech *close up* (this is, in fact, the generalized definition of the "grain" of writing) and make us hear in their materiality, their sensuality, the breath, the gutturals, the fleshiness of the lips, a whole presence of the human muzzle (that the voice, that writing, be as fresh, supple, lubricated, delicately granular and vibrant as an animal's muzzle), to succeed in shifting the signified a great distance and in throwing, so to speak, the anonymous body of the actor into my ear: it granulates, it crackles, it caresses, it grates, it cuts, it comes: that is bliss.

WAYNE C. BOOTH
b. 1921

Here, Wayne Booth situates and reflects on his work in rhetoric.

Like much of my writing, the piece here began as a speaking *assignment: one of the annual lectures given at the University of Chicago by professors trying to explain their more-or-less narrow disciplines to other specialists. Mine was the only talk in the series that seemed required to talk about itself, since rhetoric is obviously an overwhelmingly broad field that might be called "the art of talking well"—not just the art of pleasing with talk, or persuading with talk, but talking really well. How was I to explain anything as amorphous, as "soft" as that, to a pack of critically trained specialists in the "harder" sciences? Not surprisingly, the task turned out to be one of the toughest I've ever faced, and the* talk *was* written *in many drafts, long and short, over several months, as I tried to* think, *once again, about just how we might improve our talking together.*

This ambiguous relation of thinking, speaking, and writing has for several millenia in several cultures characterized the study of rhetoric. From its beginnings, years before the first great book about it was written (Aristotle's Rhetoric), *it has been defined in widely contrasting ways. Some have thought of it as simply the art of using words to win, no holds barred. Aristotle broadened it to something like "how to* think *persuasively about any and all subjects": no longer just the art of winning but the* faculty *of discovering who should win, by determining the difference between good reasons and bad. Others, especially in recent times, have stretched it even further, to become the whole art of thinking well, whether in discourse with others or in a "personal," "internal," "individual" thought that is always finally a dialogue among diverse voices. In this extension, rhetoric becomes a rival of philosophy and all other fields that claim to account, in principle, for everything. This means, of course, that it sneaks into even those fields that, like music, mathematics, physics, or computer science, claim to be most fully independent of "rhetorical" temptations. In short, I faced the task of telling all those brilliant, well-educated folks just why my field should be allowed to take charge of theirs.*

Can anyone be surprised that so far only a few experts in the sciences have paid full attention to the ways in which their work is rhetorical? (The most important, so far, is Don McCloskey's The Rhetoric of Economics.) *Is that because we imperialists have not yet learned how to make our case fully compelling?*

Other inadequate attempts of my own can be found in Modern Dogma and the Rhetoric of Assent *(1974),* Critical Understanding *(1979), and my "Response" included in a collection of essays discussing or using my work,* Keeping Company: Rhetoric, Pluralism, and Wayne Booth *(Frederick Antzcak, ed., Ohio State UP, 1993).*

The Idea of a *Uni*versity— as Seen by a Rhetorician

It is not often that a student of rhetoric faces an occasion that falls as neatly into his professional domain as this one falls into mine. The Ryerson lectures were designed as occasions for what the founders did *not* call "ecumenical rhetoric," discourse designed to bring together a community that is always tempted by modern forces to fall apart. I think I can claim, though with considerable anxiety, to be the first for whom this moment is a kind of setup: I am in effect invited to talk with you, a predetermined audience, about what the very existence of such a rhetorical occasion might mean. That is scarcely a comforting thought: it puts me on the spot in ways even more threatening than were faced by my threatened predecessors. As classical rhetoricians taught, the easiest way to guarantee failure with any perceptive audience is to be seen in advance as an expert in rhetoric. More is properly demanded where more is professed, and you can understand why I see troubles ahead.

My first problem lies of course in the very word "rhetoric." I was tempted, as I have often been in the past, to define that slippery term once and for all, but I have resisted, even though to grapple with its ambiguities would illustrate beautifully why Ryerson lecturers are notoriously nervous nellies. Just how much time should a lecturer spend claiming that, like Humpty Dumpty, he is to be the boss of definitions? Should I say, "Rhetoric on this occasion will *not* mean merely the art of winning, right or wrong, *nor* will it mean the clever use of bombast and trickery"? Should I insist that it will not even be the faculty, as Aristotle puts it, of "finding the available means of persuasion on any occasion"? Ted Schultz has recently advised me to abandon the sleazy term altogether and substitute something like "philosophy of discourse," or "theory of communication." But to abandon the term "rhetoric," with its long honorable history, just because it often suggests shoddy practices, would be like abandoning the term "philosophy," just because people talk about "the philosophy of tennis coaching," or abandoning the word "science" just because Mary Baker Eddy and the scientologists have each borrowed it for their purposes. Rather than defining it or abandoning it, suppose we just put a big question mark by whatever your own definition would now be. You may or may not, by the end, want to apply the term "rhetorical study" to what we will have been doing.

I begin with a question that the very existence of these lectures forces upon us, no matter what our field: How is it that we can gather hopefully here, year after year, to listen to one another tell about our special work, when we know in advance that most of us, most of the time, have no real hope of understanding the special work of most of the rest of us? The trustees established the Ryerson series, with the special help of the Ranneys, on the assumption that it would be a good thing if specialists lectured "to an audience from the entire university on a significant aspect" of their research. They did not say, "Please talk down to that audience," or "Kindly choose some peripheral and general question of social, political, or ethical importance." No, we are asked to speak as specialists—and to make ourselves understood.

The trustees obviously assumed that we professors ought to be able to talk with our colleagues about what we do and why we do it. They must have assumed that everyone who *professes* a subject, any subject, no matter how esoteric, ought to be able to say something intelligible about it, or through it, or with it, to the non-specialist. Clearly they hoped for something more than a series of merely ceremonial occasions, pious gatherings of hypocrites only pretending to listen. They assumed that we could follow John Simpson, say, talking of extending "space science and exploration to the third dimension—that is, to travel out of the ecliptic plane"; or Karl Weintraub talking about an "empathetic and sympathetic understanding of the past," an understanding that "gives us the burden of relative and relativized knowledge"; or Stephen Toulmin talking about "the inwardness of mental life"; or Saunders Mac Lane talking about how a mathematician deals with "fuzzy sets"; or George Stigler talking about the disharmony between sound economic principles and unsound economic practice; or—but I need not go on. You already know that the list is threateningly diverse. If we face its diversity honestly, we must wonder just how much understanding can occur across our disciplinary borderlines. Our hosts assumed that we are, in *some* sense, at *some* level, a *uni*versity, a community of inquirers who have managed to maintain *some* kind of message center or telephone exchange.

I must now risk shocking those of you who do *not* know the academy from the inside, and risk boring those of you who do, by dwelling for a bit on some of the more obvious reasons for doubting these assumptions. I ask you who are professors whether we do not have overwhelming daily proof that no one of us can understand more than a fraction of the frontline work of the rest. We are all simply shut out of almost all front parlors but our own, permitted only to do a little polite begging at the back door: "Please, sir, please give a poor beggar just a slice of nuclear physics to keep me warm, just a tiny portion of paleontology to keep up my illusion of keeping up, just a touch of cosmology—the new anthropic principle, say—to help me survive the next cocktail party." We don't like to talk about it, but we know that even Ryerson lecturers fail, at least partially, with most of their auditors. One Ryerson lecturer who has come to all of these lectures told me that he has understood only about half of what has been said: "I grasped almost nothing in a couple of the lectures," he said, "about a third in half of them, two-thirds in a few of them, and all in only one—my own."

Shocking as such a fact might seem from some perspectives, no serious scholar is likely to be at all surprised by it. Centuries have passed since that fabled moment—was it in the eighteenth century or the late seventeenth?—when the last of the Leonardo da Vincis could hope to cover the cognitive map. Since that fatal moment, whenever it was, everyone, even that polymath down the hall who is said to "know everything," has been reduced to knowing only one or two countries on the intellectual globe, granting all the other countries only the most superficial of Cook's tours.

Perhaps some of you here once shared the naive ambition that my wife and I pursued, long before we met each other. As youngsters who wanted to know everything, we once set out to read every book in the closest available library. Though both of the libraries were fortunately very small, neither of us made it even to the *M*'s, let alone the *Z*'s. And our fate is an emblem for the condition we all live in. It isn't that we don't try. The academy attracts those who aspire to omniscience. We are the kind who would like others to say of us what young Christopher Tietjens' friend says of him, in Ford Madox Ford's *Parade's End:* "Confound you, Chrissie. You know everything!"[1] Tietjens is at the time making a list, *from memory,* of errors in the new edition of the *Encyclopaedia Britannica.* But not long afterward part of Tietjens' brain, and all of his hubris, are shattered by a bomb blast in the Great War, and he is reduced, in utter humiliation, to a pathetic attempt to memorize the very *Encyclopaedia* he had once scorned. Arriving at the *K*'s, he finds, under "Koran," the saying, "The strong man when smitten is smitten in his pride" (p. 170). It is precisely in our pride that we are smitten, when for one reason or another we discover just what a pitifully small corner of the cognitive world we live in. Though we can sympathize with Tietjens' impulse, we all know that even his original sense of universal mastery, as a young genius, was illusory. Not only can no one fully understand what any good encyclopedia contains, the encyclopedias themselves are almost uniformly inadequate and misleading; ask any expert in a given field whether a reading of the encyclopedia entries in that field can educate even the cleverest of readers to genuine competence. And if this is true of our collective enterprises like encyclopedias, how much truer it is of each of us as we try individually to figure out what on earth goes on in neighboring subjects, across the hall or on the other side of the quad.

---

[1] Ford Madox Ford, *Parade's End* (four "Tietjens" novels: *Some Do Not . . .* [1924], *No More Parades* [1925], *A Man Could Stand Up*—[1926], and *The Last Post* [1928]), ed. Robie Macauley (New York, 1950), 19.

In short, the painful truth we voracious students discover, at twenty, or forty, or sixty, is that what we sometimes call the "knowledge explosion" has left us all ignorant of vast fields of knowledge that every educated man and woman *ought* to have mastered. Is it any wonder that we tend to be defensive in debate, sure that our next class or public lecture will reveal the fatal truth: we are ignoramuses, and since we call ourselves professors, scholars, even doctors, we risk exposure as frauds.

Perhaps I exaggerate. There may be in this room a few polyphilomathematico wizards who can carry on a plausible conversation with experts in as many as—shall we say, ten fields?—ten fields out of the hundreds listed in the faculty directory. (I started counting them, but soon realized that I didn't know enough in many areas even to tell what would constitute a field. Take a look sometime at the listings under "Argonne National Laboratories," or the "Department of Behavioral Sciences.") It is no doubt true that many of us can give journalistic accounts of black holes, marginal utility, polymorphous perversities, ekphrastic poetry, and the oft-repeated rise, over about twenty centuries, of the bourgeoisie. But for even the most learned among us, the circle of what we might call *participatory* understanding does not extend very far.

During the past few months, I've been asking colleagues in various disciplines about just how much they understand of other people's work, using the following test: Could you, given a week's warning, read an article or book in a given field and then enter into a serious dialogue with the author, at a level of understanding that the author would take as roughly comparable to his or her own? The answers varied widely in ambition and persuasiveness, not to say chutzpah, but you won't be surprised to learn that no one claimed to be able to understand more than a fraction of what our colleagues publish. Some were embarrassed by their confessions; most were not. Some confidently blamed the bad writing in other fields. But all confessed.

We would expect such confessions (or disguised accusations), when the fields are obviously far apart: humanists don't usually claim to meet mathematicians where they live; botanists freely confess to bafflement about particle physics. But I was a bit surprised to find that hardly anyone claims to understand all the work even within the home department. One philosopher told me that there is simply no one at this university, inside his department or out of it, who can understand his work; he is the lone inhabitant of his tiny cognitive land. His circle of fellow-understanders consists of a tiny band of similarly trained folk scattered around what we might call the known world. Another philosopher tells me that he could understand, given a week's lead time, perhaps 80 percent of what his fellow philosophers publish. He believes that perhaps even more than 80 percent of them could talk with him about his work—"Not," he adds, "that they would have *really* understood it, but at least we might be in the same ball park." A world-famous mathematician tells me that he cannot follow the proofs offered by most mathematicians; each sub-group of mathematicians has become so specialized that the other sub-groups are unable to understand them, if by "understanding" we mean being able to appraise, with full personal confidence, the validity of the proofs and thus the soundness of the conclusions. The editor of a journal in biology says that he expects to understand about fifty percent of the articles he publishes, and he adds, "I work harder at that task than most of my colleagues." The editor of a chemistry journal understands 50 percent to 80 percent of the articles he chooses to publish, but he "gets" hardly anything in most of the neighboring chemistry journals.

Obviously what my respondents have said depends on a relatively rigorous definition of "understanding." We surely ask more of ourselves than simply being able to respond, after taking in the opinions of others, with a plausible summary and an offer of our own plausible opinions. If we are to do justice to the question I am raising, we should at least for a while adhere to a more rigorous definition of "true understanding," something like this: I have understood you if and only if I can say to you, "Yes, *but*," and say it in a form that will lead you in turn to accept both my "yes" and my objections; not just my claim to have "got" your point, but my claim to have got it so well that I can raise an objection to it that you in turn must take into account. It is not enough for me to say to Professor Chandrasekhar, for example: "Oh, yes, I understand the theory of black holes. Black holes are inconceivably dense concentrations of matter; they are so dense that their gravitational force sucks in everything within range, including any photons that happen to be around, so that no light, and indeed no particles or waves of any kind, can ever emerge and therefore no information can come to us. That's why they're called *black* holes. . . ." You and I could go on like that, without even having to look anything up; that kind of understanding of black holes, or cost-benefit analysis, or ethnomethodology, or thick descriptions, or the double helix, is in the air, like a lot of other half-baked opinions we might pick up from reading the *New York Times* or *Scientific American*. I might even think I had understood black holes well enough to look the professor boldly in the eye and add a clever reservation, like this: "*But* what I think you've got wrong, Professor, is that according to *my* notion of how scientific constructs work, black holes must be considered to be no more than plausible pictures, with no necessary connection with anything we might call the reality behind the pictures. . . ." And so on. Even if my earlier description, my "yes," were roughly on the right lines, which is unlikely, Professor Chandrasekhar cannot possibly respond either to my "yes," my report, or my reservations, with anything warmer than a friendly smile as a reward for trying. I could not possibly challenge him to the point of his saying, "Yes, you've taken the point of my most recent article; you have convinced me that you are a good judge of its quality, and I therefore must take your reservations into account. Let's inquire into your objection further." But if I cannot claim that kind of understanding, in what sense do I live in the same university that honors Professor Chandrasekhar's achievements?

Lest you think I am indicting others on my behalf, I here present myself as an extreme but by no means unrepresentative example of the ignorant professor. I now serve as third reader on a dissertation being written by a young man in South Asian Studies. He is writing about a group of Indian poets, translating their poems and doing a critical poetics of their kind of poetry. Of course I cannot read the poems in the original, and I have not yet read all of his translations. What's worse, I have never read a single critical work by the non-Western critics he deals with. What on earth, then, am I doing on that committee?

Is it any wonder that when one eavesdrops on a group of experts in a given field, talking about experts in other fields, one hears a lot of contemptuous dismissal? Just listen to the chemists talking about the biologists, the biologists talking about the clinical M.D.'s, the surgeons and internists complaining about one another, the humanists talking about the social scientists, and the economists talking about everybody.

Roger Hildebrand provides what is for me the climax to my survey as he talks about his switch a few years ago from particle physics to astrophysics. To us outsiders, that might look like a small leap, really a shift within the same general field, as compared with the distance, say, between art history and chemistry. But Roger says that he had to spend the equivalent of about three full years "becoming a graduate student again" before he could feel some confidence in dialogue with frontliners in his new field—before he could judge the importance of a new article in that field. Just think how much work would be required if he decided once again to shift to microbiology, say, or constitutional law.

It is no doubt true that as we move across campus to the "softer" social sciences, through history, and on to the even floppier software occupying the brainpans of us humanists, we find a somewhat enlarged circle of those who at least claim to understand one another. The non-quantitative historians have told me that they can understand *all* of the *good* work of other non-quantitative historians. Most computer-armed prosopographers claim to understand the work of other cliometricians, and of course they claim to understand all the "easy" work of narrative historians—at least well enough to be suspicious of their inherently soft results. Lawyers all tell me that they can understand the legal arguments of all *good* lawyers. The cultural anthropologists say that they can understand everything worth reading in the social sciences. But when I press these various representatives, asking the lawyers whether they really understand the so-called critical realists, asking the cultural anthropologists whether they understand the quantitative sociologists, and so on, they often fall back on invective: "Those people are not doing true law or true anthropology." Or: "That gang have been badly trained."

Perhaps the largest circle of those who claim to understand one another would be found in English and other modern language studies. Hundreds of thousands of us profess to understand just about anything that falls into our hands. But when we look more closely at humanists' claims to membership in large circles of understanding, they appear pretty feeble. After all, in the quantitative and mathematical sciences, people tend to recognize when they have not understood one another. But we students of the human tend to think we have understood when we have not.

Here, for example, is the opening of a chapter by Jacques Derrida, the philosopher perhaps now most influential on literary studies:

> What about the voice within the logic of the supplement? within that which should perhaps be called the "graphic" of the supplement?
>
> Within the chain of supplements, it was difficult to separate writing from onanism. Those two supplements have in common at least the fact that they are dangerous. They transgress a prohibition and are experienced within culpability. But, by the economy of differance [deliberately spelled with an "a," as a special term], they confirm the interdict they transgress, get around a danger, and reserve an expenditure.[2]

Now I have worked for about a decade to become comfortable with the recondite language in which that passage is written, and I think I sort of understand it. Unlike some of my more traditional colleagues, I am utterly convinced that it is *not* nonsense, though it is opaque somewhat—more so than in the original French. Still, if I were to study the chapter that follows it carefully and then write a summary, the chances are about ninety-nine to one that Derrida would *not* say of it, "Bravo: you have understood." Just ask yourself how you have felt about the typical review or reader's report on your own carefully-wrought opus. My own response to reviews is often, "How could anyone but a moron misunderstand me so badly?"

Let me offer now a true story that summarizes our plight. Each year a committee is appointed in the Social Sciences Division to decide on the award of the annual Galler prize for the best dissertation done during that year. A couple of years ago an economist on the committee, after reading the submissions from other fields, announced that a dissertation from economics that he would now submit was superior to all the others, and should get the prize. The other committee members insisted that before granting his case they should have a chance to read it and compare it with the others.

---

[2] Jacques Derrida, "Genesis and Structure of the Essay 'On the Origin of Languages'" in *Of Grammatology*, trans. Gayatri Chakravorty Spivak (Baltimore, 1976), 165.

"No," he said, "that's impossible. You could not possibly understand it." "But how can we judge," they insisted, "if we are not allowed even to see the work?" He remained adamant, and when they refused to award the prize to a dissertation that they were not even allowed to see, he withdrew himself, and the dissertation, from the competition. He tells me now that the Department of Economics no longer even considers submitting dissertations for the prize, because they are sure that the non-quantitative "literary" types—the historians and anthropologists—simply could not recognize high quality in economics if they saw it.

Though that is clearly an extreme case, it helps make the point that even if we could create a university inhabited solely by geniuses, geniuses who, unlike most actual geniuses, were full of an infinite good will toward, and determination to understand, one another's disciplines, geniuses who would accept the assignment to work on our problem, we would find that under modern conditions of inquiry, conditions that we have no hope of changing fundamentally, none of them could come to an understanding of more than a fraction of what the others would take to be real knowledge.

Must we not admit, then, in all honesty, that we are indeed a pack of ignoramuses, inhabitants of some ancient unmapped archipelago, each of us an island—let John Donne preach as he will—living at a time before anyone had invented boats or any other form of inter-island communication?

II

I assume that many of you have long since wanted to protest against my picture. We all know that the islands are not in fact totally isolated, that somehow we have managed to invent communication systems. Though it may be true that on each island we speak a language not fully intelligible on any other, and though it may be true that some of the islands conduct active warfare against some of the others, and though some islands are in a state of civil war, the fact is that somehow we do manage to talk with one another and come to judgments that we are convinced are not *entirely* capricious. We write interdepartmental and even interdivisional memos, we indite letters of recommendation at breakneck speed and in appalling numbers, purporting to appraise the quality of colleagues whose work we don't know beans about. We appraise other scholars according to what we take to be high standards, even when we ourselves cannot state literally what the standards are. We pass judgment upon students in "related fields" and one another whenever promotion is at stake, and we seem not to suffer intolerable anxiety about our decisions. Even more shocking, in view of the plight I have described, we ask our deans and provosts and presidents to approve our judgments, and even grant the right to reverse them, implying that somehow *somebody* can be competent to judge work in *all* fields. Finally, we busy ourselves with a great deal of what we call "interdisciplinary work": degree-granting committees like Ideas and Methods, imperialistic fields like geography, anthropology, English, and rhetoric, conferences and workshops galore. None of us really thinks that *all* of these operations are totally fraudulent. We act *as if* our discussions and conferences and tenure decisions make *real* sense. Do they?

How do we actually work, as we run those of our affairs that depend on some kind of understanding different from the one I have applied so far? Do we work, as some say, only according to blind trust of friends and mistrust of enemies? Do we work according to guesses only? Are we, as some would claim, simply servants of money and power? In what sense, if any, do we employ a kind of reasoning and proof—knowledge and genuine understanding under any definition—that we might point to without shame?

After my informants of the past months have confessed their ignorance, I have asked them to tell me how they in fact operate when judging colleagues whose work they do not understand. All of them have said something like this—though never in this precise language: "We are by no means fraudulent, because we have available certain rational resources that your definition of understanding leaves out. We have learned to make use of our knowledge [one professor even called it "wisdom"] about character and how to appraise character witnesses; we have learned how to read the signs of quality even in the fields where we cannot follow the proofs. We have learned how to determine whether a referee is trustworthy, and we have learned something about how to judge the quality of a candidate's thinking, just by the way he or she writes and speaks." They have not gone on to say, though I wish we could have shared this language: "You see, what all this means is that we are experienced both as practitioners and students of—rhetoric."

When I press them further with the question, "Do you make mistakes with this kind of thinking?" the answer is always "Yes, sometimes." But nobody I've talked with has claimed that the process depends on a trust that is utterly blind, totally a matter of non-rational power-grabs or log-rolling or back-scratching or money-grubbing. Everyone, absolutely everyone, has played into this rhetorician's hands by claiming to employ a kind of thought that is not identical with what we do when proving conclusions in our front-line inquiry—and yet a kind that is still genuine thought.

Of course nobody has claimed that we offer our rhetorical proofs to each other and test them as well as we ought; indeed my main point today is that we could all employ them better, and thus improve our quality as a *university*, *if* we all studied how such peculiar yet rational persuasion works. But even in our fallen condition, even as we in our imperfection now operate, we do not perform our personal and administrative judgments on indefensible, non-scholarly grounds; we perform those judgments on grounds that are considered non-scholarly only by those who think that all knowledge is of the kind yielded by frontline specialties, only by those who embrace uncritically the criterion for understanding, and thus of knowledge, with which I began. If knowledge is confined to what experts discover at the frontline, and if understanding is confined to participation in full dialogue at the frontline, then we operate ourselves without *knowing* what we do and without *understanding* each other. If we know and understand only what we can *prove*—with empirical observation, or with statistics, or with rigorous logical deduction—we will never *know* whether a colleague is worth listening to or promoting, unless we ourselves can follow his or her proofs, in detail, and then replicate them. All else is dubious, all else is guesswork, all else is blind faith.

But one thing we all know is that we know more than that criterion implies. Though unable to tell for ourselves whether the new mathematical proof is indeed new and indeed a proof, we learn how to consider, with the eye of non-specialists, both the rhetoric of scholarship that we cannot hope fully to understand, and the rhetoric offered us *about* the scholar, the arguments offered by those who give us some reason to trust or mistrust their judgment as specialists.

We all thus implicitly aspire to mastery in three kinds of rhetoric, leading to three kinds of understanding, not just one. There are, first, the many and diverse rhetorics peculiar to each of our various frontlines. Here each small group of experts relies on what Aristotle calls *special topics* of persuasion, the often tacit convictions that are shared by all within a discipline and that are therefore available in constructing arguments within the field: the assumption, say, that photographs of bubble chambers and their interpretations can somehow be relied on; or the conventional agreements about how to deal with normal curves and chi squares, about the proper use of graphs, about what makes a sound equation, or about how to do a sensitive report of poetic scansion or a convincing analysis of sonata form in a symphony. Though these assumptions shift over time, we can at any given time rely on them without argument in their support, as we construct our arguments to our peers. I'll risk offending some of you by dubbing this frontline stuff and its workings "rhetoric-1." If calling it "hard proof" will make you happier, feel free, but I know that few specialists will want to claim that they or their successors will find themselves fifty years from now relying on the same tacit assumptions, leading to the same conclusions, that they share today.

A second kind that I call "general rhetoric," or "rhetoric-2," is what we share with members of every functioning organization or society—businesses, governments, clubs, families: the whole range of plausible or probable beliefs and modes of proof that make the world go round. Think of it as what even the most rigorous of scientists must rely on when testifying before a government committee. Here we rely on the *common,* or general topics: "More of any good thing is better than less of it—usually"; "It's wrong to lie, at least to friends and colleagues"; "Loyalty matters"; "Actions that usually produce bad consequences should be avoided." Obviously many of these are included in everyone's notion of "common sense": what *makes* sense in any argument.

Though the common topics are indispensable in every domain, they are especially prominent in our running of the university whenever we must appraise character. We all have a little storehouse of beliefs about character that we have to rely on, more or less efficiently, whenever we read a letter of recommendation, or predict the future behavior of a colleague in order to grant or deny tenure. Such common topics, "commonplaces," crop up in all public debate. "It is probable that someone who failed to carry through on her previous research plan will fail in this one; turn her down." "Ah, yes, but she was deep in the anguish of a divorce then, and she's changed a lot. I say give her the grant." "Well, but her strongest supporter is Professor Smiler, who has usually been wrong in his predictions that young colleagues are late bloomers. Why should we believe him in this case?" Or: "The truth is that Louise and Harry used to live together, and they had an angry breakup. I think—though we must say nothing of it in public—that we cannot trust his negative judgment on her scholarly ability."

Rhetoric-2 is thus the set of resources available in the functioning of all organizations, not just of universities. Arbitragers and government officers function or fail to function, depending on whether the trust they yield to their CEO's and Marine sergeants and colonels is justified. We in the university similarly succeed to the degree that our trust is granted when it should be, withheld when it should not be. The case with which rhetoric-2 can be abused accounts largely for why rhetoric has always had, and probably always *will* have, a bad press. Philosophers and moralists have often wished that it would just go away—but of course they express the wish for a purer world in the only language available to any of us when we press our wishes on the world: rhetorical argument.

There is, thirdly, a kind of rhetoric that is neither as special as the first nor as general as the second, a rhetoric relying on shared topics that are proper or special only to those within a university, but to all within that university, not to any one special group. We have no name for this peculiar stuff that we all to some degree share, but call it "the rhetoric of inquiry," or of "intellectual engagement": "academy-rhetoric," or "rhetoric-3." We learn how to judge whether the arguments in fields beyond our full competence *somehow* track, whether the style of presentation *somehow* accords with standards we recognize. We learn to sense whether a colleague, even in a quite remote field, *seems* to have mastered the tricks of the trade—not just the trade of this or that kind of economist or philosopher, but the tricks of this whole trade, the trade of learning and teaching for the sake of learning and teaching. One often hears, in the Quadrangle Club, not just the contemptuous comments I have mentioned about fools and knaves but comments like this: "What a mind that man has." "What a pleasure to argue with that woman—she never misses a stroke." "He always seems to have just the right analogy to make his point." "Have you noticed how you always come away from a conversation with him having to think through the problem in a different way?"

All three of these rhetorics are of course highly fallible. Even our many versions of rhetoric-1 are notoriously unstable, as I have already implied, shifting in threatening ways from decade to decade and field to field. But the second and third rhetorics are much more obviously fallible, indeed staggeringly so. Tough-minded appraisal of characters and witnesses through close reading of letters of recommendation and reader's reports, close listening during telephone calls and hallway conversations, careful appraisal of past records of performance—these are all dangerously unreliable, partly because charlatans can so easily mimic the proper use of the topics. If this were not so, we would not have so many successful frauds in every field. The Piltdown hoaxers, the Cyril Burts, the Darseys, the unqualified but practicing surgeons, the undiploma-ed lawyers—all the hoaxers of our world succeed as they do because they have mastered the surface conventions of all three rhetorics and through that mastery have collected or forged references testifying to high quality. We read about so many successes in this burgeoning field of pseudo-scientific conning that we are in danger of forgetting the solid and indispensable base of merely probable inferences on which it rests. The breakdowns in the system result from, and depend on, a process—the practice of producing sound conclusions from rhetorical proofs—that by its very necessities opens the door to frauds. But this is not to say that we, their dupes, could not protect ourselves better if we would study rhetoric as hard as we study lab techniques, say, or formal logic.

Again and again I have been told by my informants that "it's not really very hard to tell competent work from incompetent, even if you know nothing about the details and cannot replicate the argument or experiment." And when I then ask, "How do you *do* that?" I am told—never in this language—that "I do it using rhetorics-2 and -3—not the appraisal of frontline proofs but the careful judgment of both "general rhetoric" and "academy rhetoric." One editor told me, "Even when I know little or nothing about a special field, I can tell just by the opening paragraphs whether a would-be contributor is at least competent." What does that mean, if not that he claims to judge the author's skill in rhetorical conventions shared with other fields: skill in saying what needs saying and in not saying what should not be said; skill in implying a scholarly ethos appropriate to the subject; skill in avoiding moves that give away the novice; and so on. Though the practice and appraisal of such skills is chancy, if we ruled them out we could not operate for a day without disaster. Most of our journals would have to be scrapped, most of our grants and awards would have to be eliminated, and the university would have to surrender to total balkanization or even tribal warfare, becoming not a *uni*versity at all but a multiversity, a mere collection of research institutes warring for funds.

We can see how rhetorics-2 and -3 work, in a genuine university, by probing the grounds for our belief about the quality of any one of our more distinguished colleagues. I believe, for example, that George Stigler is really a very good economist. I would bet my next month's salary on my belief that when Stigler does economics, he is working at the highest levels of competence in his field (at least on his good days), and that in doing so he is not simply playing an esoteric power game but is actually pursuing one genuine kind of knowledge. But what's my evidence? Every bit of it, when taken by itself, is extremely chancy rhetorical inference, some of it of the second kind, some of the third, none of the first. I cannot really understand his frontline work, but when I dip into it I find enough similarities with work I do understand to give me some slight confidence. Still, my views of it are scandalously shallow. But then I start adding other bits. I've had some private conversations with George about the assumptions of economics as a field—highly general conversations, those, with me trying to put him on the defensive but always ending on the ropes, and thus increasingly impressed. Similarly, our talks about literature and about campus politics have impressed me considerably with the general quality of his reasoning, even though in themselves they tell me nothing directly about his work as an economist. I find myself admiring his more popular stuff, as in *The Economist as Preacher;*[3] not only is he a master of English style, but he offers dozens of signs that he belongs to a community of economists who respect him. Still, such reading in itself cannot tell me very much about his work as an economist. I can add to these his Nobel prize, but the fact is that it doesn't impress me much more than it probably impresses him; we all know that Nobel committees can make grotesque mistakes. The seemingly uniform esteem of his local colleagues counts most for me, but it could not in itself settle the issue; obviously whole departments and whole fields can misjudge quality. Finally, the fact of his election by his colleagues to various important university committees can again carry only slight weight, in itself.

But note that all of these weak clues point in the same direction, and they all come to a head when I hear other economists who are said to be good— note well that phrase—say that George Stigler is good and *is said to be good.* Each reason for trust is in itself slight. My confidence could be shaken quite

---

[3]George Stigler, *The Economist as Preacher and Other Essays* (Chicago, 1982).

easily by counter-testimony from someone I trust as much as I trust these witnesses, if I could find someone. It could be shaken if I discovered some obviously incompetent logic in his Ryerson lecture—his foray into the non-specialized academic rhetoric I am calling rhetoric-3. But after I have added together all the weak-but-still-pertinent reasons, it would take a good deal of contrary evidence to make me doubt his competence. What may be even more important, the half-comprehension that I gain by all of this peripheral activity adds to my own intellectual life. I take part, at a great distance, in Stigler's reasoning about economics, and I even dare from time to time to quarrel with him, ineffectually, about that weird first principle of his, the belief that people's behavior can be fully explained as the rational calculation of individual costs and benefits.

The relative weight of the three rhetorics varies from field to field, committee to committee, occasion to occasion. I once served on the Board of University Publications, and in the early spring we faced that annual ordeal, the decision about which of our colleagues should receive the Laing prize for a distinguished book. We had all read the major reviews of each eligible book, and we had all been urged to read all of the books, though I doubt that anyone had done so. Then, after preliminary balloting (based mainly, you see, on the rhetoric-3 of the reviews we had read), we were asked to read with special care those books that seemed prime contenders. In the preliminary balloting that followed, several books came out ahead of Sewall Wright's collected essays. I can remember that I had read at—I think that's the right expression—*read at* several of the essays in that monumental collection, working away dutifully because the reviews had uniformly described Wright and his book as of major importance. The essays seemed authoritative to me—that fairly small portion of them that I could understand at all. The logic, where I could follow it, made sense. The language carried authority. I found, after reading *at* four or five of the essays, that I was admiring the character who emerged from the various projects; to me it seemed obvious that this man was a serious, responsible, highly intelligent scientist. But I simply had no way of detecting for myself whether his results were original or sound or worthy to be influential, let alone worthy of the Laing prize. So, like most of the members of that board, I did not on the first round vote for Wright as number one, though he was among the highest. Rather, I voted for authors about whom I felt much more sure, because I could follow their frontline arguments.

Then in our final meeting a curious thing happened. Our late colleague Arnold Ravin spoke at some length about the true importance of Wright's work. As I remember his eloquent appeal, it went like this: "You must believe me, when I tell you that this is a major collection by a major figure, a genius who has transformed his field again and again. Believe me, though you yourselves cannot be expected to see the quality in these essays, this book is head-and-shoulders above the others on our list." Now here is where this anecdote diverges from my story of the economist and the Galler prize. *We argued back, and Ravin attempted to meet our arguments.* He gave another speech, longer and with different examples, with more testimonial quoted from other biologists, and with a repeated claim that since none of the rest of us were biologists, we were just not qualified to grasp the full cumulative importance of this record of a life's work. Finally, after an hour or so of debate, we voted decisively to give the prize to Sewall Wright, an author whose work only one person in the room could fully understand. And we had no positive evidence even of that: we had only Ravin's words as evidence that even he had understood Wright.

We voted, you see, mainly on the basis of powerful rhetoric of kinds two and three. We trusted the rhetorician because his arguments made sense to us, because they harmonized with what the other experts had told us, because they were not contradicted by what little we could infer from our own efforts at reading the essays themselves, and because we had reason to trust the judgment and integrity of Arnold Ravin.[4] Some of his arguments would have worked equally well in an insurance company's board room (rhetoric-2). His passion, for example, was not mere passion: it became hard evidence, because we felt that Ravin was not the kind of man who would fake passion like that, and passion like that could not be aroused except by an exceptional case. (So much, by the way, for the still-fashionable inclination to contrast reason and emotion; a powerful emotion, carefully appraised, can often be the hardest of evidence in this kind of reasoning.) But some of his arguments were special to this special kind of place. For example, he argued that Wright had been mainly responsible for the creation of a new discipline—a claim that would seem out of place in a business context, say, or in a psychotherapist's office. And I remember his saying that if someone a hundred years from now wanted to know both the state of that discipline and the special problems and methods it encountered at the time the book was written, the book would still live. So we all came to a choice that in retrospect still seems to me eminently sound, though I would not be shattered if some other work, neglected by us in those final moments, turned out later to be more important than Wright's.

Would we have done better to tell Arnold Ravin, "All that is *mere* rhetoric. We must vote only on and for those books that we ourselves can understand?" To say no to that route requires us to believe that there is a real difference between sound and unsound rhetorical appeals, that there is a

---

[4] After the Ryerson lecture a biologist friend said, "You know, Arnold Ravin could not have *really* understood Wright's work; it was beyond him." "Do you mean," I asked, "that we were wrong in listening to him?" "Oh, no; you were right, because *he* was right. But he was himself depending more on rhetorics-2 and -3 than you realized."

whole domain of knowledge—uncertain, chancy, elusive knowledge but knowledge nonetheless—that is important not only in the awarding of prizes and promotions but in the day-by-day intellectual life of the university. Not only does every hiring and firing, every promotion, every establishment of a new department or elimination of an old one, every choice of a dean or president, depend on such topical reasoning. Our very survival depends on our control of that kind of knowledge—that is to say, on our repertory of rhetorical practices and norms. We depend on appraising the testimony and authority and general ethos of other people, as they appraise the testimony and authority of still others, who in turn depend on others . . . and no one can say where these circles of mutual trust end, except of course when societies and universities destroy themselves by losing the arts of determining when trust is justified.

Philosophers of science like Michael Polanyi[5] and Rom Harré[6] have argued that even the "hardest" sciences, even physics and chemistry and mathematics, do *not* depend mainly on the application by each individual of so-called scientific method to all beliefs, doubting every proposition until it has been shown to be falsifiable and yet not falsified. Instead, they say, each individual scientist survives as scientist by virtue of indeterminately large networks of critical trust, based largely on assumptions shared by many or most disciplines, (rhetoric-3). Each of them must rely, as you and I do, on broad ranges of belief that no one of us could ever hope to demonstrate independently. As Polanyi puts it, we are all inherently "con-vivial," dependent for our intellectual bases, as we are in our physical lives, on living *together.* Even as specialists, he says, we live in "fiduciary" structures that we have not constructed and could never construct on our own.[7]

III

What we have arrived at here is a picture radically different from that of the archipelago of islands forced to remain incommunicado. We need another picture of how we relate as specialists. Those who worry about

---

[5] Michael Polanyi, *Personal Knowledge: Towards a Post-Critical Philosophy* (Chicago, 1958; rev. ed., New York, 1962).

[6] Rom Harré, "Science as a Communal Practice," in *Varieties of Realism: A Rationale for the Natural Sciences* (Oxford, 1986).

[7] "[W]hat earlier philosophers have alluded to by speaking of coherence as the criterion of truth is only a criterion of *stability*. It may equally stabilize an erroneous or a true view of the universe. The attribution of truth to any particular stable alternative is a fiduciary act which cannot be analysed in non-committal terms [that is, it depends on prior commitment to some enterprise shared with others]. . . . [T]here exists no principle of doubt the operation of which will discover for us which of two systems of implicit beliefs is true—except in the sense that we will admit decisive evidence against the one we do not believe to be true, and not against the other. Once more, the admission of doubt proves here to be as clearly an act of belief as does the non-admission of doubt" (Polanyi, *Personal Knowledge*, 294).

those lonely islands too often take as an ideal the impossible notion of getting more people to add more and more specialties, as if there were some hope of making each island self-sufficient. Attacking this "Leonardesque aspiration," psychologist Donald T. Campbell, in a splendid essay precisely on our subject today, suggested that the best way to combat the "ethnocentrism of disciplines," the "tribalism" and "nationalism" of specialties, would be to pursue the "fish-scale model of omniscience."[8] Picture each group of specialists as one scale in a total fish-scale, both overlapping and overlapped by the interests and competencies of adjacent specialties. The total network, or fish-scale, "knows" whatever is in fact known; though no one unit knows very much, each unit is connected to all the others, through the unbroken overlappings.[9]

Campbell hoped with this model both to relieve each of us from the anxiety to know more than anyone can possibly know, and to encourage more productive specialization in the areas where the scales overlap. The new specialties thus developed would be in one sense as narrow as the others; like everyone else in the university the new specialists would still be ignoramuses when addressing most fields. But by concentrating on hitherto-neglected connections, they would improve the efficiency of the entire fish-scale. The *university* of his model would in a sense know itself and know what it knows, while no one individual would have to feel guilty about not pursuing the impossible project of learning what the network as a whole has learned.

Campbell's model takes us in the right direction, but it may still be misleading, as a picture both of how we work at our best, and as a practice to aspire to. Unfortunately, I can't find quite as neat an image for my own notion of how we work. But suppose we imagine a fish-scale in which each separate scale is not a scale at all but some kind of organism, perhaps like an octopus, with many tentacles, some of them reaching only to one or two adjacent scales, some leaping across to the opposite sides of the whole fish, as it were. The tentacles often intertwine, and they are somehow able to send half-intelligible, scrambled, but still not worthless messages to scales in

---

[8] Donald T. Campbell, "Ethnocentrism of Disciplines and the Fish-Scale Model of Omniscience," in *Interdisciplinary Relationships in the Social Sciences*, ed. Muzafer Sherif and Carolyn W. Sherif (Chicago, 1969), 328–48. I thank Marvin Mikesell for this reference.

[9] Anxiety about the ethnocentrism of experts was not invented in recent decades. As early as 1902, Alexander R. Hohlfield, summarizing a central session of the annual meeting of the Modern Language Association, lamented "the increasing specialization of the papers" and claimed that it was "rapidly decreasing the number of occasions when a considerable proportion of those present are capable of joining in a discussion." Many a scholar has been hard-pressed to find proper analogies for our plight. Just after World War II John Erskine, describing how scholars claim to "cover" jointly fields that no one of them has mastered, recalled an ancient Irish legend: "[T]here was a tower so high that it took two persons to see to the top of it. One would begin at the bottom and look up as far as sight could reach, the other would begin where the first left off, and see the rest of the way." I owe these quotations to Gerald Graff, *Professing Literature: An Institutional History* (Chicago, 1987), 111.

unpredictable parts of the whole—well, of course the picture becomes visually absurd. But the inadequacy of pictures shouldn't surprise us, since the university is not really *much* like anything else in the universe. In my garbled image, a given physicist will not only occupy a given scale of expertise, as it overlaps adjacent fields, say mathematics and chemistry, but will also project "tentacles" across the entire network to the poets or musicians or art historians, as Professor Chandrasekhar did in his Ryerson lecture. Occupants of a given scale, a given specialty, do not hope to earn full occupancy of more than two or three further scales in a lifetime, but they not only hope for, but can achieve, a partial understanding of many. Remember: I am not yet pursuing an ideal university, only the best notion of how we ignoramuses actually work at our best. You might want to think here of professors who both occupy a single scale with high competence and extend themselves effectively into the larger network. (In one draft I began to list them by name; but the list not only risked offending by its omissions but also quickly grew too long. I wonder whether any other university can offer as many professors of the kind I have in mind.)

IV

So much is, I would argue, a roughly accurate description of why we are not *as* fraudulent as my first picture suggested. You will have noticed, however, that my description, like all descriptions of human activity, is not what the social scientists call "value-free." Even the most neutral description of any human endeavor will reveal, to the careful listener, implied judgments and exhortations, and mine is no exception. Most obviously, I have implied throughout that for people to understand one another is not only a good thing in itself, it is the sine qua non of a genuine university. It follows from that, I think, that one of our main tasks is to improve our chances for genuine understanding—understanding, of course, of all three kinds. We need to expand the size, as it were, of each fish-scale and the area of overlap among the scales. We need to encourage ourselves in the growth of tentacles reaching from scale to scale. But, even more pressingly, we need to increase our understanding of how it is that we do in fact communicate by means of those tentacles, and how we might do it better.

The lines among the three kinds of improvement will always be blurred. Mastering the special topics of most fields will lead simultaneously to some improvement in the handling of the topics common to all rational discourse. Many fields, like my own, are built largely out of the topics that are shared by all scholarly and scientific fields. But though the lines are indistinct, we are all in effect custodians of all three kinds. The ideal university that is implied by all this would obviously be one in which we all worked even more steadily, aggressively, and effectively than we do now to increase the number of moments each day when genuine understanding takes place—with a consequent improvement both in the quality of learners and in the quality of judgments passed on the learners.

What would such a university look like? Well, as some of you know, it is getting easier and easier these days to move forward and backward in time, now that Shirley MacLaine and her multiplying siblings have taught us how to achieve out-of-body experiences. I happen to have just returned this week from a visit fifty years forward, and I have brought back a little history, published by the press of a university that occupies precisely our present site (not a single new building!). It calls itself, however, the University of Polytopia—not Utopia, no-place, but Polytopia, many places. The history, dated April 22, 2037, is signed by one Raphael Hythloday, Emeritus Professor of Education. Here is a painfully shortened version of Hythloday's report.

Having decided, just fifty years ago, to become a *uni*versity and not an archipelago of mutually incomprehensible, self-congratulating isolates, our governing committees turned to a serious study of those arts that we thought had been essential to our surviving with some quality, even as late as 1987. Our first decision, arrived at not without bloodshed, was to postpone all attempts to rise one more point in the reputation polls of the *multi*versities. Deciding to be a great *uni*versity down the road a decade or two, we abandoned the attempt to cover every topic that our rivals chose to cover. We stopped adding whatever new departments or subjects our rivals added, and we stopped wooing academic stars according to their present luminosity, recognizing that any multiversity like Berkeley could beat us at both those games.[10] Instead we began to operate according to a principle that came to be known as Booth's Law: "Maximum luminosity of professors and departments is exactly like maximum luminosity in the heavenly spheres: it reaches the target millions of years after the star has burnt itself out." [Incidentally, Booth's Law applies locally as well as nationally. It means that Ryerson lecturers are chosen roughly 10.57 years too late.]

Attention to Booth's Law led us to turn to an unprecedented search, far outshining that of the MacArthur Foundation, for men and women who had managed to preserve, even as late as their thirties or early forties, some vestige of the curiosity and enthusiasm for learning that they had shown when younger. We sought out and hired the most vigorously *curious* minds we could find, regardless of their degrees and publication lists. We then turned them loose in the university as it was. We attempted no master plan, and we imposed only

---

[10] According to Graff (*Professing Literature*, 40–41), the first professor who was solicited by a rival institution on the basis of his publication list was Francis James Child, in 1876. He resisted the temptation, offered by the Johns Hopkins University, when Harvard agreed to release him from his teaching of—what else?—composition! A century later, we find ourselves spending a major part of our time on that kind of wasteful luring and responding.

two revisions of current procedures. First, all faculty members were required to teach at least half of their courses to non-specialists, graduate or undergraduate, with at least one course each year concentrating on the question of what kinds of argument are defensible, in one or more of the three rhetorics. Secondly, at tenure and promotion times the primary decision was to be made, not by a department alone, but by departmental representatives joined by a larger group from outside the department, all charged to apply one test only: Is this candidate *still curious,* still inquiring into one or more of the three rhetorics, and is it thus probable that at the age of forty, fifty, or sixty-six, he or she will still be vigorously inquiring?

The result was that we were all soon seeking, regardless of our specialties, to become masters of three rhetorics, not just one; we began to educate ourselves about where our topics, our locations, our always unpredictable problems, fit into the polytopicality that we no longer even desired to escape. Thus we did not give up on the quest for a common understanding, but the understanding we sought, as our one central value, was the one by which we still live, the one that is inherent in any attempt to live with our heterodoxies, our polytopicality: the quest for an understanding of how we understand, and why we so frequently fail to.

Many predicted that with departments no longer quite such bastions of autonomy as they had been, we would soon just fall off the national charts. But no one today will be surprised to learn that after a year or two of uncertain reputation, we quickly became famous as the national center for the study of the three rhetorics. The various publics who are always desperate for guidance in those rhetorics came to our support in such numbers that we were almost overwhelmed. Business executives and government officials came to realize that the *inter*translation of rhetorics—what we now feel comfortable in calling not "rhetoric-4" but "rhetorology"—was their own primary labor. Every scientist seeking a grant soon came to see that rhetorology was the primary resource when facing government officials and specialists in other fields. In short, The University of Polytopia found itself serving *public* needs in new and surprising ways. Money for professorships and fellowships flowed in, as our graduates became famous for the way they performed, and as our new kind of professor, recruited when young, became famous for teaching the world how to perform responsibly and effectively in its rhetorical exchanges.

No one now will be surprised by another development, but it surprised almost everyone at the time: I mean the sudden new importance of our undergraduate College, which quickly became honored as a national center for the study, not only of the three primary rhetorics, but of rhetorology. Unlike the colleges in multiversities, ours was no longer considered as somehow in conflict or competition with advanced research and instruction. Rather it was viewed as the facilitator of the most original, least imitative thinking and research. Faculty members, now required to pursue problems that arise when disciplines must make decisions together about what is worth learning and what should be taught, soon found themselves deepening their specialties as they thought about how their rhetoric-1 was or was not valuable to non-specialist undergraduates. As they considered what they knew that everybody *ought* to know, and pressed themselves about precisely where they belonged in the new Polytopia, and as they encountered solid practical problems raised by their curiosity about developing new major fields, they inescapably met with colleagues from hitherto unlikely locations. Soon it became clear that one of the most profitable challenges to the advanced expert was the planning of a staff-taught undergraduate course. Many who had thought of college teaching as a costly rival to graduate research and teaching discovered in such meetings new problems, and new disciplines for dealing with them.

The College was of course not the only center to become flushed with new importance. All of the committees and programs that had traditionally located themselves where the fish-scales overlap, and thus inevitably pursued rhetorology, found themselves with strengthened support—but also with a new and threatening pressure to probe deeper. No longer could anyone get any credit just for putting together a superficial non-understanding of two disciplines and calling the result "interdisciplinary."

Naturally enough, we soon found that every student in every program, from the freshman year to the Ph.D., was studying the question of how to improve argument, under the different requirements of the three rhetorical domains. Every field, already steeped in the frontline problems of rhetoric-1, soon included some systematic inquiry into those problems, together with inquiry into how that field could better relate itself to other fields and to the world.

No longer could anyone be forgiven for ignorantly pursuing in one field problems that had long since been solved in others. Fortunately it has now been two full decades since the following groups discovered, through rhetorology, that they were in fact studying the three rhetorics and rhetorology under other names, and that they had wasted effort in duplicating inquiry already performed elsewhere.

[I must apologize for the heavy detail that follows here. Hythloday becomes a bit cryptic, apparently feeling that he must make a little ingratiating bow, however perfunctory, toward almost every field. I have cut some of his examples and all of his tedious footnoting, and I have changed his order: with characteristic arrogance, he risked ranking fields according to his idea of their importance; with characteristic prudence, I have reranked them in simple alphabetical order.]

- anthropologists studying how root metaphors constitute societies;
- art historians quarreling about the validity of Gombrich's views of representation;
- business school professors founding centers for "decision research" and "cognition and communication," with the purpose of discovering just how minds are changed;
- classicists studying the history of the goddess Peitho, the goddess of persuasion;
- cognitive psychologists repudiating behavior modification models and studying ways in which the mind performs "constructionist" operations that escape full formalization;
- composition specialists organizing writing courses and composing books on discourse theory;

- cosmologists studying the kind of "chaos" that is actually organized;
- cultural anthropologists reducing the territory of nomothetic social science and pursuing instead what came to be called "local knowledge" and "thick descriptions";
- Divinity School professors organizing workshops in practical reason;
- economists writing entire books on the "rhetoric of economics";
- educationists protesting the reduction of pedagogy to computer models;
- Graduate Library School professors organizing seminars in communication theory;
- historians arguing for the cognitive force of narrative, or debating the "objectivity question," or urging the study of historiography;
- lawyers dealing with the appraisal of witnesses, or debating about critical realism;
- linguists pursuing, after decades of pure syntactics and semantics, a new pragmatics;
- literary critics studying the same problem under words like "irony" and "disambiguation";
- mathematicians studying fuzzy sets;
- philosophers of science studying how adherents of conflicting paradigms do actually sometimes manage to communicate across seemingly impenetrable border lines;
- professors of French studying the sources and consequences for Montaigne's kind of argument of Montaigne's kind of skepticism;
- professors of Italian rediscovering Vico's powerful new science;
- psychoanalysts and philosophers inventing a new term, "ethogenics," for the study of behavior as *generated* by persons who inescapably exhibit a character, an ethos;
- sociologists studying how people get together or fall apart through ambiguous convention;
- statisticians studying how we deal with uncertainties that escape simple numeration;
- students of "informal logic" rehabilitating many of the so-called "fallacies," such as the *argumentum ad hominem;*
- theologians and professors of Far-Eastern languages studying hermeneutics;
- urbanologists studying conflict resolution in the ghetto;

[But I must here cut another page of Hythloday's account, on down through increasingly imperialistic claims that his field covers not only urologists, Western European Studies, and the Writing Tutors program, but even the zoologists and their study of communication among our siblings, the chimpanzees.]

It was as late as 1997 [Hythloday continues] before we instituted the present requirement that every dean and provost, on taking office, enroll in a training course in the three rhetorics necessarily exercised in such offices. The course includes a study of how to appraise witnesses, with readings both from that part of legal training that deals with the subject and from that part of the classical tradition that teaches appraisal of ethos. When are we, in fact, justified in trusting a testimonial? What are the marks of a reliable letter of recommendation? Just what kinds of departmental rhetoric should a provost attend to? What are the true qualities of character that qualify a man or woman to become a citizen of the University of Polytopia? Soon we found that the bibliographies of rhetorical study, formerly consulted by few, were in universal demand. The library could not meet the demand for Aristotle's *Rhetoric;* photocopiers were kept busy duplicating the works of Cicero and Quintilian, now sold out.

Finally, we found ourselves organizing, as the major annual university-wide, College-sponsored event, the Liberal Arts Conference that has for nearly five decades now dragged departments, sometimes still kicking and screaming, into confrontation with each other about the rhetoric of the so-called disciplines and the rhetoric of the so-called interdisciplines. A key moment in that conference has come to be the annual Ryerson lecture, sponsored by the board of trustees and delivered by a faculty member who has been required, since an early date that we have not been able to discover, to address either the rhetoric of his or her discipline, as it relates to rhetorics-2 and -3, or as it relates to the rhetoric-1 of other disciplines.

A recent visitor asked us why the University of Polytopia has never followed Berkeley and Davis (in the California system), Virginia, Carnegie Mellon, Iowa, and others, in establishing a Department of Rhetoric. But is not the answer obvious? A *uni*versity run by a faculty whose members, while cultivating their own gardens, insist on looking over the garden fence and even visiting with the neighbors—such a university has no need for a department of rhetoric. With most faculty members now pursuing new specialties, discovered where previous disciplines had overlapped without their defenders' quite knowing it, just about everyone practices rhetorology in order to teach the rhetorics better.

Everyone reading this report today will know that we have not discovered, in all this innovation, any easy, cheerful harmony. New and seemingly irreconcilable differences have turned up as we have faced hitherto-unsuspected problems. And it is easy for us now, though it was hard for scholars back in 1987, to see the grand difference between our polytopian achievement and their utopian dreams. First, we have not called for or depended on any fundamental changes in human nature; we look for no great and unlikely upsurge of benevolence. Some increase in the exercise of benevolence and mutual trust does seem to have *resulted* from our changes, but the changes did not depend on them, and the kind of critical trust we exercise with one another does not depend now on loving-kindness or even everyday courtesy. Secondly, nothing we have done has required any imposition of radical structures by some powerful philosopher-president. We have always left the departmental structures intact, except where disciplinary discoveries have produced natural reshapings. In short, everything we have done is based on observing what we already did, in 1987, in coping with our pandemic polytopicality and the universal ignorance that sprang from it. We simply urged all scholars to observe how they worked when they felt best about their work—and then to pursue that best, in the service of their own deepest interests. Incidentally, one of the main intellectual rewards of all this was the abandonment, once and for all, of that old shibboleth, a Unified Language of All the Sciences. Our *uni*versity does not now exhibit, nor does it ever hope to exhibit, a single language applicable to all worthwhile inquiries. Instead, we proliferate, we multiply, we rejoice in variety. We have not, it is true, discarded Occam's razor entirely; it still does some service in the rhetoric-1 of most fields. But the law we most celebrate is no longer the law of parsimony; it is instead the law of fructification: "Never pursue a problem without at least two hypotheses—and don't despair when two or more of them survive your tests. And never forget that all human problems resist reduction to any one formulation or method of inquiry."

Well, that ends my selection from Hythloday's report from the University of Polytopia. I confess that what he has to say makes me even more uneasy than I was when I began: I am not at all clear where I might personally come out, if judged by his norms of vigorous intellectual curiosity sustained into the later years of life.

But I must also confess, abandoning now all ironies, that I do dream of living in a university somewhat more like the one he describes than the present University of Chicago. I love the life in this university as it is, but I see us as increasingly engaged in the futile pursuit of top prize as a *multi*versity. Surely it is not unrealistic, not the least bit utopian, to hope that we might resist the various temptations thrust on us by international competition, and instead set our own course, as we have often—quite miraculously, when you come to think about it—set our own course in the past.

Bibliography I: Overviews and Theories

Althusser, Louis. "Ideology and Ideological State Apparatuses." *Critical Theory since 1965*. Ed. Hazard Adams and Leroy Searle. Tallahassee: Florida State UP, 1986.

Arnold, Carroll C. "Oral Rhetoric, Rhetoric, and Literature." *Rhetoric in Transition: Studies in the Nature and Uses of Rhetoric*. Ed. Eugene E. White. University Park: Pennsylvania State UP, 1980. 157-73.

Austin, J. L. *How to Do Things with Words*. 2nd ed. Cambridge, MA: Harvard UP, 1975.

———. "Performance Utterances." *Philosophical Papers*. 3rd ed. Oxford: Clarendon, 1979.

Baird, A. Craig. *Rhetoric: A Philosophical Inquiry.* New York: Ronald, 1965.

Bakhtin, M. *The Dialogic Imagination*. Trans. Caryl Emerson and Michael Holquist. Austin: U of Texas P, 1981.

Barthes, Roland. "Authors and Writers." *Critical Essays*. Chicago: Northwestern UP, 1972. 185-93.

Bazerman, Charles. *Shaping Written Knowledge: The Genre and Activity of the Experimental Article in Science*. Madison: U of Wisconsin P, 1988.

Beale, Walter R. *A Pragmatic Theory of Rhetoric*. Carbondale: Southern Illinois UP, 1987.

Belenky, Mary F., Blythe M. Clinchy, Nancy R. Goldberger, and Jill Tarule. *Women's Ways of Knowing: The Development of the Self, Voice and Mind*. New York: Basic, 1986.

Benson, Thomas, ed. *Speech Communication in the 20th Century.* Carbondale: Southern Illinois UP, 1985.

Berlin, James A. *Rhetoric and Reality: Writing Instruction in American Colleges, 1990-1985*. Carbondale: Southern Illinois UP, 1987.

Berthoff, Ann E. "From Problem-solving to a Theory of Imagination." *College English* 33 (1972): 636-49.

Bitzer, Lloyd, and Edwin Black, eds. *The Prospect of Rhetoric: Report of the National Developmental Project*. Englewood Cliffs, NJ: Prentice, 1971.

Bizzell, Patricia. "Beyond Antifoundationalism to Rhetorical Authority: Problems Defining Cultural Literacy." *College English* 52 (1990): 661-75.

Bizzell, Patricia, and Bruce Herzberg, eds. *The Rhetorical Tradition*. Boston: Bedford, 1990.

Black, Edwin. "The Mutability of Rhetoric." *Rhetoric in Transition: Studies in the Nature and Uses of Rhetoric*. Ed. Eugene E. White. University Park: Pennsylvania State UP, 1980. 71-85.

———. "The Scope of Rhetoric Today: A Polemic Excursion." *The Prospect of Rhetoric*. Ed. Lloyd Bitzer and Edwin Black. Englewood Cliffs, NJ: Prentice, 1971. 102-03.

Black, Max. *The Labyrinth of Language*. New York: Praeger, 1968.

———. *Models and Metaphors*. Ithaca, NY: Cornell UP, 1966.

———. "More about Metaphor." *Dialectica* 31 (1977): 431-57.

Blankenship, Jane, and Hermann G. Stelzer, eds. *Rhetoric and Communication: Studies in the University of Illinois Tradition*. Urbana: U of Illinois P, 1976.

Bleich, David. "The Logic of Interpretation." *Genre* 10 (1977): 363-94.

Booth, Wayne C. *The Company We Keep: An Ethics of Fiction*. Berkeley: U of California P, 1988.

———. *Modern Dogma and the Rhetoric of Assent*. Chicago: U of Chicago P, 1974.

———. *Now Don't Try to Reason with Me: Essays and Ironies for a Credulous Age*. Chicago: U of Chicago P, 1970.

————. "The Revival of Rhetoric." *PMLA* 50 (1965): 8-12.

————. *The Rhetoric of Fiction.* Chicago: U of Chicago P, 1961.

————. *A Rhetoric of Irony.* Chicago: U of Chicago P, 1974.

Bormann, Ernest G. "Fantasy and Rhetorical Vision: The Rhetorical Criticism of Social Reality." *Quarterly Journal of Speech* 58 (1972): 396-407.

————. "Fantasy and Rhetorical Vision: Ten Years Later." *Quarterly Journal of Speech* 68 (1982): 288-305.

————. "Symbolic Convergence Theory: A Communication Formulation." *Journal of Communication* 35 (1985): 128-38.

Brummett, Barry. "On to Rhetorical Relativism." *Quarterly Journal of Speech* 68 (1982): 425-30.

————. "Some Implications of 'Process' of 'Intersubjectivity': Postmodern Rhetoric." *Philosophy and Rhetoric* 9 (1976): 21-51.

Bryant, Donald C. "Literature and Politics." *Rhetoric, Philosophy, and Literature: An Exploration.* Ed. Don M. Burks. West Lafayette, IN: Purdue UP, 1978. 95-108.

————. *Rhetorical Dimensions in Criticism.* Baton Rouge: Louisiana State UP, 1973.

————. *The Rhetorical Idiom.* Ithaca, NY: Cornell UP, 1958.

Buber, Martin. *I and Thou.* New York: Scribner's, 1958.

Burke, Kenneth. *Attitudes toward History.* Rev. 2nd ed. Los Altos, CA: Hermes, 1959.

————. *Counterstatement.* 2nd ed. Los Altos, CA: Hermes, 1953.

————. *A Grammar of Motives.* Berkeley: U of California P, 1969.

————. *Permanence and Change: An Anatomy of Purpose.* 2nd ed. Indianapolis: Bobbs-Merrill, 1965.

————. *The Philosophy of Literary Form.* 3rd ed. Berkeley: U of California P, 1973.

————. *A Rhetoric of Motives.* Berkeley: U of California P, 1969.

————. *A Rhetoric of Religion.* Boston: Beacon, 1961.

————. "Rhetoric—Old and New." *Journal of General Education* 5 (1951): 59-76.

————. "Rhetoric, Poetics, and Philosophy." *Rhetoric, Philosophy, and Literature: An Exploration.* Ed. Don M. Burks. West Lafayette, IN: Purdue UP, 1978. 15-33.

Burks, Don M., ed. *Rhetoric, Philosophy, and Literature: An Exploration.* West Lafayette, IN: Purdue UP, 1978.

Campbell, Karlyn Kohrs. "Contemporary Rhetorical Criticism: Genre, Analogs and Susan B. Anthony." *The Jensen Lectures: Contemporary Communication Studies.* Ed. John I. Sisco. Tampa: U of Southern Florida, 1983. 117-32.

————. "The Ontological Foundations of Rhetorical Theory." *Philosophy and Rhetoric* 3 (1970): 97-108.

————, and Kathleen Hall Jamieson. *Form and Genre: Shaping Rhetorical Action.* Falls Church, VA: Speech Communication Assoc., 1978.

Campbell, Paul Newell. "The *Personae* of Scientific Discourse." *Quarterly Journal of Speech* 61 (1975): 391-405.

Carleton, Walter. "What Is Rhetorical Knowledge?" *Quarterly Journal of Speech* 64 (1978): 313-28.

Cherwitz, Richard. "Rhetoric as 'A Way of Knowing': An Attenuation of the Epistemological Claims of the 'New Rhetoric.'" *Southern Speech Communication Journal* 41 (1977): 207-19.

Cherwitz, Richard A., and James W. Hikins. *Communication and Knowledge: An Investigation in Rhetorical Epistemology.* Columbia: U of South Carolina P, 1986.

Chomsky, Noam. *Aspects of the Theory of Syntax.* Cambridge, MA: MIT P, 1965.

————. "Language and the Mind." *Readings in the Theory of Grammar.* Ed. Diane D. Bornstein. Cambridge, MA: Winthrop, 1976.

————. *Language and Responsibility.* Trans. John Viertel. New York: Pantheon, 1977.

————. *Reflections on Language.* New York: Pantheon, 1975.

————. *Rules and Representations.* New York: Columbia UP, 1980.

Christensen, Francis. *Notes toward a New Rhetoric.* New York: Harper, 1967.

Clark, Katerina, and Michael Holquist. *Mikhail Bakhtin.* Cambridge, MA: Harvard UP, 1984.

Connors, Robert J. "The Rise and Fall of the Modes of Discourse." *College Composition and Communication* 32 (1981): 444-55.

————. "The Rise of Technical Writing Instruction in America." *Journal of Technical Writing and Communication* 12 (1982): 329-49.

Connors, Robert, Lisa Ede, and Andrea Lunsford. "The Revival of Rhetoric in America." *Essays on Classical Rhetoric and Modern Discourse.* Ed. Robert J. Connors, Lisa S. Ede, and Andrea A. Lunsford. Carbondale: Southern Illinois UP, 1984. 1-15.

Cooper, Charles R., and Lee Odell, eds. *Research on Composing.* Urbana, IL: NCTE, 1978.

Corbett, Edward P. J. *Selected Essays of Edward P. J. Corbett.* Ed. Robert J. Connors. Dallas: Southern Methodist UP, 1989.

————. "What Is Being Revived?" *College Composition and Communication* 18 (1967): 166-72.

Covino, William A. *The Art of Wondering: A Revisionist Return to the History of Rhetoric.* Portsmouth, NH: Heinemann, Boynton/Cook, 1988.

Crowley, Sharon. *The Methodical Imagination: Invention in Current-Traditional Rhetoric.* Carbondale: Southern Illinois UP, 1990.

Crusius, Timothy W. *Discourse: A Critique & Synthesis of the Major Theories.* New York: MLA, 1989.

Cushman, Donald P., and Phillip K. Tompkins. "A Theory of Rhetoric for Contemporary Society." *Philosophy and Rhetoric* 13 (1980): 43-67.

D'Angelo, Frank J. "The Four Master Tropes: Analogues of Development." *Rhetoric Review* 11 (1992): 91-107.

Dearin, Ray. "The Philosophical Basis of Chaim Perelman's Theory of Rhetoric." *Quarterly Journal of Speech* 55 (1969): 213-24.

de Man, Paul. "The Epistemology of Metaphor." *On Metaphor.* Ed. Sheldon Sacks. Chicago: U of Chicago P, 1979.

————. "Semiology and Rhetoric." *Allegories of Reading: Figural Language in Rousseau, Nietzsche, Rilke, and Proust.* New Haven, CT: Yale UP, 1979.

Derrida, Jacques. *Dissemination.* Trans. Barbara Johnson. Chicago: U of Chicago P, 1981.

————. *Of Grammatology.* Trans. Gayatri Spivak. Baltimore: Johns Hopkins UP, 1977.

————. *Speech and Phenomena.* Trans. David Allison. Evanston, IL: Northwestern UP, 1973.

————. *Writing and Difference.* Trans. Alan Base. Chicago: U of Chicago P, 1978.

de Saussure, Ferdinand. *Course in General Linguistics.* Trans. Wade Baskin. New York: Philosophical Library, 1959.

Dillon, George L. *Rhetoric as Social Imagination: Explorations in the Interpersonal Function of Language.* Bloomington: Indiana UP, 1986.

Duhamel, P. Albert. "The Function of Rhetoric as Effective Expression." *Journal of the History of Ideas* 10 (1949): 344-56. Rpt. in *Philosophy, Rhetoric and Argumentation.* Ed. Maurice Natanson and Henry W. Johnstone, Jr. University Park: Pennsylvania State UP, 1965. 80-92.

Eagleton, Terry. *Literary Theory: An Introduction.* Minneapolis: U of Minnesota P, 1983.

Eco, Umberto. "Metaphor." *Semiotics and the Philosophy of Language*. Trans. Christopher Paci. Bloomington: Indiana UP, 1986.

———. *The Role of the Reader: Explorations in the Semiotics of Texts*. Bloomington: Indiana UP, 1979.

———. *A Theory of Semiotics*. Bloomington: Indiana UP, 1976.

Ede, Lisa S. "Is Rogerian Rhetoric Really Rogerian?" *Rhetoric Review* 3 (1984): 40-48.

Ede, Lisa, and Andrea Lunsford. *Singular Texts/Plural Authors: Perspectives on Collaborative Writing*. Carbondale: Southern Illinois UP, 1992.

Enos, Theresa. "Reports of the 'Author's' Death May Be Greatly Exaggerated, But the 'Writer' Lives on in the Text." *Rhetoric Society Quarterly* 20 (1990): 339-46.

———, ed. *A Sourcebook for Basic Writing Teachers*. New York: Random, 1987.

Enos, Theresa, and Stuart C. Brown, eds. *Defining the New Rhetorics*. Newbury Park, CA: Sage, 1993.

Fahnestock, Jeanne, and Marie Secor. "Toward a Modern Version of Stasis." *Oldspeak/Newspeak*. Ed. Charles W. Kneupper. Urbana, IL: Rhetoric Society of America and NCTE, 1985.

Faigley, Lester. *Fragments of Rationality: Postmodernity and the Subject of Composition*. Pittsburgh: U of Pittsburgh P, 1992.

Farrell, Thomas B. "Knowledge, Consensus, and Rhetorical Theory." *Quarterly Journal of Speech* 62 (1976): 1-14.

Feyerabend, Paul. *Against Method: Outline of an Anarchistic Theory of Knowledge*. 1975. London and New York: Verso, 1978.

Fish, Stanley. "How Ordinary Is Ordinary Language?" *New Literary History* 5 (1973): 41-54.

Fisher, Walter R. "Toward a Logic of Good Reasons." *Quarterly Journal of Speech* 64 (1978): 376-84.

———, ed. *Rhetoric: A Tradition in Transition*. Michigan State UP, 1974.

Fogarty, Daniel. *Roots for a New Rhetoric*. Rpt. 1968. New York: Teachers College of Columbia U, 1959.

Foss, Sonja, Karen Foss, and Robert Trapp. *Contemporary Perspectives on Rhetoric*. 2nd ed. Prospect Heights, IL: Waveland, 1991.

Foucault, Michel. *The Archaeology of Knowledge*. Trans. A. M. Sheridan Smith. New York: Pantheon, 1972.

———. *Discipline and Punish: The Birth of the Prison*. Trans. Alan Sheridan. New York: Vintage-Random, 1979.

———. *The Order of Things: An Archaeology of the Human Sciences*. New York: Vintage, 1973.

Friedman, Maurice S. *Martin Buber: The Life of Dialogue*. New York: Harper Torchbooks, 1960.

Gadamer, Hans-George. "Man and Language." *Philosophical Hermeneutics*. Trans. and ed. David E. Linge. Berkeley: U of California P, 1976. 59-68.

———. *Philosophical Hermeneutics*. Trans. David E. Linge. Berkeley: U of California P, 1976.

Geertz, Clifford. *Local Knowledge: Further Essays in Interpretative Anthropology*. New York: Basic, 1982.

———. "Thick Description." *The Interpretation of Cultures*. New York: Basic, 1973. 3-30.

Golden, James L., Goodwin F. Berquist, and William E. Coleman. *The Rhetoric of Western Thought*. 4th ed. Dubuque, IA: Kendall/Hunt, 1989.

Grassi, Ernesto. "Remarks on German Idealism, Humanism, and the Philosophical Function of Rhetoric." *Philosophy and Rhetoric* 19 (1986): 125-33.

————. *Rhetoric as Philosophy: The Humanist Tradition.* University Park: Pennsylvania State UP, 1980.

————. "Why Philosophy Is Rhetoric." *Philosophy and Rhetoric* 20 (1987): 68–78.

Greene, Stuart. "Toward a Dialectical Theory of Composing." *Rhetoric Review* 9 (1990): 149–72.

Gregg, Richard B. "Rhetoric and Knowing: The Search for Perspective." *Central States Speech Journal* 32 (1981): 133–44.

————. *Symbolic Inducement and Knowing: A Study in the Foundations of Rhetoric.* Columbia: U of South Carolina P, 1984.

Grice, Paul. *Studies in the Ways of Words.* Cambridge, MA: Harvard UP, 1989.

Group Mu. *A General Rhetoric.* Trans. Paul B. Burrell and Edgar M. Slotkin. Baltimore: Johns Hopkins UP, 1981.

Habermas, Jürgen. *Communication and the Evolution of Society.* Trans. Thomas McCarthy. Boston: Beacon, 1979.

Hall, Stuart. "Encoding/Decoding." *Culture, Media, Language.* Ed. Stuart Hall et al. London: Hutchinson, 1980.

Halloran, Michael S. "Eloquence in a Technological Society." *Central States Speech Journal* 29 (1978): 221–27.

Hayakawa, S. I. "How Words Change Our Lives." *Symbol, Status, and Personality.* New York: Harcourt, 1963. 3–17.

Heath, Shirley Brice. *Ways with Words: Language, Life, and Work in Communities and Classrooms.* Cambridge: Cambridge UP, 1983.

Hirsch, E. D., Jr. *The Philosophy of Composition.* Chicago: U of Chicago P, 1977.

Horner, Winifred Bryan. *The Present State of Scholarship in Historical and Contemporary Rhetoric.* Rev. ed. Columbia: U of Missouri P, 1990.

Hoy, Pat C. II, Esther H. Schor, and Robert DiYanni, eds. *Women's Voices: Visions and Perspectives.* New York: McGraw, 1990.

Hudson, Hoyt H. "The Field of Rhetoric." *Quarterly Journal of Speech* 9 (1923): 167–80.

Hugenberg, Lawrence W., ed. *Rhetorical Studies Honoring James L. Golden.* Dubuque, IA: Kendall/Hunt, 1986.

Hunt, Everett Lee. "Rhetoric as a Humane Study." *Quarterly Journal of Speech* 41 (1955): 114–17.

Ijsseling, Samuel. *Rhetoric and Philosophy in Conflict.* Trans. Paul Dunphy. The Hague: M. Nijhoff, 1976.

Iser, Wolfgang. "The Reality of Fiction: A Functionalist Approach to Literature." *New Literary History* 7 (1975): 7–38.

Jakobson, Roman. "Linguistics and Poetics." *Style in Language.* Ed. Thomas Sebeok. Cambridge: MIT P, 1960. 350–77.

Jameson, Fredric. *The Prison-House of Language: A Critical Account of Structuralism and Russian Formalism.* Princeton: Princeton UP, 1972.

Johannesen, Richard L. *Contemporary Theories of Rhetoric: Selected Readings.* New York: Harper, 1971.

————, ed. *Ethics and Persuasion.* New York: Random, 1967.

Johannesen, Richard L., Rennard Strickland, and Ralph T. Eubanks, eds. *Language Is Sermonic: Richard M. Weaver on the Nature of Rhetoric.* Baton Rouge: Louisiana State UP, 1970.

Johnstone, Henry W., Jr. "From Philosophy to Rhetoric and Back." *Rhetoric, Philosophy, and Literature: An Exploration.* Ed. Don W. Burks. West Lafayette, IN: Purdue UP, 1978. 49–66.

————. "A New Theory of Philosophical Argumentation." *Philosophy and Phenomenological Research* 15 (1954): 244–52. Rpt. in *Philosophy, Rhetoric, and*

Argumentation. Ed. Maurice Natanson and Henry W. Johnstone, Jr. University Park: Pennsylvania State UP, 1965. 138-48.

———. *Philosophy and Argument.* University Park: Pennsylvania State UP, 1959.

———. "Rhetoric and Death." *Rhetoric in Transition: Studies in the Nature and Uses of Rhetoric.* Ed. Eugene E. White. University Park: Pennsylvania State UP, 1965. 1-9.

———. "Towards an Ethics of Rhetoric." *Communication* 6 (1981): 305-14.

———. *Validity and Rhetoric: A Philosophical Argument: An Outlook in Transition.* University Park, PA: Dialogue P of Man & World, 1978.

Kennedy, William J. "Voice as Frame: Longinus, Kant, Ong, and Deconstruction in Literary Studies." *Media, Consciousness, and Culture.* Ed. Bruce E. Gronbeck, Thomas J. Farrell, and Paul A. Soukup. Newbury Park, CA: Sage, 1991. 77-89.

Kent, Thomas. "Paralogic Hermeneutics and the Possibilities of Rhetoric." *Rhetoric Review* 8 (1989): 24-42.

Killingsworth, M. Jimmie, and Jacqueline S. Palmer. *Ecospeak: Rhetoric and Environmental Politics in America.* Carbondale: Southern Illinois UP, 1992.

Kimball, Bruce A. *Orators and Philosophers: A History of the Idea of Liberal Education.* New York: Teachers College P, 1986.

Kinneavy, James. "Contemporary Rhetoric." *The Present State of Scholarship in Historical and Contemporary Rhetoric.* Ed. Winifred Bryan Horner. Rev. ed. Columbia: U of Missouri P, 1990. 186-246.

———. *A Theory of Discourse.* Englewood Cliffs, NJ: Prentice, 1971.

Kneupper, Charles W., ed. *Oldspeak/Newspeak.* Urbana, IL: Rhetoric Society of America and NCTE, 1985.

Knoblauch, C. H., and Lil Brannon. *Rhetorical Traditions and the Teaching of Writing.* Upper Montclair, NJ: Boynton/Cook, 1984.

Kristeva, Julia. *The Kristeva Reader.* Ed. Toril Moi. New York: Columbia UP, 1986.

Kuhn, Thomas. "Second Thoughts on Paradigms." *The Essential Tension: Selected Studies in Scientific Tradition and Change.* Chicago: U of Chicago P, 1977. 293-319.

———. *The Structure of Scientific Revolutions.* 2nd ed. Chicago: U of Chicago P, 1970.

Lakoff, Robin. *Language and Women's Place.* New York: Harper, 1975.

Langer, Susanne. "Discursive and Presentational Forms." *Philosophy in a New Key: A Study in the Symbolism of Reason, rite, and Rite.* Cambridge, MA: Harvard UP, 1951.

Lanham, Richard A. *Literacy and the Survival of Humanism.* New Haven, CT: Yale UP, 1983.

LaTour, Bruno. *Science in Action: How to Follow Scientists and Engineers through Society.* Cambridge, MA: Harvard UP, 1987.

Lauer, Janice, and William Asher. *Composition Research: Empirical Designs.* New York: Oxford UP, 1988.

LeFevre, Karen Burke. *Invention as a Social Act.* Carbondale: Southern Illinois UP, 1987.

Leff, Michael. "In Search of Ariadne's Thread: A Review of Recent Literature on Rhetorical Theory." *Central States Speech Journal* 29 (1978): 73-91.

Liu, Huanhui. *An Outline of China's Rhetorics.* Nancang, PRC: Hundred-Flower, 1991.

Lunsford, Andrea A., and Lisa S. Ede. "Classical Rhetoric, Modern Rhetoric, and Contemporary Discourse Studies." *Written Communication* 1 (1984): 78-100.

Mailloux, Steven. *Rhetorical Power.* Ithaca, NY: Cornell UP, 1989.

Mao, LuMing R. "I Conclude Not: Toward a Pragmatic Account of Metadiscourse." *Rhetoric Review* 11 (1993): 265-89.

McKeon, Richard. *Rhetoric: Essays in Invention and Discovery.* Ed. Mark Backman. Woodbridge, CT: Ox Bow, 1987.

McKerrow, Raymie. "Critical Rhetoric: Theory and Praxis." *Communication Monographs* 56 (1989): 91–111.

McLuhan, Marshall. "At the Moment of Sputnik the Planet Became a Global Theater in Which There Are No Spectators But Only Actors." *Journal of Communication* 24 (1974): 48–58.

——. *The Gutenberg Galaxy: The Making of Typographic Man.* Toronto: U of Toronto P, 1962.

——. *Understanding Media: The Extensions of Man.* New York: McGraw, 1965.

Miller, Carolyn R. "Technology as a Form of Consciousness: A Study of Contemporary Ethos." *Central States Speech Journal* 29 (1978): 228–36.

Miller, Susan. "Classical Practices and Contemporary Basics." *The Rhetorical Tradition and Modern Writing.* Ed. James J. Murphy. New York: MLA, 1982. 46–57.

——. *Textual Carnivals: The Politics of Composition.* Carbondale: Southern Illinois UP, 1991.

Natanson, Maurice. "The Arts of Indirection." *Rhetoric, Philosophy, and Literature: An Exploration.* Ed. Don M. Burks. West Lafayette, IN: Purdue UP, 1978. 35–48.

——. "The Claims of Immediacy." *Philosophy, Rhetoric, and Argumentation.* Ed. Maurice Natanson and Henry W. Johnstone, Jr. University Park: Pennsylvania State UP, 1965. 10–19.

——. "The Limits of Rhetoric." *Quarterly Journal of Speech* 31 (1955): 133–39. Rpt. in *Philosophy, Rhetoric, and Argumentation.* Ed. Maurice Natanson and Henry W. Johnstone, Jr. University Park: Pennsylvania State UP, 1965. 93–101.

——. "Rhetoric and Philosophical Argumentation." *Quarterly Journal of Speech* 41 (1955): 133–39. Rpt. in *Philosophy, Rhetoric, and Argumentation.* Ed. Maurice Natanson and Henry W. Johnstone, Jr. University Park: Pennsylvania State UP, 1965. 149–56.

Natanson, Maurice, and Henry W. Johnstone, Jr., eds. *Philosophy, Rhetoric, and Argumentation.* University Park: Pennsylvania State UP, 1965.

Neel, Jasper. *Plato, Derrida, and Writing.* Carbondale: Southern Illinois UP, 1988.

Nelson, John S., Allan Megill, and Donald N. McCloskey, eds. *The Rhetoric of the Human Sciences.* Madison: Wisconsin UP, 1987.

Nichols, Marie Hochmuth. *Rhetoric and Criticism.* Baton Rouge: Louisiana State UP, 1963.

Norris, Christopher. *Derrida.* Cambridge, MA: Harvard UP, 1987.

North, Stephen. *The Making of Knowledge in Composition: Portrait of an Emerging Field.* Upper Montclair, NJ: Boynton/Cook, 1987.

"Octalog: The Politics of Historiography." *Rhetoric Review* 7 (1988): 5–49.

Ogden, C. K., and I. A. Richards. *The Meaning of Meaning.* 8th ed. New York: Harcourt, 1946.

Olson, David R. "From Utterance to Text: The Bias of Language in Speech and Writing." *Harvard Educational Review* 47 (1977): 257–81.

Ong, Walter J., S. J. "Literacy and Orality in Our Times." *ADE Bulletin* 58 (1978): 1–7.

——. *Orality and Literacy: The Technologizing of the Word.* London and New York: Methuen, 1982.

——. *The Presence of the Word.* New Haven, CT: Yale UP, 1971.

——. "The Province of Rhetoric and Poetic." *The Modern Schoolman* (1942): 24–27.

——. *Rhetoric, Romance and Technology.* Ithaca, NY: Cornell UP, 1971.

——. "Voice As a Summons for Belief." *Literature and Belief.* Ed. M. H. Abrams. New York: Columbia UP, 1958. 80–105.

————. "The Writer's Audience Is Always a Fiction." *PMLA* 90 (1975): 9–21.

Parker, William Riley. "Where Do English Departments Come From?" *College English* 26 (1967): 339–51.

Perelman, Chaïm. *An Historical Introduction to Philosophical Thinking.* Trans. Kenneth Brown. New York: Random, 1965.

————. *The Idea of Justice and the Problem of Argument.* New York: Humanities, 1963.

————. *The New Rhetoric and the Humanities: Essays on Rhetoric and Its Applications.* Dordrecht, Holland: D. Reidel, 1979.

————. *The Realm of Rhetoric.* Trans. William Kluback. South Bend, IN: U of Notre Dame P, 1982.

————. "Rhetoric and Philosophy." *Philosophy and Rhetoric* 1 (1968): 15–24.

————. "Value Judgments, Justifications, and Argumentation." *Philosophy Today* 6 (1961): 45–51.

————, and L. Olbrechts-Tyteca. *The New Rhetoric.* Trans. John Wilkinson and Purcell Weaver. South Bend, IN: U of Notre Dame P, 1969.

Phelps, Louise Wetherbee. *Composition as a Human Science: Contributions to the Self-Understanding of a Discipline.* New York: Oxford UP, 1988.

Polanyi, Michael. *Knowing and Being: Essays by Michael Polanyi.* Ed. Marjorie Grene. Chicago: U of Chicago P, 1969.

————. *Personal Knowledge: Towards a Post-Critical Philosophy.* Chicago: U of Chicago P, 1962.

"Polylog: Professing the New Rhetorics." *Rhetoric Review* 9 (1990): 5–35.

Popper, Karl R. "A Survey of Some Fundamental Problems." *The Logic of Scientific Discovery.* New York: Basic, 1959. 27–48.

Porter, James E. "Intertextuality and the Discourse Community." *Rhetoric Review* 5 (1986): 34–47.

Richards, I. A. *Basic English and Its Uses.* New York: Norton, 1943.

————. *Basic Rules of Reason.* London: Kegan Paul, 1933.

————. *Basic in Teaching: East and West.* London: Kegan Paul, 1935.

————. *Beyond.* New York: Harcourt, 1974.

————. *Coleridge on Imagination.* 1935. Bloomington: Indiana UP, 1960.

————. *Complementarities: Uncollected Essays.* Ed. John Paul Russo. Cambridge: Harvard UP, 1976.

————. *Design for Escape: World Education through Modern Media.* New York: Harcourt, 1968.

————. *Mencius on the Mind.* International Library of Psychology, Philosophy and Scientific Method. London: Kegan Paul, 1933.

————. *The Philosophy of Rhetoric.* New York: Oxford UP, 1936.

————. *Poetries and Sciences.* A reissue with a commentary of *Science and Poetry* (1926, 1935). New York: Norton, 1970.

————. *Poetries: Their Media and Ends.* Ed. Trevor Eaton. The Hague: Mouton, 1974.

————. *Practical Criticism: A Study of Literary Judgement.* London: Kegan Paul, 1929.

————. *Principles of Literary Criticism.* London: Kegan Paul, 1925.

————. *So Much Nearer: Essays Toward a World English.* New York: Harcourt, 1968.

————. *Speculative Instruments.* Chicago: U of Chicago P, 1955.

Richards, I. A., and Christine Gibson. *Techniques of Language Control.* Rowley, MA: Newbury, 1974.

Ricouer, Paul. "The Metaphorical Process as Cognition, Imagination, and Feeling." *On Metaphor.* Ed. Sheldon Sacks. Chicago: U of Chicago P, 1978. 141-57.
————. *The Rule of Metaphor: Multi-disciplinary Studies of the Creation of Meaning in Language.* Trans. Robert Czerny with Kathleen McLaughlin and John Costello. Toronto: U of Toronto P, 1975.
Rorty, Richard. *Contingency, Irony, and Solidarity.* Cambridge: Cambridge UP, 1989.
————. *Philosophy and the Mirror of Nature.* Princeton, NJ: Princeton UP, 1979.
Rosenblatt, Louise. *Literature as Exploration.* 3rd ed. New York: MLA, 1983.
————. *The Reader, the Text, the Poem: The Transactional Theory of the Literary Work.* Carbondale: Southern Illinois UP, 1978.
Rueckert, William H., ed. *Critical Responses to Kenneth Burke, 1924-1966.* Minneapolis: U of Minnesota P, 1969.
————. *Kenneth Burke and the Drama of Human Relations.* 2nd ed. Berkeley: U of California P, 1982.
Russo, John Paul. *I. A. Richards: His Life and Work.* Baltimore: Johns Hopkins UP, 1989.
Sacks, Sheldon. *On Metaphor.* Chicago: U of Chicago P, 1979.
Said, Edward. "The Problems of Textuality: Two Exemplary Positions." *Critical Inquiry* 4 (1978): 673-714.
Sams, Henry W. "Fields of Research in Rhetoric." *College Composition and Communication* 5 (1954): 60-65.
Schwartz, Joseph. "Kenneth Burke, Aristotle, and the Future of Rhetoric." *College Composition and Communication* 17 (1966): 210-16.
Schwartz, J., and J. Rycenga, eds. *The Province of Rhetoric.* New York: Ronald, 1965.
Schilb, John. "The History of Rhetoric and the Rhetoric of History." *PRE/TEXT* 7 (1986): 12-34.
————. "'Traveling Theory' and the Defining of New Rhetorics." *Rhetoric Review* 11 (1992): 34-48.
Scott, Robert L. "Can a New Rhetoric Be Epistemic?" *The Jensen Lectures: Contemporary Communication Studies.* Ed. John I. Sisco. Tampa: U of Southern Florida, 1983. 1-23.
————. "Intentionality in the Rhetorical Process." *Rhetoric in Transition: Studies in the Nature and Uses of Rhetoric.* Ed. Eugene E. White. University Park: Pennsylvania State UP, 1980. 39-60.
Scott, Robert L., and Donald K. Smith. "The Rhetoric of Confrontation." *Quarterly Journal of Speech* 55 (1969): 1-8.
Searle, John R. "The Logical Status of Fictional Discourse." *New Literary History* 6 (1975): 319-32.
————. *Speech Acts: An Essay in the Philosophy of Language.* New York: Cambridge UP, 1969.
Sebeok, Thomas A., ed. *Style in Language.* Cambridge, MA: MIT P, 1960.
Secor, Marie. "Perelman's Loci in Literary Argument." *PRE/TEXT* 5 (1984): 97-110.
Simons, Herbert W. "Are Scientists Rhetors in Disguise? An Analysis of Discursive Processes within Scientific Communities." *Rhetoric in Transition: Studies in the Nature and Uses of Rhetoric.* Ed. Eugene E. White. University Park: Pennsylvania State UP, 1980. 115-30.
————. *Rhetoric in the Human Sciences.* London: Sage, 1989.
————, ed. *The Rhetorical Turn: Invention and Persuasion in the Conduct of Inquiry.* Chicago: U of Chicago P, 1990.
Sisco, John I., ed. *The Jensen Lectures: Contemporary Communication Series.* Tampa: U of Southern Florida, 1983.

Smit, David W. "The Rhetorical Method of Ludwig Wittgenstein." *Rhetoric Review* 10 (1991): 31-51.

Smith, Barbara Herrnstein. *On the Margins of Discourse: The Relation of Literature and Language.* Baltimore: John Hopkins UP, 1978.

Steiner, George. *After Babel: Aspects of Language and Translation.* London: Oxford UP, 1975.

———. "Whorf, Chomsky and the Student of Literature." *New Literary History* 4 (1972): 15-34.

Steinmann, Martin, Jr., ed. *New Rhetorics.* New York: Scribner's, 1967.

———. "Rhetorical Research." *College English* 27 (1966): 16-32.

Stevenson, Charles L. "Persuasive Definitions (Parts I-II)." *Mind* 47 (1938): 331-38. Rpt. in *New Rhetorics.* Ed. Martin Steinmann, Jr. New York: Scribner's, 1967. 215-25.

Stewart, Donald. "Collaborative Learning and Composition: Boon or Bane?" *Rhetoric Review* 7 (1988): 58-83.

Tagliacozzo, George, Michael Mooney, and Donald P. Verene, eds. *Vico and Contemporary Thought.* Atlantic Highlands, NJ: Humanities, 1976.

Todorov, Tzvetan. *Mikhail Bakhtin: The Dialogical Principle.* Trans. Wlad Godzich. Minneapolis: U of Minnesota P, 1982.

———. "The Splendor and Misery of Rhetoric." *Theories of the Symbol.* Trans. Catherine Porter. Ithaca, NY: Cornell UP, 1982. 60-83.

Toulmin, Stephen. *An Examination of the Place of Reason in Ethics.* Cambridge: Cambridge UP, 1948.

———. *Human Understanding.* Vol. 1. Princeton: Princeton UP, 1972.

———. *An Introduction to Reasoning.* New York: Macmillan, 1978.

———. *The Place of Reason in Ethics.* Chicago: U of Chicago P, 1950.

———. *The Uses of Argument.* Cambridge: Cambridge UP, 1969.

Valesio, Paulo. *Novantiqua: Rhetorics as a Contemporary Theory.* Bloomington: Indiana UP, 1980.

Voloshinov, V. N. *Marxism and the Philosophy of Language.* Trans. Ladislav Matejka and I. R. Titunik. Cambridge, MA: Harvard UP, 1973.

Vygotsky, L. S. "The Prehistory of Written Language." *Mind in Society: The Development of Higher Psychological Processes.* Ed. Michael Cole, Vera John-Steiner, Sylvia Scribner, and Ellen Souberman. Cambridge, MA: Harvard UP, 1978. 105-19.

———. *Thought and Language.* Trans. Eugenia Hanfmann and Gertrude Vakar. Cambridge: MIT P, 1962.

Wallace, Karl. "The Substance of Rhetoric: Good Reasons." *Quarterly Journal of Speech* 49 (1963): 239-49.

———. "*Topoi* and the Problem of Invention." *The New Rhetoric of Chaim Perelman.* Ed. Ray Dearin. Lanham, MD: UP of America, 1989.

———. *Understanding Discourse: The Speech Act and Rhetorical Action.* Baton Rouge: Louisiana State UP, 1970.

Weaver, Richard M. *The Ethics of Rhetoric.* Chicago: Regnery, 1953.

———. *Ideas Have Consequences.* Chicago: U of Chicago P, 1948.

———. *Language Is Sermonic.* Ed. Richard Johannesen, Rennard Strickland, and Ralph T. Eubanks. Baton Rouge: Louisiana State UP, 1970.

———. *The Southern Tradition at Bay.* New Rochelle, NY: Arlington, 1968.

Welch, Kathleen E. *The Contemporary Reception of Classical Rhetoric: Appropriations of Ancient Discourse.* Hillsdale, NJ: Erlbaum, 1990.

White, Eugene E., ed. *Rhetoric in Transition: Studies in the Nature and Uses of Rhetoric.* University Park: Pennsylvania State UP, 1980.

White, Hayden. "The Discourse of History." *Humanities in Society* 2 (1979): 1-15.
———. "Historicism, History, and the Figurative Imagination." *History and Theory* 14 (1975): 48-67.
———. *Tropics of Discourse: Essays in Cultural Criticism.* Baltimore: Johns Hopkins UP, 1978.
Wichelns, Herbert A. "The Literary Criticism of Oratory." *Studies in Rhetoric and Public Speaking in Honor of James Albert Winans.* New York: Century, 1925. 181-216.
Willard, Charles Arthur. *A Theory of Argumentation.* University: U of Alabama P, 1989.
Williams, Raymond. *Keywords: A Vocabulary of Culture and Society.* New York: Oxford UP, 1976.
Winterowd, W. Ross. *Composition/Rhetoric: A Synthesis.* Carbondale: Southern Illinois UP, 1986.
———. *Contemporary Rhetoric: A Conceptual Background with Readings.* New York: Harcourt, 1975.
———. *Rhetoric: A Synthesis.* New York: Holt, 1968.
———. *The Rhetoric of the "Other" Literature.* Carbondale: Southern Illinois UP, 1990.
Witte, Stephen, et al., eds. *The Rhetoric of Doing: Essays on Written Discourse in Honor of James Kinneavy.* Carbondale: Southern Illinois UP, 1992.
Wittgenstein, Ludwig. *Philosophical Investigations.* Trans. G. E. M. Anscombe, 1953. Oxford: Basil Blackwell, 1976.
Yoos, George. "A Revision of the Concept of Ethical Appeal." *Philosophy and Rhetoric* 12 (1979): 41-58.
Young, Richard, and Alton L. Becker. "Toward a Modern Theory of Rhetoric: A Tagmemic Contribution." *Harvard Educational Review* 35 (1965): 450-68.
Zheng, Yishou. *A New Rhetorics.* Xiamen, PRC: Lujiang, 1987.

THE
NEW
RHETORICS

Commentary and Application

DONALD C. BRYANT
1905-1987

Born in New York, Donald Bryant earned his master's and his doctorate degrees in speech and English from Cornell. After teaching high school, he taught at New York State College for Teachers, Washington University, and, from 1958 until his retirement, at the University of Iowa as professor of rhetorical studies. Bryant was an internationally distinguished scholar of rhetorical theory and of British public address, concerning himself especially with the speeches, writings, life, and times of Edmund Burke in Writings and Speeches of Edmund Burke *(1939).| He also served a term as editor of* The Quarterly Journal of Speech *(1957-1959) and was president of the Speech Communication Association (1970). Bryant's definition of the functions of rhetoric is well known: "Adjusting ideas to people and people to ideas."*

Rhetoric: Its Functions and Its Scope

When a certain not always ingenuous radio spokesman for one of our large industrial concerns some years ago sought to reassure his audience on the troublesome matter of propaganda, his comfort ran thus: Propaganda, after all, is only a word for anything one says for or against anything. Either everything, therefore, is propaganda, or nothing is propaganda; so why worry?

The more seriously I take this assignment from the Editor to reexplore for the *Quarterly Journal of Speech* (1953), the ground surveyed by Hudson and Wichelns thirty years ago, and since crossed and recrossed by many another, including myself,[1] the nearer I come to a position like our friend's conclusion on propaganda. When I remember Quintilian's *Institutes* at one extreme of time, and lose myself in Kenneth Burke's "new rhetoric" at the other, I am almost forced to the position that whatever we do or say or write, or even think, in explanation of anything, or in support, or in extenuation, or in despite of anything, evinces rhetorical symptoms. Hence, either everything worth mentioning is rhetorical, or nothing is; so let's talk about

---

[1] Hoyt H. Hudson, "The Field of Rhetoric," *QJSE* 9 (April 1923): 167-80; Herbert A. Wichelns, "The Literary Criticism of Oratory," *Studies in Rhetoric and Public Speaking in Honor of James Albert Winans* (New York, 1925), pp. 181-216; Donald C. Bryant, "Some Problems of Scope and Method in Rhetorical Scholarship," *QJS* XXIII (April 1937): 182-88, and "Aspects of the Rhetorical Tradition," *QJS* 36 (April and October 1950): 169-76, 326-32.

something encompassable—say logic, or semantics, or persuasion, or linguistics, or scientific method, or poetics, or social psychology, or advertising, or salesmanship, or public relations, or pedagogy, or politics, or psychiatry, or symbolics—or propaganda.

But that is not the assignment. Others have dealt with those subjects, and have given us such illuminating definitive essays as "Speech as a Science" by Clarence Simon,[2] "The Spoken Word and the Great Unsaid" by Wendell Johnson,[3] "General Semantics[1952]" by Irving Lee,[4] and many other interpretive essays and *apologiae* for the various branches of our curricula and for the multiform captions in our departmental catalogues and organization charts. Among these, "Rhetoric and Public Address" can hardly be thought neglected over the years, at least in the *QJS* and *SM*. But perhaps we have assumed too quickly that rhetoric is now at last well understood. On the other hand, Hudson's "The Field of Rhetoric" may be inaccessible or out of date, and Burke's "new rhetoric" too cumbersome or recondite in statement, even after Marie Hochmuth's admirable exposition of it.[5] Even if all this be true, however, one can hardly hope to clarify here what may remain obscure in the work of thirty years—or twenty centuries; but in proper humility, no doubt one can try. At least, common practice seems to presume a restatement of most complex ideas about once in a generation.

I shall not undertake to summarize Hudson's or Wichelns' pioneer essays, relevant as they are to the central problem. They and certain others like Hunt's "Plato and Aristotle on Rhetoric"[6] are by now woven into the fabric of our scholarship. Nor shall I try to duplicate the coverage of my two papers on "Aspects of the Rhetorical Tradition." They can be easily reread by anyone interested.

One further limitation upon the scope of this essay seems necessary: I shall not try to present a digest of rhetoric or even an explanation of the main principles of rhetorical method. Those are also easily available, from Aristotle's *Rhetoric* to the newest textbook in persuasion. Furthermore, I intend to discuss no particular system of rhetoric, but the functions and scope which any system will embrace.

Confusion in Meaning of "Rhetoric"

Very bothersome problems arise as soon as one attempts to define rhetoric, problems that lead so quickly to hairsplitting on the one hand or cosmic inclusiveness on the other, and to ethical or moral controversy, that

---

[2] *QJS* 37 (October 1951): 281-98.

[3] *Ibid.* (December 1951): 419-29.

[4] *QJS* 38 (February 1952): 1-12.

[5] *Ibid.* (April 1952): 133-44.

[6] *Studies . . . in Honor of James Albert Winans*, pp. 3-60.

the attempt usually ends in trifling with logomachies, gloss on Aristotle, or flat frustration. *Rhetoric* is a word in common parlance, as well as in technical use in the SAA and the Chicago school of literary critics. Hence we may presume it to have meanings which must be reckoned with, however vague, various, and disparate; for a word means what responsible users make it mean. Various as the meanings are, however, one occasionally encounters uses which seem little short of perverse, in persons who ought to know better. Not long since, a doctoral candidate in the classics, who had written as his dissertation a "rhetorical" analysis of one of St. Paul's sermons, was asked how Aristotle had defined rhetoric. Though the question, it would appear, was relevant, the candidate was unable to answer satisfactorily. Whereupon the questioner was taken firmly to task by one of his fellow examiners and was told that after all rhetoric could be adequately defined as a *way of saying something*. Now of course rhetoric may be so defined, as poetic may be defined as a way of making something; but there is little intellectual profit in either definition.

Rhetoric also enjoys several other meanings which, though more common and less perverse, serve to make analysis of it difficult. In general these are the same meanings which Hudson reviewed thirty years ago: bombast; high-sounding words without content; oratorical falsification to hide meaning; sophistry; ornamentation and the study of figures of speech; most commonly among academic folk, Freshman English; and finally, least commonly of all, the whole art of spoken discourse, especially persuasive discourse. This last meaning has gained somewhat in currency in thirty years, especially among scholars in speech and renaissance literature.[7] During the same period the use of the term *rhetoric* (or the combinations *composition and rhetoric* and *grammar and rhetoric*) to label courses and textbooks in Freshman English has somewhat declined, and simultaneously the "rhetorical" content of them has declined also. The tendency now is to prefer just *Composition* or *English Composition*, or to resort to such loaded names as *Basic Writing, Effective Writing, Problems in Writing, Writing with a Purpose*, or *Communication and Analysis*.

In one of his early speeches, President Eisenhower declared that we want action from the Russians, not rhetoric, as evidence of their desire for peaceful settlement. Here is the common use of *rhetoric* to mean empty language, or language used to deceive, without honest intention behind it. Without question this use is in harmony with the current climate of meaning where what our opponents say is rhetoric, and what we say is something else.

---

[7] In his *The Ethics of Rhetoric* (Chicago: Henry Regnery, 1953), which has appeared since this article has been in proof, Richard M. Weaver of the College at the University of Chicago makes an interesting and useful effort to restore rhetoric to a central and respectable position among the arts of language and to assign it the function of giving effectiveness to truth.

Hence our attempt to define rhetoric leads almost at once into questions of morals and ethics.

Rhetoric as figures of speech or artificial elegance of language is also a healthy perennial, nurtured in literary scholarship and criticism as well as lay comment. Hence the second of the two meanings of *rhetorical* in *Webster's New Collegiate Dictionary* is "emphasizing style, often at the expense of thought." Here we encounter a second obscuring or limiting factor in our attempt at definition. We are to describe rhetoric in terms of those *elements* of a verbal composition for which it is to be held responsible. This mode of procedure has always been attractive. It can produce interesting and plausible conclusions, and it can be defended as schematically satisfying and pedagogically convenient. Thus it proved in the *trivium* of the middle ages and renaissance. If grammar has charge of the correctness of discourse, and if logic has charge of the intellectual content, then it is natural to assign to rhetoric the management of the language of discourse (or the *elocutio*), and if we do not include poetic in our system, the imaginative and emotional content also.

Another definition in the *New Collegiate Dictionary* points to the identification of rhetoric not with the elements of verbal composition but with the *forms* or *genres:* "The art of expressive speech or of discourse, orig. of oratory, now esp. of literary composition; esp., the art of writing well in prose, as disting. from versification and elocution." This approach is promising and on the whole the most popular through the ages. "Originally of oratory, now especially the art of writing well in prose—" this phrase does well enough as a general description of the scope of rhetoric in ancient Greece, as Baldwin has pointed out, when prose itself was virtually defined as oratory and history, and when even history was composed largely in the spirit of oratory. That is, rhetoric could be the art of prose when prose was predominantly concerned with the intentional, directional energizing of truth, of finding in any given situation all the available means of persuasion, and of using as many of them as good sense dictated.

Even then, however, the weakness of genres as the basis for constructing theories or writing handbooks was evident. What is the art of Plato's dialogues, which are in prose? or of Sappho's compositions, which are poems? Neither poetic nor rhetoric is adequate to either. The difficulty multiplies as variety in the kinds of compositions increases in Roman, renaissance, and modern times, and as print supplements—and often supplants—speech as the medium of verbal communication. As *poetic,* the art of imitation in language, became crystallized in Roman and renaissance learning as the theory and practice of the drama (especially tragedy) and the epic, so *rhetoric,* in Quintilian's and Cicero's theory the whole operative philosophy of civil leadership, showed in practice as the art of making winning speeches in the law courts, or later in public exhibitions. The very doctrine in rhetoric of the epideictic or ceremonial speech, as I shall show later, is excellent evidence of the weakness of the types or *genres* as the basis for definition.

All these meanings of rhetoric, in spite of their limitations, contribute something to the exposition of our subject, and the pursuit of each has yielded lucrative insights into the subject, or at least into the problem. Some of them, especially rhetoric as bombast, as excessive ornamentation, and as deceit, are evidence of the falling off of rhetoricians from time to time from the broad philosophy of the art which they inherited from the founders. For a redefinition, therefore, I know no better way of beginning than to return to that broad philosophy.

Working Definition of Rhetoric

First of all and primarily, therefore, I take rhetoric to be the *rationale of informative and suasory discourse*. All its other meanings are partial or morally-colored derivatives from that primary meaning. This rhetoric has been, at least since Aristotle; and at least since Aristotle there has existed a comprehensive, fundamental codification of its principles. It would be idolatrous to suggest that Aristotle uttered the first and last authentic words on rhetoric, or that his system is still adequate, or that it was completely satisfactory even for the Greeks of his day. Like his poetic theory, however, it enjoys unequalled scientific eminence in its field though it has sustained many additions and modifications through the centuries. Its limitations are historical rather than philosophical. Like the limitations of his poetic, the limitations of his rhetoric derive mainly from his failure to consider phenomena which had not yet occurred and to make use of learnings which had not yet been developed.

Now as then, therefore, what Aristotle said of the nature and principles of public address, of the discovery of all the available means of persuasion in any given case, must stand as the broad background for any sensible rhetorical system. Much of Aristotle's formulation, even in detail, survives ungainsaid and can only be rearranged and paraphrased by subsequent writers. Again to cite a parallel with his poetic: though the relative importance of plot in drama has shifted radically since Aristotle, when good plots are made their excellences will still be best discovered by the application of Aristotle's criteria. Similarly, though modern psychology is very different from that of the Greeks, and doubtless more scientific, modern enlightenment has produced no new method of analyzing an audience which can replace Aristotle's.

Aristotle, however, identified rhetoric with persuasion. His chief interests lay in the speaking to popular audiences in the law court and in the legislative assembly, and his system of classification and analysis obviously was framed with those types of speaking as its principal object. Some means of persuasion, however, in spite of Aristotle's comprehensive definition, are not within the scope of rhetoric. Gold and guns, for example, are certainly persuasive, and the basic motives which make them persuasive, profit and self-preservation, may enter the field of rhetoric; but applied directly to the persons to be persuaded, guns and gold belong to commerce or coercion, not to rhetoric.

No more shall we admit the persuasive use of all symbols as belonging to rhetoric. Undoubtedly the persuasive force of pictures, colors, designs, non-language sounds such as fog horns and fire alarms, and all such devices of symbolic significance is great and useful. Traffic lights, however, are not normally agents of rhetorical influence. No more, in themselves, are elephants, donkeys, lions, illuminated bottles of whiskey, or animated packs of cigarettes. Their use has a kinship to rhetoric, and when they are organized in a matrix of verbal discourse, they become what Aristotle called the extrinsic or non-artistic means of persuasion. They are instruments of the wielder of public opinion, and they are staples of two techniques which must be recognized as strongly rhetorical—advertising and propaganda. Unless we are to claim practically all interhuman activity as the field of rhetoric, however, some limits must be admitted, even within the field of persuasion. True, in the "new rhetoric" of Kenneth Burke, where the utmost extension rather than practical limit-setting is the aim, any manifestation of "identification," conscious or unconscious, is within rhetoric. Though the classic limitations of rhetoric are too narrow, others are too broad. Therefore I am assuming the traditional limitation to discourse.

Let us look now at Aristotle's apparent failure to include exposition as well as persuasion within rhetoric. Ancillary to persuasion, of course, exposition is clearly included. The idea of *demonstration,* the characteristic result of the logical mode, implies the most perfect exposition for audiences susceptible of reasoned instruction. Furthermore, another aspect of Aristotle's system admits exposition to independent status. At the expense of a slight venture into heresy (though I believe only a benign heresy) I suggest that any systematic construction of human phenomena, even Aristotle's, will either leave out something important and significant, or will include a category, however named, which is, in effect, "miscellaneous." That I think Aristotle did in discussing the rhetoric of the ceremonial or epideictic speech. The success of his categories, even so, is remarkable. The extension and effective application to the ceremonial speech in general of the principles of the persuasive speech whose end is active decision, provide very plausible coverage of that somewhat anomalous form. The three-fold, tripartite classification of speeches was too nearly perfect to abandon:

- Forensic (time, past; ends, justice and injustice; means, accusation and defense.)
- Epideictic (time, present; ends, honor and dishonor; means, praise and blame.)
- Deliberative (time, future; ends, the expedient and inexpedient; means, exhortation and dehortation.)

When the problems of what to do with time-present in the system, and with Pericles' funeral oration among the observed phenomena had to be solved, the coincidence was too attractive to be resisted. It provided for a piece of practical realism which no system should be allowed to defeat. Through that adjustment Aristotle admitted within the scope of rhetoric the predominantly literary performance on the one hand and gave an opening on the other for the primarily informative and instructional as well as the demonstrative and exhibitionistic. Through this third category rhetoric embraces, in a persuasion-centered system, the *docere* and *delectare*, the teach and delight, of the Roman and renaissance rhetoric-poetic and permits them an independent status outside their strictly ancillary or instrumental functions in persuasion.

Aristotle's system, therefore, and his rationale of effective speaking comprehend with very little violence the art of the good man skilled in speaking of Cicero and Quintilian, or Baldwin's equation of rhetoric to the art of prose whose end is giving effectiveness to truth[8]—effectiveness considered in terms of what happens to an audience, usually a popular or lay audience as distinguished from the specialized or technical audience of the scientific or dialectical demonstration. This distinction, strictly speaking, is a practical rather than a logical limitation, a limitation of degree rather than kind. No matter what the audience, when the speaker evinces skill in getting into their minds, he evinces rhetorical skill.

If the breadth of scope which I have assigned to rhetoric is implicit in Aristotle's system, the basic delimitation of that scope finds early and explicit statement there. Rhetoric is not confined in application to any specific subjects which are exclusively its own. Rhetoric is method, not subject. But if it has no special subjects, neither are all subjects within its province. In its suasory phase, at least, rhetoric is concerned, said Aristotle, only with those questions about which men dispute, that is, with the contingent—that which is dependent in part upon factors which cannot be known for certain, that which can be otherwise. Men do not dispute about what is known or certainly knowable by them. Hence the characteristic concern of rhetoric is broadly with questions of justice and injustice, of the expedient and the

---

[8] *Ancient Rhetoric and Poetic* (New York, 1924), p. 5.

inexpedient (of the desirable and undesirable, of the good and the bad), of praise and blame, or honor and dishonor.

To questions such as these and their almost infinite subsidiary questions, vital and perennial as they are in the practical operation of human society, the best answers can never be certain but only more or less probable. In reasoning about them, men at best must usually proceed from probable premise to probable conclusion, seldom from universal to universal. Hence Aristotle described the basic instrument of rhetoric, the enthymeme, as a kind of syllogism based on probabilities and signs.

Rhetoric, therefore, is distinguished from the other instrumental studies in its preoccupation with informed opinion rather than with scientific demonstration. It is the counterpart, said Aristotle, of dialectic. Strictly speaking, dialectic also may be said to attain only probability, not scientific certainty, like physics (and, perhaps, theology). The methodology, however, is the methodology of formal logic and it deals in universals. Hence it arrives at a very high degree of probability, for it admits the debatable only in the assumption of its premises. Rhetoric, however, because it normally deals with matters of uncertainty for the benefit of popular audiences, must admit probability not only in its premises but in its method also. This is the ground upon which Plato first, and hundreds of critics since, have attacked rhetoric—that it deals with opinion rather than knowledge. This is the ground also from which certain scholars have argued,[9] after some of the mediaeval fathers, that rhetoric really deals, characteristically, not with genuine probability but only with adumbration and suggestion. It is, they say, distinguished from dialectic in *degree* of probability—dialectic very high, and rhetoric very low.

The epistemological question is interesting, and in a world of philosophers where only certain knowledge was ever called upon to decide questions of human behavior, it would be the central question. Rhetoric exists, however, because a world of certainty is not the world of human affairs. It exists because the world of human affairs is a world where there must be an alternative to certain knowledge on the one hand and pure chance or whimsey on the other. The alternative is informed opinion, the nearest approach to knowledge which the circumstances of decision in any given case will permit. The art, or science, or method whose realm this is, is rhetoric. Rhetoric, therefore, is the method, the strategy, the organon of the principles for deciding best the undecidable questions, for arriving at solutions of the unsolvable problems, for instituting method in those vital phases of human activity where no method is inherent in the total subject-matter of decision. The resolving of such problems is the province of the "Good man

---

[9] For example, Craig La Drière, "Rhetoric as 'Merely Verbal' Art," *English Institute Essays—1948*, ed. by D. A. Robertson, Jr. (New York, 1949), pp. 123-52.

skilled in speaking." It always has been, and it is still. Of that there can be little question. And the comprehensive rationale of the functioning of that
good man so far as he is skilled in speaking, so far as he is a wielder of public
opinion, is rhetoric.

The Problems of Vocabulary in This Essay

Traditionally *rhetoric* and *oratory* have been the standard terms for the
theory and the product. The *rhetor* was the speaker, the addresser of the
public, or the teacher of speaking; the *rhetorician,* the teacher of rhetoric
or the formulator of the principles of rhetoric. Hence the special bias of the
terms as I use them has been and probably still is oral. That is a practical
bias and is not carelessly to be thrown away. From the beginning of publication in writing, however, essentially rhetorical performances, whether
already spoken or to be spoken, have been committed to paper and circulated to be read rather than heard—from Isocrates' *Panathenaicus* or
Christ's *Sermon on the Mount* to Eisenhower's message on the state of the
nation. Furthermore, for centuries now, especially since the invention and
cheapening of the art of printing, the agitator, the teacher, the preacher, the
wielder of public opinion has used the press quite independently of the
platform. Hence, obviously, rhetoric must be understood to be the rationale
of informative and suasory discourse both spoken and written: of Milton's
Aeropagitica as well as Cromwell's Address to the Rump Parliament; of
John Wilkes' *North Briton* as well as Chatham's speech on the repeal of the
Stamp Act; of Tom Paine's *Common Sense* as much as Patrick Henry's
Address to the Virginia Assembly; of Swift's pamphlet on the *Conduct of the
Allies* as well as Dr. Sacheverell's sermon on Passive Obedience; of George
Sokolsky's syndicated columns in the press equally with Edward R. Mur-
row's radio commentaries or Kenneth McFarland's appearances before con-
ventions of the Chambers of Commerce. I will use *rhetoric* and *rhetorical*
with that breadth of scope.

Furthermore, the terms *orator* and *oratory* have taken on, like *rhetoric*
itself, rather limited or distorted meanings, not entirely undeserved perhaps,
which make them no longer suitable for the designation of even the normal
oral rhetorical performance. *Practitioner of public address,* or some such
hyphenated monstrosity as *speaker-writer,* might be used as a generic term
for the product of rhetoric, but the disadvantages of such manipulations
of vocabulary are obvious. I am using the terms *speech* and *speaker* for
both written and oral performance and written and oral performer, unless
the particular circumstances obviously imply one or the other. Likewise, in
place of such a formula as *listener-reader,* I shall use *audience,* a usage not
uncommon anyway.

One must face still another problem of vocabulary, that of the term *rhetoric* in the three distinguishable senses in which I use it: (1) as the rationale of informative and suasory discourse, a body of principle and precept for the creation and analysis of speeches; (2) as a quality which characterizes that kind of discourse and distinguishes it from other kinds; (3) as a study of the phenomenon of informative and suasory discourse in the social context. Similarly, I fear, the term *rhetorician* will sometimes mean the formulator and philosopher of rhetorical theory; sometimes the teacher of the technique of discourse; sometimes the speaker with rhetorical intention; and finally the student or scholar whose concern is the literary or social or behavioral study of rhetoric. I have been tempted to invent terms to avoid certain of these ambiguities, such as *logology*, or even *rhetoristic* (parallel with *sophistic*), but the game would probably not be worth the candle.

In summary, rhetoric is the rationale of informative and suasory discourse, it operates chiefly in the areas of the contingent, its aim is the attainment of maximum probability as a basis for public decision, it is the organizing and animating principle of all subject-matters which have a relevant bearing on that decision. Now let us turn to the question of the subject-matters in which rhetoric most characteristically functions and of the relations it bears to special subject-matters.

Subjects of Rhetorical Discourse

Wrote Aristotle, "The most important subjects of general deliberation . . . are practically five, viz. finance, war and peace, the defense of the country, imports and exports, and legislation." This is still the basic list, though legislation now would be far more generally inclusive than it was to the Athenian assembly. In addition, within the scope of rhetorical discourse fall the subjects of forensic address—crime and its punishment and all the concerns of justice and injustice. Furthermore, the concerns of teaching, preaching—moral, intellectual, practical, and spiritual instruction and exhortation—and commercial exploitation, wherever the problems of adaptation of idea and information to the group mind are concerned, depend upon rhetorical skill for their fruition. Thus we are brought again to the position that the rhetorical factor is pervasive in the operative aspects of society.

Does this mean that the speaker must be a specialist in all subjects, as well as in rhetorical method? Cicero seemed willing to carry the demands thus far, at least in establishing his ideal orator; and this implication has been ridiculed from Plato onwards for the purpose of discrediting first the claims of the sophists and then all men "skilled in speaking." Plainly, in practice and in plausible human situations, the suggestion is absurd. Does the public speaker or the columnist or the agitator have to be a military specialist in order rightly to urge peace or war? Does the citizen have to be a dentist and a chemist and a pathologist intelligently to advocate the use of fluorine in the municipal water supply? He does not become a specialist in these fields, of course, any more than the head of an industrial plant is the technical master of the specialties of all the men who serve under him. "He attempts to learn the authorities and sources of information in each, and to develop a method which he can apply to specific problems as they arise. He learns, in any given situation, what questions to ask and to answer. The peculiar contribution of the rhetorician is the discovery and use, to the common good, of those things which move men to [understanding and] action."[10] Looked at another way, the relation of rhetoric to the subject-matters of economics, or public health, or theology, or chemistry, or agriculture is like the relation of hydraulic engineering to water, under the specific circumstances in which the engineer is to construct his dam or his pumping station or his sewage system, and in view of the specific results he is to obtain. He develops a method for determining what questions to ask and answer from all that which can be known about water. If he is a good hydraulics engineer, he will see to it that his relevant knowledge is sound, as the good speaker will see to it that his relevant knowledge of hydraulic engineering is the best obtainable if he is to urge or oppose the building of a dam in the St. Lawrence River. If either is ignorant, or careless, or dishonest, he is culpable as a man and as a rhetorician or hydraulics engineer.

It was not the scientific chronologist, the astronomer Lord Macclesfield, who secured the adoption in England of the Gregorian calendar, thoroughly as he understood the subject in all its mathematical, astronomical, and chronometrical aspects. It was the Earl of Chesterfield, learning from the chronologist all that was essential to the particular situation, and knowing rhetoric and the British Parliament, who was able to impress upon his fellows not necessarily the validity of the calculations but the desirability and the feasibility of making a change. If the truth of scientific knowledge had been left to its own inherent force with Parliament, we would doubtless be many more days out of phase with the sun than England was in 1751. As Aristotle observed in his brief and basic justification of rhetoric, truth itself has a tendency to prevail over error; but in competition with error, where skillful men have an interest in making error prevail, truth needs the help of as attractive and revealing a setting as possible. In the Kingdom of Heaven, truth may be its own sole advocate, but it needs mighty help if it is to survive in health among the nations on earth. As Fielding wrote of prudence in *Tom Jones:* "It is not enough that your designs, nay, that your actions, are intrinsically good; you must take care that they shall appear so. If your inside

---

[10] Hudson, "Field of Rhetoric," *QJSE* 9 (April 1923): 177.

be never so beautiful, you must preserve a fair outside also. This must be constantly looked to."[11]

In this sense even honest rhetoric is fundamentally concerned with appearances, not to the disregard of realities as Plato and his successors have industriously charged, but to the enforcement of realities. Rhetoric at the command of honest men strives that what is desirable shall appear desirable, that what is vicious shall appear vicious. It intends that the true or probably true shall seem so, that the false or doubtful shall be vividly realized for what it is. A bridge or an automobile or a clothes-line must not only *be* strong but must *appear* to be so. This fact has been an obstacle to the use of many new structural materials. Accustomed to an older kind, we have been reluctant to accept the adequacy of a new, more fragile-seeming substance. Hence one important reason for surrounding steel columns with stone pillars is the necessity of making them seem as strong as their predecessors. Appearances, then, must be the concern of the wielder of public opinion, the rhetorician. Through ignorance or malice, to be sure, skill in establishing appearances may be applied to deceive. This is a grave peril which must be the concern of all men of good will. Knowledge of the devices of sophistry will always be acquired by those whose purposes are bad; ignorance of them will provide no defense for the rest. No great force can be used without hazard, or ignored without hazard. The force understood, rather than the force not understood, is likely to be the force controlled. That understanding is provided by rhetoric, the technique of discourse addressed to the enlightenment and persuasion of the generality of mankind—the basic instrument for the creation of informed public opinion and the consequent expedient public action.

Occasions of Rhetorical Discourse

Whether we will or no, we cannot escape rhetoric, either the doing or the being done to. We require it. As Edmund Burke wrote, "Men want reasons to reconcile their minds to what is done, as well as motives originally to act right."[12] Whether we seek advice or give it, the nature of our talk, as being "addressed," and of the talk of which we are the audience, as being addressed to us, necessitates speaking the language of the audience or we had as well not speak at all. That process is the core of rhetoric. It goes on as genuinely, and is often managed as skillfully, over the frozen-meats counter of the local supermarket as in the halls of Congress; on the benches in front of the Boone County Court House on Saturday afternoon before election as

---

[11]Book III, Chapter 7. Modern Library Ed., p. 97.

[12]*Correspondence* (1844), I, 217.

below the benches of the Supreme Court the next Wednesday morning; around the table where a new labor contract is being negotiated as in the pulpit of Sainte-Marie de Chaillot where Bossuet is pronouncing the funeral oration upon Henriette d'Angleterre; in the Petition from Yorkshire to King George III for redress of grievances as in the Communist Manifesto or the Declaration of Independence.

As we are teachers, and as we are taught, we are involved with rhetoric. The success of the venture depends on a deliberate or instinctive adjustment of idea-through-speaker-to-audience-in-a-particular-situation. Pedagogy is the rhetoric of teaching, whether formally in the classroom or the book, or informally in the many incidental situations of our days and nights. The psychological principle, for example, that we learn through association becomes a rhetorical principle when we use it to connect one day's lesson with what has gone before. It is the same principle by which Burke attempted to establish in the minds of the House of Commons the rights of American colonists when he identified the colonists' with Englishmen, whose rights were known.

As we are readers of newspapers and magazines and all such information-giving and opinion-forming publications, and as we write for them, we are receiving or initiating rhetorical discourse, bad or good, effective or ineffective. The obligations of the journalist as investigator of the facts, as thinker about the facts, as discoverer of ideas and analyst and critic of ideas, are fundamental. They demand all the knowledge and skill that the political, scientific, and technical studies can provide. The journalist's distinctive job, however, is writing for his audience the highest grade of informative and suasory discourse that the conditions of his medium will permit. Whether editorial writer, commentator, or plain news-writer, reaching into his audience's mind is his problem. If the people who buy the paper miss the import, the paper might as well not be published. Call it *journalism* if you choose; it is the rhetoric of the press: "it is always public opinion that the press seeks to change, one way or another, directly or indirectly."[13] Seldom can the journalist wait for the solution of a problem before getting into the fray, whether the question be a more efficient way of handling municipal finances or independence for India. He must know the right questions to ask and the bases for answering them with greatest probability for his audience now. That is his rhetorical knowledge.

The same is true of the radio and television news reporter, news analyst, and commentator. He must have rhetorical skill to survive in his occupation, and he must have knowledge and integrity if his effect is to be beneficial rather than destructive to informed public opinion. His staple, also, whether

---

[13] *The Press and Society: A Book of Readings*, ed. by George L. Bird and Frederic E. Merwin (New York, 1951), preface, p. iv.

good or bad, is rhetoric. His efforts are aimed at the public mind and are significant only as they affect the public mind. If he is an honest rhetorician, he does not imply of most things, "It is so because," but only "I believe so because"; or "I recommend so because it seems probable where I cannot be sure." If he is tempted into exploiting the force of extravagant and authoritative assertion, his morals rather than his rhetoric have gone awry. Whether the use be honest or dishonest, the instrument is rhetoric.

It is obvious and commonplace that the agitator, the political speaker, the pamphleteer, the advocate, the preacher, the polemicist and apologist, the adviser of kings and princes, the teacher of statesmen, the reformer and counter-reformer, the fanatic in religion, diet, or economics, the mountebank and messiah, have enhanced the stature of a noble discourse or have exploited a degraded, shallow, and dishonest discourse. It matters not that we resort to exalted names for the one—eloquence, genius, philosophy, logic, discourse of reason; and for the other, labels of reproach and contempt—sophistry, glibness, demagoguery, chicanery, "rhetoric." That naming process itself is one of the most familiar techniques of rhetoric. The fact is that in their characteristic preoccupation with manipulating the public mind, they are one. They must not all be approved or emulated, but they must all be studied as highly significant social phenomena, lest we be ignorant of them, and hence powerless before them, for good or for ill.

Similarly, though perhaps not so easily acceptable into rhetoric, we must recognize most of what we know as advertising, salesmanship, propaganda, "public relations," and commercial, political, and national "information" services. I shall have some special consideration to give to these later. At present I merely cite them as great users of rhetoric. In this day of press, radio, and television perhaps their rhetoric is that most continuously and ubiquitously at work on the public.

Relations of Rhetoric to Other Learnings

These, then, are fundamental rhetorical situations. In them human beings are so organizing language as to effect a change in the knowledge, the understanding, the ideas, the attitudes, or the behavior of other human beings. Furthermore, they are so organizing that language as to make the change as agreeable, as easy, as active, and as secure as possible—as the Roman rhetoric had it, to teach, to delight, and to move (or to bend). What makes a situation rhetorical is the focus upon accomplishing something predetermined and directional with an audience. To that end many knowledges and sciences, concerning both what is external to audiences and what applies to audiences themselves, may be involved, many of which I have discussed in a previous essay.[14] These knowledges, however, have to be organized, managed, given places in strategy and tactics, set into coordinated and harmonious movement towards the listener as the end, towards what happens to him and in him. In short, they have to be *put to use*, for, as Bacon said, studies themselves "teach not their own use; but that is a wisdom without them, and above them, won by observation." "Studies themselves do give forth directions too much at large, except they be bounded in by experience."[15] Rhetoric teaches their use towards a particular end. It is that "observation," that "experience" codified, given a rationale. Other learnings are chiefly concerned with the discovery of ideas and phenomena and of their relations to each other within more or less homogeneous and closed systems. Rhetoric is primarily concerned with the relations of ideas to the thoughts, feelings, motives, and behavior of men. Rhetoric as distinct from the learnings which it uses is dynamic; it is concerned with movement. It *does* rather than *is*. It is method rather than matter. It is chiefly involved with bringing about a condition, rather than discovering or testing a condition. Even psychology, which is more nearly the special province of rhetoric than is any other study, is descriptive of conditions, but not of the uses of those conditions.

So far as it is method, rhetoric is like the established procedures of experimental science and like logic. As the method for solving problems of human action in the areas of the contingent and the probable, however, it does not enjoy a privilege which is at the same time the great virtue and the great limitation of science and logic—it cannot choose its problems in accordance with the current capacities of its method, or defer them until method is equal to the task. Rhetoric will postpone decision as long as feasible; indeed one of its most valuable uses in the hands of good men, is to prevent hasty and premature formulation of lines of conduct and decision. In this it is one with science—and good sense. But in human affairs, where the whole is usually greater than the most complete collection of the parts, decisions—makings up of the mind—cannot always wait until all the contingencies have been removed and solutions to problems have been tested in advance. Rhetoric, therefore, must take undemonstrable problems and do its best with them when decision is required. We must decide when the blockade is imposed whether to withdraw from Berlin or to undertake the air lift, not some time later when perhaps some of the contingencies may have been removed. And the making of the choice forever precludes trying out and testing the other possibilities under the circumstances which would have prevailed had we chosen differently at first. Likewise we must make a choice

---

[14] "Aspects of the Rhetorical Tradition" (1950), see above, note 1.

[15] "Of Studies."

on the first Tuesday in November, whether we are scientifically sure or not. In each case, rhetoric, good or bad, must be the strategy of enlightening opinion for that choice.

To restate our central idea still another way: rhetoric, or the rhetorical, is the function in human affairs which governs and gives direction to that creative activity, that process of critical analysis, that branch of learning, which address themselves to the whole phenomenon of the designed use of language for the promulgation of information, ideas, and attitudes. Though it is instrumental in the discovery of ideas and information, its characteristic function is the publication, the publicizing, the humanizing, the animating of them for a realized and usually specific audience. At its best it seeks the "energizing of truth," in order to make "reason and the will of God prevail." But except in science, and no doubt theology, the promulgation of *truth*, sure or demonstrable, is out of the question. Normally the rhetorical function serves as high a degree of probability as the combination of subject, audience, speaker, and occasion admits. Rhetoric may or may not be involved (though the speaker-writer must be) in the determination of the validity of the ideas being promulgated. Such determination will be the province in any given situation of philosophy, ethics, physics, economics, politics, eugenics, medicine, hydraulics, or bucolics. To rhetoric, however, and to no other rationale, belongs the efficiency—the validity if you will—of the relations in the idea-audience-speaker situation.

Functioning of Rhetoric

We are ready now, perhaps, if we have not been ready much sooner, to proceed to the question of how rhetoric works, what it accomplishes in an audience. Speaking generally, we may say that the rhetorical function is the *function of adjusting ideas to people and of people to ideas.* This process may be thought of as a continuum from the complete modification or accommodation of ideas to audiences (as is sometimes said, "telling people only what they want to hear") at the one extreme, to complete regeneration at the other (such perfect illumination that the "facts speak for themselves"). This continuum may, therefore, be said to have complete flattery (to use Plato's unflattering epithet) at one end and the Kingdom of Heaven at the other! Good rhetoric usually functions somewhere well in from the extremes. There, difficult and strange ideas have to be modified without being distorted or invalidated; and audiences have to be prepared through the mitigation of their prejudices, ignorance, and irrelevant sets of mind without being dispossessed of their judgments. The adjustment of ideas to people, for example, was being undertaken by the Earl of Chatham in his speech for the repeal of the Stamp Act, when he agreed that Parliament had legislative supremacy over the Colonies but that legislative supremacy did not include the right to tax without representation. And when Booker T. Washington assured the Southern white folk that they and the Negroes could be as separate as the fingers in social affairs and as united as the hand in economic, he was adjusting people to the idea of real freedom for his race.

The moral disturbances which rhetoric and rhetorical activity seem to breed do not usually result from this process of mutual accommodation itself. Most of them arise when the speaker tries so to adjust ideas to people that the ideas are basically falsified, or when he attempts so to adjust people to ideas as to deform or anesthetize the people. Report has it that after Senator Hiram Johnson had campaigned through rural New England charging that England would have three votes to one for the United States in the League of Nations, he was taxed by a critic with misrepresenting the nature of the British Empire. One could not assume, so Johnson's critic declared, that Canada and South Africa would vote with England as a single bloc. "That may be," Johnson is said to have replied, "but New England farmers do not know the nature of the British Empire, and they do know common arithmetic." That is adjusting ideas to people so far as to falsify the basic idea. In the other direction, stimulating the "Red-menace-in-the-air-we-breathe" terror in order to adjust people to the idea of giving up their right of dissent is an effort to dispossess people of their judgments.

In terms of the old, but still convenient, faculty psychology, the terms in which rhetoric is most frequently attacked—reason, imagination, passions (emotions), judgment, will—rhetoric may still be described as the method of applying "reason to imagination for the better moving of the will." To complete our broad idea of the scope of rhetoric we should add "and the better clarification of the understanding." That is Francis Bacon's succinct statement of how rhetoric functions in the audience,[16] and it is still a good one. It establishes rhetoric squarely as an instrumental learning which manages the creative powers of the whole logical-psychological man toward a single dynamic end.

Rhetoric, therefore, has the greatest possible involvement with the logical and psychological studies. These learnings must be the core of the speaker's equipment. They are the *sine qua non* in the knowledge through which rhetoric must function. In the good rhetoric which Plato described in the *Phaedrus*, after knowledge of the truth, he saw the equipment of the rhetorically skilled man to consist in knowledge of the various possible kinds of arguments, knowledge of the various kinds of souls, and knowledge of which kinds of souls will be affected by which kinds of arguments—that is,

---

[16] From *The Advancement of Learning*. See Karl R. Wallace, *Francis Bacon on Communication and Rhetoric* (Chapel Hill, 1943), p. 27.

knowledge of the rational processes and knowledge of the mutual adaptation of these processes to audiences. Furthermore, in the great counter-Platonic *Rhetoric* of Aristotle, the first Book is devoted chiefly to the rational processes of rhetoric, and the next Book is the first extant comprehensive treatise on individual and group psychology. Likewise, in one of the best of the recent books on liberal education, which is, therefore, something like a basic statement on rhetoric, Hoyt Hudson sees the fundamental equipment of the liberally educated man to require three parts: the Arm of Information, the Arm of Operative Logic, and the Arm of Imagination.[17] Of these, in practical affairs, rhetoric is based on the second and third, and the first must be the starting place of the speaker in each particular situation.

Where in this pattern, then, does emotion come in, that famous roughneck who is said to spoil the rational life and vitiate the logic of behavior? As Hudson and many others have observed, and as Bacon knew well, emotion is a derivative of both reason and imagination. Love of truth and of the good life must be the results of any genuinely rational functioning, that is, of operative logic; and vivid realization of experience, which is imagination, can hardly occur without those strong emotional accompaniments which, in practice, have given rise to the identifying of emotion with imagination. This point seems hardly to need laboring over again. Hudson's book gives it adequate coverage, and I have summarized the traditional position of rhetoric and rhetoricians on it in the essay already mentioned.[18] The position is that a complete rhetoric, and that is the kind of rhetoric which we are discussing, knows the whole man and seeks to bring to bear the whole man in achieving its ends—what he is and what he thinks he is, what he believes and what he thinks he believes, what he wants and what he tells himself he wants. Towards its special ends, rhetoric recognizes the primacy of rational processes, their primacy in time as well as in importance, as Bacon's definition implies—applying reason to the imagination. Just so poetry recognizes the primacy for its purposes of the imagination. But rhetoric has always been akin to poetry—for long periods of history it has in fact annexed poetry—in its recognition of the honest and highly important power of imagination and of that emotion which does not supplant but supports reason, and sometimes even transcends it. Thus Sir Philip Sidney and most literary theorists of the renaissance attributed to poetry the distinctly rhetorical function of using imagination to create what might be called historical fictions to give power and life to ideas. Rhetoric recognizes the strength of the fictions men live by, as well as those they live under;[19] and it aims to fortify the one and

---

[17]*Educating Liberally* (Stanford University, 1945), pp. 10 ff.

[18]Above, note 14.

[19]See the very relevant analysis of some of the fictions in the ideology of American business in C. Wright Mills, *White Collar* (New York, 1951), Ch. 3, "The Rhetoric of Competition."

explode the other. Rhetoric aims at what is *worth* doing, what is *worth* trying. It is concerned with *values,* and values are established with the aid of imaginative realization, not through rational determination alone; and they gain their force through emotional animation.

We have observed that psychology, human nature, has been a staple of rhetorical learning through the ages. No doubt, therefore, scientific psychology will have more and more to contribute to modern rhetoric. The first notable attempt to ground rhetoric in a systematic modern psychology was made by George Campbell in his *Philosophy of Rhetoric* (1776), in which he stated as his purpose

> to exhibit . . . a tolerable sketch of the human mind; and, aided by the lights which the poet and the orator so amply furnish, to disclose its secret movements, tracing its principal channels of perception and action, as near as possible, to their source: and, on the other hand, from the science of human nature, to ascertain with greater precision, the radical principles of that art, whose object it is, by the use of language, to operate on the soul of the hearer, in the way of informing, convincing, pleasing, moving, or persuading.[20]

That same purpose governs our contemporary writers of treatises and textbooks on public speaking, argumentation, and persuasion, and most of them include as up-to-date a statement as possible of the psychological and the rational bases of rhetoric. It is a commonplace that of the studies recently come to new and promising maturity, psychology, especially social psychology, and cultural anthropology have much to teach modern rhetoric and to correct or reinterpret in traditional rhetoric. The same may be said of the various new ventures into the study of meaning, under the general head of semantics. How language *means* is obviously important to the rationale of informative and suasory discourse. Nevertheless, in spite of I. A. Richards' book,[21] the theory of meaning is not *the* philosophy of rhetoric, any more than is the psychology of perception. Rhetoric is the organizer of all such for the wielding of public opinion.

Advertising, Salesmanship, and Propaganda

Now that we have sketched the rhetorical process functioning at its best for the exposition and dissemination of ideas in the wielding of public opinion, with the ethical and pathetic modes of proof in ancillary relation to the logical, with the imagination aiding and reenforcing the rational, let us turn

---

[20] 7th ed. (London, 1823), pp. vii–viii.
[21] *The Philosophy of Rhetoric* (New York, 1936).

to some of the partial, incomplete, perhaps misused, rhetorics which I have already mentioned briefly.

It is axiomatic that men do not live by reason alone or even predominantly, though reason is such a highly prized commodity and stands in so high a repute even among the unreasoning and unreasonable, that men prefer to tell themselves and to be told that they make up their minds and determine their choices from reason and the facts. Intellectual activity, both learning and thinking, is so difficult that man tends to avoid it wherever possible. Hence education has almost always put its first efforts into cultivating the reasonable portion of the mind rather than the imaginative or emotional. Furthermore, the strength and accessibility of imaginative and emotional responses is so great in spite of education that though men seldom make effective reasonable decisions without the help of emotion, they often make, or appear to make, effective emotional decisions without the help of rational processes or the modification of reasonable consideration. Inevitably, therefore, the available reason in rhetorical situations will vary tremendously, and the assistance which imagination must provide towards the moving of the will must vary accordingly. Except in Swift's unexciting land of the Houyhnhnms, however, imagination will always be there.

Ever since men first began to weave the web of words to charm their fellows, they have known that some men can impose their wills on others through language in despite of reason. Almost as long, other men have deplored and feared this talent. If the talent were wholly a matter of divine gift and were wholly unexplainable, the only alternative to succumbing to the orator would be to kill him. In time it appeared, however, that this skill could be learned, in part at least, and could be analyzed. Thus if it were good, men could learn to develop it further; and if it were bad, they could be armed in some measure against it. Hence rhetoric, and hence the partial rhetoric of anti-reason and pseudo-reason. And hence the appeal of such rhetorical eruptions as Aldous Huxley's total condemnation of oratory in *The Devils of Loudon.*[22] His indictment of public speakers is indeed skillful, and ought to be taken seriously. If the talent of his golden-voiced Grandiers be indeed magic, then we will have to agree that the fate of man before such wizards is hopeless. Rhetoric teaches, however, that the method and the power of this kind of discourse can be analyzed, at least in large part, and if its subtleties cannot be wholly *learned* by every ambitious speaker, the characteristics of its operation can be understood, and if understood, then controlled, for better or for worse.[23]

---

[22] (New York, 1952), pp. 18–19.

[23] Observe the tradition of rhetoric as a systematic study, summarized in my "Aspects of Rhetorical Tradition," *QJS* 36 (April 1950): 169–72.

The oratory which Huxley would extirpate presents a rewarding approach to the rhetoric of advertising and propaganda, of which it is the historic prototype. In them the techniques of suggestion, reiteration, imaginative substitution, verbal irrelevance and indirection, and emotional and pseudological bullying have been developed beyond, one might hazard a guess, the fondest dreams of the sophists and the historic demagogues. This development does not represent a change in intention from them to our contemporaries, but an advance in knowledge and opportunity and media.

If you have a soap or a cigarette or a social order for quick, profitable sale, you do not neglect any method within your ethical system of making that sale. That is the paramount problem of the advertiser and the propagandist, and their solutions are very much alike. They are rhetorical solutions, at their best very carefully gauged to the mass audience, adapted to special audiences, and varying basically only as the initial sale or the permanent customer is the principal object. What advertising is in commerce, propaganda is in politics, especially international politics. Neither scorns reason or the likeness of reason, the rhetoric of information and logical argument, if the message and the audience seem to make that the best or only means to the sale. Neither, on the other hand, prefers that method to the shorter, quicker ways to unconsidered action. They concentrate—forcibly where possible, rhetorically where necessary—on the exclusion of competing ideas, on the short-circuiting or by-passing of informed judgment. By preference they do not seek to balance or overbalance alternative ideas or courses of action; they seek to obliterate them, to circumvent or subvert the rational processes which tend to make men weigh and consider. As Adlai Stevenson said, slogans, the common staple of advertising and propaganda, "are normally designed to get action without reflection."

That advertising should enjoy a happier reputation than propaganda in a competitive, commercial-industrial nation such as the United States, which is only just now learning the term *psychological warfare,* is not to be wondered at. We do not have a public service institution for the defensive analysis of advertising, like the Institute of Propaganda Analysis, which assumed that propaganda is something from which we must learn to protect ourselves. The ethical superiority of our advertising is no doubt a compliment to our dominant business code—and to our laws. Still, if one wishes to know what the ungoverned rhetoric of advertising can be, he may get a suggestion by listening to some of what is beamed to us from certain radio stations south of the border.

The kinship of advertising and salesmanship, and their somewhat denatured relatives "public relations" and "promotion," to conventional public address, the established vehicle of rhetoric, may be embarrassing at times, but it must be acknowledged. The family resemblance is too strong to be ignored and too important to be denied. The omnipresence of the rhetoric of advertising, as I have suggested, gives it a standing which must be reckoned with, no matter what opinion the student of public address may hold of it. The rhetoric of public address, in this country at least, must function, whether or no, in a public mind which is steeped in the rhetoric of advertising, a rhetoric whose dominating principles must be recognized as adaptations of a portion of the fundamentals of any rhetoric. One need only compare a textbook or handbook of advertising methods with standard, conventional rhetorics—textbooks in public speaking and persuasion— especially in the handling of such topics as interest, suggestion, and motivation, to be convinced of the coincidence of method if not of philosophic outlook. Many times in adult evening classes in public speaking, have I heard speeches on the secrets of successful salesmanship, and as often have I found myself being offered a more or a less competent parody of certain portions of our textbook, which for some reason the student had omitted to read. Not by mere chance, one must confess, does the non-academic public take great interest in the four "miracle" courses to be found among the offerings of many universities—advertising, salesmanship, psychology, and effective speaking. Nor is it remarkable, though one may think it deplorable, that appearances of the officers of our national government before the mass audience of the citizens are characteristic products of the country's leading advertising agencies.

Likewise propaganda and its brother "information" borrow and refine upon certain portions of rhetoric. No doubt it serves a useful purpose to identify propaganda with the vicious forces in the modern world, with the German Government of World War I and with the Nazi and Soviet totalitarianisms of the present time. At the same time, however, it would be the better part of wisdom to recognize that most of the major techniques of this propaganda are long-known rhetorical techniques gone wrong, that propaganda is not a new invention which we have no ready equipment for combatting, let alone fumigating and using for our honorable ends. The understanding of propaganda will be founded in the understanding of rhetoric first of all, whatever else may be necessary.[24] Both Ross Scanlan and Kenneth Burke have demonstrated the enlightenment which can come from the application of rhetorical criticism to both the internal and external propaganda of the Nazis;[25] and two articles by Scanlan and Henry C. Youngerman in the first issue of *Today's Speech* (April, 1953) are grounded on the assumption of a close kinship between rhetoric (or its corollary, "public

---

[24] See, for example, Everett L. Hunt, "Ancient Rhetoric and Modern Propaganda," *QJS* 37 (April 1951): 157-60.

[25] Burke, *The Philosophy of Literary Form* (1941), pp. 191-220; Scanlan, "The Nazi Party Speaker System, I & II," *SM* 16 (August 1949), 82-97, 17 (June 1950), 134-48; "The Nazi Rhetorician," *QJS* 27 (December 1951); 430-40.

address") and propaganda.[26] In fact, one of Scanlan's concluding statements indirectly makes both the identification and the basic distinction: "Today it is to be hoped that America will find means to match enemy propaganda in effectiveness without sacrificing the standards of morality and intellect that distinguish democracy from the totalitarian order."

Rhetoric as a Method of Inquiry

More than once in the preceding pages I have in passing assigned to rhetoric a secondary function of the discovery of ideas, contributory to its prime function of the popularizing of ideas. That is the consequence of the division of *inventio,* the term applied in Roman rhetoric to the systematic investigative procedures by which rhetoric sought to turn up all the relevant arguments or considerations in any given situation. As part of *inventio,* for example, the elaborate doctrine of *status* was developed, through which by the application of analytical criteria it was possible to determine just what was the core, the central issue in any given case, just what had to be proved as a *sine qua non,* and where the lines of argument for proving it would lie if they were available. In general the division of *inventio* constituted a codification of the *topoi* or *places where arguments are to be found;* for instance, in *fact past, fact future, more and less, etc.* Rhetoric, thus, as we have said, provides scientific assistance to the speaker in discovering what questions to ask and how to go about answering them. It serves the speaker as laboratory procedures for analysis serve the chemist—by systematic inventory it enables him to determine with reasonable completeness what is present and what is absent in any given case.

We need not be surprised, therefore, that so useful a method tended to be incorporated into other arts and sciences where its original provenience was often forgotten. Historically, some of the studies to profit greatly from this borrowing from rhetoric have been the law, theology, logic, and poetic.[27] The Polandizing of rhetoric, one of the characteristic phenomena of its history, accounts in large part for the splinter meanings and the distortions which we have seen as typical of its current and historic significance. It has been the fate of rhetoric, the residual term, to be applied to the less intellectual segments of itself, while its central operating division, *inventio,* has been appropriated by the studies and sciences which rhetoric serves.

---

[26] "Two Views of Propaganda," pp. 13–4; "Propaganda and Public Address," pp. 15–7.

[27] See Richard McKeon, "Rhetoric in the Middle Ages," *Critics and Criticism, Ancient and Modern,* ed. R. S. Crane (Chicago, 1952), pp. 260–96, reprinted from *Speculum,* January 1942; and Marvin T. Herrick, "The Place of Rhetoric in Poetic Theory," *QJS* 36 (February 1948): 1–22.

The functions of a complete rhetoric, however, have usually been opera-tive under whatever temporary auspices as the whole art of discourse, even as they were in the renaissance tripartite grammar-logic-rhetoric. This splin-tering may go so far towards specialism, however, that the investigative function of rhetoric, the method of *inventio,* may be diverted from that to which it most properly applies. This diversion may very well be the ten-dency today, where a complete rhetoric hardly exists as a formal discipline except in those classically oriented courses in public speaking, debate, group discussion, argumentation, and persuasion whose central focus is on *inventio*—the investigation and discovery of lines of argument and basic issues. Mostly rhetoric today survives, as we have seen, under other names and special applications in those specialties which contribute to it or draw upon it or appropriate selectively from its store of method—psychology, advertising, salesmanship, propaganda analysis, public opinion and social control, semantics, and that which is loosely called "research" in common parlance.

May I attempt in summary of this matter to bring rhetoric back to its essential investigative function, its function of discovery, by quoting from Isocrates, the Athenian politico-rhetorical philosopher, and from Edmund Burke, the eighteenth-century British statesman-orator? Wrote Isocrates in the *Antidosis,* "With this faculty we both contend against others on matters that are open to dispute and seek light for ourselves on things which are unknown; for the same arguments which we use in persuading others when we speak in public, we employ when we deliberate in our thoughts."[28] Twenty-two centuries later, the young Burke included in his notebook digest of the topics of rhetoric, which he headed "How to Argue," the following succinct, Baconian statement about the functions of *inventio:*

> To invent Arguments without a thorough knowledge of the Subject is clearly impossible. But the Art of Invention does two things—
> 1. It suggests to us more readily those Parts of our actual knowledge which may help towards illustrating the matter before us, &
> 2. It suggests to us heads of Examination which may lead, if pursued with effect into a knowledge of the Subject.
>
> So that the Art of Invention may properly be considered as the method of call-ing up what we do know, & investigating that of which we are ignorant.[29]

---

[28] *Isocrates,* trans. George Norlin (Loeb Classical Library, New York, 1929), II, 327.

[29] From an original manuscript among the Wentworth-Fitzwilliam papers in the Sheffield City Library, used with the kind permission of Earl Fitzwilliam and the trustees of the Fitz-william settled estates.

Rhetoric in Education

If the burden of the preceding pages is not misplaced, the importance of rhetoric in the equipment of the well-educated member of society can hardly be in doubt. I am not inclined, therefore, especially in this journal, to offer to demonstrate the desirability of speech as an academic study. Our conventions and our journals have been full of such demonstration for, lo, these thirty years.[30] If enlightened and responsible leaders with rhetorical knowledge and skill are not trained and nurtured, irresponsible demagogues will monopolize the power of rhetoric, will have things to themselves. If talk rather than take is to settle the course of our society, if ballots instead of bullets are to effect our choice of governors, if discourse rather than coercion is to prevail in the conduct of human affairs, it would seem like arrant folly to trust to chance that the right people shall be equipped offensively and defensively with a sound rationale of informative and suasory discourse.

In general education, especially, rhetoric would appear to deserve a place of uncommon importance. That is the burden of a recent article by Dean Hunt of Swarthmore. Rhetoric is the organon of the liberal studies, the formulation of the principles through which the educated man, the possessor of many specialties, attains effectiveness in society.[31] A complete rhetoric is a structure for the wholeness of the effective man, the aim of general education. But, as Dean Hunt concludes, the rhetorician himself must not become a technical specialist:

> He will keep his wholeness if he comes back again and again to Aristotle, but he must supplement those conceptions with what modern scientists have added to the mirror for man; he must illuminate the classical rhetoric with psychology, cultural anthropology, linguistics and semantics, special disciplines, perhaps, but disciplines in which he can lean heavily on interpreters who speak to others than their professional colleagues. Departments of speech which have emphasized training in rhetoric have a new opportunity to establish their place in general education. Their very claim to wholeness has been a source of distrust in an atmosphere of specialism. If now they can relate themselves to newer conceptions in the sciences, social sciences, and humanities, they can show that the ideal of the good man skilled in speaking is like the sea, ever changing and ever the same.[32]

So much for rhetoric in education as a study directed at the creation and at the analysis and criticism of informative and suasory discourse—at the

---

[30] See, for example, one of the latest, W. N. Brigance, "General Education in an Industrial Free Society," *QJS* 38 (April 1952), esp. p. 181.

[31] "Rhetoric and General Education," *QJS* 35 (October 1949): 275, 277.

[32] *Ibid.*, 279.

ability, on the one hand, "to summon thought quickly and use it forcibly,"[33] and on the other to listen or read critically with the maximum application of analytical judgment.

Rhetoric would appear thus to be in certain senses a literary study, or as Wichelns wrote, at least "its tools are those of literature." It is a literary study as it is involved in the creative arts of language, of informing ideas. It is a literary study also as it contributes substantially to literary scholarship. Not only have literature and literary theory been persistently rhetorical for long periods—during much of the renaissance, for example, the seventeenth and eighteenth centuries in England, and for most of the short history of American literature—but writers and readers until fairly recently had been so generally educated in rhetoric that it provided the vocabulary and many of the concepts in terms of which much literature was both written and read. Clark's *Milton at St. Paul's School* may be cited as one conclusive demonstration of the importance of rhetoric in renaissance education and its importance in renaissance literature. This importance is now being recognized by literary scholars, and rhetoric is taking on considerable proportions in their studies, especially among those who are studying the renaissance. Myrick's study of Sir Philip Sidney as a literary craftsman,[34] for example, demonstrates how thoroughly Sidney was schooled in rhetoric and how carefully he constructed his defense of poetry on familiar rhetorical principles. If Myrick has been in error in his construction of the specific genealogy of Sidney's rhetoric, the fact of Sidney's rhetorical system is nevertheless in no doubt.

The plain truth is that whatever the inadequacies in specific cases of the analytical method ingrained in our educated ancestors, they *had* method, the method of formal rhetoric; whereas a general characteristic of our contemporary education is that it inculcates *no* method beyond a rather uncertain grammar and a few rules of paragraphing and bibliography. Rigidity of method is doubtless a grievous obstacle to the greatest fulfillment of genius in either belles lettres or public address; but the widespread impotence and ineptitude even of our best-educated fellows when faced with the problem of constructing or analyzing any but the most rudimentary expository or argumentative discourse, much less a complicated literary work, are surely worse. Rhetoric supplies the equipment for such practical endeavor in the promulgation of ideas, and twenty centuries have learned to use it to supplement and perfect chance and natural instinct.

That such method has at times become sterile or mechanical, that at other times it has been put to uses for which it was least adapted is amusing, perhaps lamentable, but not surprising. The remote uses to which rhetorical

---

[33] Herbert A. Wichelns, "Public Speaking and Dramatic Arts," in *On Going to College: A Symposium* (New York: Oxford University Press, 1938), p. 240.

[34] Kenneth O. Myrick, *Sir Philip Sidney as a Literary Craftsman* (1935).

methods of analysis and description have been put, in the absence of a more appropriate method, are well illustrated by the following passage from Sir John Hawkins' *History of Music,* first published in the late eighteenth century:

> The art of invention is made one of the heads among the precepts of rhetoric, to which music in this and sundry instances bears a near resemblance; the end of persuasion, or affecting the passions being common to both. This faculty consists in the enumeration of common places, which are revolved over in the mind, and requires both an ample store of knowledge in the subject upon which it is exercised, and a power of applying that knowledge as occasion may require. It differs from memory in this respect, that whereas memory does but recall to the mind the images or remembrance of things as they were first perceived, the faculty of invention divides complex ideas into those whereof they are composed, and recommends them again after different fashions, thereby creating variety of new objects and conceptions. Now, the greater the fund of knowledge above spoken of is, the greater is the source from whence the invention of the artist or composer is supplied; and the benefits thereof are seen in new combinations and phrases, capable of variety and permutation without end.[55]

From its lapses and wanderings, however, rhetoric when needed has almost always recovered its vitality and comprehensive scope, by reference to its classic sources. But that it should be ignored seems, as Dean Hunt suggests, hardly a compliment to education.

Rhetoric as a serious scholarly study I have treated in my former essay, and I shall not go over the same ground again. That there is a body of philosophy and principle worth scholarly effort in discovery, enlargement, and reinterpretation is beyond question, and fortunately more competent scholars each year are working at it. Rhetorical criticism and the study of rhetoric as a revealing social and cultural phenomenon are also gaining ground. New and interesting directions for research in these areas are being explored, or at least marked out; they are based on newly developed techniques and hitherto neglected kinds of data. One might mention, for example, those new approaches listed by Maloney:[56] the quantitative content analysis as developed by Lasswell; the qualitative content analysis as used by Lowenthal and Guterman; figurative analysis such as applied to Shakespeare by Caroline Spurgeon; and intonational analysis. Extensive and provocative suggestions are to be found in quantity in the text and bibliography of Brembeck and Howell's *Persuasion: A Means of Social Control,*[57] especially in Part VI. Lucrative also

---

[55] (2 vols., London, 1875), I, xxv.

[56] "Some New Directions in Rhetorical Criticism," *Central States Speech Journal* 4 (February 1953): 1–5.

[57] (New York, 1952).

are the new attempts at the analysis of the rhetoric of historical movements, such as Griffin's study of the rhetoric of the anti-masonic movement and others under way within the Speech Association of America. Elsewhere in this issue Thonssen's review of recent rhetorical studies illustrates amply both the new and the traditional in rhetorical scholarship; and the section on rhetoric in the annual Haberman bibliography is convincing evidence of the vitality of current enterprise.[38]

Though new avenues, new techniques, new materials such as the foregoing are inviting to the increasing numbers of scholars whose interests and abilities—to say nothing of their necessities—lie in rhetorical research, especially those new directions which lead to rhetoric as a cultural, a sociological, a social-psychiatric phenomenon, the older literary-historical-political studies are still neither too complete nor too good. In any event, each new generation probably needs to interpret afresh much of the relevant history of thought, especially the thought of the people as distinguished from what is commonly considered the history of ideas. For this the scholarship of rhetoric seems particularly adapted. Towards this purpose, I find no need to relocate the field of rhetorical scholarship as envisioned by Hudson and Wichelns, nor to recant from the considerations which I outlined in the *QJS* in 1937.[39] One may find it reassuring to observe, however, that much which was asked for in those essays has since then been undertaken and often accomplished with considerable success. Especially is this true of the study of public address in its bulk and day-to-day manifestations: in the movement studies, the "case" studies, the sectional and regional studies, the studies of "debates" and "campaigns" such as the debates on the League of Nations and the campaigns for conservation.

There remains much to do, nevertheless, and much to re-do in the more familiar and conventional areas of research and interpretation. The editing and translation of rhetorical texts is still far from complete or adequate. The canon of ancient rhetoric is, to be sure, in very good shape, and when Caplan's translation of the *Ad Herennium* is published in the Loeb Library there will hardly be a major deficiency. In post-classical, mediaeval, and renaissance rhetoric the situation is not so good, though it is improving. There are still too few works like Howell's *Rhetoric of Alcuin and Charlemagne* and Sister Therese Sullivan's commentary on and translation of the fourth book of St. Augustine's *De Doctrina*. Halm's *Rhetores Minores*, for example, is substantially unmolested so far.

English and continental rhetoric of the sixteenth, seventeenth, and eighteenth centuries is slowly appearing in modern editions by scholars who

---

[38] "A Bibliography of Rhetoric and Public Address," ed. F. W. Haberman, formerly appearing annually in the *QJS*, latterly in *SM*.

[39] See above, note 1.

know rhetoric as the theory of public address. Our bibliographies show increasing numbers of these as doctoral dissertations, most of which, alas, seem to be abandoned almost as soon as finished. Only a few works of the sort, like Howell's *Fénelon,* represent mature, published work.

In the history and historical analysis of rhetoric, nothing of adequate range and scope yet exists. Thonssen and Baird's *Speech Criticism,* ambitious as it is, is only a beginning. The general history of rhetoric, and even most of the special histories, have yet to be written. Works now under way by Donald I. Clark and Wilbur S. Howell will make substantial contributions, but rhetoric from Corax to Whately needs far fuller and better treatment than it gets in the series of histories of criticism by the late J. W. H. Atkins.

Towards the study of the rhetorical principles and practice of individual speakers and writers the major part of our scholarly effort seems to have been directed. The convenience of this kind of study is beyond question and is hard to resist, either in public address or in literature. And this is as it should be. The tendency to write biographies of speakers, however, rather than rhetorico-critical studies of them, must be kept in check, or at least in proportion. Again for reasons of convenience, if not also of scholarly nationalism, the studies of American speakers are proportionately too numerous. British and foreign public address is still far too scantily noticed by competent rhetorical scholars.

Rhetoric and Poetic

This would not be the place, I think, even if Professor Thonssen's review of rhetorical works were not appearing in this same issue of the *QJS,* for a survey of rhetorical scholarship. The preceding paragraphs are intended only as a token of decent respect to accomplishment and progress in a discrete and important branch of humane scholarship. A further area where rhetorical scholarship may be very profitably pursued, however, perhaps deserves some special consideration.

Even if it were not for the contributions of Kenneth Burke, the study of rhetoric in literature and of the relation of the theory of rhetoric to the theory of poetic would be taking on renewed importance at the present time. The lively revival of rhetorical study in renaissance scholarship which I have mentioned is only one phase of the problem. A renewed or increased interest in satire, deriving in part, perhaps, from the excellent work which of late has been done on Swift, leads directly to rhetoric. The rhetorical mode is obviously at the center of satire, and any fundamental analysis of satire must depend upon the equipment for rhetorical analysis. Likewise a complete dramatic criticism must draw upon rhetoric, both practically and philosophically. The internal rhetoric of the drama was specifically recognized by

Aristotle when he referred readers of the *Poetics* to the *Rhetoric* for coverage of the element of *dianoia,* for the analysis of speeches in which agents try to convince or persuade each other. What, however, is the external rhetoric of the drama? What is the drama intended to do to an audience? Herein lies the question of the province of poetic as opposed to the province of rhetoric. When Antony addresses the Roman citizens in *Julius Caesar,* the existence of an internal rhetoric in the play is clear enough; the relation between Antony and his stage audience is unmistakably rhetorical. But what of the relation between Antony and the audience in the pit, or the Antony-stage-audience combination and the audience in the pit? The more we speculate about the effect of a play or any literary work on an audience, the more we become involved in metaphysical questions in which rhetoric must be involved.

Much contemporary poetry or pseudopoetry in any generation is rhetorical in the most obvious sense—in the same sense as the epideictic oration. It "pleases" largely by rhetorical means or methods. It "reminds" us of experience instead of "organizing" or "creating" experience. It appeals to our satisfaction with what we are used to; it convinces us that what *was* still may be as it was, that old formulas are pleasantest if not best. It is not so much concerned with pointing up the old elements in the new, even, as establishing the identity of the old and the contemporary. "What oft was thought, but ne'er so well expressed" is a distinctly rhetorical attainment, and it would not have occurred to Pope to suppose that the poetic and the rhetorical were antithetical, if indeed they were separable. Though sporadically the effort of critics and theorists has been to keep *rhetoric* and *poetic* apart, the two rationales have had an irresistible tendency to come together, and their similarities may well be more important than their differences. When the forming of attitude is admitted into the province of rhetoric, then, to Kenneth Burke, rhetoric becomes a method for the analysis of even lyric poetry. Hence a frequent term in certain kinds of literary analysis now is *poetic-rhetoric,* as for example in the first two sentences in Ruth Wallerstein's analysis of two elegies: "I want this paper to consider two poems, John Donne's elegy on Prince Henry and Milton's *Lycidas,* in the light that is shed on them by seventeenth-century rhetoric-poetic as I understand it. Both the significance of that rhetoric and the test of my view of it will reside in its power to illuminate the poems."[40]

Undoubtedly there are basic differences between *poetic* and *rhetoric,* both practical and philosophical, and probably these differences lie both in the kind of method which is the proper concern of each and the kind of effect on audiences to the study of which each is devoted. The purely poetic

---

[40] "Rhetoric in the English Renaissance: Two Elegies," *English Institute Essays, 1948,* p. 153.

seeks the creation or organization of imaginative experience, probably providing for reader or audience some kind of satisfying spiritual or emotional therapy. The rhetorical seeks a predetermined channeling of the audience's understanding or attitude. Poetry works by representation; rhetoric by instigation. The poetic is fulfilled in creation, the rhetorical in illumination. "An image," wrote Longinus, "has one purpose with the orators and another with the poets; . . . the design of the poetic image is enthralment, of the rhetorical, vivid description. Both, however, seek to stir the passions and the emotions. . . . In oratorical imagery its best feature is always its reality and truth."[41] Poetry, declared Sir Philip Sidney, cannot lie because it affirms nothing; it merely presents. Rhetoric not only presents but affirms. That is its characteristic. Both poetic and rhetoric attain their effects through language. If the poet's highest skill lies in his power to make language do what it has never done before, to force from words and the conjunction of words meanings which are new and unique, perhaps it is the highest skill of the speaker to use words in their accepted senses in such a way as to make them carry their traditional meanings with a vividness and effectiveness which they have never known before.

Summary

In brief we may assign to rhetoric a four-fold status. So far as it is concerned with the management of discourse in specific situations for practical purposes, it is an instrumental discipline. It is a literary study, involving linguistics, critical theory, and semantics as it touches the art of informing ideas, and the functioning of language. It is a philosophical study so far as it is concerned with a method of investigation or inquiry. And finally, as it is akin to politics, drawing upon psychology and sociology, rhetoric is a social study, the study of a major force in the behavior of men in society.

---

[41] Trans. Rhys Roberts, sec. 15.

RICHARD OHMANN
b. 1931

Richard Ohmann has taught at Wesleyan University since earning his 1960 PhD from Harvard University. Editor of College English *from 1966–1978, he is currently a member of the editorial group of* Radical Teacher, *a journal he helped launch. Ohmann is known for his Marxist ideas in politics, language and literature, and mass culture. Long associated with cultural studies, he speaks and writes on rhetoric in the context of social issues. For further understanding of Ohmann's views, see* English in America *(1976),* Politics of Letters *(1987), and "Graduate Students, Professionals, Intellectuals" (*College English, *March 1990).*

In Lieu of a New Rhetoric

The warriors of Homer regularly spoke "winged words," or so Lang, Leaf, and Myers translated the formula in the version of the *Iliad* that college freshmen used to read. The measured speech of a bard had even greater force: when Demodocus sang of the Trojan War in the court of Alcinous, he was "stirred by a god," and his tale made Odysseus weep. Anglo-Saxon heroes, under the influence, perhaps, of a sterner climate, tended to speak "stidum wordum"; for a more grandiloquent speaker the formula might be "word-hord onleac." Greek or Germanic, these heroes of oral epic wielded an awesome power when they spoke: among pre-literate peoples, apparently, skilled rhetoric approximated to magic; certainly it was an expression of charisma on a plane with heroic deeds. Plato seems to have preserved Homer's attitude toward rhetoric, though he tempered awe with distrust, and assigned the rhetorician powers of evil as great as his power to move the soul in pursuit of the Good.

The more analytic Aristotle domesticated rhetoric by enclosing it in a reassuring system of rules and procedures. And like ethics, metaphysics, and poetics, rhetoric maintained a formulation close to Aristotle's for a good long time. Most rhetorical treatises, down through those of George Campbell, Hugh Blair, and Archbishop Whately in the eighteenth and nineteenth centuries, took it as their main business to supply a portfolio of strategies and devices of argumentation and oratory, however imposing the rubrics under which these strategies were arrayed.

Great though the difference is between rhetoric as mysterious power and rhetoric as calculated procedure, these two conceptions share one feature which, for my present purposes, is the most important one: both take rhetoric to be concerned, fundamentally, with *persuasion*. The practical rhetorician—the orator—seeks to impel his audience from apathy to action or from old opinion to new, by appealing to will, emotion, and reason. The theoretical rhetorician—the rhetor—sets down methods of persuasion. And the novice—the student—learns the tricks, almost as he would learn a new language, proceeding from theory through imitation to practice.

Writers in the field have been saying for a hundred years that this notion of rhetoric shows marks of weariness, and that a new rhetoric is in the offing. Perhaps the expectation has sublimed itself into a belief; in any case, rhetoricians have lately taken to using the phrase "new rhetoric" as if it had a reference like that of the word "horse," rather than that of the word "hippogriff." I am not at all sure that the wings have done more than sprout.

But if *the* new rhetoric has yet to appear, there is no shortage of new ideas about rhetoric: even the briefest survey of definitions and positions uncovers a somewhat bewildering variety. I. A. Richards has it that rhetoric "should be a study of misunderstanding and its remedies," "a persistent, systematic, detailed inquiry into how words work."[1] Richards' definition branches two ways. His stress on inquiry and system is behind the definition offered by Daniel Fogarty in a book called *Roots for a New Rhetoric:* rhetoric is "the science of recognizing the range of the meanings and of the functions of words, and the art of using and interpreting them in accordance with this recognition."[2] The other side of Richards' definition, its therapeutic intent, is second cousin to the conception of rhetoric (or anti-rhetoric?) implied by the work of Korzybski and Hayakawa: the rhetorician, in their view, should work to quiet the insistent clamor of words, which, if left to themselves, tend to drown out experience and reality. Kenneth Burke takes a different line: according to him, "The key term for the 'new' rhetoric would be *'identification.'* "[3] Rhetoric should build on the "consubstantiality" of men, their shared modes of feeling, thought, and action. Its goal is cooperation. Richard Weaver argues that rhetoric is the "intellectual love of the Good," and that it "seeks to perfect men by showing them better versions of themselves."[4] The newest book on the subject, *Rhetoric and Criticism,* by Marie Hochmuth Nichols, tells us that rhetoric is "the theory and the practice of the verbal mode of presenting judgment and choice, knowledge and feeling. . . . It works in the area of the contingent, where alternatives are possible."[5] And, to make an end, Northrop Frye calls rhetoric "the social aspect of the use of language."[6]

[1] I. A. Richards, *The Philosophy of Rhetoric* (New York, 1936), pp. 3, 23.

[2] Daniel Fogarty, S. J., *Roots for a New Rhetoric* (New York, 1959), p. 130.

[3] Kenneth Burke, "Rhetoric—Old and New," *The Journal of General Education* 5 (April 1951): 203.

[4] Richard M. Weaver, *The Ethics of Rhetoric* (Chicago, 1953), p. 25.

[5] Marie Hochmuth Nichols, *Rhetoric and Criticism* (Baton Rouge, 1963), p. 7.

[6] Northrop Frye, *The Well-Tempered Critic* (Bloomington, Ind., 1963), p. 39.

Clearly, the meaning of "rhetoric" is not clear. We have here one of those infinitely expandable and contractable notions—such as "democracy" and "virtue"—that can be suited to the exigencies of the moment. (I have not even mentioned hostile definitions—rhetoric is propaganda, or lying.) I do not propose to add a definition to the ample supply already available. Nor will the "new" rhetoric make its dramatic appearance by the end of this paper. Instead, I would like to suggest one way in which contemporary ideas of rhetoric, however disparate, resemble each other more than any of them resembles older ideas.

Whereas classical rhetoric, in practice if not always in theory, accepts persuasion as its domain, writers on rhetoric since the romantic period have increasingly strayed from this well-traveled province, or at least enlarged its boundaries. Persuasion is but one use of language, as Richards pointed out; modern theorists have wished to incorporate others: communication, contemplation, inquiry, self-expression, and so on. They have moved away from the simple and convenient picture of a wily speaker or writer attempting to sway a passive or refractory audience, and turned their attention to the whole spectrum of linguistic processes. As a corollary, they have looked less at specific tropes and tactics, and more at rhetorical *patterns,* whole works, and basic features of meaning.

Let me try to outline, schematically but in somewhat greater detail, the relationship of current theories to older ones. In the first place, traditional rhetoric, as I have noted, tends to conceive the task of eloquence in terms of overcoming resistance, to a course of action, an idea, a judgment. There is an intimate link between rhetoric and action, rhetoric and decision. The speaker is, in some manner, to impose his will upon the audience. Modern rhetoric lowers the barrier between speaker or writer and audience. It shifts the emphasis toward cooperation, mutuality, social harmony. Its dynamic is one of joint movement toward an end that both writer and audience accept, not one of an insistent force acting upon a stubborn object. Theorists like Kenneth Burke conceive of the discourse as itself a form of action, not simply an inducement to action.

Second, classical rhetorical theory assumed that the speaker or writer knows in advance what is true and what is good; he tries to convey a truth, or enjoin a moral commitment, at which he has previously arrived. Modern rhetoricians tend to see truth and attitude as inseparable from the discourse. Truth is not a lump of matter, decorated and disguised, but finally delivered intact; rather it is a web of shifting complexities whose pattern emerges only in the process of writing, and is in fact modified *by* the writing (form is content). Thus in the newer view rhetoric becomes the *pursuit*—and not simply the transmission—of truth and right.

The third shift in our conception of rhetoric follows from the second. As rhetoric absorbs truth, it splits off from conscious stratagem. The writer does not begin in secure command of his message, and try to deck it out as beguilingly as possible; he sets his own ideas and feelings in order only as he writes. Thus canny persuasion actually threatens good rhetoric, for the writer who manipulates his audience is in danger of deceiving himself. If rhetoric is self-discovery, candor is not merely an incidental virtue in the writer, but a necessary condition of his labor.

Fourth, another corollary: as theorists from Pater and Symons on have stripped rhetoric of guile, they have naturally come to conceive the finished product as a revelation of the writer's mind and of his moral character. The style may always have been the man, but now the equation holds by fiat. In this point, rhetorical theory has accompanied post-romantic critical theory in general: the writer holds the mirror up, not only to nature or to the audience, but to himself. Rhetorical theory supplies a justification for the critical methods that trace the writer's psyche in his imagery, his tone, his syntax. As Northrop Frye puts it, "genuine speech is the expression of a genuine personality."[7]

"Because it takes pains to make itself intelligible," Frye continues, "it assumes that the hearer is a genuine personality too—in other words, wherever it is spoken it creates a community." Modern rhetorical theories make the same claim for writing that Frye makes for speech, and his notion of "community" leads to my fifth and final point. The community that a piece of genuine writing creates is one, not only of ideas and attitudes, but of fundamental modes of perception, thought, and feeling. That is, discourse works within and reflects a conceptual system, or what I shall call (for want of a term both brief and unpretentious) a world view. Experience, subtle shape-changer, is given form only by this or that set of conceptual habits, and each set of habits has its own patterns of linguistic expression, its own community.

It is easy to postulate a hierarchy of world views and corresponding communities. Most generally, there is the set of conceptual modes (seeking causes, categorizing) that belong to the community of all men, and are perhaps dictated by our biological makeup. Culture and language organize men into smaller communities. The speaker of an Indo-European language does not come at experience in the same way as a speaker of Chinese (so runs the Whorfian hypothesis, still disputed, but compelling). The world view of a language community divides into special world views that characterize smaller subgroups—speakers of a certain dialect, professional groups, people of a given educational background, writers for *Time* or for the *New York Review*—and each group has its characteristic idiom. Still more particular is the world view of a single writer (or even of a single work), those ways of

---

[7] *The Well-Tempered Critic*, p. 41.

experiencing that reflect themselves in his unique employment of language, that lead him to begin his story with "Call me Ishmael" instead of "It is a truth universally acknowledged that a single man in possession of a good fortune, must be in want of a wife." Recent stylistic studies, more than rhetorical theories, work from the premise that rhetorical practice grows out of deep intellectual and moral habits.

This, roughly, is the core of views and assumptions about rhetoric that emerges from a good deal of recent work on the subject. Let me repeat a cautionary word: there is nothing approximating unanimity in current definitions. Certainly this or that rhetorician would quarrel with this or that point in my summary. But for the purposes of this paper my summary need not lay claim to comprehensiveness. It is enough that the assumptions I have listed are ones to which I myself adhere, and that they are shared in large part by many people who teach or write about rhetoric today.

• • •

Our primary subject is the college curriculum in English, not the bodies of theory behind it, and I want to spend the rest of the available space sketching out some ways in which the curriculum might respond to the rhetorical theory I have described. Though I shall recommend a few new approaches, my proposals do not imply wholesale abandonment of traditional emphases. Rather, I hope to suggest how the things many of us already teach under the heading of rhetoric or composition or communication might find a comfortable place within a framework that derives from modern rhetorical theory.

But before theory abducts us altogether, let it be admitted that the freshman course must confront one hard reality: some of our students (their numbers vary from place to place, but they exist everywhere) do not control the English language well enough to make rhetoric a genuine possibility for them. Rhetoric, pursued in the grotesque idiolect of an ill-trained freshman, is not a phenomenon for which the average instructor can generate much enthusiasm; and no amount of rhetorical theory can remove the necessity of reinforcing the student's grammar and his rapport with words and idioms. Several years ago a student of mine began her first freshman paper (an essay on language) like this: "Mankind perpetuates themselves by means of a fundamental cooperative act that bears the word-name of language." Now, there are, certainly, rhetorical maladies in this sentence, aside from the *double-entendre*. The "Mankind . . ." opening establishes a relationship of writer and audience that no freshman can hope to sustain, and the instructor might have something to say about the portentousness of the final clause. But most would think that the failure of grammatical agreement and the neologism, "word-name," are prior concerns. The red pencil is a perennial solution, to be sure, but I believe that the red pencil does more good if the student understands its rationale. The freshman course, then, might well begin with some direct study of language. I do not mean an abbreviated course in linguistics or a survey of English grammar, but an attempt to give the student some notion of what his language is and what limits there are to the torment he can impose upon it.

The student should have a brief but systematic introduction to the concept of linguistic structure, to the intricate regularity of patterns in English, to the operation of form classes, to immediate constituent analysis, and to the grammatical signals of meaning. It is in the context of such a discussion that the question of usage may most profitably be raised. The student should see that rules are not made up by grammarians, that a dialect is a set of conventions, always changing but with traditional provenance. He should be aware of the ways in which his own dialect differs from standard written English, and should realize that to master standard written English is to become capable of participating in a linguistic community of considerable importance in our culture. If he approaches the subject this way he will discover in grammar more than mystery and arbitrariness; he may even develop a respect for the extraordinary system he imperfectly controls, and a posture of courtesy toward it.

A treatment of semantics should follow the study of structure. It should include such familiar topics as denotation and connotation, ambiguity, abstraction, the effect of context on the meaning of a word, and the extension of meaning through metaphor. These subjects lead easily into that of synonymy and the consequences of choosing one word over another. And the course might move, finally, from lexical alternatives to syntactic alternatives—to the stylistic differences, for instance, among

1. Just how Parliament functions is a tricky but explorable question.
2. Just how does Parliament function? This is a tricky question, but an explorable one.
3. The question "just how does Parliament function?" is tricky but explorable.
4. It is a tricky question just how Parliament functions. But it is an explorable question.

And so on. The machinery of transformational grammar will be useful here to those instructors who know something of it, but not essential. One way or another the student should be made aware of the abundance of syntactic patterns available to him. If this happens, he will find it easy to extricate himself from those impasses that occur when he has begun a sentence or a paragraph infelicitously; and he may for the first time get a sense of genuine stylistic choice.

With the treatment of stylistic variation the course will have slid imperceptibly into rhetoric: it will have moved from language to *uses* of language, from *langue* to *parole*. If this focus is made explicit, the student will be prepared to consider intelligently the differences (partly structural, partly semantic) among the traditional types of written discourse: definition, description, classification, analysis, comparison, narration, and so on. He can also study modes of coherence and order as special uses of language, and then move naturally to the major types of proof. This section of the course is given over to distinctions.

But most of the rhetorical theory I have drawn on insists or implies that such distinctions are secondary, and that the central concerns of rhetoric are the same for description and comparison, narrative and argument, induction and deduction. If so, the heart of the freshman course should be an attempt to confront problems inherent in *all* expository writing. The drift of modern theory, as outlined above, suggests a four-part framework for the consideration of such problems.

1. The relationship between a piece of writing and its content. If content becomes tangible and complete only in the process of writing, the novice should study the ways in which rhetoric modulates meaning. The use of example, the process of generalization, the deployment of value-laden terms, the ethics of precision: these and other similar topics can conveniently be managed at this point in the course.
2. The relationship between a piece of writing and its author. How do his awareness and his attitudes evolve in the course of composition? How are they reflected in his prose? If the student can come to see his choice of emphatic device, metaphor, tone, economy, and the like as self-defining and self-revealing, that understanding will go some way toward convincing him that rhetoric has consequences he should care about—that verbal form has an importance barely hinted at by the notion of correctness.
3. The relationship between a piece of writing and its audience. The student should also discover that verbal forms carry an appeal to the audience for assent to more than the ideas. The writer asks his reader to share, for the nonce or for good, an attitude, a habit of mind, a set of values, a concept of civility, a way of being human. To see rhetoric as a means of alliance, a search for what Burke calls "identification," is to come at problems of tone, emotional distance, diction, and the like in a mood of high seriousness.
4. World views. Through the three pedagogical steps just outlined, it will scarcely be possible to ignore world views, as modifying content, as implicated in the student's definition of himself, and as shared with an audience. I suggest—and this is my only radical departure from recent tradition—that the freshman course come finally to an explicit discussion of world views. That the world is not conceptually available to all men in

the same way, that we organize experience differently, that writing, like all uses of language, reflects one or another mode of experiencing—these ideas are both important and, to a freshman, strange; and they seem to me to infuse the rhetorical theory that has lately been emerging, as well as much of the literary criticism. We can hardly expect to transmute freshmen (or ourselves) into skilled analytic philosophers, but I think we can sketch out to some purpose competing ways of conceptualizing action, mind, the past, cause, space, society, etc. (If this sounds absurdly ambitious, remember that it is no more than we attempt when, for instance, we try to analyze with students the "world" of a novel or a play.) Admittedly, a freshman is not likely to make dramatic advances in composition as a direct result of such a study: the benefits are more remote. The student who understands that world views differ, and that he himself employs one, has prepared himself for the informed encounter with experience that precedes good writing. He becomes a voting citizen of his world, rather than a bound vassal to an inherited ontology.

A required course must earn its slot in the curriculum by demonstrating its general educational worth, not merely its heuristic value within a particular discipline; I think that the course outlined here meets the broader test. But it is worth pointing out that students going on from such rhetorical training to do work in literature would take along some useful equipment. They would possess already a considerable critical vocabulary, the more valuable because evolved through application to their own writing. They would have some formal background in language, and hence a sensitivity to the medium of literature. They would be thoroughly instructed in the concept of the speaker's or narrator's "voice." And they would be prepared, through their work on world views, to apprehend the ordering of experience peculiar to a literary work, to an author, to a genre, or to an historical period. Theories of rhetoric have always been close to theories of literature, and in this matter our century is no exception.

• • •

Can a freshman course on this model cope with the inevitable and ordinary deficiencies in writing which our students bring with them each fall? I see no reason to think that the view of rhetoric here proposed is incompatible with the humbler virtues of good writing. If anything, the student who sees rhetoric as implicated with his own identity, with integrity, with community, and with an interpretation of experience should be especially ready to grant the importance of choosing words with care. The trouble with composition courses is less often in the substance of what is taught than in the intellectual framework provided for that substance, and in the motivation offered for mastering it. Though we are not likely to invest rhetoric with magic again, perhaps, by accepting the pedagogical implications of our convictions, we can at least justify to ourselves and our students the privileged place of rhetorical instruction, now as two thousand years ago, in education.

ROBERT L. SCOTT
b. 1928

Robert Scott is professor of speech communication at the University of Minnesota, Minneapolis. The piece reprinted here was directed primarily to college professors specializing in rhetorical theory and criticism in departments of speech, speech communication, or communication. Scott intended it as a counterargument against the common defenses that these sorts of rhetoricians make in adapting current practice to classical rhetorical thought, principally to the dominant interpretation of Plato's views on rhetoric and to glosses on Aristotle's supposed defense of rhetoric. These adaptations, Scott believed, undercut rhetoric rather than sustained it. The essay, however, has taken on a life that has ranged beyond his intentions. Arguing about the "epistemic" character of rhetoric has become something of a cottage industry and has put its stamp on a good deal of work that does not even feature the key term. Anyone interested in the essay reprinted here might want to follow up with "Rhetoric as Epistemic: Ten Years Later" (Central States Speech Journal 27 [1976]: 258-68) or "Rhetoric Is Epistemic: What Difference Does That Make?" in Defining the New Rhetorics *(Enos and Brown, eds., Sage, 1993, 120-36). The latter essay will direct readers to collateral work.*

On Viewing Rhetoric as Epistemic

> Every beginning is against nature: the beginning is a leap and nature does not make leaps.
>
> Pierre Thévenaz[1]

Rhetoric is among the oldest of the arts of Western civilization. As the familiar tradition informs us, it sprung up in the fifth century B.C., during the aftermath of democratic revolts in several Greek *poleis* on the island of Sicily. But professing rhetoric seems always eventually to lead to embarrassment. In Plato's dialogue, Socrates' questions soon silence Gorgias leaving young Polus to inquire, "Then what do you think rhetoric is?" In one way or another Socrates' answer has had a way of echoing through history.

At best good men grant rhetoric a slight role but grudgingly. A few years ago, Arthur Larson, cast in the role of rhetorician by virtue of his appointment as Director of the United States Information Agency, found himself

---

[1] "The Question of the Radical Point of Departure in Descartes and Hussert," in *What Is Phenomenology? and Other Essays,* edited with an introduction by James M. Edie, trans. by James M. Edie, Charles Courtney, and Paul Brockelman (Chicago, 1962), p. 96.

trying to explain the importance of his mission to a Senate subcommittee. There creeps throughout the testimony the feeling that undertaking to persuade others is not quite right. Recall that Socrates remarks in responding to Polus that Gorgias has not made his profession altogether clear,[2] and consider Senator Fulbright's statement to Larson: "Well, this is a very interesting subject. I would not want to minimize the difficulty, either, by simply saying that you have not made it clear. Certainly all members of Congress have struggled with it. . . . It is a very difficult thing to sit here in peacetime and feel that it is constructive."[3]

Fulbright's remark goes to the heart of the matter. Invoking those well known arguments of Aristotle's from the opening chapter of his *Rhetoric* do no good for clearly the art of persuasion is granted sufferance only on the grounds that men are not as they ought to be. Were all men able as some men are to reason soundly from true premises, then rhetoric would be superfluous.

The assumption that has spanned the centuries from that dialogue in Athens to the one in Washington, D.C., is that men can possess truth. If indeed one can, in the sense that "truth" is ordinarily taken, then rhetoric is of limited value. If some men can possess truth, and others understand truth, then what need the former do but present truth to the latter? Only in unusual circumstances, for example, as Fulbright's statement implies, in time of war, or for those incapable of responding to right reason, may rhetoric be sanctioned.

Accepting the notion that truth exists, may be known, and communicated leads logically to the position that there should be only two modes of discourse: a neutral presenting of data among equals and a persuasive leading of inferiors by the capable. The attitude with which this position may be espoused can vary from benevolent to cynical, but it is certainly undemocratic. Still the contemporary rhetorician is prone to accept the assumption, to say, in effect, "My art is simply one which is useful in making the truth effective in practical affairs," scarcely conscious of the irony inherent in his statement.

It is absurd, of course, to typify in a few paragraphs the attitude that has dominated rhetoric. But inasmuch as my purpose is to set forth a different position as a starting point for rhetoric, a longer consideration would be inappropriate. My undertaking can be described as philosophizing about rhetoric. The result will not be the discovery of a fresh starting point; I

---

[2] Plato, *Gorgias* 463.

[3] *Hearing Before the Subcommittee of the Committee on Appropriations United States Senate, Eighty-fifth Congress, First Session on H. R. 6871, Making Appropriations for the Departments of State and Justice, the Judiciary and Related Agencies for the Fiscal Year Ending June 30, 1958*, p. 530.

merely hope to clarify through a fresh analysis a way which has always been open and sometimes chosen, but seldom in a clear, incisive manner.

Obviously I take as a sufficient meaning for "philosophy" that indicated by Maurice Natanson who sees it as a study of beginnings, which is to say that every discipline starts with some assumptions and that it is the business of philosophy to discover those assumptions and to study their meanings.[4]

My point of departure will be drawn from the work of Stephen Toulmin. Interestingly, Toulmin's book, *The Uses of Argument,* has had a remarkably potent influence on rhetorical theory and teaching in this decade, but rhetoricians have borrowed from the third chapter of that book, "The Layout of Arguments," tending to ignore the larger concern of which that analysis is a part.

I

Plato's Socrates confronted Gorgias with a choice: "Shall we, then, assume two kinds of persuasion, the one producing belief without certainty, the other knowledge?"[5] The choice seems simple enough, but the grounds involved need examining.

The terms "certainty" and "knowledge" confront one with what has become known as epistemology. It is to a fundamental inquiry about epistemology that Stephen Toulmin directs his analysis in the book mentioned. He argues that the question "How do I know?" is an ambiguous one. In one sense it seems to ask, "How do my senses work?" and is a physio-psychological question. As such, it requires the compilation of data which can be analyzed in an empirical fashion—*a posteriori*. This is not, however, the fashion in which epistemologists have worked. Their methods have been speculative or at least abstract and *a priori*. The goal has been to obtain some standard or standards to satisfy the question, "How can I be certain of my conclusions?"

Toulmin suggests that we can set aside the psychological aspects of the central question, "How do I know?" This is not to say that these aspects are unimportant; it simply is a maneuver to allow us to concentrate on the philosophical aspects; he sees these as logical.

The quest for certainty presents a question which is often begged simply by entering into epistemological discussion. The question may be posed, "What do you mean by *certain?*" To say, "I am certain that the sun will rise

⁴ "Rhetoric and Philosophical Argumentation," *Quarterly Journal of Speech* 48 (February 1962): 28.

⁵ *Gorgias* 454.

tomorrow," may be to make a common statement which will probably not elicit argument, unless one is engaged in an epistemological discussion. (The fact that this example is often used in logic textbooks is evidence supporting Toulmin's disposition to see epistemology, considered philosophically, as basically an inquiry into logic.) But to say, "The sun will not rise tomorrow," does not contradict the grounds on which most people feel certain that the sun will rise. Our conclusion, based on experience, does not follow necessarily from true premises. This is to say that we are *not* certain by the standard required.

The only sort of arguments which will answer the demands of certainty made in epistemological speculation are those arguments which Toulmin calls analytic. It is questionable (although Toulmin does not put the matter in this fashion) whether or not analytic arguments should be called arguments at all since the word "argument" suggests the drawing of conclusions which are somehow fresh, new, unknown or unaccepted otherwise. Consider Toulmin's model analytic argument:

Anne is Jack's sister;
All Jack's sisters have red hair;
So Anne has red hair.[6]

The conclusion of this argument, Toulmin says quite rightly, might better be introduced with the phrase "in other words" rather than "so" or "therefore." If the argument is to be analytic, the premise, "All Jack's sisters have red hair," can only be asserted in the presence of his sisters, including Anne.

Toulmin contrasts analytic arguments with arguments he calls substantial. He claims that analytic arguments, which have been taken to be the model to which philosophic arguments ought to be held, are rare. I am inclined to believe that they are non-existent, that is, that they can be indicated only with special sorts of notational systems which can never make existential claims. In terms of Toulmin's example, if one is not in the presence of Anne, then the conclusion makes a claim about a present condition on the basis of past experience, i.e., all Jack's sisters *had* red hair when last we saw them. To deny the conclusion is not to contradict the truth of the premises. If one is in Anne's presence, then no argument is necessary.

The famous illustrative syllogism concerning Socrates' mortality is ambiguous. If the major premise, "All men are mortal," is taken as a statement about our past experience, then the argument is not analytic; as a matter of fact, the argument turns out to be quite like that one from which we conclude that the sun will rise tomorrow. On the other hand, if we take the premise to be one defining what we mean in part by "man," then I would have to say that we have no argument; Toulmin would say, at least, that we

---

[6] See *Uses of Argument* (Cambridge, 1958), pp. 123–30, 222–32.

have no substantial argument. In the case of taking the premise to be a definition, we could define men as being purple, and our argument is as good analytically. The rejoinder, "But men are not purple," appeals to a non-analytic criterion.

As Toulmin sees them, substantial arguments involve some sort of type shift, that is, the conclusion contains an element not present in the premises, e.g., "cause" or "other minds." The type shift Toulmin concentrates on, and one which in my opinion is crucial, is the shift in time. In substantial arguments a shift in time always occurs. If a shift in time does not occur, then one is simply reporting what is present, not arguing. That one is able to report, that is, share his perceptions with others, may be called into question if the analytic ideal is taken as the criterion for knowing.[7]

The observations thus far made lead us to believe that analytic arguments must be tenseless; they cannot exist in time.[8] The certainty demanded must arise from what has been true, is true, and shall be true, which is to say that it must be settled once and for all—immutable, changeless. Can there be substantial truths, that is, statements with content, not empty, which can be used in analytic argument? If so, then they must be stated in time and cannot be stated in time. Technically this is the conclusion of a *reductio ad absurdum.* The possibility of such truths can be rejected on formal grounds.

Although the possibility may be rejected formally, one may accept the conclusion labeled as invalid. One may not follow the reasoning or not accept the grounds. These possible responses underscore the use of the word "truth" in the foregoing paragraph. One might argue that "truth" is not coincident with the analytic ideal. It is possible but difficult to use the word without the freight of the analytic ideal. This strong tendency to associate one with the other should make us suspicious of a rhetoric which claims to be based on truth.

By "truth" one may mean some set of generally accepted social norms, experience, or even matters of faith as reference points in working out the contingencies in which men find themselves. In such cases the word might be better avoided, for in it the breath of the fanatic hangs threatening to transmute the term to one of crushing certainty. If truth is somehow both prior and substantial, then problems need not be worked out but only classified and disposed of. Unwittingly, one may commit himself to a rhetoric which tolerates only equals, that is, those who understand his "truths" and consequently the conclusions drawn from them; such a rhetoric approaches

---

[7] "If a genuine claim to knowledge must be backed by an analytic argument, then there can be no authentic claim to knowledge in such fields as these. The future, the past, other minds, ethics, even material objects: about all of these we ought, strictly speaking, to admit that we *know* nothing." *Ibid.,* p. 231.

[8] Cf. *ibid.,* p. 235.

those who are not able to take its "truths" at face value as inferiors to be treated as such.

The attractiveness of the analytic ideal, ordinarily only dimly grasped but nonetheless powerfully active in the rhetoric of those who deem truth as prior and enabling, lies in the smuggling of the sense of certainty into human affairs.

II

In order to press further into the possibilities presented by rejecting prior and enabling truth as the epistemological basis for a rhetoric, I shall make several observations about the adaptations of Toulmin's concepts by contemporary rhetorical theorists. The earliest and most thorough use of his concepts has been made by Douglas Ehninger and Wayne Brockriede.[9] They have adapted Toulmin's form for "laying out" argument, holding it to be a more clear and complete pattern than the traditional syllogism, without pushing further into the philosophic issues for which Toulmin's scheme of analysis is preparatory. In this respect, Ehninger and Brockriede do not differ from others who have used Toulmin's "layout" in speech textbooks.

One might argue that these further issues are irrelevant to the interests of rhetorical theorists, although one of the purposes of this paper is to show that such a position is untenable. Furthermore, Ehninger and Brockriede take care to indicate a point of view toward debate which might be well described as a philosophical foundation for their treatment of rhetorical concepts. Although there is no evidence that their treatment owed anything to Toulmin, their description of debate as cooperative critical inquiry[10] is nonetheless congruent with some of the implications of his criticism of analytic argument as he applies it to epistemology.

When Ehninger and Brockriede describe debate as cooperative critical inquiry, they may be interpreted as taking a radical departure from the typical point of view. If debate is critical inquiry, then it is not simply an effort to make a preconceived position effective. It would be absurd for anyone who begins with the attitude that he possesses truth, in the sense in which I began this essay, to embark on any genuine enterprise of cooperative critical inquiry. Of course these statements do not mean that Ehninger

---

[9] *Decision by Debate* (New York, 1963). Also Wayne Brockriede and Douglas Ehninger, "Toulmin on Argument: An Interpretation and Application," *Quarterly Journal of Speech* 46 (February 1960): 44–53.

[10] See *Decision by Debate,* preface and chapter two. See also Douglas Ehninger, "Decision by Debate: A Re-Examination," *Quarterly Journal of Speech* 45 (October 1959): 282–87.

and Brockriede reject investigation before speaking or the use by speakers of experience, references to social norms, or even to articles of faith. What these statements do suggest is that truth is not prior and immutable but is contingent. Insofar as we can say that there is truth in human affairs, it is in time; it can be the result of a process of interaction at a given moment. Thus rhetoric may be viewed not as a matter of giving effectiveness to truth but of creating truth. *in hictmmnt/cmtxt*

Ehninger and Brockriede's debate-as-cooperative-critical-inquiry is one vantage point from which to see rhetoric as epistemic. This notion is most coherent when it is taken as *normative* rather than as *descriptive*. When so taken, it calls for a commitment to a standard and several matters become clear: one may be committed and, being human, fall short of the standard; further, one may make use of the attributes associated with the standard without at all being committed to it.

I have already suggested that Ehninger and Brockriede may err in not examining their philosophic position in light of the disclosures toward which Stephen Toulmin leads. I am now arguing that they err in presenting their fundamental position as *descriptive* of debate. A confusion arises from their attempt to describe the process of debate (the title of their second chapter is "The Process of Debate") as the "rationale of debate as an instrument for settling inferential questions critically."[11] As a description this statement is plainly contrary to much of our experience; we commonly use the word "debate" to refer to situations in which anything but cooperative critical inquiry is occurring. The confusion may be cleared away if we recognize that Ehninger and Brockriede's ideal is *one* of the uses of the process of debate to which men may be committed. They do argue that the process tends to assure this use, but that it *tends toward* rather than *determines* such a use is clear. As a matter of fact, the authors modify their statements at times, e.g., "the highest tradition of debate,"[12] and are driven finally to explain that "any control, internal or external, may, of course, be circumvented, or debate may be so ineptly practiced that much of its effectiveness is lost. Such failure, however, is human and is not to be charged against debate as a method."[13] But just as the failure is not to be charged against the method neither should the success, i.e., debate at its "highest tradition," be attributed to the process itself rather than the human commitment and the energy and skill to make that commitment meaningful.

The direction of analysis, from Toulmin through Ehninger and Brockriede, leads to the conclusion that there is no possibility in matters relevant to human interaction to determine truth in any *a priori* way, that truth can

---

[11] *Decision by Debate*, p. 15.

[12] *Ibid.*, p. viii.

[13] *Ibid.*, p. 17.

arise only from cooperative critical inquiry. Men may have recourse to some universal ideas in which they are willing to affirm their faith, but these must enter into the contingencies of time and place and will not give rise to products which are certain.

III

This analysis has led toward the tragic view of life: man who desires certainty understands that he cannot be certain and, moreover, that he must act in dissonant circumstances. One of the great symbols of man, Faust, sits in his chamber at the point of suicide early in Goethe's drama. He is vastly learned in all four of the great professions, but he is certain only that he cannot be certain.[14]

Later Faust sits translating the Bible. He is working on the beginning of the Gospel according to St. John. The troublesome word is *logos,* which he renders as "word," then "mind," then "power," then "act."[15]

The word *logos* and its derivatives have long had a suggestion of divinity about them. For the ancient Greeks, it was often an expression for "universal mind"; and it retains something of this sense in Plato. Man could know because he was identified with the substance of God, that is, the universal mind. From the universal mind (*logos*), man's mind (*logos*) can reason (*logos*) to bring forth speech (*logos*). The wonderful ambiguity of *logos* retains the identity, that is, truth.

All of this may be quite right, the Greek Sophist Protagoras said in effect, but I have no way of knowing that it is.[16] All I have is experiences, and my experiences, being finite, cannot reveal the infinite to me. The argument of the Greek sophist Gorgias for his famous three propositions (nothing is; if anything is, it cannot be known; if anything is and can be known, it cannot be communicated)[17] may be interpreted as an attempt to show that man can be certain of no absolute standard. We may be aware of the attributes of

---

[14] My paraphrase is intended to underscore the argument I have been making. Walter Kaufmann translates:

Called Master of Arts, and Doctor to boot,
For ten years almost I confute
And up and down, wherever it goes.
I drag my students by the nose—
And see that for all our science and art
We can know nothing. It burns my heart.

(Goethe's *Faust,* ll. 360–65. Garden City, New York, 1962).

[15] *Wort! . . . Sinn! . . . Kraft! . . . Tat!* (ll, 1225–37).

[16] See Mario Untersteiner, *The Sophists,* trans. Kathleen Freeman (Oxford, 1954), pp. 27–8.

[17] *Ibid.,* pp. 146–56.

our experiences, but there is no way for us to recognize any attribute which is essential among experiences. (Gorgias' inquiry was into the reality of that primary attribute, *being* itself.) There may be some quality (value, norm, standard) which identifies all experiences with all others, or some with some others, but we cannot make such identifications with absolute certainty.

In human affairs, ours is a world of conflicting claims. Not only may one person contradict another, but a single person may find himself called upon to believe or act when his knowledge gives rise to directives which are dissonant. He may be caught, for example, in a conflict of duty toward his family and his country. As a father, he may reason that he ought keep a well-paying job to provide for the material necessities of his children and by his presence help guide them during their immaturity. As a citizen, he may reason that he is obligated to lower his income and remove his presence from his home to serve in the armed forces. He may decide that his duty to country must take precedence and even that in following the demands of that duty he will in many ways serve his family, but although he is able to make such a decision, the rightness of the decision does not obviate the responsibilities generated by the rejected claim.

The illustrative example can be easily modified into other quite common sets of circumstances: a draft board considering a particular case, arguments concerning the policy of the draft, or even war as a particular or general policy. All these questions must be settled by specific men in specific circumstances. Even taking uncritically the dictates of some past solution is to take that solution in a particular circumstance.

The sophists facing their experiences found consistently not *logos* (in this context we might read "a simple explanation" or "a solitary moral imperative") but *dissoi logoi*, that is, contradictory claims.[18] From another point of view, Stephen Toulmin gives a similar suggestion: "Practice forces us to recognize that general ethical truths can aspire at best to hold good in the absence of effective counterclaims: conflicts of duty are an inescapable feature of the moral life."[19]

My argument is not that one has the choice to act on prior truth or to act to create truth. One may act assuming that the truth is fixed and that his persuasion, for example, is simply carrying out the dictates of that truth, but he will be deceiving himself. Pierre Thévenaz' statement summarizes this point of view: "The phenomenon of expression cannot be reduced to *logos;* it is both more fundamental and more general. Man acts and speaks *before he knows.* Or, better, it is *by acting* and *in action* that he is enabled to know."[20]

---

[18] *Ibid., passim.*

[19] Toulmin, p. 117.

[20] "What Is Phenomenology?" *op cit.,* p. 33.

IV

The attractiveness of the notion that first one must know the truth and that persuasion at its best is simply making the truth effective rests in large part on man's desire to be ethical. "How can I assure myself that my actions are good?" is the question with which he nags himself. The question is a good one. The position I have argued is not one that sets it aside but one that holds that the question cannot be answered in the abstract and that whatever principles one holds are only guides in acting consistently with moral demands.

The point of view that holds that man cannot be certain but must act in the face of uncertainty to create situational truth entails three ethical guidelines: toleration, will, and responsibility. I shall suggest why these principles follow from the point of view set forth.

If one can be certain, then one needs no commands or urgings (either from oneself or from others) to act. Failure to act can only be a sign of a momentary misunderstanding or of a flawed intellect. In either case, there is no good reason to tolerate disagreement. As a matter of fact, if one can be certain, tolerating deviations from the demands of certainty may itself be deemed evil.

On the other hand, uncertainty, taking truth as a toehold to climb into the yet-to-be-created rather than as a program to unfold regardless of the circumstances, demands toleration. It would be inconsistent with one's starting point and one's quest to act otherwise. When one's undertaking involves the belief and action of others, one spoils his own potentiality for *knowing*, by Thévenaz' criterion at least, if one fails to respect the integrity of the expression and action of others.

This demand, the *sine qua non* of a democratic state, is called by Karl Popper one of "the most important principles of humanitarian and equalitarian ethics." His phrasing of the principle is "tolerance towards all who are not intolerant and who do not propagate intolerance."[21]

If one cannot be certain, however, then one must either withdraw from the conflicts of life or find some way to act in the face of these conflicts. He must say with Gorgias, "I know the irreconcilable conflicts, and yet I act."[22]

---

[21] *The Open Society and Its Enemies: Volume I, The Spell of Plato* (New York, 1963), p. 235.

[22] Untersteiner, pp. 181-82: "If Gorgias speaks of the many virtues and not of absolute virtue, he did not deny 'the formal concept of a supreme ethical law'; rather, Gorgias' ethical concept was intended especially to overcome the rigidity of an absolute concept which historical experience also had shown to be contradictory. To make virtue possible in the active turmoil of life, Gorgias detaches it from the empyrean of an abstraction overruled by the incessant reproduction of the antitheses, and makes it relative. In the face of all idealistic dogmatism he stands for the inner turmoil of a tragic decision which gives so profound a meaning to life."

That man can so act, he knows from experience. What is true for that man does not exist prior to but in the working out of its own expression. Although this working out may not always involve attempts to communicate with others, such attempts are commonly involved, and thus we disclose again the potentiality for rhetoric to be epistemic. Inaction, failure to take on the burden of participating in the development of contingent truth, ought to be considered ethical failure.

If one can act with certainty of truth then any effects of that action can be viewed as inevitable, that is, determined by the principles for which the individual is simply the instrument; the individual acting is not responsible for the pain, for example, that his actions may bring to himself or to others. The man who views himself as the instrument of the state, or of history, or of certain truth of any sort puts himself beyond ethical demands, for he says, in effect, "It is not I who am responsible."

On the contrary, one who acts without certainty must embrace the responsibility for making his acts the best possible. He must recognize the conflicts of the circumstances that he is in, maximizing the potential good and accepting responsibility for the inevitable harm. If the person acts in circumstances in which harm is not an ever-present potential, then he is not confronted by ethical questions. Such circumstances are apt to be rare in human interaction. Looking to the future in making ethical decisions, we must be prepared to look to the past. "Certainly nothing can justify or condemn means except results," John Dewey has argued. "But we must include consequences impartially. . . . It is willful folly to fasten upon some single end or consequence [or intention] which is liked and to permit the view of that to blot from perception all other undesired and undesirable consequences."[23] To act with intentions for good consequences, but to accept the responsibilities for all the consequences in so far as they can be known is part of what being ethical must mean. " 'That which was' is the name of the stone he cannot move." The Soothsayer tells Zarathustra of man. To redeem the past, man must learn "to recreate all 'it was' into 'thus I willed it.' "[24]

Perhaps a final example is necessary. Consider a story from his youth told by the Italian novelist Ignazio Silone.[25] Briefly, he and other village boys were taken to a puppet show by their parish priest. During the performance a devil-puppet suddenly turned to ask the children where a child-puppet was hiding. Rather than reporting "under the bed," the children lied. The priest was upset, for lying was contrary to the precepts he had taught them. His demands for truth were not met. "But," the children protested, "the truth is

---

[23] *Human Nature and Conduct* (New York, 1922), pp. 228–29.

[24] *Thus Spoke Zarathustra*, Part II. See *The Portable Nietzsche*, trans. Walter Kaufmann (New York, 1954), p. 251.

[25] See *The God that Failed*, ed. Richard Crossman (New York, 1952), pp. 84–6.

that there was the devil on one side and a child on the other. We wanted to help the child."

At best (or least) truth must be seen as dual: the demands of the precepts one adheres to and the demands of the circumstances in which one must act. The children had to act and acted to maximize the good potential in the situation. In chastising the children, as he did, the priest had to act also. He also had to make what he could of the situation as well as of his precepts. One may doubt that insisting repeatedly only that "a lie is always a lie," in the face of the children's question, "Ought we to have told the devil where the child was hiding, yes or no?" as Silone reports, the priest did make maximum the good and minimum the harm potential in the situation.[1]

Man must consider truth not as something fixed and final but as something to be created moment by moment in the circumstances in which he finds himself and with which he must cope. Man may plot his course by fixed stars but he does not possess those stars; he only proceeds, more or less effectively, on his course. Furthermore, man has learned that his stars are fixed only in a relative sense.

In human affairs, then, rhetoric, perceived in the frame herein discussed, is a way of knowing; it is epistemic. The uncertainty of this way may seem too threatening to many. But the other way of looking at the world offers no legitimate role to rhetoric; if one would accept that way, then one may be called upon to act consistently with it.

DOUGLAS EHNINGER
1913–1979

Born in Indiana, Douglas Ehninger received his MA in speech from Northwestern University and his PhD in 1949 from Ohio State University. He taught at Purdue University, Case Western Reserve University, George Washington University, the University of Virginia, and the University of Florida before his 1961–1979 tenure at the University of Iowa. In addition to serving in various editorial positions with the Quarterly Journal of Speech, *the* Journal of the American Forensic Association, *and* Philosophy and Rhetoric, *Ehninger was also editor of* Southern Speech Journal *(1954–1957) and* Speech Monographs *(1960–1962). Ehninger is known especially for his scholarship in modern and contemporary rhetorical theory and the theory and practice of argument.*

On Systems of Rhetoric

I

In this paper I shall be concerned with rhetorical systems as systems.

A rhetoric I define as an organized, consistent, coherent way of talking about practical discourse in any of its forms or modes. By practical discourse I mean discourse, written or oral, that seeks to inform, evaluate, or persuade, and therefore is to be distinguished from discourse that seeks to please, elevate, or depict. An organized, consistent, coherent way of talking about something, in line with my present purpose, I call a system. In this sense, not only the rhetoric embodied in a single treatise, but also the rhetoric embodied collectively in the treatises of a given place or period constitutes a system, and may be spoken of as such.

In the remarks that follow I shall be concerned with the second of these possibilities. Specifically, I shall attempt to describe the rhetorics of three historical periods in terms broad enough to exhibit their essential characteristics as systems, and then to suggest certain practical uses of an analysis conducted at this level.

It would be naive to suppose that in the characterizations I offer it will be easy to walk a line between the obvious on the one side and the disputable or false on the other. Nor do I expect that the formulations I advance or the inferences I draw will escape criticism. Because not all of the rhetorical treatises of a period fall into a mold, an attempt to treat that period as a system means that one must select from diverse possibilities the trends and emphases that are dominant. Because any one treatise, insofar as it pretends to completeness, is a complex construct, involving a delicate balance among ethical, aesthetic, semantic, and pragmatic elements, attempts to fit it into a pattern inevitably invite refutation by the citation of isolated passages.

But while the hazards are sizable the rewards beckon. Unlike microscopic sightings, which atomize and divide, a macroscopic view extending over an entire genus of treatises submerges differences and details so as to call forth the common characteristics of rhetorical systems as organized wholes—the parts of which they are composed, the joints at which they are articulated, and the weaknesses to which they are prone.

Of these advantages, however, I shall speak further in the final section of this paper. Initially, I turn to the task of characterizing the rhetorics of three historical periods in terms broad enough to display their common nature as systems. I chose as case studies for my investigation what I regard as the three crucial eras in the development of Western rhetorical thought—the classical period, the late eighteenth century, and the period extending from the early 1930's to the present time.

II

The rhetoric of the classical period arose out of a two-fold problem or need.

First, with the development of democratic institutions in the city states of Sicily and Greece, speechmaking as an activity found new avenues of expression and gained in importance until it came to be regarded as an art form as well as a social instrument. What was this phenomenon upon which men depended for the making of laws, the administration of justice, and the honoring of heroes? What was the essential nature of the speech act? Of what parts did this act consist? Upon what faculties or arts did it depend? How could it systematically be described and talked about? And, second, how could proficiency in the important business of performing this speech act be taught in a society where every man must act as his own lawyer and his own legislator? How might instruction in speechmaking be methodized and imparted to the masses?

These two needs, as limited and shaped by the social and intellectual milieu in which the new activity of speechmaking found itself, were the decisive factors in determining the nature of the classical rhetoric. Because this rhetoric operated in an aural world it became the art of science of oral rather than of written discourse. Because its principal functions were to argue the relative merits of laws and policies and to attack or defend from attack in the courtroom, it became primarily the art of persuasion. Because skill in speaking had to be imparted to the masses rhetoric was written with an eye to easy prescription and stressed the development of mechanical or "artificial" procedures and routines. Because speaking was regarded as a fine art as well as a practical tool, rhetoric was given both aesthetic and pragmatic dimensions.

But while all of these properties and others must be recognized in a full description of the classical rhetoric, the one characteristic which perhaps most adequately distinguishes it as a system is its basically grammatical nature. For, without denying other achievements, it still must be said that the central concern and principal contribution of the classical rhetoric were the development of the syntax of the speech act—the delineating and naming of the parts of that act and the tracing of the permutations and combinations of which these parts permit. And this emphasis is entirely understandable. Before the classical writers could consider the pragmatic or aesthetic aspects of speechmaking, they first had to determine what the act of speaking entailed and to devise a grammar for talking about its parts and their relationships.

The work of the classical rhetoricians in devising such a grammar was admirable. So well, indeed, did they perform this task that even today any system of rhetoric which fails to encompass the basic terms and relationships which they isolated is properly regarded as incomplete. They defined or located the speech act itself in two important ways: first, methodologically, by distinguishing rhetoric from grammar, logic, and poetic; and second, substantively, by exploring the relations rhetoric bears to politics and ethics. They divided the speech act into its functional parts of speaker, speech, and audience-occasion, and speculated upon the relative importance of each of these parts in determining the success of the whole. They distinguished among the kinds or types of speeches which they found in the world about them—the legislative, judicial, and epideictic—and described the characteristic uses of each. They recognized the various arts or "offices" upon which oral communication depends—invention, disposition, style, memory, and delivery—and they assigned a specific function to each. As sub-classifications within the various *officia*, they devised vocabularies for discussing types of proofs, characters of style, and the parts of a speech. And, finally, they arranged this grammar into a pattern which permitted its easy acquisition by the aspiring student.

But while as a grammatically centered and pedagogically oriented system the classical rhetoric had strengths, its focus on grammar and pedagogy also made for weaknesses.

First, in their desire to draw lines between phenomena which by nature blend into another—to divide, compartmentalize, and name—the ancients gave if not a false, at least a painfully oversimplified picture of the relationships between invention and disposition and invention and style. Indeed, save perhaps in the case of delivery—and even here modern studies in paralanguage give grounds for doubt—the divisions among all the *officia* tend to be artificial rather than real.

Second, in their desire to render the art of speaking teachable, and teachable to the average man, the classical writers were led to depend too much on preprocessed materials and modes of expression; to reduce to formula or routine, matters inherently incapable of such reduction; to provide, as in the *status* and the topics, purely "artificial" substitutes for knowledge and cogitation—substitutes which by converting *noesis* to rote might equalize individual differences in industry and ability.

Third, and most important, in their emphasis upon the speech act as such and hampered by the primitive psychology and epistemology with which they worked, as a group the classical writers tended either to scant or to present a patently naive account of the relation between the speech act and the mind of the listener.

III

Whereas the rhetoric of the classical period was basically "grammatical" in nature, the rhetoric of the period we now are to examine is best described as "psychological." For it was the major contribution of the "new British rhetoric" of the later eighteenth century, as embodied principally in such works as Lord Kames' *Elements of Criticism* (1761), John Ogilvie's *Philosophical and Critical Observations* (1774), George Campbell's *Philosophy of Rhetoric* (1776), and Joseph Priestley's *Lectures on Oratory and Criticism* (1777), that it corrected the major deficiency of the classical system by working out a series of detailed statements concerning the relation between the communicative act and the mind of the listener-reader.

And here, too, the new emphasis or interest arose in response to a felt need and was shaped by the environment in which that need emerged. For as Locke and his successors among the British empiricists began to develop more sophisticated systems of psychology and epistemology, not only did the ancients' lack of attention the message-mind relationship seem a more glaring deficiency, but many of the traditional assumptions concerning how men know or are persuaded no longer were acceptable.

So far as the student of rhetorical systems is concerned, it is immaterial that most of the doctrines which the new rhetoricians chose as groundings for their work—the faculty and associational psychologies, the common sense philosophy, and the like—no longer are fashionable. What is important is that, taking these doctrines as premises, the British rhetoricians of the period worked out a more sophisticated statement of the message-mind relationship than had hitherto been possible, and that here again the statement was shaped by the environment in which the need arose.

In their effort to carry rhetoric beyond the grammar of the speech act, with its attendant pedagogical rules and cautions—to bring it, as Campbell said, to a "new country" where rules might be validated by checking them against those principles of the human understanding from whence they sprang[1]—the architects of the new system gave rhetoric an epistemological rather than a grammatical or a logical starting point. Instead of approaching rhetoric through an analysis of what might be said on behalf of a cause, as had the ancients, they approached it through an analysis of the mind of the listener-reader, premising their doctrine upon assumptions concerning the ways in which men come to know what they know, believe what they believe, and feel what they feel. From such an analysis, they assumed, the radical principles of rhetoric could be inferred and, as Campbell said, validated. In short, whereas the ancients had built a subject- or substance-centered rhetoric, the eighteenth-century theorists built an audience-centered one. They classified speeches in terms of the effect the speaker sought to produce upon his listener—"to enlighten the understanding, to please the imagination, to move the passions, or to influence the will."[2] They categorized proofs according to the ways in which listeners come to believe—by experience, analogy, testimony, and the calculation of chances.[3] They fused the traditional areas of invention and arrangement into the broader concept of the conduct or "management" or a discourse and included in this rubric all of the grosser resources, both substantive and methodological, by which the listener could be persuaded.[4] They rejected the view that rhetoric is a "counterpart" of dialectic or logic, and declared it to be an "off-shoot" of logical studies. Then, with rhetoric dependent upon logic for its routines of analysis and proof, they took the bold step of ruling the tasks of search and discovery entirely out of the art, and of substituting in their stead a new doctrine of invention conceived of as the framing and use of proofs that had previously been derived.[5]

How shall we evaluate this "new" rhetoric? Although now largely dated, there can be little question, I think, but that on the whole it was a remarkable achievement and represented a level of sophistication not envisioned by the ancients. At the same time, however, it is equally clear that this new system, as had the classical rhetoric, suffered from too intense a preoccupation with one aspect of the communication spectrum. While the ancients had focused on the grammar of the speech act at the expense of exploring how that act is related to the listener, so the eighteenth-century writers focused on the speaker-listener relationship at cost of developing an improved grammar of the act itself. Consequently, as in the case of Priestley,[6] they gave the traditional concepts new tortured meanings, or like Campbell they accepted the ancient grammar and buried it in their works—de-emphasized it until the parts of the speech act and the arts or offices upon which the act depends tended to lose identity as discrete units.

Even more important, however, in their preoccupation with the message-mind relationship the architects of the "new" rhetoric gave insufficient attention to another vital dimension of a complete and rounded theory of communication. And this is the role that practical discourse plays in society—the function it performs and should perform in promoting social cohesion and exercising social control.

In two different senses the "new" rhetoric of the eighteenth century was almost entirely an armchair construct—a product of the study rather than of the forum. First, it was largely unrelated to and uninterested in speaking and writing as they existed in the world about it. It was a hypothetical or "if, then" rhetoric—a self-contained theoretical study which might equally well exist if actual discourses never were or never had been composed. Campbell, who in the *Philosophy* defends the study of "eloquence" on the ground that it furnishes the quickest, surest, and pleasantest way to knowledge of the human mind, reserves most of his practical advice on speaking for the strangely unphilosophical *Lectures on Systematic Theology and Pulpit Eloquence* (1807). Joseph Priestley regards his *Lectures on Oratory* as a practical illustration of the associational psychology of David Hartley.[7] And Hugh Blair, by allying rhetoric with *belles lettres,* places that discipline at the service of the critic as well as of the speaker or writer.[8]

Finally, and more briefly, as one might imagine of a system that largely predates the development of experimental techniques of investigation and verification, the "new" rhetoric was armchair in the sense that for the most part it consisted of inferences drawn from premises based upon intuition or common sense.

IV

The third and last of the period systems we are to examine extends from the early 1930's to the present time, and encompasses developments which, for the most part, have occurred here in the United States.

If the classical rhetoric may be characterized as "grammatical" and the "new" rhetoric of the eighteenth century as "psychological," the rhetoric of our third period may best be described as "social" or "sociological." For while as a system contemporary rhetoric is unusually complex and embraces many specialized strands of interest, all of these strands find unity in the fact that at bottom they view rhetoric as an instrument for understanding and improving human relations.

Like systems of the past, the contemporary system arises out of a felt need and is shaped by the intellectual and social milieu in which rhetoric today finds itself. And here the need is simple but compelling. From the personal to the national and international levels tensions and breakdowns in human relations now, as never before, may result not only in maladjusted personalities or in misunderstanding among individuals, but in depressions, wars, and the suicide of the race itself.

Under such circumstances it is natural that rhetoric as a form of verbal interaction among persons and groups should be concerned with the part it can play in promoting human understanding and in improving the processes by which man communicates with man.

This motive is reflected in the thinking of Kenneth Burke, who argues that because language is symbolic action rhetorical analysis can throw light upon human relations and motives generally, while rhetoric as a social force arising out of an atmosphere of divisiveness can promote consubstantiality and peace through the process of identification.[9] Similarly, it underlies I. A. Richards' definition of rhetoric as a study of the causes and remedies of misunderstanding and accounts for his interest in metaphor and in "comprehending."[10]

Proponents of group discussion, under the influence of Dewey's instrumentalism and the exploration of the group dynamists, seek to implement the ideal of improved human relations by developing a specialized rhetoric of reflective problem solving. Students of communication theory, influenced by the terminology and insights of the electronics engineers, believe that an understanding of transmission systems will help to eliminate many of the blockages that occur when man speaks to man. The General Semanticists profess to find in a neuter or feckless mode of communication a cure for many of the world's social ills. Writers on argument, aware that traditional proof patterns are inapplicable to disputes on moral issues, seek a logic of "ought propositions," drawn with a particular eye to the problems of "conflict resolution."

But these workers and others throughout the broad field of contemporary rhetoric do not find unity only in their concern with the social aspects of improved communication. They are bound still more closely together by their common belief that at the root of many of the misunderstandings which impair or block communications are man's language and his habits of using and abusing it—a conviction bolstered by the growing realization that language is not a pliable medium which through struggle may be molded to one's will, but rather is itself a shaping force which goes far toward determining how man will conceive of himself and of his world.

Therefore, while the ancients centered principally upon methods for analyzing the substance or subject matter of a "cause" and while the eighteenth-century framers of the "new" rhetoric emphasized the message-mind relationship, contemporary writers find a locus of interest in language as the vehicle by which the message is transmitted. Beyond this, however, they recognize that while language is the central instrument of human communication, other symbol systems, some of which lie beneath the sender's or receiver's threshold of awareness, also may carry messages which influence thought or behavior.

This new focus, no less than the ones which preceded it, has had both desirable and undesirable results. The encompassment within rhetoric of appeals which are at least partially "unconscious"[11] has extended the traditional range of that science, and in so doing has provided a more comprehensive picture of the role which rhetorical forces play in promoting social cohesion and effecting social control. On the other hand, since this extension carried to its fullest would render any stimulus-response situation rhetorical, rhetoric is in danger of losing its identity as a discrete discipline. Indeed, even today it is moot to dispute whether one may with profit talk of a rhetoric of clothes, or of social status, or, for that matter, of a rhetoric of the stoplight.[12]

And, second, the current interest in vehicles of message transmission, coupled with the premium which quantitative studies in communication research place upon ever more effective transmission, threatens the concern which a sound rhetoric should have for message content and for the ethical and aesthetic dimensions of communication. If a rhetoric is to pretend to completeness, it must be concerned not only with means, but with ends. Besides asking what does communicate and persuade, it must ask what should persuade and what that which persuades should persuade to. Moreover, because at bottom ethical and pragmatic considerations are inseparable from the problem of form, a complete rhetoric also must have an aesthetic dimension.

If, then, as there is reason to suspect, the present emphasis on the vehicle of transmission may threaten the integrity of rhetoric as a bounded discipline or impair those relations which guarantee its character as a humane subject, it may be well in the future to watch this development with more than ordinary care.

V

As I remarked at the outset, this paper has two purposes: (1) to attempt to describe the rhetorics of three periods in terms broad enough to exhibit their essential characteristics as systems, and (2) to suggest some of the uses of an analysis conducted at this level. Having described the three rhetorics, I now inquire into the uses which such analysis may have.

First, I would argue that attempts to characterize the rhetorics of various places or periods at the systems level are useful because they introduce a healthy and much needed relativism into studies still too much dominated by the notion of the classical rhetoric as a preferred archetype from which all departures are greater or lesser aberrations.

As our survey has suggested, the collective rhetorics of a period, as well as the rhetoric embodied in a single treatise, are time- and culture-bound. Systems of rhetoric arise out of a felt need and are shaped in part by the intellectual and social environment in which the need exists. No matter how sound internally or how imposing architecturally a given system may be—no matter how much its ethical or aesthetic groundings may arouse our admiration—to regard it as a universally applicable paradigm is to overlook a fundamental fact concerning the very nature of rhetoric.

From this it follows that the continuing dialogue on the question, What is rhetoric? except as an academic exercise, is largely profitless. If there is no one generic rhetoric which, like a Platonic Idea, is lurking in the shadows awaiting him who shall have the acuteness to discern it, the search for a defining quality can only end in error or frustration. It would serve the cause of rhetorical studies in general, I think, if instead of continuing this dialogue we openly adopted the plural of the noun and spoke of the history or theory of "rhetorics."

But more important than any reform in notation which might be effected by the laying of the one-rhetoric myth is the fact that a view which allows for many rhetorics rather than a single preferred one pointedly reminds us that in the final analysis the worth of a rhetorical system cannot be divorced from pragmatic considerations. It cannot be merely good or bad; it must be good or bad for something. Abstractly considered, a system geared to the Platonic ideal of communicating truth in order to make men better is to be ranked above one devoted to the ornamenting of language or the trick of persuasion, and without doubt every "good" rhetoric has as its ultimate purpose the communication of "truth." But, at the same time, a rhetoric which conceives of truth as a transcendent entity and requires a perfect knowledge of the soul as a condition for its successful transmittal automatically rules itself out as an instrument for doing the practical work of the world, and for this reason is less preferable than a system geared to the communication of contingent truths as established by probable rather than apodeictic proofs. In short, the problem of evaluating a rhetoric is a complex one, calling for a delicate balancing of the ideal with the utilitarian and for a precarious adjustment of ends to means. A study of rhetorical systems as systems, I believe, may contribute to our understanding of this fact.

Second, I would contend that analysis of the sort here attempted is useful because it helps to clarify the roles which form and substance play in the creation of a rhetoric. Our discussion appears to show that while the form a rhetoric assumes is a joint product of need and environment, its content or subject matter in each case is supplied by all or some of the constituents of the communication process. Indeed, if a system of rhetoric did not have these constituents as its subject matter, it would not be a system of rhetoric but a system of another sort.

Because systems of rhetoric share in part or in whole the same content or substance, no matter how much they vary in form or purpose they have inescapable elements of commonality. Therefore, looked at from one point of view they are different rather than alike, while from another they are alike rather than different. It is, I suggest, a failure on the part of the disputants to make clear how they are viewing a rhetoric which lies at the basis of the wearisome controversy concerning the classical or non-classical orientation of the rhetorics of George Campbell or Kenneth Burke.[13] In any event, by making their respective points of view clear, the parties to this argument almost certainly could narrow the area of dispute.

Third, analysis of rhetorics at the systems level, I believe, is useful because it directs attention to the dangers and difficulties involved in constructing a rhetoric. And surely this information is helpful both in evaluating systems of the past and in building systems to meet the changing needs of the future.

Because even by the loose definition adopted here a system is an organized and coherent way of looking at something, unless an account of the communication process has a distinctive emphasis or focus—is ordered in terms of a hierarchy of ends and is marked by a distinguishing method—it is not a system but a random collection of observations and precepts. And yet it would appear from our discussion that emphasis in one direction may lead to unwarranted de-emphasis in another. For if the classical rhetoric focused on the grammar of the speech act at the expense of exploring the message-mind relationship, and if the "new" rhetoric of the eighteenth century emphasized this relationship at the cost of advancing the grammar of the act, so the concern of contemporary theorists with the vehicle of transmission and its more efficient use threatens to detract interest from the crucial problem of message content.

In a different vein, our analysis underscores the fact that he who would construct a rhetoric of any sort must draw lines and erect boundaries where in fact none exist, and hence to this extent always must give an unreliable account of the territory and processes he attempts to map. On at least two counts practical discourse resists systematizing. First, human communication itself is a process—a fluid, on-going, circular movement without a definite beginning, middle, or end. In order to talk about communication at all not only must one arbitrarily slice off a segment of the whole, but he must momentarily stop or freeze motion within this segment, thus imposing a false stasis upon a kinetic phenomenon. And, second, discourse resists systematizing for the quite different reason that the several arts or skills upon which writing or speaking depends cannot be compartmentalized. Style glides imperceptibly into invention on the one hand and disposition on the other, while memory, as Ramus suggested,[14] is dependent on both, and invention and disposition, as the formulary rhetoric recognized, may perform interchangeable functions.[15] It is, I think, no exaggeration to say that a system of rhetoric never has and that very probably none ever will satisfactorily solve the foregoing problems.

And finally under this head, an analysis on the systems level confirms that while a distinctive grammar must lie at the basis of every rhetorical system a narrow focus upon grammar is the least healthy and productive way of regarding rhetoric. Because rhetorical concepts may profitably be divided into only a limited number of ways, after these possibilities have been exhausted innovation must consist of pointless elaborations and refinements. Hence, with the passage of time the distinctions drawn by a grammatically oriented rhetoric tend to become needlessly minute, its rules are multiplied beyond warrant, and ever growing areas of doctrine are reduced to formula and routine.[16] If rhetoric is to have status as a humane discipline, clearly it must develop its psychological and social dimensions. In proportion as it does so, however, our analysis also indicates that rhetoric may become a challenging and illuminating field for study—one worthy of attention by the best minds of an age. The great rhetorical systems of the past and present stand as testimony to this fact.

Fourth and last, I would argue the usefulness of examining rhetorics as systems for what such study may suggest concerning a possible metasystem of rhetorics and the promise which this metasystem holds for the future. For as our analysis suggests—and as I believe an examination of additional systems would confirm—while in one sense the major rhetorics of the Western world may properly be described as revolutionary, in another sense they may perhaps be regarded as *evolutionary.* Although each of the systems we have examined overthrew the premise or starting point of its predecessor for a premise that was radically different and distinctively its own, it also appears that in each case the new starting point not only corrected a deficiency in the preceding system but encompassed that system to pass beyond it. Just as the "new" rhetoric of the eighteenth century, though it accepted much of the classical grammar, raised its sights above the grammatical to develop an account of the message-mind relationship, so contemporary theorists accept the crucial position which this relationship must occupy in a fruitful rhetoric, and entertain the still broader purpose of exploring the social significance of the communication act in all its forms and uses.

Whether in the long view all major systems of rhetoric tend to correct deficiencies in their predecessors and to pass beyond them is a complex question, and one which cannot be divorced from a careful consideration of the social and intellectual environment in which each system arises. It would seem, however, that through the ages, and despite occasional setbacks, rhetorics have constantly become both richer in content and more embracing in scope. Perhaps the central lesson to be learned from an analysis of the rhetorics of various periods considered as systems is that while the final word on rhetorics never has and probably never will be said, there is reason for optimism concerning the future of rhetoric as a discipline—reason to believe that as man's knowledge grows and his attempts to talk about practical discourse in a coherent and consistent fashion improve, rhetorics ever will become more penetrating and more fruitful.

Notes

1. George Campbell, *The Philosophy of Rhetoric,* ed. Lloyd Bitzer (Carbondale, Ill., 1963), p. li.
2. *Ibid.,* p. 1.
3. *Ibid.,* pp. 50-58. Cf. Richard Whately, *Elements of Rhetoric,* ed. Douglas Ehninger (Carbondale, Ill., 1963), pp. 46-108.
4. Hugh Blair, *Lectures on Rhetoric and Belles Lettres,* ed. Harold Harding, 2 vols. (Carbondale, Ill., 1965), II, 127-15, etc.
5. Whately, pp. 4, 35-167 *passim.*
6. Joseph Priestley, *Lectures on Oratory and Criticism,* ed. Vincent M. Bevilacqua and Richard Murphy (Carbondale, Ill., 1965), *Lectures* II-IV, VI-VIII, etc.
7. *Ibid.,* Preface, p. i.
8. See Blair, *Lectures,* XX-XXIV, XXXV-XLVII *passim.*
9. Kenneth Burke, *A Rhetoric of Motives* (New York, 1950), pp. xiv-xv.
10. I. A. Richards, *The Philosophy of Rhetoric* (New York, 1936), pp. 3, 89-138; *Speculative Instruments* (Chicago, 1955), pp. 17-38.
11. See Kenneth Burke, "Rhetoric—Old and New," *Journal of General Education,* V (April 1951), 203. "If I had to sum up in one word the difference between the 'old' rhetoric and a 'new' (a rhetoric reinvigorated by fresh insights which the 'new' sciences contributed to the subject), I would reduce it to this: The key term for the old rhetoric was 'persuasion' and its stress was upon deliberate design. The key term for the new rhetoric would be 'identification,' which can include a partially 'unconscious' factor in appeal."
12. See Donald C. Bryant, "Rhetoric: Its Functions and Scope," *Quarterly Journal of Speech,* XXXIX (December 1953), 405.
13. See, for example, Douglas McDermott, "George Campbell and the Classical Tradition," *Quarterly Journal of Speech,* XLIX (December 1963), 403-409.
14. See *P. Rami Scholarum Dialecticarum, seu Animadversionum in Organum Aristotelis, libri XX,* Recens emendati per Joan. Piscatorem Argentinensem (Frankfurt, 1581), p. 593.
15. See Wilbur Samuel Howell, *Logic and Rhetoric in England, 1500-1700* (Princeton, N.J., 1956), pp. 138-145.
16. Besides the excessive refinements worked by the classical rhetoricians in the areas of invention and disposition, the sixteenth-century rhetoric of style may be taken as an example of this tendency; for this rhetoric, in its concern to distinguish and name all possible deviations from the normal and usual patterns of expression, was no less grammatical in nature than was the routinized rhetoric of the ancients.

S. MICHAEL HALLORAN
b. 1939

*This essay and a companion titled "Tradition and Theory in Rhetoric" (*Quarterly Journal of Speech *62) were drawn from the first chapter of S. Michael Halloran's dissertation, "A Rhetoric of the Absurd: The Use of Language in the Plays of Samuel Beckett" (Rensselaer Polytechnic Institute, 1973). Halloran says that that chapter was a sort of grudging afterthought, written to satisfy what seemed at the time unreasonable demands of his committee. It is appropriately ironic, he notes, that his subsequent work derives more clearly from the concerns of that last-written first chapter, particularly its treatment of* ethos, *than from his interests in Samuel Beckett and the theater of the absurd. For a retrospective of some of the issues addressed in "On the End of Rhetoric," see "Further Thoughts on the End of Rhetoric" in* Defining the New Rhetorics *(Enos and Brown, eds., Sage, 1993).*

On the End of Rhetoric, Classical and Modern

I

Edward P. J. Corbett defines the classical tradition of rhetoric as extending from the fifth century B.C. down to the close of the eighteenth century A.D.[1] There are in actuality many distinct theories of rhetoric that arose during this period, but they are unified by a single cultural ideal. That ideal was stated by the Greeks in the word *arete*, signifying the quality of excellence in all modes of human endeavor, a quality valued above any specialized talent because it was considered the foundation of good citizenship. In Rome, the ideal was most succinctly stated by Quintilian, who described the perfect orator as "a good man skilled in speaking." The master of rhetoric was the man who had interiorized all that was best in his culture and applied this knowledge in public forums, influencing his fellow citizens to think and act in accord with their common cultural heritage. He was the man of such broad knowledge and general competency that he could apply

---

[1] Edward P. J. Corbett, "Survey of Rhetoric" in *Classical Rhetoric for the Modern Student* (New York: Oxford University Press, 1965), pp. 535–68.

the accumulated wisdom of the culture to the particular case in a sufficiently logical fashion to move his hearers' minds (*logos*), and with enough emotional force to engage their passions (*pathos*). The name for the third of the traditional modes of rhetorical appeal, *ethos,* indicates the importance of the orator's mastery of the cultural heritage; through the cogency of his logical and emotional appeals he became a kind of living embodiment of that heritage, a voice of such apparent authority that the word spoken by this man was the word of communal wisdom, a word to be trusted for the weight of the man who spoke it and the tradition he spoke for.

Classical rhetoric, then, rested on the assumption that wisdom is open and publicly available. In principle if not in fact, the individual was assumed to be capable of knowing everything worth knowing. The orator was a polymath rather than a specialist. This is why Aristotle sees the common lines of argument—those applicable to any sort of argument, such as the possible and the impossible—as being of more central concern to rhetoric than the special lines of argument which apply only to particular fields of argumentation. The world of classical rhetoric—its complex of images and values and the motives for action that arise from them—was a known world, a world in which common sense prevailed over specialized knowledge.

The Renaissance was in an important sense the rebirth of a culture built upon this rhetorical ideal of the man who took all knowledge as his province, wore his learning with grace and dignity, and wielded his universal mastery in the forum of practical affairs.[2] The Middle Ages had been anti-rhetorical in that knowledge had been arcane, pursued and preserved in the isolation of the monastery. Renaissance figures such as Petrarch, Erasmus, and Francis Bacon virtually reincarnated the classical ideal of a culture so publicly knowable that it could be embodied in a single man. These men aspired to becoming the living *ethos* of their age, and one might argue that they succeeded. What is important, however, is the existence of the ideal rather than the possibility of its realization.

The image of the politically and socially active polymath as a cultural ideal survived through the Enlightenment. As serious amateurs of science, writers of considerable talent, and politically engaged men, Voltaire in Europe and Benjamin Franklin in America were inheritors of the tradition of Petrarch, Erasmus, and Bacon, who in turn were descendents of Cicero. But while eighteenth-century science was still in a state where the amateur could make a significant contribution, Newton was in the process of raising it to the level of a highly specialized activity, accessible only to the man who will subordinate all other interests to it, cultivating what Whitehead has called a

---

[2] The influence of the Ciceronian rhetorical tradition on Italian humanists of the fourteenth- and early fifteenth-centuries is traced in Jerrold E. Seigel, *Rhetoric and Philosophy in Renaissance Humanism* (Princeton: Princeton University Press, 1968).

"celibacy of the intellect." Appropriately, Newton himself was not a poly-math but a one-sided eccentric with no taste at all for the public contro-versies in which Quintilian's good man would exercise his skill in speaking.

The tradition of classical rhetoric, then, is defined principally by the image of the Orator as a cultural idea. He appears in Greece as the man who possesses *arete*, in Rome as "the good man skilled in speaking," later as The Renaissance Man, and later still as the Enlightenment's "man of reason." He takes all knowledge as his province, becomes a kind of living repository of the accumulated wisdom of the culture, and puts what he knows to practi-cal use in guiding the conduct of human affairs. The existence of such a cul-tural model implies certain assumptions about the world, namely that it is knowable, that values are coherent, that wisdom is public and can be fully mastered by one man, who in turn can relate the accumulated wisdom of mankind to the particular case at hand in a clear and persuasive fashion.

II

Today the image of the Orator as a cultural ideal seems thoroughly dead. Should a Demosthenes or a Cicero arise in the modern world, he might well be reduced to tormented gurgling, like the Orator who appears at the end of Eugene Ionesco's *The Chairs*. Where could he begin the process of *inventio*, of scanning the communal wisdom of our culture for arguments pertinent to the particular case at hand? From what premises would his argument pro-ceed? What common values could he assume in his audience? The Orator is speechless because the assumptions about knowledge and the world on which his activity must be based are no longer valid.

It is of interest that George Steiner, who sees the modern world as having evolved a "post-culture," finds the roots of this modern malaise in what he calls "the great ennui" that followed the disappointment of the romantic-utopian hopes of the late eighteenth and early nineteenth centuries.[3] He thus sees the "post-culture" as having been born just this side of the point Corbett defines as the end of the period of classical rhetoric. Steiner has long been preoccupied with Nazis, particularly with their ability to appreci-ate great literature and art, and at the same time indulge in the barbarity of the "final solution." Steiner does not say so, but this phenomenon might well be taken as defining the death of the tradition of classical rhetoric. Quintil-ian's perfect orator was a "good man" largely because he was so intimately acquainted with Homer and Vergil, and this acquaintance was not merely a matter of feeling the beauty of their poetry, but of embodying the virtues

---

[3] George Steiner, *In Bluebeard's Castle* (New Haven: Yale University Press, 1971), pp. 1-26.

they articulated. The ancients went to poetry not merely for delight, but for instruction also. What Steiner remarks in the Nazis' attitude toward art and literature is nothing more than their ability to see a picture or a poem as an artifact totally removed from the concerns of everyday life. In doing so, they were merely following the counsel of post-romantic aestheticism:

> Never attempt to make the images of great art the companions of your daily life; do not permit their mute splendor to pervade your everyday dreams. Rather, keep them apart from the dust and trivialities of daily life and linger with them only in the rare moments of elevated joy of living.[4]

As a source of knowledge and value pertinent to the conduct of life, art has been declared null.

Science likewise has been dominated by the ideal of disinterestedness and thus largely negated as a source of values pertinent to human affairs. This is not to deny the obvious fact that science has profound implications for the way we live, or that there are certain values implicit in the conduct of science. Certainly Jacob Bronowski makes a very persuasive case in *Science and Human Values* for his claim that the practice of science has reinforced certain important values, such as respect for truth and diversity of opinion. Yet even granting all Bronowski's claims, it remains true that the drive of modern science toward specialization and exactness has tended to remove the scientist from the arena of practical decisions on contingent human affairs, first because such matters are outside his specialty, and second because they are by definition inexact. At best, the scientist becomes an advisor making his "input" in turn with many other specialists to some decision-making machine (human or otherwise) whose "output" no one individual scientist can be fully identified with.

Indeed, it is not quite true, as Bronowski seems to believe, that even those minimal values he is concerned with are generated by the practice of empirical science. In his work as a scientist, a man must cultivate what Bronowski calls "the habit of truth," but once he leaves his laboratory he may and frequently does become as self-deceptive and prevaricating as anyone else. Scientific work demands that certain values be preserved within the walls of the laboratory and the pages of the journals, but it does not examine the nature of these values or otherwise pursue them per se. Nor does it demand that they apply outside the highly stylized framework of science itself. Faced with a question of how one ought to behave outside the laboratory, the scientist becomes like the man who assaulted Samuel Beckett and replied when asked why he had stabbed a total stranger, *"Je ne sais pas."*[5] Modern science has

---

[4] Georg Mehlis, "The Aesthetic Problem of Distance," in Susanne K. Langer (ed.) *Reflections on Art* (New York: Oxford University Press, 1961), p. 82 (Mehlis' essay first published in 1917).

[5] The story is recounted in Martin Easlin, *The Theatre of the Absurd* (Garden City: Doubleday and Company, Inc. 1969), p. 17.

made it possible to prolong and manipulate life in the most marvelous ways, but when asked in the particular case whether and how one ought to use these powers, the scientist can only shrug, *"Je ne sais pas."* His province is general laws, not particular cases.

One could go on listing the many ways in which modern man has been denied the possibility of achieving knowledge on which he can base his life; the decline of religion would be another important theme. But our concern is simply to point out that the cultural ideal upon which the tradition of classical rhetoric rested is today moribund if not dead. There have been efforts to revive it, one of the most ambitious and interesting being the Great Books movement started at the University of Chicago. What this amounts to is an attempt to create more or less by fiat a comprehensive yet coherent and manageable canon of books constituting all that is most worth knowing in our culture. One reads the books and, with the Syntopicon at hand to jog the memory, one becomes a twentieth-century Erasmus. The fact that the whole effort seems more like a wholesome amusement than a serious educational task suggests the futility of trying to resurrect the classical ideal. Nick Carraway, in Fitzgerald's *The Great Gatsby,* put it well when he referred to the modern day polymath as "that most limited of all specialists, the well-rounded man."

The assumptions about knowledge and the world that informed classical rhetoric are no longer tenable. External reality is paradoxical; our very effort to know something of the physical environment alters that which we seek to know so that the object-as-known is not the same as the object we set out to know. Our values seem arbitrary, contradictory, and ultimately groundless. The wisdom our culture has accumulated is arcane and available only in narrow portions governed by specialists who speak mysterious and intimidating languages. What those specialists know is so intricate that the ordinary citizen must simply accept their conclusions on faith. The modern world is less akin to the cozy study pictured in magazine advertisements for subscriptions to the Great Books than to the endless succession of compartments filled with undecipherable books described by Jorge Luis Borges in "The Liberty of Babel." Like the hero of that story, modern man searches for the "catalogue of catalogues" that will unlock the mystery of the library and make sense of the world once more.

What, then, happens to the discipline of rhetoric in such a situation? There are those who would resurrect the classical tradition more or less intact. Mortimer Adler's *How to Read a Book* is one example; Corbett's *Classical Rhetoric for the Modern Student* is another. Yet, sound as they are, such texts have a musty, antiquarian air about them, as if their authors had succeeded in blotting out a hundred years or so of modern history. Corbett can note President Kennedy's use of asyndeton in the line ". . . we shall pay any price, bear any burden, meet any hardship, support any friend, oppose any foe to assure the survival and the success of liberty." But he cannot note the irony these words take on in the context of the decade that followed President Kennedy's inaugural. Indeed, one gets the impression that the authors of such books would pick out classical commonplaces and figures of speech with the same detached skill whether the text under analysis were a speech by George Wallace, Malcolm X, Winston Churchill, or Adolph Hitler.

It might be argued that a technique for rhetorical analysis ought to deal with any text by whatever speaker or author in precisely the same manner and with precisely the same attitude of detachment. And certainly in the world of the classical rhetorician—a world shaped by the common knowledge and shared values of a relatively stable culture—this is correct.

But Adolph Hitler and Malcolm X, despite their having inhabited the same planet, did not live in the same world. As Deeley in Harold Pinter's recent play *Old Times* says, with a self-destructive irony characteristic of modern man, ". . . the word world possesses emotional political sociological and psychological pretensions and resonances which I prefer as a matter of choice to do without, or shall I say steer clear of, of if you like to reject." To inhabit a world is to possess images of how things are beyond the reach of one's immediate experience, images that have implications for how one experiences the immediate, and that generate values which make claims on the conduct of one's life. In the absence of a world given by a stable and coherent cultural tradition, man is compelled to construct his own. To open one's own world to others is to run the risk of discovering its inadequacy or falsehood, and thus to be compelled to reconstruct it. Many men, like Deeley, "prefer . . . to steer clear of" this risk, reducing language to superficial banter. Some, like Beckett's assailant, are themselves unaware of the shape of their world, and so can only answer *"Je ne sais pas"* when asked why they live as they do.

A number of modern rhetorical theorists have clearly been responding to the cultural scene sketched above. I. A. Richards, for instance, suggested nearly forty years ago in *The Philosophy of Rhetoric* that rhetoric should be "a study of misunderstanding and its remedies." In other words, it is no longer valid to assume that speaker and audience live in the same world and to study the techniques by which the speaker moves his audience to act or think in a particular way. One must turn instead to the more fundamental problem of why the gap between the speaker's and audience's worlds is so broad and how one might bridge it successfully. Maurice Natanson and Henry Johnstone both place great emphasis upon the element of risk involved in genuine argumentation.[6] Natanson, for instance, distinguishes between an argument to convince and an argument to persuade: the former

---
[6] Maurice Natanson & Henry W. Johnstone, Jr. (eds.), *Philosophy, Rhetoric, and Argumentation* (University Park, Pa.: Pennsylvania State University Press, 1965); see especially "Introduction One" and "Introduction Two," by Johnstone and Natanson respectively, pp. 1-19.

is little more than an intellectual game, like a debate contest, with nothing of real importance at stake; in an argument to persuade, however, one's complete existentiality is at risk, including the immediate world of feeling and perception. If, for example, a white supremacist is persuaded that his racism is reprehensible, he must learn to perceive the black man he sees on the street in an entirely new way. Johnstone argues that it is only through the existential risk of rhetoric that one transcends the boundaries of immediate experience, and thus it is through rhetoric that the self and its world are constituted. Not to engage in rhetoric is not to be human.

Kenneth Burke likewise redefines rhetoric in the context of what Steiner calls the "post-culture." While Burke draws heavily on Aristotle and in fact sees himself as a neo-Aristotelian, his insistence in *A Rhetoric of Motives* that the key term for a modern rhetoric is not persuasion but identification indicates a profound shift of emphasis. To persuade a man, in the Aristotelian sense, is to move him to act or think in a certain way on a certain topic, the topic and the other terms of the argument being assumed as preconditions of the persuasive effort. To achieve identification, or, as Burke also calls it, consubstantiality, is to enter into that very condition assumed as the precondition of persuasion. It is to articulate an area of shared experience, imagery, and value; it is to define my world in such a way that the other can enter into that world with me. Burke is thus in accord with Johnstone, who defines rhetoric as "the evocation and maintenance of the consciousness required for communication."[7] That consciousness consists in establishing the proper distance from the object, setting it in contrast to the welter of sensory impressions of which we are, strictly speaking, unconscious; rhetoric thus strives toward the establishment of a certain order in the stream of consciousness, an order that constitutes the identification or consubstantiality between the speaker and audience.

The conflict in terminology between Burke and Natanson points up an important problem that arises in the study of rhetoric as we are here discussing it. Natanson sees persuasion as the object of rhetoric, insisting only that this term be distinguished from conviction, which he sees as a purely intellectual state with no existential implications. Burke relegates the Aristotelian notion of persuasion to a subsidiary position in his view of rhetoric, emphasizing instead his own term, identification. The problem is one of existential commitment to the implications of an argument, or more simply of the seriousness with which one takes an argument. For Aristotle, the problem apparently did not arise; when both speaker and audience are assumed to inhabit the same world, it is sufficient that both attend to the argument. But when speaker and audience inhabit different worlds, it becomes possible for both to hear without listening. The speaker may hear

---

[7] Henry W. Johnstone, Jr., *The Problem of the Self* (University Park, Pa.: Pennsylvania State University Press, 1970), p. 121.

himself in an attitude of intellectual detachment and smugness, never listening for the nuances of his words, never asking whether he is willing to live the implications of what he says. The audience likewise is detached, hearing the speaker's argument but never allowing it to touch his life, never measuring the images articulated in the speech against the contours of his own world. It is possible, in other words, for both speaker and audience to hear the speech in the way an aesthete looks at a painting by a currently fashionable artist. In Sartrean terms, both speaker and audience are liable to the rhetorical equivalent of bad faith. The apparent conflict between Natanson and Burke on the proper object of rhetoric is resolved by this notion. Both are concerned to rule out of the province of rhetoric speech heard and spoken in bad faith. Identification, as Burke means it, and persuasion, as Natanson means that, are possible only if both speaker and audience enter into the rhetorical transaction as a serious existential commitment.

Richard Weaver, in his interpretation of Plato's *Phaedrus*,[8] focuses on this element of seriousness in rhetorical speech. Weaver interprets the three speeches in the dialogue on the subject of the relative excellence of lovers and non-lovers as allegories on three modes of speech. The first speech in praise of the non-lover, attributed to Lysias, is interpreted by Weaver as a defense of language devoid of rhetorical inclination, the sort of language Philip Wheelwright calls steno-language. The first of the two speeches attributed to Socrates, in which he purports to handle Lysias' own theme more eloquently by attacking the lover, is in Weaver's view an attack on the kind of rhetoric that seeks to persuade by deception, half-truth, and trickery. The final speech, in which Socrates presents his own view that the lover is in fact more excellent than the non-lover, becomes a defense of the rhetoric that seeks honestly to give effectiveness to truth. The faithfulness of this allegorical interpretation to Plato's intention in writing the dialogue is not the question of primary concern to Weaver. What is of interest is Weaver's own understanding of the nature of rhetoric. Divested of its mythological and idealistic implications, the "divine madness" Weaver sees as informing true rhetoric, the kind defended in Socrates' second speech, is very like the seriousness, or existential commitment, we spoke of above as prerequisite to a rhetoric that aims to achieve identification.

The title of the book in which Weaver's essay originally appeared, *The Ethics of Rhetoric*, suggests at what point such notions as "divine madness," "seriousness," or "existential commitment," fit into a theory of rhetoric that maintains roots in the classical tradition. *Ethos*, most simply defined as the persuasive appeal growing out of the character of the speaker, is acknowledged by Aristotle to be "the most potent of all the means to persuasion."

---

[8] Richard Weaver, "The *Phaedrus* and the Nature of Rhetoric," in *The Ethics of Rhetoric* (Chicago: Henry Regnery Company, 1953), pp. 3–26.

For the ancients, *ethos* consisted in the degree to which the speaker embodied the virtues most revered by the culture, the degree to which he had apparently internalized all that was best in the tradition that defined the shared world of speaker and audience. Ideally, the hearer would perceive in the speaker the living embodiment of all his own highest aspirations, and the speaker's voice would thus become the voice of the hearer's own best self, the ideal self defined by his education in the common wisdom of the culture. In our time of fragmentation and isolation, *ethos* is generated by the seriousness and passion with which the speaker articulates his own world, the degree to which he is willing and able to make his world open to the other, and thus to the possibility of rupture. If, as Johnstone argues, rhetoric is the means whereby the self and its world are constituted, *ethos* is the measure of one's willingness to risk one's self and world by a rigorous and open articulation of them in the presence of the other.

III

As we noted above, efforts to define the classical tradition of rhetoric in terms of the genre(s) of discourse it encompasses seem inadequate. It is the position of this study that all such efforts are inadequate, yet it must be admitted that efforts persist to define rhetoric by marking out the canon of discourse that is its legitimate province. One of the more recent and interesting of these attempts is James R. McNally's proposal that rhetoric be defined as "(1) sign-behavior exhibiting a pragmatic concentration of meaning or (2) the study of such behavior."[9] McNally is here invoking Charles Morris' theory of signs, within which *pragmatics* deals with the relationships between signs and the people who use them; the other two branches of Morris' semiotic are *semantics*, the study of the relationships between signs and what they signify; and *syntactics*, the study of the relationships among signs themselves. McNally suggests that statements of alleged fact, such as "The Yankees won three pennants in the 1950's," exhibit a semantic concentration of meaning; statements about the symbolic universes of science or literature, such as "Pi = 3.1416" or "Rhett Butler got his revenge," exhibit a syntactic concentration of meaning. Exhortations to act or think in a particular way, such as "Cubism is ugly" or "Do not lie," exhibit a pragmatic concentration of meaning, and thus the canon of discourse constituting the legitimate province of rhetoric would consist of such statements.

---

[9] James R. McNally, "Toward a Definition of Rhetoric," *Philosophy and Rhetoric* 3 (Spring 1970): 77.

As McNally himself notes, no statement is such that its meaning falls entirely within one of his three areas of semiotic. To an ardent fan, the statement that "The Yankees won three pennants in the 1950's" may be charged with value, and hence would have meaning on the pragmatic dimension. The emotive, hence evaluative and pragmatic significance of "Rhett Butler got his revenge" is even more complex, particularly if one raises questions about such matters as the literary sophistication of the one who makes or hears the statement, or the place of a notion like male chauvinism in his/her world. As Bronowski points out in "The Abacus and the Rose," whether one chooses to equate Pi with 3.1, 3.14, 3.1416, or 3.141592 . . . implies value judgments about the situation in which the equation is made.[10] Hence, McNally's notion of semantic concentration; realizing that no statement can be fully identified with one of the three areas and no others, he falls back on the idea that the meaning of a given statement will fall mostly in one or another area. Rhetoric, according to McNally, is properly concerned with language whose meaning falls mostly in the area of pragmatics. Literature falls outside the province of rhetoric, since its meaning falls mostly in the area of semantics.

It is important to note that McNally departs from the thinking of Morris on this point. Morris claims that poetry is "an example of discourse which is appraisive-valuative": "its primary aim is to cause the interpreter to accord to what is signified the preferential place in his behavior signified by the appraisors."[11] Thus within McNally's definition of rhetoric, Morris himself would clearly make of literature an instance of rhetoric.

Yet in order to draw literature into the province of rhetoric it is not necessary to accept Morris' idea of what literature is, an idea that, as Philip Wheelwright points out in *The Burning Fountain*, is not adequate to the sophisticated reader's experience. If, as we have suggested, rhetoric has to do with the way in which one defines one's world and self, then literature falls quite readily within the province of rhetoric. Jacques Maritain's philosophy of art as developed in *Creative Intuition in Art and Poetry* proceeds from the notion that art in general and poetry in particular reveal both things and creative subjectivity—both the world and the self. Albert Hofstadter's *Truth and Art* goes further, asserting that it is through language, of which all art is an instance, that the world and the self are brought into being. One is reminded inevitably of Johnstone's position that it is through the existential risk of rhetoric that both the world and the self are constituted, and thus that one becomes human. "All language," says Hofstadter,

---

[10] In Jacob Bronowski, *Science and Human Values*, revised ed. (New York: Harper and Row, 1965), p. 89; the measurement in question in "The Abacus and the Rose" is not Pi, but the wavelength of the sun.

[11] Quoted in Philip Wheelwright, *The Burning Fountain* (Bloomington, Ind.: Indiana UP, 1968), p. 65.

"articulates human being." Prior to this articulation there are only things and brute existence. In this process of articulation, which is both a giving shape to the outer and an uttering of the inner, both the self and the world are formed, and in that region of self/world human being is realized.

The function of art in giving shape to the world has long been recognized, implicitly if not explicitly, and in fact is a central element of the foundation upon which tradition of classical rhetoric, as described above, was built. It was largely by knowing a canon of art and literature that the orator came to know the world he shared with his audience, and thus the values he could argue from. If the orator wanted to know what the culture's ideal of manhood was, and how he could use the definition of man as a commonplace from which to argue, he could look to Homer. Literature gave reality to the ideals upon which the stability of the culture was based. Indeed, one might see Plato's dismissal of poets from his Republic as growing out of a variation of this notion. Believing in an objectively real realm of ideas discoverable through philosophy, Plato feared the power of poets to make alternative, and hence false ideas attractive.

A particularly striking illustration of the ancients' recognition of the role of literature, especially dramatic literature, in defining the world is Aristophanes' *The Frogs*. Written subsequent to the death of Euripides, the last of the three great tragedians, during a period of political and moral chaos in Athens, *The Frogs* is Aristophanes' version of how the crumbling world might be put back together again. The god Dionysus goes to the underworld to find and bring back the greatest of the dead tragedians, who it is assumed will somehow be able to bring order into the chaos that seems to be consuming Athens. Aeschylus is held to be the greatest of the tragedians because he gives expression to the noblest ideals. Indeed, the very presence of Aeschylus is so effective that the character of Dionysus undergoes a striking change in the course of the play; a ridiculous and cowardly figure at the beginning, thus signifying the state to which Athenian society has fallen, he regains his dignity once he meets with the three tragedians.

It is important to point out that the idea of literature as giving shape to one's self/world is quite different from notions of literature as propaganda. When Morris identifies the aim of literature as "caus[ing] the interpreter to accord to what is signified by the appraisers," he reduces literature to the level of propaganda, as Wheelwright correctly asserts. In the first place, propaganda is aimed at "causing" the desired behavior (or attitude), and thus the propagandist feels no obligation regarding the freedom of the audience. Moreover, for the propagandist the desired outcome is never in question; he knows what it is he wishes his audience to do, think, or feel. For him there is no existential quest, no serious commitment to the discovery/creation of his authentic self/world. The rhetorical dimension on which one distinguishes literature from propaganda is therefore *ethos*. It remains now for us to define just what sort of study of literature is properly rhetorical.

Perhaps the one feature of discourse that has remained a constant emphasis of rhetorical theories from ancient Greece down to the present is that it is addressed. Rhetorical discourse is discourse spoken to an audience. This remains so even if one person becomes both speaker and addressee; if a single person is divided on a given issue, the symbolic means by which he seeks to resolve his inner conflict are subject to rhetorical analysis precisely because the person addresses himself, becoming his own audience. A rhetorical analysis of a work of literature would therefore focus on the work as something addressed to a readership.

It is because of their concern with language as addressed to an audience that rhetorics of the past have accorded a central place to conventions of style and argument such as commonplaces and figures of speech. Language is communicative because it is conventionalized, because it is an organized system of repeatable patterns which can be combined and permuted in ways that provide speaker and audience with presuppositions about what can be said without limiting their creative potential in determining what actually is said. Lacking conventionalized patterns, language would become wholly private or even chaotic. At its most fundamental level, the system of conventions is described by the lexicon and grammar of a given language. A rhetoric (to be distinguished from "rhetoric" in the same way that "a grammar" differs from "grammar") moves beyond this fundamental level, providing more subtly nuanced conventions in the form of commonplaces and figures. A complete rhetoric—which would be an ideal at least as difficult to realize as a complete grammar—together with the lexicon and grammar it is built upon, might be taken as constituting the world shared by the speaker and audience for whom the rhetoric functions. A measure of the complex formality of the Elizabethan world is the nearly two hundred figures of speech defined in Peacham's *The Garden of Eloquence* (1577).

Deprived of a given world, the modern author is likewise deprived of a given rhetoric. To the extent that he must articulate his own world in such a way that his readers can enter it with him, he must likewise invent the commonplaces and figures that are the rhetorical lineaments of that world. Rhetorical analysis of such literature is the effort to discover the conventions established by a given work or group of works, and thus to trace the outlines of the world articulated by it, particularly as that world is made open to the audience.

IV

This essay has presented a view of rhetoric, classical and modern, centering on the concepts "world" and "self." According to this view, modern rhetoric is distinguished by its emphasis on the responsibility of the speaker (or author) to articulate his own world, and thereby his own self. The seriousness with which he undertakes this task, hence the rigor and passion with which he discloses his world to the audience, is his *ethos*. In this view, literature is of interest to the rhetorician, since it is most importantly a medium in which a man articulates his world and self.

It should finally be noted that the view of rhetoric herein presented encompasses literature because it likewise encompasses all uses of language. Language is always a disclosure—more or less deliberate, profound, and honest—of the one who speaks, of his personal view of the world. There is always a dimension of *ethos* in language, even when it is the evasive *ethos* of bureaucratic language or the dispassionate *ethos* of science. The improbable uses of the passive voice that mar bureaucratise, for example, are rhetorical conventions that articulate a self—the timid self of the bureaucrat who hides his opinion behind "It is believed that. . . ." The concept of *ethos* is crucial to rhetoric because the object of rhetoric is *man speaking*. The end of rhetorical analysis is to discover a man in his words, whether that man is the Ciceronian Orator or the lonely modern anti-hero.

Terry Eagleton is currently a fellow of Linacre College at Oxford University. He is of Catholic, working-class origins, and, in the 1960s, was involved in a project to reconcile Marxism and Catholicism, which led to the short-lived journal Slant. *He is also a former student (at Cambridge University) of Raymond Williams, whom he alternately attacks and praises, because Eagleton prefers a much more overt and politically directed Marxism than Williams posits. Eagleton's critical work on literature (and later on linguistics and rhetoric) began in the tradition of the British New Left during the late 1960s. But he soon responded to the influence of European structuralist and poststructuralist theory, especially as it was refracted through Louis Althusser and Pierre Machery. Debates generated by these writers are reflected in Eagleton's* Myths of Power: A Marxist Study of the Brontes *(1975),* Criticism and Ideology *(1976), and* Marxism and Literary Criticism *(1976). Later, Eagleton became critical of the Althusserian sense of the "relative autonomy" of cultural predictions from economic determinations, especially in view of the increased drift to the Right in the governments of Western democracies in the late 1970s and the 1980s. These concerns led him to write works, as he says, "more preoccupied with questions of experience and the subject, with that of difference or heterogeneity which escapes formalization, with humour, the body and the 'carnivalesque,' with cultural politics rather than textual science." These interests are reflected in* Walter Benjamin *(1981),* The Rape of Clarissa *(1982),* Literary Theory: An Introduction *(1983),* Against the Grain *(1986), and* The Ideology of the Aesthetic *(1990).*

Conclusion: Political Criticism

In the course of this book we have considered a number of problems of literary theory. But the most important question of all has as yet gone unanswered. What is the *point* of literary theory? Why bother with it in the first place? Are there not issues in the world more weighty than codes, signifiers and reading subjects?

Let us consider merely one such issue. As I write, it is estimated that the world contains over 60,000 nuclear warheads, many with a capacity a thousand times greater than the bomb which destroyed Hiroshima. The possibility that these weapons will be used in our lifetime is steadily growing. The approximate cost of these weapons is 500 billion dollars a year, or 1.3 billion dollars a day. Five per cent of this sum—25 billion dollars—could drastically, fundamentally alleviate the problems of the poverty-stricken Third World.

Anyone who believed that literary theory was more important than such matters would no doubt be considered somewhat eccentric, but perhaps only a little less eccentric than those who consider that the two topics might be somehow related. What has international politics to do with literary theory? Why this perverse insistence on dragging politics into the argument?

There is, in fact, no need to drag politics into literary theory: as with South African sport, it has been there from the beginning. I mean by the political no more than the way we organize our social life together, and the power-relations which this involves; and what I have tried to show throughout this book is that the history of modern literary theory is part of the political and ideological history of our epoch. From Percy Bysshe Shelley to Norman N. Holland, literary theory has been indissociably bound up with political beliefs and ideological values. Indeed literary theory is less an object of intellectual enquiry in its own right than a particular perspective in which to view the history of our times. Nor should this be in the least cause for surprise. For any body of theory concerned with human meaning, value, language, feeling and experience will inevitably engage with broader, deeper beliefs about the nature of human individuals and societies, problems of power and sexuality, interpretations of past history, versions of the present and hopes for the future. It is not a matter of *regretting* that this is so—of *blaming* literary theory for being caught up with such questions, as opposed to some "pure" literary theory which might be absolved from them. Such "pure" literary theory is an academic myth: some of the theories we have examined in this book are nowhere more clearly ideological than in their attempts to ignore history and politics altogether. Literary theories are not to be upbraided for being political, but for being on the whole covertly or unconsciously so—for the blindness with which they offer as a supposedly "technical," "self-evident," "scientific" or "universal" truth doctrines which with a little reflection can be seen to relate to and reinforce the particular interests of particular groups of people at particular times. The title of this section, "Conclusion: Political Criticism," is not intended to mean: "Finally, a political alternative," it is intended to mean: "The conclusion is that the literary theory we have examined is political."

It is not only, however, a matter of such biases being covert or unconscious. Sometimes, as with Matthew Arnold, they are neither, and at other times, as with T. S. Eliot, they are certainly covert but not in the least unconscious. It is not the fact that literary theory is political which is objectionable, nor just the fact that its frequent obliviousness of this tends to mislead: what is really objectionable is the nature of its politics. That objection can be briefly summarized by stating that the great majority of the literary theories outlined in this book have strengthened rather than challenged the assumptions of the power-system some of whose present-day consequences I have just described. I do not mean by this that Matthew Arnold supported nuclear weapons, or that there are not a good many literary theorists who would not dissent in one way or another from a system in which some grow rich on profits from armaments while others starve in the street. I do not believe that many, perhaps most, literary theorists and critics are not disturbed by a world in which some economies, left stagnant and lopsided by generations of colonial exploitation, are still in fee to Western capitalism through their crippling repayments of debts, or that all literary theorists would genially endorse a society like our own, in which considerable private wealth remains concentrated in the hands of a tiny minority, while the human services of education, health, culture and recreation for the great majority are torn to shreds. It is just that they would not regard literary theory as at all relevant to such matters. My own view, as I have commented, is that literary theory has a most particular relevance to this political system: it has helped, wittingly or not, to sustain and reinforce its assumptions.

Literature, we are told, is vitally engaged with the living situations of men and women: it is concrete rather than abstract, displays life in all its rich variousness, and rejects barren conceptual enquiry for the feel and taste of what it is to be alive. The story of modern literary theory, paradoxically, is the narrative of a flight from such realities into a seemingly endless range of alternatives: the poem itself, the organic society, eternal verities, the imagination, the structure of the human mind, myth, language and so on. Such a flight from real history is in part understandable as a reaction to the antiquarian, historically reductionist criticism which held sway in the nineteenth century; but the extremism of this reaction has been nevertheless striking. It is indeed the *extremism* of literary theory, its obstinate, perverse, endlessly resourceful refusal to countenance social and historical realities, which most strikes a student of its documents, even though "extremism" is a term more commonly used of those who would seek to call attention to literature's role in actual life. Even in the act of fleeing modern ideologies, however, literary theory reveals its often unconscious complicity with them, betraying its elitism, sexism or individualism in the very "aesthetic" or "unpolitical" language it finds natural to use of the literary text. It assumes, in the main, that at the centre of the world is the contemplative individual self, bowed over its book, striving to gain touch with experience, truth, reality, history or tradition. Other things matter too, of course—this individual is in personal relationship with others, and we are always much more than readers—but it is notable how often such individual consciousness, set in its small circle of relationships, ends up as the touchstone of all else. The further we move from the rich inwardness of the personal life, of which literature is the supreme exemplar, the more drab, mechanical and impersonal existence becomes. It is a view equivalent in the literary sphere to what has been called possessive individualism in the social realm, much as the former attitude may shudder at the latter: it reflects the values of a political system which subordinates the sociality of human life to solitary individual enterprise.

I began this book by arguing that literature did not exist. How in that case can literary theory exist either? There are two familiar ways in which any theory can provide itself with a distinct purpose and identity. Either it can define itself in terms of its particular *methods* of enquiry; or it can define itself in terms of the particular *object* that is being enquired into. Any attempts to define literary theory in terms of a distinctive method is doomed to failure. Literary theory is supposed to reflect on the nature of literature and literary criticism. But just think of how many methods are involved in literary criticism. You can discuss the poet's asthmatic childhood, or examine her peculiar use of syntax; you can detect the rustling of silk in the hissing of the *s*'s, explore the phenomenology of reading, relate the literary work to the state of the class-struggle or find out how many copies it sold. These methods have nothing whatsoever of significance in common. In fact they have more in common with other "disciplines"—linguistics, history, sociology and so on—than they have with each other. Methodologically speaking, literary criticism is a non-subject. If literary theory is a kind of "metacriticism," a critical reflection on criticism, then it follows that it too is a non-subject.

Perhaps, then, the unity of literary studies is to be sought elsewhere. Perhaps literary criticism and literary theory just mean any kind of talk (of a certain level of "competence," clearly enough) about an object named literature. Perhaps it is the object, not the method, which distinguishes and delimits the discourse. As long as that object remains relatively stable, we can move equably from biographical to mythological to semiotic methods and still know where we are. But as I argued in the Introduction, literature has no such stability. The unity of the object is as illusory as the unity of the method. "Literature," as Roland Barthes once remarked, "is what gets taught."

Maybe this lack of methodological unity in literary studies should not worry us unduly. After all, it would be a rash person who would define geography or philosophy, distinguish neatly between sociology and anthropology or advance a snap definition of "history." Perhaps we should celebrate the plurality of critical methods, adopt a tolerantly ecumenical posture and rejoice in our freedom from the tyranny of any single procedure. Before we become too euphoric, however, we should notice that there are certain problems here too. For one thing, not all of these methods are mutually compatible. However generously liberal-minded we aim to be, trying to combine structuralism, phenomenology and psychoanalysis is more likely to lead to a nervous breakdown than to a brilliant literary career. Those critics who parade their pluralism are usually able to do so because the different methods they have in mind are not all that different in the end. For another thing, some of these "methods" are hardly methods at all. Many literary critics dislike the whole idea of method and prefer to work by glimmers and hunches, intuitions and sudden perceptions. It is perhaps fortunate that this way of proceeding has not yet infiltrated medicine or aeronautical engineering; but even so one should not take this modest disowning of method altogether seriously, since what glimmers and hunches you have will depend on a latent structure of assumptions often quite as stubborn as that of any structuralist. It is notable that such "intuitive" criticism, which relies not on "method" but on "intelligent sensitivity," does not often seem to intuit, say, the presence of ideological values in literature. Yet there is no reason, on its own reckoning, why it should not. Some traditional critics would appear to hold that other people subscribe to theories while they prefer to read literature "straightforwardly." No theoretical or ideological predilections, in other words, mediate between themselves and the text: to describe George Eliot's later world as one of "mature resignation" is not ideological, whereas to claim that it reveals evasion and compromise is. It is therefore difficult to engage such critics in debate about ideological preconceptions, since the power of ideology over them is nowhere more marked than in their honest belief that their readings are "innocent." It was Leavis who was being "doctrinal" in attacking Milton, not C. S. Lewis in defending him; it is feminist critics who insist on confusing literature with politics by examining fictional images of gender, not conventional critics who are being political by arguing that Richardson's Clarissa is largely responsible for her own rape.

Even so, the fact that some critical methods are less methodical than others proves something of an embarrassment to the pluralists who believe that there is a little truth in everything. (This theoretical pluralism also has its political correlative: seeking to understand everybody's point of view quite often suggests that you yourself are disinterestedly up on high or in the middle, and trying to resolve conflicting viewpoints into a consensus implies a refusal of the truth that some conflicts can be resolved on one side alone.) Literary criticism is rather like a laboratory in which some of the staff are seated in white coats at control panels, while others are throwing sticks in the air or spinning coins. Genteel amateurs jostle with hard-nosed professionals, and after a century or so of "English" they have still not decided to which camp the subject really belongs. This dilemma is the product of the peculiar history of English, and it cannot really be settled because what is at stake is much more than a mere conflict over methods or the lack of them. The true reason why the pluralists are wishful thinkers is that what is at issue in the contention between different literary theories or "non-theories" are competing ideological strategies related to the very destiny of English studies in modern society. The problem with literary theory is that it can neither beat nor join the dominant ideologies of late industrial capitalism. Liberal humanism seeks to oppose or at least modify such ideologies with its distaste for the technocratic and its nurturing of spiritual wholeness in a hostile world; certain brands of formalism and structuralism try to take over the technocratic rationality of such a society and thus incorporate themselves into it. Northrop Frye and the New Critics thought that they had pulled off a synthesis of the two, but how many students of literature today read them? Liberal humanism has dwindled to the impotent conscience of bourgeois society, gentle, sensitive and ineffectual; structuralism has already more or less vanished into the literary museum.

The impotence of liberal humanism is a symptom of its essentially contradictory relationship to modern capitalism. For although it forms a part of the "official" ideology of such society, and the "humanities" exist to reproduce it, the social order within which it exists has in one sense very little time for it at all. Who is concerned with the uniqueness of the individual, the imperishable truths of the human condition or the sensuous textures of lived experience in the Foreign Office or the boardroom of Standard Oil? Capitalism's reverential hat-tipping to the arts is obvious hypocrisy, except when it can hang them on its walls as a sound investment. Yet capitalist states have continued to direct funds into higher education humanities departments, and though such departments are usually the first in line for savage cutting when capitalism enters on one of its periodic crises, it is doubtful that it is only hypocrisy, a fear of appearing in its true philistine colours, which compels this grudging support. The truth is that liberal humanism is at once largely ineffectual, and the best ideology of the "human" that present bourgeois society can muster. The "unique individual" is indeed important when it comes to defending the business entrepreneur's right to make profit while throwing men and women out of work; the individual must at all costs have the "right to choose," provided this means the right to buy one's child an expensive private education while other children are deprived of their school meals, rather than the rights of women to decide whether to have children in the first place. The "imperishable truths of the human condition" include such verities as freedom and democracy, the essences of which are embodied in our particular way of life. The "sensuous textures of lived experience" can be roughly translated as reacting from the gut—judging according to habit, prejudice and "common sense," rather than according to some inconvenient, "aridly theoretical" set of debatable ideas. There is, after all, room for the humanities yet, much as those who guarantee our freedom and democracy despise them.

Departments of literature in higher education, then, are part of the ideological apparatus of the modern capitalist state. They are not wholly reliable apparatuses, since for one thing the humanities contain many values, meanings and traditions which are antithetical to the state's social priorities, which are rich in kinds of wisdom and experience beyond its comprehension. For another thing, if you allow a lot of young people to do nothing for a few years but read books and talk to each other then it is possible that, given certain wider historical circumstances, they will not only begin to question some of the values transmitted to them but begin to interrogate the authority by which they are transmitted. There is of course no harm in students questioning the values conveyed to them: indeed it is part of the very meaning of higher education that they should do so. Independent thought, critical dissent and reasoned dialectic are part of the very stuff of a humane education; hardly anyone, as I commented earlier, will demand that your essay on Chaucer or Baudelaire arrives inexorably at certain pre-set conclusions. All that is being demanded is that you manipulate a particular language in acceptable ways. Becoming certificated by the state as proficient in literary studies is a matter of being able to talk and write in certain ways. It is this which is being taught, examined and certificated, not what you personally think or believe, though what is thinkable will of course be constrained by the language itself. You can think or believe what you want, as long as you can speak this particular language. Nobody is especially concerned about what you say, with what extreme, moderate, radical or conservative positions you adopt, provided that they are compatible with, and can be articulated within it. Literary studies, in other words, are a question of the signifier, not of the signified. Those employed to teach you this form of discourse will remember whether or not you were able to speak it proficiently long after they have forgotten what you said.

Literary theorists, critics and teachers, then, are not so much purveyors of doctrine as custodians of a discourse. Their task is to preserve this discourse, extend and elaborate it as necessary, defend it from other forms of discourse, initiate newcomers into it and determine whether or not they have successfully mastered it. The discourse itself has no definite signified, which is not to say that it embodies no assumptions: it is rather a network of signifiers able to envelop a whole field of meanings, objects and practices. Certain pieces of writing are selected as being more amenable to this discourse than others, and these are what is known as literature or the "literary canon." The fact that this canon is usually regarded as fairly fixed, even at times as eternal and immutable, is in a sense ironic, because since literary critical discourse has no definite signified it can, if it wants to, turn its attention to more or less any kind of writing. Some of those hottest in their defence of the canon have from time to time demonstrated how the discourse can be made to operate on "non-literary" writing. This, indeed, is the embarrassment of literary criticism, that it defines for itself a special object, literature, while existing as a set of discursive techniques which have no reason to stop short at that object at all. If you have nothing better to do at a party you can always try on a literary critical analysis of it, speak of its styles and genres, discriminate its significant nuances or formalize its sign-systems.

Such a "text" can prove quite as rich as one of the canonical works, and critical dissections of it quite as ingenious as those of Shakespeare. So either literary criticism confesses that it can handle parties just as well as it can Shakespeare, in which case it is in danger of losing its identity along with its object; or it agrees that parties may be interestingly analysed provided that this is called something else: ethnomethodology or hermeneutical phenomenology, perhaps. Its own concern is with literature, because literature is more valuable and rewarding than any of the other texts on which the critical discourse might operate. The disadvantage of this claim is that it is plainly untrue: many films and works of philosophy are considerably more valuable than much that is included in the "literary canon." It is not that they are valuable in different ways: they could present objects of value in the sense that criticism defines that term. Their exclusion from what is studied is not because they are not "amenable" to the discourse: it is a question of the arbitrary authority of the literary institution.

Another reason why literary criticism cannot justify its self-limiting to certain works by an appeal to their "value" is that criticism is part of a literary institution which constitutes these works as valuable in the first place. It is not only parties that need to be *made* into worthwhile literary objects by being treated in specific ways, but also Shakespeare. Shakespeare was not great literature lying conveniently to hand, which the literary institution then happily discovered: he is great literature because the institution constitutes him as such. This does not mean that he is not "really" great literature—that it is just a matter of people's opinions about him—because there is no such thing as literature which is "really" great, or "really" anything, independently of the ways in which that writing is treated within specific forms of social and institutional life. There are an indefinite number of ways of discussing Shakespeare, but not all of them count as literary critical. Perhaps Shakespeare himself, his friends and actors, did not talk about his plays in ways which we would regard as literary critical. Perhaps some of the most interesting statements which could be made about Shakespeare drama would also not count as belonging to literary criticism. Literary criticism selects, processes, corrects and rewrites texts in accordance with certain institutionalized norms of the "literary"—norms which are at any given time arguable, and always historically variable. For though I have said that critical discourse has no determinate signified, there are certainly a great many ways of talking about literature which it excludes, and a great many discursive moves and strategies which it disqualifies as invalid, illicit, non-critical, nonsense. Its apparent generosity at the level of the signified is matched only by its sectarian intolerance at the level of the signifier. Regional dialects of the discourse, so to speak, are acknowledged and sometimes tolerated, but you must not sound as though you are speaking another language altogether. To do so is to recognize in the sharpest way that critical discourse is power. To be on the inside of the discourse itself is to be blind to this power, for what is more natural and non-dominative than to speak one's own tongue?

The power of critical discourse moves on several levels. It is the power of "policing" language—of determining that certain statements must be excluded because they do not conform to what is acceptably sayable. It is the power of policing writing itself, classifying it into the "literary" and "non-literary," the enduringly great and the ephemerally popular. It is the power of authority *vis-à-vis* others—the power-relations between those who define and preserve the discourse, and those who are selectively admitted to it. It is the power of certificating or non-certificating those who have been judged to speak the discourse better or worse. Finally, it is a question of the power-relations between the literary-academic institution, where all of this occurs, and the ruling power-interests of society at large, whose ideological needs will be served and whose personnel will be reproduced by the preservation and controlled extension of the discourse in question.

I have argued that the theoretically limitless extendibility of critical discourse, the fact that it is only arbitrarily confined to "literature," is or should be a source of embarrassment to the custodians of the canon. The objects of criticism, like those of the Freudian drive, are in a certain sense contingent and replaceable. Ironically, criticism only really became aware of this fact when, sensing that its own liberal humanism was running out of steam, it turned for aid to more ambitious or rigorous critical methods. It thought that by adding a judicious pinch of historical analysis here or swallowing a non-addictive dose of structuralism there, it could exploit these otherwise alien approaches to eke out its own dwindling spiritual capital. The boot, however, might well prove to be on the other foot. For you cannot engage in an historical analysis of literature without recognizing that literature itself is a recent historical invention; you cannot apply structuralist tools to *Paradise Lost* without acknowledging that just the same tools can be applied to the *Daily Mirror.* Criticism can thus prop itself up only at the risk of losing its defining object; it has the unenviable choice of stifling or suffocating. If literary theory presses its own implications too far, then it has argued itself out of existence.

This, I would suggest, is the best possible thing for it to do. The final logic move in a process which began by recognizing that literature is an illusion is to recognize that literary theory is an illusion too. It is not of course an illusion in the sense that I have invented the various people I have discussed in this book: Northrop Frye really does exist, and so did F. R. Leavis. It is an illusion first in the sense that literary theory, as I hope to have shown, is really no more than a branch of social ideologies, utterly without any unity or identity which would adequately distinguish it from philosophy, linguistics, psychology, cultural and sociological thought; and secondly in the sense that the one hope it has of distinguishing itself—clinging to an object named literature—is misplaced. We must conclude, then, that this book is less an introduction than an obituary, and that we have ended by burying the object we sought to unearth.

My intention, in other words, is not to counter the literary theories I have critically examined in this book with a literary theory of my own, which would claim to be more politically acceptable. Any reader who has been expectantly waiting for a Marxist theory has obviously not been reading this book with due attention. There are indeed Marxist and feminist theories of literature, which in my opinion are more valuable than any of the theories discussed here, and to which the reader may like to refer in the bibliography. But this is not exactly the point. The point is whether it is possible to speak of "literary theory" without perpetuating the illusion that literature exists as a distinct, bounded object of knowledge, or whether it is not preferable to draw the practical consequences of the fact that literary theory can handle Bob Dylan just as well as John Milton. My own view is that it is most useful to see "literature" as a name which people give from time to time for different reasons to certain kinds of writing within a whole field of what Michel Foucault has called "discursive practices," and that if anything is to be an object of study it is this whole field of practices rather than just those sometimes rather obscurely labeled "literature." I am countering the theories set out in this book not with a *literary* theory, but with a different kind of discourse—whether one calls it of "culture," "signifying practices" or whatever is not of first importance—which would include the objects ("literature") with which these other theorists deal, but which would transform them by setting them in a wider context.

But is this not to extend the boundaries of literary theory to a point where any kind of particularity is lost? Would not a "theory of discourse" run into just the same problem of methodology and object of study which we have seen in the case of literary studies? After all, there are any number of discourses and any number of ways of studying them. What would be specific to the kind of study I have in mind, however, would be its concern for the kinds of *effects* which discourses produce, and how they produce them. Reading a zoology textbook to find out about giraffes is part of studying zoology, but reading it to see how its discourse is structured and organized, and examining what kind of effects these forms and devices produce in particular readers in actual situations, is a different kind of project. It is, in fact, probably the oldest form of "literary criticism" in the world, known as rhetoric. Rhetoric, which was the received form of critical analysis all the way from ancient society to the eighteenth century, examined the way discourses are constructed in order to achieve certain effects. It was not worried about whether its objects of inquiry were speaking or writing, poetry or philosophy, fiction or historiography: its horizon was nothing less than the field of discursive practices in society as a whole, and its particular interest lay in grasping such practices as forms of power and performance. This is not to say that it ignored the truth-value of the discourses in question, since this could often be crucially relevant to the kinds of effect they produced in their readers and listeners. Rhetoric in its major phase was neither a "humanism," concerned in some intuitive way with people's experience of language, nor a "formalism," preoccupied simply with analyzing linguistic devices. It looked at such devices in terms of concrete performance—they were means of pleading, persuading, inciting and so on—and at people's responses to discourse in terms of linguistic structures and the material situations in which they functioned. It saw speaking and writing not merely as textual objects, to be aesthetically contemplated or endlessly deconstructed, but as forms of *activity* inseparable from the wider social relations between writers and readers, orators and audiences, and as largely unintelligible outside the social purposes and conditions in which they were embedded.

Like all the best radical positions, then, mine is a thoroughly traditionalist one. I wish to recall literary criticism from certain fashionable, new-fangled ways of thinking it has been seduced by—"literature" as a specially privileged object, the "aesthetic" as separable from social determinants, and so on—and return it to the ancient paths which it has abandoned. Although my case is thus reactionary, I do not mean that we should revive the whole range of ancient rhetorical terms and substitute these for modern critical language. We do not need to do this, since there are enough concepts contained in the literary theories examined in this book to allow us at least to make a start. Rhetoric, or discourse theory, shares with Formalism, structuralism and semiotics an interest in the formal devices of language, but like reception theory is also concerned with how these devices are actually effective at the point of "consumption"; its preoccupation with discourse as a form of power and desire can learn much from deconstruction and psychoanalytical theory, and its belief that discourse can be a humanly transformative affair shares a good deal with liberal humanism. The fact that "literary theory" is an illusion does not mean that we cannot retrieve from it many valuable concepts for a different kind of discursive practice altogether.

There was, of course, a reason why rhetoric bothered to analyze discourses. It did not analyze them just because they were there, any more than most forms of literary criticism today examine literature just for the sake of it. Rhetoric wanted to find out the most effective ways of pleading, persuading and debating, and rhetoricians studied such devices in other people's language in order to use them more productively in their own. It was, as we would say today, a "creative" as well as a "critical" activity: the word "rhetoric" covers both the practice of effective discourse and the science of it. Similarly, there must be a reason why we would consider it worthwhile to develop a form of study which would look at the various sign-systems and signifying practices in our own society, all the way from *Moby Dick* to the Muppet show, from Dryden and Jean-Luc Goddard to the portrayal of women in advertisements and the rhetorical techniques of Government reports. All theory and knowledge, as I have argued previously, is "interested," in the sense that you can always ask why one should bother to develop it in the first place. One striking weakness of most formalist and structuralist criticism is that it is unable to answer this question. The structuralist really does examine sign-systems because they happen to be there, or if this seems indefensible is forced into some rationale—studying our modes of sense-making will deepen our critical self-awareness—which is not much different from the standard line of the liberal humanists. The strength of the liberal humanist case, by contrast, is that it is able to say why dealing with literature is worth while. Its answer, as we have seen, is roughly that it makes you a better person. This is also the weakness of the liberal humanist case.

The liberal humanist response, however, is not weak because it believes that literature can be transformative. It is weak because it usually grossly overestimates this transformative power, considers it in isolation from any determining social context, and can formulate what it means by a "better person" only in the most narrow and abstract of terms. They are terms which generally ignore the fact that to be a person in the Western society of the 1980s is to be bound up with, and in some sense responsible for, the kinds of political conditions which I began this Conclusion by outlining. Liberal humanism is a suburban moral ideology, limited in practice to largely interpersonal matters. It is stronger on adultery than on armaments, and its valuable concern with freedom, democracy and individual rights are simply not concrete enough. Its view of democracy, for example, is the abstract one of the ballot box, rather than a specific, living and practical democracy which might also somehow concern the operations of the Foreign Office and Standard Oil. Its view of individual freedom is similarly abstract: the freedom of any particular individual is crippled and parasitic as long as it depends on the futile labour and active oppression of others. Literature may protest against such conditions or it may not, but it is only possible in the first place because of them. As the German critic Walter Benjamin put it: "There is no cultural document that is not at the same time a record of barbarism." Socialists are those who wish to draw the full, concrete, practical applications of the abstract notions of freedom and democracy to which liberal humanism subscribes, taking them at their word when they draw attention to the "vividly particular." It is for this reason that many Western socialists are restless with the liberal humanist opinion of the tyrannies in Eastern Europe, feeling that these opinions simply do not go far enough: what would be necessary to bring down such tyrannies would not be just more free speech, but a workers' revolution against the state.

What it means to be a "better person," then, must be concrete and practical—that is to say, concerned with people's political situations as a whole—rather than narrowly abstract, concerned only with the immediate interpersonal relations which can be abstracted from this concrete whole. It must be a question of political and not only of "moral" argument: that is to say, it must be *genuine* moral argument, which sees the relations between individual qualities and values and our whole material conditions of existence. Political argument is not an alternative to moral preoccupations: it is those preoccupations taken seriously in their full implications. But the liberal humanists are right to see that there is a *point* in studying literature, and that this point is not itself, in the end, a literary one. What they are arguing, although this way of putting it would grate harshly on their ears, is that literature has a *use*. Few words are more offensive to literary ears than "use," evoking as it does paperclips and hairdryers. The Romantic opposition to the utilitarian ideology of capitalism has made "use" an unusable word: for the aesthetes, the glory of art is its utter uselessness. Yet few of us nowadays would be prepared to subscribe to *that:* every reading of a work is surely in some sense a use of it. We may not use *Moby Dick* to learn how to hunt whales, but we "get something out of it" even so. Every literary theory presupposes a certain use of literature, even if what you get out of it is its utter uselessness. Liberal humanist criticism is not wrong to use literature, but wrong to deceive itself that it does not. It uses it to further certain moral values, which as I hope to have shown are in fact indissociable from certain ideological ones, and in the end imply a particular form of politics. It is not that it reads the texts "disinterestedly" and then places what it has read in the service of its values: the values govern the actual reading process itself, inform what sense criticism makes of the works it studies. I am not going to argue, then, for a "political criticism" which would read literary texts in the light of certain values which are related to political beliefs and actions; all criticism does this. The idea that there are "non-political" forms of criticism is simply a myth which furthers certain political uses of literature all the more effectively. The difference between a "political" and "non-political" criticism is just the difference between the prime minister and the monarch: the latter furthers certain political ends by pretending not to, while the former makes no bones about it. It is always better to be honest in these matters. The difference between a conventional critic who speaks of the "chaos of experience" in Conrad or Woolf, and the feminist who examines those writers' images of gender, is not a distinction between non-political and political criticism. It is a distinction between different forms of politics—between those who subscribe to the doctrine that history, society and human reality as a whole are fragmentary, arbitrary and directionless, and those who have other interests which imply alternative views about the way the world is. There is no way of settling the question of which politics is preferable in literary critical terms. You simply have to argue about politics. It is not a question of debating whether "literature" should be related to "history" or not: it is a question of different readings of history itself.

The feminist critic is not studying representations of gender simply because she believes that this will further her political ends. She also believes that gender and sexuality are central themes in literature and other sorts of discourse, and that any critical account which suppresses them is seriously defective. Similarly, the socialist critic does not see literature in terms of ideology or class-struggle because these happen to be his or her political interests, arbitrarily projected on to literary works. He or she would hold that such matters are the very stuff of history, and that in so far as literature is an historical phenomenon, they are the very stuff of literature too. What would be strange would be if the feminist or socialist critic thought analyzing questions of gender or class was merely a matter of academic interest—merely a question of achieving a more satisfyingly complete account of literature. For why should it be worth doing this? Liberal humanist critics are not merely out for a more complete account of literature: they wish to discuss literature in ways which will deepen, enrich and extend our lives. Socialist and feminist critics are quite at one with them on this: it is just that they wish to point out that such deepening and enriching entails the transformation of a society divided by class and gender. They would like the liberal humanist to draw the full implications of his or her position. If the liberal humanist disagrees, then this is a political argument, not an argument about whether one is "using" literature or not.

I argued earlier that any attempt to define the study of literature in terms of either its method or its object is bound to fail. But we have now begun to discuss another way of conceiving what distinguishes one kind of discourse from another, which is neither ontological or methodological but *strategic*. This means asking first not *what* the object is or *how* we should approach it, but *why* we should want to engage with it in the first place. The liberal humanist response to this question, I have suggested, is at once perfectly reasonable and, as it stands, entirely useless. Let us try to concretize it a little by asking how the reinvention of rhetoric that I have proposed (though it might equally as well be called "discourse theory" or "cultural studies" or whatever) might contribute to making us all better people. Discourses, sign-systems and signifying practices of all kinds, from film and television to fiction and the languages of natural science, produce effects, shape forms of consciousness and unconsciousness, which are closely related to the maintenance or transformation of our existing systems of power. They are thus closely related to what it means to be a person. Indeed "ideology" can be taken to indicate no more than this connection—the link or nexus between discourses and power. Once we have seen this, then the questions of theory and method may be allowed to appear in a new light. It is not a matter of starting from certain theoretical or methodological problems: it is a matter of starting from what we want to *do,* and then seeing which methods and theories will best help us to achieve these ends. Deciding on your strategy will not pre-determine which methods and objects of study are most valuable. As far as the object of study goes, what you decide to examine depends very much on the practical situation. It may seem best to look at Proust and *King Lear,* or at children's television programmes or popular romances or avant-garde films. A radical critic is quite liberal on these questions: he rejects the dogmatism which would insist that Proust is always more worthy of study than television advertisements. It all depends on what you are trying to do, in what situation. Radical critics are also open-minded about questions of theory and method: they tend to be pluralists in this respect. Any method or theory which will contribute to the strategic goal of human emancipation, the production of "better people" through the socialist transformation of society, is acceptable. Structuralism, semiotics, psychoanalysis, deconstruction, reception theory and so on: all of these approaches, and others, have their valuable insights which may be put to use. Not all literary theories, however, are likely to prove amenable to the strategic goals in question: there are several examined in this book which seem to me highly unlikely to do so. What you choose and reject theoretically, then, depends upon what you are practically trying to do. This has always been the case with literary criticism: it is simply that it is often very reluctant to realize the fact. In any academic study we select the objects and methods of procedure which we believe the most important, and our assessment of their importance is governed by frames of interest deeply rooted in our practical forms of social life. Radical critics are no different in this respect: it is just that they have a set of social priorities with which most people at present tend to disagree. This is why they are commonly dismissed as "ideological," because "ideology" is always a way of describing other people's interests rather than one's own.

No theory or method, in any case, will have merely one strategic use. They can be mobilized in a variety of different strategies for a variety of ends. But not all methods will be equally amenable to particular ends. It is a matter of finding out, not of assuming from the start that a single method or theory will do. One reason why I have not ended this book with an account of socialist or feminist literary theory is that I believe such a move might encourage the reader to make what the philosophers call a "category mistake." It might mislead people into thinking that "political criticism" was another sort of critical approach from those I have discussed, different in its assumptions, but essentially the same kind of thing. Since I have made clear my view that all criticism is in some sense political, and since people tend to give the word "political" to criticism whose politics disagrees with their own, this cannot be so. Socialist and feminist criticism are, of course, concerned with developing theories and methods appropriate to their aims: they consider questions of the relations between writing and sexuality, or of text and ideology, as other theories in general do not. They will also want to claim that these theories are more powerfully explanatory than others, for if they were not there would be no point in advancing them as theories. But it would be a mistake to see the particularity of such forms of criticism as consisting in the offering of alternative theories or methods. These forms of criticism differ from others because they define the object of analysis differently, have different values, beliefs and goals, and thus offer different kinds of strategy for the realizing of these goals.

I say "goals" because it should not be thought that this form of criticism has only one. There are many goals to be achieved, and many ways of achieving them. In some situations the most productive procedure may be to explore how the signifying systems of a "literary" text produce certain ideological effects; or it may be a matter of doing the same with a Hollywood film. Such projects may prove particularly important in teaching cultural studies to children; but it may also be valuable to use literature to foster in them a sense of linguistic potential denied to them by their social conditions. There are "utopian" uses of literature of this kind, and a rich tradition of such utopian thought which should not be airily dismissed as "idealist." The active enjoyment of cultural artifacts should not, however, be relegated to the primary school, leaving older students with the grimmer business of analysis. Pleasure, enjoyment, the potentially transformative effects of discourse is quite as "proper" a topic for "higher" study as is the setting of puritan tracts in the discursive formations of the seventeenth century. On other occasions what might prove more useful will not be the criticism or enjoyment of other people's discourse but the production of one's own. Here, as with the rhetorical tradition, studying what other people have done may help. You may want to stage your own signifying practices to enrich, combat, modify or transform the effects which others' practices produce.

Within all of this varied activity, the study of what is currently termed "literature" will have its place. But it should not be taken as an *a priori* assumption that what is currently termed "literature" will always and everywhere be the most important focus of attention. Such dogmatism has no place in the field of cultural study. Nor are the texts now dubbed "literature" likely to be perceived and defined as they are now, once they are returned to the broader and deeper discursive formations of which they are part. They will be inevitably "rewritten," recycled, put to different uses, inserted into different relations and practices. They always have been, of course; but one effect of the word "literature" is to prevent us from recognizing this fact.

Such a strategy obviously has far-reaching institutional implications. It would mean, for example, that departments of literature as we presently know them in higher education would cease to exist. Since the government, as I write, seems on the point of achieving this end more quickly and effec-tively than I could myself, it is necessary to add that the first political priority for those who have doubts about the ideological implications of such departmental organizations is to defend them unconditionally against gov-ernment assaults. But this priority cannot mean refusing to contemplate how we might better organize literary studies in the longer term. The ideo-logical effects of such departments lie not only in the particular values they disseminate, but in their implicit and actual dislocation of "literature" from other cultural and social practices. The churlish admission of such practices as literary "background" need not detain us: "background," with its static, distancing connotations, tells its own story. Whatever would in the long term replace such departments—and the proposal is a modest one, for such experiments are already under way in certain areas of higher education— would centrally involve education in the various theories and methods of cultural analysis. The fact that such education is not routinely provided by many existing departments of literature, or is provided "optionally" or marginally, is one of their most scandalous and farcical features. (Perhaps their other most scandalous and farcical feature is the largely wasted energy which postgraduate students are required to pour into obscure, often spuri-ous research topics in order to produce dissertations which are frequently no more than sterile academic exercises, and which few others will ever read.) The genteel amateurism which regards criticism as some spontaneous sixth sense has not only thrown many students of literature into understand-able confusion for many decades, but serves to consolidate the authority of those in power. If criticism is no more than a knack, like being able to whis-tle and hum different tunes simultaneously, then it is at once rare enough to be preserved in the hands of an elite, while "ordinary" enough to require no stringent theoretical justification. Exactly the same pincer movement is at work in English "ordinary language" philosophy. But the answer is not to replace such dishevelled amateurism with a well-groomed professionalism intent on justifying itself to the disgusted taxpayer. Such professionalism, as we have seen, is equally bereft of any social validation of its activities, since it cannot say why it should bother with literature at all other than to tidy it up, drop texts into their appropriate categories and then move over into marine biology. If the point of criticism is not to interpret literary works but to master in some disinterested spirit the underlying sign-systems which generate them, what is criticism to do once it has achieved this mastery, which will hardly take a lifetime and probably not much more than a few years?

The present crisis in the field of literary studies is at root a crisis in the definition of the subject itself. That it should prove difficult to provide such a definition is, as I hope to have shown in this book, hardly surprising. Nobody is likely to be dismissed from an academic job for trying on a little semiotic analysis of Edmund Spenser; they are likely to be shown the door, or refused entry through it in the first place, if they question whether the "tradition" from Spenser to Shakespeare and Milton is the best or only way of carving up discourse into a syllabus. It is at this point that the canon is trundled out to blast offenders out of the literary arena.

Those who work in the field of cultural practices are unlikely to mistake their activity as utterly central. Men and women do not live by culture alone; the vast majority of them throughout history have been deprived of the chance of living by it at all, and those few who are fortunate enough to live by it now are able to do so because of the labour of those who do not. Any cultural or critical theory which does not begin from this single most important fact, and hold it steadily in mind in its activities, is in my view unlikely to be worth very much. There is no document of culture which is not also a record of barbarism. But even in societies which, like our own as Marx reminded us, have no time for culture, there are times and places when it suddenly becomes newly relevant, charged with a significance beyond itself. Four such major moments are evident in our own world. Culture, in the lives of nations struggling for their independence from imperialism, has a meaning quite remote from the review pages of the Sunday newspapers. Imperialism is not only the exploitation of cheap labour-power, raw materials and easy markets but the uprooting of languages and customs—not just the imposition of foreign armies, but of alien ways of experiencing. It manifests itself not only in company balance-sheets and in airbases, but can be tracked to the most intimate roots of speech and signification. In such situations, which are not all a thousand miles from our own doorstep, culture is so vitally bound up with one's common identity that there is no need to argue for its relation to political struggle. It is arguing against it which would seem incomprehensible.

The second area where cultural and political action have become closely united is in the women's movement. It is in the nature of feminist politics that signs and images, written and dramatized experience, should be of special significance. Discourse in all its forms is an obvious concern for feminists, either as places where women's oppression can be deciphered, or as places where it can be challenged. In any politics which puts identity and relationship centrally at stake, renewing attention to lived experience and the discourse of the body, culture does not need to argue its way to political relevance. Indeed one of the achievements of the women's movement has been to redeem such phrases as "lived experience" and "the discourse of the body" from the empiricist connotations with which much literary theory has invested them. "Experience" need now no longer signify an appeal away from power-systems and social relations to the privileged certainties of the private, for feminism recognizes no such distinction between questions of the human subject and questions of political struggle. The discourse of the body is not a matter of Lawrentian ganglions and suave loins of darkness, but a *politics* of the body, a rediscovery of its sociality through an awareness of the forces which control and subordinate it.

The third area in question is the "culture industry." While literary critics have been cultivating sensibility in a minority, large segments of the media have been busy trying to devastate it in the majority; yet it is still presumed that studying, say, Gray and Collins is inherently more important than examining television or the popular press. Such a project differs from the two I have outlined already in its essentially defensive character: it represents a critical reaction to someone else's culture ideology rather than an appropriation of culture for one's own ends. Yet it is a vital project nevertheless, which must not be surrendered to a melancholic Left or Right mythology of the media as impregnably monolithic. We know that people do not after all believe all that they see and read; but we also need to know much more than we do about the role such effects play in their general consciousness, even though such critical study should be seen, politically, as no more than a holding operation. The democratic control of these ideological apparatuses, along with popular alternatives to them, must be high on the agenda of any future socialist programme.

The fourth and final area is that of the strongly emergent movement of working-class writing. Silenced for generations, taught to regard literature as a coterie activity beyond their grasp, working people over the past decade in Britain have been actively organizing to find their own literary styles and voices. The worker writers' movement is almost unknown to academia, and has not been exactly encouraged by the cultural organs of the state; but it is one sign of a significant break from the dominant relations of literary production. Community and cooperative publishing enterprises are associated projects, concerned not simply with a literature wedded to alternative social values, but with one which challenges and changes the existing social relations between writers, publishers, readers and other literary workers. It is because such ventures interrogate the ruling *definitions* of literature that they cannot so easily be incorporated by a literary institution quite happy to welcome *Sons and Lovers,* and even, from time to time, Robert Tressell.

These areas are not alternatives to the study of Shakespeare and Proust. If the study of such writers could become as charged with energy, urgency and enthusiasm as the activities I have just reviewed, the literary institution ought to rejoice rather than complain. But it is doubtful that this will happen when such texts are hermetically sealed from history, subjected to a sterile critical formalism, piously swaddled with eternal verities and used to confirm prejudices which any moderately enlightened student can perceive to be objectionable. The liberation of Shakespeare and Proust from such controls may well entail the death of literature, but it may also be their redemption.

I shall end with an allegory. *We* know that the lion is stronger than the lion-tamer, and so does the lion-tamer. The problem is that the lion does not know it. It is not out of the question that the death of literature may help the lion to awaken.

E. D. HIRSCH, JR.
b. 1928

Educated at Cornell and Yale Universities, E. D. Hirsch is best known as an educational reformer. After a long career in literary studies and a recognized book on literary criticism, Validity in Interpretation *(1967), he expressed his intention to join the rhetoric and composition discourse community with* The Philosophy of Composition *(1977). Since then, he has involved himself in various assessment and literary projects, most notably by becoming president of the Cultural Literacy Foundation in 1987. Hirsch has been regularly attacked not so much for his basic views about cultural literacy, but for the list of essentials appended to his* Cultural Literacy: What Every American Needs To Know *(1987).*

Cultural Literacy

For the past twelve years I have been pursuing technical research in the teaching of reading and writing. I now wish to emerge from my closet to declare that technical research is not going to remedy the national decline in our literacy that is documented in the decline of verbal SAT scores. We already know enough about methodology to do a good job of teaching reading and writing. Of course we would profit from knowing still more about teaching methods, but better teaching techniques alone would produce only a marginal improvement in the literacy of our students. Raising their reading and writing levels will depend far less on our methods of instruction (there are many acceptable methods) than on the specific contents of our school curricula. Commonsensical as this proposition might seem to the man in the street, it is regarded as heresy by many (I hope by ever fewer) professional educators. The received and dominant view of educational specialists is that the specific materials of reading and writing instruction are interchangeable so long as they are "appropriate," and of "high quality."

But consider this historical fact. The national decline in our literacy has accompanied a decline in our use of common, nationwide materials in the subject most closely connected with literacy, "English." From the 1890s to 1900 we taught in English courses what amounted to a national core curriculum. As Arthur Applebee observes in his excellent book *Tradition and Reform in the Teaching of English*, the following texts were used in those days in more than 25 percent of our schools: *The Merchant of Venice, Julius Caesar,* "First Bunker Hill Oration," *The Sketch Book, Evangeline,* "The Vision of Sir Launfal," "Snow-Bound," *Macbeth,* "The Lady of the Lake,"

Hamlet, "The Deserted Village," Gray's "Elegy," "Thanatopsis," *As You Like It.* Other widely used works will strike a resonance in those who are over fifty: "The Courtship of Miles Standish," "Il Penseroso," *Paradise Lost,* "L'Allegro," "Lycidas," *Ivanhoe, David Copperfield, Silas Marner,* etc., etc. Then in 1901 the College Entrance Examination Board issued its first "uniform lists" of texts required to be known by students in applying to colleges. This core curriculum, though narrower, became even more widespread than the earlier canon. Lest anyone assume that I shall urge a return to those particular texts, let me at once deny it. By way of introducing my subject, I simply want to claim that the decline in our literacy and the decline in the commonly shared knowledge that we acquire in school are causally related facts. Why this should be so and what we might do about it are my twin subjects.

That a decline in our national level of literacy has occurred few will seriously doubt. The chief and decisive piece of evidence for it is the decline in verbal SAT scores among the white middle class. (This takes into account the still greater lowering of scores caused by an increased proportion of poor and minority students taking the tests.) Now scores on the verbal SAT show a high correlation with reading and writing skills that have been tested independently by other means. So, as a rough index to the literacy levels of our students, the verbal SAT is a reliable guide. That is unsurprising if we accept the point made by John Carroll and others that the verbal SAT is chiefly a vocabulary test, for no one is surprised by a correlation between a rich vocabulary and a high level of literacy. A rich vocabulary is not a purely technical or rote-learnable skill. Knowledge of words is an adjunct to knowledge of cultural realities signified by words, and to whole domains of experience to which words refer. Specific words go with specific knowledge. And when we begin to contemplate how to teach specific knowledge, we are led back inexorably to the contents of the school curriculum, whether or not those contents are linked, as they used to be, to specific texts.

From the start of our national life, the school curriculum has been an especially important formative element of our national culture. In the schools we not only tried to harmonize the various traditions of our parent cultures, we also wanted to strike out on our own within the dominant British heritage. Being rebellious children, we produced our own dictionary, and were destined, according to Melville, to produce our own Shakespeare. In this self-conscious job of culture making, the schools played a necessary role. That was especially true in the teaching of history and English, the two subjects central to culture making. In the nineteenth century we held national conferences on school curricula. We formed the College Board, which created the "uniform lists" already referred to. The dominant symbol for the role of the school was the symbol of the melting pot.

But from early times we have also resisted this narrow uniformity in our culture. The symbol of the melting pot was opposed by the symbol of the stew pot, where our national ingredients kept their individual characteristics and contributed to the flavor and vitality of the whole. That is the doctrine of pluralism. It has now become the dominant doctrine in our schools, especially in those subjects, English and history, that are closest to culture making. In math and science, by contrast, there is wide agreement about the contents of a common curriculum. But in English courses, diversity and pluralism now reign without challenge. I am persuaded that if we want to achieve a more literate culture than we now have, we shall need to restore the balance between these two equally American traditions of unity and diversity. We shall need to restore certain common contents to the humanistic side of the school curriculum. But before we can make much headway in that direction, we shall also need to modify the now-dominant educational principle that holds that any suitable materials of instruction can be used to teach the skills of reading and writing. I call this the doctrine of educational formalism.

The current curriculum guide to the study of English in the state of California is a remarkable document. In its several pages of advice to teachers I do not find the title of a single recommended work. Such "curricular guides" are produced on the theory that the actual contents of English courses are simply vehicles for inculcating formal skills, and that contents can be left to local choice. But wouldn't even a dyed-in-the-wool formalist concede that teachers might be saved time if some merely illustrative, non-compulsory titles were listed? Of course; but another doctrine, in alliance with formalism, conspires against even that concession to content—the doctrine of pluralism. An illustrative list put out by the state would imply official sanction of the cultural and ideological values expressed by the works on the list. The California Education Department is not in the business of imposing cultures and ideologies. Its business is to inculcate "skills" and "positive self-concepts," regardless of the students' cultural backgrounds. The contents of English should be left to local communities.

This is an attractive theory to educators in those places where spokesmen for minority cultures are especially vocal in their attack on the melting-pot idea. That concept, they say, is nothing but cultural imperialism (true), which submerges cultural identities (true) and gives minority children a sense of inferiority (often true). In recent years such attitudes have led to attacks on teaching school courses exclusively in standard English; in the bilingual movement (really a monolingual movement) it has led to attacks on an exclusive use of the English language for instruction. This kind of political pressure has encouraged a retreat to the extreme and untenable educational formalism reflected in the California curriculum guide.

What the current controversies have really demonstrated is a truth that is quite contrary to the spirit of neutrality implied by educational formalism.

Literacy is not just a formal skill; it is also a political decision. The decision to *want* a literate society is a value-laden one that carries costs as well as advantages. English teachers by profession are committed to the ideology of literacy. They cannot successfully avoid the political implications of that ideology by hiding behind the skirts of methodology and research. Literacy implies specific contents as well as formal skills. Extreme formalism is misleading and evasive. But allow me to illustrate that point with some specific examples.

During most of the time that I was pursuing research in literacy I was, like others in the field, a confirmed formalist. In 1977 I came out with a book on the subject, *The Philosophy of Composition,* that was entirely formalistic in outlook. One of my arguments, for instance, was that the effectiveness of English prose as an instrument of communication gradually increased, after the invention of printing, through a trial-and-error process that slowly uncovered some of the psycholinguistic principles of efficient communication in prose. I suggested that freshmen could learn in a semester what earlier writers had taken centuries to achieve, if they were directly taught those underlying psycholinguistic principles. (With respect to certain formal structures of clauses, this idea still seems valid.) I predicted further that we could learn how to teach those formal principles still more effectively if we pursued appropriately controlled pedagogical research.

So intent was I upon this idea that I undertook some arduous research into one of the most important aspects of writing pedagogy—evaluation. After all, in order to decide upon the best methods of inculcating the skills of writing, it was essential to evaluate the results of using the different teaching methods. For that we needed non-arbitrary, reliable techniques for evaluating student writing. In my book I had made some suggestions about how we might do this, and those ideas seemed cogent enough to a National Endowment for the Humanities panel to get me a grant to go forward with the research. For about two years I was deeply engaged in this work. It was this detailed engagement with the realities of reading and writing under controlled conditions that caused me finally to abandon my formalistic assumptions. (Later I discovered that experimentation on a much bigger scale had brought Richard C. Anderson, the premier scholar in reading research, to similar conclusions.)

The experiments that changed my mind were, briefly, these: To get a non-arbitrary evaluation of writing, we decided to base our evaluations on actual audience effects. We devised a way of comparing the effects of well-written and badly written versions of the same paper. Our method was to pair off two large groups of readers (about a hundred in each group), each of which, when given the *same* piece of writing, would read it collectively with the same speed and comprehension. In other words, we matched the reading skills of these two large groups. Then, when one group was given a good version and the other given a degraded version, we measured the overall effect of these stylistic differences on speed and accuracy of comprehension. To our delight, we discovered that good style did make an appreciable difference, and that the degree of difference was replicable and predictable. So far so good. But what became very disconcerting about these results was that they came out properly only when the subjects of the papers were highly familiar to our audiences. When, later in the experiments, we introduced unfamiliar materials, the results were not only messy, they were "counterintuitive," the term of art for results that go against one's expectations. (Real scientists generally like to get counterintuitive results, but we were not altogether disinterested onlookers and were dismayed.) For what we discovered was that good writing makes very little difference when the subject is unfamiliar. We English teachers tend to believe that a good style is all the more helpful when the content is difficult, but it turns out that we are wrong. The reasons for this unexpected result are complex, and I will not pause to discuss them at length, since the important issues lie elsewhere.

Briefly, good style contributes little to our reading of unfamiliar material because we must continually backtrack to test out different hypotheses about what is being meant or referred to. Thus, a reader of a text about Grant and Lee who is unsure just who Grant and Lee are would have to get clues from later parts of the text, and then go back to re-read earlier parts in the light of surer conjectures. This trial-and-error backtracking with unfamiliar material is so much more time-consuming than the delays caused by a bad style alone that style begins to lose its importance as a factor in reading unfamiliar material. The contribution of style in such cases can no longer be measured with statistical confidence.

The significance of this result is, first of all, that one cannot, even in principle, base writing evaluations on audience effects—the only nonarbitrary principle that makes any sense. The reading skill of an audience is not a constant against which prose can be reliably measured. Audience reading skills vary unpredictably with the subject matter of the text. Although we were trying to measure our prose samples with the yardstick of paired audiences, the contrary had, in effect, occurred; our carefully contrived prose samples were measuring the background knowledge of our audiences. For instance, if the subject of a text was "Friendship," all audience pairs, everywhere we gave the trials, exhibited the same differentials. Also, for all audiences, if the subject was "Hegel's Metaphysics," the differential between good and bad writing tended to disappear. Also, so long as we used university audiences, a text on Grant and Lee gave the same sort of appropriate results as did a text on friendship. But for one community college audience (in, no less, Richmond, Virginia) "Grant and Lee" turned out to be as unfamiliar as "Hegel's Metaphysics"—a complacency-shattering result.

While the variability of reading skills within the same person was making itself disconcertingly known to me, I learned that similar variability was showing up in formal writing skills—and for the same reasons. Researchers at the City University of New York were finding that when a topic is unfamiliar, writing skill declines in all of its dimensions—including grammar and spelling—not to mention sentence structure, parallelism, unity, focus, and other skills taught in writing courses. One part of the explanation for such results is that we all have limited attention space, and cannot pay much heed to form when we are devoting a lot of our attention to unfamiliar content. But another part of the explanation is more interesting. Part of our skill in reading and in writing is skill not just with linguistic structures but with words. Words are not purely formal counters of language; they represent large underlying domains of content. Part of language skill is content skill. As Apeneck Sweeney profoundly observed: "I gotta use words when I talk to you."

When I therefore assert that reading and writing skills are content-bound, I mean also to make the corollary assertion that important aspects of reading and writing skills are *not* transferable. Of course some skills *are* carried over from task to task; we know that broad strategies of reading and writing can become second nature, and thereby facilitate literary skills at all levels. But the content-indifferent, how-to approach to literacy skills is enormously oversimplified. As my final example of this, I shall mention an ingenious experiment conducted by Richard C. Anderson and his colleagues at the University of Illinois. It, too, was an experiment with paired audiences and paired texts. The texts were two letters, each describing a wedding, each of similar length, word-familiarity, sentence complexity, and number of idea units. Each audience group was similarly paired according to age, educational level, marital status, sex, professional specialty, etc. Structurally speaking, the texts were similar and the audiences were similar. The crucial variables were these: one letter described a wedding in America, the other a wedding in India. One audience was American, the other Indian. Both audiences read both letters. The results were that the reading skills of the two groups—their speed and accuracy of comprehension—were very different in reading the two linguistically similar letters. The Americans read about an American wedding skillfully, accurately, and with good recall. They did poorly with the letter about the Indian wedding. The reverse was the case with the group of Indian readers. Anderson and his colleagues concluded that reading is not just a linguistic skill, but involves translinguistic knowledge beyond the abstract sense of words. They suggested that reading involves both "linguistic-schemata" (systems of expectation) and "content-schemata" as well. In short, the assumptions of educational formalism are incorrect.

Every writer is aware that the subtlety and complexity of what can be conveyed in writing depends on the amount of relevant tacit knowledge that can be assumed in readers. As psycholinguists have shown, the explicitly stated words on the page often represent the smaller part of the literary transaction. Some of this assumed knowledge involves such matters as generic conventions, that is, what to expect in a business letter, a technical report, a detective story, etc. An equally significant part of the assumed knowledge—often a more significant part—concerns tacit knowledge of the experiential realities embraced by the discourse. Not only have I gotta use words to talk to you, I gotta assume you know *something* about what I am saying. If I had to start from scratch, I couldn't start at all.

We adjust for this in the most casual talk. It has been shown that we always explain ourselves more fully to strangers than to intimates. But, when the strangers being addressed are some unknown collectivity to whom we are writing, how much shall we then need to explain? This was one of the most difficult authorial problems that arose with the advent of printing and mass literacy. Later on, in the eighteenth century, Dr. Johnson confidently assumed he could predict the knowledge possessed by a personage whom he called "the common reader." Some such construct is a necessary fiction for every writer in every literate culture and subculture. Even a writer for an astrophysics journal must assume a "common reader" for the subculture being addressed. A newspaper writer must also assume a "common reader" but for a much bigger part of the culture, perhaps for the literate culture as a whole. In our own culture, Jefferson wanted to create a highly informed "common reader," and he must have assumed the real existence of such a personage when he said he would prefer newspapers without government to government without newspapers. But, without appropriate, tacitly shared background knowledge, people cannot understand newspapers. A certain extent of shared, canonical knowledge is inherently necessary to a literate democracy.

For this canonical information I have proposed the term "cultural literacy." It is the translinguistic knowledge on which linguistic literacy depends. You cannot have the one without the other. Teachers of foreign languages are aware of this interdependency between linguistic proficiency and translinguistic, cultural knowledge. To get very far in reading or writing French, a student must come to know facets of French culture quite different from his own. By the same token, American children learning to read and write English get instruction in aspects of their own national culture that are as foreign to them as French. National culture always has this "foreignness" with respect to family culture alone. School materials contain unfamiliar materials that promote the "acculturation" that is a universal part of growing up in any tribe or nation. Acculturation into a national literate culture might be defined as learning what the "common reader" of a newspaper in a literate culture could be expected to know. That would include knowledge of certain values (whether or not one accepted them), and knowledge of such things as (for example) the First Amendment, Grant and Lee, and DNA. In our own culture, what should these contents be? Surely our answer to that should partly define our school curriculum. Acculturation into a literate culture (the minimal aim of schooling; we should aim still higher) could be defined as the gaining of cultural literacy.

Such canonical knowledge could not be fixed once and for all. "Grant and Lee" could not have been part of it in 1840, or "DNA" in 1940. The canon changeth. And in our media-paced era, it might change from month to month—faster at the edges, more slowly at the center, and some of its contents would be connected to events beyond our control. But much of it is within our control and is part of our traditional task of culture making. One reassuring feature of our responsibilities as makers of culture is the implicit and automatic character of most canonical cultural knowledge; we get it through the pores. Another reassuring aspect is its vagueness. How much do I *really* have to know about DNA in order to comprehend a newspaper text directed to the common reader? Not much. Such vagueness in our background knowledge is a feature of cultural literacy that Hilary Putnam has analyzed brilliantly as "the division of linguistic labor." An immensely literate person, Putnam claims that he does not know the difference between a beech tree and an elm. Still, when reading those words he gets along acceptably well because he knows that under the division of linguistic labor somebody in the culture could supply more precise knowledge if it should be needed. Putnam's observation suggests that the school curriculum can be vague enough to leave plenty of room for local choice regarding what things shall be studied in detail, and what things shall be touched on just far enough to get us by. This vagueness in cultural literacy permits a reasonable compromise between lockstep, Napoleonic prescription of texts on the one side, and extreme laissez-faire pluralism on the other. Between these two extremes we have a national responsibility to take stock of the contents of schooling.

Although I have argued that a literate society depends upon shared information, I have said little about what that information should be. That is chiefly a political question. Estimable cultures exist that are ignorant of Shakespeare and the First Amendment. Indeed, estimable cultures exist that are entirely ignorant of reading and writing. On the other hand, no culture exists that is ignorant of its own traditions. In a literate society, culture and cultural literacy are nearly synonymous terms. American culture, always large and heterogeneous, and increasingly lacking a common acculturative curriculum, is perhaps getting fragmented enough to lose its coherence as a culture. Television is perhaps our only national curriculum, despite the justified complaints against it as a partial cause of the literacy decline. My hunch is that this complaint is overstated. The decline in literacy skills, I have suggested, is mainly a result of cultural fragmentation. Within black culture, for instance, blacks are more literate than whites, a point that was demonstrated by Robert L. Williams, as I learned from a recent article on the SAT by Jay Amberg (*The American Scholar,* Autumn 1982). The big political question that has to be decided first of all is whether we *want* a broadly literate culture that unites our cultural fragments enough to allow us to write to one another and read what our fellow citizens have written. Our traditional, Jeffersonian answer has been yes. But even if that political decision remains the dominant one, as I very much hope, we still face the much more difficult political decision of choosing the contents of cultural literacy.

The answer to this question is not going to be supplied by theoretical speculation and educational research. It will be worked out, if at all, by discussion, argument, and compromise. Professional educators have understandably avoided this political arena. Indeed, educators should *not* be left to decide so momentous an issue as the canonical contents of our culture. Within a democracy, educational technicians do not want and should not be awarded the function that Plato reserved for philosopher kings. But who is making such decisions at a national level? Nobody, I fear, because we are transfixed by the twin doctrines of pluralism and formalism.

Having made this technical point where I have some expertise, I must now leave any pretense of authority, except as a parent and citizen. The question of guidance for our national school curriculum is a political question on which I have only a citizen's opinion. For my own part, I wish we could have a National Board of Education on the pattern of the New York State Board of Regents—our most successful and admirable body for educational leadership. This imposing body of practical idealists is insulated by law from short-term demagogic pressures. It is a pluralistic group, too, with representation for minority as well as majority cultures. Its influence for good may be gauged by comparing the patterns of SAT scores in New York with those in California, two otherwise comparable states. To give just one example of the Regents' leadership in the field of writing, they have instituted a requirement that no New Yorker can receive a high school diploma before passing a statewide writing test that requires three types of prose composition.

Of course I am aware that the New York Regents have powers that no National Board in this country could possibly gain. But what a National Board could hope to achieve would be the respect of the country, a respect that could give it genuine influence over our schools. Such influence, based on leadership rather than compulsion, would be quite consistent with our federalist and pluralist principles. The Board, for instance, could present broad lists of suggested literary works for the different grades, lists broad enough to yield local freedom but also to yield a measure of commonality in our literary heritage. The teachers whom I know, while valuing their independence, are eager for intelligent guidance in such matters.

But I doubt that such a Curriculum Board would ever be established in this country. So strong is our suspicion of anything like a central "ministry of culture," that the Board is probably not a politically feasible idea. But perhaps a consortium of universities, or of national associations, or of foundations could make ongoing recommendations that arise from broadly based discussions of the national curriculum. In any case, we need leadership at the national level, and we need specific guidance.

It would be useful, for instance, to have guidance about the *words* that high school graduates ought to know—a lexicon of cultural literacy. I am thinking of a special sort of lexicon that would include not just ordinary dictionary words, but would also include proper names, important phrases, and conventions. Nobody likes word lists as objects of instruction; for one thing, they don't work. But I am not thinking of such a lexicon as an object of instruction. I am thinking of it rather as a guide to objects of instruction. Take the phrase "First Amendment," for instance. That is a lexical item that can hardly be used without bringing in a lot of associated information. Just what *are* the words and phrases that our school graduates should know? Right now, this seems to be decided by the makers of the SAT, which is, as I have mentioned, chiefly a vocabulary test. The educational technicians who choose the words that appear on the SAT are already the implicit makers of our national curriculum. Is then the Educational Testing Service our hidden National Board of Education? Does it sponsor our hidden national curriculum? If so, the ETS is rather to be praised than blamed. For if we wish to raise our national level of literacy, a hidden national curriculum is far better than no curriculum at all.

Where does this leave us? What issues are raised? If I am right in my interpretation of the evidence—and I have seen no alternative interpretation in the literature—then we can only raise our reading and writing skills significantly by consciously redefining and extending our cultural literacy. And yet our current national effort in the schools is largely run on the premise that the best way to proceed is through a culturally neutral, skills-approach to reading and writing. But if skill in writing and in reading comes about chiefly through what I have termed cultural literacy, then radical consequences follow. These consequences are not merely educational but social and political in their scope—and that scope is vast. I shall not attempt to set out these consequences here, but it will be obvious that acting upon them would involve our dismantling and casting aside the leading educational assumptions of the past half century.

WALTER R. **FISHER**

b. 1931

As a graduate student at the University of Iowa, where I earned my doctorate in 1960, I pursued ways of interpreting and assessing human communication compatible with the best thinking of the twentieth century, convinced at the same time that this could not be done by ignoring the best thought from previous ages. Examples of this effort include my essays, "A Motive View of Communication" (1970), where I sought to reformulate rhetorical genres, and "Toward a Logic of Good Reasons" (1978), in which I proposed a rational scheme for considering the reasonableness of values in human communication. This latter line of thinking led eventually to Human Communication as Narration: Toward a Philosophy of Reason, Value, and Action *(1987, 1989), which contains the fullest statement of what I call the narrative paradigm and its attendant logic, narrative rationality. Since the book appeared, I have applied these constructs in examinations of historical writing (a brief essay), community, and scientific discourse. I believe my work provides a logic not apparent in Kenneth Burke's writings and a more specific, useful logic than that offered by Chaim Perelman. My work can also be seen as a resistance to the insistence that human communication/human relations are to be understood best in regard to ideology, power, desire, language games, or totalitarian impulses that pervade discourse. I believe that these are real or potential forces in human transactions, but that their affirmation or actual appearance in practices do not escape the relevance of reason—to determine their truthfulness or merit for belief or action in specific rhetorical situations. My current interest is to extend my project to include ethics, which until now has been an implicit concern throughout my work.*

Narration as a Human Communication Paradigm: The Case of Public Moral Argument

The corrective of the scientific rationalization would seem necessarily to be a *rationale of art*—not, however, a performer's art, not a specialist's art for some to produce and many to observe, but an art in its widest aspects, an *art of living.*

Kenneth Burke

When I wrote "Toward a Logic of Good Reasons" (Fisher, 1978), I was unaware that I was moving toward an alternative paradigm for human communication. Indications of it are to be found in the assumption that *"Humans as rhetorical beings are as much valuing as they are reasoning animals"* (p. 376) and in the conception of good reasons as *"those elements that provide warrants for accepting or adhering to the advice fostered by any form of communication that can be considered rhetorical"* (p. 378). While the assumption does not seriously disturb the view of rhetoric as practical reasoning, the conception implies a stance that goes beyond this theory. The logic of good reasons maintains that reasoning need not be bound to argumentative prose or be expressed in clear-cut inferential or implicative structures: Reasoning may be discovered in all sorts of symbolic action—nondiscursive as well as discursive.

That this is the case was demonstrated in an exploration of argument in *Death of a Salesman* and *The Great Gatsby* (Fisher & Filloy, 1982). The authors concluded that these works provide good reasons to distrust the materialist myth of the American Dream (Fisher, 1973, p. 161), for what it requires to live by it and for what it does not necessarily deliver even if one lives by it "successfully." This finding confirms Gerald Graff's thesis that a theory or practice of literature that denies reference to the world, that denies that literature has cognitive as well as aesthetic significance, is a *Literature Against Itself* (Graff, 1979). In other words, "some dramatic and literary works do, in fact, argue" (Fisher & Filloy, 1982, p. 343).

The paradigm I was moving toward did not become entirely clear until I examined the current nuclear controversy, where the traditional view of rationality did not serve well, and I read Alasdair MacIntyre's *After Virtue: A Study in Moral Theory* (1981). What impressed me most about the book was the observation that "man is in his actions and practice, as well as in his fictions, essentially a story-telling animal" (p. 201). Given this view, "enacted dramatic narrative" (p. 200) is the "basic and essential genre for the characterization of human actions" (p. 194). These ideas are the foundation of the paradigm I am proposing—the narrative paradigm. Thus, when I use the term "narration," I do not mean a fictive composition whose propositions may be true or false and have no necessary relationship to the message of that composition. By "narration," I refer to a theory of symbolic actions—words and/or deeds—that have sequence and meaning for those who live, create, or interpret them. The narrative perspective, therefore, has relevance to real as well as fictive worlds, to stories of living and to stories of the imagination.

The narrative paradigm, then, can be considered a dialectical synthesis of two traditional strands in the history of rhetoric: the argumentative, persuasive theme and the literary, aesthetic theme. As will be seen, the narrative paradigm insists that human communication should be viewed as historical as well as situational, as stories competing with other stories constituted by good reasons, as being rational when they satisfy the demands of narrative probability and narrative fidelity, and as inevitably moral inducements. The narrative paradigm challenges the notions that human communication—if it is to be considered rhetorical—must be an argumentative form, that reason is to be attributed only to discourse marked by clearly identifiable modes of inference and/or implication, and that the norms for evaluation of rhetorical communication must be rational standards taken essentially from informal or formal logic. The narrative paradigm does not deny reason and rationality; it reconstitutes them, making them amenable to all forms of human communication.

Before going further, I should clarify the sense in which I use the term "paradigm." By paradigm, I refer to a representation designed to formalize the structure of a component of experience and to direct understanding and inquiry into the nature and functions of that experience—in this instance, the experience of human communication. Masterman designates this form of paradigm "metaphysical" or as a "metaparadigm" (1970, p. 65; see also Kuhn, 1974). Since the narrative paradigm does not entail a particular method of investigation, I have not used a designation that might be suggested: "narratism." The narrative perspective, however, does have a critical connection with "dramatism," which will be discussed later.

Consistent with Wayne Brockriede's concept of perspectivism (1982), I shall not maintain that the narrative paradigm is the only legitimate, useful way to appreciate human communication or that it will necessarily supplant the traditional rational paradigm of human decision-making and action. As already indicated, I will propose the narrative paradigm as an alternative view. I do not even claim that it is entirely "new." W. Lance Bennett has published a book with Martha S. Feldman, *Reconstructing Reality in the Courtroom* (1981), and two essays that directly bear on the present enterprise, one concerning political communication (Bennett, 1975) and one on legal communication (Bennett, 1978; see also, Farrell, 1983; Gallie, 1964; Hawes, 1978; Mink, 1978; Schrag, 1984; Scott, 1978; Simons, 1978). Except for these studies, I know of no other attempt to suggest narration as a paradigm. There is, of course, a tradition in rhetorical theory and pedagogy that focuses on narration as an element in discourse and as a genre in and of itself (e.g., Ochs & Burritt, 1973). In addition, there is an increasing number of investigations involving storytelling (e.g., Kirkwood, 1983). Here again, narration is conceived as a mode, not a paradigm, of communication.

The context for what is to follow would not be complete without recognition of the work done by theologians and those interested in religious discourse. The most recent works in this tradition include Goldberg (1982) and Hauerwas (1981). It is worth pausing with these studies as they foreshadow several of the themes to be developed later. Goldberg claims that:

a theologian, regardless of the propositional statements he or she may have to make about a community's convictions, must consciously strive to keep those statements in intimate contact with the narratives which give rise to those convictions, within which they gain their sense and meaning, and *from which they have been abstracted.* (p. 35)

The same can be said for those who would understand ordinary experience. The ground for determining meaning, validity, reason, rationality, and truth must be a narrative context: history, culture, biography, and character. Goldberg also argues:

Neither "the facts" nor our "experience" come to us in discrete and disconnected packets which simply await the appropriate moral principle to be applied. Rather, they stand in need of some narrative which can bind the facts of our experience together into a coherent pattern and it is thus in virtue of that narrative that our abstracted rules, principles, and notions gain their full intelligibility. (p. 242)

Again, the statement is relevant to more than the moral life; it is germane to social and political life as well. He observes, as I would, that "what counts as meeting the various conditions of justification will vary from story to story . . ." (p. 246). I will suggest a foundation for such justifications in the discussion of narrative rationality.

With some modifications, I would endorse two of Hauerwas' (1981) 10 theses. First, he claims that "The social significance of the Gospel requires recognition of the narrative structure of Christian convictions for the life of the church" (p. 9). I would say: The meaning and significance of life in all of its social dimensions require the recognition of its narrative structure. Second, Hauerwas asserts that "Every social ethic involves a narrative, whether it is conceived with the formulation of basic principles of social organization and/or concrete alternatives" (p. 9; see also Alter, 1981; Scult, 1983). The only change that I would make here is to delete the word "social." Any ethic, whether social, political, legal or otherwise, involves narrative.

Finally, mention should be made of the work on narration by such scholars as Derrida (1980), Kermode (1980), and Ricoeur (1980). Especially relevant to this project are essays by White (1980; see also, White, 1978), Turner (1980), and Danto (1982; see also Nelson, 1980; Todorov, 1977).

Purpose

If I can establish that narration deserves to be accepted as a paradigm, it will vie with the reigning paradigm, which I will refer to as the rational world paradigm. In truth, however, the narrative paradigm, like other paradigms in the human sciences, does not so much deny what has gone before as it subsumes it.

The rational world paradigm will be seen as one way to tell the story of how persons reason together in certain settings. For now, it is enough that the narrative paradigm be contemplated as worthy of co-existing with the rational world paradigm.

I shall begin by characterizing and contrasting the two paradigms. I shall then examine the controversy over nuclear warfare, a public moral argument, noting particular problems with the rational world paradigm and indicating how the narrative paradigm provides a way of possibly resolving them. Following this discussion, I shall reconsider the narrative paradigm and conclude with several implications for further inquiry. Needless to say, this essay does not constitute a finished statement. It offers a conceptual frame which, I am fully aware, requires much greater development for it to be considered compelling. At this point, as I have suggested, it is sufficient that it receive serious attention. From such attention, a fuller, more persuasive statement should emerge.

The Rational World Paradigm

This paradigm is very familiar, having been in existence since Aristotle's *Organon* became foundational to Western thought. Regardless of its historic forms, the rational world paradigm presupposes that: (1) humans are essentially rational beings; (2) the paradigmatic mode of human decision-making and communication is argument—clear-cut inferential (implicative) structures; (3) the conduct of argument is ruled by the dictates of situations— legal, scientific, legislative, public, and so on; (4) rationality is determined by subject matter knowledge, argumentative ability, and skill in employing the rules of advocacy in given fields; and (5) the world is a set of logical puzzles which can be resolved through appropriate analysis and application of reason conceived as an argumentative construct. In short, argument as product and process is *the* means of being human, the agency of all that humans can know and realize in achieving their *telos*. The philosophical ground of the rational world paradigm is epistemology. Its linguistic materials are self-evident propositions, demonstrations, and proofs, the verbal expressions of certain and probable knowing.

The actualization of the rational world paradigm, it should be noted, depends on a form of society that permits, if not requires, participation of qualified persons in public decision-making. It further demands a citizenry that shares a common language, general adherence to the values of the state, information relevant to the questions that confront the community to be arbitrated by argument, and an understanding of argumentative issues and the various forms of reasoning and their appropriate assessment. In other words, there must exist something that can be called public or social knowledge and there must be a "public" for argument to be the kind of force envisioned for it (Bitzer, 1978; Farrell, 1976). Because the rational world paradigm has these requirements and because *being rational* (being competent in argument) *must be learned,* an historic mission of education in the West has been to generate a consciousness of national community and to instruct citizens in at least the rudiments of logic and rhetoric (Hollis, 1977, pp. 165–166; Toulmin, 1970, p. 4).

Needless to say, the rational world paradigm, which is by and large a heritage of the classical period, has not been untouched by "modernism." The impact of modernism has been recounted and reacted to by many writers (Barrett, 1979; Booth, 1974; Gadamer, 1981, 1982; Lonergan, 1958; MacIntyre, 1981; Rorty, 1979; Schrag, 1980; Sennett, 1978; Toulmin, 1972, 1982; Voegelin, 1952, 1975). The line of thought that has done most to subvert the rational world paradigm is, along with existentialism, naturalism. One of its schools starts with physics and mathematics and makes the logical structure of scientific knowledge fundamental; the other school, involving biology, psychology, and the social sciences, adapts this structure and conception of knowledge to the human sciences. According to John Herman Randall, Jr.:

> The major practical issue still left between the two types of naturalism concerns the treatment of values. The philosophies starting from physics tend to exclude questions of value from the field of science and the scope of scientific method. They either leave them to traditional non-scientific treatment, handing them over, with Russell, to the poet and mystic; or else with the logical empiricists they dismiss the whole matter as "meaningless," maintaining with Ayer, that any judgment of value is an expression of mere personal feeling. The philosophies of human experience—all the heirs of Hegel, from dialectical materialism to Dewey—subject them to the same scientific methods of criticism and testing as other beliefs; and thus offer the hope of using all we have learned of scientific procedure to erect at last a science of values comparable to the science that was the glory of Greek thought. (1976, p. 651)

It is clear: With the first type of naturalism, there can be neither public or social knowledge nor rational public or social argument, for both are permeated by values. As Habermas notes, "the relationship of theory to practice can now only assert itself as the purposive rational application of techniques assured by empirical science" (Habermas, 1967, p. 254; Heiddegger, 1972, pp. 58–59).

With the second type of naturalism, one can hope with Randall that it produces the work he sees possible in it. But the fact is that no science of values has appeared or seems likely to do so; further, Dewey (1927) himself noted the eclipse of the "public" and doubted its reemergence. His hope was the development of "communities." Interestingly, 55 years later, MacIntyre concludes *After Virtue* with the observation: "What matters at this state is the construction of local forms of community within which civility and the intellectual and moral life can be sustained" (1981, p. 245).

The effects of naturalism have been to restrict the rational world paradigm to specialized studies and to relegate everyday argument to an irrational exercise. The reaction to this state of affairs has been an historic effort to recover the rational world paradigm for human decision-making and communication by: (1) reconstituting the conception of knowledge (e.g., Bitzer, 1978; Farrell, 1976; Habermas, 1973; Lyne, 1982; McGee & Martin, 1983; Polanyi, 1958; Ziman, 1968); (2) reconceptualizing the public—in terms of rational enterprises, fields, and/or communities (e.g., McKerrow, 1980a,b; Toulmin, 1958, 1972; Toulmin, Rieke & Janik, 1979; Willard, 1982; see also the first 19 essays in Ziegelmueller & Rhodes, 1981); (3) formulating a logic appropriate for practical reasoning (e.g., Fisher, 1978; Perelman & Olbrechts-Tyteca, 1969; Toulmin, 1958; Wenzel, 1977); and (4) reconceiving the conceptions of validity, reason, and rationality (e.g., Apel, 1979; Ehninger, 1968; Farrell, 1977; Fisher, 1980; Gottlieb, 1968; Johnstone, 1978; McKerrow, 1977, 1982). Many of the studies cited here intimate, if not specifically state, proposals for reconstructing the concept of argument itself. Writers explicitly working on this task include Brockriede (1975, 1977), Burleson (1981), Jacobs and Jackson (1981), McKerrow (1981), O'Keefe (1977, 1982), Wenzel (1980), and Willard (1978).

The motive underlying these various studies, and the movement of which they are an energizing force, is, as I have suggested, to repair the rational world paradigm so that it once again will serve everyday argument. One may well applaud the motive and the movement and yet ask two questions: (1) Has the reformation been successful? (2) Is there a more beneficial way to conceive and to articulate the structures of everyday argument? It is too early to answer the first question with finality but one cannot deny that much useful work has been done, especially in establishing at least the semblance of rationality for fields of argument. I shall maintain, however, that similar progress has not been made in the arena where argument is most general and is most obviously concerned with values, public moral argument, as the examination of the nuclear controversy will show later.

This failure suggests to me that the problem in restoring rationality to everyday argument may be the assumption that the reaffirmation of the rational world paradigm is the only solution. The position I am taking is that another paradigm, the narrative paradigm, may offer a better solution, one that will provide substance not only for public moral argument, but also all other forms of argument, for human communication in general. My answer to the second question, then, is: "Yes, I think so." Adoption of the narrative paradigm, I hasten to repeat, does not mean rejection of all the good work that has been done; it means a rethinking of it and investigating new moves that can be made to enrich our understanding of communicative interaction. Representative of the good work that has already been done on public argument are essays by Cox (1981), Goodnight (1980), Hynes, Jr. (1980), Lucaitas (1981), Pryor (1981), Sillars and Ganer (1982), and Zarefsky (1981).

The Narrative Paradigm

Many different root metaphors have been put forth to represent the essential nature of human beings: *homo faber, homo economous, homo politicus, homo sociologicus,* "psychological man," "ecclesiastical man," *homo sapiens,* and, of course, "rational man." I now propose *homo narrans* to be added to the list.

Preliminary to an attempt to delineate the presuppositions that structure the narrative paradigm, I should indicate how the *homo narrans* metaphor relates to those that have preceded it. First, each of the root metaphors may be held to be the master metaphor, thereby standing as the ground, while the others are manifest as figures. In the terminology of the narrative perspective, the master metaphor sets the plot of human experience and the others the subplots. When any of the other metaphors are asserted as the master metaphor, narration is as it is considered now: a type of human interaction—an activity, an art, a genre, or mode of expression.

Second, when narration is taken as the master metaphor, it subsumes the others. The other metaphors are then considered conceptions that inform various ways of *recounting* or *accounting for* human choice and action. Recounting takes the forms of history, biography, or autobiography. Accounting for takes the forms of theoretical explanation or argument. Recounting and accounting for can be also expressed in poetic forms: drama, poetry, novel, and so on. Recounting and accounting for are, in addition, the bases for all advisory discourse. Regardless of the form they may assume, recounting and accounting for are stories we tell ourselves and each other to establish a meaningful life-world. The character of narrator(s), the conflicts, the resolutions, and the style will vary, but each mode of recounting and accounting for is but a way of relating a "truth" about the human condition.

Third, the *homo narrans* metaphor is an incorporation and extension of Burke's definition of "man" as the "symbol-using (symbol-making, symbol-misusing) animal" (Burke, 1968, p. 16; Cassirer, 1944, p. 26; see also Langer, 1953, pp. 264 ff). The idea of human beings as storytellers indicates the generic form of all symbol composition; it holds that symbols are created and communicated ultimately as stories meant to give order to human experience and to induce others to dwell in them to establish ways of living in common, in communities in which there is sanction for the story that constitutes one's life. And one's life is, as suggested by Burke, a story that participates in the stories of those who have lived, who live now, and who will live in the future. He asks: "Where does the drama get its materials?" I would modify the question to read: "Where do our narratives get their materials?" And, I would accept his answer:

From the "unending conversation" that is going on in history when we are born. Imagine that you enter a parlor. You come late. When you arrive, others have long preceded you, and they are engaged in a heated discussion, a discussion too heated for them to pause and tell you exactly what it is about. In fact, the discussion had already begun long before any of them got there, so that no one present is qualified to retrace for you all the steps that had gone before. You listen for awhile, until you decide that you have caught the tenor of the argument; then you put in your oar. Someone answers; you answer him; another comes to your defense; another aligns himself against you, to either the embarrassment or gratification of your opponent, depending upon the quality of your ally's assistance. However, the discussion is interminable. The hour grows late, you must depart. And you do depart, with the discussion still vigorously in process. (Burke, 1957, pp. 94–97; for a discussion of the nature of conversation as narration, see MacIntyre, 1981; Campbell & Stewart, 1981).

As Heidegger observes, "We are a conversation . . . conversation and its unity support our existence" (Heidegger, 1949, p. 278; Gadamer, 1982, pp. 330 ff; Rorty, 1979, pp. 315 ff).

To clarify further the narrative paradigm, I should specify how it is related to Bormann's (1972) concepts of "fantasy themes" and "rhetorical visions," and to the Frentz and Farrell (1976) language action paradigm. Fantasy, Bormann holds, is a technical term, meaning "the creative and imaginative interpretation of events that fulfills a psychological or rhetorical need" (1983, p. 434). Fantasy themes arise "in group interaction out of a recollection of something that happened to the group in the *past* or a dream of what a group might do in the *future*" (1972, p. 397). When woven together, they become composite dramas, which Bormann calls "rhetorical visions" (1972, p. 398). From the narrative view, each of these concepts translates into dramatic stories constituting the fabric of social reality for those who compose them. They are, thus, "rhetorical fictions," constructions of fact and faith having persuasive force, rather than fantasies (Fisher, 1980). Nevertheless, without getting into the problem of how group-generated stories become public stories, I would note that Bormann (1973) and others have demonstrated that "rhetorical visions" do exist (e.g., Bantz, 1975; Kidd, 1975; Rarick, Duncan & Porter, 1977). I take this demonstration as partial evidence for the validity of the narrative paradigm. (For further empirical evidence, see Bennett, 1978; Campbell, 1984.)

With minor adaptation, I find no incompatibility between the narrative paradigm and the language action paradigm. Indeed, language action is meaningful only in terms of narrative form (Ricoeur, 1976). What Frentz and Farrell (1976) designate as "form of life" and "encounters"—implicit matters of knowledge, aesthetic expectations, institutional constraints, and propriety rules—can be considered the forces that determine the structure of narratives in given interpersonal environments. What they call an "episode," a "rule-conforming sequence of symbolic acts generated by two or more actors who are collectively oriented toward emergent goals," can be thought of as the process by which one or more authors generate a short story or chapter—deciding on plot, the nature of characters, resolutions, and their meaning and import for them and others (p. 336).

I do not want to leave the impression that the narrative paradigm merely accommodates the constructs of Bormann, Frentz and Farrell. Their work enriches the narrative paradigm. I shall rely specifically on the language action paradigm in what follows.

The presuppositions that structure the narrative paradigm are: (1) humans are essentially storytellers; (2) the paradigmatic mode of human decision-making and communication is "good reasons" which vary in form among communication situations, genres, and media; (3) the production and practice of good reasons are ruled by matters of history, biography, culture, and character along with the kinds of forces identified in the Frentz and Farrell language action paradigm; (4) rationality is determined by the nature of persons as narrative beings—their inherent awareness of *narrative probability*, what constitutes a coherent story, and their constant habit of testing *narrative fidelity*, whether the stories they experience ring true with the stories they know to be true in their lives (narrative probability and narrative fidelity, it will be noted, are analogous to the concepts of dramatic probability and verisimilitude; as MacIntyre [1981, p. 200] observes, "The difference between imaginary characters and real ones is not in the narrative form of what they do; it is in the degree of their authorship of that form and of their own deeds"); and (5) the world is a set of stories which must be chosen among to live the good life in a process of continual recreation. In short, good reasons are the stuff of stories, the means by which humans realize their nature as reasoning-valuing animals. The philosophical ground of the narrative paradigm is ontology. The materials of the narrative paradigm are symbols, signs of consubstantiation, and good reasons, the communicative expressions of social reality.

The actualization of the narrative paradigm does not require a given form of society. Where the rational world paradigm is an ever-present part of our consciousness because we have been educated into it, the narrative impulse is part of our very being because we acquire narrativity in the natural process of socialization (Goody & Watt, 1962–1963; Krashen, 1982). That narrative, whether written or oral, is a feature of human nature and that it crosses time and culture is attested by historian White: "far from being one code among many that a culture may utilize for endowing experience with meaning, narrative is a metacode, a human universal on the basis of which trans-cultural messages about the shared reality can be transmitted . . . the absence of narrative capacity or a refusal of narrative indicates an absence of refusal of meaning itself" (1980, p. 6); by anthropologist Turner: "if we regard narrative ethically, as the supreme instrument for building 'values' and 'goals,' in Dilthey's sense of these terms, which motivate human conduct into situational structures of 'meaning,' then we must concede it to be a universal cultural activity, embedded in the very center of the social drama, itself another cross-cultural and transtemporal unit in social process" (1980, p. 167); and by linguist-folklorist Dell Hymes: "the narrative use of language is not a property of subordinate cultures, whether folk, or working class, or the like, but a universal function" (1980, p. 132; see also Barthes, 1977; Ong, 1982).

Gregory Bateson goes so far as to claim that "If I am at all fundamentally right in what I am saying, then *thinking in terms of stories* must be shared by all mind or minds, whether ours or those of redwood forests and sea anemones" (1979, p. 14). And Burke observes that "We assume a time when our primal ancestors became able to go from SENSATIONS to *WORDS*. (When they could duplicate the experience of tasting an orange by saying 'the taste of an orange,' that was WHEN STORY CAME INTO THE WORLD)" (1983, p. 1).

In theme, if not in every detail, narrative, then, is meaningful for persons in particular and in general, across communities as well as cultures, across time and place. Narratives enable us to understand the actions of others "because we all live out narratives in our lives and because we understand our own lives in terms of narratives" (MacIntyre, 1981, p. 197).

Rationality from this perspective involves, as I have proposed, the principles of narrative probability and narrative fidelity. These principles contrast with but do not contradict the constituents of rationality I have outlined earlier (Fisher, 1978, 1980). They are, in fact, subsumed by the narrative paradigm. The earlier notion was attuned to the rational world paradigm and essentially held that rationality was a matter of argumentative competence: knowledge of issues, modes of reasoning, appropriate tests, and rules of advocacy in given fields. As such, rationality was something to be learned, depended on deliberation, and required a high degree of self-consciousness. Narrative rationality does not make these demands. It is a capacity we all share. It depends on our minds being as Booth (1974, pp. 114–137) represents them in *Modern Dogma and the Rhetoric of Assent*, a key point of which is: "Not only do human beings successfully infer other beings' states of mind from symbolic clues; we know that they characteristically, in all societies, build each other's minds. This is obvious knowledge—all the more genuine for being obvious" (p. 114). The operative principle of narrative rationality is identification rather than deliberation (Burke, 1955, pp. 20–46).

Narrative rationality differs from traditional rationality in another significant way. Narrative rationality is not an account of the "laws of thought" and it is not normative in the sense that one must reason according to prescribed rules of calculation or inference making. Traditional rationality posits the way people think when they reason truly or with certainty. MacIntyre notes,

"To call an argument fallacious is always at once to describe and to evaluate it" (1978, p. 258). It is, therefore, a normative construct. Narrative rationality is, on the other hand, descriptive, as it offers an account, an understanding, of any instance of human choice and action, including science (Gadamer, 1982; Heidegger, 1972; Holton, 1973; Ramsey, 1969). At the same time, it is a basis for critique, because it implies a praxis, an ideal democratic society (McGee, Scult & Kuntz, 1983). Traditional rationality implies some sort of hierarchical system, a community in which some persons are qualified to judge and to lead and some other persons are to follow.

For the sake of clarity, I should note that, while the narrative paradigm provides a radical democratic ground for social-political critique, it does not deny the legitimacy (the inevitability) of hierarchy. History records no community, uncivilized or civilized, without key storymakers/storytellers, whether sanctioned by God, a "gift," heritage, power, intelligence, or election. It insists, however, that the "people" do judge the stories that are told for and about them and that they have a rational capacity to make such judgments. It holds, along with Aristotle (1954, bk. 1, ch. 1, 1355^{a}20) that the "people" have a natural tendency to prefer the true and the just. Neither does the narrative paradigm deny that the "people" can be wrong. But, then, so can elites, especially when a decision is social or political. And neither does the theory deny the existence and desirability of genius in individuals or the "people" to formulate and to adopt new stories that better account for their lives or the mystery of life itself. The sort of hierarchy condemned by the narrative praxis is the sort that is marked by the will to power, the kind of system in which elites struggle to dominate and to use the people for their own ends or that makes the people blind subjects of technology.

Narrative rationality, then, is inimical to elitist politics, whether facist, communist, or even democratic—if traditional rationality is the prevailing societal view. And this seems to be the case with American democracy, as subsequent examination of the nuclear controversy will show. The prevalent position is that voters are rational if they know enough about public issues, are cognizant of argumentative procedures, forms, and functions, and weigh carefully all the arguments they hear and read in a systematic, deliberative process. Contrary to this notion is that of V. O. Key, Jr. In a classic study of presidential voting between 1936 and 1960, he concluded that "voters are not fools," which is what they must be considered if measured by traditional rationality. His data led him to conclude that the American electorate is not "straitjacketed by social determinants or moved by subconscious urges triggered by devilishly skillful propagandists." They are moved by their perceptions and appraisals of "central and relevant questions of public policy, of governmental performance, and of executive personality" (1966, pp. 7–8). These perceptions and appraisals of political discourse and action become stories, narratives that must stand the tests of probability and fidelity. And these stories are no less valuable than the stories constructed by persons who are rational in the traditional way. There is no evidence to support the claim that "experts" know better than anyone else who should be elected president.

Obviously, as I will note later, some stories are better than others, more coherent, more "true" to the way people and the world are—in fact and in value. In other words, some stories are better in satisfying the criteria of the logic of good reasons, which is attentive to reason and values. Persons may even choose not to participate in the making of public narratives (vote) if they feel that they are meaningless spectators rather than co-authors. But, all persons have the capacity to be rational in the narrative paradigm. And, by and large, persons are that—at least in the fashioning of their daily lives. Persons do not have the capacity to be equally rational in the rational world paradigm. Because persons have the capacity of narrative rationality, it is reasonable to have juries of lay persons and popular elections, as Bennett (1978; Bennett & Feldman, 1981) has well demonstrated. I want to stress, however, that narrative rationality does not negate traditional rationality. It holds that traditional rationality is only relevant in specialized fields and even in those arenas narrative rationality is meaningful and useful.

Certain other features of the narrative paradigm should be noted before moving to the case of public moral argument. First, the paradigm is a ground for resolving the dualisms of modernism: fact-value, intellect-imagination, reason-emotion, and so on. Stories are the enactment of the whole mind in concert with itself. Second, narratives are moral constructs. As White asserts: "Where, in any account of reality, narrativity is present, we can be sure that morality or a moral impulse is present too" (1980, p. 26; Benjamin, 1969). Third, the narrative paradigm is consonant with the notion of reason proposed by Schrag: "Reason, as the performance of vision and insight, commemoration and foresight, occasions the recognition of a process of meaning-formation that gathers within it the logic of technical reason and the *logos* of myth" (1980, p. 126). The appropriateness and validity of this view of reason for the narrative paradigm is supported by Angel Medina (1979). In a statement that reiterates several of the points I have made, he writes:

> it is necessary to define our reason primarily as biographical, that is, above all narrative and then symbolic. Human reason is narrative because it extends from its inception and in every one of its acts toward the foreshadowing of its total course. It is symbolic in that the major aim in the formation of this totality is its own self-presentation within the dialogue of consciousness. The meaning of my whole life is communicative; it emerges, as such, for the benefit of another consciousness when I attempt to present myself totally to it. Reciprocally, the meaning of another life becomes a totality only when received fully within my life. (p. 30)

And, fourth, as I will attempt to show, the narrative paradigm offers ways of resolving the problems of public moral argument.

The Case: Public Moral Argument

It should be apparent by now that I think that MacIntyre's (1981) *After Virtue* is a remarkable work. Equally remarkable, in its own way, is Jonathan Schell's (1982) *The Fate of the Earth.* Schell's book is exemplary of contemporary moral argument intended to persuade a general audience, the "public." His concluding argument is:

> Either we will sink into the final coma and end it all or, as I trust and believe, we will awaken to the truth of our peril, a truth as great as life itself, and, like a person who has swallowed a lethal poison but shakes off his stupor at the last moment and vomits the poison up, we will break through the layers of denials, put aside our faint-hearted excuses, and rise up to cleanse the earth of nuclear weapons. (p. 231)

The validity of Schell's argument is not the question here. Our concern is its reception, which reveals the limits, perhaps the impossibility, of persuasive moral argument in our time, given the rational world paradigm.

Critical response to *The Fate of the Earth* is of two sorts. The first is celebratory. Reviewers in this group are obviously in sympathy with the book's moral thrust, its depiction of the results of nuclear war and its call for action—for life instead of death—but not with every detail of its argument. Although reviewers in this group include distinguished figures from a variety of professions: journalists Walter Cronkite, James Reston, and James Kilpatrick; historians Harrison Salisbury, John Hersey, and Henry Steele Commager; and politicians Barry Commoner, W. Averell Harriman, and Walter Mondale; none is a current member of the federal administration or the defense establishment. Each of them bears witness to an attitude—opposition to nuclear annihilation—but none testifies to the technical merits of Schell's representation of "deterrence theory," his inferences about its meaning in regard to strategy and tactics, or his conclusions about national sovereignty. They, like Schell, are not "experts" in the field in which the argument is made. They, like Schell, are active in the realm of rhetorical knowledge, in the sphere of social-political policy and behavior (Bitzer, 1978; Farrell, 1976).

Reviewers in the second group, on the other hand, are purveyors of ideological, bureaucratic, or technical arguments. Such arguments may overlap, be used by the same arguer, but each is distinguished by a particular privileged position: political "truth," administrative sanction, or subject matter expertise. The thrust of the ideological argument is that one violates ultimate "facts," is fundamentally wrong-headed; the bureaucratic argument stresses feasibility in regard to administrative approval; and the technical argument alleges ignorance of the "facts," that opponents are "unrealistic," meaning they do not have a firm grasp on reality. These are, of course, the lines of refutation or subversion. Their opposites would be constructive arguments of affirmation or reaffirmation.

The subversive pattern of ideological, bureaucratic, and technical arguments is evident in the following attacks on Schell's reasoning. McCracken (1982) labels Schell an "alarmist" and concludes: "The danger is that Mr. Schell's followers may triumph and bring about a freeze that by making present inequities permanent will prove destabilizing in the short run and in the long run productive of both redness and deadness" (p. 905). Focusing on the linch-pin arguments of *The Fate of the Earth* (Schell's interpretation of deterrence theory and his suggested solution of abolishing national sovereignty), Hausknecht (1982) first cites Alexander Haig and then observes that "It is not hard to imagine Ronald Reagan saying, 'Okay, so it may be the end of the species, but we can't let the bastards get away with it.'" In regard to Schell's solution, he concludes that "Successful political action demands significant but realizable goals" (p. 284). The same charge is leveled by Pierre (1982), who approves the moral force of Schell's position but then charges "Schell provides no realistic alternative to our nuclear policy based on the concept of deterrence. His argument—that knowledge that nuclear weapons can extinguish mankind must be the new deterrent in a disarmed world—is very weak" (p. 1188).

The strategy of these reviews is clear: reaffirmation of the moral concern, subversion of the reasoning. The tactics are also obvious: juxtapose Schell's reasoning with what is right-headed, what is approved by the administration, or what is "realistic." Insofar as there is merit in these "arguments," it lies not in the way they foreclose dialogue but in their narrative probability and narrative fidelity. Yet, this is not their intended appeal or effect. The effects are to discredit Schell as an arguer and to dismiss his argument as unfounded. Public moral argument is thus overwhelmed by privileged argument. Put another way, it is submerged by ideological and bureaucratic arguments that insist on rival moralities and technical argument which denudes it of morality altogether, making the dispute one for "experts" alone to consider (see Farrell & Goodnight, 1981).

The question that arises at this point is: What happens when "experts" argue about moral issues in public? Before considering this question, however, it is essential to sketch the general characteristics of "public moral argument."

Public moral argument is to be distinguished from reasoned discourse in interpersonal interactions and arguments occurring in specialized communities, such as theological disputes, academic debates, and arguments before the Supreme Court. The features differentiating *public* moral argument from such encounters are: (1) It is publicized, made available for consumption and persuasion of the polity at large; and (2) it is aimed at what Aristotle called "untrained thinkers," or, to be effective, it should be (1954, bk. I, ch. 2, 1357ª10). Most important *public* moral argument is a form of controversy that inherently crosses fields. It is not contained in the way that legal, scientific, or theological arguments are by subject matter, particular conceptions of argumentative competence, and well recognized rules of advocacy. Because this is so and because its realm is public-social knowledge, *public* moral argument naturally invites participation by field experts and is dominated by the rational superiority of their arguments. *Public* moral argument, which is oriented toward what ought to be, is undermined by the "truth" that prevails at the moment. The presence of "experts" in *public* moral arguments makes it difficult, if not impossible, for the public of "untrained thinkers" to win an argument or even judge them well—given, again, the rational world paradigm.

Public *moral* argument is moral in the sense that it is founded on ultimate questions—of life and death, of how persons should be defined and treated, of preferred patterns of living. Gusfield (1976) designates such questions as "status issues." Their resolution, he writes, indicates "the group, culture, or style of life to which the government and society are publicly committed" (p. 173). In addition to nuclear warfare, desegregation would be included in the category as well as abortion and school prayer.

Public moral *argument* refers to clearcut inferential structures, in the rational world paradigm, and to "good reasons," in the narrative paradigm. Public moral *argument* may also refer to public controversies—disputes and debates—about moral issues. The nuclear warfare controversy is an obvious case in point, but so are the others mentioned above. One could add disputes over pornography, ERA, and crime and punishment. This characterization of public moral *argument* is attentive to argument as product and as process (Wenzel, 1980).

The problem posed by the presence of experts in public moral argument is illustrated by the dispute between Hans Bethe and Edward Teller over the 1982 nuclear freeze proposition in California. Their positions were published in the *Los Angeles Times* (1982, October 17, Part IV, pp. 1–2), so they were public. They obviously concerned a moral issue and they were reasoned statements. Both persons are credible. Which one is to be believed and followed? Who in the general public could contend with them? Teller answers the second question in unequivocal terms: "The American public is ignorant, even of the general ideas on which they [nuclear weapons] are based" (p. 2). Here is revealed the fate of non-experts who would argue about nuclear warfare. Only experts can argue with experts and their arguments—while public—cannot be rationally questioned. As Perelman (1979) notes, rationality in and of itself forecloses discussion and debate. In the audience of experts, the public is left with no compelling reason, from the perspective of the rational world paradigm, to believe one over the other. One is not a judge but a spectator who must choose between actors. From the narrative paradigm view, the experts are storytellers and the audience is not a group of observers but are active participants in the meaning-formation of the stories.

It may be asked at this point: How is it that freeze referendums were approved in eight out of nine states and in 28 cities and counties in 1982? One answer is "fear," the "most intelligent feeling of our time" (Wieseltier, 1983, p. 7). Another answer is "distrust," distrust of those responsible for the development, deployment, and use of nuclear weapons. This answer is, I believe, more accurate. It does not deny the existence of fear. It insists on the "rationality" of those who voted for and against the referendum. Those who opposed the referendum did so because of a basic distrust of Soviet leaders and a fundamental trust of our own. What I am saying is that there are good reasons for trust and distrust, that the response of voters was rational, given the narrative paradigm. The good reasons that are expressed in public moral argument relate to issues not accounted for in the rational world paradigm. These issues include the motivations and values of the characters involved in the ongoing narrative of nuclear warfare, the way in which they conceive and behave in respect to the conflict, and the narrative probability and narrative fidelity of the particular stories they tell, which may well take the form of "reasoned argument." Experts and lay persons meet on common ground, given the narrative paradigm. As Toulmin observes, "a scientist off duty is as much an 'ordinary' man as a tinker or a bus-conductor off duty" (1982, p. 81).

From the narrative perspective, the proper role of the expert in public moral argument is that of a counselor, which is, as Benjamin (1969) notes, the true function of the storyteller. His or her contribution to public dialogue is to impart knowledge, like a teacher, or wisdom, like a sage. It is not to pronounce a story that ends all storytelling. The expert assumes the role of public counselor whenever she or he crosses the boundary of technical knowledge into the territory of life as it ought to be lived. Once this invasion is made, the public, which then includes the expert, has its own criteria for determining whose story is most coherent and reliable as a guide to belief and action. The expert, in other words, then becomes subject to the demands of narrative rationality. Technical communities have their own conceptions and criteria for judging the rationality of communication. But, as Holton (1973) has demonstrated, the work even of scientists is inspired by stories; hence, their discourse can be interpreted usefully from the narrative perspective. Holton writes tellingly of the "nascent moment" in science, the impulse to do science in a particular or in a new way, and how science is informed by "themes"—thematic concepts, methods, and hypotheses inherited from Parmenides, Heraclitus, Pythagoras, Thales, and others (pp. 28–29; see also Ong, 1982, p. 140).

Viewed from the perspective of the rational world paradigm, Schell's case, his argument and its reception, evokes despair. If one looks to MacIntyre's *After Virtue* for relief, one will be disappointed and disheartened further, for he provides the historical and philosophical reasons for the fate of *The Fate of the Earth* and similar such arguments. His own argument is that "we still, in spite of the efforts of three centuries of moral philosophy and one of sociology, lack any coherent, rationally defensible statement of a liberal individualist point of view" (1981, p. 241). He offers some hope with the idea that "the Aristotelian tradition can be restated in a way that restores intelligibility and rationality to our moral and social attitudes and commitments." He observes, however, "the new dark ages" are "already upon us." The "barbarians are not waiting beyond the frontiers; they have already been governing us for quite some time. And it is our lack of consciousness of this that constitutes part of our predicament. We are waiting not for Godot, but for another—doubtless very different—St. Benedict" (p. 245).

The reasons for this state of affairs are: (1) The rejection of a teleological view of human nature and the classical conception of reason as embodied in Aristotelian logic and rhetoric; (2) the separation of morality from theological, legal, and aesthetic concerns; and (3) the evolution of the individualistic sense of self and the rise of emotivism. The consequence of these movements is a situation in which ethical arguments in public are rendered ineffectual because of "conceptual incommensurability."

A case in point is protest—where advocates of reform argue from a position of "rights" and those who oppose them reason from the stance of "utility." MacIntyre observes:

> the facts of incommensurability ensure that protestors can never win an *argument;* the indignant self-righteousness of protestors arises because the facts of incommensurability ensure equally that the protestors can never lose an argument either. Hence, the *utterance* of protest is characteristically addressed to those who already *share* the protestors' premises. . . . This is not to say that protest cannot be effective; it is to say that protest cannot be *rationally* effective. (p. 69)

Thus, when arguers appealing to justice and equality contend with adversaries who base their case on success, survival, and liberty, they talk past each other.

From the perspective of the narrative paradigm, the dynamic of this situation is that rival stories are being told. Any story, any form of rhetorical communication, not only says something about the world, it also implies an audience, persons who conceive of themselves in very specific ways. If a story denies a person's self-conception, it does not matter what it says about the world. In the instance of protest, the rival factions' stories deny each other in respect to self-conceptions and the world. The only way to bridge this gap, if it can be bridged through discourse, is by telling stories that do not negate the self-conceptions people hold of themselves.

It may be germane to note at this point that narrative as *a mode of discourse* is more universal and probably more efficacious than argument for nontechnical forms of communication (Fisher, 1982, p. 304). There are several reasons why this should be true. First, narration comes closer to capturing the experience of the world, simultaneously appealing to the various senses, to reason and emotion, to intellect and imagination, and to fact and value. It does not presume intellectual contact only. Second, one does not have to be taught narrative probability and narrative fidelity; one culturally acquires them through a universal faculty and experience. Obviously, one can, through education, become sophisticated in one's understanding and application of these principles. But, as Gadamer observes, "I am convinced of the fact that there are no people who do not 'think' sometime and somewhere. That means there is no one who does not form general views about life and death, about freedom and living together, about the good and about happiness" (1981, p. 58; see also Ogden, 1977, p. 114; Lonergan, 1958, xiv-xv, xxii-xxx). In other words, people are reflective and from such reflection they make the stories of their lives and have the basis for judging narratives for and about them. On the other hand, appreciation of argument requires not only reflection, but also specialized knowledge of issues, reasoning, rules of rationality, and so on. Third, narration works by suggestion and identification; argument operates by inferential moves and deliberation. Both forms, however, are modes of expressing good reasons—given the narrative paradigm—so the differences between them are structural rather than substantive.

Summary and Conclusions

This essay began as a study of public moral argument—the nuclear controversy. It was undertaken with the rational world paradigm well in mind. The results of my analysis were disturbing not only in what I found to be the inevitable subversion of *The Fate of the Earth* and similar such arguments, but also in that the rational world paradigm was at least partly responsible for that fate. Then came MacIntyre's (1981) *After Virtue*. Reflection set in and the narrative paradigm came out of it.

I was concerned with the concept of technical reason and the way it rendered the public unreasonable; with the idea of rationality being a matter of argumentative competence in specialized fields, leaving the public and its discourse irrational; with the apparent impossibility of bridging the gaps between experts and the public and between segments of the public; and with the necessity to learn what was supposed to be of the essence of persons—rationality—so that one class of citizens can always be superior to another.

Although I do not mean to maintain that the narrative paradigm resolves these problems out of existence, I do think that it provides a basis for reconsideration of them. Before that, I am aware, the narrative paradigm itself needs further scrutiny. I know that I do not need to tell critics how to do their work—the examination of my representation of the rational world paradigm, the presuppositions of the narrative paradigm and its relationship to other constructs, my concept of public moral argument, and the analysis of the specific case. I welcome the "stories" the critics will tell.

In closing, I should like to make two additional comments. First, I think that the concepts of public and social knowledge should be reconceived in light of the narrative paradigm. The effect would be to give shape to these ideas as identifiable entities in the discourse of the citizenry, to give public knowledge a form of being. To consider that public-social knowledge is to be found in the stories that we tell one another would enable us to observe not only our differences, but also our commonalities, and in such observation we might be able to reform the notion of the "public."

Second, and closely related to the discovery of our communal identity, is the matter of what makes one story better than another. Two features come to mind: formal and substantive. Formal features are attributes of narrative probability: the consistency of characters and actions, the accommodation of auditors, and so on. In epistemological terms, the question would be whether a narrative satisfied the demands of a coherence theory of truth. The most compelling, persuasive stories are mythic in form (Campbell, 1973; Cassirer, 1944, 1979, p. 246; Eliade, 1963). Substantive features relate to narrative fidelity. Bormann has proposed two concepts pertinent to the problem of narrative fidelity: "corroboration" (1978) and "social convergence" (1983, p. 436). These concepts concern how people come to adhere to particular stories. They do not solve the problem of narrative fidelity because both suggest that narratives are valid by virtue of consensus and provide no criteria by which one can establish that one narrative is more sound than another. While there is work to be done on the problem, I think the logic of good reasons is the most viable scheme presently available by which narratives can be tested. Its application requires an examination of reasoning and "inspection of facts, values, self, and society" (Fisher, 1978, p. 382). In epistemological terms, narrative fidelity is a matter of truth according to the doctrine of correspondence. Though the most engaging stories are mythic, the most helpful and uplifting stories are moral. As John Gardner wrote, "Moral action is action that affirms life" (1978, p. 23).

One may get the impression that the conception of rationality I have presented leads to a denial of logic. It does, but only as logic is conceived so that persons are considered irrational beings. With Heidegger (1973, p. 170), I would assert that "To think counter to logic does not mean to stick up for the illogical, but only means to think the *logos*, and its essence as it appeared in the early days of thought; i.e., to make an effort first of all to prepare such an act of re-flecting (*Nachdenka*)." In an earlier essay, I attempted to make such an effort by showing the relationship of the logic of good reasons to Aristotle's concept of "practical wisdom" (Fisher, 1980, pp. 127–128).

Application of narrative rationality to specific stories may further clarify its nature and value. From the perspective of narrative rationality, Hitler's *Mein Kampf* must be judged a bad story. Although it has formal coherence in its structure, as McGuire (1977) demonstrated, it denies the identity of significant persons and demeans others. It also lacks fidelity to the truths humanity shares in regard to reason, justice, veracity, and peaceful ways to resolve social-political differences. On the other hand, one may cite the cosmological myths of Lao-tse, Buddha, Zoroaster, Christ, and Mohammed which satisfy both narrative probability and narrative fidelity for those cultures for whom they were intended—and many others across time and place. Far from denying the humanity of persons, they elevate it to the profoundest moral and metaphysical level the world has known. One could also cite such works as the *Iliad, The Odyssey,* the tragedies of Aeschylus, Sophocles, Euripides, Virgil's *Aeneid,* Dante's *Commedia,* the plays of Shakespeare, and the novels of Tolstoy, Melville, Thomas Mann, and James Joyce. One could point to the lives of Jesus, Socrates, Lincoln, and Ghandi. Regarding political discourse, one could mention many of the speeches and writings of Adlai Stevenson and Winston Churchill. While these classic manifestations of religious, social, cultural, and political life have been celebrated by persons' committed to traditional rationality, it has been because they have not restricted themselves to "logic" but have recognized and responded to the values fostered by them, by their reaffirmation of the human spirit as the transcendent ground of existence.

For a more detailed illustration of how narrative probability and fidelity can be usefully applied, I offer this brief analysis of *The Epic of Gilgamesh,* "the finest surviving epic poem from any period until the appearance of Homer's *Iliad:* and it is immeasurably older" (Sandars, 1982, p. 7). It is, in fact, 1500 years older.

The story, in sum, is as follows: Gilgamesh, the King of Urak, two-thirds god and one-third man, is possessed of a perfect body, unbounded courage, and extraordinary strength. He is a hero, a tragic hero, the "first tragic hero of whom anything is known" (Sandars, 1982, p. 7). His youth is spent in pursuit of fame as the means of immortality.

He is restless, with no one to match his appetites and physical feats. His people ask the gods to create a companion for him, which they do in Enkidu. Enkidu is Gilgamesh's counterpart in strength, energy, and exuberance for life. After a wrestling match, they become inseparable, brothers in every way but birth. Gilgamesh learns what it means to love.

Because Enkidu begins to lose his physical prowess—he had been an inhabitant of the wilds and ran with animals—Gilgamesh proposes that they pursue and slay Huwawa, a terrible monster. At first, Enkidu is reluctant but is chided into joining the quest. The monster is met, subdued, and, because of an insult, is slain by Enkidu.

When they return to Urak, the goddess, Ishtar, proposes to Gilgamesh. He not only refuses her, but he and Enkidu heap scorn upon her. She goes to her father, Anu, and asks him to have the bull of heaven kill Gilgamesh. But Gilgamesh and Enkidu kill the bull instead. It appears at this point that the "brothers" cannot be defeated by man, monsters, or the gods.

It turns out, however, that in killing Huwawa, Gilgamesh and Enkidu incurred the wrath of Enlil, guardian of the forest in which the monster lived. Enlil demands the death of Gilgamesh, but the sun god intervenes and Enkidu is doomed and dies.

With Enkidu's death, the world of Gilgamesh is shattered. He has not only lost his loving companion, he must now directly confront the fact of death. Up to this point, he has lived as a willful child, acting as though the meaning of life is a matter of dominating it.

At first, Gilgamesh refuses to accept Enkidu's death as real. He becomes obsessed with death and starts a quest to learn the secret of immortality. His journey is tortured and long. He finally arrives, after incredible hardships, at the island of Utanapishtim and asks him how one gains eternal life. Utanapishtim suggests that he try not to sleep for six days and seven nights. But he soon falls asleep, for seven days, a form of living death. He is awakened and realizes there is no escape from death. He resigns himself to his fate, the fate of all humankind, and returns home. On his return he learns to value the wall he has built around the city; immortality is, he apparently concludes, to be found in the monuments that one leaves behind.

The story provides good reasons to accept not only this truth, but others as well: Life is fullest when one loves and is loved; death is real; and maturity is achieved by accepting the reality of death. We learn these truths by dwelling in the characters in the story, by observing the outcomes of the several conflicts that arise throughout it, by seeing the unity of characters and their actions, and by comparing the truths to the truths we know to be true from our own lives. In other words, the story exhibits narrative probability and fidelity across time and culture (Jacobsen, 1976).

Finally, I do not mean to maintain that "knowledge of agents" is superior to "knowledge of objects." With Toulmin, I would hold that "A decent respect for each kind of knowledge is surely compatible with conceding the legitimate claims of the other" (1982, p. 244). With knowledge of agents, we can hope to find that which is *reliable* or *trustworthy;* with knowledge of objects, we can hope to discover that which has the quality of *veracity.* The world requires both kinds of knowledge.

Karl Wallace was right: "One could do worse than characterize rhetoric as the art of finding and effectively presenting good reasons" (1963, p. 248). MacIntyre is also right:

> The unity of human life is the unity of a narrative quest. Quests sometimes fail, are frustrated, abandoned or dissipated into distractions; and human lives may in all these ways also fail. But the criteria for success or failure in a human life as a whole are the criteria of success or failure in a narrated or to-be-narrated quest. (1981, p. 203)

And that quest is "for the good life" for all persons.

Works Cited

Baier, A. (1983). Secular faith. In S. Hauerwas & A. MacIntyre (Eds.), *Revisions: Changing perspectives on moral philosophy* (pp. 203–221). Notre Dame: University of Notre Dame Press.

Bormann, E.G. (1978). The tentative and the certain in rhetoric: The role of corroboration on the rigidity or flexibility of rhetorical visions. Paper presented at the annual meeting of the Central States Speech Association, Minneapolis.

Dijk, T.A. (1976). Philosophy of action and theory of narrative. *Poetics, 5,* 287–388.

Farrell, T.B., & Goodnight, G.T. (1981). Accidental rhetoric: The root metaphor of Three Mile Island. *Communication Monographs, 48,* 271–300.

Fisher, W.R. (1973). Reaffirmation and subversion of the American dream. *The Quarterly Journal of Speech, 9,* 160–169.

Fisher, W.R., & Burns, R.D. (1964). *Armament and disarmament: The continuing dispute.* Belmont, CA: Wadsworth Publishing.

Gadamer, H.G. (1980). *Dialogue and dialectic: Eight hermeneutical essays on Plato* (P. Christofer Smith, Trans.). New Haven, CT: Yale University Press.

McKerrow, R.E. (1982). Rationality and reasonableness in a theory of argument. In J.R. Cox & C.A. Willard (Eds.), *Advances in argumentation theory and research* (pp. 105–122). Carbondale, IL: Southern University Press.

Wieseltier, L. (1983, January 10 and 17). The great nuclear debate. *The New Republic,* 7–38.

Willard, C.A. (1982). Argument fields. In J.R. Cox & C.A. Willard (Eds), *Advances in argumentation theory and research* (pp. 24–77). Carbondale, IL: Southern Illinois University Press.

Ziegelmueller, G., & Rhodes, J. *Dimensions of argument: Proceedings of the second conference on argumentation.* Annandale, VA: Speech Communication Association.

ANDREA A. LUNSFORD
b. 1942

LISA S. EDE
b. 1947

Andrea Lunsford and Lisa Ede met as graduate students at Ohio State University in the early 1970s. They cannot recall whether their pleasure in one another's company or their shared interest in composition and rhetoric first brought them together, but since the mid-1970s the two have combined a close friendship with frequent collaborative writing projects. "On Distinctions between Classical and Modern Rhetoric" is one of their early collaborative efforts. In this essay, Ede and Lunsford challenge the tendency of scholars to emphasize the distinctions between classical and contemporary rhetoric and argue instead that scholars might more productively focus on their similarities. Lunsford and Ede said that the inclusion of this essay here provided an opportunity for them to reflect on the changes in their thinking in the last two decades. Although they still agree with their essay's basic position, if they were writing "On Distinction . . ." today, they would attempt to acknowledge the ways in which the postmodern critique has both complicated and enriched our understanding of the rhetorical tradition. They would also avoid the occasional sexist references to "man" that, in retrospect, seem glaringly inappropriate. Their most recent collaborative work is Singular Texts/Plural Authors: Perspectives on Collaborative Writing *(1990).*

On Distinctions between Classical and Modern Rhetoric

The tentative emergence of a modern or a "new" rhetoric has been characterized by the attempt both to recover and reexamine the concepts of classical rhetoric and to define itself *against* that classical tradition. The works of Richard Weaver, Richard McKeon, Kenneth Burke, Donald Bryant and, later, Albert Duhamel, Chaim Perelman, and Edward P. J. Corbett helped draw attention to major tenets and values of the classical system. Daniel Fogarty's important *Roots for a New Rhetoric* (1959) stands at a metaphorical crossroads, affirming the continuing need for a viable rhetoric and sketching in the broad outlines of a "new" rhetoric that would meet that need:

[The new rhetoric] will need to broaden its aim until it no longer confines itself to teaching the art of formal persuasion but includes formation in every

397

kind of symbol-using . . . ; it will need to adjust itself to the recent studies in the psychology and sociology of communication; and, finally, it will need to make considerable provision for a new kind of speaker-listener situation.[1]

The years since 1959 have witnessed numerous attempts to define modern rhetoric more fully—attempts that consistently have rested on distinctions drawn between classical rhetoric and an emerging "new" system.[2] We believe that focusing primarily on distinctions between the "old" and the "new" rhetoric has led to unfortunate oversimplifications and distortions. Consequently, our purpose in this essay is to survey the distinctions typically drawn between classical and modern rhetoric, to suggest why these distinctions are inaccurate and, most importantly, to note the compelling similarities between classical and modern rhetoric. These similarities, we believe, can help clarify the features essential to any dynamic theory of rhetoric.

Although stated in widely varying terms, the distinctions persistently drawn between classical and modern or "new" rhetoric fall under four related heads. Images of man and of society provide one area frequently cited as distinguishing the two rhetorical periods. According to many definers of new rhetoric, the classical tradition, and especially Aristotle, defined man as a "rational animal" who dealt with problems of the world primarily through logic or reason and who lived during a time characterized by stable values, social cohesion, and a unified cultural ideal.[3] In contrast, modern rhetoric defines man as essentially a "rhetorical" or "symbol-using" or "communal" animal who constitutes the world through shared and private symbols.[4] And this modern man is said to live not in a simple, cohesive society but in an aleatoric universe in which generally agreed upon values and unifying norms are scarce or nonexistent.[5] In such a universe, it is argued, the bases of classical rhetoric are simply inadequate.

The second distinction often drawn between classical and contemporary rhetoric—that classical rhetoric emphasizes logical proofs while modern rhetoric stresses emotional (or psychological) proofs—is closely related to the first. Young, Becker, and Pike argue, for example, that Aristotle's image of man as a rational animal had a direct influence on his rhetoric: "Underlying the classical tradition is the notion that although men are often swayed by passions, their basic and distinguishing characteristic is their ability to reason. . . . [Thus for classical rhetoricians] logical argument . . . was the heart of persuasive discourse."[6] According to Douglas Ehninger, this preference for logical proof is also evident in classical invention, which focuses on the analysis of subject matter at the expense of a concern for "the basic laws of human understanding." As a result, Ehninger notes, a successful classical orator has to be "an expert logician," while the modern speaker or writer needs, in contrast, to be "a keen student of practical psychology."[7]

A third often-cited distinction between the two periods concerns the rhetor-audience relationship, a relationship said to be characterized in the classical period by manipulative, antagonistic, one-way or unidirectional communication.[8] The new rhetoric is conversely said to posit not an antagonistic but a cooperative relationship between rhetor and audience, one based upon empathy, understanding, mutual trust, and two-way or "dialogic" communication.[9] In *Rhetoric: Discovery and Change,* for instance, Young, Becker, and Pike reject what they see as the classical model of "skillful verbal coercion" and introduce instead a "Rogerian rhetoric" of "enlightened cooperation."[10] In his 1967 and 1968 essays describing systems of rhetoric, Douglas Ehninger labels the new rhetoric "social" or "sociological" and argues that it is an "instrument for understanding."[11]

The final distinction often drawn between the two periods is inextricably related to the rhetor-audience relationship just described. This distinction results from identifying the goal of classical rhetoric as persuasion, while the goal of the new rhetoric is identified as communication. In his widely influential 1936 study, *The Philosophy of Rhetoric,* I. A. Richards articulates this view:

> Among the general themes of the old Rhetoric [which he associates with Aristotle] is one which is especially pertinent to our inquiry. The old Rhetoric was an offspring of dispute; it developed as the rationale of pleadings and persuadings; it was the theory of the battle of words and has always been itself dominated by the combative impulse.[12]

Wilbur Samuel Howell, whose works on sixteenth-, seventeenth-, and eighteenth-century rhetoric have become standard texts, also identifies persuasion as the goal of classical rhetoric and specifically argues that the "new" eighteenth-century rhetoric explicitly embraced exposition and communication as goals.[13] Recent articles by Otis Walter, Richard Ohmann, Herbert Simons, Douglas Ehninger, Richard Young, and Paul Bator describe classical (and often specifically Aristotelian) rhetoric as emphasizing success or winning above all else, often depicting rhetors as attempting to coerce or impose their will on others.[14] In Ohmann's words, classical rhetoric is "concerned, fundamentally, with *persuasion.* The practical rhetorician—the orator—seeks to impel his audience from apathy to action or from old opinion to new, by appealing to will, emotion, and reason. And the novice . . . learns the tricks."[15] Most of these writers claim that the new rhetoric, on the other hand, stresses not coercive persuasion but communication, understanding, and reduction of threat through dialogue.

Table 1 summarizes the four distinctions which are persistently drawn between classical and modern rhetoric. Of the many points which could be made about these distinctions, one seems particularly crucial: they resolve to two contradictory claims about the nature of classical rhetoric. The first two distinctions, which view the classical image of man as a rational being and the logical proofs as supreme, discount classical rhetoric as too rationalistic.[16] The latter two, which present the rhetor-audience relationship in classical rhetoric as antagonistic and unidirectional and its goal as persuasion (in the narrowest, most limited sense), discount classical rhetoric as too dependent upon emotional manipulation and coercion.

Table 1
Major Distinctions Typically Drawn between
Classical and Modern Rhetoric

Classical Rhetoric	Modern Rhetoric
1. Man is a rational animal living in a society marked by social cohesion and agreed-upon values.	1. Man is a symbol-using animal living in a fragmented society.
2. Emphasis is on logical (or rational) proofs.	2. Emphasis is on emotional (or psychological) proofs.
3. Rhetor-audience relationship is antagonistic, characterized by manipulative one-way communication.	3. Rhetor-audience relationship is cooperative, characterized by emphatic, two-way communication.
4. Goal is *persuasion*.	4. Goal is *communication*.

This disconcerting contradiction is perhaps the strongest evidence that the conventional understanding of classical rhetoric, as embodied in the above distinctions, is seriously flawed. The resulting confusion has led not only to major distortions and misrepresentations of classical rhetoric, but to critical misunderstandings of our own potential system as well. Although we believe a strong argument can be made that these distinctions distort classical rhetoric in general, space restrictions do not permit us to make such a case here.[17] Instead, we have chosen to use Aristotle as the locus of our discussion because the Aristotelian theory is the most complete of all classical rhetorics and, more importantly, because many current misconceptions grow out of a limited reading of Aristotle's *Rhetoric*. In particular, we wish to argue that the distinctions we have outlined reflect two major problems: 1) a failure to relate Aristotle's *Rhetoric* to the rest of his philosophy; and 2) serious, persistent misunderstandings about the nature and function of the *pisteis* and of the *enthymeme* in Aristotelian rhetoric.

One of the most essential characteristics of Aristotle's philosophical system is its integration. It is no accident, for example, that Aristotle begins his work on rhetoric by carefully noting its relationship with dialectic. As William M. A. Grimaldi observes in his *Studies in the Philosophy of Aristotle's Rhetoric*, Aristotle in this work "insists from the outset upon showing the relation of his comments to his work on dialectic, epistemology, ethics, and even metaphysics. . . . Throughout the analysis his constant explicit and implicit reference to his own philosophical work clearly reveals that he was working with his own philosophical system in mind."[18]

A recent article by Christopher Lyle Johnstone on "An Aristotelian Trilogy: Ethics, Rhetoric, Politics, and the Search for Moral Truth" demonstrates how the failure to relate Aristotle's analysis of rhetoric to his discussion of ethics and politics has resulted in critical misinterpretations of Aristotle's intent.[19] As an example, Johnstone cites the often-quoted passage in the *Rhetoric* in which Aristotle emphasizes the necessity of "putting the judge in 'a certain' or 'the right' frame of mind," a statement often used as evidence that Aristotle advocates crass emotional manipulation (p. 9). What commentators have failed to recognize is that in the *Nicomachean Ethics* Aristotle consistently uses the same phrase to mean "the *morally* right condition, the state in which emotion is amenable to rational guidance" (p. 9). This emphasis on rational guidance should not, however, be interpreted as support for the view that Aristotle advocates an exclusively rational rhetoric since the end of rhetoric, as Aristotle clearly indicates, is *krisis* (judgment), "an activity of the practical intellect, and thus one directed by *logos* and *pathos* functioning in a complementary relationship. As a result 'the right frame of mind' can only be taken to refer to that emotional state that, when joined by reason in the process of judging or deciding, makes intelligent and responsible choice possible" (pp. 9–10).[20]

This example is symptomatic of the misunderstandings that can occur when commentators ignore the fundamental connections among Aristotle's writings. Lawrence Rosenfield makes a similar point in "Rhetorical Criticism and an Aristotelian Notion of Process," which explores the relationship between Aristotle's concept of process, or "the way in which an object acquires characteristics or properties," and his concept of animism.[21] Basic to Rosenfield's argument is his assertion that "the essential contribution of the concept of animism to Aristotle's notion of process is that of dynamic interaction between an agent and an object undergoing change" (p. 4). As a result, Rosenfield questions whether in Aristotelian rhetoric "the figure which best captures the communicator's role . . . is not that of a puppeteer, who manipulates his audience according to his skill at persuasion, but that of a mid-wife who focuses and directs energies inherent in the listener himself" (p. 8). In fact, Aristotle's metaphysics intrinsically rejects exploitive or "monologic" communication from speaker to listener (p. 15).

As even this brief discussion should suggest, investigations of the relationship between Aristotle's rhetorical and philosophical writings can help us locate alternatives to previous interpretations of the *Rhetoric* which have, simplistically, tended to characterize that work as exclusively committed either to rational or emotional appeals. In order fully to resolve the reductive dilemma posed by these contradictory interpretations, however, we must finally turn to the *Rhetoric* itself, particularly to the *pisteis* and the *enthymeme*. For much of the confusion surrounding the *Rhetoric* can be traced, finally, to an inadequate understanding of the nature of and interrelationships among Aristotle's methods of proof.

As William Grimaldi observes, the traditional conception of the nature and role of the *pisteis* is that they are "three independent modes of rhetorical demonstration: non-logical (or quasi-logical) demonstration by the use of *ethos* and *pathos,* and logical demonstration by means of the *enthymeme,* the syllogism of rhetoric" (*Studies,* p. 65).[22] Such a view encourages the conflict between the role of reason and emotion in the *Rhetoric* which has complicated interpretations of that work and led to the contradiction noted above. For if the *pisteis* are viewed as discrete, separable elements of discourse, then *logos* and its tool the *enthymeme* may be isolated and crowned supreme (as some commentators have done). Or *pathos* may hold sway instead, resulting in a view of rhetoric as overly emotional and manipulative. The solution to this dilemma must be to replace an oversimplified notion of the *pisteis* as elements that can be added to discourse—rather like ingredients in a recipe—with a more complex understanding of the inseparable strands that link people engaged in discourse.

In his *Studies in the Philosophy of Aristotle's Rhetoric* and *Aristotle, Rhetoric I: A Commentary,* William Grimaldi articulates such an enriched, corrective perspective.[23] His complex argument cannot be fully described here, but particularly central to his discussion are: 1) his analyses of the multiple uses of the words *pistis* and *pisteis* in the original text[24] and of the pre-Aristotelian history of the word *enthymeme;* and 2) his discussion of the relationship of the *eide* and *koinoi topoi* to the *pisteis* (*logis, ethos,* and *pathos*) and of these *pisteis* to *enthymeme* and *paradeigma* (example). The resulting analysis represents a powerful alternative explication of the basic method of rhetorical discourse as outlined in the *Rhetoric.* In this method, the *enthymeme* is not a mere tool of *logos,* nor do the three *pisteis* of *logos, ethos,* and *pathos* function independently of one another. Rather, they interact in the *enthymeme* and *paradeigma,* the two central methods of rhetorical demonstration—the former deductive, the latter inductive. Thus Grimaldi clarifies our understanding of the *enthymeme,* broadening its generally accepted definition as the limited tool of *logos* to one of the two modes of inference through which rhetor and audience together move toward *krisis.*

Grimaldi's analysis thus dissolves the apparent contradiction between reason and emotion in the *Rhetoric* and demonstrates that the contradictory interpretations of classical rhetoric we described earlier represent a false dichotomy. Aristotle's *Rhetoric* is neither an abstract theoretical treatise in praise of *logos* nor a handbook of manipulative emotional tricks. Rather, through the *enthymeme,* which (along with *paradeigma*) integrates and organizes the *pisteis* of *logos, ethos,* and *pathos,* Aristotle develops a system of language use whereby individuals unite all their resources—intellect, will, and emotion—in communicating with one another. The *Rhetoric,* then, acknowledges that we are moved to *krisis* not just by knowledge but by emotion as well: "In rhetorical discourse the audience must be brought not only to knowledge of the subject but knowledge as relevant and significant for they are either indifferent, opposed, or in partial agreement. . . . If the whole person acts then it is the whole person to whom discourse in rhetoric must be directed" (*Studies*, pp. 146–47).

An understanding of how Aristotle's *Rhetoric* relates to his entire philosophical system and of how the *enthymeme* and the *pisteis* function in the *Rhetoric* suggests that the characterization of classical rhetoric summarized in Table 1 is inadequate and misleading. The first distinction, which posits classical man as solely a rational being living in a stable society seems particularly oversimplistic. As our discussion of the *enthymeme* indicates, the rational man of Aristotle's rhetoric is not a logic-chopping automaton but a language-using animal who unites reason and emotion in discourse with others. Aristotle (and indeed, Plato and Isocrates as well) studied the power of the mind to gain meaning from the world and to share that meaning with others.[25] And far from being a highly stable society marked by agreement on all values, Aristotle's Greece was one of upheaval: old beliefs in the gods were increasingly challenged, the political structure of the Greek city state system was under attack, and the educational system was embroiled in deep controversy.[26]

Equally inadequate is the second distinction, held by those who argue that classical rhetoric privileges logical proofs. As we have seen, such a view oversimplifies Aristotle's own complex analysis of the nature of reason, ignoring his careful discrimination of the speculative and practical intellect. In addition, this distinction misrepresents the nature and function of the *enthymeme* and the *pisteis*.

If *logos*, *ethos*, and *pathos* are dynamically related in the *enthymeme*, the third traditional distinction, which characterizes the rhetor-audience relationship in classical rhetoric as antagonistic and unidirectional, is equally unacceptable. Further support to this position is given by Lawrence Rosenfield's discussion of Aristotle's concept of process and by Lloyd Bitzer's analysis of the *enthymeme* in "Aristotle's Enthymeme Revisited," which argues that since "enthymemes occur only when speaker and audience jointly produce them . . . [they] intimately unite speaker and audience and provide the strongest possible proofs."[27] Far from being "one-way," "manipulative," or "monological," Aristotle's rhetoric provides a complete description of the dynamic interaction between rhetor and audience, an interaction mediated by language. Seen in the light of Aristotle's entire system of thought, the rhetorical elements of rhetor, audience, and subject matter are dynamic, interlocking forces.

Finally, if the relationship between the rhetor and the audience in Aristotle's system is indeed dynamic and interdependent, then the goal of Aristotelian rhetoric can hardly be persuasion in the narrow or pejorative sense in which it is used by those who equate persuasion with manipulation and coercion. We suggest that a much more accurate way to describe Aristotle's concept of the goal of rhetoric is as an interactive means of discovering meaning through language.[28] It is, as Richard Hughes notes in "The Contemporaneity of Classical Rhetoric," "a generative process," one in which the rhetor "is both investigator and communicator."[29] As Grimaldi observes, rhetoric was for Aristotle "the heart of the process by which man tried to interpret and make meaningful for himself and others the world of the real" (*Studies*, p. 54). This process may be termed "persuasion," only in the broad sense that all language is inherently persuasive. In his discussion of the function of rhetoric, Kenneth Burke says that "there is no chance of our keeping apart the meanings of persuasion, identification ('consubstantiality') and communication." We have thus, Burke notes, "come to the point at which Aristotle begins his treatise on rhetoric."[30]

In spite of the large body of scholarship which should have kept us from drawing misleading distinctions, the view of classical rhetoric as manipulative, monologic, and rationalistic persists. We believe that we, therefore, must also come back to Aristotle, to a richer understanding of how his theory can enrich and illuminate our own. Indeed, major distinctions between Aristotelian and contemporary rhetoric do exist, but these distinctions are

Table 2
Similarities and Qualifying Distinctions between
Classical and Modern Rhetoric

1. Both classical and modern rhetoric view man as a language-usage animal who unites reason and emotion in discourse with another.
   Qualifying distinction:
   Aristotle addresses himself primarily to the oral use of language; ours is primarily an age of print.
2. In both periods rhetoric provides a dynamic methodology whereby rhetor and audience may jointly have access to knowledge.
   Qualifying distinction:
   According to Aristotle, rhetor and audience come into a state of knowing which places them in a clearly defined relationship with the world and with each other, mediated by their language. The prevailing modernist world view compels rhetoric to operate without any such clearly articulated theory of the knower and the known.
3. In both periods rhetoric has the potential to clarify and inform activities in numerous related fields.
   Qualifying distinction:
   Aristotle's theory establishes rhetoric as an art and relates it clearly to all fields of knowledge. Despite the efforts of modern rhetoricians, we lack any systematic, generally accepted theory to inform current practice.

more fundamental than those traditionally cited. While we shall note these distinctions, we wish to stress what we believe are compelling similarities between the two rhetorics, similarities which draw contemporary rhetoric closer to the classical system rather than further away from it. Our understanding of these similarities and of the profound distinctions which must accompany them, as outlined in Table 2, will help us identify those qualities which must characterize any vital theory of rhetoric.

One similarity between classical and modern rhetoric is their shared *concept of man as a language-using animal who unites reason and emotion in discourse with another.* Central to this concept is the role of language in the creation of knowledge or belief and its relationship to the knowing mind. We have already demonstrated the ways in which Aristotle's *Rhetoric* unites reason and emotion. In addition, Aristotle's works on logic, ethics, and epistemology as well as the *Rhetoric* demonstrate that Aristotle recognized the powerful dynamism of the creating human mind. These works further indicate that Aristotle was aware of man's ability to use symbols and that he viewed language as the medium through which judgments about the world are communicated.

Modern theories, of course, also posit language as the ground of rhetoric. This view is articulated in Burke's famous statement that rhetoric "is rooted in an essential function of language itself, a function that is wholly realistic, and is continually born anew; the use of language as a symbolic means of inducing cooperation in beings that by nature respond to symbols."[31] Theorists as dissimilar as I. A. Richards, Chaim Perelman, and Wayne Booth hold parallel views on the relation between language and rhetoric.

As expected in rhetorics removed by twenty-three hundred years, however, Aristotle's system of language use differs from ours. The resultant distinction between the two periods is potentially profound: Aristotle addressed himself primarily to oral discourse; modern rhetorics have addressed themselves primarily to written discourse. Our understanding of the historical and methodological ramifications of the speaking/writing distinction has been hampered by the twentieth-century split among speech, linguistics, philosophy, and English departments. Despite the work of scholars such as Walter Ong, Kenneth Burke, and Jacques Derrida, many questions about the relationship of speech and writing remain unanswered and, in some cases, unexplored.[32]

The second major similarity we find between Aristotelian and modern rhetoric is the view of rhetoric as a *techne or dynamic methodology through which rhetor and audience, a self and an other, may jointly have access to knowledge.*[33] We have already examined Aristotle's concept of the *enthymeme* and the ways in which it united speaker and audience, *logos, ethos,* and *pathos,* in the pursuit of knowledge leading to action. In modern theory, particularly the work of Kenneth Burke, rhetoric provides the means through which we may both achieve identification with an other and understand that identification through the attribution of motives. Similarly, Chaim Perelman's rhetorical system posits rhetoric as the process through which rhetor and audience gain access to knowledge.

We believe that such a view of rhetoric as creative or epistemic must characterize any viable, dynamic rhetoric and, indeed, any other view reduces the role of rhetoric to a "naming of parts" or to stylistic embellishment, reductions characteristic of many rhetorical theories. But this basic similarity should not mask an equally important distinction between classical and modern rhetoric. As we have seen, this distinction concerns not the notion of man, the nature of proof, the speaker-audience relationship, nor the goal of rhetoric. Instead, this distinction concerns the nature and status of knowledge.[34]

In Aristotle's system, knowledge may be either of the necessary or the contingent. Knowledge of the necessary or universal, *episteme*, operates in the realm of the theoretical or scientific. Breaking with Plato, Aristotle admits of another kind of knowledge, that of the contingent. Such knowledge, *doxa*, is the way of knowing contingent reality (that is, the world around us that is both characterized and limited by change). Rhetoric's realm is limited to the contingent, and the connections among language, thought, and that reality are grounded in an epistemology which posits reality independent of the knower. In short, rhetoric uses thought and language to lead to judgment (*krisis*) as the basis of action in matters of this world. And for Aristotle, that world of contingent reality, though itself in a state of flux, could be understood by systematic application of the intellect because that reality was itself thought to be informed by stable first principles.

Modern rhetorical theory rests on no such fully confident epistemology, nor does knowledge enjoy such a clearly defined status. In fact, we are in radical disagreement over what "knowledge" may be, though we generally agree on man's ability to communicate that disagreement. Hence, for the modern period, connections among thought, language, and reality are thought to be grounded not in an independent, charitable reality but in the nature of the knower instead, and reality is not so much discovered or discoverable as it is constituted by the interplay of thought and language. Though we lack a fully articulated theory, Kenneth Burke, Richard Weaver, and Wayne Booth offer intensive investigations into the rhetoric of this interplay; and works in disciplines as diverse as anthropology, language philosophy, literary criticism, philosophy, psychology, and the physical sciences suggest that, as Michael Polanyi says in the opening of *Personal Knowledge,* "We must inevitably see the universe from a center lying within ourselves and speak about it in terms of a human language shaped by the exigencies of human intercourse. Any attempt rigorously to eliminate our human perspective from our pictures of the world must lead to absurdity."[35]

Rhetoric's grounding in language and its potential ability to join rhetor and audience in the discovery of shared (communicable) knowledge suggests a third compelling similarity between classical and modern rhetoric: *in both periods rhetoric has the potential to clarify and inform activities in numerous related fields.* By establishing rhetoric as the *antistrophos* or corollary of dialectic,[36] Aristotle immediately places rhetoric in relation to other fields of knowledge, and these relationships are painstakingly worked out in the *Organon.* Rhetoric, poetics, and ethics all involve *doxa,* knowledge of contingent, shifting reality. Hence, rhetoric is necessarily useful in addressing complex human problems in any field where certainty is unachievable.

In addition, Aristotle's *Rhetoric* provided a theory that was intimately related to practice. For the Greeks, and indeed for the Romans who followed them, rhetoric was a practical art of discourse which played a central role in education and in the daily affairs of citizens. Aristotle's work established a theoretical relationship among belief, language, and action; Isocrates, Cicero, and Quintilian all adapted and acted out that theory, Quintilian using it as a basis for a rhetoric which would serve as a way of knowing and a guide to action throughout a person's life.

From the time of Quintilian, the history of rhetoric has been haunted by a whittling away of domain, a compartmentalization of its offices, and a frequent dramatic separation of theory and practice. The most obvious instance of rhetoric's diminution is Ramus' assignment of *inventio* and *dispositio* to logic, thus leaving rhetoric with a concern only for style. Even George Campbell and Alexander Bain, both of whom attempted to ground rhetoric in a full psychology, did not fully admit invention into the province of rhetoric. Not until philosophers began to recapture the crucial conception of language as a meaning-making activity, an essential element in the social construction of reality, has rhetoric had the opportunity to regain some of its lost status and scope, to inform both education and ordinary behavior and thus clarify a number of related fields.

Why, thus far at least, has this opportunity not been realized? A partial answer to this question must lie in what we see as a final qualifying distinction between classical and modern rhetorics. Aristotle's theory is revolutionary in that it establishes rhetoric as an art and relates it clearly to all fields of knowledge. Despite the efforts of modern rhetoricians, we lack any such systematic theory to inform current practice. In fact, our age has witnessed a curious divorce between rhetorical theory and practice and an extreme fragmentation of our discipline. Earlier in this essay, we alluded to the large body of rhetorical "theory" which argues that modern rhetoric is characterized by understanding, mutual sharing, and two-way communication. Yet how well does such theory account for or describe twentieth-century rhetorical practice, which has surely reached new heights (or depths) of manipulative use of language?

The position of rhetorical theory and practice in education is equally fragmented. While theorists in speech departments consider the theoretical concept of "dialogic communication," their counterparts in English departments struggle over abstruse questions of intentionality in literary texts, and scholars in linguistics departments strive to describe the abstract grammar of a sentence. Meanwhile, instruction in rhetorical practice—speaking, writing, and reading—is usually relegated to graduate students and part-time instructors and looked upon as menial "service." As a result, most of our textbooks offer compendia of "how-to" tips but fail to ground that advice in a theoretical framework that would relate language, action, and belief.[37]

Such a situation is a far cry from Aristotle's elegant theory, from Cicero's powerful statesmanship, or from Quintilian's masterful pedagogy. But if our failure to articulate a systematic theory which informs current practice is great, our need is even greater. We believe that the work of such theorists as Kenneth Burke, Chaim Perelman, Wolfgang Iser, Richard Weaver, and Wayne Booth offers a modern ground for the reunion of rhetorical theory and practice. But such a reunion demands that we attempt to reinstate rhetoric at or near the center of our curriculum, as the art of using language in the creation—and sharing—of knowledge and belief.

One way to begin this task is by eschewing the false distinctions that have been drawn persistently between classical and modern rhetoric and by building instead on their powerful similarities. If we see Aristotle's *Rhetoric* as a work which unites rhetor and audience, language and action, theory and practice, then we have a model for our own *antistrophos*. If rhetoric is to reach its full potential in the twentieth century as an informing framework for long-divorced disciplines and for instruction and conduct in reading, writing, and speaking, then we must define ourselves not in opposition to but in consonance with the classical model.

Notes

1. Daniel Fogarty, S.J., *Roots for a New Rhetoric* (New York: Russell and Russell, 1959), p. 130.
2. We are thinking particularly of Otis M. Walter, "On Views of Rhetoric, Whether Conservative or Progressive," *Quarterly Journal of Speech* 49 (Dec. 1963): 367–82; rpt. in *Contemporary Theories of Rhetoric,* ed. Richard Johannesen (New York: Harper and Row, 1971), pp. 18–38; Richard Ohmann, "In Lieu of a New Rhetoric," *College English* 26 (Oct. 1961): 17–22, rpt. in Johannesen, pp. 63–71; Wayne E. Brockriede, "Toward a Contemporary Aristotelian Theory of Rhetoric," *Quarterly Journal of Speech* 52 (Feb. 1966): 33–40, rpt. in Johannesen, pp. 39–49; Herbert W. Simons, "Toward a New Rhetoric," *Pennsylvania Speech Annual* 24 (Sept. 1967): 7–20, rpt. in Johannesen, pp. 50–62; Douglas Ehninger, "On Rhetoric and Rhetorics," *Western Speech* 31 (1967): 242–49, and "On Systems of Rhetoric," *Philosophy and Rhetoric* 1 (Summer 1968): 431–44, rpt. in *Contemporary Rhetoric,* ed. Douglas Ehninger (Glenview, Ill.: Scott, Foresman and Co., 1972), pp. 49–58; Howard Martin and Kenneth Andersen, *Speech Communication: Analyses and Readings* (Boston: Allyn and Bacon,

1968); Richard Young, Alton Becker, and Kenneth Pike, *Rhetoric: Discovery and Change* (New York: Harcourt, Brace, and World, 1970); S. Michael Halloran, "On the End of Rhetoric, Classical and Modern," *College English* 36 (Feb. 1975): 621-31, and "Tradition and Theory in Rhetoric," *Quarterly Journal of Speech* 62 (Oct. 1976): 234-41; Robert L. Scott, "A Synoptic View of Systems of Western Rhetoric," *Quarterly Journal of Speech* 61 (Dec. 1975): 439-47, and its companion piece of the same title by Douglas Ehninger, 448-53; Richard Young, "Paradigms and Problems: Needed Research in Rhetorical Invention," in *Research on Composing*, ed. Charles Cooper and Lee Odell (Urbana, Ill.: NCTE, 1978), pp. 28-48; Frank Zappen, "Carl R. Rogers and Political Rhetoric," *Pre-Text* 1 (Spring-Fall 1980): 95-113; and Paul Bator, "Aristotelian and Rogerian Rhetoric," *College Composition and Communication* 31 (Dec. 1980): 427-32.

3. See, for example, Ehninger, "A Synoptic View of Systems of Western Rhetoric," 452; Young, Becker, and Pike, *Rhetoric: Discovery and Change*, p. 6; Halloran, "Tradition and Theory in Rhetoric," 236; and Zappen, "Carl R. Rogers and Political Rhetoric," 98.

4. These definitions stem primarily from Kenneth Burke's profound efforts to articulate a contemporary rhetoric, though Burke in no way upholds or sets forth the problematic distinctions we have previously detailed. For a discussion of man as communal, see Young, Becker, and Pike's *Rhetoric: Discovery and Change*, pp. 7-9, and the articles on dialogic communication listed in note 9.

5. Halloran, "On the End of Rhetoric, Classical and Modern," 624.

6. *Rhetoric: Discovery and Change*, p. 6. This notion is reiterated by Paul Bator in "Aristotelian and Rogerian Rhetoric."

7. Douglas Ehninger, "George Campbell and the Revolution in Inventional Theory," *Southern Speech Journal* 15 (May 1950): 274.

8. See, for example, Robert L. Scott, "Dialogue and Rhetoric," in *Rhetoric and Communication*, ed. J. Blankenship and H. G. Stelzner (Urbana: Univ. of Illinois Press, 1976), p. 101; David B. Strother, "Communication and Human Response: A Heuristic View," also in the Blankenship and Stelzner volume; and Paul Bator, "Aristotelian and Rogerian Rhetoric," previously cited in note 2. *Rhetoric: Discovery and Change* also perpetuates this view.

9. Richard I. Johannesen, "The Emerging Concept of Communication as Dialogue," *Quarterly Journal of Speech* 57 (1971): 373-82; John Stewart, "Foundations of Dialogic Communication," *Quarterly Journal of Speech* 64 (1978): 183-201; John Poulakos, "The Components of Dialogue," *Western Speech* 38 (1974): 199-212; Floyd Matson and Ashley Montagu, eds., *The Human Dialogue* (New York: Macmillan, Free Press, 1967); Frank Keller and Charles Brown, "An Interpersonal Ethic for Communication," *Journal of Communication* 16 (1968): 73-81.

10. *Rhetoric: Discovery and Change*, pp. 8-9.

11. Ehninger, "On Systems of Rhetoric," in *Contemporary Rhetoric*, p. 53.

12. I. A. Richards, *The Philosophy of Rhetoric* (New York: Oxford Univ. Press, 1936), p. 24.

13. Wilbur Samuel Howell, *Eighteenth-Century British Logic and Rhetoric* (Princeton, N.J.: Princeton Univ. Press, 1971), pp. 441-42.

14. See note 2 for full citations.

15. Ohmann, "In Lieu of a New Rhetoric," rpt. in *Contemporary Theories of Rhetoric*, p. 64.

16. They do so often in reference to Aristotle's condemnation, early in Book 1, of *pathos* in the hands of the technographers. Yet Aristotle by no means denies that

pathos is part of the rhetorical art. He is rather questioning the misuse of *pathos* by these technographers. See William Grimaldi, *Aristotle, Rhetoric I: A Commentary* (Bronx, N.Y.: Fordham Univ. Press, 1980), p. 7.

17. As we were completing this essay, we were fortunate to receive a copy of an article by Floyd D. Anderson, "The Classical Conception of Communication as Dialogue." Professor Anderson makes a very persuasive argument in his essay for all of classical rhetoric as sharing what we argue is an Aristotelian view of communication. We are indebted to Professor Anderson for sharing his insights with us.

18. William M. A. Grimaldi, *Studies in the Philosophy of Aristotle's Rhetoric* (Wiesbaden: Frans Steiner Verlag, 1972), p. 18. Subsequent references will be cited in the text as *Studies.*

19. Christopher Lyle Johnstone, "An Aristotelian Trilogy: Ethics, Rhetoric, Politics, and the Search for Moral Truth," *Philosophy and Rhetoric* 13 (Winter 1980): 1–24. Subsequent references will be cited in the text.

20. The failure to read the *Rhetoric* in light of Aristotle's other works is further exacerbated by difficulties in translation. In "The Greekless Reader and Aristotle's *Rhetoric,*" Thomas M. Conley demonstrates that Lane Cooper's popular translation is seriously flawed in a number of places. In particular, Conley argues that where Aristotle discusses the importance of getting the "judge into the right frame of mind," the Greek does not "express the one-way view of persuasion" usually inferred. *Quarterly Journal of Speech* 65 (1979): 75.

21. Lawrence W. Rosenfield, "Rhetorical Criticism and an Aristotelian Notion of Process," *Quarterly Journal of Speech* 33 (Mar. 1966): 1–16. Subsequent references will be cited in the text.

22. Douglas Ehninger notes, for example, in his discussion of "Campbell, Blair, and Whately Revisited," *Southern Speech Journal* 28 (Spring 1963): 169–82, that in classical rhetorical theory the *pisteis* "were viewed as autonomous. Each was considered as complete in itself, and as entirely capable of effecting conviction without the aid of the others" (172).

23. Grimaldi, *Aristotle, Rhetoric I: A Commentary.* Subsequent references will be cited in the text and notes as *Commentary.*

24. The heart of Grimaldi's analysis reveals that the Greek word for *pisteis* is used by Aristotle to indicate both *logos, pathos,* and *ethos* (the *entechnic pisteis*) and *enthymeme* and *paradeigma* (the *apodeictic pisteis*). See especially the Appendix, "The Role of the *Pisteis* in Aristotle's Methodology," *Commentary,* pp. 319–56.

25. See Aristotle, *The "Art" of Rhetoric,* trans. John Henry Freese (Cambridge: Harvard Univ. Press, Loeb Classical Library, 1926), 1355a 27–28, 1395b 31–1396a 4, 1402a 33.

26. We are indebted to Michael Halloran for pointing out that the oratory of fourth-century B.C. Athens reveals much about contemporary cultural turmoil.

27. Lloyd Bitzer, "Aristotle's Enthymeme Revisited," *Quarterly Journal of Speech,* 15 (Dec. 1959), 108.

28. Grimaldi makes essentially the same point: "As soon as it is understood that rhetoric for Aristotle is an activity which engages the whole person in an effort to communicate meaning by way of language a major obstacle toward understanding the *Rhetoric* is removed" (*Studies,* p. 53).

29. Richard Hughes, "The Contemporaneity of Classical Rhetoric," *College Composition and Communication* 16 (1965): 158–59.

30. Kenneth Burke, *A Rhetoric of Motives* (1950; rpt. Berkeley: Univ. of California Press, 1969), p. 46.

31. Ibid., p. 43.
32. In "Rhetoric in the American College Curriculum: The Decline of Public Discourse" *Pre/Text* 3 (1982): 245-69, Michael Halloran traces the move from oral discourse to written discourse in American colleges and draws a number of provocative and insightful conclusions about the results of that move.
33. Grimaldi provides an illuminating discussion of the relationship of *techne* to *dynamis* in *Commentary,* pp. 5-6.
34. Among the articles we have read which draw distinctions between classical and modern rhetoric, Michael Halloran's works cited in note 2 deal substantively with this epistemological difference.
35. Michael Polanyi, *Personal Knowledge: Towards a Post-Critical Philosophy* (Chicago: Univ. of Chicago Press, 1962), p. 3.
36. Otis Walter has recently argued that the opening sentence of the *Rhetoric* be interpreted as "Rhetoric must follow the lead of an informed, searching and brilliant intellect" and that this sentence is the most significant in the *Rhetoric* because it "carries Aristotle's revolutionary intent, because it suggests his concern for knowing, [and] because it contains the ethical case for knowledge." Such an interpretation fits well with, and indeed supports, our view of Aristotle's concept of rhetoric and its relationship to knowledge and human action. See "The Most Important Sentence in Aristotle's Rhetoric," *Rhetoric Society Quarterly* 12 (1982): 18-20.
37. In "An Adequate Epistemology for Composition: Classical and Modern Perspectives," also in this volume, John Gage presents a persuasive discussion of how the concept of the enthymeme has been reduced to sterile formulae in modern texts, and he goes on to show how a fuller understanding of Aristotle's enthymeme can provide the kind of theoretical framework we are calling for here.

JIM W. CORDER
b. 1930

The editors think it appropriate to have Jim Corder, given his particular ethos, speak in his own voice.

I was born in West Texas, in Jayton, a small town of some 600 souls. That doesn't include Mr. Boone Bilberry. He drank a little, sometimes turned fuzzy around the edges, and the Baptists said he didn't have a soul to count. Since, I have traveled the length and breadth of Kent County and Stonewall County, with occasional fearful expeditions elsewhere. I did graduate work at the University of Oklahoma, took the PhD in 1958, and came to Texas Christian University, where I have been since, though it's sometimes hard to tell, for I sometimes vanish before my very eyes. I have been chair of the English department, dean of the College of Arts and Sciences, and associate vice-chancellor, but I returned full-time to the English department some years ago. They told me that if I plugged away I would eventually get steady work.

I came to the study of rhetoric late, as many my age did, having concentrated in graduate school on Restoration and eighteenth-century English literature. I taught Dryden and Pope and Johnson (or like to imagine that I did) long before I thought about rhetoric. More or less self-taught, therefore poorly taught, I think that much of my learning in rhetoric has been erratic and sporadic, unsystematic and inadequate. Sometimes, I not only don't know, I don't even suspect. I like to think about and around and once in a while through rhetoric, but I don't think of myself as a rhetorician. I'd rather be called by my name, if I'm to be called at all. I have committed papers and even composition textbooks with the word rhetoric in their titles, as if I knew and were composing a rhetoric. I'm no longer much interested in such enterprises, unless I can at the same time think about and understand a little the rhetoric I'm already in whenever I say or write anything about rhetoric. Since I can't fix either myself or rhetoric, I'd rather think about two or three small rhetorics, remembering to take the word as plural, trying to understand, for example, the consequences for rhetoric if one thinks of all speakers as remnants or leftovers, or trying to understand the consequences for rhetoric if one decides, momentarily say, that all rhetoric is nostalgic, resonant with regret and loss, or trying to understand how one might make a rhetoric yonder on the other side of regret and loss.

Argument as Emergence, Rhetoric as Love

1

In a recent review in *The New York Times Book Review,* A. G. Mojtabai said, "We are all authors. Adding here, deleting there, we people the world with our needs: with friends, lovers, ciphers, enemies, villains—and heroes" (March 3, 1985, 7). All authors, to be sure, we are more particularly narrators, historians, tale-tellers. Going through experience, hooking some version of it to ourselves, accumulating what we know as evidence and insight, ignoring what does not look like evidence and insight to us, finding some pieces of life that become life for us, failing to find others, or choosing not to look, each of us creates the narrative that he or she is. We tell our lives and live our tales, enjoying where we can, tolerating what we must, turning away to re-tell, or sinking into madness and disorder if we cannot make (or re-make) our tale into a narrative we can live in. Each of us forms conceptions of the world, its institutions, its public, private, wide, or local histories, and each of us is the narrative that shows our living in and through the conceptions that are always being formed as the tales of our lives take their shape. In this history-making, as E. L. Doctorow says, "there is no fiction or non-fiction as we commonly understand the distinction" ("False Documents," *American Review* 26 [1977]: 215-32). There is only our making, sometimes by design, sometimes not. None of us lives without a history; each of us is a narrative. We're always standing some place in our lives, and there is always a tale of how we came to stand there, though few of us have marked carefully the dimensions of the place where we are or kept time with the tale of how we came to be there.

The catch is that, though we are all fiction-makers/historians, we are seldom all that good at the work. Sometimes we can't find all that's needed to make the narrative we want of ourselves, though we still make our narrative. Sometimes we don't see enough. Sometimes we find enough and see enough and still tell it wrong. Sometimes we fail to judge either the events within our narrative or the people, places, things, and ideas that might enter our narrative. Sometimes we judge dogmatically, even ignorantly, holding only to standards that we have already accepted or established. We see only what our eyes will let us see at a given moment, but eventually make a narrative of ourselves that we can enjoy, tolerate, or at least not have to think about too much. Every so often, we will see something we have not seen before, and then we have to nudge, poke, and re-make our narrative, or we decide we can either ignore the thing seen or whittle it to shape the narrative we already have. We are always seeing, hearing, thinking, living, and saying the fiction that we and our times make possible and tolerable, a fiction that is the history we can assent to at a given time. But not only can we not always be good narrators/historians, we also cannot be thorough at the work. We never quite get the narrative all said: we're always making a fiction/history that always has to be re-made, unless we are so bound by dogma, arrogance, and ignorance that we cannot see a new artifact, hear a new opinion, or enter a new experience in our narrative.

When I say that we make the fictions that are our lives, I mean to identify a human activity, not a foolish or evil one. History as fiction may become evil, of course, if we refuse to see any history except the one we've already accepted or if we try to force that history upon others. At any rate, making the fiction of our lives—not at all the same as discovering a way to present an objective, externally verifiable history, which is not possible, anywhere— is not by nature limited, valueless, ignorant, despicable, or "merely subjective." It is human. It is what we do and are, even if we think we are doing and being something else. Even if we imagine that we are learning what can be known "out there," some truths that are fixed and forever, we are after all creating our narratives "in here," ourselves always agents for what can be known. We are always, as the rhetorician might say, inventing the narratives that are our lives.

As I have already suggested, we are always standing somewhere in our narratives when we speak to others or to ourselves. When we use language, some choices have already been made and others must be made. Our narratives, which include our pasts, accompany us and exist in our statements and exercise their influence whether or not we are aware of the influence. Before we speak, we have lived; when we speak, we must continually choose because our mouths will not say two words simultaneously. Whether consciously or not, we always station ourselves somewhere in our narratives when we use language. This means that invention always occurs. The process of invention may occur in a conscious, deliberate way, but it will occur, even if at some subterranean level. Any statement carries its history with it. We may speak without knowing all of our narratives, but the history is there. If the history of a statement someone else makes isn't apparent to us as hearers, then we have to go and find it. If we are talking to someone and that person says something we don't understand, or something that offends us, or something we cannot easily agree to, then we have to start searching that person's history until we begin to understand what led him or her to speak just so. Sometimes we do less well: if the history isn't there for us, we don't learn it, but instead make it up to suit ourselves. If we learn or make up another's narrative so that it becomes part of our narrative, then we can live in some peace with the other. If the other's narrative will not enter our own, then something else happens, to which I'll return in a moment.

While the language that lets us invent our narratives and be human is a great gift, its capacities will not extend infinitely. Language comes out of us a word at a time; we cannot get all said at once. We open ourselves as we can to insight and experience and say what we can, but what we say will invariably be incomplete. Two words cannot occupy the same space at the same time; two messages cannot fully occupy the same space at the same time. Language enforces a closure: we must say one thing or the other; we choose, and make our narrative. To be sure, having lived, thought, and spoken, we can open ourselves again to insight and experience and evidence and try to say it all again. But what will come out will be the fiction we can make at the time. We cannot make all that was and is and shall be into an is of the moment's speaking. Whatever we can get into our heads we will make into the narratives that will be our truths unless we learn again.

2

Each of us is a narrative. A good part of the time we can live comfortably adjacent to or across the way from other narratives. Our narratives can be congruent with other narratives, or untouched by other narratives. But sometimes another narrative impinges upon ours, or thunders around and down into our narratives. We can't build this other into our narratives without harm to the tales we have been telling. This other is a narrative in another world; it is disruptive, shocking, initially at least incomprehensible, and, as Carl Rogers has shown us, threatening.

When this happens, our narratives become indeed what they are perpetually becoming—arguments. The choosing we do to make our narratives (whether or not we are aware of the nature of our choosing) also makes our narratives into arguments. The narratives we tell (ourselves) create and define the worlds in which we hold our beliefs. Our narratives are the evidence we have of ourselves and of our convictions. Argument, then, is not something we *make* outside ourselves; argument is what we are. Each of us is an argument. We always live in, through, around, over, and under argument. All the choices we've made, accidentally or on purpose, in creating our histories/narratives have also made us arguments, or, I should go on to say, sets of congruent arguments, or in some instances, sets of conflicting arguments.

3

Each of us is an argument, evidenced by our narrative. What happens, then, if the narrative of another crushes up against our own—disruptive, shocking, incomprehensible, threatening, suddenly showing us into a narrative not our own? What happens if a narrative not our own reveals to us that our own narrative was wanting all along, though it is the only evidence of our identity? What happens if the merest glimpse into another narrative sends us lurching, stunned by its differentness, either alarmed that such differentness could exist or astonished to see that our own narrative might have been or might yet be radically otherwise than it is? Do we hold our narratives? Keep telling the story we have been telling? At all costs?

We react, of course, in many different ways. Sometimes we turn away from other narratives. Sometimes we teach ourselves not to know that there are other narratives. Sometimes—probably all too seldom—we encounter another narrative and learn to change our own. Sometimes we lose our plot, and our convictions as well; since our convictions belong to our narratives, any strong interference with our narrative or sapping of its way of being will also interrupt or sap our convictions. Sometimes we go to war. Sometimes we sink into madness, totally unable to manage what our wit or judgment has shown us—a contending narrative that has force to it and charm and appeal and perhaps justice and beauty as well, a narrative compelling us to attention and toward belief that we cannot ultimately give, a contending narrative that shakes and cracks all foundations and promises to alter our identity, a narrative that would educate us to be wholly other than what we are. Any narrative exists in time; any narrative is made of the past, the present, and the future. We cannot without potential harm shift from the past of one narrative into the present and future of another, or from the past and present of one narrative into the future of another, or from the future we are narrating into a past that is not readily ours. How can we take that one chance I mentioned just now and learn to change when change is to be cherished? How can we expect another to change when we are ourselves that other's contending narrative?

4

Let there be no mistake: a contending narrative, that is, an argument of genuine consequence because it confronts one life with another is a threat, whether it is another's narrative become argument impinging upon or thundering into ours, or our own, impinging upon the other's. A contending narrative, I'd suggest, is a threat more consequential than Carl Rogers has shown us. In *On Becoming a Person* (Boston: Houghton Mifflin Company, 1961), Rogers proposes that "significant learning . . . takes place when five conditions are met":

- when the client perceives himself as faced by a serious problem;
- when the therapist is a congruent person in the relationship, able to *be* the person he *is;*

- when the therapist feels an unconditional positive regard for the client;
- when the therapist experiences an accurate emphatic understanding of the client's private world and communicates this;
- when the client to some degree experiences the therapist's congruence, acceptance, and empathy.

Rogers had earlier applied his thinking more directly to rhetoric, announcing his belief that a sense of threat usually blocks successful communication. As he put it, "the major barrier to mutual interpersonal communication is our very natural tendency to judge, to evaluate, to approve or disapprove, the statement of the other person" ("Communication: Its Blocking and Its Facilitation," paper delivered at Northwestern University's Centennial Conference on Communication, Oct. 11, 1951, reprinted in Richard E. Young, Alton L. Becker, and Kenneth L. Pike, *Rhetoric: Discovery and Change* [New York: Harcourt, Brace, and World, 1979], 284-89). If we refrain from evaluating and instead "listen with understanding," according to Rogers, we will "see the expressed idea and attitude from the other person's point of view . . . sense how it feels to him . . . achieve his frame of reference in regard to the thing he is talking about" (285). When we are immersed in the attitudes, ideas, and beliefs of the other person, we "will find the emotion going out of the discussion, the differences being reduced, and those differences which remain being of a rational and understandable sort" (286).

Such insights have been enormously valuable in recent years. Some (Maxine Hairston, for example) believe that Rogers' work has brought a new dimension to rhetoric after all these centuries, changing our way of thinking about argument. Others believe that Rogers' views are assumed by Aristotle, as Andrea Lunsford put it, to be "the foundation which is necessary before successful argumentation begins" ("Aristotelian vs. Rogerian Argument: A Reassessment," *College Composition and Communication* [May, 1979]: 146-51). Lunsford singles out two texts that propose methods of organizing Rogerian argument. Young, Becker, and Pike (283) suggest the following method:

First: an introduction to the problem and a demonstration that the opponent's position is understood.
Second: a statement of the contexts in which the opponent's position may be valid.
Third: a statement of the writer's position, including the contexts in which it is valid.
Fourth: a statement of how the opponent's position would benefit if he were to adopt elements of the writer's position.

In *A Contemporary Rhetoric* (Boston: Houghton Mifflin and Co., 1974, 210-11), Maxine Hairston presents another Rogerian pattern:

1. a brief, objectively phrased statement of the issue.
2. a complete and impartially worded summary of your audience's opinions on the issue, demonstrating that you have made an honest effort to understand how they feel and why they feel that way. It would be useful to mention the values that underlie these opinions.
3. an objective statement of your opinions on the issue, along with your reasons for feeling as you do. Here again it would be useful to give the values on which you base your opinions.
4. an analysis of what your opinions have in common.
5. a proposal for resolving the issue in a way that injures neither party.

Such insights added to those of Carl Rogers, I'll say again, have been highly valuable. They lead to patterns of argument that may even work, part of the time, in some settings. But they won't do. They do not, I believe, face the flushed, feverish, quaky, shaky, angry, scared, hurt, shocked, disappointed, alarmed, outraged, even terrified condition that a person comes to when his or her narrative is opposed by a genuinely contending narrative. Then it is one life or another, perhaps this life or none.

I want to pause a little to suggest some of the reasons that I think Rogers and others who have applied his work have not gone far enough, though this is not the place for a full critique, even if I could give it. First, we should remember, Rogers is talking about the therapist-client relationship, and much of what he says rises from that context. Since it takes two to tango, and since at least one of the participants in this context is already intent upon *not* being an adversary, then conflict may be resolved and mutual communication may ensue. The therapist-client relationship, I'd suggest, even at its prickliest, is simply not going to produce the stress and pain that can occur when contending narratives meet. It is by its nature more amenable to discussion and resolution, and the rules or conditions I cited earlier are, at any rate, *game* rules, as my colleague, Professor James Baumlin, has pointed out. In the passage I cited earlier, Rogers is talking about a client who already has a need (he or she is faced by a serious problem), and the therapist is already a congruent person in the relationship. Rogers proposes for the therapist an "unconditional positive regard," but straight away recommends that all take emotion out of discussions and reduce differences. If one holds another in "unconditional positive regard," that regard, I believe, includes both emotions and differences. They cannot be reduced, though their force may be diminished for a moment; such energy is always conserved. If emotions do go out of the discussion—and I don't think they do—it is only after time and care. What each must face in contention before emotions and differences dwindle is something in the other altogether more startling: a horror, a wrong, a dishonesty (as each sees the other), a shock, an outrage, or perhaps a beauty too startling and stunning to see. As for the texts that propose patterns of Rogerian arguments, I'd say that the recommended designs are altogether commendable and will sometimes work, so long as the argument isn't crucial to the nature of the narratives involved. Where arguments entail identity, the presentation of "a statement of how the opponent's position would benefit if he were to adopt elements of the writer's position" is about as efficacious as storming Hell with a bucket of water or trying to hide the glories of Heaven with a torn curtain. If I cannot accept the identity of the other, his kindness in offering me benefits will be of no avail. As for offering a "proposal for resolving the issue in a way that injures neither party," I'd say that in the arguments that grip us most tightly, we *do* injure the other, or the other injures us, or we seem about to injure each other, except we take the tenderest, strongest care. Paul Bator ("Aristotelian and Rogerian Argument," *College Composition and Communication* [Dec., 1980]: 427-32) acknowledges that Rogerian strategy works most effectively when students "encounter non-adversary writing situations." "Under the Rogerian schema," he continues, "students can be encouraged to view their writing as a communicative first step—one designed to build bridges and win over minds—rather than being prompted to view the essay only as a finished product serving as an ultimate weapon for conversion."

I am suggesting that the arguments most significant to us are just where threat occurs and continues, just where emotions and differences do not get calmly talked away, just where we are plunged into that flushed, feverish, quaky, shaky, angry, scared, hurt, shocked, disappointed, alarmed, outraged, even terrified condition I spoke of a little earlier. Then what do we do?

5

To make the kind of contention or opposition I am trying to discuss a little clearer, I should add another term. I have been talking about contending narratives, or identities. Let me now add what I hope has been suggested all along: let us suppose that in this contention each narrator is entirely *steadfast*, wholly intent upon preserving the nature and movement of his or her narrative, earnest and zealous to keep its identity. I think we have not fully considered what happens in argument when the arguers are steadfast.

If Ms. Smith is steadfast in conviction and is outfitted with what she takes to be good evidence and sound reasoning, that means that she is living a narrative that is congruent with her expectations and satisfying to her needs. But if she speaks to Mr. Jones, who is at opposites and equally steadfast, who is his own satisfying narrative, then it's likely that Ms. Smith's evidence will not look like evidence to Mr. Jones, and Ms. Smith's reasoning will not look like reasoning. Evidence and reason are evidence and reason only if one lives in the narrative that creates and regards them.

That seems to picture a near-hopeless prospect.

Sometimes it is, at least for long periods of time. Sometimes we don't resolve oppositions, but must either remain apart or live as adversaries with the other. But the prospect doesn't have to be hopeless, at least not permanently.

What can change it? What can free us from the apparent hopelessness of steadfast arguments opposing each other? I have to start with a simple answer and hope that I can gradually give it the texture and capacity it needs: we have *to see* each other, *to know* each other, *to be present to* each other, *to embrace* each other.

What makes that possible? We have to change the way we talk about argument and conceive of argument.

6

I'm not ready to go on yet. I want to try to place my interest in argument, and perhaps I can do that by comparing my interest to those of Carl Rogers, to whom I am clearly much indebted. Rogers extrapolates from therapist-client relationships to public communication relationships. The base from which he works (the therapist-client relationship) gives him a setting in which civil understanding is a goal to be reached through mutual communication transactions. He does recognize the potentially threatening effect of alien insights and ideas. Young, Becker, and Pike show that the Rogerian strategy "rests on the assumption that a man holds to his beliefs about who he is and what the world is like because other beliefs threaten his identity and integrity" (7). In the Rogerian view, as Paul Bator puts it, carefully reasoned arguments "may be totally ineffectual when employed in a rhetorical situation where the audience feels its beliefs or values are being threatened. No amount of reasoned argument will prompt the audience to consider the speaker's point of view if the audience senses that its opinions are somehow being 'explained away'" (428). Followers of Rogers see in Aristotle's *Rhetoric* an antagonistic speaker-audience relationship; they do not find this in Rogers, for, as Bator says, "Generation and control of audience expectation do not attract Rogers" (428). As I have already suggested, given the therapist-client relationship he starts from, Rogers is appropriately enough interested in rhetorical contexts that do not involve advocacy. As Rogers says, "If I can listen to what [the other person] can tell me, if I can understand how it seems to him, if I can see its personal meaning for him, if I can sense the emotional flavor which it has for him, then I will be releasing potent forces of change in him" (285–86). Since he is customarily talking about a mutual communication transaction, Rogers is often as concerned with the audience as with the speaker. A speaker, Bator says, "must be willing to achieve the frame of reference of the listener even if the values or views held by the other are antithetical to the speaker's personal code of ethics. A necessary correlate of acceptance (of the other's view) is understanding, an understanding which implies that the listener accepts the views of the speaker without knowing cognitively what will result. Such understanding, in turn, encourages the speaker to explore untried avenues of exchange" (428). Looking for the therapist-client relationship, Rogers sees the therapist/communicator as an understanding audience. He expects that the therapist-as-audience will not only accept, but also understand the feelings and thoughts of the client-as-speaker. When the therapist understands the feelings and thoughts that seem so horrible or weak or sentimental or bizarre to the client, when the therapist understands and accepts the client, then the therapist frees the client to explore deep experience freely. As each understands and accepts the other, then they may move toward the truth.

This, I would gladly agree, is the way we ought to argue, each accepting, understanding, and helping the other. However, I think the significant arguments that crowd us into each other are somewhat less kindly composed. I want to get to the place where we are threatened and where the setting doesn't seem to give us opportunity to reduce threat and to enter a mutual search for congruence and regard. I want to get to the place where we are advocates of contending narratives (with their accompanying feelings and thoughts), where we are adversaries, each seeming to propose the repudiation or annihilation of what the other lives, values, and is, where we are beyond being adversaries in that strange kind of argument we seldom attend to, where one offers the other a rightness so demanding, a beauty so stunning, a grace so fearful as to call the hearer to forgo one identity for a startling new one.

7

What can free us from the apparent hopelessness of steadfast arguments contending with each other, of narratives come bluntly up against each other? Can the text of one narrative become the text of another narrative without sacrifice? If there is to be hope, we have to see each other, to know each other, to be present to each other, to embrace each other.

What makes that possible? I don't know. We can start toward these capacities by changing the way we talk about argument and conceive of argument.

It may be helpful, before I go on, if I try to explain a little more fully the kind of occasion I mean to refer to, the kind of setting in which contention generates that flushed, feverish, quaky, shaky, angry, scared, hurt, shocked, disappointed, alarmed, outraged, even terrified condition I have mentioned. Of course I cannot imagine, let alone explain or describe, all the oppositions that can occur. Perhaps I can by illustration at least suggest the kind of occasion that I want to talk about. I mean such occasions as these: let two people confront each other, each holding views antithetical to the sacred values and images of the other, one an extreme advocate of the current Pro-Life movement, the other an extreme advocate of the current movement to leave free choice open to women in the matter of abortion, each a mockery of the other; let two parties confront each other, zealous advocates of one contending that farmers must learn to stand on their own without government support, and zealous advocates of the other contending that the government, by withdrawing support, will literally kill farmers; let two tribes go to war for ancient reasons not entirely explicable to themselves or to outsiders, each a denial of the other, as in various current Middle East crises; let two nations confront each other in what sometimes appears to be a shocked and total inability to understand or even to recognize each other, as in continuing conflicts between the United States and Russia, wherever these conflicts happen to be located, whether in East Germany or in Nicaragua; let a beautiful Jewish woman encounter an aged captain of guards for Dachau; let some man confront an affirmation of life he has not been able to achieve; let an honest woman encounter cruel dishonesty; let a man encounter a narrative so beautiful but different that he cannot look; let two quite different narratives converge in conflict inside the head of a single lonely man or woman.

Given such occasions, what do we do in argument? Can we hope for happy resolution? I don't know. I do think the risk in argument is greater than we have learned from Aristotle or Rogers. What can we do, then?

We can start, as I suggested earlier, by changing the way we talk about argument.

As we presently understand, talk about, and teach argument, it is, whatever our intentions, *display* and *presentation.* We entice with an exordium and lay in a background. We present a proposition. We display our proofs, our evidence. We show that we can handle and if need be refute opposing views. We offer our conclusion. That is display and presentation. The same thing is true of proposed plans for Rogerian argument, as in the passages I cited earlier from Young, Becker, and Pike and from Maxine Hairston.

But argument is not something *to present* or *to display.* It is something *to be.* It is what we *are,* as I suggested earlier.

We are the argument over against another. Another is the argument over against us. We live in, through, around, and against arguments. To display or to present them is to pretend a disengagement that we cannot actually achieve and probably should not want to achieve. Argument is not display or presentation, for our engagement in it, or identity with it, will out. When argument is taken as display or presentation, then it eventually becomes a matter of my poster against yours, with the prize to the slickest performance.

If we are to hope for ourselves and to value all others, we must learn that argument is emergence.

8

Argument is emergence toward the other. That requires a readiness to testify to an identity that is always emerging, a willingness to dramatize one's narrative in progress before the other; it calls for an untiring stretch toward the other, a reach toward enfolding the other. It is a risky relevation of the self, for the arguer is asking for an acknowledgment of his or her identity, is asking for witness from the other. In argument, the arguer must plunge on alone, with no assurance of welcome from the other, with no assurance whatever of unconditional positive regard from the other. In argument, the arguer must, with no assurance, go out, inviting the other to enter a world that the arguer tries to make commodious, inviting the other to emerge as well, but with no assurance of kind or even thoughtful response. How does this happen? Better, how can it happen?

It can happen if we learn to love before we disagree. Usually, it's the other way around: if we learn to love, it is only after silence or conflict or both. In ancient times, I was in the United States Army. I spent the better part of 1951 and 1952 in Germany. In those years, American troops were still officially regarded as an Occupation Force, with certain privileges extended, such as free transportation. One service provided was a kind of rental agency in many large cities. On pass or on leave, one could go to this agency and be directed to a room for rent (very cheap) in a private home. Since I was stationed only ten or twelve miles away, I often went to Heidelberg when I had just a weekend pass or a three-day pass. On one such occasion I went to Heidelberg, stopped in at the agency, and got directions to a room that was available. I found the address, a large brownstone just a block off the main street, met the matron of the house, and was taken to a small bedroom on the third floor that would be mine for a couple of days. I left shortly thereafter to go places and do things, paying no particular attention to the room except to notice it was clean and neat. The next morning was clear and bright and cool; I opened the windows and finally began to see the room. A picture on one wall startled me, more, stunned me.

On the kitchen wall in my parents' home in Texas there was a picture of my older brother, taken while he was in what was known as the Air Corps in

World War II. It was a posed shot of the sort that I suppose most airmen had taken at one time or another to send home to the folks. In the picture, my brother is wearing the airman's favorite of that time, a leather jacket with knit cuffs and a knit band about the waist. He is wearing the old-fashioned leather cap with ear flaps and goggles, and there is a white scarf around his neck, one end tossed over his shoulder. Behind him there is a Consolidated-Vultee B-24.

The picture on the wall in the bedroom in Heidelberg showed a young man wearing a leather jacket with knit cuffs and a knit band about the waist. He wore an old-fashioned leather cap with ear flaps and goggles, and there is a white scarf around his neck, one end tossed over his shoulder. Behind him there was an airplane; it was a Focke-Wulfe 190. He might have been my brother. After a while, I guess I realized that he *was* my brother.

The television news on March 7, 1985, showed a memorial service at Remagen, Germany, marking the fortieth anniversary of the American troops' capture of the Remagen bridge, which let them cross the Rhine. No major world leaders were there, but veterans from both sides had come to look and take notice of the day. American and German veterans who had fought there wept and hugged each other and shook hands.

In the mid-fifties, another group of veterans met, to commemorate the fortieth anniversary of the end of battle at Verdun, that hellish landscape where over a million men died to gain or to preserve two or three miles of scrubby country, where no birds sang. They shook hands; they embraced; they wept; they sang an old song that begins, "Ich hatte ein kamaraden."

After a while, the hated dead can be mourned, and the old enemy can be embraced.

In these instances, we waited to love (or at least to accept) until long after silence and grim conflict. (I've not lost my head altogether: some conflicts will not be resolved in time and love—there's always that captain of guards from Dachau.) Often, we don't learn to love (or at least to accept) at all. All precedents and examples notwithstanding, I'll still insist that argument—that rhetoric itself—must begin, proceed, and end in love.

9

But how is this to happen? How will we argue, or teach argument taken in this way? I don't know, but I'll chance some suggestions.

a. The arguer has to go alone. When argument has gone beyond attempts made by the arguer and by the other to accept and understand, when those early exploratory steps toward mutual communication are over, or when all of these stages have been bypassed altogether—as they often will be—then the arguer is alone, with no assurance at all that the other or any audience will be kindly disposed. When argument comes to advocacy or to adversarial confrontation, the mutuality that Rogers describes will probably not occur. At the point of advocacy, most particularly at the crisis point in adversarial relationships, the burden is on the maker of the argument as he or she is making the argument. At the moment of heat (which may last twenty seconds or twenty years and which may be feverish and scary), the arguer in all likelihood will not know whether or not the other, the audience, will choose to take the role of the well-disposed listener or the kindly therapist. The arguer, alone, must see in the reverence owed to the other, discover and offer all grace that he or she can muster, and, most especially, extend every liberty possible to the other. The arguer must hold the other wholly in mind and yet cherish his or her own identity. *Then,* perhaps, the arguer and the other may be able to break into mutuality.

b. The arguer must at once hold his or her identity and give it to the other, learning to live—and argue—provisionally. In "Supposing History Is a Woman—What Then?" (*The American Scholar,* Autumn, 1984), Gertrude Himmelfarb remarks:

> Whatever "truth or validity" adheres to history . . . does not derive, as the conventional historian might assume, from an "objective" world, a world of past events waiting to be discovered and reconstructed by the historian. For there is no objective world, no historical events independent of the experience of the historian, no events or facts which are not also ideas.

We must keep learning as speakers/narrators/arguers (and as hearers). We can learn to dispense with what we imagined was absolute truth and to pursue the reality of things only partially knowable. We can learn to keep adding pieces of knowledge here, to keep rearranging pieces over yonder, to keep standing back and turning to see how things look elsewhere. We can learn that our narrative/argument doesn't exist except as it is composed and that the "act of composition can never end," as Doctorow has said.

c. As I have just suggested, we arguers can learn to abandon authoritative positions. They cannot be achieved, at any rate, except as in arrogance, ignorance, and dogma we convince ourselves that we have reached authority. We should not want to achieve an authoritative position, anyway. An authoritative position is a prison both to us and to any audience.

d. We arguers can learn the lessons that rhetoric itself wants to teach us. By its nature, invention asks us to open ourselves to the richness of creation, to plumb its depths, search its expanses, and track its chronologies. But the moment we speak (or write), we are no longer open; we have chosen, whether deliberately or not, and so have closed ourselves off from some possibilities. Invention wants openness; structure and style demand closure. We are asked to be perpetually open and always closing. If we stay open, we cannot speak or act; if we stand closed, we have succumbed to dogma and rigidity. Each utterance may deplete the inventive possibilities if a speaker falls into arrogance, ignorance, or dogma. But each utterance, if the speaker having spoken opens again, may also nurture and replenish the speaker's inventive world and enable him or her to reach out around the other. Beyond any speaker's bound inventive world lies another: there lie the riches of creation, the great, unbounded possible universe of invention. All time is there, past, present, and future. The natural and the supernatural are there. All creation is there, ground and source for invention. The knowledge we have is formed out of the plentitude of creation, which is all before us, but must be sought again and again through the cycling process of rhetoric, closing to speak, opening again to invent again. In an unlimited universe of meaning, we can never foreclose on interpretation and argument. Invention is a name for a great miracle—the attempt to unbind time, to loosen the capacities of time and space into our speaking. This copiousness is eternally there, a plentitude for all. Piaget remarked that the more an infant sees and hears, the more he or she wants to see and hear. Just this is what the cycling of rhetoric offers us: opening to invention, closing to speak, opening again to a richer invention. Utterances may thus be elevated, may grow to hold both arguer and other.

e. We still need to study. There is much about argument that we still have not learned, or that we have not acknowledged. If we are accurate in our evaluation of what happens in conflict, I think we will have to concede that most of what happens is bad. If we know that accurately, we'll be a step farther than we were toward knowing how to deal with contention and the hurts that rise from conflict and argument. We have not at any time in our public or personal histories known consistently how to deal with conflicts, especially when each side or party or view arises normally according to its own variety of thought—and there is no arguer who does not believe that his or her view is a just consequence of normal thought and need. In discourse and behavior, our ways of resolving conflicts have typically been limited and unsatisfactory. When opposing views, each issuing by its own normal processes from its own inventive world, come together in conflict because each wants the same time and space, we usually have only a few ways of handling the conflict:

1. one view prevails, the other subsides;
2. advocates of the two views compromise;
3. the need for action prompts arbitrary selection of one of the two views, even if both are appealing and attractive;
4. we are paralyzed, unable to choose;
5. we go to war; or
6. occasionally, the advocates of one side learn gladly from those of the other and gladly lay down their own views in favor of the other.

To be sure, there are other patterns for resolving conflicts that I haven't had wit enough to recognize; I'd reckon, however, that most are unrewarding to some or all. Once a view emerges—that is, once an inventive process has become structure and style—it cannot wholly subside, as in (1), though it must seem to do so; required by force or expediency to subside, it does not subside but persists underground, festering. Compromise, as in (2), is likely to leave parts of both views hidden away and festering. Deliberate choice between two appealing views, as in (3), leaves the unchosen to grow and compete underground, generating a cynicism that undercuts the chosen argument. Paralysis, as in (4), clearly gives no view gain, though each remains, eating away at the paralyzed agent. War, physical or psychological, is plainly not an appropriate human resolution. In most of these instances there is a thwarted or misplaced or submerged narrative, a normality that may grow wild because it is thwarted, misplaced, or submerged. We have not learned how to let competing normalities live together in the same time and space. We're not sure, we frail humans, that it is possible.

f. The arguer must go alone, unaided by any world of thought, value, and belief except the one that he or she composes in the process of arguing, unassisted by the other because the other is over in a different place, being realized in a different narrative. In my mind, this means that the burden of argument is upon the *ethos* of the arguer. *Ethos,* of course, is a term still poorly understood. Among others, Bator objects to any concentration upon *ethos* because it seems to be "related primarily to adversary situations calling for argumentative strategies designed to persuade others," because "the speaker may be concerned particularly with enhancing her own image or character rather than addressing the issue at hand" (428). Ideally, Bator believes, the subject or problem "is viewed within the audience's framework of values, not simply from the writer's assumptions or premises. The *ethos* of the writer is not the main focus of attention, nor is it the primary means of appeal" (431). This view omits considering the likelihood that *ethos* occurs in various ways; the term does not require to be defined as it has formerly been defined. A genuinely provocative and evocative *ethos* does, in fact, hold the audience wholly in mind, does view matters both as the arguer sees them and as others see them. The self-authenticating language of such an *ethos* issues an invitation into a commodious universe. Argument is partial; when a speaker argues a proposition or develops a theme or makes an assertion, he or she has knowingly or not chosen one proposition, one theme, one assertion from all available. When we speak, we stand somewhere, and our standing place makes both known and silent claims upon us. We make truth, if at all, out of what is incomplete or partial. Language is a closure, but the generative *ethos* I am trying to identify uses language to shove back the restraints of closure, to make a commodious universe, to stretch words out beyond our private universe.

g. We must pile time into argumentative discourse. Earlier, I suggested that in our most grievous and disturbing conflicts, we need time to accept, to understand, to love the other. At crisis points in adversarial relationships, we do not, however, have time; we are already in opposition and confrontation. Since we don't have time, we must rescue time by putting it into our discourses and holding it there, learning to speak and write not argumentative displays and presentations, but arguments full of the anecdotal, personal, and cultural reflections that will make us plain to all others, thoughtful histories and narratives that reveal us as we're reaching for the others. The world, of course, doesn't want time in its discourses. The world wants the quick memo, the rapid-fire electronic mail service; the world wants speed, efficiency, and economy of motion, all goals that, when reached, have given the world less than it wanted or needed. We must teach the world to want otherwise, to want time for care.

10

Rhetoric is love, and it must speak a commodious language, creating a world full of space and time that will hold our diversities. Most failures of communication result from some willful or inadvertent but unloving violation of the space and time we and others live in, and most of our speaking is tribal talk. But there is more to us than that. We can learn to speak a commodious language, and we can learn to hear a commodious language.

PAULO FREIRE

b. 1921

DONALDO MACEDO

b. 1950

*To the Brazilian educator Paulo Freire, the purpose of education is human libera-
tion. His innovative ideas about adult literacy and his success as a teacher in
empowering students through critical consciousness led first to his imprisonment
and then to his forced exile from Brazil in 1964. Returning in 1980 to continue
his work, he became minister of education. The principle underlying Freire's pedagogy is that only by becoming literate—"saying the word"—can people throw off
their oppressors—thus "transforming the world." Known for his dialogical method
of teaching, Freire delineates his Marxist rhetoric in* Education for Critical Consciousness *and* Pedagogy of the Oppressed *(1990). In the following dialogue, one
of three in* Literacy, *Freire and coauthor Donaldo Macedo (who teaches at the University of Massachusetts, Boston) discuss connections among literacy, culture, and
education, and examine the issue of literacy in the United States. Their purpose,
in part, is to stimulate and encourage us to engage in a critical dialogue ourselves
about the nature of our work.*

The Illiteracy of Literacy in the
United States

Macedo: It is ironic that in the United States, a country that prides itself on being the first and most advanced within the so-called "first world,"
over 60 million people are illiterate or functionally illiterate. According to
Jonathon Kozol's book *Illiterate America* (1985), the United States is in
forty-ninth place among the 128 countries of the United Nations in terms
of literacy rate. How can a country that considers itself a model of democracy tolerate an educational system that contributes to such a high level of
illiteracy?

Freire: The first reaction to these data should be one of shock. How can
this be possible? But this would still be a reaction at the affective level. Let us
think a bit about this phenomenon. The first question might be, did this
huge sector of the population, the illiterate or functionally illiterate, ever go
to school? In Latin America you have a number of people who are illiterate
because they were socially forbidden to go to school. And you have another

large population of illiterates who went to school. If this large illiterate sector of the population never went to school, the shock that I mentioned before is exacerbated by the immense contradiction this implies, given the United States' high level of modernization. Further, we have to consider whether illiterates did go to school and whether they were untouched by the school to the extent that they remained illiterate (apparently they were not touched, but, actually, they *were* touched), and whether they left school or they were left by the school.

I am inclined to think that this large population of illiterates in the United States went to school and then were expelled from school. How were they expelled? Were they thrown out by decree because they did not learn how to read and write? I believe that the school did not operate in this overt a manner.

This brings us to a point that is once again political and ideological in nature. And let us not forget the question of power, which is always associated with education. Our speculations should provoke those who are in the school systems to react to the following notion as absurd, nonrigorous, and purely ideological. The notion is: this large number of people who do not read or write and who were expelled from school do not represent a failure of the schooling class; their expulsion reveals the triumph of the schooling class. In fact, this misreading of responsibility reflects the schools' hidden curriculum. (Henry Giroux has written brilliantly on this subject, and I urge readers to consult his work.)

Curriculum in the broadest sense involves not only the programmatic contents of the school system, but also the scheduling, discipline, and day-to-day tasks required from students in schools. In this curriculum, then, there is a quality that is hidden and that gradually incites rebelliousness on the part of children and adolescents. Their defiance corresponds to the aggressive elements in the curriculum that work against the students and their interests.

School authorities who repress these students might argue that they are only responding to the students' aggressiveness. In fact, students are reacting to a curriculum and other material conditions in schools that negate their histories, cultures, and day-to-day experiences. School values work counter to the interests of these students and tend to precipitate their expulsion from school. It is as if the system were put in place to ensure that these students pass through school and leave it as illiterates.

This type of thinking typifies many well-intentioned educators who are not yet able to comprehend the internal mechanisms of the dominant ideology that so influences the school atmosphere. Because of the rebelliousness of children and adolescents who leave school or who are truants and refuse to engage in the intellectual activity predetermined by the curriculum, these students end up refusing to comprehend the word (not their own word, of course, but the word of the curriculum). They thus remain distant from the practice of reading.

Macedo: Let's clarify what you refer to as intellectual activity from the dominant point of view, so as not to preclude other intellectual activities that are generated and sustained by these students. We should emphasize that these students can, and in fact do, engage in frequent intellectual activities, but these are activities generated from their own perspective. That is, they define their own activities.

Freire: It is difficult to understand these issues outside of an analysis of power relations. Only those who have power, for example, can define what is correct or incorrect. Only those who have power can decide what constitutes intellectualism. Once the intellectual parameters are set, those who want to be considered intellectuals must meet the requirements of the profile dictated by the elite class. To be intellectual one must do exactly what those with the power to define intellectualism do.

The intellectual activity of those without power is always characterized as nonintellectual. I think this issue should be underscored, not just as a dimension of pedagogy, but a dimension of politics, as well. This is difficult to do in a society like that of the United States, where the political nature of pedagogy is negated ideologically. It is necessary to negate the political nature of pedagogy to give the superficial appearance that education serves everyone, thus assuring that it continues to function in the interest of the dominant class.

This mythical universality of education to better serve humanity leads many times to blame the students themselves for dropping out. It is their decision if they want to remain and succeed in school.

Once you accept the political dimension of education, it becomes difficult to accept the education, it becomes difficult to accept the dominant class's conclusion: that the dropouts are to blame. The more you deny the political dimension of education, the more you assume the moral potential to blame the victims. This is somewhat paradoxical. The many people who pass through school and come out illiterate because they resisted and refused to read the dominant word are representative of self-affirmation. This self-affirmation is, from another point of view, a process of literacy in the normal, global sense of the term. That is, the refusal to read the word chosen by the teacher is the realization on the part of the student that he or she is making a decision not to accept what is perceived as violating his or her world.

In the end, what you have is a separation between teacher and students along class lines. Even though we recognize that it is very difficult to do an analysis of class in a complex society like that of the United States, we cannot deny that class division exists.

Macedo: In general, educators in the United States deemphasize the issue of social class as it pertains to education. In fact, most of the studies concerning the unacceptable number of illiterates in the school system treat the problem from a technocratic perspective. And the remedies proposed tend to be technocratic as well. Although some educators may describe a possible correlation between the high dropout rate and the low socioeconomic background of students, this correlation remains at a level of description. More often than not, U.S. educators in general and literacy experts in particular fail to establish political and ideological linkages in their analyses that could illuminate the reproductive nature of schools in this society. For example, conservative educators such as Secretary of Education William Bennett call for a back-to-basics approach as they blindly embrace competency-based curricula. Although the rigidity of the competency-based approach may benefit the white-and upper-class students, I doubt that it will remedy the illiteracy problem that plagues the majority of subordinate groups in the United States. Panaceas such as more student-contact hours for reading and math and a better salary base for teachers will perpetuate those ideological elements that negate students' life experiences. As a result, students react by refusing to read what the curriculum has decided they should read.

There is no guarantee that more of the same approach, which fundamentally lacks equity and sensitivity for the culture of the subordinate groups, will diminish the resistance of students as they refuse to read the "chosen" word. When curriculum designers ignore important variables such as social-class differences, when they ignore the incorporation of the subordinate cultures' values in the curriculum, and when they refuse to accept and legitimize the students' language, their actions point to the inflexibility, insensitivity, and rigidity of a curriculum that was designed to benefit those who wrote it.

By giving teachers token salary increases, one is paternalistically placating the majority of teachers, who find themselves in an increasingly powerless position as they confront a reductionist system that aims to further de-skill them. These approaches and their related proposals tend to overlook the material conditions with which teachers struggle in their attempt to survive the overwhelming task of teaching material that is politically and ideologically at odds with the subordinate students' reality.

These approaches and proposals fail to examine the lack of time teachers have to perform a task that, by its very nature, should involve thinking and reflection. Moreover, the intellectual dimension of teaching is never celebrated by a system whose main objective is to further de-skill teachers and reduce them to mere technical agents who are destined to walk unreflectively through a labyrinth of procedures. So my question is, do you think that these educators are aware that their proposals will exacerbate the equity gap that is already victimizing a great number of "minority" students?

Freire: Let's first clarify the term "minority."

Macedo: I use the term in the U.S. context. I am also aware that it is contradictory in nature.

Freire: Exactly. Do you see how ideologically impregnated the term "minority" is? When you use "minority" in the U.S. context to refer to the majority of people who are not part of the dominant class, you alter its semantic value. When you refer to "minority" you are in fact talking about the "majority" who find themselves outside the sphere of political and economic dominance.

Macedo: If Kozol is correct, the 60 million illiterates and functional illiterates that he documents in *Illiterate America* do not constitute a minority class. These 60 million should not be added to other sizable groups who learn how to read but who are still not part of dominant political and economic spheres.

Freire: In reality, as with many other words, the semantic alteration of the term "minority" serves to hide the many myths that are part of the mechanism sustaining cultural dominance.

Macedo: Let us move on to our second question. I think it is of paramount importance to analyze how subordinate cultures are produced in the classroom. We need to understand the antagonistic relationships between subordinate cultures and the dominant values of the curriculum. Take, for example, the resistance to speaking the required standard dialect of the curriculum. The dominant curriculum is designed primarily to reproduce the inequality of social classes, while it mostly benefits the interests of an elite minority. How can North American progressive educators capitalize on the antagonistic cultural elements produced in subordinate students' acts of resistance, and how can educators launch a literacy campaign that would enable students to comprehend their world so they can later read it? That is, is it possible to use students' rebelliousness as a platform from which they can transcend the mechanistic nature of literacy imposed on them by a curriculum that demands only the mechanical codification and decodification of graphemes and phonemes to form words that further alienate them?

Freire: Your question is absolutely fundamental. Theoretically, the answer to it is of value not only in the U.S. context, but also in the Brazilian context, as well as in other areas where there are clear class divisions and tensions. The major difference lies in how to design and implement programs that meet the different needs of each context. I would find it easier to answer your question within the Brazilian context. At any rate, theoretically your question necessarily takes us to the important issue of whether it is possible to develop a critical literacy program within the institutional space, which contradicts and neutralizes the fundamental task required by the dominant power of the schools. That is, we need to discuss the reproduction of the dominant ideology, an important issue that has been clearly and amply discussed by Henry Giroux and other North American educators, as well.

Theories of reproduction tend to fall into a type of mechanical exaggeration in which they interpret the real and concrete fact that the educational system reproduces dominant ideology. Within the educational system there is another task to be executed by conscious educators, independent of the wishes of the dominant class. The educational task, from the perspective of the dominant class, is to reproduce its ideology. But the educational task that contradicts the reproductionist process cannot be carried out by anyone who opts for the status quo. This task has to be carried out by the educator, who in fact refuses to maintain the inequality inherent within the status quo.

The progressive educator rejects the dominant values imposed on the school because he or she has a different dream, because he or she wants to transform the status quo. Naturally, transforming the status quo is much more difficult to do than maintaining it. The question that you raised has to do exactly with this theory. As I have said, the educational space reproduces the dominant ideology. However, it is possible within educational institutions to contradict imposed dominant values.

The reproduction of the dominant ideology necessarily implies an opaque reality. The unveiling of reality falls within the space for possible change in which progressive and politically clear educators must operate. I believe that this space for change, however small, is always available. In the United States, where society is much more complex than in Brazil, the task of emphasizing reality is more difficult. In this process it is necessary for educators to assume a political posture that renounces the myth of pedagogical neutrality.

These educators cannot reduce themselves to being pure education specialists. They cannot be educators who are concerned with only the technical dimensions of bilingualism, for example, without a thorough understanding of the political and ideological implications of bilingualism and multiculturalism in the United States. Educators must become conscious individuals who live part of their dreams within their educational space.

Educators cannot work successfully by themselves; they have to work collaboratively in order to succeed in integrating the cultural elements produced by the subordinate students in their educational process. Finally, these educators have to invent and create methods in which they maximize the limited space for possible change that is available to them. They need to use their students' cultural universe as a point of departure, enabling students to recognize themselves as possessing a specific and important cultural identity.

The successful usage of the students' cultural universe requires respect and legitimation of students' discourses, that is, their own linguistic codes, which are different but never inferior. Educators also have to respect and understand students' dreams and expectations. In the case of black Americans, for example, educators must respect black English. It is possible to codify and decodify black English with the same ease as standard American English. The difference is that black Americans will find it infinitely easier to codify and decodify the dialect of their own authorship. The legitimation of black English as an educational tool does not, however, preclude the need to acquire proficiency in the linguistic code of the dominant group.

Macedo: Beyond the linguistic code issue, educators must understand the ways in which different dialects encode different world views. The semantic value of specific lexical items belonging to black English differs radically, in some cases, from the reading derived from the standard, dominant dialect. The first important issue is that black Americans' linguistic code not only reflects their reality, but also their lived experience in a given historical moment. Terms that encapsulate the drug culture, daily alienation, the struggle to survive the substandard and inhumane conditions of ghettos—these constitute a discourse black Americans find no difficulty in using.

It is from this raw and sometimes cruel reality that black students can begin to unveil the obfuscation that characterizes their daily existence inside and outside the schools. Their language is, therefore, a powerful tool demystifying the distorted reality prepackaged for them by the dominant curriculum. As we will discuss in the last chapter of this book, language should never be understood as a mere tool of communication. Language is packed with ideology, and for this reason it has to be given prominence in any radical pedagogy that proposes to provide space for students' emancipation.

Freire: It is by the use of all dimensions of students' language, taste, and so forth that you and the students are able to arrive at the programmatic contents that attend to the immediate interests of those in power. You don't tell those in a dependent and oppressed position that, for example, they have no say in the substance of scientific study because this type of curricular requirement interests only students of the dominant class. Subordinate students also need the skills gained through studying the dominant curriculum. However, these skills should never be imposed at the sacrifice of a thorough understanding of reality, which enables students to develop a positive self-image before grappling with the type of knowledge that is outside their immediate world.

It is only after they have a firm grasp on their world that they can begin to acquire other knowledge. To acquire the selected knowledge contained in the dominant curriculum should be a goal attained by subordinate students in the process of self and group empowerment. They can use the dominant knowledge effectively in their struggle to change the material and historical conditions that have enslaved them. But they must never allow the knowledge that benefits the dominant class to domesticate themselves or, as in some cases, to turn them into little oppressors. The dominant curriculum must gradually become dominated by the dependent students so as to help them in their struggle for social equity and justice.

This vision is political and not merely *epistemological*. That is, in the case of black Americans, they need to master fully standard English in order to fight effectively for their preservation and their full participation in society. But that does not mean that standard American English is more beautiful or superior to black English. The notion of linguistic superiority is artificially imposed.

Macedo: Then standard English can be viewed as a weapon against the oppressive forces that use this dominant dialect as a way to maintain the present social order. We should also point out that critical mastery of the standard dialect can never be achieved fully without the development of one's voice, which is contained within the social dialect that shapes one's reality.

Freire: Exactly. This is what I mean by the necessary political and ideological dimensions in any pedagogy that proposes to be critical. The question of methods is directly linked to the creative and inventive capacity of political educators. Creativity obviously requires risk taking. The educational tasks that we have discussed so far can be carried out through a thorough understanding of the political and ideological nature of educators, and through a willingness to be creative and to take the risks that will allow this creativity to flourish. In highly modernized societies like that of the United States, I have noticed that people carry with them a long capitalistic historical experience that sustains a general theme of human existence always evolving from fear—the fear, for instance, of not getting tenure, the fear that conditions educators to be well behaved for many years so they can get tenure. Many years afterward, if they are not given tenure, they remain domesticated in fear of losing their second chance at tenure. If they are refused tenure, they become preoccupied only with trying to understand what possible misconduct led to the tenure denial. If they are granted tenure, of course, there is no reason to change the behavior for which they were bestowed the gift of tenure.

Macedo: I agree, but I think it is important to understand this fear of taking risks or being inventive, and the societal mechanisms that generate it. In some cases, mainstream educators sacrifice educational and moral principles to help sustain a status quo that they have identified as uncreative, just so they can receive the reward of tenure or personal social advancement. This compromise is connected to a lack of political clarity, which in the long run impedes any possibility for these educators to engage in an educational praxis leading to conscientization. Can you discuss this problem of political clarity among educators in highly modernized societies, such as the United States?

Freire: Before elaborating on what you refer to as "political clarity," let us first define this concept. I will try to explain what I sometimes refer to as "political clarity," before an action," something necessary in the evolvement process of political praxis.

Our first concern has to do with the adverb *before* used in the expression "before an action." This *before* refers to a certain action, let us say action A, to be realized as a political task in the process of struggle and transformation. This *before* does not refer to just any form of action to achieve clarity in "reading" reality. Its understanding requires us to prolong our critical and radical experience in the world. Understanding the world's sensibility does not take place outside our practice, that is, the lived practice or the practice upon which we reflect.

In the final analysis, what I have been calling "political clarity" cannot be found in the purely mechanical repetition, for example, of formal criticisms of U.S. imperialism or in the recitation (no less mechanical) of Marx's phrases. This type of intellectual posture does not relate to my notion of political clarity.

Political clarity is necessary for more profound engagement in political praxis, and it is emphasized in that praxis. This conception was well captured by Frei Betto, in a book we recently completed together in Brazil. According to Betto, a politicized person (a person who more or less has political clarity) is one who has transcended the perception of life as a pure biological process to arrive at a perception of life as a biographical, historical, and collective process.

In this moment, this person conceptualizes what Betto calls "a clothesline of information." On the clothesline we may have a flux of information and yet remain unable to link one piece of information with another. A politicized person is one who can sort out the different and often fragmented pieces contained in the flux. This person has to be able to sift through the flux of information and relate, for example, Pinochet and Reagan, or understand the ideological content of the term "freedom fighters" as it is applied to the *Contras* in their effort to sabotage the revolutionary process in Nicaragua. This person sees the ideology in the concept "terrorism" as applied to the military action against a cruel dictatorship that maintains a highly proficient death squad killing thousands of innocent women, children, and other civilians. Noam Chomsky, for instance, succinctly analyzes American policy in Latin America in *Turning the Tide,* pointing to the contradictions in the U.S. intervention.

Political clarity is possible to the extent that we reflect critically on day-to-day facts, and to the extent that we transcend our sensibilities (the capacity to feel them or to take notice of them) so as to progressively gain a more rigorous understanding of the facts. Even before this, still at the level of sensibility, we can begin to become clearer politically. This happens in Betto's biographical, historical, and collective process (described above).

For me, one of the possibilities we have working with a group of intellectuals, students, for example, is to challenge them to understand the social and historical reality, not of a given fact, but of a fact that is ongoing. Reality in this sense is the process of becoming.

We need to challenge students to understand that, as knowing subjects (sometimes of existing knowledge, sometimes of objects to be produced), our relation to knowable objects cannot be reduced to the objects themselves. We need to reach a level of comprehension of the complex whole of relations among objects. That is, we need to challenge them to treat critically the "clothesline of information" with which they are working.

Whether we work at the university level or in adult education literacy, whether involved in the pure sensibility of facts or in the pursuit of a more rigorous comprehension of facts, one of the difficulties in the critical treatment of the different "pieces" of information on the "clothesline" is that there are always obstacles that obfuscate political clarity. If it were not for these ideological obstacles, how could we explain the ease with which we accept President Reagan's pronouncements that a weak and poor country like Grenada poses a threat to the gigantic power of the United States?

Political clarity always implies a dynamic comprehension between the least coherent sensibility of the world and a more coherent understanding of the world. Through political practice the less coherent sensibility of the world begins to be surpassed and more rigorous intellectual pursuits give rise to a more coherent comprehension of the world. I find this transition to a more coherent sensitivity one of the fundamental moments in any educational praxis that attempts to go beyond the pure description of reality.

We need political clarity before we can understand the political action of eradicating illiteracy in the United States or any other place. Educators who do not have political clarity can, at best, help students read the word, but they are incapable of helping them read the world. A literacy campaign that enables students to read the world requires political clarity.

Macedo: Many educators in the United States have attempted to put into practice your theory of literacy. They often complain that you do not give any "how-to" information for putting into practice your theoretical ideas and your experiences in other areas of the world, particularly Africa and Latin America. First, do you find that these criticisms are valid? If not, can you address the anxieties of many well-intended educators who, perhaps, still feel captive to an educational culture of how-to manuals?

Freire: There are two parts to this question. The first refers to my reticence in telling educators what to do. The second deals with my lack of direction in the theories I have proposed.

Let's consider the first part. What is generated in any practice? Experiences and practices can be neither exported nor imported. It follows that it is impossible to fulfill someone's request to import practices from other contexts. How can a culture of a different history and historical time learn from another culture? How can a society learn from the experience of another, given that it is impossible to export or import practices and experiences?

When I ask these questions, I do not mean that it is impossible to learn from others' practices. Amilcar Cabral, who loved African culture, said that one's respect for African culture does not mean that one should ignore positive elements of other cultures, which may prove vital for the development of African culture. When I speak of the impossibility of exporting practices, I am not denying the validity of foreign practices. Nor am I negating the necessity for interchange. What I am saying is that they should be reinvented.

Macedo: Explain in concrete terms how one reinvents one's practice and experience.

Freire: You must have a critical approach to the practice and experience to be reinvented.

Macedo: What do you mean by a critical approach?

Freire: To approach others' practices and experiences critically is to understand the validity of social, political, historical, cultural, and economic factors relative to the practice and experience to be reinvented. In other words, reinvention demands the historical, cultural, political, social, and economic comprehension of the practice and proposals to be reinvented.

This critical process applies to the reading of books as well. For example, how can one apply Lenin to the Latin American context without making an effort to have a critical, political, and historical comprehension of the moment in which Lenin wrote? I cannot simply get by on Lenin's written text concerning a certain Russia at a certain time. In the preface to a new edition of his text, Lenin called attention to the necessity of having a critical comprehension of the moment in which he wrote the text. In our own case, it is also necessary to understand the historical, political, social, cultural, and economic moment, the concrete conditions that led Lenin to create the text in the first place. I cannot, then, simply use Lenin's text and apply it literally to the Brazilian context without rewriting it, without reinventing it.

Macedo: What would this rewriting consist of?

Freire: To the extent that I understand the parameters of the struggle in the Russia of Lenin's time, I can begin to understand what is happening in Brazil today. I can begin to see how valid certain general principles are so they can be reinvented. Other principles may have to be adapted for our context. I think it is impossible to read any text without a critical comprehension of the context to which the text refers.

Let's turn to your question of why I refuse to give so-called how-to recipes. When a North American educator reads my work, does not necessarily agree with all I say (he or she could not agree with me on everything, after all), but feels touched by my writings, rather than merely following me, he or she should begin practice by trying to critically comprehend the contextual conditions of where I worked. This educator must fully understand the economic, social, cultural, and historical conditions that culminated, for example, in the writing of *Pedagogy of the Oppressed.*

Educators must also investigate all of these conditions in their own contexts. When one thinks about the context that generated *Pedagogy of the Oppressed* and also thinks about one's own context, one can begin to re-create *Pedagogy of the Oppressed.* If educators are faithful to this radical reinvention, they will understand my insistence that learners assume the role of knowing subjects; that is, subjects who know alongside the educator, who is also a knowing subject. This is the principle of taking an epistemological, philosophical, pedagogical, and political stance.

It is one thing to read my work in order to identify with my positions and decide whether they are valid. But one ought not to do the same things I did in my practice.

In essence, educators must work hard so that learners assume the role of knowing subjects and can live this experience as subjects. Educators and learners do not have to do the exact same things I did in order to experience being a subject. That is because the cultural, historical, social, economic, and political differences that characterize two or more contexts will begin to play a role in the definition of the tense relationship between the educator and the learner, that is, the so-called values of a particular society. It is for this reason that I refuse to write a how-to manual or provide a step-by-step recipe.

I could not tell North American educators what to do, even if I wanted to. I do not know the contexts and material conditions in which North American educators must work. It is not that I do not know how to say what they should do. Rather, I do not know what to say precisely because my own viewpoints have been formed by my own contexts. I don't deny that I can make a contribution to U.S. educators. I think I have done so when visiting the United States and participating in concrete discussions with various groups about their projects. At these discussions I have suggested that, given my experience, I may be able to facilitate their work. But I cannot write a text that is filled with universal advice and suggestions.

When some educators criticize me on this point they reveal how influenced they are by the dominant ideology they are fighting against, and how they fail to understand the ways in which they reproduce it.

I once suggested to a group of U.S. students that they consider the following for their masters theses: how many texts were there in the United States in 1984, for instance, on how to make friends, get a good job, develop skills; that is, texts that primarily give recipes? These texts are explained in terms of the general context that generates them. There are many educators who welcome this type of text, which in essence contributes to further deskilling. I refuse to write such texts, because my political convictions are opposed to the ideology that feeds such domestication of the mind.

For me, my major task in the United States, or elsewhere, is to say: Look, my political position is A, B, C. This political position requires that I maintain consistency between my discourse and my practice. This involves narrowing the distance between the two. Narrowing the distance between discourse and practice is what I call "coherence."

In any context I speak about my own practice, and upon reflection I articulate my practice theoretically. From here on, I have to challenge other educators, including those in my own country, to take my practice and my reflections as the object of their own reflections and analyze their context so they can begin to reinvent them in practice. This is my role as an educator; not to arrogantly pretend to be an educator of educators in the United States.

Macedo: This lack of coherence you talked about is a problem. Even though some North American educators agree with you theoretically, in practice they find themselves still conditioned by the dominant ideology. It could be that the failure to establish harmony between theory and practice leads to a head-on collision with the coherence necessary to maintain a succinct view of the political and pedagogical project at hand. It could be they unknowingly reproduce elements of the dominant ideology, which contradicts the fundamental principles of your theory.

Freire: Exactly. And this does not happen only in the United States, of course; it happens in Brazil as well. The distance that exists in Brazil between educators' revolutionary discourse and their practice is enormous. It is very common to find intellectuals who authoritatively discuss the right of the subordinated classes to liberate themselves. The mere act of talking about the working class as objects of their reflections smacks of elitism on the part of these intellectuals. There is only one way to overcome this elitism, which is also authoritarian and implies an inconsistency in intellectuals' revolutionary discourse. These intellectuals ought to stop speaking *about* and start speaking *with* the working classes. When educators expose themselves to the working classes, they automatically begin to become reeducated.

Macedo: They would also begin to understand and respect the cultural production of the working class; for example, their various forms of resistance as concrete aspects of culture.

Freire: Exactly.

Macedo: It is also important to stress, for instance, that the understanding of subordinated groups' cultural production is indispensable in any attempt to develop a type of emancipatory literacy. To do otherwise would be to develop pedagogical structures under the guise of a radical pedagogy that has hidden goals for assimilating students into ideological spheres of the dominant class. Critical to appreciating subordinated groups' culture is the element of resistance and how to use it as a platform that enables students to become literate in their own history and lived experiences.

Freire: You have touched upon an important point that Henry Giroux elaborates so eloquently in his writing: the problem of resistance. One of the learning tasks of educators who consider themselves progressive (for me, "revolutionary" is the preferred term) should be the critical comprehension of the different levels of resistance on the part of the subordinated classes, that is, the levels of their resistance given the levels of confrontation between them and the dominant classes.

Understanding these forms of resistance leads you to a better appreciation of their language; and, in fact, you cannot comprehend their resistance without grasping the essence of their language. Language makes explicit the ways in which people have been resisting. In other words, language gives you a glimpse of how people survive.

Understanding resistance leads to appreciating the "astuteness" of the oppressed classes as a way to defend themselves against the dominant. This astuteness is social to the degree that it is part of the social network of the oppressed class. This astuteness is explicit through the use of their language, artworks, music, and even in their physiology. The oppressed body develops immunization to defend itself against the harsh conditions to which it is subjugated. If this were not so, it would be impossible to explain how millions of Latin Americans and Africans continue to survive in subhuman conditions. Under similar conditions, you or I would not last more than a week. Our bodies have never had to develop the immune system to combat that type of harsh reality.

Again, understanding the oppressed's reality, as reflected in the various forms of cultural production—language, art, music—leads to a better comprehension of the cultural expression through which people articulate their rebelliousness against the dominant. These cultural expressions also represent the level of possible struggle against oppression.

For example, there are extraordinary murals and graffiti art in most U.S. cities populated by the working class and, more tragically, the jobless class. These are both cultural and political expressions. I visited Chicago with an artist who used these forms and he told me about black artists who paint on building walls depictions of the day-to-day existence of the oppressed classes. Though highly artistic and thus aesthetic, they are also a political act.

These artworks are an astute method that the dominated classes use to denounce their unjust and often oppressive domination. They denounce through artistic expression and sometimes they hide their denunciation with artistic expression. It is this context of oppression that triggers the oppressed classes' need to be astute and to resist. Giroux is correct: any radical pedagogy must first understand fully the dynamics of resistance on the part of learners. Last year, for instance, an interesting book was published in Brazil: *The Feasts of the People: Pedagogy of Resistance*. The author analyzes various cultural expressions, people's different festive moments, not as pure folkloric expressions, but as cultural expressions through which they also express their resistance.

Cultural understanding from this point of view is fundamental for the radical educator. The basic difference between a reactionary and a radical educator relates to manifestations of resistance. The reactionary educator is interested in knowing the levels of resistance and the forms it takes so that he or she can smother this resistance. A radical educator has to know the forms and ways in which people resist, not to hide the reasons for resistance, but to explicate at the theoretical level the nature of this resistance.

Macedo: A radical educator should not remain at the level of theory exclusively. He or she should use resistance as a tool that will enable students to become literate in their culture as well as in the codes of the dominant classes.

Freire: The difference between reactionary and radical educators is that the reactionary wants to know about resistance to hide or suppress it, and the radical wants to know about resistance to understand better the discourse of resistance, to provide pedagogical structures that will enable students to emancipate themselves.

Macedo: Could you now address the second part of my question, on the lack of direction in your proposals?

Freire: As an educator, you can only maintain a nondirective posture if you attempt a deceitful discourse; that is, a discourse from the perspective of the dominant class. Only in this deceitful discourse can an educator talk about a lack of direction. Why? I think this is because there is no real education without a directive. To the extent that all educational practice brings with it its own transcendence, it presupposes an objective to be reached. Therefore practice cannot be nondirective. There is no educational practice that does not point to an objective; this proves that the nature of educational practice has direction.

Let's now pose a question on epistemology and philosophy. The directional nature of educational practice that leads to a particular objective has to be lived by educators and learners. In other words, how can an educator behave in his educational practice in view of the directive nature of education? First, if this educator defends in practice the notorious position of those who wash their hands of such issues (somewhat like Pontius Pilate), he washes his hands and says in effect: "Since I respect students and I am not directive, and since they are individuals deserving respect, they should determine their own direction." This educator does not deny the directive nature of education that is independent of his own subjectivity. He simply denies himself the pedagogical, political, and epistemological task of assuming the role of a subject of that directive practice. He refuses to convince his learners of what he thinks is just. This educator, then, ends up helping the power structure.

What other viable methods are there relative to the directive nature of education? Another method would be to combat the situation I just described, that is, to combat laissez faire. The educator must help learners get involved in planning education, help them create the critical capacity to consider and participate in the direction and dreams of education.

The authoritarian educator is correct, even though he is not always theoretically explicit when he says that there is no education that is nondirective. I would not disagree with this educator; but I would say that he is authoritarian to the extent that he makes his own objectives and dreams the directives that he gives to learners in his educational practice. He is authoritarian because, as subject of the educational practice, he reduces learners to objects of the directives he imposes.

Which position or method is substantially democratic or, as I call it, radically democratic or revolutionary? The radically democratic view does not contain in its spontaneity the polar opposite of authoritarianism. After all, authoritarianism does not contain the polar opposite of spontaneity. For example, I am not going to be authoritarian so as not to be a laissez-faire educator. So as not to be an authoritarian, I am not going to be a laissez-faire educator.

Once more we fall into the theoretical framework of a pedagogical radicality as proposed by Giroux. We see that the correct way to assume the direction of education is to avoid reducing learners to a minority led by educators. On the contrary, the direction of education lies in the presentation of this problem to learners, a problem that is political, epistemological, and pedagogical. The problem of the directiveness and nature of education once more focuses on the issue of subjectivity, the role of education in the reconstruction of the world.

What are the roles of the educator and the learner? It cannot be merely that the learner follows the educator blindly. The role of an educator who is pedagogically and critically radical is to avoid being indifferent, a character-istic of laissez-faire educators. The radical has to be an active presence in educational practice. But the educator should never allow his or her active and curious presence to transform learners' presences into shadows of the educator's presence. Neither can the educator be the shadow of learners. The educator has to stimulate learners to live a critically conscious presence in the pedagogical and historical process.

PATRICIA BIZZELL
b. 1948

Born in Chicago and educated at Wellesley College, Patricia Bizzell in 1975 took her PhD at Rutgers University in English literature. She was assistant director of writing programs at Rutgers from 1975–1978, at which time she went to Holy Cross, where she is currently Professor of English and Director of Writing Programs (a peer-tutoring facility and a writing-across-the-curriculum program). She is perhaps best known for using the concept of "discourse community" to advance a social constructionist view of writing. "Arguing about Literacy" was one of several essays written in the late 1980s and early 1990s in which she pursued a dual agenda. She wanted to struggle not only against the cultural literacy work of E. D. Hirsch, Jr., but also against the tacks taken by many of his critics, which she saw as quietistic. She wanted a sort of third way that allows us to avow our ideological agendas or moral values in our teaching without recourse to foundational justifications. She suggested that this way might be rhetorical, the term pointing to an ongoing consensual process that would work to forestall oppression in classroom exercises of authority. She eventually named this approach "rhetorical authority" (in "Beyond Anti-Foundationalism to Rhetorical Authority," College English, 1990), a concept she is still working to develop.

Arguing about Literacy

I

Arguments about literacy typically take the same form. One kind of literacy holds a commanding position, that which comprises the ways of using language valued by the academy and the upper social classes with which it is associated. The dominance of this academic literacy is challenged by people who have made their way into the schools but whose native tongues are at a relatively greater remove from the academic dialect, whose preferred modes of developing ideas conflict with the linear logic and impersonal posture of academic debate, and whose cultural treasures are not included in the academic canon. These challenges of academic literacy typically come from social groups at some remove from the upper classes—that is, from the lower classes, foreign born, non-white, and/or female.

Although they have won some battles, these oppositional forces seem to have lost the war. For example, on the college level they have effected change in isolated instances: perhaps through instituting a pluralistic method of holistic essay exam scoring that avoids penalizing nonstandard dialect writers; perhaps through getting selections from "minority" artists included in reading anthologies. But the requirement that students master academic literacy in order to continue their educations is still institutionalized in the great majority of writing programs in this country (see Applebee; Baron; Finegan).

Yet this view of the monolithic power of academic literacy is misleading, and itself politically oppressive. I suspect that historical study of academic literacy would show the steady influence of oppositional forces for change. The academic literacy that is now required of American college students is, I suspect, more pluralistic than that enforced at the turn of the century. It is not my purpose to prove this here; because I think of myself professionally as a supporter of the opposition, I certainly do not mean to suggest that no further change is needed. I simply wish to suggest that change is possible; indeed, this possibility is implied by the argumentative tack typically taken by defenders of the status quo, of academic literacy as it is presently constituted.

Typically, people arguing this position have sought to draw attention away from the social class basis of academic literacy. Rather, they have sought arguments that rest on some supposedly transcendent standards, standards preserved above the merely political. Such "foundationalist" arguments, as contemporary philosophers and literary theorists have taught us to call them, aim to end debate, and with it, the embarrassing questions about who holds the political power to decide what constitutes good language use.

In this essay I examine some of these apolitical arguments for the academic status quo. First I discuss arguments adduced from social science research in what I might call literal literacy, that is, the study of what happens when people who were previously completely illiterate learn elementary reading and writing. We rarely see such people in American colleges. Then I look at work on so-called cultural literacy, most notably that of E. D. Hirsch, Jr., which seeks to be more responsive to the actual situation in our colleges by posing the "literacy problem" in terms of competing bodies of knowledge, but which nevertheless attempts to resolve debate in a way that conceals political implications. Finally I argue for a view of literacy—and thus implicitly defend a way of arguing about literacy—that is based on a properly rhetorical understanding of history and knowledge.

II

Social science research in literacy assumes that some kind of decisive change takes place when individuals and societies acquire literacy. Jack Goody summarizes these changes as:

the move from myth to history, from magic to science, status to contract, cold to hot [an allusion to Lévi-Strauss's "raw/cooked" distinction], concrete to abstract, collective to individual, ritual to rationality. (3)

Yet the social science approach to literacy is not as dichotomizing as Goody's characterization suggests. Social science research tends to focus on how these changes occur within individuals, changes in the ways they think and interact with the world, but also to consider these cognitive changes as conditioned by the social contexts in which literacy is used. Hence there is no monolithic concept of what happens when any individual or society, regardless of the historical circumstances, acquires literacy. Social science research in literacy is moving toward a more pluralistic view of "multiple literacies" (Scribner and Cole) or a "continuum of orality and literacy" (Tannen; see also Heath).

Research on literacy, however, has come into the debate on college reading and writing by way of the work of humanists who study literacy, such as classical philologist Eric Havelock and literary critic Walter Ong. In examining changes attendant upon literacy, humanists tend to focus on the changes occurring within discourse—stylistic changes—and to infer from the discourse the cognitive and cultural changes accompanying it. Humanists tend to dichotomize non-literate and literate states of being, and to reify the two states into all-embracing conceptual universes of orality and literacy (see Ong).

Among literacy scholars, the humanist position is called the "Great Cognitive Divide" theory of literacy. According to this theory, an oral culture, in which speech is the sole medium of verbal exchange, is characterized in its verbal style and in its thinking by parataxis, the simple juxtaposition of ideas; by concrete imagery that appeals to the senses and the emotions; by ritualized references to authority in the form of proverbs, epithets, incantations, and other formulae; and by an agonistic posture in disputation.

According to the humanists, this "orality" can be changed only through mastery of alphabetic literacy, in which symbols are assigned to phonemes rather than to syllables or whole concepts. Alphabetic literacy is more "efficient" than non-alphabetic systems because a much smaller number of symbols represents a much greater number of words, with much less ambiguity, thus enabling more people to master the system more quickly, and allowing textual content to be more varied without the need to codify it in orthodox formulae for easy recognition. Hence alphabetic literacy gives rise to the following characteristics of style and thinking: hypotaxis, the subordination of one idea to another in logical hierarchies; generalizations that appeal to reason and text-assisted memory for validation; and a dialectical relation to authority, encouraging the on-going, disinterested criticism of ideas.

Humanists argue that the single set of changes they see as characteristic of all literacy is always attendant upon the acquisition of literacy and is independent of social variables. They assert that the change from oral thinking to literate thinking can be achieved only through acquisition of alphabetic literacy, and that it is always achieved when alphabetic literacy has been acquired. These two assertions, however, have not been confirmed among variously literate contemporary peoples. Social scientists describe a wider variety of changes than do humanists and link particular changes to features of the particular social situation in which literacy is used. Some forms of alphabetic literacy do not convey all the cognitive changes associated with "Great Divide" literate thinking (see Heath); and some forms of non-alphabetic literacy do encourage some aspects of literate thinking (see Scribner and Cole).

This is not to say that social science scholarship on literacy has disproved the humanist "Great Divide" idea. Rather, the conflict between social scientists' and humanists' findings suggests that they are not looking at the same data. Specifically, social science research has found that the changes accompanying literacy most closely conform to the humanists' expectations when the literacy has been learned in a Western-type secular school. This match suggests that the orality/literacy dichotomy of the humanists has been derived from studying a subset of all possible literate texts, namely those texts that reflect the kinds of thinking induced by academic literacy.

Typically, however, humanist literacy scholars do not acknowledge their conflation of literacy and academic literacy. Thus not only do they reduce all possible cognitive gains attendant upon literacy acquired in various social circumstances to the narrow set of abilities associated with academic literacy, but they also foster arguments that any cognitive gains to be had from any kind of literacy are available only from mastery of academic literacy.

Such arguments have been used in aid of requiring students to learn Standard English because this dialect is preferred in academic literacy. Thomas J. Farrell argues native speakers of Black English score lower than whites on I.Q. tests and do poorly in school because Black English is essentially an oral, not a literate, language. These students' difficulties would be remedied, he claims, by teaching them Standard English; mastering the copula and other elements in the grammatical "alphabet" of Standard English would automatically enable them to think "literately"—that is, in ways sanctioned by academic literacy. In making this argument, Farrell ignores the fact that the Black English-speaking students he is discussing are not in fact totally illiterate—for example, they read well enough to take the tests upon whose results Farrell's case depends so heavily. Farrell does not recognize the existence of any literate abilities here because the students have not mastered the literate abilities that count for him, namely those associated with academic literacy.

III

The concept of "cultural literacy" has emerged as a corrective to "Great Divide" literacy theories. This concept suggests that all literacy is in fact cultural literacy—that is, that no symbol system in and of itself induces cognitive changes. A cultural context is necessary to invest the features of the system with meaning, to give them the significance that then induces changes in thinking. An alphabet, or a standard grammar, does not somehow structurally force changes in the user's mental apparatus. Rather, such changes flow from the cultural significance attached to mastering the alphabet or the grammar—the kinds of knowledge and social roles open to those who have achieved mastery and so on.

The development of E. D. Hirsch's thought on literacy illustrates how the need for a concept of cultural literacy arises. Hirsch's first major contribution is *The Philosophy of Composition* (1977). Here, like other defenders of the status quo, he attempts to resolve the debate over what should constitute academic literacy by establishing a definition that transcends social contexts and the local ideological agendas to which they give rise. "An authentic ideology of literacy," Hirsch claims, "inheres in the subject itself, and should guide our teaching of it" (xiii).

Hirsch deduces his "privileged ideology" of literacy from psycholinguistic research on memory and information processing, which he interprets as describing the characteristics of an ideally efficient language. He asserts that these characteristics may largely be found in formal written Standard English. Hirsch thus suppresses ideology both in the reasons he gives for teaching Standard English and in the results he hopes to gain from such teaching. He argues in favor of requiring all students to master Standard English because of its cognitive status as the most "communicatively efficient" form of the language. And his predictions of cognitive gains from mastery, like the arguments of humanist literacy scholars for alphabetic literacy, attribute these gains to the formal structure of the symbol system—like the alphabet, Standard English is more "efficient"—rather than to any contextual influences.

Moreover, Hirsch seeks to require mastery not merely of Standard English, but of a particular style of writing Standard English, a style encapsulated in the maxims of Strunk and White's well-known manual, which he recommends. His argument for the cognitive superiority of a clear, concise style of Standard English, like the humanists' argument for the cognitive characteristics of literate style, fails to notice that this style is socially situated. Hirsch's preferred verbal style, and the humanists' literate style, both appear upon further analysis to be the preferred style and thought patterns of academics, not necessarily of all literate people. In short, Hirsch's candidate for privileged ideology of literacy is not as context-free as he claims: it is an academic ideology of literacy.

Many critics have noted problems with the theory of literacy Hirsch defends in *The Philosophy of Composition* (see Bizzell and Herzberg). So has Hirsch. In this book, Hirsch defines a concept of "relative readability" that, he claims, enables him to measure the communicative efficiency of any text. He received a grant from the National Endowment for the Humanities to test the applicability of this concept. His experiments changed his mind. Hirsch and his associates at the University of Virginia "systematically degraded" academic texts (selections from Will and Ariel Durant, Bruce Catton, and others) to render them more difficult according to the standards of relative readability (Hirsch, "Culture and Literacy" 38–42). They then asked different groups ("literate adults" [38], community college basic writing students and others) to read either the degraded text or the original and to answer some comprehension questions.

Hirsch expected to find, of course, that the original texts, those that rated higher in relative readability, would generate better comprehension scores than the degraded texts. Instead, test results were unpredictable—until Hirsch realized the comprehension scores were tied more closely to the readers' prior knowledge of the subject discussed in the reading selection than to the stylistic features of the selection. If prior knowledge, which is conditioned by the reader's social background, affects readability, then social context in general must affect literacy in general much more than Hirsch had thought when he wrote *The Philosophy of Composition*.

Hirsch has explicitly rejected what he calls the "formalist" bias of his book in his essay "Cultural Literacy" (161). He abandons a "Great Divide" approach to literacy in defining "cultural literacy" as "the translinguistic knowledge on which linguistic literacy depends. You can't have one without the other" (165). He argues that "without appropriate, tacitly shared background knowledge" no audience can understand a text, whether the text is an astrophysics journal or a daily newspaper (165). Hirsch uses the term "canonical" to refer to this necessary knowledge, thus suggesting it is essential not only to reading comprehension, but also to membership in the social group that constitutes the audience for the text that the knowledge renders intelligible. Any audience, whether for an astrophysics journal or a daily newspaper, will have its canonical knowledge that, as a common possession of the group, helps the group to cohere, to distinguish itself from others, and to exclude or initiate outsiders.

To this point, Hirsch's "cultural literacy" position sorts well with the social-science approach to literacy. Hirsch suggests that different audiences have different bodies of shared knowledge that enable them to read the texts of their group. In other words, he is describing multiple literacies, and his notion of canonical knowledge helps to explain where multiple literacies come from. The understanding that prior knowledge conditions language use is of the utmost importance. This insight goes far to prevent the "diagnosis" of unsuccessful college writers as cognitively deficient (see Bizzell; Rose). Instead, as David Bartholomae has shown, we can see them as beginners in academic discourse, trying to find a way to use language for their own purposes in a community whose knowledge they do not yet fully share.

But when Hirsch turns to pedagogy, he begins once again to argue prescriptively. He begins his "Cultural Literacy" essay with this implied causal statement: "The national decline in our literacy has accompanied a decline in our use of common, nationwide materials in the subject most closely connected with literacy, 'English'" (159). Hirsch then invokes the turn-of-the-century practice of teaching from lists of authors, first established (although Hirsch does not say so) by Harvard University. While he names them at length, Hirsch denies he wants to recommend a return to the particular texts that made up these lists (159–60). But he returns to the idea of uniform lists in his recommendation for the formation of a "National Curriculum Board" that could establish new lists for contemporary schools (167–68). Indeed, Hirsch has recently established a Cultural Literacy Foundation with the avowed purpose of designing standardized tests of students' knowledge, tests intended to be used to shape school curricula.

What exactly is wrong with defining cultural literacy in terms of a common list? Opponents question the social and political biases that would inform the process of choosing works for the list (see Warnock). But Hirsch claims that his list is fair and representative (he developed a list, recently published in book form, with the aid of grants from Exxon and the National Endowment for the Humanities; note that Hirsch's continued success in receiving financial support for his work suggests its potential broad influence). In addition to canonical literature, Hirsch includes non-literary references such as the Declaration of Independence, minority figures such as Frederick Douglass, and popular culture items such as Pinocchio. By and large, however, the concessions to popular and minority cultures appear to be few. The core of the list is the core of Western high culture.

Hirsch does not deny that "choosing the contents of cultural literacy" requires a "difficult political decision" (167). Moreover, he seems to rule out any transcendent principles for deciding what works belong on the list—a departure from his habitual practice—admitting instead that selection will proceed by "discussion, argument, and compromise" (167). He does not want to require that every American school teach every work on the list—

local selectivity and addition would be allowed, within some limits, presumably. He thus attempts to forestall critics who would argue that his dream for a national curriculum is totalitarian, racist, sexist, and laden with social class prejudice.

Nevertheless, the function of history in Hirsch's argument points to the argument's crucial weakness: his idea of how canonical knowledge gets established. One cannot argue with Hirsch's choices of items for his list without tackling this issue first. Hirsch justifies his concentration on Western high or academic culture on grounds that this is our tradition: "no culture exists that is ignorant of its own traditions" (167). At this point Hirsch turns from the question of how this particular tradition got to be *the* tradition, concentrating instead on the need for *some* tradition to unite an increasingly fragmented society. He hopes that we Americans will decide we want "a broadly literate culture that unites our cultural fragments enough to allow us to write to one another and read what our fellow citizens have written" (167). To want this, as Hirsch himself points out, is to adopt the traditional point of view, "Our traditional, Jeffersonian answer" (167).

History functions at this crucial point in the argument in several ways. First, history is depicted as presenting us with the core curriculum of Western academic culture, essentially as a *fait accompli*. We are not now in a position to argue about the canonical status of most of the works on Hirsch's putative list, for they have been established by the impersonal force of history. Hirsch does not depict modern people as completely powerless before the force of history. We can add works to the canon, for instance. But no matter how unfair we now think the processes of history to have been, when we see how history has systematically excluded certain social groups from representation in the high culture, we can do nothing about those injustices now.

More importantly, history blocks our examining the attitudes that compel us to submit to it. One such attitude is that those cultural subgroups not presently represented in the academic canon are "fragmentary" and in need of unification. In short, the academic canon is now performing for Hirsch exactly the same function that Standard English did in *The Philosophy of Composition:* he imagines that it has been granted by history the power to transcend and hence to control local cultural canons. Hirsch detaches the academic canon from its own social origins, which are systematically suppressed—for example, in his forgetting to mention that the turn-of-the-century lists he admires were first promulgated by Harvard, a highly race-, sex-, and class-determined institution.

Moreover, Hirsch assumes that history has granted the academic canon the right to exercise this power over other cultures, through establishing canonical ways of thinking and of using language, canonical values, verbal styles, and mindsets as the "most important" to our national culture. This kind of valorizing of the canon resembles the process whereby humanist literacy scholars establish the importance of literate ways of thinking and of using language. Hirsch links the two arguments when he says: "Estimable cultures exist that are ignorant of Shakespeare and the First Amendment. Indeed, estimable cultures exist that are entirely ignorant of reading and writing" (167). Humanist literacy scholars frequently protest, as Hirsch does here, that their oral/literate dichotomy is not meant to imply any absolute inferiority of oral culture. They simply claim that the cognitive abilities fostered by literate culture are necessary now, the world over. Similarly, Hirsch does not wish to claim that everyone ignorant of his academic canon is inferior. But everyone ignorant of this canon in America is inferior because knowledge of this canon is necessary to enter the national literate forums— as defined by Hirsch.

Hence, "history" in Hirsch's argument becomes a cover term, concealing not only the process whereby certain texts achieve canonical status but also the process whereby attitudes towards the very existence of any canon, and its function in society, become ingrained. Hirsch adopts a determinist view of the power of history. He seems to say that both the content of the academic canon and our attitudes about the rightness of its dominance have been fixed by the past life of the society that has formed us. We may be able to make minor changes, but basically, we must submit. If one believes this, then there is no objection to teaching in the most indoctrinating fashion possible. What students lack is canonical knowledge: let's give it to them.

IV

How can we avoid the "foundationalism" of humanist literacy work and of cultural literacy work such as Hirsch's when we argue about literacy? I would like to suggest a rhetorical view that offers both a better understanding of how to argue and a better understanding of literacy itself. First how to argue: from a rhetorical point of view, one is never able to prove an opponent wrong absolutely, to present evidence that demonstrates the opponent's error and one's own correctness for all times and places. This is the kind of proof sought in "foundationalist" arguments. Rather, from a rhetorical point of view, what one does when arguing is to seek to persuade a particular audience, in a particular time and place. An argument is provisionally correct if it carries the day, but is always subject to dialectical revision.

This rhetorical view of argument means that in framing an argument, what one needs is not absolute truth or unimpeachable evidence, but rather means of persuasion that will move this particular audience. Rhetoric has traditionally been defined as the study of the means of persuasion. "Means" of persuasion can vary from enthymemes to gestures that express a speaker's ethos to tropes that are presumed to have some affect built into them structurally. The study of these means of persuasion has two ends: first, to call them to the communicator's attention, and second, to investigate *what* they mean in a given rhetorical situation. Aristotle notes, for example, that appeals to prudence will move old men, but not young ones. To understand how to use the means of persuasion effectively the rhetorician needs to know the audience well. This can mean knowing the audience's age and social condition, the audience's personal interests, and more, the audience's values.

I would argue that this focus on the means of persuasion implies not only a notion of the provisionality of all arguments but also a view of literacy as something local, something shared in a social context. The rhetorical investigation of audience entails attempting to share the canonical knowledge that constitutes the group as an audience. In other words, it is research into the group's cultural literacy. In classical times, such study appeared to be the study of universal human nature because rhetoricians typically had to do with a single, homogeneous audience. Increasingly since the Renaissance, however, rhetoric has sought to deal with the pluralism of the modern condition. Rhetoricians may very well have to deal with audiences whose shared knowledge seems quite alien at first. Thus the study of contemporary audiences has come to seem like comparative anthropology, while tracing the development of shared knowledge over time calls for discursively sophisticated historical study. In other words, rhetoric's commitment to understanding the means of persuasion has led, especially in modern, pluralistic times, into the historical and comparative study of ideologies.

I do not intend to suggest, however, that such study raises rhetoric above ideology. That would leave me open to a charge rhetoricians have faced ever since Plato, namely that they are fundamentally dishonest because they try to be in a community without being of it—to use some of its shared knowledge to achieve their own purposes while preserving a cynical distance on the world-view implied by the knowledge. The best answer to this charge was suggested by the Sophists, namely that rhetoric itself creates all knowledge (see Gronbeck; Engnell). Knowledge is not a content conveyed by rhetoric; knowledge is what ensues when rhetoric is successful, when rhetorician and audience reach agreement. If this is true, then by the same token, rhetoricians cannot share a community's knowledge while remaining unchanged. Rhetoricians' own world-views will be influenced to the extent that they assimilate the community's knowledge to their own discourse.

In other words, when you argue with someone, your own thinking is inevitably influenced by what you have to do to persuade the other person. All arguments are not only ideological, but dialectical. Hirsch's approach to the "problem of canon formation" is weakened by ignoring this aspect of argumentation. For him canon formation entails simply figuring out what texts (in the broadest sense) are in fact the most influential. Hirsch rules out any "merely ideological" attack on a work's canonical status. If it is in the canon now, it can be dislodged only if one can "prove" that it has not in fact had such influence. But current debates among literary critics over canon formation have been much more ideological than this. For example, feminist critics have argued that works by women writers should be moved into the canon in order to change the ideological bent of scholarship, to correct its male chauvinism. At the same time, many of these feminist arguments are couched in an argumentative style sanctioned by the male-dominated literary-critical tradition and designed explicitly to appeal to such readers. The feminists have been influenced by the audience with whom they are arguing—as some feminists, in turn, have noted and deplored!

Fundamentally, Hirsch sees ignorance of the canon in terms of a problem in deciphering literary allusions. He does not do justice to the value of his own insight concerning the crucial importance of knowledge to participation in discourse, for he does not consider the possibility that the very ability to count allusions depends on the canonical knowledge one already has. The researchers compiling the common list will be guided in their perceptions of what is frequently cited by what they can recognize on the basis of their own education. The researchers' own cultural assumptions will predetermine what will be perceived as "important." An example of this kind of circular reasoning about influence can be found in Hirsch's "Cultural Literacy" essay, in which, as I noted earlier, he cites Thomas Jefferson as an authority to support his view that a canon including Jefferson's Declaration of Independence should be imposed on all American schools.

If we see the production of literacy as a collaborative effort—if we adopt a rhetorical perspective on literacy, which dialectically relates means of persuasion to audience's canonical knowledge—then we need a pedagogy much less prescriptive than Hirsch's or Farrell's. Teaching academic literacy becomes a process of constructing academic literacy, creating it anew in each class through the interaction of the professor's and the students' cultural resources. I would argue that this is in fact what happens, very slowly—hence the increasing pluralism in academic literacy noted earlier.

But if one wishes to foster this process, to support oppositional forces as I said I did, then the problem with this model of the dialectical formation of academic literacy is that professor and students do not appear to be equal partners in the collaboration. The professor automatically has more persuasive power for what he or she wants to include in academic literacy, simply by virtue of the social power his or her position provides over the students. A larger version of this problem has emerged in connection with the concept of "interpretive communities" in reader-response literary criticism and writing across the curriculum work: when the professor initiates students into currently acceptable methods of responding to texts—or into the practices of any other academic discipline—isn't he or she simply forcing conformity to these practices? Even if we understand disciplinary practices to be developed by human beings, the master practitioners in the field, rather than to be discovered in some absolute form, independent of human agency, isn't the result for the student the same, namely submission? Can change occur only when the material world erupts into the academic community and forces an adjustment—but not as a result of the initiatives of any human newcomers?

I do not know that anyone has yet articulated a truly collaborative pedagogy of academic literacy, one that successfully integrates the professor's traditional canonical knowledge and the students' non-canonical cultural resources. Certainly I cannot do so. It is extremely difficult to abrogate in the classroom, by a collective act of will, the social arrangements that separate professors and students outside the classroom. Integration has not been achieved if students are simply allowed to express affective responses to canonical knowledge as conveyed by the professor; or if the professor simply abdicates the role of guide to tradition and encourages the students to define a course agenda from their own interests. For example, we might expect Richard Rorty to favor a pedagogy that raises questions about canonical knowledge and opens the academy to new cultural resources. This has been his project in his own scholarly work. Yet in discussing pedagogy, even Rorty can find no way around an unequal relation between professor and students.

Rorty argues that we should "give students a chance for intellectual hero-worship" by depicting the "great men" of traditional intellectual history not as geniuses in touch with transcendent truth, but as "fighters against their time" who "were taking on the problems which the community around them had inherited" and "inventing new forms of communal life by inventing new songs, new discourses, new polities" (10). To be sure, this approach historicizes intellectual work and emphasizes its discursive basis. But students are cast very much in a subordinate role, as worshippers, and whom they are worshipping is made clearer later in the same essay, in which Rorty notes with approval: "In practice, the content of core curricula is whatever books the most influential members of the faculty of a given institution all happen to have liked, or all like to teach—the books which give them the greatest pleasure" (12).

In other words, students are to be seduced into cultural literacy by their admiration, first, for the master practitioners who are directing their lives in the classroom, and second, for their masters' intimate friends to be found in great books. Rorty uses the term "eroticism" to characterize the teacher-student relationship he desires. Of course, this is meant as an ironic commentary on Plato, but Rorty's version of cultural literacy itself evokes the homoeroticism of the *Phaedrus*. It seems quite appropriate that throughout his essay, Rorty uses the masculine pronoun exclusively to refer to the masters and their worshippers.

It's not that I wish to inveigh against any pleasure resulting from reciprocal acts of teaching and learning, or, more important, against Plato's vision in the *Phaedrus* of an education that reaches the whole person, not intellect alone. Rather, I simply wish to show how difficult it can be to make education truly reciprocal, and not something done to one person by another. Rorty's model inevitably takes on these instrumental overtones, and typically, they are accompanied by elitist implications such as attend Platonic homoeroticism. The masters, too, learned to love their favorites from their own teachers.

Such a closed system would indeed seem to support the view that only a radical change in historical circumstances, an eruption of the material world, can force changes in the academic canon. Once change has been initiated by impersonal forces, students may find the opportunity to act on their own cultural agendas—some newcomers may find that they are better equipped to deal with the crisis, precisely because they have not yet learned to view the world in the currently traditional academic ways, than are the convention-bound masters. If we are forced to this conclusion about the possibility of change, must we give up trying to be actively oppositional? Must we simply passively await an opportunity that may never come?

We have to be careful here not to fall back into a "foundationalist" way of arguing about change. If the power of an individual to effect change is qualified, if opportunities for oppositionally motivated change are contingent upon historical circumstances "erupting" into the academic community, this does not mean that change is now out of human hands. Rather, we should understand that change is always immanent but becomes evident when the time is right—and when those who wish to effect change are willing and able to engage in the rhetorical processes that make change happen. That is, those who support change must persuade other members of the academic community that the prevailing notion of academic literacy needs revision. We should not expect those with a critical perspective on prevailing notions to be any more able to transcend historical circumstances than the supporters of the dominant culture are—to wish for this power is to fantasize avoiding the rhetorical process.

We also have to be careful not to resurrect a determinist view. The opportunities historical circumstances present for cultural change may be very difficult to access for individuals—but not for groups. You can't act alone, perhaps, but you can act with others with whom you make common cause. Again, this view is congenial to the rhetorical perspective—persuasion is not based on idiosyncratic values but on what is shared. A truism worth repeating is that only through collective effort have changes been effected in the academic canon so far—whether we speak of theoretical shifts such as the rise and fall of New Criticism, or changes in the subject of study such as feminist-motivated revision of the textual canon. I need not advocate, then, the creation of oppositional discourses within the academy—people working out their relations to the changing historical circumstances are creating them all the time. I do advocate, however, the recognition that this process constitutes "normal" intellectual life. The crucial moment in the inculcation of cultural literacy will be finding ways to persuade our students to participate in this life with us.

References

Applebee, Arthur N. *Tradition and Reform in the Teaching of English: A History.* Urbana: NCTE, 1974.

Baron, Dennis. *Grammar and Good Taste: Reforming the American Language.* New Haven: Yale UP, 1982.

Bartholomae, David. "Inventing the University." *When a Writer Can't Write: Studies in Writer's Block and Other Composing Process Problems.* Ed. Mike Rose. New York: Guilford, 1985. 134-65.

Bizzell, Patricia. "Cognition, Convention, and Certainty: What We Need to Know about Writing." *PRE/TEXT* 3 (1982): 213-44.

Bizzell, Patricia, and Bruce Herzberg. "'Inherent' Ideology, 'Universal' History, 'Empirical' Evidence, and 'Context-Free' Writing: Some Problems in E. D. Hirsch's *The Philosophy of Composition.*" *MLN* 95 (1980): 1181-1202.

Engnell, Richard A. "Implications for Communication of the Rhetorical Theory of Gorgias of Leontini." *Western Speech* 37 (1973): 175-84.

Farrell, Thomas J. "I.Q. and Standard English." *College Composition and Communication* 34 (1985): 470-84.

Finegan, Edward. *Attitudes Toward English Usage.* New York: Teacher's College, 1980.

Goody, Jack. *The Domestication of the Savage Mind.* Cambridge: Cambridge UP, 1977.

Gronbeck, Bruce. "Gorgias on Rhetoric and Poetic: A Rehabilitation." *Southern Speech Communication Journal* 38 (1972): 27-38.

Havelock, Eric. *The Literate Revolution in Greece and Its Cultural Consequences.* Princeton: Princeton UP, 1982.

Heath, Shirley Brice. *Ways With Words: Language, Life, and Work in Communities and Classrooms.* Cambridge: Cambridge UP, 1983.

Heller, Scott. "Author Sets Up Foundation to Create 'Cultural Literacy' Tests." *The Chronicle of Higher Education* 5 (Aug. 1987): 2.

Hirsch, E. D., Jr. "Cultural Literacy." *American Scholar* 52 (1982-83): 159-69.

———. "Culture and Literacy." *Journal of Basic Writing* 3 (Fall/Winter 1980): 27-47.

———. *The Philosophy of Composition.* Chicago: U of Chicago P, 1977.

Hirsch, E. D., Jr., Joseph Kett, and James Trefil. *Cultural Literacy: What Every American Needs to Know.* Boston: Houghton, 1987.

Ong, Walter J. *Orality and Literacy: The Technologizing of the Word.* New York: Methuen, 1982.

Rorty, Richard. "Hermeneutics, General Studies, and Teaching." *Synergos: Selected Papers from the Synergos Seminars* 2 (1982): 1-15.

Rose, Mike. "The Language of Exclusion: Writing Instruction at the University." *College English* 47 (1985): 341-59.

Scribner, Sylvia, and Michael Cole. *The Psychology of Literacy.* Cambridge: Harvard UP, 1981.

Tannen, Deborah. "The Oral/Literate Continuum of Discourse." *Spoken and Written Languages: Exploring Orality and Literacy.* Ed. Deborah Tannen. Norwood, NJ: Ablex, 1982. 1-16.

Warnock, John. "Cultural Literacy: A Worm in the Bud?" *ADE Bulletin* 82 (Winter 1985): 1-7.

JAMES A. BERLIN
b. 1942

Like most English department rhetorical theorists of his generation, James Berlin was trained in literary studies, receiving a PhD in Victorian literature at the University of Michigan in 1975. His formal entry into rhetorical studies came during a postdoctoral seminar in rhetorical invention conducted by Richard Young at Carnegie Mellon University during the 1978-79 school year. Berlin has since worked in the history and theory of rhetoric. His Writing Instruction in Nineteenth-Century American Colleges *was published in 1984 and* Rhetoric and Reality: Writing Instruction in American Colleges, 1900-1985 *in 1987. Both works attempt to relate developments in classroom rhetorics to larger economic and political events. Most recently, Berlin has turned his attention to the converging concerns of rhetoric and cultural studies, arguing that the latter is working to rediscover the material force of language in the play of human affairs; that is, the rhetorical dimension of discourse. He joined Michael Vivion to edit* Cultural Studies in the English Classroom *(1993), and he is completing a manuscript on a rhetorical approach to English studies titled* Rhetorics, Poetics, and Cultures: Refiguring College English Studies. *Berlin teaches in the English department at Purdue University.*

Poststructuralism, Cultural Studies, and the Composition Classroom: Postmodern Theory in Practice

The uses of postmodern theory in rhetoric and composition studies have been the object of considerable abuse of late. Figures of some repute in the field—the likes of Maxine Hairston and Peter Elbow—as well as anonymous voices from the Burkean Parlor section of *Rhetoric Review*—most recently, TS, a graduate student, and KF, a voice speaking for "a general English teacher audience" (192)—have joined the chorus of protest. The charges have included willful obscurity, self-indulgence, elitism, pomposity, intellectual impoverishment, and a host of related offenses. Although my name usually appears among the accused, I am sympathetic with those undergoing the difficulties of the first encounter with this discussion. (I exclude Professor Hairston in her irresponsible charge that its recent contributors in *College English* are "low-risk Marxists who write very badly" [695] and who should be banned from NCTE publications.) I experienced the same

461

frustration when I first encountered the different but closely related language of rhetoric and composition studies some fifteen years ago. I wondered, for example, if I would ever grasp the complexities of Aristotle or Quintilian or Kenneth Burke or I. A. Richards, not to mention the new language of the writing process. A bit later I was introduced to French poststructuralism, and once again I found myself wandering in strange seas, and this time alone. In reading rhetoric, after all, I had the benefit of numerous commentators to help me along—the work of Kinneavy and Lauer and Corbett and Emig, for example. In reading Foucault and Derrida in the late seventies, on the other hand, I was largely on my own since the commentaries were as difficult as the originals, and those few that were readable were often (as even I could see) wrong. Nonetheless, with the help of informal reading groups made up of colleagues and students, I persisted in my efforts to come to terms with this difficult body of thought. I was then, as now, convinced that both rhetorical studies and postmodern speculation offered strikingly convergent and remarkably compelling visions for conducting my life as a teacher and a citizen. It is clear to me that rhetoric and composition study has arrived as a serious field of study because it has taken into account the best that has been thought and said about its concerns from the past and the present, and I have found that postmodern work in historical and contemporary rhetorical theory has done much to further this effort.

I will readily admit that discussants in postmodern theories of rhetoric have been more concerned with advancing this immensely rich vein of speculation than they have with communicating with the novice. But I think it is a mistake to condemn them for this. Contrary to what KF, the hard-working general English teacher, has asserted, teaching writing is not a "relatively simple and straightforward task" (192). As the intense effort that has been given this activity in the 2500-year history of Western education indicates, communication is at once extremely important in the life of a society and extremely complex (see the histories of Kennedy or Corbett or Vickers, for example). Those who wish to come to grips with this complexity cannot be expected to write exclusively for the uninitiated, a move that would hopelessly retard the development of any discussion. A new rhetoric requires a new language if we are to develop devices for producing and interpreting discourse that are adequate to our historical moment. I would argue that those working today at the intersections of rhetoric and postmodern theory are beginning to generate rhetorics that in conception and pedagogical application promise to be counterparts to the greatest accomplishments of the past—of an Aristotle (who once sounded strange next to Plato) or an Isocrates (who sounded strange next to Gorgias) or to Campbell (who sounded strange next to Ward). Eventually (and sooner than we might imagine, I expect), those interested in rhetoric will be talking and thinking in the new terminologies emerging today, finding them just as comfortable as the language of cognitive rhetoric or expressionist rhetoric. Still, this does not help the overworked composition teacher or the new graduate student who is eager to explore the significance of this new speculation for theory and the classroom but is not sure where to start.

In this essay I want to present as clearly as I know how some of the central features of postmodern theory that workers in rhetoric have found especially relevant to their efforts. Since covering the field as whole would require more space than I have here, however, I want to restrict myself to considering the ways these postmodern conceptions are counterparts to discussions in social-epistemic rhetoric. I will also include a description of a freshman course I have designed that is the result of my theoretical studies, a course that combines methods of cultural studies (itself a product of postmodern thought coupled with a progressive politics) with the methods of social-epistemic rhetoric in a beginning composition class. My intent is to demonstrate that the complexities of theory have immediate pedagogical applications, and that one of the efforts of composition teachers must be to discover these. Indeed, I will argue that the merger of theory and classroom practice in a uniquely new relation is one of the results of (what I should perhaps now call) postmodern rhetorical theory.

The Postmodern

John Schilb has explained that postmodernism "can designate a critique of traditional epistemology, a set of artistic practices, and an ensemble of larger social conditions" (174). Here the focus will be on the first, particularly on that body of thought that has emerged in what is loosely called structuralist and poststructuralist theory (sometimes called the "language division" of postmodern speculation). In "Rhetoric Programs after World War II: Ideology, Power, and Conflict," I attempt to outline the ways certain branches of rhetorical studies in the US, particularly of the epistemic variety, have paralleled the trajectory of structuralist and poststructuralist developments both at home and abroad. In this section I would like to explore the important features of postmodernism in which this is most apparent; in the next I will trace their uses in social-epistemic rhetoric. The significant postmodern developments fall into three general categories: the status of the subject; the characteristics of signifying practices; the role of master theories in explaining human affairs.

The unified, coherent, autonomous, self-present subject of the Enlightenment has been the centerpiece of liberal humanism. From this perspective the subject is a transcendent consciousness that functions unencumbered by social and material conditions of experience, acting as a free and rational agent who adjudicates competing claims for action. In other words, the individual is regarded as the author of all her actions, moving in complete freedom in deciding how she will live. This perception has been challenged by the postmodern conception of the subject as the product of social and material conditions. Here the subject is considered the construction of the various signifying practices, the uses of language, of a given historical moment (see, for example, Benveniste, Barthes, Foucault). This means that each person is formed by the various discourses, sign systems, that surround her. These include both everyday uses of language in the home, school, the media, and other institutions, as well as the material conditions that are arranged in the manner of languages—that is, semiotically (like a sign system), such as the clothes we wear, the way we carry our bodies, the way our school and home environments are arranged. These signifying practices then are languages that tell us who we are and how we should behave in terms of such categories as gender, race, class, age, ethnicity, and the like. The result is that each of us is heterogeneously made up of various competing discourses, conflicted and contradictory scripts, that make our consciousness anything but unified, coherent, and autonomous. At the most everyday level, for example, the discourses of the school and the home about appropriate gender behavior ("Just say 'No'") are frequently at odds with the discourse provided by peers and the media ("Go for it"). The result is that we are made up of subject formations or subject positions that do not always square with each other.

Signifying practices then are at the center of the formation of the "subject" and of "subjectivities"—terms made necessary to avoid all the liberal humanist implications of talking about the "individual." But the conception of signifying practices, of language, is itself radically altered in this scheme. A given language is no longer taken to be a transparent medium that records an externally present thing-in-itself, that is, it is not a simple signaling device that stands for and corresponds to the separate realities that lend it meaning. Language is instead taken to be a pluralistic and complex system of signifying practices that construct realities rather than simply presenting or re-presenting them. Our conception of material and social phenomena then are fabrications of signifying, the products of culturally coded signs. Saussure, the prime originator of structuralism in Europe, first demonstrated the ways language functions as a set of differences: Signifiers derive meaning not in relation to signifieds, to external referents, but in relation to other signifiers, the semiotic systems in which they are functioning. For example, just as the sound "t" is significant in English because it contrasts with "d"—making for a difference in meaning between "to" and "do"—a term, such as "man," has significance in a given discourse because it contrasts with another term, such as "woman" or "boy" or "ape." And just as the sounds of a language are culturally variable, so are its terms and their structural relations. A sign thus has meaning by virtue of its position relative to another sign or signs within a given system, not to externally verifiable certainties. Most important, these signs are arranged in a hierarchy so that one is "privileged," that is, considered more important than its related term. For example, Alleen Pace Nilsen has shown that terms in English that are gender specific almost invariably involve positive connotations in the case of males and negative connotation in the case of females (master/mistress, sir/madam, chef/cook, for example). Such hierarchies, once again, are not universal but are culturally specific.

Roland Barthes has shown the ways that signs form systems (semiotic systems) that extend beyond natural language to all realms of a culture, for example, film, television, photography, food, fashion, automobiles, and on and on (see *Mythologies*). He presents a method for analyzing and discussing the semiosis (sign production) of texts as they appear in virtually all features of human behavior. Michel Foucault has indicated the manner in which different "discursive regimes," elaborate systems of signifying systems, forge knowledge/power formations that govern action during successive stages of history. (He does so, furthermore, while denying any master regime or narrative unfolding over time, a matter to be considered shortly.) Finally, Jacques Derrida has shown the attempt of philosophy to establish a foundation, an essential presence, for its systems in a realm outside of language, an effort to avoid the role of signification, of discourse, in all human undertakings. From the postmodern perspective, then, signifying practices shape the subject, the social, and the material—the perceiver and the perceived.

These antifoundational, antiessentialist assaults on Enlightenment conceptions of the subjects and objects of experience are extended to postulates of grand narratives of the past or present—that is, the stories we tell about our experiences that attempt to account for all features of it (its totality) in a comprehensive way. Jean-François Lyotard has been the central figure in denying the possibility of any grand metanarrative that might exhaustively account for human conditions in the past or present. Like Foucault, he renounces the totalizing discourse of such schemes as Hegelianism or Marxism or the faith in scientific progress or the invisible hand of economic law. All are declared language games that are inherently partial and interested, intended to endorse particular relations of power and to privilege certain groups in historical struggles. Against this totalizing move, Lyotard argues for a plurality of particular narratives, limited and localized accounts that attempt to explain features of experience that grand narratives exclude. The structuralist and poststructuralist analyses of sign systems look for the binary opposites of key terms, the marginalized terms that often go unmentioned. (This is why they use the term *foreground*: it refers to putting the concealed and unacknowledged term in a binary structure forward so that the *complete* significance of the term can be examined in a given discourse.) Similarly, postmodern studies of cultures of the past and present look for what is left out, what exists on the unspoken margins of the culture. This moves attention to such categories as class, race, gender, and ethnicity in the unfolding of historical events. This is often history from the bottom up, telling the stories of the people and events normally excluded from totalizing accounts.

Social-Epistemic Rhetoric

Those familiar with social-epistemic rhetoric can readily see its convergence with postmodern conclusions about language and culture. I have discussed this rhetoric at length in *Rhetoric and Reality,* "Rhetoric and Ideology in the Writing Class," and elsewhere. Here I wish to offer a look at the ways in which it converges with postmodern speculation in providing a mutually enriching theoretical synthesis. To say this differently, poststructuralism provides a way of more fully discussing elements of social-epistemic rhetoric that are fully operative within it; at the same time, social-epistemic rhetoric provides poststructuralism with methods for discussing the production and reception of texts—and especially the former—that have been a part of its effort. I will show these convergences in discussing the elements of the rhetorical situation—interlocutor, conceptions of the real, audience, and language—as they are being conceived in social-epistemic rhetoric informed by poststructuralism. I should also mention that this development is bringing social-epistemic rhetoric, particularly, as I will show, in the classroom, very close to the work of cultural studies as it has been discussed by the Birmingham Center for Contemporary Cultural Studies.

We have already seen that the subject of the rhetorical act cannot be regarded as the unified, coherent, autonomous, transcendent subject of liberal humanism. The subject is instead multiple and conflicted, composed of numerous subject formations or positions. From one perspective this is a standard feature of many historical rhetorics in their concern with the *ethos* of the speaker, her presentation of the appropriate image of her character through language, voice, bearing, and the like. For a contemporary rhetoric, the writer and reader, the speaker and listener (and more of their commutability of function shortly), must likewise be aware that the subject (the producer) of discourse is a construction, a fabrication, established through the devices of signifying practices. This means that great care must be taken in choosing the subject position that the interlocutor wishes to present, and equally great care must be taken in teaching students the way this is done. In other words, it will not do to say, "Be yourself," since all of us possess multiple selves, not all of which are appropriate for the particular discourse situation. This is not, it should be noted, to deny that all of us display a measure of singularity. As Paul Smith argues, the unique place of each of us in the network of intersecting discourses assures differences among us as well as possibilities for originality and political agency. This does not mean, however, that anyone can totally escape the discursive regimes, the power/knowledge formations, of the historical moment. Political agency but never complete autonomy is the guiding formulation here.

But if the subject, the sender, is a construct of signifying practices in social-epistemic rhetoric, so are the material conditions to which the subject responds, the prime constituents of the message of discourse. (I am of course relying on Burke's formulation of language as symbolic action to be distinguished from the sheer motion of the material, as well as on the work of Barthes and Foucault). This is not to deny the force of the material in human affairs: people do need to provide for physiological needs, to arrange refuge from the elements, and to deal with eventual physical extinction. However, all of these material experiences are mediated through signifying practices. Only through language do we know and act upon the conditions of our experience. Ways of living and dying are finally negotiated through discourse, the cultural codes that are part of our historical conditions. These conditions are of an economic, social, and political nature, and they change over time. But they too can only be known and acted upon through the discourses available at any historical moment. Thus the subject who experiences and the material and social conditions experienced are discursively constituted in historically specific terms.

The mediation of signifying practices in the relations of subjects to material conditions is especially crucial. From the perspective offered here, signifying practices are always at the center of conflict and contention. In the effort to name experience, different groups are constantly vying for supremacy, for ownership and control of terms and their meanings in any discourse situation. As Stuart Hall, a past director of the Birmingham Center, has pointed out, a given language or discourse does not automatically belong to any class, race, or gender. Following Volosinov and Gramsci, he argues that language is always an arena of struggle to make certain meanings—certain ideological formulations—prevail. Cultural codes thus are constantly in conflict: they contend for hegemony in defining and directing the material conditions of experience as well as consciousness itself. The signifying practices of different groups thus compete in forwarding different agendas for the ways people are to regard their historical conditions and their modes of responding to them, and these signifying practices are thus always a scene of battle (Hall, "The Rediscovery of 'Ideology'").

The receiver of messages, the audience of discourse, obviously cannot escape the consequences of signifying practices. The audience's possible responses to texts are in part a function of its discursively constituted social roles. These roles are often constructed with some measure of specificity as membership in a specific discourse community—in a particular union or profession, for example. But these roles are never discretely separate from other subject positions the members of an audience may share or, on the other hand, occupy independent of each other. In other words, members of an audience cannot simply activate one subject position and switch off all others. Thus, audiences must be considered both as members of communities and as separate subject formations. The result is that the responses of the audience as a collective and as separate subjects are never totally predictable, never completely in the control of the sender of a coded message or of the coded message itself. As Stuart Hall has demonstrated, audiences are capable of a range of possible responses to any message. They can simply accommodate the message, sharing in the codes of the sender and assenting to them. The audience can completely resist the message, rejecting its codes and purposes and turning them to other ends. Finally, the receiver can engage in a process of negotiation, neither accommodating alone nor resisting alone, instead engaging in a measure of both (Hall, "Encoding/Decoding").

The work of rhetoric, then, is to study the production and reception of these historically specific signifying practices. In other words, social-epistemic rhetoric will enable senders and receivers to arrive at a formulation of the conception of the entire rhetorical context in any given discourse situation, and this will be done through an analysis of the signifying practices operating within it. Thus in composing a text, a writer will engage in an analysis of the cultural codes operating in defining her role, the roles of the audience, and the constructions of the matter to be considered. These function in a dialectical relation to each other so that the writer must engage in complex decision-making in shaping the text to be presented. By dialectic I mean they change in response to each other in ways that are not mechanically predictable—not presenting, for example, simply a cause-effect relation but a shifting affiliation in which causes and effects are mutually interactive, with effects becoming causes and causes effects simultaneously. The reader of the text must also engage in a dialectical process involving coded conceptions of the writer, the matter under consideration, and the role of the receiver of the text in arriving at an interpretation of the text. Writing and reading are thus both acts of textual interpretation and construction, and both are central to social-epistemic rhetoric. More of this reading/writing relationship will be taken up later. First I would like to consider the role of ideology in rhetoric.

As I have indicated throughout, signifying practices are never innocent: they are always involved in ideological designations, conceptions of economic, social, political, and cultural arrangements and their relations to the subjects of history within concrete power relations. Ideology is not here declared a mystification to be placed in binary opposition to truth or science. The formulation invoked is instead derived from Louis Althusser as elaborated in Goran Therborn's *The Ideology of Power and the Power of Ideology*. This conception places ideology within the category of discourse, describing it as an inevitable feature of all signifying practices. Ideology then becomes closely imbricated with rhetoric, the two inseparably overlapped however distinguished for purposes of discussion. From this perspective, no claims can be offered as absolute, timeless truths since all are historically specific, arising in response to the conditions of a particular time and place. Choices in the economic, social, political, and cultural are thus based on discursive practices that are interpretations—not mere transcriptions of some external, verifiable certainty. Thus the choice is never between ideology and absolute truth, but between different ideologies. Some are finally judged better ("truer") than others on the basis of their ability to fulfill the promises of democracy at all levels of experience—the economic, social, political, and cultural—providing an equal share of authority in decision-making and a tolerance for difference.

Ideology addresses or interpellates human beings. It provides the language to define the subject, other subjects, the material and social, and the relation of all of these to each other. Ideology addresses three questions: what exists, what is good, what is possible? The first, explains Therborn, tells us "who we are, what the world is, what nature, society, men and women are like. In this way we acquire a sense of identity, becoming conscious of what is real and true." Ideology also provides the subject with standards for making ethical and aesthetic decisions: "*what is good,* right, just, beautiful, attractive, enjoyable, and its opposites. In this way our desires become structured and normalized." The very configurations of our desires, what we will long for and pursue, are thus shaped by ideology. Finally, ideology defines the elements of expectation: "*what is possible* and impossible: our sense of the mutability of our being-in-the-world and the consequences of change are hereby patterned, and our hopes, ambitions, and fears given shape" (18). This is especially important since the recognition of the existence of a condition (homelessness, for example) and the desire for its change will go for nothing if ideology indicates that a change is simply not possible (the homeless freely choose to live in the street and cannot be forced to come inside). All three are further implicated in power relations in groups and in society, in deciding who has power and in determining what power can be expected to achieve.

Finally, ideology always brings with it strong social and cultural reinforcement, so that what we take to exist, to have value, and to be possible seems necessary, normal, and inevitable—in the nature of things. And this goes for power as well since ideology naturalizes certain authority regimes—those of class, race, and gender, for example—and renders alternatives unthinkable, in this way determining who can act and what can be accomplished. Finally, ideology is always inscribed in the discourses of daily practice and is plural-istic and conflicted. Any historical moment displays a wide variety of com-peting ideologies and each subject displays permutations of these conflicts, although the overall effect is to support the hegemony of dominant groups.

All of this has great consequences for the writing classroom. Given the ubiquitous role of discourse in human affairs, instructors cannot be content to focus exclusively on teaching the production of academic texts. Our busi-ness must be to instruct students in signifying practices broadly conceived—to see not only the rhetoric of the college essay but the rhetoric of the institution of schooling, of the work place, and of the media. We must take as our province the production and reception of semiotic codes broadly conceived, providing students with the heuristics to penetrate these codes and their ideological designs on our formation as the subjects of our experi-ence. Students must come to see that the languages they are expected to speak, write, and embrace as ways of thinking and acting are never disinter-ested, always bringing with them strictures on the existent, the good, the possible, and regimes of power.

If rhetoric is to be a consideration of signifying practices and their ideo-logical involvement—that is, their imbrication in economic, social, political, and cultural conditions and subject formation—then the study of signs will of course be central. A large part of the business of this rhetoric will be to provide methods for describing and analyzing the operations of significa-tion. Just as successive rhetorics for centuries furnished the terms to name the elements involved in text production and interpretation for the past (inventional devices, arrangement schemes, stylistic labels for tropes and fig-ures), social-epistemic rhetoric will offer a terminology to discuss these activities for contemporary conditions and conceptual formulations. Struc-turalism, poststructuralism, and rhetoric have all begun this effort, and workers in semiotics have profited from them. It is composition teachers, however, who are best situated to develop ways of analyzing and discussing discourse to enable students to become better writers and readers. (After all, most of the important rhetorics of the past were written by teachers: Socrates, Plato, and Aristotle all taught the counterpart of freshman compo-sition.) This leads to a consideration of the relation of reading and writing, of text production and text interpretation.

As I have already indicated, social-epistemic rhetoric demands revised models of reading and writing. Both composing and interpreting texts become instances of discourse analysis and, significantly, negotiation. Indeed, the very acts of writing and reading are themselves verbally coded discursive procedures which guide the production and interpretation of meanings, making a certain range more likely to appear and others more improbable. This exclusionary coding is apparent, for example, in reflecting on the directives for text production and reception provided in certain expressionist rhetorics. For these, only personal and metaphoric accounts can be regarded as authentic discourse, and, unlike current-traditional rhetoric, any attempt to be rational, objective, and dispassionate is considered a violation of the self and of genuine writing. In addition, for social-epistemic rhetoric, writing and reading become acts of discourse analysis as both the sender and receiver attempt to negotiate the semiotic codes in which each is situated—that is, the signifying practices that make up the entire rhetorical context. Composing and reception are thus interactive since both are performances of production, requiring the active construction of meaning according to one or another coded procedure. The opposition between the active writer and the passive reader is displaced since both reading and writing are considered constructive. It will be the work of rhetoric and composition teachers, then, to develop lexicons to articulate the complex coding activity involved in writing and reading, and this leads us to the classroom.

The Classroom

The recommendations of the new rhetoric proposed here become clearest in considering pedagogy. For social-epistemic rhetoric, teaching is central, not an afterthought through which practice is made to conform with the more important work of theory. Instead, the classroom becomes the point at which theory and practice engage in a dialectical interaction, working out a rhetoric more adequate to the historical moment and the actual conditions of teacher and students. From this perspective, all teachers of rhetoric and composition are regarded as intellectuals engaging in theoretical and empirical research, the two coming to fruition in their interaction within the classroom. Indeed, as Patricia Donahue and Ellen Quandahl have argued, composition teachers are through this interaction striving to create a new variety of academic discourse. The teacher's duty here is to bring to bear rhetorical theory as broadly defined in this essay within the conditions of her students' lives. The teacher will in this act develop methods for producing and receiving texts, including strategies for negotiating and resisting signifying practices, that are best suited for the situations of her students. These of course will be recommended to other teachers, but only as example and guideline, not pronouncements from on (theoretical) high. The uses of postmodern theory in rhetoric will then be in the hands of teachers, not prescribed in advance by "outside experts."

This role as intellectual, furthermore, has an important political dimension, involving the transformation and improvement of present social and political arrangements. As I have emphasized elsewhere, social-epistemic rhetoric grows out of the experience of democracy in the US, carrying with it a strong antifoundational impulse (*Rhetoric and Reality*, "Rhetoric and Ideology"). Knowledge/power relationships are regarded as human constructions, not natural and inevitable facts of life. All institutional arrangements are humanly made and so can be unmade, and the core of this productive act is found in democracy and open discussion.

The social-epistemic classroom thus offers a lesson in democracy intended to prepare students for critical participation in public life. It is dedicated to making schools places for individual and social empowerment. Schools after all are places, as Aronowitz and Giroux remind us, "of struggle over what forms of authority, orders of representation, forms of moral regulation, and versions of the past should be legitimated, passed on, and debated" (32). The teacher must then recognize and resist inequities in our society—the economic and social injustices inscribed in race, ethnic, and gender relations, relations that privilege the few and discriminate against the many. This classroom is dialogic, situating learning within the realities of the students' own experience, particularly their political experience. The dialogic classroom is designed to encourage students to become transformative intellectuals in their own right. Studying signifying practices will require a "critical literacy." As Ira Shor explains: "Critical literacy invites teachers and students to *problematize* all subjects of study, that is, to understand existing knowledge as historical products deeply invested with the value of those who developed such knowledge." For this teacher, all learning is based in ideology, and signifying practices—the production and reception of texts—must challenge dominant ideological formations. In Shor's terms, the study of discourse must go "beneath the surface to understand the origin, structure, and consequences of any body of knowledge, technical process, or object under study" (24). Students thus research their own language, their own society, their own learning, examining the values inscribed in them and the ways these values are shaping their subjectivities and their conceptions of their material and social conditions.

The Course

I would now like to turn to a course in freshman composition that will demonstrate the operations of the social-epistemic rhetoric described here. This effort locates the composing process within its social context, combining the methods of semiotic analysis in considering cultural codes with the recommendations of the rhetoric I have outlined. As will be apparent, it is allied with attempts to refigure English studies along the lines of cultural studies, a matter I have discussed in "Composition Studies and Cultural Studies" and "Composition and Cultural Studies: Collapsing the Boundaries." Since I devised the syllabus for this course to be shared with teaching assistants in my mentor group at Purdue and since my report here is based on our shared experience over the past three years, I will use the plural pronoun in referring to the effort. (I would also like to thank them for their cooperation throughout.)

The course is organized around an examination of the cultural codes— the social semiotics—that are working themselves out in shaping consciousness in our students and ourselves. We start with the personal experience of the students, but the emphasis is on the position of this experience within its formative context. Our main concern is the relation of current signifying practices to the structuring of subjectivities—of race, class, and gender formations, for example—in our students and ourselves. The effort is to make students aware of cultural codes, the competing discourses that are influencing their formations as the subjects of experience. Our larger purpose is to encourage students to resist and to negotiate these codes—these hegemonic discourses—in order to bring about more democratic and personally humane economic, social, and political arrangements. From our perspective, only in this way can they become genuinely competent writers and readers.

We thus guide students to locate in their experience the points at which they are now engaging in resistance and negotiation with the cultural codes they daily encounter. These are then used as avenues of departure for a dialogue. It is our hope that students who can demystify the subtle devices of persuasion in these cultural codes will be motivated to begin the re-forming of subjectivities and social arrangements, a re-forming which is a normal part of democratic political arrangements. We also want to explore the wide range of codes that students confront daily—print, film, television—in order to prepare them to critique their experiences with these codes. As Donald Morton and Mas'ud Zavarzadeh explain, this "critique (not to be confused with criticism) is an investigation of the enabling conditions of discursive practices" (7). Its purpose is to locate the ideological predispositions of the semiotic codes that we encounter and enact in our lives, seeing their commitment to certain conceptions of the existent, the good, and the possible. The course then explores these coded discourses in the institutional forms—the family, the school, the work place, the media—that make them seem natural and timeless rather than historically situated social constructions.

The course consists of six units: advertising, work, play, education, gender, and individuality. Each unit begins with a reading of essays dealing with competing versions of the significance of the topic of the unit. For example, the unit on education includes an analysis of US schools by a diverse range of observers: William Bennett, Jonathon Kozol, John Dewey, and James Thurber. These essays are often followed with a film dealing with school experiences—for example, *Risky Business* or *Sixteen Candles* or

The Breakfast Club. A videotape of a current television program about schools—for example, *Beverly Hills, 90210*—is also often included. The important consideration is not the texts in themselves but the texts in relation to certain methods of interpreting them.

Students are provided a set of heuristics (invention strategies) that grow out of the interaction of rhetoric, structuralism, poststructuralism, semiotics, and cultural studies (again, especially of the Birmingham Center variety). While those outlined here have been developed as a result of reading in Saussure, Peirce, Lévi-Strauss, Barthes, Gramsci, Raymond Williams, Stuart Hall, and others, an excellent introduction to them for teachers and students can be found in John Fiske's *Introduction to Communication Studies.* (Diana George and John Trimbur's *Reading Culture* will perform a similar function for composition classrooms.) In examining any text—print, film, television—students are asked to locate the key terms in the discourse and to situate these within the structure of meaning of which they form a part. These terms of course are made up of the central preoccupations of the text, but to determine how they are working to constitute experience their functions as parts of coded structures—a semiotic system—must be examined. The terms are first set in relation to their binary opposites as suggested by the text itself. (This of course follows Saussure's description of the central place of contrast in signification and Lévi-Strauss's application of it.) Sometimes this opposition is indicated explicitly, but often it is not. It is also important to note that a term commonly occupies a position in opposition to more than one other term.

For example, we sometimes begin with a 1981 essay from *The Wall Street Journal,* "The Days of a Cowboy are Marked by Danger, Drudgery, and Low Pay," by William Blundell. (This essay is most appropriate for the unit on work, but its codes are at once so varied and so accessible to students that it is a useful introduction to any unit.) We first consider the context of the piece, exploring the characteristics of the readership of the newspaper and the historical events surrounding the essay's production, particularly as indicated within the text. The purpose of this is to decide what probably acted as key terms for the original readers. The essay focuses on the cowboss, the ranch foreman who runs the cattle operation. The meaning of "cowboss" is established by seeing it in binary opposition to the cowboys who work for him as well as the owners who work away from the ranch in cities. At other times in the essay, the cowboss is grouped together with the cowboys in opposition to office workers. Through the description of labor relations on the ranch, the cowboys are also situated in contrast to urban union workers, but the latter are never explicitly mentioned. Finally, the exclusively masculine nature of ranching is suggested only at the end of the essay when the cowboss's wife is described in passing as living apart from the ranch on the cowboss's own small spread, creating male/female domain binary. All of these binaries suggest others, such as the opposition of nature/civilization, country/city, cowboy/urban cowboy, and the like. Students begin to see that these binaries are arranged hierarchically, with one term privileged over the other. They also see how unstable these hierarchies can be, however, with a term frequently shifting valences as it moves from one binary to another— for example, cowboy/union worker but cowboss/cowboy. It is also important to point out that this location of binaries is of course not an exact operation and that great diversity appears as students negotiate the text differently. Their reasons for doing so become clear at the next level of analysis.

These terms are then placed within the narrative structural forms suggested by the text, the culturally coded stories about patterns of behavior appropriate for people within certain situations. These codes deal with such social designations as race, class, gender, age, ethnicity, and the like. The position of the key terms within these socially constructed narrative codes are analyzed, discussed, and written about. It is not too difficult to imagine how these are at work in the binaries indicated above. The narratives that cluster around the figure of the cowboy in our culture are quickly detected in this essay—for example, patterns of behavior involving individuality, freedom, and independence. These, however, are simultaneously coupled with self-discipline, respect for authority (good cowboys never complain), and submission to the will of the cowboss. Students have little difficulty in pointing out the ways these narratives are conflicted while concurrently reinforcing differences in class and gender role expectations. Of particular value is to see the way the essay employs narratives that at once disparage the *Wall Street Journal* readers because they are urban office workers while enabling them to identify with the rugged freedom and adventure of the cowboys, seeing themselves as metaphorically enacting the masculine narrative of the cowboss in their separate domains. In other words, students discover that the essay attempts to position the reader in the role of a certain kind of masculine subject.

These narrative patterns at the level of the social role are then situated within larger narrative structures that have to do with economic, political, and cultural formulations. Here students examine capitalist economic narratives as demonstrated in this essay and their consequences for class, gender, and race relations and roles both in the work place and elsewhere. They look, for example, at the distribution of work in beef production with its divisions between managers and workers, thinkers and doers, producers and consumers. They also consider the place of narratives of democracy in the essay, discussing the nature of the political relations that are implied in the hierarchies of terms and social relations presented. It should be clear that at these two narrative levels considerable debate results as students disagree about the narratives that ought to be invoked in interpreting the text, their relative worth as models for emulation, and the degree to which these narratives are conflicted. In other words, the discussion emerging from the use of these heuristics is itself conflicted and unpredictable.

Thus, the term as it is designated within a hierarchical binary is situated within narratives of social roles, and these roles are located within more comprehensive narratives of economic and political formations in the larger society. The point of the interpretation is to see that texts—whether rhetorical or poetic—are ideologically invested in the construction of subjectivities within recommended economic, social, and political arrangements. Finally, as should now be clear, this hermeneutic process is open-ended, leading in diverse and unpredictable directions in the classroom. And this is one of its strengths as it encourages open debate and wide-ranging speculation.

After some experience with written and video texts, students apply these heuristics to their personal experiences in order to analyze in essay form the effect of an important cultural code on their lives. The students select the topic and content of the essay, but they must do so within the context of the larger theme of each unit. Thus, in the unit on education, students must choose some feature of their school experience from the past or present that has been of particular personal significance. The students must then locate points of conflict and dissonance in the cultural codes discovered, although they are not expected to resolve them. For example, students often choose to write about their experiences in high school athletics in order to discuss the conflicted codes involved in the emphasis on personal versus team success, winning versus learning to accept defeat, discipline versus play, and the like. The roles the students learn to assume in sports are examined in terms of such categories as gender, age, race, and group membership. Some students have explored the differences in the experiences of male and female athletes. Here they commonly examine the narratives appropriate to the behavior of each as recommended by dominant cultural codes about sports. These role definitions and performances are then placed within larger narratives having to do with life experiences, such as vocational aspirations, career objectives, marriage plans, and the like. Students at this point often discover the parallels between the contrasting experiences of males and females in high school sports and the contrasting experiences of males and females in career tracks. Once again, the various levels of conflict are explored, both within the expectations for each gender and across the genders, although, once again, students are not expected to resolve them. It should also be noted that conflicts also appear as students disagree in discussions about the codes that are being recommended within ·'
sports activities. These incidents reinforce the point that ···'
always negotiated so that students produce the··
duce them; that is, students do no· ·'

often reshaping them to serve their own agendas. And of course incidents of resistance are frequently discussed as students report their defiance of required roles—for example, refusing to engage in some humiliating hazing ritual against those declared "losers."

As students develop material through the use of the heuristic and begin to write initial drafts of their essays, they discover the culturally coded character of all parts of composing. Students must learn to arrange their materials to conform to the genre codes of the form of the essay they are writing—the personal essay, the academic essay, the newspaper essay, for example. (Students could also be asked to create other kinds of texts—short stories, poems, videos—although we have not done so in our composition course. Here the genre codes of each would again be foregrounded.) These essay genres conform to socially indicated formal codes that students must identify and enact, and they, of course, carry great consequences for meaning. A given genre encourages certain kinds of messages while discouraging others. Next, at the level of the sentence, stylistic form comes into play, and the student must again learn to generate sentence structures and patterns of diction that are expected of the genre employed. It is important that students be made aware of the purposes of these codes, both practical and ideological. In other words, expecting certain formal and stylistic patterns is not always a matter of securing "clear and effective communication." As all writing teachers know, most errors in grammar and spelling do not in themselves interfere with the reader's understanding. The use of "who" for "whom," for example, seldom creates any confusion in reference. These errors instead create interferences of a social and political nature.

Finally, I would like to restate a point on the interchangeability of reading and writing made earlier. In enacting the composing process, students are learning that all experience is situated within signifying practices, and that learning to understand personal and social experience involves acts of discourse production and interpretation, the two acting reciprocally in reading and writing codes. Students in the class come to see that interpretation involves production as well as reproduction, and is as constructive as composing itself. At the same time, they discover that the more one knows about a text—its author, place of publication, audience, historical context—the less indeterminate it becomes and the more confident the reader can be in interpreting and negotiating its intentions. Similarly, the more the writer understands the entire semiotic context in which she is functioning, the greater will be the likelihood that her text will serve as a successful intervention in an ongoing discussion. After all, despite the inevitable slippages that appear in the production and interpretation of codes, people do in fact communicate with each other daily to get all sorts of work done effectively. At the same time, even these "effective" exchanges can be seen to harbor contradictions that are concealed or ignored. These contradictions are important to discover for the reader and writer because they foreground the political unconscious of decision making, a level of unspoken assumptions that are often repressed in ordinary discourse. It is here that the betrayals of democracy and the value of the individual are discovered despite the more obvious claims to the contrary.

The purpose of social-epistemic rhetoric is finally political, an effort to prepare students for critical citizenship in a democracy. We want students to begin to understand that language is never innocent, instead constituting a terrain of ideological battle. Language—textuality—is thus the terrain on which different conceptions of economic, social, and political conditions are contested with consequences for the formation of the subjects of history, the very consciousness of the historical agent. We are thus committed to teaching writing as an inescapably political act, the working out of contested cultural codes that affect every feature of experience. This involves teachers in an effort to problematize students' experiences, requiring them to challenge the ideological codes they bring to college by placing their signifying practices against alternatives. Sometimes this is done in a cooperative effort with teachers and students agreeing about the conflicts that are apparent in considering a particular cultural formation—for example, the elitist and often ruthlessly competitive organization of varsity sports in high schools. Students are able to locate points of personal resistance and negotiation in dealing with the injustices of this common social practice. At other times, students and teachers are at odds with each other or, just as often, the students are themselves divided about the operation and effects of conflicting codes. This often results in spirited exchange. The role of the teacher is to act as a mediator while ensuring that no code, including her own, goes unchallenged.

This has been a lengthy introduction to the intersections of postmodern discourse theory and rhetoric. Even so, it only begins to explore the possibilities, as can be seen, for example, in the excellent new collection, *Contending with Words: Composition and Rhetoric in a Postmodern Age*, edited by Patricia Harkin and John Schilb. (This volume arrived while I was putting the finishing touches on this piece.) These essays share with mine the confidence that postmodern speculation has much to offer writing teachers. None, furthermore, suggests that it is a savior come to redeem us from our fallen ways. All see rhetoric and composition as engaged in a dialectic with the new speculation, the result being the enrichment of both. Indeed, these essays confirm what I have long maintained: The postmodern turn in recent discussions in the academy is an attempt to restore the place of rhetoric in the human sciences. In it we find an ally in our work of creating a critically literate citizenry, and we ought not to reject it just because it speaks a nonstandard dialect.

Works Cited

Aronowitz, Stanley, and Henry A. Giroux. *Education Under Siege*. South Hadley, MA: Bergin and Garvey, 1985.

Barthes, Roland. *Mythologies*. Trans. Annette Lavers. New York: Hill and Wang, 1972.

Benveniste, Emil. *Problems in General Linguistics*. Trans. Mary Elizabeth Meek. Coral Gables: U of Miami P, 1971.

Berlin, James A. "Composition and Cultural Studies." *Composition and Resistance*. Ed. Mark Hurlbert and Michael Blitz. Portsmouth, NH: Heinemann-Boynton/Cook, 1991. 47-55.

———. "Composition Studies and Cultural Studies: Collapsing the Boundaries." *Into the Field: The Site of Composition Studies*. Ed. Anne Ruggles Gere. New York: MLA, 1992.

———. "Rhetoric and Ideology in the Writing Class." *College English* 50 (1988): 477-94.

———. *Rhetoric and Reality: Writing Instruction in American Colleges, 1900-1985*. Carbondale, IL: Southern Illinois UP, 1987.

———. "Rhetoric Programs After World War II: Ideology, Power, and Conflict." *Rhetoric and Ideology: Compositions and Criticisms of Power*. Ed. Charles W. Kneupper, Arlington, TX: Rhetoric Society of America, 1989.

Blundell, William E. "The Days of a Cowboy are Marked by Danger, Drudgery, and Low Pay." *Wall Street Journal* 10 June 1981: A1+.

Burke, Kenneth. *Language as Symbolic Action*. Berkeley: U of California P, 1966.

Corbett, Edward P.J. *Classical Rhetoric for the Modern Student*. New York: Oxford UP, 1965.

Derrida, Jacques. *Of Grammatology*. Trans. Gayatri Spivak. Baltimore: Johns Hopkins UP, 1976.

Donahue, Patricia, and Ellen Quandahl. *Reclaiming Pedagogy: The Rhetoric of the Classroom*. Carbondale, IL: Southern Illinois UP, 1989.

Dowst, Kenneth. "The Epistemic Approach: Writing, Knowing, and Learning." *Eight Approaches to Teaching Composition*. Ed. Timothy Donovan and Ben W. McClelland, Urbana: NCTE, 1980.

Elbow, Peter. "Reflections on Academic Discourse." *College English* 53 (1991): 135-55.

Fiske, John. *Introduction to Communication Studies*. 2nd ed. London: Routledge, 1990.

Foucault, Michel. *Power/Knowledge: Selected Interviews and Other Writings: 1972-1977*. Ed. Colin Gordon. Trans. Colin Gordon et al. New York: Pantheon, 1980.

George, Diana, and John Trimbur. *Reading Culture*. New York: Harper Collins, 1992.

Hairston, Maxine C. "Comment and Response." *College English* 52 (1990): 694-96.

Hall, Stuart. "Encoding/Decoding." *Culture, Media, Language*. Ed. Stuart Hall et al. London: Hutchinson, 1980.

———. "The Rediscovery of 'Ideology': Return of the Repressed in Media Studies." *Culture, Society and the Media*. Ed. Michael Gurevitch et al. London: Routledge, 1982.

Harkin, Patricia, and John Schilb, eds. *Contending with Words: Composition and Rhetoric in a Postmodern Age*. New York: MLA, 1991.

Hodge, Robert, and Gunther Kress. *Social Semiotics*. Ithaca, NY: Cornell UP, 1988.

Johnson, Richard. "What Is Cultural Studies Anyway?" *Social Text* 16 (1986-87): 38-80.

Kennedy, George A. *Classical Rhetoric and its Christian and Secular Tradition from Ancient to Modern Times.* Chapel Hill: U of North Carolina P, 1980.

KF. "Putting on the Dog: Heuristics, Paradigms, and Hermeneutics." *Rhetoric Review* 10 (1991): 187-93.

Knoblauch, C. H., and Lil Brannon. *Rhetorical Traditions and the Teaching of Writing.* Upper Montclair, NJ: Boynton/Cook, 1984.

Morton, Donald, and Mas'ud Zavarzadeh. *Theory/Pedagogy/Politics: Texts for Change.* Urbana: U of Illinois P, 1991.

Nilsen, Alleen Pace. "Sexism in English: A Feminist View." *Perspectives: Turning Reading into Writing.* Ed. Joseph J. Comprone. Boston: Houghton, 1987.

Schilb, John. "Cultural Studies, Postmodernism, and Composition." *Contending with Words: Composition and Rhetoric in a Postmodern Age.* Ed. Patricia Harkin and John Schilb. New York: MLA, 1991. 173-88.

Scott, Robert L. "On Viewing Rhetoric as Epistemic." *Central States Speech Journal* 18 (1967): 9-16.

Shor, Ira. "Educating the Educators: A Freirean Approach to the Crisis in Education." *Freire for the Classroom.* Ed. Ira Shor. Portsmouth, NH: Heinemann-Boynton/Cook, 1987. 7-32.

Smith, Paul. *Discerning the Subject.* Minneapolis: U of Minnesota P, 1988.

Therborn, Goran. *The Ideology of Power and the Power of Ideology.* London: Verso, 1980.

TS. "Joining the Conversation." *Rhetoric Review* 10 (1991): 175-86.

Vickers, Brian. *In Defence of Rhetoric.* Oxford: Clarendon, 1988.

Bibliography II: Commentary and Application

Annas, Pamela J. "Style as Politics: A Feminist Approach to the Teaching of Writing." *College English* 47 (1985): 360-71.

Arnold, Carroll C. "Perelman's New Rhetoric." *Quarterly Journal of Speech* 26 (1970): 87-92.

———. "Some Preliminaries to English-Speech Collaboration in the Study of Rhetoric." *Rhetoric: Theories for Application.* Papers presented at the 1965 Convention of the National Council of Teachers of English. Champaign, IL: NCTE, 1967. 30-36.

Aronowitz, Stanley, and Henry A. Giroux. *Education under Siege.* South Hadley, MA: Bergin & Garvey, 1985.

Bailey, Dudley. "A Plea for a Modern Set of Topoi." *College English* 26 (1964): 111-16.

Bailey, Richard W. "Current Trends in the Analysis of Style." *Style* 1 (1967): 1-14.

Baldwin, Charles Sears. "The College Teaching of Rhetoric." *Educational Review* 48 (June 1914): 1-14.

Bator, Paul G. "The 'Good Reasons' Movement: A 'Confounding' of Dialectic and Rhetoric." *Philosophy and Rhetoric* 21 (1988): 38-47.

Beale, Walter H. "Richard M. Weaver: Philosophical Rhetoric, Cultural Criticism, and the First Rhetorical Awakening." *College English* 52 (1990): 626-40.

Berlin, James A. "Composition and Cultural Studies." *Composition and Resistance.* Ed. Mark Hurlbert and Michael Blitz. Portsmouth, NH: Heinemann, Boynton/ Cook, 1991.

———. "Rhetoric and Ideology in the Writing Class." *College English* 50 (1988): 477-94.

Berthoff, Ann E. "Abstraction as a Speculative Instrument." *The Territory of Language.* Ed. Donald A. McQuade. Carbondale: Southern Illinois UP, 1986. 227-37.

———. *Forming/Thinking/Writing.* Portsmouth, NH: Boynton/Cook, 1982.

———. "I. A. Richards and the Audit of Meaning." *New Literary History* 14 (1982): 63-79.

———. "I. A. Richards and the Philosophy of Rhetoric." *Rhetoric Society Quarterly* 10 (1980): 195-210.

———. "The Problem of Problem Solving." *College Composition and Communication* 22 (1971): 237-42.

———, ed. *Reclaiming the Imagination: Philosophical Perspectives for Writers and Teachers of Writing.* Upper Montclair, NJ: Boynton, 1981.

Bilsky, Manuel. "I. A. Richards' Theory of Metaphor." *Modern Philology* 50 (1952): 130-37.

Bitzer, Lloyd F. "Functional Communication: A Situational Perspective." *Rhetoric in Transition: Studies in the Nature and Uses of Rhetoric.* Ed. Eugene E. White. University Park: Pennsylvania State UP, 1980. 21-38.

———. "Rhetoric and Public Knowledge." *Rhetoric, Philosophy, and Literature: An Exploration.* Ed. Don M. Burks. West Lafayette, IN: Purdue UP, 1978. 67-93.

———. "The Rhetorical Situation." *Philosophy and Rhetoric* 1 (1968): 1-14.

Bizzell, Patricia. *Academic Discourse and Critical Consciousness.* Pittsburgh: U of Pittsburgh P, 1992.

———. "Beyond Anti-foundationalism to Rhetorical Authority: Problems Defining Cultural Literacy." *College English* 50 (1988): 141–53.

———. "Cognition, Convention, and Certainty: What We Need to Know about Writing." *PRE/TEXT* 3 (1982): 213–43.

———. "Power, Authority, and Critical Pedagogy." *Journal of Basic Writing* 10 (1991): 54–70.

Black, Edwin. *Rhetorical Criticism: A Study in Method.* New York: Macmillan, 1965.

Booth, Wayne. "The Rhetorical Stance." *College Composition and Communication* 14 (1963): 139–45.

———. *The Vocation of a Teacher: Rhetorical Occasions, 1967–1988.* Chicago: U of Chicago P, 1988.

Brent, Doug. "Young, Becker and Pike's 'Rogerian' Rhetoric: A Twenty-Year Reassessment." *College English* 53 (1991): 452–66.

Brockriede, Wayne, and Douglas Ehninger. "Toulmin on Argument: An Interpretation and Application." *Quarterly Journal of Speech* 46 (1960): 44–53.

Brown, Stuart C. "I. A. Richards' New Rhetoric: Multiplicity, Instrument, and Metaphor." *Rhetoric Review* 10 (1992): 218–31.

Bruffee, Kenneth. "Social Construction, Language, and the Authority of Learning: A Bibliographic Essay." *College English* 48 (1986): 773–90.

———. "Writing and Reading as Collaborative or Social Acts." *The Writer's Mind: Writing as a Mode of Thinking.* Ed. Janice N. Hays, Phyllis A. Rother, Jon R. Ramsey, and Robert D. Foulke. Urbana, IL: NCTE, 1983. 159–69.

Coe, Richard M. "Rhetoric 2001." *Freshman English News* 3 (1974): 1–13.

———. "Beyond Diction: Using Burke to Empower Words—and Wordlings." *Rhetoric Review* 11 (1993): 368–77.

Coles, William E., Jr. *The Plural I—and After.* Portsmouth, NH: Heinemann, Boynton/Cook, 1988.

Consigny, Scott. "Rhetoric and Its Situations." *Philosophy and Rhetoric* 7 (1974): 175–86.

Cooley, J. C. "On Mr. Toulmin's Revolution in Logic." *Journal of Philosophy* 56 (1959): 297–319.

Corbett, Edward P. J. "A New Look at Old Rhetoric." *Rhetoric: Theories for Application.* Papers presented at the 1965 Convention of the National Council of Teachers of English. Ed. Robert M. Gorrell. Champaign, IL: NCTE, 1967. 16–22.

———. "The Rhetoric of the Open Hand and the Closed Fist." *College Composition and Communication* 20 (1969): 288–96.

Corbett, Edward P. J., James L. Golden, and Goodwin F. Berquist, eds. *Essays on the Rhetoric of the Western World.* Dubuque, IA: Kendall/Hunt, 1990.

Corder, Jim W. "Hunting for *Ethos* Where They Say It Can't Be Found." *Rhetoric Review* 7 (1989): 299–316.

———. "On the Way, Perhaps, to a New Rhetoric but Not There Yet, and if We Do Get There, There Won't Be There Anymore." *College English* 47 (1985): 162–70.

Crismore, Avon, and Rodney Farnsworth. "Mr. Darwin and His Readers: Exploring Interpersonal Metadiscourse as a Dimension of *Ethos.*" *Rhetoric Review* 8 (1989): 91–111.

Crosswhite, James. "Universality in Rhetoric: Perelman's Universal Audience." *Philosophy and Rhetoric* 22 (1989): 157–73.

Crowley, Sharon. "A Plea for the Revival of Sophistry." *Rhetoric Review* 7 (1989): 318–34.

Dasenbrock, Reed Way. "J. L. Austin and the Articulation of a New Rhetoric." *College Composition and Communication* 38 (1987): 291–305.

Dearin, Ray, ed. *The New Rhetoric of Chaim Perelman: Statement & Response.* Lanham, MD: UP of America, 1989.

Donahue, Patricia, and Ellen Quandahl. *Reclaiming Pedagogy: The Rhetoric of the Classroom.* Carbondale: Southern Illinois UP, 1989.

Dowst, Kenneth. "The Epistemic Approach: Writing, Knowing, and Learning." *Eight Approaches to Teaching Composition.* Ed. Timothy Donovan and Ben W. McClelland. Urbana, IL: NCTE, 1980. 65-86.

Elbow, Peter. *Embracing Contraries: Explorations in Teaching and Learning.* New York: Oxford UP, 1986.

———, ed. "Expressive Writing." Spec. issue of *PRE/TEXT* 11 (1990): 1-154.

———. *Writing with Power.* New York: Oxford UP, 1981.

———. *Writing without Teachers.* New York: Oxford UP, 1973.

Emig, Janet. "Writing as a Mode of Learning." *College Composition and Communication* 28 (1977): 122-28.

Enos, Theresa. *Learning from the Histories of Rhetoric: Essays in Honor of Winifred Bryan Horner.* Carbondale: Southern Illinois UP, 1993.

Faigley, Lester. "Competing Theories of Process: A Critique and a Proposal." *College English* 48 (1986): 527-42.

Feehan, Michael. "Kenneth Burke's Discovery of Dramatism." *Quarterly Journal of Speech* 65 (1979): 405-11.

Flynn, Elizabeth A., and Patrocinio P. Schweickart, eds. *Gender and Reading: Essays on Readers, Texts, and Contexts.* Baltimore: Johns Hopkins UP, 1986. 31-62.

Freedman, Aviva, and Ian Pringle, eds. *Reinventing the Rhetorical Tradition.* Ottawa: Canadian Council of Teachers of English, 1980.

Freire, Paulo. *Pedagogy of the Oppressed.* Trans. Myra Bergman Ramos. New York: Continuum, 1990.

———. *The Politics of Education: Culture, Power, and Liberation.* Trans. Donaldo Macedo. South Hadley, MA: Bergin & Garvey, 1985.

Fulkerson, Richard P. "Kinneavy on Rhetorical and Persuasive Discourse: A Critique." *College Composition and Communication* 35 (1984): 43-56.

Gearhart, Sally Miller. "The Womanization of Rhetoric." *Women's Studies International Quarterly* 2 (1979): 195-201.

Gibson, Walker. *Tough, Sweet, and Stuffy: An Essay on Modern American Prose Styles.* Bloomington: Indiana UP, 1975.

Giroux, Henry, and Stanley Aronowitz. *Education under Siege: The Conservative, Liberal, and Radical Debate over Schooling.* London: Routledge and Kegan Paul, 1986.

———. *Postmodern Education: Politics, Culture, and Social Criticism.* Minneapolis: U of Minnesota P, 1991.

Gorrell, Robert M., ed. *Rhetoric: Theories for Application.* Papers presented at the 1965 Convention of the National Council of Teachers of English. Champaign, IL: NCTE, 1967.

———. "Very Like a Whale—A Report on Rhetoric." *College Composition and Communication* 16 (1965): 138-43.

Graves, Richard L., ed. *Rhetoric and Composition: A Sourcebook for Teachers and Writers.* Rev. 2nd ed. Upper Montclair, NJ: Boynton/Cook, 1984.

Hairston, Maxine. "The Winds of Change: Thomas Kuhn and the Revolution in the Teaching of Writing." *College Composition and Communication* 33 (1982): 76-88.

Harris, Joseph. "The Idea of Community in the Study of Writing." *College Composition and Communication* 40 (1989): 11-22.

Hart, Roderick P., and Don M. Burks. "Rhetorical Sensitivity and Social Interaction." *Speech Monographs* 39 (1972): 75-91.

Holland, L. Virginia. *Counterpoint: Kenneth Burke and Aristotle's Theories of Rhetoric.* New York: Philosophical Library, 1959.

Johannesen, Richard L. "The Emerging Concept of Communication as Dialogue." *Quarterly Journal of Speech* 27 (1971): 373-82.

————. "Richard Weaver's View of Rhetoric and Criticism." *Southern Speech Journal* 32 (1966): 133-45.

Karis, Bill. "Conflict in Collaboration: A Burkean Perspective." *Rhetoric Review* 8 (1989): 113-26.

Kinneavy, James E. "The Basic Aims of Discourse." *College Composition and Communication* 20 (1969): 297-313.

Kirsch, Gesa, and Duane Roen, eds. *A Sense of Audience in Written Communication.* Newbury Park, CA: Sage, 1990.

Kneupper, Charles. "Teaching Argument: An Introduction to the Toulmin Model." *College Composition and Communication* 29 (1978): 237-41.

Lassner, Phyllis. "Feminist Responses to Rogerian Argument." *Rhetoric Review* 8 (1990): 220-32.

Long, Richard. "The Role of Audience in Chaim Perelman's *New Rhetoric.*" *Journal of Advanced Composition* 4 (1983): 107-17.

Murphy, James J., ed. *The Rhetorical Tradition and Modern Writing.* New York: MLA, 1982.

Murray, Donald. *Write to Learn.* Fort Worth: Holt, 1990.

Nichols, Marie Hochmuth. "Kenneth Burke and the 'New Rhetoric.'" *Quarterly Journal of Speech* 38 (1952): 133-44.

Phelps, Louise Wetherbee. *Composition as a Human Science: Contributions to the Self-Understanding of a Discipline.* New York: Oxford, 1988.

Poulakos, John. "The Components of Dialogue." *Western Speech Journal* 38 (1974): 199-212.

Reynolds, Nedra. "*Ethos* as Location: New Sites for Understanding Discursive Authority." *Rhetoric Review* 11 (1993): 325-38.

Rich, Adrienne. "When We Dead Awaken: Writing as Re-vision." *On Lies, Secrets, and Silence: Selected Prose 1966-1978.* New York: Norton, 1979.

Richards, I. A. *How to Read a Page: A Course in Effective Reading with an Introduction to a Hundred Great Words.* New York: Norton, 1942.

————. *Interpretation in Teaching.* New York: Harcourt, 1938.

Rogers, Carl. "Communication: Its Blocking and Its Facilitation." *Rhetoric: Discovery and Change.* Richard Young, Alton Becker, and Kenneth Pike. New York: Harcourt, 1970. 284-89.

Rohman, D. Gordon. "Pre-Writing: The Stage of Discovery in the Writing Process." *College Composition and Communication* 16 (1965): 106-12.

Royer, Daniel J. "New Challenges to Epistemic Rhetoric." *Rhetoric Review* 9 (1991): 282-97.

Schuster, Charles I. "Bakhtin as Rhetorical Theorist." *College English* 47 (1985): 594-607.

Scott, Robert L. "Chaim Perelman: Persona and Accommodation in *The New Rhetoric.*" *PRE/TEXT* 5 (1984): 89-95.

————. "On *Not* Defining 'Rhetoric.'" *Philosophy and Rhetoric* 6 (1973): 81-96.

————. "On Viewing Rhetoric as Epistemic: Ten Years Later." *Central States Speech Journal* 27 (1976): 258-66.

Secor, Marie J. "Perelman's *Loci* in Literary Argument." *PRE/TEXT* 5 (1984): 97-110.

Shor, Ira. *Critical Teaching and Everyday Life.* Chicago: U of Chicago P, 1987.

———. *Culture Wars*. Boston: Routledge and Kegan Paul, 1986.

———. *Empowering Education*. Chicago: U of Chicago P, 1992.

———. *Freire for the Classroom: A Sourcebook for Liberatory Teaching*. Portsmouth, NH: Heinemann, Boynton/Cook, 1987.

Spellmeyer, Kurt. "Foucault and the Freshman Writer: Considering the Self in Discourse." *College English* 51 (1989): 715–29.

Stewart, Donald C. "Some History Lessons for Composition Teachers." *Rhetoric Review* 3 (1985): 134–44.

Stratman, James F. "Teaching Written Argument: The Significance of Toulmin's Layout for Sentence-Combining." *College English* 44 (1982): 718–34.

Tate, Gary, ed. *Teaching Composition: 12 Bibliographical Essays*. 2nd ed. New York: Oxford, 1987.

Tate, Gary, and Edward P. J. Corbett. *The Writing Teacher's Sourcebook*. 2nd ed. New York: Oxford, 1988.

Trimbur, John. "Consensus and Difference in Collaborative Learning." *College English* 51 (1989): 602–16.

Vatz, Richard E. "The Myth of the Rhetorical Situation." *Philosophy and Rhetoric* 6 (1973): 154–61.

Wallace, Karl. "An Ethical Basis of Communication." *Speech Teacher* 4 (1955): 1–9.

Winterowd, W. Ross. "The Purification of Literature and Rhetoric." *College English* 49 (1987): 57–73.

———. "Reading (and Rehabilitating) the Literature of Fact." *Rhetoric Review* 8 (1989): 44–59.

Young, Richard E., Alton L. Becker, and Kenneth L. Pike. *Rhetoric: Discovery and Change*. New York, Harcourt, 1970.

Acknowledgments

Mikhail M. Bakhtin. "Toward a Methodology for the Human Sciences." From *Speech Genres and Other Late Essays*. Ed. Caryl Emerson and Michael Holquist. Copyright 1986 University of Texas. Reprinted by permission of the University of Texas Press.

Roland Barthes. From *The Pleasure of the Text* by Roland Barthes, translated by Richard Miller. Copyright 1982 by Farrar, Straus & Giroux. Reprinted by permission of Farrar, Straus & Giroux, Inc.

James Berlin. "Poststructuralism, Cultural Studies, and the Composition Classroom: Postmodern Theory in Practice." Originally appeared in *Rhetoric Review,* 11 (1992). Reprinted by permission.

Patricia Bizzell. "Arguing about Literacy." Appeared originally in *College English,* February 1988. Copyright 1988 by the National Council of Teachers of English. Reprinted with permission.

Wayne C. Booth. "The Idea of a *University*—as Seen by a Rhetorician." From *The Vocation of a Teacher: Rhetorical Occasions 1967-1988.* Chicago: University of Chicago Press, 1988. Copyright © 1988 by The University of Chicago. Reprinted by permission of The University of Chicago Press and the author.

Donald C. Bryant. "Rhetoric: Its Functions and Its Scope." Originally appeared in *Quarterly Journal of Speech,* 39 (1953). Pages 3-36. Reprinted by permission of the Speech Communication Association.

Kenneth Burke. "Definition of Man." From *Language as Symbolic Action: Essays on Life, Literature, and Method,* by Kenneth Burke. Copyright 1968 by the University of California. Reprinted by the University of California Press.

Jim W. Corder. "Argument as Emergence, Rhetoric as Love." Originally appeared in *Rhetoric Review,* 4 (1985). Reprinted by permission.

Terry Eagleton. "Conclusion: Political Criticism." From *Literary Theory: An Introduction* by Terry Eagleton. Copyright © 1983 by the University of Minnesota. Reprinted by permission of the University of Minnesota Press.

Douglas Ehninger. "On Systems of Rhetoric." Originally appeared in *Philosophy and Rhetoric,* 1 (1968). Pages 131-144. Reprinted by permission of The Pennsylvania State University Press.

Walter R. Fisher. "Narration as a Human Communication Paradigm: The Case of Public Moral Argument." Appeared originally in *Communication Monographs* 51 (1984). Copyright © 1984 by the Speech Communication Association. Reprinted by permission of the Speech Communication Association and the author.

Michel Foucault. "What is an Author?" From *Language, Counter-Memory, Practice: Selected Essays and Interviews with Michel Foucault.* Translated from the French by Donald F. Bouchard and Sherry Simon, and edited by Donald F. Bouchard. Copyright © 1977 by Cornell University. Used by permission of the publisher, Cornell University Press.

Paulo Freire and Donaldo Macedo. "The Illiteracy of Literacy in the United States." From *Literacy: Reading the Word and the World.* Copyright 1987 by Bergin and Garvey. Reprinted by permission of the publisher.

Ernesto Grassi. "Rhetoric and Philosophy." Appeared originally in *Philosophy and Rhetoric* 9 (1976), pages 200-16. Copyright 1976 by The Pennsylvania State University. Reproduced by permission of The Pennsylvania State University Press.

Jürgen Habermas. "Intermediate Reflections: Social Action, Purpose Activity, and Communication." From *The Theory of Communicative Action* by Jürgen Habermas. Copyright © 1984 by Beacon Press. Reprinted by permission of Beacon Press.

S. M. Halloran. "On the End of Rhetoric, Classical and Modern." Appeared originally in *College English,* February 1975. Copyright 1975 by the National Council of Teachers of English. Reprinted with permission.

E. D. Hirsch. "Cultural Literacy." Reprinted from *The American Scholar,* Volume 52, Number 2, Spring 1983. Copyright © 1983 by the author. By permission of the publisher.

Andrea A. Lunsford and Lisa S. Ede. "On Distinctions between Classical and Modern Rhetoric." From *Essays on Classical Rhetoric and Modern Discourse.* Ed. Robert J. Connors, Lisa S. Ede, and Andrea A. Lunsford. Copyright 1984. Reprinted by permission of the authors.

Richard McKeon. "The Uses of Rhetoric in a Technological Age: Architectonic Productive Arts." From *The Prospect of Rhetoric: Report of the National Development Project.* Ed. Lloyd F. Bitzer and Edwin Black. © 1971. Reprinted by permission of Zahava K. McKeon.

Richard Ohmann. "In Lieu of a New Rhetoric." Appeared originally in *College English,* October 1964. Copyright 1964 by the National Council of Teachers of English. Reprinted with permission.

Chaïm Perelman. "The New Rhetoric: A Theory of Practical Reasoning." From *Great Ideas Today,* 1970. © 1970 Encyclopaedia Britannica, Inc. Reprinted with permission.

Michael Polanyi. "Scientific Controversy." From *Personal Knowledge* by Michael Polyani. Copyright © 1962 by the University of Chicago. Reprinted by permission of The University of Chicago Press.

I. A. Richards. From *How to Read a Page* and *Speculative Instruments,* by I. A. Richards. Cambridge University Press. Reprinted by permission of the Master and Fellows, Magdalene College, Cambridge.

Ferdinand de Saussure. "Nature of the Linguistic Sign." Reprinted from *A Course in General Linguistics* by Ferdinand de Saussure by permission of The Open Court Publishing Company.

Robert L. Scott. "On Viewing Rhetoric as Epistemic." Originally appeared in *Central States Speech Journal,* Nr. 18, 1967. Pages 9-17. Reprinted by permission of the Central States Communication Association.

Stephen Toulmin. "The Layout of Arguments." From *The Uses of Argument,* by Stephen Toulmin. Cambridge University Press. Reprinted by permission of the Master and Fellows, Magdalene College, Cambridge.

Richard M. Weaver. "The Cultural Role of Rhetoric." Reprinted by permission of Louisiana State University from *Visions of Order: The Cultural Crisis of Our Time* by Richard M. Weaver. Copyright © 1964 by Louisiana State University Press.

Index of Authors and Titles